PICARESQUE NARRATIVE, PICARESQUE FICTIONS

PICARESQUE NARRATIVE, PICARESQUE FICTIONS

A Theory and Research Guide

ULRICH WICKS

GREENWOOD PRESS
New York • Westport, Connecticut • London

Library of Congress Cataloging-in-Publication Data

Wicks, Ulrich, 1942–
    Picaresque narrative, picaresque fictions : a theory and research
guide / Ulrich Wicks.
        p.   cm.
    Bibliography: p.
    Includes index.
    ISBN 0–313–24934–2 (lib. bdg. : alk. paper)
    1. Fiction—History and criticism.   2. Picaresque literature—
History and criticism.   I. Title.
PN3428.W53   1989
809.3—dc19   88–15493

British Library Cataloguing in Publication Data is available.

Library of Congress Catalog Card Number: 88–15493
ISBN: 0–313–24934–2

First published in 1989

Greenwood Press, Inc.
88 Post Road West, Westport, Connecticut 06881

Printed in the United States of America

∞

The paper used in this book complies with the
Permanent Paper Standard issued by the National
Information Standards Organization (Z39.48–1984).

10 9 8 7 6 5 4 3 2 1

To Barbara, Elisabeth, and Stephen

Nothing in the world is more constant
than inconstancy itself.

—*Simplicius Simplicissimus* (III, 8)

Contents

Preface

We might ask, in general, for whom should a literary term be defined? The expert? The casual reader? All those readers in between? Everyone? The question of audience, which governs all writing, troubled me long after my threefold goal was clear: to describe picaresque narrative with both careful attention to its historical development as a genre and to its persistent appeal as an archetypal narrative structure; to propose a genre construct of picaresque narrative; and to explore the usefulness of generic awareness in the act of reading by describing, in varying depths proportionate to their exemplary traits, a number of specific fictions that collectively illustrate the full narrative spectrum of the picaresque mode. Before long, I realized that my imaginary reader, my constructed audience, my *Vuestra Merced*, was myself. Let me explain this apparent presumptuousness, worthy of a narrating picaro himself.

When I began to study picaresque fiction, after being stunned by a first encounter with *Lazarillo de Tormes* in a graduate course on the Spanish novel, I wished I had a book of the kind I have here tried to write. At that time there was very little available from a generic and comparative perspective. As I pursued the subject, books and articles appeared from everywhere, and soon the picaresque was a hot, even controversial, topic among academic critics and scholars. Years later, after a number of superb and illuminating studies of the picaresque from a variety of angles, the book I had wished for still had not been written. So here I am, still trying to make sense of the picaresque to myself.

It may well be that such is the motivation behind all critical writing, as it is behind genre theory itself: to construct the extra-text that helps guide all other texts into an order within which individual texts can be properly understood. The paradox of the absent book is that, having now explored the critical territory that I wished were covered in that book, I no longer need this one. I therefore present it to any readers who, like me then, are now wishing for a reference book that will help guide them through the confusing ubiquity of "picaresque" in contemporary critical and popular usage.

A wide-ranging study such as this led me of necessity into genres, periods, languages, and other territories in which I need guidance myself, and such errors of fact and of judgment that have resulted from my audacity in roaming so far and wide are entirely my fault, and not those of the critics and authors I present. In part I, except for a few instances, I have annotated all quotations parenthetically by author's name or title plus page number; full bibliographical information appears in the list of works cited following chapter 4. Part II is deliberately discontinuous; it is designed as a vagabondage of reading, appropriate to the fictions it discusses, and I hope the reader browses as he or she needs to. Except where noted, all annotations in part II refer to the select bibliographies following each entry. In order to make each entry self-standing, I have had to allow some bibliographical duplication from entry to entry, especially of those works that themselves cover a number of the fictions. In part II, I have not given original language editions with any consistency because I have not assumed a bilingual reader. Throughout I have tried to avoid the à la mode and *à la page* terminology of currently fashionable critical theory. Many of these terms remistify rather than clarify, even within the academy, to all but a few. When literary theory and criticism do not speak to the same audience that is reading literature, something is very wrong.

Brief portions of part I and a small section of part II were previously published in different form. I thank the editors of *Genre, PMLA, College Literature*, and *Mosaic* for permission to adapt portions of previously published work in this book. My debt to all the scholars and critics who have illuminated the picaresque from their perspectives will be evident from the frequency with which I quote them to make points that I could not hope to articulate more insightfully myself.

I am fortunate to have had the conscientious and patient editorial guidance of Marilyn Brownstein, Maureen Melino, Beverly Miller, and Penny Sippel of Greenwood Press.

PART I

A THEORY OF PICARESQUE NARRATIVE

CHAPTER 1
The Picaresque Genre

It has become a critical commonplace in generic theory to make an obligatory acknowledgment of vicious circularity before being forced to proceed within it. The frustration of this part of the hermeneutic task is succinctly put by Paul Hernadi (paraphrasing Günther Müller) in *Beyond Genre* (1972): "How can I define tragedy (or any other genre) before I know on which works to base the definition, yet how can I know on which works to base the definition before I have defined tragedy?" (2). Inside this circle is still another problem, which Alastair Fowler in *Kinds of Literature* (1982) calls "ineradicable knowledge": "In order to reconstruct the original genre, we have to eliminate from consciousness its subsequent states. For the idea of a genre that informs a reader's understanding is normally the latest, most inclusive conception of it that he knows. And unless he can unknow this conception, it seems that he cannot recover meanings that relate to the genre's earlier, 'innocent' states" (261). The first of these activities is essentially synchronic, seeking to create a paradigm or hypothetical *Ur*-type in the context of which individual works might be better understood. The second is primarily diachronic, aiming to trace the evolution of an identifiable genre or type in specific historical contexts. Together such literary activities only formalize theoretically and critically what is absolutely unsuppressible in even the most cursory acts of reading: trying to assimilate a new text into the familiar community of our accumulated reading experiences.

Even the child reading (or being read) her first stories gropes for connections, for the most rudimentary generic signals. In the act of reading, a text yields meaning only in the context of its co-texts from other acts of reading; these co-texts in turn alter their meanings and slightly rearrange themselves with the addition of every new text. The reading of each new text is therefore of necessity also a rereading of already familiar texts; the reading of the new and this rereading of the old often combine to form an extratext, a generic construct, or type, or kind against which the strangely new text can be familiarized while simultaneously reassessing the old texts. The reading experience is always implicitly and sometimes explicitly generic, and the whole of genre theory springs from this dynamic process, which T. S. Eliot in his "Tradition and the Individual Talent" (1917) captured in an assertion that itself resonates like the phenomenon it describes: "What happens when a new work of art is created is something that happens simultaneously to all the works of art which preceded it" (50). Fifty years later, Eliot's statement finds an echo in Julia Kristeva's description of the structuralist concept of *intertextuality*, as quoted in Jonathan Culler's *Structuralist Poetics* (1975): "Every text takes shape as a mosaic of citations, every text is the absorption and transformation of other texts" (139). Culler himself adds, "A work can only be read in connection with or against other texts, which provides a grid through which it is read and structured by establishing expectations which enable one to pick out salient features and give them a structure." Both Eliot's statement and the structuralist variations of it describe the creation and reception of literary texts as a process of continual generic readjustment, of constant reformulation of the literary frame of reference within which we read.

The very imprecision and circularity of Eliot's assertion ("what happens . . . is something that happens") are particularly appropriate to a phenomenon that is always process. Just when we think we have the "what" pinned down, the "something" proves elusive and forces us back to reformulate the "what," which in turn impels us to reassess the "something," and so on. The circle is not vicious after all, for it is hardly closed. As more texts are added to the collectivity of experienced texts, it resembles more an ever-expanding spiral, with each new text (or new reading of a previously read text) at its center for the duration of the reading. The centrifugal force of the new reading and the centripetal force of all accumulated readings (the "ineradicable memory") automatically—and dynamically—interact, creating the generic process that leads to an understanding of texts in the only way that we can understand them: in relation to other texts.

Or should lead. Genre theory, unfortunately, has more often than not in literary history been rigidly prescriptive rather than flexibly descriptive, for both maker and reader. When genre theory exists primarily as a pigeonholing or classification system for its own sake, it soon becomes tiresome to all but the hyperorganized reader, as individual literary works are coerced through formulaic reduction into available slots. Rigid genre theory actually undermines literature by squelching what we most admire in literary texts: the innovative, the unpredictable, the experimental—in short, the new, for which there may be no existing pigeonhole. When genre theory cannot or will not do what individual texts are constantly doing, then one of the two must make way for the other; either the new text is rejected as an unacceptable mutation, or genre theory must refine or expand its categories.

When literature thrives on experimentation, as it has in the twentieth century, prescriptive genre theory must make room or else make way. That the latter has been the case—that the theory of genres has not been at the center of literary study and reflection in this century—is diagnosed by René Wellek at the beginning of his "Genre Theory, the Lyric, and *Erlebnis*" (1967): "Clearly this is due to the fact that in the practice of almost all writers of our time genre distinctions matter little: boundaries are being constantly transgressed, genres combined or fused, old genres discarded or transformed, new genres created, to such an extent that the very concept has been called in doubt" (225). If genre theory adapted itself to what Wellek describes literature as doing—if, that is, it conceived of itself in Eliot's terms or along the lines of structuralist conceptions of intertextuality—it could again be at the heart of literary study, where in fact it should be, given that the act of reading is inherently generic.

If every act of reading is fundamentally, inherently, and inescapably generic and yet genre theory is not at the center of literary study, then somewhere theory must have gotten seriously out of whack with practice. It did so primarily by not changing as literature itself changes. This is precisely the point Fowler makes in refuting those who hold genre theory to be irrelevant because they misapprehend genres as simple and immutable permanent forms, established once and for all:

But . . . genres are actually in a continual state of transmutation. It is by *their* modification, primarily, that individual works convey literary meaning. Frequent adjustments in genre theory are needed, therefore, if the forms are to continue to mediate between the flux of history and the canons of art. Thus, to expect fixed forms, immune to change yet permanently corresponding to literature, is to misunderstand what genre theory undertakes (or should undertake). (*Kinds of Literature*, 24; emphasis mine)

As Fowler suggests, genre theory must be conceived in rhythm with what actually happens in our individual acts of reading, which are only superficially guided by a genre theory that limits itself to the prescriptively taxonomic or the historically cartographic. When genre theory acknowledges the rudimentary generic groping of the reading experience itself, it can help us understand a text as the act of reading blends imperceptibly into interpretation. Here, too, generic identity is absolutely fundamental. It is also unavoidably consequential, as E. D. Hirsch points out in *Validity in Interpretation* (1967) when he says that "an interpreter's preliminary generic conception of a text is constitutive of everything that he subsequently understands, and that this remains the case unless and until that generic conception is altered" (74). It is this process of constant alteration that generic theory should concern itself with, as Thomas Kent proposes in *Interpretation and Genre* (1986) when he calls for a holistic theory of genre that will attempt to see each text as both an unchanging body of words and a continually developing cultural artifact: "The holistic genre critic, then, should see both the part and the whole, the synchronic and the diachronic conventional elements, constantly interacting together to form new patterns of meaning, and generating a descriptive model of this kind of activity requires a substantial shift in attitude about the critic's role in the study of literary texts" (27). Yet such a shift would only bring critical theory into line with literary practice; it would simply and rightfully acknowledge what actually happens to and in the text as it is being made and whenever it is being received. The term *holistic genre theory* ought to be something of a redundancy, but its necessity for Kent's purpose emphasizes how fragmenting and distancing our received concepts of genre have become when we bring them into our actual encounters with literary texts. Genre theory that has a healthy respect for how literature actually works should by its very nature be holistic, always keeping the text and its kind in a carefully balanced and mutually respectful relationship, which Rosalie Colie in her conclusion to *The Resources of Kind* (1973) captures in an almost aphoristic way: "Significant pieces of literature are worth much more than their kind, but they are what they are in part by their inevitable kind-ness" (128).

What concept of kind-ness was going through the mind of the reader in 1554 who picked up a slim volume called *La vida de Lazarillo de Tormes y de sus fortunas y adversidades*? And what kinds of kind-ness had been at work in the mind and imagination of the anonymous author when he wrote it a year or two earlier? What prompted 1599 readers of the first part of *Guzmán de Alfarache* to make a conscious connection with *Lazarillo*? How aware were these readers of the generic newness of what they were reading, and how consciously did they have to sift through their accumulated reading experiences in order to assimilate these new texts? What generic signals were the texts themselves giving these readers? Was it only something as crude as mere content or subject matter? Who, in fact, were these first readers, and how did they respond interpretively to these fictions?

Unfortunately, the further back in literary history we go, the more elusively hypothetical the answers to such questions become. Thus far, we know relatively little about the actual readers of the fictions that soon came to be called picaresque. We know that *Lazarillo* was considered to be a subversive book. (In 1559 it was placed on the *Index Librorum Prohibitorum*, a list of books forbidden by Church authority to be read by Roman Catholics.) We know that *Guzmán* became an unprecedented best-seller. In the wake of the popularity of *Guzmán*, *Lazarillo* was reissued at least nine times in the four years between 1599 and 1603—as many editions as there had been in the whole forty-five years since its initial publication. King Philip II had died in 1598, and the new reign of his son Philip III resulted in some relaxation of censorship. For several years, then, until the publication of the first part of *Don Quixote* in 1605, *Lazarillo de Tormes* and *Guzmán de Alfarache* must have been the most talked-about books of the decade, if not of the century. But the actual composition of this sizable literate audience has not yet been explored. It seems reasonable to conclude that almost none of this large readership coincided with the lower class, among whom were the hordes of vagrants and beggars roaming the roads of Spain and congregating in some cities in such huge numbers that they had to be periodically expelled. The poor, as Lionel Trilling has said, do not read about the poor. One may imagine then, as Helen H. Reed does in *The Reader in the Picaresque Novel* (1984), a reading public comprised of aristocrats, courtiers, *conversos*, country gentry, the urban bourgeoisie, clergy, students, some women, and virtually no *pícaros*. . . . No doubt the individual novels varied in their appeal to different social groups as well as to different tastes, but the early picaresque novel might be described as a new genre in search of a readership, or a genre in the process of formation that created its own readership. (17–18)

That it was a democratic intended readership we know from the hypothetical readers set up in the prologues to both *Lazarillo* and *Guzmán*. Lazarillo not only addresses a specific narratee ("Vuestra Merced"), to whom he has been asked to explain his life, but he also invites a homogeneous readership to listen in, as it were, for "anybody can read my story and enjoy it." Alemán in *Guzmán* provides two direct addresses to readers—one "al Vulgo," the other "al discreto lector"—and then adds a "Declaration for the Understanding of this Book," which is addressed to all readers. No actual reader is going to admit belonging to the mob at whom the first prologue is aimed, and so Alemán shapes his readers by making them feel privileged, above the incorrigible rabble—a narrating strategy that justifies his subject matter by short-circuiting any objections to it. Ironically, the reader becomes part of an in-group looking at society's down and out. In both *Lazarillo* and *Guzmán*, all readers ("anybody") are discreet; this flattery aimed at the self-images of readers makes them paradoxically both willing and wary participants in a narrative confidence game that enables picaresque narration to function between author and reader.

In two of his three addresses to readers in the 1599 first part, Alemán uses *pícaro* (which does not occur in *Lazarillo*), a word choice he would come to regret by the time he published the second part of *Guzmán de Alfarache* in 1604, when he has Guzmán (in the sixth chapter of book 1) lament the epithet by which he has been known since writing the first part. The etymology of *pícaro* is troublesome. Corominas (1954–1957) dates its first appearance in 1525 in the expression *pícaro de cozina* ("kitchen boy," or "scullion"), a relatively neutral word with none of the associations Guzmán is complaining about. But around 1545, the meaning of *pícaro* shifted from designating a lowly profession to describing immoral and antisocial behavior. In Eugenio de Salazar's *Carta del Bachiller de Arcadia* (1548), *pícaros* are explicitly contrasted with courtiers. In a morality play of that time, the word is used in a context clearly of mischief and wrongdoing. Harry Sieber in *The Picaresque* (1977) suggests that the semantic shift may have had something to do with the vast armies of pike-men (*picas secas* and/or *piqueros secos*, from the verb *picar*) needed in Spain's defense of its territories. Some of them were recruited from among criminals, and many deserted. "Deserting soldiers . . . attempted to return home, begging and stealing on the way. It is possible that some of the deserters carried their previous military title of *piquero* with them into 'civilian' life" (6). Another explanation for the later meaning of *pícaro* is by association with Picardy, a region near Flanders where Spain was engaged in wars from 1587 to 1659. To a Spaniard, a Picard was a rogue. Whatever its precise origins, the word *pícaro* achieved wide currency by the end of the sixteenth century. In dictionaries compiled in 1570 and 1593, a *pícaro* is defined as a shabby man without honor. This was the popular meaning of the word when Alemán applied it to his literary creation, and from then on the meaning of the word has been inextricably bound up with the various literary characters who are called *pícaros*. A dramatic interlude called *Testamento del pícaro pobre*, which must have been written before 1605, when the author to whom it has been attributed (Pedro Láinez) died, has a sonnet in praise of the picaresque life; it begins, "Gozar de libertad, vivir contento" ("to enjoy freedom, to live content"), which emphasizes the picaro's outsider status positively as a freedom from responsibility and tiresome social obligations. A similar tone dominates a poem from about the same time, *La vida del pícaro*, in which "sólo el pícaro muere bien logrado,/que desde que nació, nada desea" ("only a picaro dies successful, because from birth he desired nothing"). By 1611 in Covarrubias's *Tesoro de la lengua castellana*, as Bjornson points out in *The Picaresque Hero in European Fiction* (1977), the word *pícaro* meant a vulgar, rootless person willing to perform menial tasks, but there begins to be associated with him "a characteristic freedom from duty and responsibility" (262).

A year after Guzmán de Alfarache complained of his epithet, Cervantes published the first part of *Don Quixote*, in the twenty-second chapter of which Quixote encounters the galley slave Ginés de Pasamonte, who says that he is writing a book:

> "It's so good," replied Ginés, "that Lazarillo de Tormes will have to look out, and so will everything in that style that has ever been written or ever will be. One thing I can promise you, is that it is all the truth, and such well-written, entertaining truth that there is no fiction that can compare with it."
>
> "And what is the title of the book?" asked Don Quixote.
>
> "*The Life of Ginés de Pasamonte*," replied that hero.
>
> "Is it finished?" asked Don Quixote.
>
> "How can it be finished," replied the other, "if my life isn't? What is written begins with my birth and goes down to the point when I was sent to the galleys this last time." (Trans. J. M. Cohen, 176–77)

There are two allusions here: a direct one to Lazarillo and an indirect one to Guzmán de Alfarache, who writes while serving a sentence in the galleys. Not only is an explicit link made between *Lazarillo* and *Guzmán*, but a sense of genre distinctly emerges in Ginés's comparing his effort with "everything in that style" that has been or is yet to be written. Ginés de Pasamonte the writer is generically conscious of his narrative task, and the genre he is actively being shaped by and shaping is the emerging picaresque genre as thus far articulated in *Lazarillo de Tormes* and *Guzmán de Alfarache*. "One witnesses here," writes Claudio Guillén in "Genre and Countergenre" (1971), "the spontaneous discovery of a class by a reader-critic belonging to the most vast of the audiences. . . . Ginés, as a reader neither cultured nor ignorant, as a layman (or *ingenio lego*), combines a bold ability to recognize novelty with the generic mentality of his time, that is, with an immoderate fondness for classification, be it within or without the pale of traditional poetics'' (*Literature as System*, 151–52). The essential point here is that Ginés is not merely expressing the imitative urge of a hack copycat; he is not spinning off *Lazarillo* but rather improving on the kind or ''style'' or class of which he sees *Lazarillo* as a specific example (Cervantes's word is actually *género*, but it did not then mean ''genre'' in the modern sense). Ginés has a strong, if rudimentary, sense of genre, both diachronically and synchronically, as he posits the future development of this kind of fiction. And Cervantes assumed that his own readers would catch the allusions and understand the implications without further explanation.

This passage from *Don Quixote* establishes as strongly as any contemporary evidence can a generic awareness of the emerging picaresque genre in both writers and readers. The passage also emphasizes major characteristics of the structure, content, style, and readership of works in that genre. A work of this kind is, first of all, a *vida*, and thus narrated by its protagonist; as such, it is true to life in the sense of being empirically valid, as compared to the chivalric romances, which were not and which the emerging picaresque must have dealt a considerable blow (when Cervantes has a friend in his prologue to part 1 of *Don Quixote* describe the book as ''una invectiva contra los libros de caballerías,'' he may have been beating a dying or already dead horse). When Ginés insists on the need to live out his life before writing about it, he emphasizes the empirical impulse in this kind of writing. A *vida* is, moreover, chronological in structure. It should be entertaining and well written. Its content is determined by the shady, shifty—even criminal—behavior of characters like Ginés de Pasamonte himself (who later validates his status as a picaro by turning the galley slaves against Don Quixote, stealing Sancho's donkey, and robbing the priest and barber; in disguise as Maese Pedro in part 2, he reappears as a full-fledged trickster). And, finally, such *vidas* can be read—and indeed written—by everybody, including the Ginés de Pasamontes of the world: the ''anybody'' Lazarillo addresses in his prologue.

Even if we accept the by-now almost conventional interpretation of the Ginés de Pasamonte episode in *Don Quixote* as expressing Cervantine hostility against the new picaresque narrative form (as expounded perhaps most influentially in Carlos Blanco Aguinaga's 1957 article, ''Cervantes y la picaresca. Notas sobre dos tipos de realismo''), we have to assume that in the dialogue between Ginés and Don Quixote, Cervantes is relying absolutely on a rudimentary generic awareness on the part of his readers. As reader Ginés converses with reader Quixote, their exchange is listened to by a third: the readers of *Don Quixote* who, whether they interpret the discussion as critical parody or not, are nevertheless expected to bring to it an intertextual and intergeneric awareness of the picaresque, which is as necessary for understanding this episode as an even more fundamentally assumed generic familiarity with the chivalric romances is for the whole of *Don Quixote*. Thus, by 1605, the emerging picaresque is already ''defined''—implicitly, if not explicitly—as a distinctly recognizable kind of writing, and it is so defined by a picaro himself. By 1605, a huge (by any previous standard) audience has been responding to, and by that very response further engendering, a specific narrative type, if not a literary genre in the formal sense of a traditional literary kind familiar to educated Renaissance readers. A regulative concept must have been at work, though its "poetics" will remain informal for several more centuries, until literary historians in the nineteenth century begin to formulate it a posteriori.

Through Ginés de Pasamonte, Cervantes gives us the first theory of the picaresque, defining it aesthetically by its autobiographical form, sociologically by its democratic readership—and authorship, and even ideologically by its subject matter—which is clearly subversive, given Ginés's arrogant character, his past behavior, and his present and future behavior as revealed in the tricks he will play on Don Quixote. The seasoned criminal, reader of picaresques and would-be author of them, confronts the self-deluded *hidalgo*, reader of romances who anticipates an *historiador* writing his life even as he sets out on his first sally. Having read *Lazarillo*, Ginés must see in Quixote much of the equally deluded *hidalgo* in the third chapter of that work; reading *Don Quixote*, Cervantes's reader cannot avoid making the connection. Lazarillo sees through his *hidalgo* (though with a great deal of sympathy) as much as Ginés sees through his. In their stances, the two picaros represent a new order defying an old. Their upstart tone must have satisfied a need in what Guillén suggests was the core audience of the picaresque: "the discontented middle class" (*Literature as System*, 144).

With the appearance of López de Ubeda's *La pícara Justina* in that same year, the picaresque as a narrative genre is firmly established, for *Justina* is among other things a parody of picaresque fiction itself. Parody assumes its audience's familiarity with the conventions of the literary tradition or specific work that is its parodic object, and *Justina* works successfully only in contextuality with *Guzmán de Alfarache* and *Lazarillo de Tormes*. In addition to its conscious (and self-conscious) parody, which demands generic awareness in the reader, and its introduction of a picara, or female rogue, *Justina* is also significant in the picaresque tradition for a more or less extratextual contribution, which has been much reproduced and from which a number of critics have drawn important conclusions about the picaresque genre: the frontispiece to its first edition, which depicts "La nave de la vida picaresca" (the ship of picaresque life). On board, the principal figures are Guzmán, Justina, and Celestina (Justina's literary "mother"); Lazarillo is by himself in a little rowboat connected by a rope to the larger vessel. Classical divinities, proverbial sayings, allegorical figures, and pictorial emblems constituting the paraphernalia of the picaresque life complete the crowded scene. We can derive a number of moralistic readings from this interesting engraving, some of them mutually contradictory; and the perspective is such that we cannot be entirely sure if Lazarillo is towing the ship. But what is most significant in this picture is that Lazarillo, Guzmán, and Justina are all inside the same frame. In both this engraving and its text, *La pícara Justina* establishes its genre; by bringing two superficially unlike texts into contact with a third—itself—*Justina* forces readers into seeking out deeper similarities, in the course of which they cannot avoid constructing a generic type, or abstract extratext, which governs all three. Once the third text acknowledges as models the first and second texts, generic identity and awareness regulate both the writing and the reading of the fiction, and a genre exists.

The works belonging to this genre were not fully enumerated until the late nineteenth century, when Fonger de Haan and Frank Wadleigh Chandler published their doctoral dissertations on the picaresque. The generally accepted canon of Spanish picaresque fictions was established by Angel Valbuena Prat who in 1943 produced a two-thousand-page anthology, *La novela picaresca española*. This anthology, which has gone through more than a half-dozen editions, contains twenty-three works of fiction in their entirety. In addition to *Lazarillo, Guzmán*, and *Justina*, Valbuena Prat includes Juan de Luna's *Segunda parte de Lazarillo de Tormes* (1620) and Juan Martí's *Segunda parte de Guzmán de Alfarache* (1602), published under the pseudonym Mateo Luján de Sayavedra; and four *novelas ejemplares* by Cervantes: "La ilustre fregona," "Rinconete y Cortadillo," "El casamiento engañoso," and "Coloquio de los perros" (published in 1613 but written earlier). The other works anthologized are Salas Barbadillo, *Le hija de Celestina* (1612); Vicente Espinel, *Vida de Marcos de Obregón* (1618); Quevedo, *El Buscón* (1626); Carlos García, *La desordenada codicia de los bienes ajenos* (1619); Jerónimo de Alcalá, *Alonso, mozo de muchos amos* (*El donado hablador*) (1624, 1626); Alonso de Castillo Solórzano, *La niña de los embustes, Teresa de Manzanares* (1632), *Adventuras del Bachiller Trapaza* (1637), and *La garduña de Sevilla* (1642); María de Zayas, "El castigo de la miseria" (1637); Guevara, *El diablo Cojuelo* (1641); Antonio Enriquez Gomez, *Vida de don Gregorio Guadaña* (part of *El siglo pitagórico*, 1644); the anonymous *Vida y hechos de Estebanillo Gonzalez* (1646); Francisco Santos, *Periquillo el de las gallineras* (1688); and Torres Villarroel, *Su vida* (1743, 1752, 1758). There is considerable lack of consensus among scholars that this collection indeed constitutes a generic canon. Torres Villarroel's *Vida* and Santos's *Periquillo el de las gallineras*, for example, are almost universally rejected as picaresques, or just simply ignored, while Guevara's *El diablo Cojuelo* is, more properly speaking and as Valbuena Prat himself says in his introduction, a formal satire with picaresque characteristics. The critical emphasis among scholars has been and continues to be overwhelmingly on *Lazarillo, Guzmán*, and *El Buscón*, with *Justina* trailing behind, and even lesser attention to the other writers except, perhaps, for Cervantes. As the only collection of its kind in any language, *La novela picaresca española*, immensely useful and helpful as it is, has proved frustrating to critics looking there for a clear genre definition. Putting twenty-three works together inside the same covers does not yield as strong a sense of generic identity as did putting Lazarillo, Guzmán, and Justina inside the same frame in the frontispiece to *Justina*, which Valbuena Prat also uses as his frontispiece.

In his "Zur Chronologie und Verbreitung des spanischen Schelmenromans"

(1928), Helmut Petriconi chronologically lists thirty-seven works of fiction published between 1528 (*La lozana andaluza*) and 1680 (*Trabajo del vicio*) and in a parallel chronology lists the thirty-one editions of *Lazarillo de Tormes* published between 1554 and 1664. With a basic definition of the picaresque guiding his selection of fictional works, Petriconi demonstrates that there is a thoroughly traceable development, which peaks around 1620. *Lazarillo* continues to be widely read as new picaresque fictions appear, reinforcing its position as generic prototype and suggesting a generic impulse in readers to connect with what must have been perceived even then as the earliest text in the tradition.

Among a certain group of readers, the picaresque even became what today we would call trendy. Bjornson says that picaresque life as viewed by the upper-class reader "exercised an undeniable appeal in the increasingly secular atmosphere at Philip III's court, where women even adopted the custom of disguising themselves in ragged clothes and claiming to be dressed 'a lo picaresco' (in picaresque fashion)" (*The Picaresque Hero in European Fiction*, 69). Works that parodied the picaresque, such as *La pícara Justina* and *El Buscón* (the latter already circulating in manuscript before *Justina* was published), were thus intended in large part as in-jokes for a highly select audience, and the more frivolous picaresques, like the adventure stories of Salas Barbadillo and Castillo Solórzano, were aimed at a leisure-class readership seeking vicarious excitement. It has therefore sometimes been argued that highly self-conscious, even precious, works such as *Justina* and *El Buscón* and superficially derivative works such as *La hija de Celestina* and *La garduña de Sevilla*, for example, cannot be considered genuine picaresques. Specifically targeted for an elite audience, such works either caricature their genre through clever exaggeration of its characteristics or seek to cash in on the genre's success by spinning off its most popular conventions. Such arguments, valid though they may be in some cases, are primarily value judgments of individual works rather than generic assessments. In the end, such a line of thinking leaves us with a genre comprised of a mere two or three works. But a new genre does not remain naive for long; after *Lazarillo* and *Guzmán*, generic self-consciousness itself becomes a major convention of the picaresque genre. A genre would be truly sterile if every work in it recapitulated the prototype. Genres evolve through the tension between generic constraints and the demands of the unique work, a tension that itself may become the center of interest, as it does in *Justina* and *El Buscón*, or that may be erased altogether in favor of emphasizing and embellishing those characteristics of the genre that were proving most popular, as it is in the superficial imitations. Both kinds of generic perpetuation rely on and in turn enhance the reader's generic awareness. A parody is probably one of the most revealing things that can happen to a genre. By their very act of expending clever literary force against a grouped body of literary works, parodies like *Justina* and *El Buscón* sharpen the reader's sense of the genre being spoofed—just as we have a better grasp, for example, of the gothic novel after reading Jane Austen's *Northanger Abbey* or just as through *Don Quixote* we get an excellent sense of what a *libro de caballería* is without ever having read one. The copycat works are equally revealing generically. By their formulaic reduction of generic conventions, they can give us a more coherent understanding of a genre than can the more complex and creative works in that genre.

When Guzmán de Alfarache becomes Justina's husband in *La pícara Justina* in 1605, the picaresque genre has fully emerged in Spanish literature. The frontispiece to the book explicitly connects both of them with Lazarillo. In that same year, readers were also meeting Ginés de Pasamonte, whose life closely resembles Guzmán's and whose literary goal is to surpass *Lazarillo de Tormes* when he finishes writing his own *vida*. In the course of the development of the picaresque genre, both *Lazarillo* and *Guzmán* remain exemplary fictions; they continue together to be the generic prototypes, providing the models against which many subsequent works measure themselves, no matter how freely they play variations on the genre through self-conscious parody, unauthorized continuation, exploitive mimicking, and epigonic imitation. In 1646, the picaro in *Vida y hechos de Estebanillo González, hombre de buen humor* still measures his work (albeit ironically) against the generic models when he claims to be writing a "true" story, not "la fingida Guzmán de Alfarache, ni la fabulosa de Lazarillo de Tormes."

The enormous popularity of the picaresque in Spain soon spread to other European countries as translations made the major works widely accessible to English, French, German, and Italian readers who could not read Spanish. By the middle of the seventeenth century, the picaresque was an international literary phenomenon as translations gave way to narrative attempts to perpetuate the genre while simultaneously integrating it with indigenous literary conditions and conventions. In 1655 in England there was Head's *The English Rogue*, with a dedicatory verse that mentions *Lazarillo, Guzmán*, and *El Buscón*. In 1669 Germany produced its own major contribution to the picaresque genre in Grimmelshausen's *The Adventurous Simplicissimus*, which was just as explicitly influenced by Aleman's work (through Albertinus's translation) and a year later spun off one of its minor characters into *The Runagate Courage*, with a formidable picara who is successor to Justina and predecessor of Moll Flanders and whose birth out of the pages of *Simplicissimus* is the obverse of Guzmán's absorption into the pages of *La pícara Justina*. In 1683 and 1690, respectively, according to A. A. Parker in *Literature and the Delinquent*, appeared *The Dutch Rogue, or Guzman of Amsterdam* and *Teague O'Divelly, or The Irish Rogue*. In the eighteenth century, the picaresque underwent a significant transformation as Lesage in France shaped the Spanish tradition his own way in *The Adventures of Gil Blas* (1715, 1724, 1735). It is his version of the picaresque that became normative throughout the rest of the century and well into the nineteenth, especially in English literature. Lesage's English translator was Smollett, who was primarily responsible for establishing *Gil Blas* as the picaresque prototype, although in his own *The Adventures of Ferdinand Count Fathom* (1753) he made explicit references to *Guzmán de Alfarache* and Petronius's *The Satyricon* in addition to *Gil Blas*. In the early nineteenth century, Sir Walter Scott perpetuated the French model; he and Smollett were responsible for many of the major misconceptions of the picaresque that still haunt theory and criticism in English. The confusion was confounded by the English novelists' love for Cervantes, and in using both *Don Quixote* and *Gil Blas* as models for their own fiction, the eighteenth-century novelists created a case of literary mistaken identity that continues today in the misapprehension of *Don Quixote* as a picaresque novel even among well-read critics, an error that Hispanists (despite their own lack of unanimity about the nature of the Spanish picaresque genre) would never make. Although the original Spanish picaresques continue to be read—there is evidence that Defoe read them, and in Fielding's *The History of the Life of the Late Mr. Jonathan Wild the Great* (1743) Wild cites *The Spanish Rogue* (that is, *Guzmán*) as his favorite book—the indigenous narrative tradition of the criminal biography shapes whatever influence they may have had as distinctly as *Gil Blas* had shaped them.

Meanwhile, in 1822 there was *Der deutsche Gil Blas*, so titled by Goethe, and at midcentury there was even a *Russian Gil Blas*, by Vassily Narezhny. In the New World, Mexican writer José Joaquín Fernández de Lizardi wrote *The Itching Parrot (Vida y hechos de Periquillo Sarniento*, 1816, 1830), which alludes directly to *Periquillo el de las gallineras*; and a century later, also in Mexico, José Rubén Romero in *The Futile Life of Pito Pérez (La vida inútil de Pito Pérez*, 1938) alluded to both when Pito referred to himself as a Periquillo. Toward the end of the nineteenth century in the United States, William Dean Howells suggested that the picaresque might provide the appropriate narrative structure for rendering the American experience, but Howells read *Lazarillo* through *Don Quixote* and conjured up an image true to neither, like the earliest American attempt to mix the Cervantine and the picaresque, Brackenridge's *Modern Chivalry*, the first two volumes of which had appeared a century before (1792). Nonetheless, a stable sense of the historical Spanish picaresque genre persisted, even in otherwise casual and unpretentious fictions like, for example, *The Picaroons* (1904), by Gelett Burgess and Will Irwin, which is prefaced by this note:

Picaroon—a petty rascal; one who lives by his wits; an adventurer. The Picaresque Tales, in Spanish literature of the beginning of the Seventeenth Century, dealt with the fortunes of beggars, imposters, thieves, etc., and chronicled the Romance of Roguery. Such stories were the precursors of the modern novel. The San Francisco Night's Entertainment is an attempt to render similar subjects with an essentially modern setting. (*The Picaroons*, p. v)

In the twentieth century, such self-conscious use of tradition continued. Mann's *Confessions of Felix Krull*, composed over a forty-year period, was written directly in the tradition of *Simplicissimus*. Oskar in Günter Grass's *The Tin Drum* (1959) is a direct descendant of the drummer boy Simplicissimus. Hans Schmetterling, the character in Alfred Kern's only peripherally picaresque

Le Clown (1957), is referred to by the circus performers as "our Simplicissimus" and runs into Felix Krull in Paris. John Hawkes has acknowledged Quevedo as a major influence on his fiction. Camilo José Cela continues Lazarillo's life almost four hundred years later, in his *Nuevas andanzas y desventuras de Lazarillo de Tormes* (1944). At midcentury in the United States, works such as Saul Bellow's *The Adventures of Augie March* (1953), Donleavy's *The Ginger Man* (1955), Ellison's *Invisible Man* (1952), Kerouac's *On the Road* (1957), Purdy's *Malcolm* (1959), and Pynchon's *V.* (1963) were linked back to Nathanael West's *The Dream Life of Balso Snell* (1931) and *A Cool Million* (1934) to signal the apparent emergence of a contemporary American picaresque as an assertive strand of twentieth-century narrative. In Canada, there is Mordecai Richler's *The Apprenticeship of Duddy Kravitz* (1959). In England, fictions like Kingsley Amis's *Lucky Jim* (1954), Malcolm Bradbury's *Eating People Is Wrong* (1959), and John Wain's *Hurry on Down* (1953) were grouped with such works as Evelyn Waugh's *Decline and Fall* (1928), eliciting similar speculations about a "neopicaresque" in contemporary British fiction. In Germany, *Felix Krull* and *The Tin Drum*, already linked extra- and intertextually with *Simplicissimus*, were compared to a whole roster of new fictions, including Heinrich Böll's *The Clown* *(Ansichten eines Clowns*, 1963). The new fiction there was studied under such titles as "Picaro Today," "The Return of the Picaros," and "The Eternal Simplicissimus." In Spanish literature itself, the persistence of the picaresque in twentieth-century fiction is demonstrated by the more than one hundred pages devoted to this topic in the proceedings of what billed itself as the First International Congress on the Picaresque (Madrid, July 1976), edited by Manuel Criado de Val as *La picaresca: Orígenes, Textos y Estructuras* (1979). In addition to Cela and Pio Baroja, writers like Ricardo León (*Los Centauros*, 1912), Juan Antonio de Zunzunegui (*La vida como es*, 1954), Sebastián Juan Arbó (*Martín de Caretas*, 1955), Darío Fernández-Flórez (*Lola, espejo oscuro*, 1950), and Juan Goytisolo (*Fiestas*, 1958) wrote fictions often explicitly rooted, through generic self-reference or indirect allusion, in the seventeenth-century Spanish picaresque narrative tradition. Among fictions written in French, Alfred Kern's *Le Clown* tries deliberately to be picaresque, and in France, too, there is talk of a *renaissance du roman picaresque* as critics look at Kern and at some of the new fictions being produced in Germany, England, and the United States.

Even this sketchiest of surveys over three and a half centuries of several major literatures makes it clear that the picaresque genre of *siglo de oro* Spain left a historically robust and geographically diverse narrative legacy. This culturally very coded narrative structure, which emerged, peaked, and declined under specific social, economic, political, religious, and literary conditions in Spain over the relatively short span of the first three decades of the seventeenth century (there being no genre until *Guzmán* and *Lazarillo* together created it in 1599), proved universally appealing to readers and writers outside Spain and has continued, despite a number of sea-changes, with traceable continuity up to the present. Today book reviewers, literary critics, and even film critics call works "picaresque" with such frequency that any objective observer of the literary and film scenes cannot help but conclude that the picaresque is a thriving contemporary narrative form. Such an observer would also automatically assume that the term's ubiquity reflected unanimity about its meaning. But, in fact, disagreement about the precise nature of the Spanish picaresque genre, the definition of the concept *picaresque*, and the narratological usefulness of the term *picaresque novel* has never been more intense than it is now in the immediate wake of the perceived surge of contemporary picaresque fictions, as a brief survey of the picaresque in literary scholarship will illustrate.

CHAPTER 2
The Picaresque Genre in Literary Scholarship

The outer dimensions of the full range of critical approaches to the picaresque can be measured both diachronically and synchronically by the juxtaposition of the following two passages, written almost a century apart. The first is from an anonymous essay, "Picaresco Romances," which appeared in *The Southern Review* in 1867:

But . . . why disinter these fossil remains of an extinct literature? The picaresco novel is as dead as the dodo: why disturb its bones? We answer that a fossil literature is at least as interesting as a fossil fauna.

The second is from Walter Allen's *The English Novel* (1954), and it both reflects and in turn is reflected in any number of literary dictionaries, handbooks, and surveys of the history of the novel:

If the word "picaresque" is now stretched, as it commonly is, to mean any novel in which the hero takes a journey whose course plunges him into all sorts, conditions, and classes of men, *The Pilgrim's Progress* is not so different in form from the conventional picaresque novel. (18)

We might call the first approach extrinsic or historistic because it tends to see picaresque narrative primarily in its historical context as a segment in the development of the novel and as an episode of the social and literary history of Spain; it is primarily positivistic and sees picaresque fiction diachronically as a predominantly closed phenomenon. The second approach is intrinsic (as opposed to extrinsic) and formal (as opposed to historistic), and it sees picaresque narrative synchronically as an open phenomenon because it tends to lift the picaresque out of its geographic location in space and its historical location in time and sees it as a developing and influential form or convention that writers have at their disposal or as a tradition inside of which writers may work and on which they may build.

The range of possibilities between them has yielded few universally acceptable syntheses, despite a sizable and still growing body of scholarship during the last three decades. It sometimes seems that in the process of clarifying some particular aspect of the picaresque, each new critical work contributes simultaneously to the theoretical disarray of the concept as a whole, until at one extreme the very existence of a historical picaresque genre is called into question, while at the other extreme the term *picaresque* is so diminished from its historical origins that it becomes critically meaningless. To want to use the term with even a minimum of historical consciousness and a modicum of literary-critical conscientiousness now requires sifting through an increasingly unsortable number of puzzle pieces, only to find that no coherent picture emerges even as the number of pieces multiplies. While such insubstantiality and inconstancy are thematically essential in the world rendered in those fictions we call picaresque, they are useless attributes in critical tools.

Complicating this problematic situation even more is the tendency toward value judgment, which straddles both extremes. While value judgments are necessary (indeed, implicit) in studies of individual works, we find them here applied to an entire narrative type. Standing toward the closed end of the critical spectrum, Sir Walter Scott in his 1827 essay on Defoe brushes off what he calls the "Romance of Roguery" as a "coarse species of amusement" that is dangerous to the lower classes and that we feel ashamed reading, no matter how much we may be amused. Well over a century later, about as far to the open end of the spectrum as one can get, R. W. B. Lewis in *The Picaresque Saint: Representative Figures in Contemporary Fiction* (1959) explores a number of fictions that virtually no one else has called picaresque, explaining that "the genre of fiction which has re-emerged to carry the adventures of the picaresque saint is the old and sometimes disreputable genre of the picaresque novel—the traditional account of the journeying rogue" (34). And a note before the title page of the English translation of Alfred Kern's *The Clown* (trans. Gerard Hopkins, 1960) says in the last paragraph: "A good circus story is wellnigh irresistible, but this is also much more; a picaresque novel raised to the level of literature." For Hispanists, on the other hand, no matter how much they themselves may be in disagreement about the nature of the genre, it is often a matter of pride to acknowledge Spain's contribution to the evolution of narrative forms. In *Literature and the Delinquent* (1967), Parker's overall purpose is to argue for due recognition of the picaresque: "The history of the modern European novel should be rewritten with a truer perspective" (137). Manuel Criado de Val's huge 1979 anthology *La picaresca* in the opening sentence of the preface calls the picaresque "the most original Spanish contribution to the world of literary culture" (9). Such assessments, which range from merely grudging acceptance of the existence of the form to polemics about its seminal importance for all subsequent European fiction, further distort the concept.

The mainstream of what has been written about picaresque fiction is the historically oriented approach, which sees it as a closed episode in the literary history of *siglo de oro* Spain and, in related forms of fiction, in the literary histories of England, France, and Germany as well. Often too extrinsic, often buried in documentation and burdened with philological luggage, this approach treads the path between art and life rather carelessly. At its best, it has left us with insights into the total situation of the picaresque, and out of it has come most of what we know and understand about it in its historical context in Spain and its influence on other literatures.

In the latter half of the nineteenth century, the picaresque was treated in short historical sketches that served as introductions to the texts of the fictions themselves, such as Buenaventura Carlos Aribau's "Novela picaresca" in *Novelistas anteriores a Cervantes*; the third volume of the *Biblioteca de autores españoles* (1858); in short historical surveys such as Henry Butler Clarke's "The Spanish Rogue-Story (Novela de Picaros)" (1898); or in histories of the novel, such as F. M. Warren's *A History of the Novel Previous to the Seventeenth Century* (1895). The plan was usually (1) a characterization of the type, (2) a theory of its origins, (3) a plot synopsis of each of the major works, and (4) a review of their imitators outside Spain. Warren devoted a whole chapter to the "picaresco novel" and called it the first form of realistic writing (287): "In the career of the picaro, the despised third estate avenged itself for the successes of Amadis and Palmerin" (289). According to Warren, the social conditions of Spain engendered picaresque fiction, creating a hero driven by hunger and insecurity. The English picaresque, on the other hand (and he refers specifically to Nashe's *Unfortunate Traveller*), created an adventurer for the sake of adventure, a "rough, rollicking Englishman type who at bottom is a solid, round uncorrupted Anglo-Saxon, whose sins are the result of his ungoverned temperament and not of his perverted moral judgment" (342). Jean J. Jusserand in *The English Novel in the Time of Shakespeare* (1890) treats the English picaresque as wholly rooted in the Spanish and speaks of "the barrenness of the greater part of the picaresque romances" (293). George Ticknor in his *History of Spanish Literature* (1891) more or less summarizes the consensus when he writes: "Taken as a class, they [the Spanish picaresque fictions] constitute a singular exhibition of character, and are, in fact, as separate and national in their air as anything in the whole body of modern literature" (III, 109). Among the first to devote an entire book to the subject was Javier Garriga in his *Estudio de la novela picaresca* (1891), in which he sees it as an exclusively Spanish manifestation of the *novela de costumbres*, or novel of manners, and he refers to it (in a phrase that will become an epithet) as the "tragedy and the epic of hunger" (22).

The focus of these and other early studies is primarily on the social milieu, on the literary climate that provoked a reaction against romances, and on the peculiar indigenousness of picaresque fiction to Spain. Outside of Spain, they suggest, the picaresque invariably changed its makeup or became something else entirely, or was merely conscious imitation of Spanish models. An extreme example of the sociological approach is Rafael Salillas's *El delincuente español* (1898), which studies various social types in their environments and emphasizes picaresque life and literature as peculiarly nationalistic qualities of Spain. Salillas also bases much of his study on what he conceives to be the three special qualities of "the Spanish soul": *caballeresca, picaresca,* and *religiosa.*

Any treatment of the picaresque, however, must begin with Frank Wadleigh Chandler's *Romances of Roguery* (1899), the first standard work on the subject and still among the most comprehensive. It laid the foundation for almost all subsequent criticism. Chandler's subtitle, *An Episode in the History of the Novel,* indicates his direction and his focus. Even further subtitled, *Part I: The Picaresque Novel in Spain,* it was to be followed by a study of the picaresque in France, Germany, Holland, and England, but this part was never completed. For Chandler, "the picaresque tale was indigenous to Spain" (3), but its elements had existed earlier and elsewhere in literature. The *Golden Ass* of Apuleius, except for the absence of roguery in the hero, is an important model because it supplied the form, though the content of the picaresque was a slow and independent growth of the Middle Ages. *The Dance of Death,* the *Roman de Renart,* parts of the *Decameron,* and *Till Eulenspiegel* all used picaresque subject matter in embryo. At the heart of the picaresque tale for Chandler was a special notion of the hero:

The romance of roguery, in fact, rather evolved negatively from the notion of the anti-hero. . . . Into the gap created by the recoil from the hero of fiction stepped the anti-hero of society—the Spanish picaro. He was the parody incarnate of the elder hero, the central figure of an opera-bouffe. But because observation and a return to nature were concerned in his very being, the picaro transcended other anti-heroes. They might contrast one fantasy with another; he must contrast the obviously real with the fantastic. A study of actual life was thus his aim, observation the method, and the most striking things of everyday experience the subject, as those of imaginary experience had been the matter of antecedent types. (14–15)

In form, Chandler goes on, the picaresque tale proved "the lowest type of book organism." Its unity "was an inferior unity, not that of time or place of action, but merely the identity of the hero" (16). The spirit of the antihero's story was necessarily satirical and corrective, and Spain was his landscape. Spain, with feudalism crumbling in the transition from a medieval to a modern state, was filled with class confusion. Royal employment alone was worth having, and the only gateways to advancement were the church, the government, or the army. "Even the ignorant and the boors disdained to stoop to the patient business of life" (21). The exile of the Jews and the ultimate expulsion of the Moriscos by Philip III in 1609 severely damaged the labor force in Spain, for they were the only groups who had not succumbed to the contempt for work. Adventure lay across the ocean in Spain's new lands. The stay-at-home, "if he would not work or starve, must pluck the elated wanderer" (23), and so the rogue with his deceptive measures went to work. Exhaustion and drainage as a result of its reaches abroad, internal mismanagement, expanding ecclesiastical power, the gypsy problem—all combined to make Spain ripe for a landscape of vagabondage and beggary:

The rogue of literature was only what he claimed to be. His creator brought him forward to expose in effigy the vices of the day. Taken from life, to be met with on the street at every turning, he was the best instrument for satire to be found. . . . Thus social conditions in Spain in the sixteenth and seventeenth centuries furnished an ample pretext for making the literary reaction expressive of a social one. The decadence presented all the material to inspire a corrective fiction; and the peculiar form of that fiction was determined both by the foregoing literary development from which it recoiled and by the social facts and failures which it emphasized. (42–44)

The Spanish rogue, according to Chandler, is "everything in what he does, nothing in character" (46). He stands "midway between the mere jester and the villain; he is neither the court fool nor the pirate, but he has actual and literary affiliations with both" (46). "Life to him is a problem to avoid, not to solve" (50). "He is the person to whom things happen" (52).

A similar characterization of the picaro was made two decades later by H. E. Watts in his "Quevedo and His Works, with an Essay on the Picaresque Novel" (1927). Watts defined the picaro as

one who was at odds with the world—a remnant left over in the making of society—a survival of the age gone by. Of his order were all the broken men of the time—a time in which there was much breaking of men—those who lived by their wits on the witless, the mumpers and beggars, strolling quacks, sham pilgrims. . . . The picaro was the adventurer who had missed his chance in the general scramble, who did not or could not go to Flanders or to America, or who, having been, had returned empty. He was the *conquistador* out of date—the gold-seeker run to seed. (29, 31)

But because picaresque fictions were primarily *libros de entretenimiento*, Chandler says, the society the picaro traverses is the main thing, and it is seen through the picaro's eyes: "We do not so much look at the rogue as borrow his eyes with which to look at the world" (60). Chandler describes this society and the various social types that repeatedly appear—students, hermits, doctors, priests, pilgrims, gypsies, innkeepers, actors, and so on—summarizing the emphasis on the social canvas when he writes that

so thorough a canvass of society for its own sake as the Spanish romances of roguery offered was scarcely again to be had. The novel of manners refined meant the study of manners already beginning to succumb to the personal interest, and for that reason the picaresque tale of the Spaniards in its very crudity is a mine of curious detail, and of value chiefly as such. (183)

Dividing the Spanish picaresque fictions into several stages, Chandler concludes that the picaresque finally decayed because "the fundamental conception of a rascal serving, defrauding, and satirizing masters, traversing all society to describe its faults and foibles, if excellent, was too eccentric to endure when the zest of novelty had worn away" (368). Moreover, a literature of villains "can never be more than a negative, transient literature" (369). In Spain, the romance of roguery "had lived its day and fulfilled its mission" (394). Its development abroad was to lead to a different kind of fiction: the subordination of observation and intrigue to the personal interest in France and the supplanting of the personal by the deeper interests of morals and of character in England, where "the scene of conflict was shifted to the conscience" (396). The Spanish novels developed not into a new or different picaresque fiction but through "the perfected novel of manners to the modern novel of character" (397).

Chandler must be looked at in some detail because most of his ideas have had wide currency, especially among non-Hispanists, and continue to do so in many dictionaries of literary terms and in the capsule definitions that form the core of received opinions about the rise of the novel in Europe. Contemporary with Chandler's work, though actually written earlier (1895), is Fonger de Haan's *An Outline of the History of the Novela Picaresca in Spain* (1903). De Haan's method is similar to Chandler's; he examines the same literary antecedents, and he too finds the picaro's origin in actual society. His definition of the genre has had equally wide currency:

It is the prose autobiography of a person, real or imaginary, who strives by fair means and by foul to make a living, and in relating his experience in various classes of society points out the evils which come under his observation. (8)

De Haan's is the positivistic approach at its purest, because for him picaresque fiction is not so much a fictional type to be considered with aesthetic criteria as it is a "mine of information concerning the habits, customs, ways of thinking, of dressing, of eating and drinking, of seeking diversion, of travelling, etc., of all classes in Spain during the time of the Habsburghs" (66). He calls finally for a "sort of encyclopedia of our knowledge" gathered from them, a *kultur-geschichtliche* treatment of the subject. In a comparative review of Chandler and de Haan in *Revue hispanique* in 1903, James Fitzmaurice-Kelly wrote that "Professor de Haan's work seems to be more serviceable, more exact, more suggestive, and better written than Professor Chandler's."

Between them, Chandler and de Haan mapped out the territory that subsequent critical work has, to a great extent, made use of. They investigated with great thoroughness the social and literary backgrounds, attempted a definition of the genre, gave plot synopses of the major works, and explored the reasons for the decline of picaresque fiction and its direct influence on other literatures. Before them, there had been only one major comparative study, Albert Schultheiss's *Der Schelmenroman der Spanier und seine Nachbildungen* (1893), and it was much more limited in scope than Chandler's and de Haan's work. During the first half of the twentieth century, studies of the picaresque would rarely be so comprehensive; now critics tend to discuss aspects of picaresque fiction rather than the whole of it. Typical directions following Chandler and de Haan are studies of themes such as Guzmán Alvarez's *El amor en la novela picaresca española* (1958); studies of direct influence such as Martin Hume's *Spanish Influence on English Literature* (1905), Hubert Rausse's *Zur Geschichte des spanischen Schelmenromans in Deutschland* (1908), and Manuel García Blanco's *Mateo Alemán y la novela picaresca alemana* (1928); studies of the Spanish national character or soul, like Manuel de Montolíu's *El alma de España y sus reflejos en la literatura del siglo de oro* (1942) or Gerald Brenan's section on the picaresque in his *The Literature of the Spanish People* (1951):

These [picaresque] novels depict as a rule a child growing up under sordid conditions and making his way through the world where everything is hostile and dangerous. He has no arms but his mother wit: by using it he becomes a criminal, but essentially he is innocent and well-intentioned and it is the wickedness of the world that corrupts him. Conversion and submission to the Church will enable him at the end of the book to be saved, but meanwhile what holds the attention is the contrast between the solitary, struggling individual and the hostile world around him. I believe that the awareness of this contrast is one of the things most deeply ingrained in the Spanish character. The Spanish soul is a border castle, adapted for defence and offence in a hostile land: *soberbia*, or pride, and an eternal suspiciousness are its most ingrained qualities, together with a distrust of any but its own skill or weapons. But what the garrison feels all the time is loneliness. (174)

In the chapter "Der Ritter als Schelm oder die Novela Picaresca" in his *Geschichte der spanischen Nationalliteratur in ihrer Blütezeit* (1929), Ludwig Pfandl distinguished among three kinds of picaresque forms in the *siglo de oro* narratives of Spain. First, there is the "idealistic-satirical," in which the writer seeks to express a certain nationalistic idea or concept (*El Buscón, Guzmán de Alfarache*); second, the "realistic-optimistic," in which an understanding of the national problem is not very marked, and thus this form lacks the deeper meaning of the first—it interests itself primarily in providing entertainment through portraying the likeable qualities of the contemporary social world (*La hija de Celestina, Estebanillo González, La pícara Justina*); and, third, the "descriptive-novelistic," in which the colorful description of milieu moves to the foreground and provides a transitional form toward certain novelistic developments (*Marcos de Obregón*, the works of Castillo Solórzano). Such internal groupings, or subgenres, within the picaresque genre are made by a number of critics and literary historians, though the principles of subdivision differ somewhat in each case.

There are, furthermore, studies of the baroque context, such as Enrique Moreno Báez's *Lección y sentido del "Guzmán de Alfarache"* (1948) and Werner Beck's *Die Anfänge des deutschen Schelmenromans: Studien zur frühbarocken Erzählung* (1957), which sees the "Schelmenroman als desillusionistischer Weltspiegel" (71) and the picaro in Alemán as "Verkörperung einer Art von Zeitkrankheit." Ildefonso Pereda Valdés's *La novela picaresca y el pícaro en España y America* (1950) studies the real-life picaro, as Salillas had done earlier. Sometimes Chandler's ground is covered again, though more hastily, as in Guillermo Rojas Carrasco's *La novela picaresca en la literatura española* (1919). There is an emphasis on biography in George Haley's *Vicente Espinel and Marcos de Obregón, A Life and Its Literary Representation* (1950) and Antonio Papell's *Quevedo; su tiempo, su vida, su obra* (1947). Américo Castro in his "Perspectiva de la novela picaresca," published in *Hacia Cervantes* (1967), was the first to suggest that Mateo Alemán was a *converso*, or converted Jew, thus initiating a continuing line of interpretation that the picaresque reflected the convert's resentment against the society that rejected him. Frutos Gómez in "El antihéroe y su actitud vital (Sentido de la novela picaresca)" (1950) interprets picaresque fiction from the period perspective, seeing it as a degenerated literary attempt to embody the ideals of the reforming movements influenced by Erasmus's *Praise of Folly*. Some historical causes of the decline of the picaresque are studied in Peter Dunn's *Castillo Solórzano and the Decline of the Spanish Novel* (1952), Samuel Gili Gaya's "Apogeo y desintegración de la novela picaresca" (1953), and William Atkinson's "Studies in Literary Decadence: The Picaresque Novel" (1927). Etymological studies such as Nykl's "Pícaro" (1929), Spitzer's "Pícaro," which comments on Nykl (1930), and May's " 'Pícaro': A Suggestion" (1952); contemporary problems of censorship, such as Moldenhauer's "Spanische Zensur und Schelmenroman" (1927); direct literary sources, as in Ford's "Possible Foreign Sources of the Spanish Novel of Roguery" (1913) and Kirkpatrick's "The First Picaresque Romance" (1928); studies of the rise of realism, like Gustave Reynier's *Le Roman réaliste au XVIIe siècle* (1914); and publication histories such as Petriconi's "Zur Chronologie und Verbreitung des spanischen Schelmenromans" (1928) are further aspects of the historical context of picaresque fiction that this mainstream of scholarship in the picaresque has explored. A so-called "Nueva interpretación de la novela picaresca" (1937) by Miguel Herrero is primarily historistic; he sees the picaresque as a low-life vision that was prevalent in other countries as well, but Spain expressed its vision in literature, while other countries expressed theirs in the visual arts. For Herrero, the picaresque is "un producto seudoasético, hijo de las circunstancias peculiares del espíritu español," which made of the autobiographical confessions of sinners an "instrumento de corrección."

A reevaluation of the prevalent historical focus is Alexander A. Parker's *Literature and the Delinquent: The Picaresque Novel in Spain and Europe 1599–1753* (1967), which is an attempt to look at the picaresque from a new angle. It is the vagueness of the term *picaresque* and what he finds included in the category, as well as excluded from it, that concern him. His aim is "to suggest than an important section of the history of the European novel needs to undergo revision." His first step is to reject *rogue* as an equivalent for *pícaro*, substituting for it the term *delinquent*, by which he means "an offender against the moral and civil laws, not a criminal." The distinguishing feature of the picaresque for Parker is "the atmosphere of delinquency" (6). He wants to do away with four misleading assumptions that have helped to prevent the best of the Spanish works from getting their share of serious attention in the sphere of comparative literature. These assumptions, as summarized by Parker, constitute the heart of the mainstream closed approach:

The first is the belief that the picaresque genre arose in Spain because Spain at that time was the country in which social conditions were most conducive to the production of delinquents in large numbers. The second is the assumption that the picaresque novels are essentially comic, since their authors turned to the real-life phenomenon of the delinquent in order to produce a satirical counterblast to the romances. The third is the belief that, since the novels were born out of prevailing social conditions, the society they portray is more important than the individual characters they present as protagonists. The last misconception is that, since the novels are essentially humorous and deal with unsavory material, they have no real moral interest, any avowed moral intentions being hypocritical, or at best conventional, lip-service to social propriety. The first of these assumptions is practically universal; the other three derive from Chandler. (9)

One by one, Parker argues against the validity of these received assumptions, arriving finally at his own thesis: that the picaresque arises "as an exposition of the theme of freedom, including the concept of moral freedom" (14), as a " 'truthful' literature in response to the explicit demands of the Counter-Reformation" (22), and that the emergence of the genre in Spain is explained more satisfactorily by this literary-cultural background "than by economic conditions, Jewish *conversos*, or qualities in the national character" (24). In his study of the major works, Parker explores the guilt, existential anguish, suffering, and tragedy in delinquency—the delinquency of the individual against society, the collective delinquency of mankind against God—which for him constitute the main picaresque tradition.

Himself reacting against historistic and sociological approaches, Parker nevertheless works within the same perspective; he reorients the concept of the picaresque within that focus. His approach is essentially closed; he excludes examination of a possible ahistorical tradition: "It may or may not be useful to call such novels as *Huckleberry Finn, Felix Krull*, or *Augie March* 'picaresque,' but they do not form part of the rise or fall of the historically definable *genre* that is my theme" (vi).

At the other extreme of the scholarship spectrum is a trend that might be called "open" or ahistorical because it sees the picaresque as a basic narrative structure that may have flowered in Spain during a particular period but is essentially a universal narrative type. While not rejecting sociopolitical perspectives and period contexts, this approach tends more toward the formalistic, examining works themselves for technique and meaning, and in general evading the controversy about genre. In Hans Robert Jauss's "Ursprung und Bedeutung der Ich-Form im *Lazarillo de Tormes*" (1957), for example, the autobiographical form receives attention as an important narrative technique. Francisco Rico's *La novela picaresca y el punto de vista* (1970), translated by Charles Davis and Harry Sieber as *The Spanish Picaresque Novel and the Point of View* (1984), is a thorough attempt to define the picaresque genre on the basis of narrative technique. Edward Friedman's *The Antiheroine's Voice: Narrative Discourse and Transformations of the Piscaresque* (1987) is a study that combines feminist concerns with a study of the function of narrative discourse in picaras from *Justina* to the twentieth century. Rather than using the texts as evidence for or against the existence of a genre, the texts themselves are formally analyzed, even deconstructed.

One of the central concerns of this more synchronic approach to the picaresque is the establishment of a universal narrative type: Is there a narrative form that can be called picaresque apart from (though not denying) literary-historical ties to a particular place, time, or cultural milieu? Is there a distinction to be made between the picaresque genre (a historical manifestation) and the picaresque narrative tradition (an ahistorical narrative "deep structure")? As these issues are explored, the scope becomes much more comparative. This approach, too, began in the nineteenth century. James Fitzmaurice-Kelly, for example, suggested in *A History of Spanish Literature* (1898) that *Lazarillo* "set a fashion that spread to all countries, and finds a nineteenth-century manifestation in the pages of *Pickwick*. . . . Whoever wrote the book, he fixed forever the type of the comic prose epic as rendered by the needy, and he did it in such wise as to defy all competition" (158–60). Waldo Frank in "The First Rogue" (1926) wrote that the true heirs of the Spanish picaro "are his collateral and remote descendants of a modern world in which once again energy has become aspirant and religious. They are the heroes of Stendhal. Above all, they appear in Russia—that other extreme of Europe which touches Spain in the domain of the spirit: the buyer of 'Dead Souls' of Gogol, the mystic criminals of Dostoievski" (561).

For the diffuseness and dilution that sometimes mar the extremes of this approach we must go again to Chandler, whose two-volume *The Literature of Roguery* (1907) is the source of its major conceptions, as *Romances of Roguery* is for the approaches at the other extreme. In this later work, Chandler surveyed rogue literature in Holland, France, and Germany, and then turned his attention to England, with a vast survey of the rogue figure in jest books, criminal biographies, beggar books, and coney-catching pamphlets, and their transformations in the works of Nashe, Chettle, Head, and Kirkman, and through the eighteenth century (Defoe, Fielding, Smollett) to Scott, Bulwer-Lytton, and Dickens, and finally to roguery in contemporary fiction (Twain, Kipling) and the literature of crime detection. In the course of his survey, he ventured a more precise definition of the picaresque than he had done in *Romances of Roguery*:

As conceived in Spain and matured in France, the picaresque novel is the comic biography (or more often the autobiography) of an anti-hero who makes his way in the world through the service of masters, satirizing their personal faults, as well as their trades and professions. It possesses, therefore, two poles of interest—one, the rogue and his tricks; the other, the manners he pillories. (I, 5)

The very breadth of Chandler's study diffuses the concept of the picaresque. It is now merely a type within the larger body of rogue literature that Chandler calls a genre and that is determined primarily by subject matter. Opening up the concept to generically unmanageable scope, Chandler is ultimately responsible— as he was for the historical approach—for the confusingly loose concept of the picaresque that is the extreme of the open or ahistorical approach.

Reacting against this other seminal work of Chandler's, as Parker was to react against *Romances of Roguery*, Claudio Guillén in *The Anatomies of Roguery*

(1987; written as a dissertation at Harvard in 1953) tries to compensate for de Haan and Chandler's failure to "underline sufficiently the emergence of a novelistic form from the general body of roguish literature" (iv). The two main difficulties in the attempts to define the picaresque, Guillén says, have been "the failure to limit the subject of inquiry by making generic distinctions and distinguishing the novelistic form from such related works as the anatomies of roguery" and the fallacy of "assigning to the whole the quality of the part—for example, the psychology of the hero, characteristics of structure or types of subject-matter" (377).

Robert Alter's *Rogue's Progress: Studies in the Picaresque Novel* (1964) builds on Guillén's statement in *The Anatomies of Roguery* that "the basic situation of the picaresque novel is the solitude of its principal character in the world" (383). Alter studies only one Spanish work (*Lazarillo*) and then moves to *Gil Blas, Tom Jones, Moll Flanders, Peregrine Pickle*, and the "Heirs of the Tradition" (Stendhal, Thackeray, Twain, Bellow, Mann, and Cary). Alter's statement of purpose summarizes well this broader tendency in scholarship to view the picaresque beyond historical confines:

In some recent criticism . . . there is a tendency to see "picaresque" as a broad ahistorical category—like "comic," "tragic," "satiric," "bucolic"—which is applicable to works of literature of all ages. . . . There seems little point in using a term like "picaresque" without a serious sense of responsibility to the definite historical phenomenon from which the term derives. And yet I think there is a sound intuition behind these broader applications of the term, for it seems reasonable to assume that the picaresque novel is not simply a long-finished episode in Western literature but rather a permanent addition to the storehouse of literary resources, capable of regenerating and transforming itself in a surprising variety of new environments. (viii–ix)

Alter's book appeared after the beginning of a marked upsurge in criticism on the picaresque, and so "Rogue's Progress" took its place among studies exploring "uses and mutations of the picaresque," "the picaresque saint," "variations on picaresque," "der ewige Simplizissimus," the "Wiederkehr der Schelme," the "renaissance du roman picaresque," and its "actualité." The last two years of the decade saw no fewer than seven book-length studies: Edmond Cros, *Protée et le gueux*; Wilfried van der Will, *Pikaro heute*; Stuart Miller, *The Picaresque Novel*; R. L. Giddings, *The Tradition of Smollett*; and Parker's *Literature and the Delinquent*, all published in 1967, which also saw the publication of Robert Scholes's *The Fabulators* and Ronald Paulson's *The Fictions of Satire*, both with long sections on the picaresque; and a translation of Marcel Bataillon's work as *Pícaros y picaresca* in Spain as Bruno Schleussner's *Der neopikareske Roman* and Helmut Heidenreich's *Die pikarische Welt* both appeared in Germany in 1969. Anthologies of picaresque fiction in German, French, and Italian (but not in English) translation were published, and the sixth edition of Valbuena Prat's *La novela picaresca española* appeared. On average, a dissertation or two on the picaresque was indexed every year during the 1960s in *DAI* (Dissertation Abstracts International).

In the midst of this surge, Heidenreich's *Pikarische Welt* (1969), the first anthology of criticism on the picaresque, provided much-needed orientation in, as well as perspectives on, what had now become a confusing proliferation of scholarship. Heidenreich's compilation includes essays representing every possible approach to the picaresque, including Ihad Hassan's "The Anti-Hero in Modern British and American Fiction" (1958), which had been responsible for some of the stretching of the term in contemporary contexts. In his introduction, Heidenreich poses the questions that motivated the anthology and guided the selection of its contents: Are we dealing here with a specific area of the genre "novel," or with subject matter rooted in wider literary and extraliterary spheres? Should we continue to use a term that defines a temporally and geographically located narrative type (a term that, moreover, has firmly established itself in the major literary languages) for everything between *The Satyricon* and *The Good Soldier Schweik* that shows similarities? Heidenreich claims that much of the problem stems from the relatively late acceptance of novelistic fiction into the sanctioned literary genres. The extremely conservative aesthetic doctrines prevalent in Spain and the hybrid nature of picaresque fiction made it difficult to consider the picaresque as literature at all. As a result, the picaresque never achieved independent literary status, a condition that remained until the middle of the nineteenth century, when scholars began to treat the picaresque as a distinct literary type. By the 1890s, the concept *novela picaresca* (and its German, French, and English equivalents) was well established, after scholars had concerned themselves in the preceding decades with the biographical, textual, and linguistic problems inherent in the preparation of authoritative texts. By the turn of the century, then, three distinct critical tendencies had emerged: the positivistic, which saw the picaresque novel as a deliberate antiromance and as a sociohistorical document of the decadent times; the period perspective, which explored the picaresque in the light of Renaissance and baroque characteristics and consequently saw the fiction didactically as an ideological weapon of humanism and the Counter-Reformation, with the picaro ushering in a new image of man; and Castro's theory that the picaresque reflected the discontent of the racial outsider or *converso*. As literature of social protest, as didactic proselityzing, and as literary revenge of the persecuted outsider, the picaresque could now be taken seriously, leading to a more thorough investigation of the formal aspects of picaresque fiction. A concentration on technique and other aesthetic concerns, with the work as center of attention, has now emerged in place of the sweeping generalizations about the genre as a whole, which often approached the fiction from the perspectives of social history, art history, theology, philosophy, and other extraliterary fields.

Miller in *The Picaresque Novel* tried to construct an "ideal genre type," showing how a number of coherent formal devices unite to produce a specific picaresque content and emotional response. Using plot, pattern, and rhythm as his major divisions and examining a limited number of works (*El Buscón, Guz-*

mán, Simplicissimus, Gil Blas, Moll Flanders, and *Roderick Random*), Miller explores the major narrative devices to arrive finally at his definition:

A picaresque novel is a novel with an episodic plot. The episodic plot, together with the Fortune pattern, the accident motif, and the rush of events pattern, projects a universe in a state of chaos. This universe is different from worlds implied by patterns of action in romance, comedy, tragedy, and the realistic novel because the plot patterns in these types of fiction are different. . . . [The picaro's] internal chaos is externally reflected in his protean roles. This instability of personality is seen in the picaresque novel as a reflection of the outer chaos discovered by the plot patterns. The picaresque character is not merely a rogue, and his chaos of personality is greater than any purely moral chaos. It reflects a total lack of structure in the world, not merely a lack of ethical or social structure. (131)

Although Miller's book elicited some harsh reviews, its attempt to describe a genre type is a step in the right direction. He avoids the historical narrowness that governs one extreme approach, and he stays away from an overly broad concept at the other extreme. More important, he concentrates on narrative technique more than on subject matter and on reader response well before it becomes fashionable. Curiously, Miller was criticized for an undue emphasis on the picaro's existential condition, yet Miller himself rejected any contemporary picaresque except for Ellison's *Invisible Man*. Paradoxically, a genre definition with useful applicability to contemporary fiction while not violating the historical genre is rigidly confined by the author himself to the picaresque in its ''classical period'' with explicit doubts that the so-called revival of picaresque in contemporary fiction conforms ''to the traditional patterns of the picaresque enough to assign them to the genre'' (132–33).

At the other extreme is a conception such as that of Paul West in his two-volume *The Modern Novel* (1963), which gives a completely structureless definition of the picaresque. West sees the picaresque as a dominant form in contemporary fiction because it ''repudiates the organizing mind and exemplifies inability to use the immediate literary past,'' and ''it gives the iconoclast, as well as the man who can connect nothing with nothing, an ideal medium. When a coherent world-view is lacking, the picaresque can still make points with the minimum of manipulation and communicate the flavour of experiences that seem incapable of being interpreted'' (140). This means, apparently, that when there is nothing to say, the picaresque can say it—a complete reversal of the Spanish picaresque, which had plenty to say. Such a concept is fairly typical of the tendency to stretch the term until it becomes so far removed from any historical grounding that it loses any regulative concept of genre. Even Wellek and Warren in their highly influential *Theory of Literature* (1948) merely echo a definition that could be found in any dozens of studies of fiction at midcentury: ''In the picaresque novel, the chronological sequence is all there is: this happened and then that. The adventures, each an incident, which might be an independent tale, are connected by the figure of the hero'' (215). For years, critics of fiction and

compilers of literary handbooks had been handing such label-like definitions
back and forth whenever something "episodic" tied together by an "antihero"
needed a name, and the way was paved for the diffusion of the concept into the
context of contemporary fiction, yielding a definition like West's, which in
making the picaresque express meaninglessness becomes itself meaningless as
any kind of definition, an absurd circle.

Frustrated, W. M. Frohock in a series of articles in the late 1960s attacked
the extremes of the open approach. In "The Idea of the Picaresque" (1967), he
concludes that "comparative literature as a discipline accepts an obligation to
use critical terms responsibly," and contemporary approaches to the picaresque
were falling short of that standard. One solution would be to confine usage of
picaresque to those works clearly belonging to the tradition, "but only a pedant
would, or could attempt this, and an alternative solution must be found. This
solution is, on the basis of the evidence, to use the term when we feel we must
but with the realization that when we use it we can count on being misunderstood"
(52). In the more polemical "The Failing Center: Recent Fiction and the Picaresque Tradition" (1969), Frohock doubts whether the idea of the picaresque
can help us to understand what has happened in contemporary fiction and whether
it is worth "the sacrifice of an established critical concept" (69). In an interview
with Gerber and Gemmett ("Picaresque and Modern Literature: A Conversation
with W. M. Frohock," 1970), he repeats his essential skepticism, pointing out
furthermore that the real dilemma in current usage of the term is in applying
only one or two characteristics of the picaresque in order to make the whole
picaresque, a problem Guillén had already perceived in his *Anatomies of Roguery*.
Such partial usage of the concept could actually be obscuring other important
aspects of the works that may lead to a better definition of what is going on in
the new fiction. "I doubt that taking over the concept of the picaresque really
helps much. What we have is a new kind of literature" (197).

Scholarship on the picaresque continues to flourish in the 1970s and 1980s
and it would take a book-length study to survey it all. Non-Hispanists, after
having to rely far too long on Chandler and a few scattered items, now have a
growing bibliography to refer to, although the Spanish fictions, with the exception
of *Lazarillo* and *El Buscón*, are still mostly inaccessible. Harry Sieber's concise
but comprehensive *The Picaresque* came out in 1977, followed a year later by
his *Language and Society in "Lazarillo de Tormes,"* a study of "the modes of
operation that exist between the text and the language with which it is produced"
(viii). Richard Bjornson's *The Picaresque Hero in European Fiction* (also 1977)
studies the same literary-historical ground Parker did (*Lazarillo* to Smollett) but
from a wider and less polemical perspective:

During the two-hundred-year period in which picaresque fiction flourished, European
society was undergoing significant changes in social organization; as the feudal order
declined in most countries, the increasingly important middle classes began to provide a
dynamic but often frustrated impetus toward a redefinition of established aristocratic
values and modes of perception. Picaresque novels written against the background of

these conflicting ideologies manifest numerous different attitudes toward the rise of bourgeois individualism, but because the essential picaresque situation involves the paradigmatic confrontation between an isolated individual and a hostile society, these novels
almost invariably reflect a world view defined in terms of the author's position on precisely
this question. (4)

Bjornson's close readings of almost all of the works in Valbuena Prat's anthology
are not intended to culminate in a definition of a genre type but rather in a
"dynamic model" flexible enough to encompass works in their specific historical
contexts while simultaneously identifying shared characteristics that would go
to make up an ideal genre type. Bjornson's focus is on three of the most significant
aspects of such a model: the lower-class wandering hero, the structural conventions that become associated with the telling of his story, and the ideological
and moral assumptions of each work itself.

In 1979 two important books on the picaresque appeared in English—Peter
N. Dunn's *The Spanish Picaresque Novel* and Alexander Blackburn's *The Myth
of the Picaro*—and they could not be more different. Dunn's is a survey, free
of any single controlling approach, for the non-Hispanist, that makes Chandler's
work obsolete. Blackburn's is the widest-ranging study yet of the picaresque in
all of its transformations; he studies works that others have excluded or stopped
short of confronting. Of the books published so far on twentieth-century picaresque (like Schleussner's and van der Will's), Blackburn's is the most securely
anchored in the historical picaresque. He focuses on what he calls "the fundamental situation of the literary picaro [which] is the loneliness of an individual
isolated *within* society" (19) and explores the transformation of this elemental
human condition over four centuries in the literature of Spain, England, France,
Germany, Russia, and the United States. In the 1980s Ife's *Reading and Fiction
in Golden-Age Spain* (1985) and Reed's *An Exemplary History of the Novel*
(1981) provide new insights into the emergence of novelistic forms and the
picaresque's role in it; 1986 saw the publication of the first anthology of criticism
in English, with *Upstarts, Wanderers or Swindlers: Anatomy of the Picaro, A
Critical Anthology*, by Gustavo Pellón and Julio Rodríguez-Luis, whose purpose
is clearly stated in their introduction:

We believe that any clear understanding of the picaresque novel must be grounded on a
solid acquaintance with a body of international criticism which represents various approaches, but whose major concern is to comprehend the evolution of the Spanish picaresque. It is only after examining how the Spanish picaresque has been understood by
Spanish and foreign scholars that we may be able to make sense out of the system of
diachronic as well as synchronic relations that characterizes the study of the picaresque
genre and to begin to deduce some general laws about the existence and evolution of a
picaresque mode. (10)

Coming almost two decades after Frohock's initial critical alert, such a syn-
thesizing methodology seems the most sensible way to reconcile the sometimes
mutually negating approaches we have been briefly surveying here. But achieving

a solid acquaintance with this body of criticism is becoming less and less manageable as it grows in size and diversity in half a dozen languages. While our
knowledge about the picaresque in Spain has never been more extensive or
comprehensive, our sense of a definable picaresque genre seems to become more
and more elusive—the literary equivalent, perhaps, of obscuring the forest by
paying too much attention to three or four trees.

In the last chapter of *The Spanish Picaresque Novel*, Peter Dunn surveys the
major generic theories that have been proposed or are implied in some of the
exemplary critical studies devoted to the picaresque, and none strikes him as
wholly satisfactory. The crucial problem, he suggests, resides in the one common
characteristic that the Spanish fictions share: "not conformity to a model, but
discomformity. Those works which we can see were most original are most
antagonistic to their predecessors in the way that they make shared formal elements signify something radically different" (144). In a later essay, "Cervantes
De/Re-Constructs the Picaresque" (1982), Dunn concludes (for the time being)
that "both genre theory and literary history are in disarray," "that we can no
longer talk usefully about 'the picaresque novel' as a well defined genre," and
that it is time to begin "deconstructing that nineteenth-century invention, the
picaresque, and the criticism that has kept it in place" (131). Howard Mancing
in "The Picaresque Novel: A Protean Form" (1979) suggests that the attempt
to arrive at a genre concept that will include fictions beyond the Spanish and
their immediate imitators is doomed to frustration: "Proteus has ultimately assumed so many forms that he is literally undistinguishable in a crowd; in fact,
he is the crowd" (197). Frank J. Kearful in "Spanish Rogues and English
Foundlings: On the Disintegration of Picaresque" (1971) asserts that the picaresque in Spain "fully exhausted its own possibilities" and that "positing a
platonically ideal, mythic 'picaresque,' of which the Spanish is but a local,
temporal, manifestation, may be an interesting intellectual exercise but it has
little use for practical literary criticism or genuine literary history" (384). Most
radical of all, Daniel Eisenberg in "Does the Picaresque Novel Exist?" (1979)
calls for abandonment of the term, on the basis that a genre in any coherent
sense of the word never existed in reality, not even in *siglo de oro* Spain, and
that continued usage of the term distorts the individual works that are said to
belong to such a genre by forcing on them characteristics that they do not really
share.

These observations bring us back full and frustrating circle to the discussion
of generic theory. Mancing, Kearful, and Eisenberg to some extent demonstrate
and thus validate Dunn's diagnosis that genre theory is in disarray, for their
expectations of genre theory are that it be rigidly what in literary practice it
cannot be: a prescriptive pattern into which individual works neatly fit. Were
such a pigeonhole to exist, it would indeed violate the integrity of the individual
work that slips relatively easily into such a mold. The ease of fit would itself
become a criterion of value for both the genre and the work. Inclusion and
exclusion would become, inevitably, value judgments that could not help but

distort individual works, and the works that conformed most exactly to the contours of the generic mold would confirm the existence of their genre while simultaneously destroying their own uniqueness and originality. The work that occupies this generic space most precisely, without gaps or bulges, is the prototype of its genre, for in such a conception of genre there can be only one individual work that can be generically pure. And it follows from this that the prototypical work would also become the measure of value for other individual works. The more closely other individual works share qualities with such an authentic model, the more imitative, derivative, unoriginal, and inauthentic they will be judged to be. A genre thus conceived negates its very reason for being, which is to help us understand how individual works work in an intertextual order or system. When a prototype is made to "guard" its generic "space," so to speak (as *Guzmán* is for Bataillon, as *El Buscón* is for Parker, as *Lazarillo* is for many others), all individual works approaching that space will be driven away to varying distances from the closed literary gate; their permitted proximity will depend on their generic aggressiveness, which in turn will determine their literary status as individual works. Such a genre concept paradoxically makes genre serve uniqueness through exclusion, thereby cancelling itself out as a genre. Such kind-ness is hardly kind to other texts.

What is a picaresque novel? Is novel X a picaresque novel? Perhaps we have been asking generic questions the wrong way, in futile search of answers that literary works, unlike classifiable objects in the material world, can never supply. Perhaps our questions ought to be more on the order of: What do the contemporaneous fictions X, Y, and Z seem to share in spite of their obvious dissimilarities? Is fiction A, at a later or earlier historical moment, functioning narratively in the same or similar ways as X, Y, and Z? The process is automatic for the reader (and the writer), and it should be given its due in generic theory, which since the Renaissance has not been adequate to the emergence of new literary forms because it wants Aristotelian certainty in a universe of texts that assert their individuality over their literary ancestry. Neither *Lazarillo* nor *Guzmán* occupies the generic space that has been called "the picaresque novel" for so long. What happened when *Guzmán* attracted *Lazarillo* to itself at the beginning of the seventeenth century in Spain was the construction of a prototype, fiction P, from both of them. Fiction P created the genre, and fiction P exists as a real text in literary history as much as the texts *Lazarillo* and *Guzmán* do. A genre and its prototype are a construct, an extratext—a fiction—and this fiction is more dynamically active in the creation of new fictions than are the individual fictional texts from which it was constructed. Moreover, fiction P itself changes every time it helps engender a new fiction, which in turn also changes all previously existing texts related to P; when *El Buscón* and *La pícara Justina* appear, the whole contextuality of fiction P, *Lazarillo*, and *Guzmán* reshapes itself to accommodate them. Fiction P is always paradigmatic, prototypical, and protean (and, in this specific instance, picaresque) and intersects each text of a syntagmatic sequence of fictions. Rather than trying out texts by jamming them into a generic space already occupied exclusively by one privileged text, a genre prototype so conceived and constructed might prove more adequate in our critical discourses about texts as orders. Pursuing fiction P will be the subject of the next two chapters.

CHAPTER 3
The Picaresque Mode

At the turn of the seventeenth century in Spain, the picaresque was narratively novel, but it was not yet a novel. Linking the terms *picaresque* and *novel* has perhaps done more to thwart a generic definition of the picaresque than have, on the one hand, a too rigid sense of genre, and on the other, a postromantic distrust of genre theory itself. Cervantes was consciously writing *novelas*—"Yo soy el primero que he novelado en lengua castellana," he asserts in the preface to his *Novelas ejemplares* (1613)—but his model was Boccaccio's self-styled *novelle* of the *Decameron*, which were "new" because they did not retell traditional stories and which Cervantes combined with the Spanish tradition of the *ejemplo*. When we use the term *novel* today, we quite clearly do not mean narratives of that kind. Yet we are not clear about what we do mean by the term. The search for a valid generic concept of the novel has intensified during the last several decades, as even a cursory glance through the pages of such journals as *Genre* and *Novel* will verify; a *Genre* special topics issue (spring 1981), for example, was called *Novel vs. Fiction: The Contemporary Reformation*, and studies such as Gustavo Pérez Firmat's "The Novel as Genres" (1979)—an exemplary approach to genre theory—reminds us that the novel "is not one but many genres, as many genres as there have been groups of conventions designated by the word" (289) and that the concept *novel* "is an extended individual, a text of texts, constituted from the generic properties of those works we call novels" (269). In the first chapter of his *The Fantastic: A Structural Approach to a Literary Genre* (*Introduction à la littérature fantastique*, 1970), Tzvetan Todorov suggests an approach to genre that Pérez Firmat uses as a springboard for his own. Todorov asserts that literature is a language whose every utterance is ungrammatical at the moment of enunciation; each new text modifies its class or genre by changing the very grammar or generic convention in which it speaks. Todorov also claims that in literary criticism, one does not need to examine all the members of a class in order to abstract the properties of that class; and, most important, Todorov distinguishes two kinds of genres: theoretical (which are deduced from a theory of literature) and historical (which are arrived at from an observation of the facts of literature). Theoretical genres can be subdivided into simple (characterized by a single genre-specific feature) and complex (characterized by a combination of features). Moreover, historical genres are subsets of complex theoretical genres. The task of generic criticism for Todorov is to understand literature through its kinds while maintaining a careful balance between the empirical and the abstract, between the practical and the theoretical; theoretical genres must be verified by real texts that exist in literature, and historical genres must be looked at in the context of a coherent theory.

The term *picaresque novel* is the nineteenth-century literary equivalent of a kind of back formation. In Todorov's terms, it is a theoretical genre (simple or complex, depending on the critic) that insists on applying historically later narrative phenomena to a historical genre whose dominant verifiable feature is whatever seventeenth-century Spanish writers and readers understood by the first part of the term. It is what was perceived in the concept "picaresque" that should be the goal of genre theory first of all; and while there may well be such a literary species as the picaresque novel that we can verify in eighteenth-century French and English literature, it is a distinct historical genre of its own. Studies that try to explain picaresque fiction as a novelistic phenomenon are therefore obscuring the historical picaresque genre by coercing our scant knowledge of it into a theoretical genre composed of features abstracted from subsequent narrative forms. Such a procedure, which makes of any syntagmatic point in literary history a paradigm for earlier points, is not in the spirit of responsibly useful genre theory because it leads inevitably to the even more damaging obfuscation of genre through assessment by value. Proclaiming that *Lazarillo de Tormes* is the first modern novel or that Homer is the first novelist (*The Odyssey* has, in fact, been called the first picaresque novel) is to damage the reading experience beyond repair. Even the literarily naive reader is done a disservice by being given generic signals that prove unequal to the task of regulating the flow of responses to the text or, more likely and worse, that prove the text inadequate to the generic expectation. Used in such contexts, of course, *novel* is an honorific more than a generic term. But the problem of novel as a genre concept is an even greater one than the problem of a picaresque genre, and it should be the first order of business in pursuit of fiction P to separate *novel* from *picaresque* unless (and, historically, until) such a term as *picaresque novel* becomes theoretically necessary to designate a specific genre or subgenre of the novel. Used to designate narrative fictions before the eighteenth century, *picaresque novel* is literary-historically anachronistic and generically sloppy.

The search for a picaresque genre concept has fluctuated between two extremes, which ultimately cancel themselves and each other out: a rigidly historical approach that seeks a genre so pure that no two texts together can verify it, and an ahistorical approach that posits a genre concept so inclusive that its many texts in their diversity invalidate it. Out of all the effort that has been expended in this search, only a handful of critics has managed to transcend, through persuasive synthesis, the historical demands for generic purity on the one hand and the theoretical and practical desire for generic plenitude on the other. Of these, three in particular have proposed concepts of the picaresque that attempt to reconcile the theoretical with the historical in such a way that each informs the other. Although they do not necessarily share, or even make explicit, some major assumptions and premises (about the nature of narrative, about genre theory, even about the meanings of certain critical terms) on which their arguments rely, they have in common, first, the mutual goal of defining the picaresque in such a way that the historical and the theoretical do not violate each other; and, second, they try to satisfy the needs of the genre theorist as well as the literary historian and practicing critic for a definition that adds to our literary understanding by explaining a specific narrative kind, clarifying particular narrative developments in the history of literature, and illuminating our experience with certain individual texts.

The first of these has been widely influential: Claudio Guillén's "Toward a Definition of the Picaresque" (1962), incorporated in expanded form into his *Literature as System* (1971), where it can be read in the context of his wider concerns about genre theory. For Guillén, a genre "is an invitation to form," which looks backward to the literary works that already exist and forward in the direction of the future writer and informed critic (109). A genre "is not a mere aspect of a work but one of its principles of unity" (386). Moreover, "looking backward, a genre is a descriptive statement concerning a number of related works. Looking forward, it becomes . . . an invitation to the matching (dynamically speaking) of matter and form" for the writer (111). The Renaissance theorist, Guillén says, "would usually regard as a species what is today considered a genre—a species resulting from the introduction of certain particulars or differentiae into the genus," and "the confusion of modern genre theory is partly due to the fact that what we now call genre was once considered more specific than generic and that we are left without an accepted term for genus" (117). But this development has also broken the link between genus and species, making it possible to "speak of genus in different ways (i.e., of universals, 'ultimates,' 'types,' *Naturformen, Grundhaltungen*) and of species as well (i.e., genres, or modes, or styles) without retaining the traditional assumption that the two need be logically and genealogically related" (119). Guillén illustrates one essential difference between genus and species, or rather between universals and genres:

More problems are raised than solved by the writer's determination, vis-à-vis the blank page, to "tell a story" [that is, to compose within one of the universals, such as narrative, as opposed to lyric or drama]. But let us suppose that he is facing a particular genre like the picaresque novel. Let us say—hastily—that the picaresque model can be described in the following way: it is the fictional confession of a liar. This is already a provocative notion. Besides, the writer knows that the picaresque tale begins not *in medias res* but with the narrator's birth, that it recounts in chronological order the orphaned boy's peregrinations from city to city, and that it usually ends—that is, it can end—with either the defeat or the conversion of the "inner" man who both narrates and experiences the events. What is at stake now, it seems to me—what is being constructively suggested—is not the presentation [that is, the demands of the universal, in this case narrative] but the informing drive (in Viëtor's words, *Gestaltungsdrang*) that makes the whole work possible. Within the process of writing, the "radicals" and the "universals" fulfill their function at a very early stage; details of rhetoric and style play essential but partial and variegated roles; and only the generic model is likely to be effective at the crucial moment of total configuration, construction, *com-position*. (120)

In the creation of the fictional work, it is genre that plays the *form*-ative part, and it must follow from this model of the composing act that a similar process must occur in the mind of the reader interested in the genealogical relations among literary texts, in literature as system.

Guillén's definition of the picaresque is governed entirely by its potential usefulness, not its validity as an absolute norm to which we might be tempted to subordinate actual works. And he wants it to be useful in two distinct ways: "as a procedure for ordering the continuum of individual literary facts; and as a critical perspective, perhaps fruitful at the moment of reading" (74). From a historical point of view, he asserts, the early existence of a picaresque genre is undeniable. But "no work embodies completely the picaresque genre. The genre is not, of course, a novel any more than the equine species is a horse. A genre is a model—and a convenient model to boot: an invitation to the actual writing of a work, on the basis of certain principles of composition" (72). At the beginning of his essay, Guillén posits four distinct sets or classes within which his definition is to proceed:

It may be useful to distinguish between the following: the picaresque genre, first of all; a group of novels, secondly, that deserve to be called picaresque in the strict sense—usually in agreement with the original Spanish pattern; another group of novels, thirdly, which may be considered picaresque in a broader sense of the term only; and finally, a picaresque myth: an essential situation or significant structure derived from the novels themselves. (71)

Having established these crucial procedural, generic, and critical premises, Guillén then singles out eight distinguishing features of the picaresque: (1) a dynamic psychosociological situation (or series of situations) focused on a *pícaro*, an orphan, a "half-outsider," who can "*neither join nor actually reject his fellow men*" (80; Guillén's italics); (2) a pseudo-autobiographical form of narration with "a double perspective of self-concealment and self-revelation" (82); (3) a partial and prejudiced narrative viewpoint that "offers no synthesis of human life" (82); (4) a total view that is reflective, philosophical, and critical on religious or moral grounds, tending toward the *roman à thèse*; (5) a stress on the material level of existence, on "sordid facts, hunger, money" (83); (6) observation of a number of collective conditions such as social classes, professions, *caractères*, cities, and nations, providing "a standing invitation to satire"

(83); (7) a horizontal movement through space and a vertical movement through society; and (8) an episodic structure that makes a picaresque fiction "formally open, so to speak, and idelogically closed" (85). Some of these overlap a great deal (for example, 3 with 4, 4 with 6, and 6 with 7), but sharper demarcations or a reduced group of condensed features would blur useful distinctions in works that, for example, demonstrate feature 6 but not 4, which would tell us something about its picaresqueness that combining 4 and 6 into one could not, because the latter would be more exclusive and much less discretionary. Guillén's target, after all, is "a series of literary works, not a definition" through an ordering that is "tentative and empirical" (74).

Although elsewhere in *Literature as System*, Guillén rejects mechanical or visual models because "our subject is a certain type of *mental* order, characterized by the functional importance of the relationships obtaining between its various parts" (378), it is tempting to try to schematize his concept of the picaresque, which he maps out across an overlapping grid that he himself refers to visually as "concentric" circles (93) (figure 1). Such a visualization, despite its inadequacies in including all the coordinates of Guillén's carefully structured ordering concept, has at least the virtue of accounting for the degree of a work's generic purity (how much it demonstrates the essential features of the genre) and of its generic plenitude (how picaresque features function in fictions from other narrative genres). Moreover, it has diachronic and syntagmatic as well as synchronic and paradigmatic dimensions if further refined.

A second major attempt at a comprehensive theory of the picaresque is André Jolles's "Die literarischen Travestien: Ritter—Hirt—Schelm" (1931), given relative accessibility only through its inclusion (in a German version by Otto Görner) by Helmut Heidenreich in his 1969 anthology *Pikarische Welt* (pp. 101–18). Jolles says that we try to escape the pressures of culture through a special kind of self-metamorphosis that takes us above society, below it, or outside it into realms that we have learned to call in literary terms the heroic (or romance), the picaresque, and the pastoral (or bucolic), respectively. In imaginatively becoming a knight (*Ritter*) or great hero, we wish to rise above society, exercising our yearning for consummation and order. In imaginatively becoming a rogue or picaro (*Schelm*), we sink below, satisfying our desires to avoid order and custom. And in imaginatively becoming a shepherd (*Hirt*), we move close to a gentle, hospitable nature and thus exist in a kind of arcadia outside the demanding world of culture, civilization, and society. These "represent in their totality our yearning to escape temporarily from society, to change our necessities, and to become someone else without completely ceasing to be ourselves. These represent, too, the only three possibilities open to us for this flight. Outward, upward, and downward—these are the three dimensions" (my trans., Heidenreich, p. 112).

Jolles uses the word *travesty* in its etymological sense: "to disguise," from the Latin *trans* ("over," "across") plus *vestire* ("to dress," "attire"), free of the common usage of the word as a derogatory term meaning "sham" or "burlesque." He means it in a neutral sense as designating the process through which

Figure 1

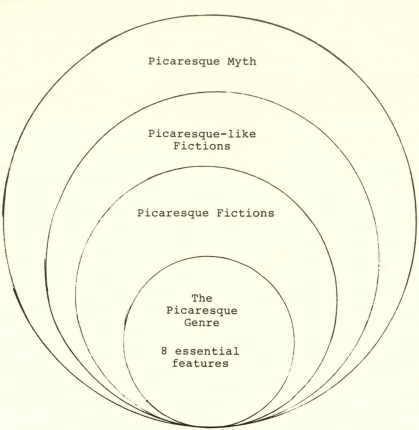

we disguise our real selves by way of "dressing" ourselves (and our selves) in the favorite "masks" or roles that literature offers. As high-minded, courageous knight, we despise the simple shepherd and the cunning rogue; as satisfied shepherd, we show disdain for the rogue's inconstancy and the knight's thirst for honor; as bohemian rogue, we scorn the narrowness and dullness of bucolic life and the chimeras of knighthood. Rogue and knight both represent the adventurous and mobile life as opposed to the peace-loving and place-bound shepherd; knight and shepherd defend their noble names against the rogue, who stands in disrepute; rogue and shepherd taste the joy of life, whereas the knight exerts and torments himself. By way of travesty,

Man, dissatisfied with culture and civilization, seeks an opportunity to leave culture, society, or community behind—he wants to metamorphose himself. But he wants to transform himself in a manner which will not require him to divorce himself totally from himself: the possibility of a return cannot be omitted. Three directions lie open for him, and with these three directions the range of possibilities is exhausted. As soon as he enters upon one of these directions, he finds a completely ordered world, a world with its own requisites and laws, a world which is consistent down to its smallest detail—a literary world. In order to attain this world, he must disguise himself, or, to express it more precisely, he must transform himself into a literary personage—a knight, a shepherd, or a rogue. (My trans., Heidenreich, p. 117)

The directions upward, downward, and outward, Jolles says, are without doubt ethical directions. But the travesty remains play—literary play—insofar as we temporarily avoid the constraints of reality by transcending it (the knight), leaving it (the shepherd), or losing it (the rogue). Knight, shepherd, and rogue are the "three safety-valves of our culture" and where culture presses, "the safety-valves take effect." If they did not, most of us would more often be inclined to break the oppressive bonds of culture, society, and community. Jolles goes so far as to suggest that the three figures and their realms provide a preventative, through literary form, of actual social unrest.

Jolles limits himself in his examples to fictions from the seventeenth century in which he sees as the three dominant types the pastoral, the picaresque, and the heroic romance. These three types, Jolles says, recur whenever and wherever we go in literature: "They belong to the permanent inventory of literature." Such a conception of the picaresque as one of several major types (or universals) of narrative is broad enough to include both the concept of a historically defined picaresque genre and the concept of picaresque fiction in the more flexible sense, and it thus complements Guillén's effort by exploring the realm that used to be called genus, or a transitional class between genus and species, between universal type and genre.

Jolles's conception of literature resembles Northrop Frye's in *The Educated Imagination* (1964)—"The world of literature is a world where there is no reality except that of the human imagination" (96)—and in it we seem to be looking up or down, at a wish fulfillment dream or an anxiety dream, which focus together and "become a fully conscious vision" (102). Such a conception of fictional worlds provides a transition to the third major attempt at a broader genre concept of the picaresque: that of Robert Scholes in his "Towards a Poetics of Fiction: An Approach through Genre" (1969), which he later incorporated into his *Structuralism in Literature* (1974), where he follows his discussion with an admiring consideration of Guillén's approach to genre in general and to the picaresque in particular.

Scholes proposes a spectrum of ideal types of narrative fiction, which he calls *modes*. Fictional modes are defined by the qualities of the world that the storyteller renders. There are three possible relationships between any fictional world and our world of actual experience: a world fictionally rendered can be (1) better than the world of experience, (2) worse than it, or (3) more or less equal to it; these are visions or perspectives that we have learned to call, respectively, romantic, satiric, and realistic. Fiction can give us, then, the heroic world of romance, the degraded world of satire, or the mimetic world of history, respectively. These three modes are the middle and end points of a spectrum of fictional possibilities, which has seven modes in all:

satire	picaresque	comedy	history	sentiment	tragedy	romance

Romance, for example, presents superhuman types in an ideal world. Satire portrays subhuman grotesques enmeshed in chaos. Picaresque presents a protagonist enduring a world that is chaotic beyond ordinary human tolerance, but it is a world closer to our own experiential one, or "history," than are the worlds of romance or satire. "Our 'real' world (which we live in but never understand)," Scholes says, "is ethically neutral. Fictional worlds, on the other hand, are charged with values. They offer us a perspective on our own situation, so that by trying to place them we are engaged in seeking our own position" (133). This spectrum must be seen as a system of shades that individual works of fiction have combined in various ways.

Scholes goes on to refine this spectrum in order to accommodate complex fictional mixtures like *Don Quixote* and, more important, to allow for a diachronic dimension that will help explain the emergence of specific narrative genres—in particular, the novel. He distinguishes modal theory from generic criticism by suggesting that the term *genre* be reserved for the study of individual works in their relationships to specific and historically identifiable traditions. Generic study begins in "the thick of the phenomena," trying to group works in a way that will relate them to the ideal types as well as to a vertical (that is, historical) continuum of tradition, without sacrificing the uniqueness of the particular work. The ideal act of reading is thus a process of passing "through insensible gradations from a modal to a generic awareness, to a final sense of the unique qualities of the individual work, as distinguished from those most like it" (138–39). Scholes then discusses Guillén's essay as a model of how to close that "disturbing space"—the "gap between generic knowledge and modal ideas."

A modal perspective, as Scholes proposes it, is thus the largest, most comprehensive perspective we can have on narrative, itself one of what Wellek and Warren would call the "ultimate kinds" of literature. We begin from a position that allows us to see the entire narrative spectrum with its infinite range of possibilities along the scale from satire to romance (like the spectrum of light with its undetectable blending of one color into the next, an analogy Scholes also uses elsewhere). The spectrum itself is not an inflexible pigeonholing system. It accounts for shades and mixtures, and therefore we can see in any particular work of narrative fiction how several of the ideal types are mixed together to achieve the uniqueness of that work. By grouping works in a continuum, we can also see which particular mode or mixture of modes tends to assume a more significant role in a particular epoch of literary history than the other modes.

A modal perspective can help to shape our aesthetic response to the concrete work before us. It can orient for us the context of that work in terms of all the fictional possibilities along the spectrum. To recognize that a particular work belongs, say, to romance (or that the romance mode dominates it) is to channel our response to—and thus our expectations of—that work. Modal recognition allows us to group the particular work with other works from our total experience of fiction that function in a similar way. And modal awareness readjusts our expectations of the individual modes themselves by making us see the way a particular work makes use of—and thus changes—those very expectations. What this larger perspective implies for our more immediate problem of picaresque fiction is a different approach, one that begins above and beyond historical considerations and moves gradually toward the more specific and particular problems of historical context, tradition, and influence.

This concept of modes as ideal fictional types—as irreducible narrative types, we might say, or primitive narrative forms—is not in itself a critical tool, but it is the beginning of one: a large, overall perspective on fiction based on a spectrum of possible fictional worlds and the kinds of characters who are created to inhabit those worlds. Modal awareness allows us to see the general fictional makeup of the individual narrative work. Modes do not specifically impose a form (except telling a story, or narration itself) and are thus prenovelistic; they are applicable to fiction anytime, anywhere. Since the picaresque is here posited as one of the modes, we would expect to find it in widely varying degrees in much fiction that could not by even the most generous generic measure be considered picaresque fictions proper.

Recognizing picaresque as one of the basic modes is an extraordinarily useful leap in bridging the critical impasse that contemporary criticism has been struggling to get through in the midst of an ever-broadening use of the term *picaresque*. The recurrent tendency to use the term in all sorts of general ways argues for its necessity as one of the basic fictional modes. Empirical evidence alone would indicate that there is some basic fictional situation that cannot be explained except with *picaresque*. A mode concept of the picaresque reconciles the extremes of generic purity and generic plenitude; it accounts both for a specific kind of narrative whose exclusive preoccupation is an exploration of the fictional world posited by the picaresque and for a primitive fictional possibility that may be present in all sorts of varying degrees of mixture in many other works of fiction. The picaresque mode is the dimly recognized and unarticulated common denominator underlying all those assessments that genre purists find so irritating, from Walter Allen's comment on *The Pilgrim's Progress* to the latest film or book review calling a work "picaresque." Such modal recognition is dramatically illustrated when, for example, a work entirely forgotten by literary history is rediscovered centuries later, as happened with the 1976 publication of *The Adventures of Jonathan Corncob, Loyal American Refugee* (1787). Modal recognition of the work's position in the fictional spectrum was instant; more precise generic articulation will take considerably more critical resources.

Guillén, Jolles, and Scholes in their different ways all synthesize the critical extremes that in their dogged irreconcilability have plagued scholarship on the picaresque for over a century. Jolles and Scholes are charting the fictional territory in similarly structural ways. For Jolles, the formal structures of his universal fictional types exist in response to human needs that experience does not satisfy—thus the appeal in picaresque of what Robert Heilman in his "Variations on Picaresque (*Felix Krull*)" (1958) aptly calls the "catharsis of rascality," the "secret inclination to discontinuity, to hit-and-run raids on life, the impulse to shun the long and exacting unity, to live instead by episodes." For Scholes, the modal structures by their very difference from experience help us to make sense of experience—and they serve genre theory and literary history by making us "more sympathetic and open to the varieties of fiction, old and new" (138) and expanding our vision beyond a novel-focused one. Guillén, who works through to a more complete genre concept, nevertheless makes room for the universals of Scholes and Jolles. His "picaresque myth" coincides with their universals in his conceiving it as "being connected particularly with the reader's or critic's understanding of its larger significance—his ultimate appreciation, independent of any particular work, of the theme as a whole" (100). All three therefore map out the limits of the fictional grid on which any investigation into the picaresque must take place; they provide the modal and structural coordinates that govern our investigations into individual texts and groupings of texts. We might call this mapped fictional space the picaresque mode.

Unfortunately, *mode* is an even more troublesome term critically than *genre* is, and a random sampling of its usage will yield a dismaying lack of common ground. In *The Anatomy of Criticism* (1957), Northrop Frye uses it to mean a conventional power of action assumed about the chief characters in fiction, while F. K. Stanzel uses it to mean one of three constitutive elements that define a narrating process (*A Theory of Narrative*, 1979). Guillén uses it synonymously with *universals* (*Literature as System*, 387, for example), while Fowler in *Kinds of Literature* sees modes as successors to obsolete fixed kinds (167) and defines *mode* as "a selection or abstraction from kind" (56). Modal terms "tend to be adjectival" and "never imply a complete external form" (106–7). Scholes means by it a basic fictional structure or situation defined by the quality of the fictional world rendered and the relationship between the protagonists and their fictional surroundings, not by any "form of story customarily associated with the term" (133). In a hierarchy of literary kinds, modes would thus come somewhere between the genus or universal and the specific genre. For our purposes here, let us consider a mode as a subdivision of *narrative*, as a simple fictional macrostructure defined by one essential characteristic.

But like *mode* itself, the terminology used to designate individual modes is problematic. Edith Kern points out in "The Romance of Novel/Novella" (1968) that " 'novel' has become the generic term for all long fictitious prose narratives. Even retroactively, it has usurped the place of 'romance,' which now designates only a particular kind of long narrative, although it was once applicable to all of them. 'Romance' has been supplanted by 'novel' to such an extent that modern critics unflinchingly speak of chivalric and picaresque 'novels' where earlier critics would have used the term 'romance' " (511). This development is particularly troublesome in the context of picaresque fiction because it does not discriminate among generic levels. Hierarchically, the romance mode is "larger" or more encompassing than any specific romance genre. It is a problem originating in the beginning of the criticism on the picaresque in English. Chandler's title was *Romances of Roguery*, and one of his assumptions about the emergence of picaresque fiction was that "the romance of roguery . . . evolved negatively from the notion of the anti-hero," even though "the picaresque novels in Spain had little direct invective against the romances of shepherds and chivalry" (14, 76). Throughout his book, Chandler uses the phrase "romances of roguery" at least seventy times, and there is no indication that he meant it any differently from the phrase "picaresque novel," which he uses at least thirty times. In fact, Chandler indiscriminately uses "picaresque fiction," "picaresque narrative," "picaresque tale," "novel of rogues," and others synonymously, making no generic distinctions between *novel* and *romance*. Although *romance* did once encompass all prose fiction (retained in the German *Roman* and the French *roman*), by Chandler's time a distinction had developed. From Homer's gates of ivory and horn in *The Odyssey* (XIX), to Clara Reeve's distinction between *novel* and *romance* in *The Progress of Romance* (1785), to Hawthorne's preface to *The House of the Seven Gables* (1851), a crude generic distinction has been functional in narrative literature between fictions portraying idealized worlds and fictions attempting to render reality.

Like *picaresque*, which is used historically to designate a special episode in the evolution of fictional forms and ahistorically to designate a universal kind of narrative, *romance* refers both to a specific group of medieval and Renaissance fictions and to a universal kind of fiction with certain characteristics. (In Spanish literature, *romance* refers to a specific kind of ballad in the fifteenth and sixteenth centuries, but that usage does not concern us here, though it illustrates once more the frustrations of literary terminology.) It seems sensible as a way out of the confusion to call the broader uses of each term *modes* and the narrower historical uses *genres*. Mode designates a fictional construct characterized by the qualities of the world it renders (as in Scholes's spectrum). A fiction in the romance mode offers a word-world-construct in which harmony, integration, and perfection prevail: dreamlike wish fulfillment. The picaresque mode offers a word-world-construct in which disharmony, disintegration, and chaos prevail: nightmarish anxiety.

If the concept of a picaresque mode, thus conceived, has been implicit in most critical approaches to picaresque fiction, it has been explicit in the critical commonplace that the picaresque evolved as an antitype to romance. Histories of Spanish literature have always emphasized the picaresque as a comic or satiric antitype to chivalric or pastoral romances, and such contrasts have made their way into almost all generic definitions in one form or another. Ortega y Gasset in "La picardía original de la novela picaresca" (1915) even extends such a comparison sociologically by talking about a literature of the noble classes and a literature of the plebians; the theme of "love and fantasy" was developed in chivalric fiction and the theme of resentment and criticism in the picaresque. Stuart Miller in *The Picaresque Novel* (1967) contrasts picaresque with romance: "The pattern and meaning of the romance plot contrast absolutely with the episodic plot of the picaresque novel" (12), adding a formal concept of narrative structure to the modal concept of the quality of the fictional world. Scholes and Kellogg in *The Nature of Narrative* (1966) trace the evolution of narrative forms from the time of the epic, after which narrative tends to dissolve into two antithetical types: the empirical and the fictional. Where the epic storyteller's allegiance had been to a *mythos* or traditional plot, the empirical type of narrative replaces this allegiance to tradition with allegiance to reality. Empirical narratives can be either historical, which owes its allegiance to truth of fact, or mimetic, which owes its allegiance to truth of sensation and environment. The fictional type of narrative replaces allegiance to the *mythos* with allegiance to the ideal, and it can be either romantic, which is determined by an aesthetic impulse to portray an ideal world of beauty in which poetic justice prevails, or didactic, which is ruled by an intellectual and moral impulse. Picaresque fiction, they say, "is the comic antitype of the romance. It approaches the mimetic, but for comic and satiric purposes mainly. It sets the contemporary world and a first-person narrator up against the never-never world and impalpable narrator of romance" (75). And A. A. Parker in *Literature and the Delinquent* (1967) says that "the first Spanish novels can indeed be considered, historically, as reactions against pastoral novels and novels of chivalry, but as alternatives not as satires"; the picaresque arose "as a reaction to the romances—not as satire or parody, but as a deliberate alternative, a 'truthful' literature in response to the explicit demands of the Counter-Reformation" (19, 22).

Fowler says that "genres may have several mutual relations, such as inclusion, mixture (tragicomedy), antigenre inversion (romance and picaresque), and contrast (sonnet and epigram)" (216). Later, discussing the concept of "contrasting genres" in the context of intergeneric relations, he suggests one kind of contrast in which genres have a "converse relation comparable with the semantic converseness of 'buy' and 'sell.' These pairs of antigenres include romance and picaresque romance, novel and antinovel. . . . Here the one antonym implies the presence of the other" (252). And finally, Barbara Babcock in " 'Liberty's a Whore': Inversions, Marginalia, and Picaresque Narrative" (1978) makes a crucial point that is rarely, if ever, given much consideration in generic discussions of the picaresque: that the picaresque embodies the romance at the same time as it inverts it. "The code which is being broken is always implicitly there, for the very act of deconstructing reconstructs and reaffirms the structure of romance," and thus the reader receives at least two competing generic signals: "this is a romance" and "this is a picaresque antiromance" (99). Such concepts of anti- and countergenre require modal macrostructures of the kind that Scholes has developed.

Yet it is precisely because of such anti- and countergeneric conversion, inversion, and embodiment that generic macrostructures like the spectrum of fictional modes raise as many problems as they seek to solve, in addition to the confusion resulting from their being forced to use terms from an inadequate critical vocabulary that is itself a major obstacle to generic precision. One such problem results from the affinity a mode has for its neighbors on the spectrum. Picaresque often blends with satire, yielding hasty generic identifications such as, say, Voltaire's *Candide* as a picaresque, which is more misleading than helpful. Picaresque frequently looks toward comedy, a mixture that if superficially taken as a basic genre characteristic can obscure the severity of the picaresque worldview and leads to such generic distortions as, say, calling *Tom Jones* picaresque. Romance is picaresque's almost polar opposite on the spectrum, and their generic antithesis is a staple of received critical opinion. If, however, we take a close look at some specific picaresque fictions, we notice that the relationship between picaresque and romance is a good deal more complex than a mere antithesis would require. Apart from the obvious structural similarities between picaresque and romance (for example, episodes, adventures, journeys, and unifying characters) and the occasional inclusion of a romance within picaresque (the story of Daraxa and Ozmin, for example, in part one, book I, chapter 8 of *Guzmán de Alfarache*), how do we integrate the following into any modal-generic concept?

1. What do we do with the "communities of roguery" that appear recurrently in picaresque? These brotherhoods of thieves, like the ones in Brecht's *Three-Penny Opera* and Fritz Lang's *M*, may serve as a satirical inversion of the social order; but, paradoxically, these brotherhoods are much more ordered and structured than the social order they ostensibly undermine. We know that beggar books were a popular subgenre, but when such structures become part of picaresque proper, what do they mean? In Rome, Guzmán tells about a charter concerning "The Laws and Ordinances that are inviolably to be observed amongst Beggars" (One, III, 2), the general and superintendent of whom is called "the Prince of Roguerie, and the Arch-begger of Christendome." Pablos in *El Buscón* joins a group of beggars who are just as rigidly ordered, and we find a similar organization in Cervantes's "Rinconete and Cortadillo." In García's *La desordenada codicia*, there is an elaborate genealogy of thieves, which is an outrageous justification of thieves, as the romance hero's lineage justifies his prowess and goodness. García traces thievery and thieves back to Adam (whose sin thieves partake of) and to Lucifer, the first thief, who stole from God. In *The English Rogue*, Meriton Latroon refers to his "comrogues" and talks about a brotherhood of rogues in which an elaborate hierarchy exists. In Ellison's *Invisible Man*, the hero joins a Brotherhood, which "was a world within a world" and which orders existence: "Life was all pattern and discipline" (ch. 17). And in *The Tin Drum*, Oskar becomes the leader of a group of pranksters called "The Dusters," for whom he serves as an embodiment of Jesus. Simplicissimus juxtaposes a real battle with his own version of war against the fleas that are attacking him (II, ch. 28); and he has a vision of a tree on which everyone has his designated place in a hierarchy of oppression that is all too metaphorically true of the Thirty

Years' War landscape Grimmelshausen's character must cope with. Are these orders antisocieties or perverse romance structures of order within a disordered world?

2. What about the larger pattern of picaresque, which Parker, connecting picaresque with pastoral and mystical writings, calls "the circle of existence"? Guzmán inherits original sin from his father and must find his way back to God the Father through a delinquent life. Simplicissimus begins life in total innocence in an edenic forest and ends it, alone, converted, on a paradisiacal island. Along the way, he experiences a romance—not just as a story, as Guzmán does, but as an absorbing, dynamic event: the Mummelsee, a paradise below the earth (V, ch. 10–16). We can find this circle in contemporary picaresque too—for example, in *Invisible Man*, where the picaro is ejected from college, "this Eden" (ch. 5), and flung into the chaos of Harlem. This "circle of existence," as Parker describes it, has a lot in common with what Frye calls the "Genesis-apocalypse myth" in the Bible in which "Adam is cast out of Eden, loses the river of life and the trees of life, and wanders in the labyrinth of human history until he is restored to his original state by the Messiah" (*Anatomy*, 191). This is one of the central myths of quest romance, which leads to the next question.

3. Is not the essential picaresque pattern a quest for "home"—home in the sense of material and social success (*Lazarillo*), or in the spiritual sense of union with God (as in *Guzmán* and *Simplicissimus*), or even in the mythic sense of a return to Paradise? Hesse's *Knulp* deals with such cosmic homesickness, and Karl in Kafka's *Amerika* finds "The Nature Theatre of Oklahoma." Oskar in *The Tin Drum* yearns to get back to the umbilical cord. It might even be said that contemporary picaresque, especially, is a fictional exploration of exile from and search for home. It may well be that our twentieth-century interest in the picaresque has its origins in picaresque's implicit romance desire more than in its explicit depiction of disorder and chaos. Frye defines romance as "the nearest of all literary forms to the wish-fulfillment dream" and adds that "the perenially child-like quality of romance is marked by its extra-ordinarily persistent nostalgia, its search for some kind of imaginative golden age in time or space." At its most naive, "it is an endless form in which a central character who never develops or ages goes through one adventure after another until the author himself collapses" (*Anatomy*, 186).

4. Is not the strong didactic or moral and intellectual impulse of picaresque a romance characteristic? Guzmán creates a deliberate tension between the appeal of personal experience and sensation and the allegiance to an ideal of moral conduct in a world shaped by God, which is also true of Simplicissimus. Alemán and Grimmelshausen are, on the narrative level, writing essentially philosophical works, pointing out directly the illustrative quality of the represented life. Mimetic portrayal of ugly life and moralizing ideas of conduct provide a continuous tension and dualism that in modal-generic terms means romance versus picaresque. Otis H. Green in *Spain and the Western Tradition* (1965) points out that in "all the works of the period there remains intact the belief in an over-all

harmony—Christian with Platonic overtones—in the ultimate goodness of God's universe, the ultimate justice of His will. The paths trod by mankind have a destination which is none other than the chief end of man as defined by Christian doctrine in all centuries'' (IV, 283).

5. Isn't the picaro's impulse to tell the story itself a yearning for order? Shaping one's *vida* in words satisfies the form completion impulse to impose aesthetic and moral order on the chaotic past, which is re-membered now as a structure. The re-membering "I" tries to piece together again the dis-membered, as Oskar Seidlin points out in "Picaresque Elements in Thomas Mann's Work" (1951). This "I" tries to balance the chaos of experience-as-lived with the moral order now-being-contemplated. In *Guzmán* and *Simplicissimus*, we are suspended between two modes, romance and picaresque; the picaro's role in the narrating process is thus a kind of double exposure, superimposing the shaping artist over the unstable succession of beings he was in the past. This double exposure can itself be doubly exposed, as when the artist-self yearns for chaos, and the rootless self yearns for order, as Robert Jay Lifton observes in "Protean Man" (1968) when he describes two contemporary behavioral patterns—the "mode of transformation" (the need to disrupt all things and make them constantly new) and "the mode of restoration" (the yearning for a mythical past of perfect harmony)—and notes that one behavior can actually engender the other so that there is transformationism in restoration and restorationism in transformation.

6. If we consider the picaro as a literary version of the trickster archetype in myth, what then is his role in the total scheme of things? According to Kerényi in "The Trickster in Relation to Greek Mythology" (1954), "Disorder belongs to the totality of life, and the spirit of this disorder is the trickster. His function in an archaic society, or rather the function of his mythology, of the tales told about him, is to add disorder to order and so make a whole, to render possible, within the fixed bounds of what is permitted, an experience of what is not permitted," a function that picaresque "has consciously taken over" (185). At the end of the trickster myth, says Jung in "On the Psychology of the Trickster-Figure" (1954), "the savior is hinted at." Jung emphasizes the therapeutic effect of the trickster's function, and in this respect his view of the picaresque coincides with that of André Jolles. Moreover, as Heilman points out, the picaro always finds willing victims and thus gratifies our desires to be tricked, as well as to participate vicariously in the tricking itself.

7. Finally, exactly how has the picaresque merged with other narrative types in the evolution of narrative forms? Eichendorff's *Memoirs of a Good-for-Nothing* is a curious synthesis of the picaresque-fragmented world of wandering existence and its deceiving appearances on the one hand, and the ordered, harmonized, and divine world of romance on the other. Picaresque is both parodied and contrasted with romance, and romance is parodied and contrasted with picaresque. That the random world of chance and disorder should turn out to have been ordered by an elaborately designed plot is romance's mockery of picaresque. Yet is the romance plot at the end of Eichendorff's work really so

different from the predicted plot in *Lazarillo de Tormes* that allows the blind
man to foretell exactly the outcome of Lazarillo's life (he says that Lazarillo
will have much to do with horns and wine)? Smollett's *Roderick Random* and
Ferdinand, Count Fathom begin as picaresque and end, with marvelous coincidences, as romances. In *Guzmán* and in *Simplicissimus*, on the other hand,
the picaresque and romance visions are so thoroughly fused that it is hard to
separate them. In the Bildungsroman of late eighteenth- and early nineteenth-
century German literature, what at first appears to be a disconnected picaresque
world slowly takes shape as an emerging world of order and moral goodness, a
modal blending that provides the basis for Ralph Freedman's "The Possibility
of a Theory of the Novel" (1968). For Felix Krull and for Gulley Jimson in
The Horse's Mouth, art itself provides a romance vision to counteract a world
in flux. And in *The Tin Drum* two Oskars are telling stories about at least two
Oskars of the past, a blend of Dionysian and Apollonian visions that is yet
another variation on the modal mixture of romance with picaresque.

Most of these examples demonstrate the integration of romance into picaresque, not the inversion or conversion or mere embodiment of romance inside
picaresque. Perhaps the picaro has more to do with Amadís and other romance
heroes than being their negative image or antitype (an antithetical notion of
romance and picaresque that has become entrenched since Chandler coined the
term *antihero*). Perhaps the picaro is another version of the romance hero,
differing from him only in circumstance and the kind of world he can act in.
Yet the romance world is often fraught with unexpected danger, potential disharmony, and apparent fragmentation. It may well be that if every explicit
picaresque contains within itself an implicit romance, so every romance contains
within itself an implicit picaresque or satire.

Let us return to the Ginés de Pasamonte episode in *Don Quixote*. In freeing
the galley slaves, Don Quixote acts according to a higher concept of justice than
that which operates in the "real" world. He says, "It seems to me a hard case
to make slaves out of those whom God and nature made free." Quixote's romance
vision and Ginés's picaresque stance are in sharp contrast here, but they also
implicate each other. The picaresque episode of the galley slaves takes place
within a structure of romance perceived and projected by Don Quixote on to it.
Significantly, Ginés reappears in part II (24–26) as Maese Pedro, who performs
a puppet show romance that Don Quixote demolishes, a reversal of roles from
their encounter in part I. If the story of Ginés de Pasamonte is a picaresque
inside a satire that is also a romance, then we perhaps ought to look more closely
at the romances (and satires) within the picaresque. The makeup of picaresque
narrative is more complex than the vast majority of our definitions let on. Romance visions of order are integrated into the picaresque in a way that makes the
concept of fictional antitypes false. For Guzmán and Simplicissimus, in fact,
the narrative vehicle is in tone, stance, and temporal vantage point distinctly
romance-like. Picaresque implies romance rather than opposes it, either by integrating it, as in *Guzmán* and *Simplicissimus*, or by invoking it by superimposing

its fictional world through the picaro's yearning. Even the darkest of picaresque worlds, as in Cèline's *Journey to the End of the Night*, evokes it through its absence. All picaresques display it in this central paradox; they are narratively integrative (even therapeutic) while fictionally disintegrative; they give disorder order.

These questions and problems are not raised to debunk the modal approach as a legitimate starting point for a generic inquiry into the picaresque. On the contrary: modal approaches such as the ones proposed by Jolles, Scholes, and Guillén (in his concept of a "picaresque myth") seem to be precisely the way to begin. The issues raised demonstrate, however, that even at this relatively general level of generic inquiry, numerous problems exist; even these rough preliminary distinctions at a comparatively simple level of type differentiation cannot be made as cleanly as we might wish. To move from them, from "the heady, conceptual wheeling and dealing of modal criticism," as Scholes says (138), "to the painstaking historical study of generic traditions is a descent indeed." The problems that exist at the modal level will persist—and multiply manyfold—as we move into the thick of the phenomena, the texts themselves. Only they can provide the building blocks for constructing our hypothetical fiction P. The picaresque mode, as conceived by Scholes, Jolles, and Guillén, has provided the foundation.

CHAPTER 4
The Nature of Picaresque Narrative

Vuelve a nacer mi vida con la historia. "With this Story, my life now liv's againe." When Guzmán de Alfarache says this in a dedicatory verse (by "el licenciado Arias") to part I, he is narratively enacting the fictional macrostructure that the concept picaresque mode only describes. The fiction that is the picaresque mode yields the narrative microstructure that is *Guzmán de Alfarache*. In the thick of the phenomena between the individual text and the mode is where fiction P must be constructed. Any individual fictional text is likely to be a mixture dominated by a single mode, and it is also a specific narrative enactment. Constructing our hypothetical fiction P will therefore entail constant paradigmatic traversing of the distance between the extratexts (the genre, fiction P, and the mode) and the individual texts, as well as syntagmatic back and forth along a historical continuum of texts. These synchronic and diachronic coordinates focus a context for each individual text even as they accommodate readjustment by each text. A modal-generic approach like the one suggested in chapter 3 is a continuing process of refinement and discrimination, moving from the widest possible perspective and narrowing down to the single text or beginning with the textual phenomena and opening out. As a means of identifying and describing a specific narrative kind, modal-generic theory should not concern itself with inclusion or exclusion according to rigid rules that themselves may have been derived from texts that subsequently are perceived not to adhere to them. The extratext is precisely extra, and it must never interfere with the integrity of the individual text. In all this, the aim is to see and understand a specific narrative genre and its tradition so that we may be critically equipped to respond appropriately to the individual text. In other words, the construction of fiction P should be useful in our experience of narrative texts, which is what any literary term or concept should be first of all.

For the specific problem of the picaresque, the modal-generic approach allows a perspective that is broad enough to recognize the larger fictional mixtures in any particular work—picaresque elements in *Don Quixote*, for example, or picaresque characteristics in *The Adventures of Augie March*—and specific enough to account for a particular group of works that share enough attributes to make them identifiable as belonging to a specific genre, to which *Don Quixote* and *Augie March* do not belong. Such an approach satisfies the impulse to literary order that is engendered by perceived similarities in reading two or more individual texts in the first place. Fiction P always exists in individual acts of reading, but it may not always have been systematically constructed. The modal-generic approach provides blueprints for such a construct. What, then, does fiction P look like? What is its nature? In the major characteristics of its nature that follow, no single element should be considered proprietary over fiction P or the picaresque genre. This is not a hierarchy of decreasingly significant elements so much as it is an aggregate of essential characteristics that function together to produce the nature of picaresque narrative. Moreover, some of these terms have become part of the increasingly specialized vocabulary of narratology (*macro-* and *microstructure*, for example, were developed narratologically by Teun A. van Dijk), but in all except a few cases, common literary usage does not conflict with the narratologically stipulative meanings of terms such as *theme* or *motif*. The attributes outlined should collectively give us what we might call ''the total picaresque fictional situation,'' or fiction P.

PICARESQUE MODE/PANORAMIC STRUCTURE

The essential picaresque situation, the fictional world mapped out in the picaresque mode, is that of an unheroic protagonist, worse than we, caught up in a chaotic world, worse than ours, in which he is on an eternal journey of encounters that allow him to be alternately both victim of that world and its exploiter. By way of contrast, the essential romance situation—the fictional world mapped out by the romance mode—is that of a heroic protagonist in a world marvelously better than ours in which he is on a quest that confronts him with challenges, each ending in a moral victory leading toward a final ordered and harmonious cosmos. If the romance mode satisfies our impulse for vicarious participation in harmony, order, and beauty, then the picaresque mode satisfies our impulse for a vicarious journey through chaos and depravity. In picaresque, we participate in the tricks essential to survival in chaos and become victims of the world's tricks, just as in romance we participate in overcoming the dangerous obstacles necessary for the establishment of harmony and order and become recipients of harmony's rewards. In *El Buscón*, we roll in excrement with Pablos one minute, are thrashed with him the next, and indulge with him in his tricks on the world. In book I of Spenser's *Faerie Queene*, we expose ourselves along with the Redcrosse Knight to Despair and other gruesome obstacles, knowing that ultimately this will win the restoration of Una's kingdom and the reward of Una herself. Our journey into romance is a finite one ending in a goal unattainable in our own world of experiential flux. Our journey into picaresque is an infinite foray into a world that is forever falling apart, disintegrating. Romance satisfies our craving for divine harmony, integration, beauty, order, goodness, and ultimate fulfillment. Picaresque satisfies our darker yearnings for demonic disharmony, ugliness, disintegration, disorder, evil, and the gaping abyss. A romance vision is constantly present (by its experiential absence) in the picaresque world, and in some fictions (*Guzmán, Simplicissimus*, eighteenth-century French and English fiction) it even supplants it. Picaresque always looks toward romance.

The fictional macrostructure of the picaresque implies a narrative macrostructure, the panoramic, which is commensurate with the kind of world the picaresque mode renders. Smollett is a convenient illustration here because he seems to have been fully conscious of these two macrostructural features. He is aware of panoramic structure when in his dedication to *Ferdinand, Count Fathom* he writes: "A novel is a large diffused picture, comprehending the characters of life, disposed in different groups, and exhibited in various attitudes, for the purposes of a uniform plan, and general occurrence, to which every individual figure is subservient." And he is aware of the picaresque landscape when he claims in his preface to *Roderick Random* that Lesage's *Gil Blas*, because of the lack of seriousness in the main character, "prevents that generous indignation which ought to animate the reader, against the sordid and vicious disposition of the world."

NARRATIVE RHYTHM

The external rhythm of picaresque narrative is what we might call the Sisyphus rhythm. Guzmán writes: "And being come now to the height of all my labors and paines-taking, and when I was to have received the reward of them, and to take mine ease after all this toyle, the stone rolled down, and I was forced like Sisiphus, to beginne the world anew, and to fall afresh to my work." *Volver de nuevo*, or "to beginne the world anew," is the picaro's existential condition. *Subir la piedra*, to climb Sisyphus's mountain, demands an eternal "falling afresh" to the task of survival in the landscape of the discontinuous, paralleled narratively by a continuously dis-continuous (episodic) form.

The internal rhythm of the picaresque is the rhythm within each episode, which usually follows this pattern: (1) a confrontation (self-willed or forced by "fortune" or adversity, the picaro's cosmic scapegoat) out of need, (2) some scheme to satisfy that need (if only for revenge), (3) a complication that endangers the picaro's existence, and (4) the extrication (or entanglement if he is caught). Lazarillo's efforts to get the key from the priest in chapter 2 illustrate such a rhythm, which is basic to the typical episode of picaresque fiction. It is a simple pattern, tightly organized, with cause-and-effect relationships and a plotted beginning, middle, and end, but it is only within the episode that the picaresque has such organized plots. The narrative as a whole is a succession of such episodic rhythms. The episodes individually and collectively illustrate the perpetual rhythm of the picaresque, which is continuous dis-integration. The external

Sisyphus rhythm is consecutive, while the internal rhythm of each episode is consequential; working together, they alternately harmonize the disharmonic and disharmonize the harmonic.

PICARESQUE POINT OF VIEW

Guillén says that the absence of the first-person form "prevents a story . . . from being picaresque in the full sense" (*Literature as System*, 93), while Parker finds that Aleman "was handicapped by his use of autobiographical form" (*Literature and the Delinquent*, 35); Rico bases his generic distinction between a picaresque proper and what he calls "narratives with a *pícaro*" solely on the presence or absence of first-person narration (*The Spanish Picaresque Novel and the Point of View*, 86). Exploration of point of view in narrative has moved to the center of narrative theory, and the profuse activity has so far produced a number of approaches that illuminate the picaresque narrating situation, which is as tricky as the picaro himself. Of these, Boris Uspensky's in *A Poetics of Composition* (1970) provides a structural approach that may help to clarify some of the technical complexities of point of view, which are compounded by the fact that it is simultaneously a structure—it has spatial (where?) and temporal (when?) dimensions—and an attitude: it has emotional and intellectual effects. Uspensky transcends the simplistic distinction between first- and third-person points of view by suggesting we approach the problem somewhat differently:

We may consider point of view as an ideological and evaluative position; we may consider it as a spatial and temporal position of the one who produces the description of the events (that is, the narrator, whose position is fixed along spatial and temporal coordinates); we may study it with respect to perceptual characteristics; or we may study it in a purely linguistic sense (as, for example, it relates to such phenomena as quasi-direct discourse). . . . For our purposes, these planes will be designated as the plane of ideology, the plane of phraseology, the spatial and temporal plane, and the psychological plane. (6)

In the considerable wake of the path-breaking studies of Wayne Booth and Norman Friedman, we are learning a great deal about how point of view functions in a text, and one of the things that we are learning is that distinctions between person are not as revealing as the kinds of distinctions Uspensky suggests instead (he does not even focus on person as such). In focusing attention on discourse as much as on textual narration, this branch of narratology has taught us to be sensitive to textual meaning on the one hand and to textual significance (a distinction insisted on by E. D. Hirsch) on the other in ways that are just beginning to be explored in the critical approaches to the picaresque.

The concepts of the implied author and the implied reader, for example, are essential to explaining what is happening narrationally in *Lazarillo de Tormes*. The implied author (constructed from signals within the text) really makes any first-person narrative into a third-person discourse by letting us see beyond what Lazarillo himself narrates directly. Or conversely, the implied author in a third-person narration really becomes a first-person narrator in his relationship to the reader on the level of discourse, as happens in Kafka's *Amerika*. Ultimately, distinctions based on person do not hold up to intensive narratological scrutiny. In an approach such as Uspensky's, both internal and external points of view are possible on a number of levels. Moreover, the narrator can shift points of view on any level, even within a short narrative unit such as a paragraph, from an internal to an external perspective, from the space and time dimensions of the action to a spatial-temporal point above and beyond them, from the attitudes of characters themselves to the narrator's attitudes about them, and so on. Conceived of in this way, point of view is a multileveled, constant shifting of perspectives, attitudes, and relationships.

Picaresque narrative has been most often and most characteristically rendered through the voice of the picaro himself, and this narrational situation creates a number of narrative conditions we must be alert to. We have to distinguish, for example, between an experiencing "I" and a narrating "I," or between a remembered "I" and a remembering "I": the narrator is quite literally remembering the dis-membered. As readers, moreover, we suspend our disbelief that anyone should be able to recall such specific details; we consent, that is, to the "convention of perfect memory," as Romberg calls it. The distance between the plane of narration and the plane of action depends on the position in time of the narrator; all events are related to it in varying degrees of temporal distance. But this distance or narrative space is not only temporal, for in it the narrator has a great deal of manipulatively rhetorical power. He not only depicts and analyzes himself at any chronological point through the psychological being he is at the time of narration, but he also plays with narrative distance and comments on the narrating process (the difficulty of remembering, the difference between what he was then and what he is now, and so on). He is both reflective and reflexive narratively. Sequential and associational patterns are fused in our awareness (and his awareness) of the process of narration. Although the plane of action is in the past in relation to the plane of narration, the awareness of narrative distance is often destroyed by what has been called the fictive present. Moreover, there is a temporal span on the plane of narration; the narrating act itself accumulates during the time of the narration and becomes part of the past that is being narrated. And finally, the recreative act itself can work against narrative distance by asserting the primacy of the narrating "I" as the only reality; there is no real distinction between past and present self because the past self exists only insofar as the present self creates it.

There are, too, the distances between the picaro and the implied author and the distance between the picaro and the reader, which Oskar Seidlin describes:

The discrepancy between the wretched, lowly Picaro who does not amount to anything in this world, and the effrontery with which he dares to say "I," is in itself a piece of *blague*, of persiflage and roguery, probably felt much more keenly than today in the sixteenth and seventeenth centuries when the weight and dignity of a person depended heavily on his status in life, although the conviction that it is presumptuous to write one's autobiography is by no means dead today and unwittingly leads to the question: "Who is he, after all, to claim our attention for his 'I'?" (192)

Such a provoking, I-dare-you-to-read-me gesture engages the reader and is part of picaresque narrative strategy, which, as Ife says, creates a dynamic relationship between reader and text: "author, protagonist, and reader become entangled in a web of irony from which no one escapes" (*Reading and Fiction in Golden-Age Spain*, 91).

The picaresque narrative act is both an aesthetic shaping and a moral reshaping of disordered fragments. If the picaro's life has been a welter of paradoxically continuous disintegrations, the narrative act is an attempt to integrate and make aesthetic, psychological, and moral sense of the dismembered past. Like the panoramic world it depicts, picaresque narration needs narrating space to convey both that world and its own process of presenting that world. Narrative distance, a dimension of point of view, provides that space.

Ultimately the picaro's narration is itself a trick, a lure, the narrative analogue of the tricks he has played to survive. Robert Heilman has said that shallowness is the key to the picaresque; there is incongruity between the depth of probing that the confessional narrative form implies and the actually shallow surface skimming that picaresque life portrays. Just as the adaptable picaro can in life play the social games in order to perpetrate his tricks of survival, so he can play the literary game of presenting himself in conventional dress and moral attire, only to focus on the chaotic, unconventional, and amoral life itself. Picaresque narration is thus a narrative version, between the picaro and the reader-victim, of the tricks in the picaro's life experiences, between the picaro and his landscape, as rendered in the fiction that emerges from the narrative act of telling. Narrative distance thus alerts us to "watch out" for ourselves, as the picaro early in life learns from hard knocks to watch out for himself, to distance ourselves from too much solicitous identification with the picaro's narrated past and too ready and uncritical acceptance of the morality of the picaro's present act of narration. Paying attention to all the dimensions of narrative distance provides our means of steering our way through the narrative hypocrisy that is part of the picaresque point of view.

In sum, then, narrative distance describes the narrating situation essential to picaresque narrative. It accounts for the temporal, spatial, psychological, moral, and aesthetic dimensions operating in the picaro's narrative act. And it accounts for the reader's distance from the picaro along those same planes, a distance that varies from very close to very far and implies an ethical distance within the reader, who may be closer to the unreformed and unconverted Guzmán of the past than to the converted and moralizing Guzmán of the present. Thematically, too, narrative distance reflects one of the larger themes of the picaresque: alienation, separation (from past, from reader, from self), and aloneness. First-person narration, the most intimate form of storytelling, is used in the service of alienation; even the narrative act does not integrate the exluded picaro into a stable order of things. And rhetorically, narrative distance reflects the internal rhythm of picaresque when through verbal prestidigitation it tries to manipulate the reader. Even in the narrative act, the picaro is still up to his old tricks. He assumes yet another role and becomes a trickster of narration, a verbally manipulative rogue. Simplicissimus learns early in life that "the foolish world wants to be fooled," and Felix Krull observes, "He who really loves the world shapes himself to please it," two assessments that, though they seem superficially to contradict one another, really implicate each other, for the world is pleased when it is deceived, a desire fiction gratifies well.

One further aspect of picaresque narration needs particular emphasizing, and it responds to the often-made and thus tiresome comment that picaresques do not "end" or conclude, that they just stop, or that they have no end until the picaro dies (which, ironically, could never itself be part of the narrative unless another narrator entered in); as far as his own narration is concerned, the picaro's death as a conclusion or ending is extratextual. Such a view is of the same order as the equally frequent observation about picaresques being primitive narrative organisms because they are "merely" episodic. Such originally analytical statements cannot help but become evaluative in a still novel-centered view of narrative fiction, and as such they have blinded many a reader—and many a critic— to complete readings of picaresque texts. Yet the panoramic-episodic structure and the Sisyphus rhythm are singularly appropriate to the fictional world rendered in picaresque; form matches subject matter precisely. Closer attention to picaresque narrative processes will also reveal their appropriateness to the rendering of the picaresque view of experience: a picaresque narrative ends at its beginning (or begins at its end), when narrative distance ceases to exist—that is, at the point when the picaro had decided to narrate his life. This "end" pervades the entire work and provides the vantage point from which every aspect of the work must be studied. Picaresque narrative begins from and then propels itself circularly toward its starting point. Simplicissimus begins his story in a cave on a desert island and brings his story to that cave; Guzmán narrates from and up to his sentence in the galleys; Lazarillo tells his story in defense of his case, which engenders, justifies, and completes his tale; and Ellison's Invisible Man is in his underground hole during the whole of his story. We have to remember, too, that picaresques climax with a self-perceived and -externalized change, which may take the form of explicit conversion (as in *Guzmán* and *Simplicissimus*) or some kind of moral or psychological rehabilitation (as in *Invisible Man*), or simply moral awareness suppressed by defiance (as in *Lazarillo*) or resignation (as in *El Buscón*). While such endings may not have the finality and resolving completeness of a romance ending, they are the starting points and the endings of picaresque narration (which is not at all the same as saying they are why the author produced the text). Picaresques are neither structurally nor narratively primitive.

THE PICARO/PICARA

The picaro is a pragmatic, unprincipled, resilient, solitary figure who just manages to survive in his chaotic landscape, but who, in the ups and downs, can also put that world very much on the defensive. The picaro is a protean figure who can not only serve many masters but play different roles, and his essential character trait is his inconstancy (of life roles, of self-identity), his own personality flux in the face of an inconstant world. "Nothing in the world is more constant than inconstancy itself," Simplicissimus discovers. "Would any man see Proteus?" wrote Edw. Burton to the translator in part two of Mabbe's version of *Guzmán*, "Guzmán is all the World; know him alone / And then yee know a Multitude in One." Through experience, too, the picaro develops a kind of internal gyroscope, what might be called a picaresque equilibrium, yet another paradox, as the insider-outsider situation of the picaro socially is one. Stuart Miller in *The Picaresque Novel* calls the picaro a being of "apersonality." The picaro is an orphan, Claudio Guillén says: "In the history of narrative forms, *Lazarillo de Tormes* represents the first significant appearance of the myth of the orphan. All later picaresque novels will build on this same highly suggestive situation" (*Literature as System*, 79). Moreover, he is a blank slate: "All values must be rediscovered by him anew, as if by a godless Adam." But despite the savvy he soon acquires, part of him remains engagingly innocent.

Picaros far outnumber picaras in the texts generally considered to be picaresque (and therefore I use the masculine pronouns and *picaro* to refer to the picaresque protagonist as a type, reserving *picara* for specific female characters such as Grimmelshausen's Courage and Defoe's Moll Flanders and Roxana). The relative paucity of picaras could well reflect a patriarchical literary establishment, which has simply not acknowledged such female figures over the centuries. More likely is Julio Rodríguez-Luis's assertion in his "*Pícaras*: The Modal Approach to the Picaresque" (1979) that the scarcity of picaras is a reflection of woman's lack of mobility: "Consequently, we are left with empty characters, or at most with caricatures of the *pícaro*, until the time in history when it becomes possible for a woman of low birth to move up in society with a certain degree of freedom, thus allowing the *pícara* . . . to achieve real depth in her literary characterization" (43). Moreover, all of the pre-twentieth-century picaras were created by male authors, resulting in a male voice-over whose discourse subjugates the picara's voice as much as society restricts her movement—a phenomenon just now being studied, most recently (and thoroughly) by Edward H. Friedman in his *The Antiheroine's Voice: Narrative Discourse and Transformations of the Picaresque* (1987): "The feminine picaresque accentuates the ironic voice-over. The intrusion of the author in the narrative (*La pícara Justina*), the man's voice claiming to be a woman's (*Teresa de Manzanares*), and the silencing of the antiheroine (*La hija de Celestina, La garduña de Sevilla*) parallel the relegation of women in society. Similarly, the editing and censorship of Moll Flanders's manuscript correspond to eighteenth-century social conditioning," while in a contemporary work like Erica Jong's *Fanny* (1980) "the play of voices comes full circle to all but eliminate the male perspective" (228).

That most picaresque protagonists have been male is, most probably, attributable to extraliterary factors. In terms of the character's function within the narrative structures we call picaresque, there is no reason why this protagonist must be male or female: the archetypal Trickster had attributes of both sexes.

THE PICARO-LANDSCAPE RELATIONSHIP

Our attention here is focused on the protagonist's interaction with society, a basic novelistic situation, and its typical pattern, in step with the internal rhythm of picaresque, is a movement from exclusion to attempted inclusion and back to exclusion: outside, inside, outside, resolved finally by a kind of self-exclusion through spiritual, moral, or psychological conversion, which in effect turns the tables on the world by renouncing it, as it had always rejected the picaro. As a deracinated being, the picaro is always looking for a home. But from society's point of view, he is an upstart, and this is true of all levels of society, none of which make room for him. He is truly outside. While he may reflect in his origins the fears of a social class priding itself on honor and purity of blood, his outsiderdom approaches what Camus called "cosmic homelessness" (cited by Lewis, *The Picaresque Saint*, 26). Lazarillo's early realization of *solo soy*— "I must keep awake because I'm on my own and I've got to look after myself"— is echoed by Pablos in *El Buscón* ("Pablos, you've got to wake up. Watch out for yourself. You know your father and mother can't do it for you") and by Guzmán: "Well, when I saw how the world went, and that there was no helpe for it; I pluckt up my spirits, set a good face on the matter, and drew strength out of weaknesse." The interaction between the picaro and society results in a dualization of the picaro: he is perceived by society as a disrupter of established social rhythms who must be kept out, and by himself as the plaything of fortune. Guillén observes a distinction between inner and outer man: "An inner man (embracing all the richness and subtlety of one's private thoughts and judgments) affirms his independence from an outer man (the patterns of behavior, the simplicity of the social role)," and considers this division of the hero "one of the most significant achievements of the picaresque, and perhaps its most substantial contribution to the thematics of the modern novel" (*Literature as System*, 89).

GALLERY OF HUMAN TYPES

These appear as human inhabitants of the landscape and often represent a cross-section of society both vertically and horizontally. As representatives of social orders or institutions, they are frequently satiric objects: the schoolmaster Cabra ("Goat") in *El Buscón*; the blind man, squire, and priest in *Lazarillo*. The panoramic landscape, the picaro's frequent change of master and locale, and the picaro's outside point of view all work together to make such a varied satiric gallery of human types verisimilar in the picaresque fictional world. Felix Krull travels not only horizontally but vertically through society quite literally when he is an elevator operator in a hotel (a job Karl Rossman in Kafka's *Amerika* also holds). Such a gallery, tied together by a wandering observer, however, does not in itself constitute a picaresque. If none or only a few of the other essential features are absent, the work is probably a formal satire. In picaresque, the gallery is important for the way it is observed by the picaro, not for the portrait itself as such. What Pablos perceives in the schoolmaster is his own outrageous wit and linguistic cleverness in drawing the portrait; what Lazarillo observes in the squire reflects his own humanity, perhaps even a kind of leveling of social class distinctions into one level of the human condition. The focus is always on the observer in picaresque; in full satire it is on the satiric object.

PARODY

Already with the third and fourth major picaresques (*El Buscón, La pícara Justina*) self-consciousness is coded into the genre, as Quevedo and López de Ubeda use the form against itself, as *Lazarillo* and *Guzmán* had been using it against chivalric romances. Implied parody of romance continues in such devices as the communities of rogues that persist even into latter-day picaresques. *The Tin Drum* is, among other things, a parody of the romance-like Bildungsroman, as *Invisible Man* is a parodic reversal of the quintessentially American romance, the Horatio Alger myth. Generic self-reference enters the picaresque narrative tradition with *Justina* and *El Buscón* and is rarely absent after that. And the kind of self-reflexiveness that can lead to self-parody is already evident in Quevedo's preface to *El Buscón*.

BASIC THEMES

Picaresque narrative tends to be discursively philosophical and meditative and fictionally antiphilosophical. What it asserts on the level of discourse it often contradicts or cancels out on the level of story. There is a constant tension between what is narrated and the narrating attitude of the narrator, making us suspect the sincerity of conversions, for example (the most notorious example being *Moll Flanders*). The conceptual discursive intent conflicts with the obvious relish with which the narrator launches into the hurly-burly of his sordid life; he works against his ostensible purpose by dwelling on the very things that his narration is supposed to prove worthless.

One major and overtly proclaimed theme is *desengaño*, or disillusionment (or Vanity of vanities), especially in *Simplicissimus*, but the philosophical seriousness with which it is worked out becomes problematic as soon as we examine narrative distance in any depth. This theme is problematic right up to our own day. Ellison's picaro is devastated, not spiritually strengthened, by his discovery of the callously manipulative truth behind an apparently good facade. And Felix Krull is horrified when he deconstructs stage illusion by visiting the actor Müller-Rosé backstage, and he quickly decides never to go behind the scenes again.

Another major picaresque theme is freedom, which the picaresque explores partly as the paradoxical entrapment in freedom. The picaro is freed not of his own will from the confines of ordinary social life, and he roams the landscape (which is paralleled on the narrative level by his desire to free himself from his life by turning it into art, which, paradoxically, entraps him in his life once more). Although the freedom is imposed on him, the picaro learns to relish it. Guzmán, though he is as quick as any other picaro to blame his lot on "fortune" or on what he calls (in Mabbe's version) his "squint-eyed Starre," realizes nevertheless the paradox of his freedom:

In these Morall and outward things, thou hast a kinde of free-will conferred upon thee, whereby thou maist (if thou wilt) governe both thy selfe, and thy actions. Thy starre cannot constraine thee, nor all the heavens joyned together with all the force and power that they have, cannot compell thee against thy will. It is thou that forcest thy selfe to leave what is good, and to apply thy selfe to that which is evill, following thy dishonest desires, whence these thy crosses and calamities come upon thee. (One, III, 10)

Karl Rossmann in Kafka's *Amerika*, when told he is free, replies, " 'Yes, I'm free,' said Karl, and nothing seemed more worthless than his freedom" (ch. 5).

Another picaresque theme is hunger, which emphasizes the picaro's struggle for the barest minimum level of physical sustenance. This theme grows primarily out of the fiction rather than the discourse and is as a result much more strongly embodied by being enacted rather than discoursed. Hunger is what Lazarillo's life is all about. After he has been with the impoverished squire for several days and received nothing to eat, he is sent out with money to buy food. Along the way he encounters a funeral procession, with a woman wailing, "Oh, my darling husband, where are they taking you? To the sad and accursed place, to the gloomy and dark dwelling, to the domain where there is no food or drink!" Lazarillo interprets the woman's words in terms of his own experiential situation, and he tells the squire they are bringing a body to his house. This incident is a vivid example of how a fundamental picaresque theme can be meaningfully portrayed in the particularity of a concretized incident on the story level. But even on the level of discourse, the theme has power. Guzmán says on one desperate occasion, "It is good to have a father, it is good to have a mother; but to have meat to put in a mans mouth, is better then them both" (One, II, 1). In contemporary picaresque, hunger remains a central thematic concern of the human condition as reflected in a picaro's experience. Orwell uses as epigram to *Down and Out in Paris and London* a quotation from Chaucer: "O scathful harm, condition of poverte!" Even Felix Krull, whose origins are upper middle class, goes hungry for a while.

Two other major picaresque themes are solitude, which arises from the picaro's essential condition in the world and his fundamental aloneness in the midst of teeming life (he is, to use Guillén's phrase, the "half-outsider," who can neither reject nor join his fellow human beings); and gullibility, arising from what the picaro learns in his relationship with the landscape when he tries to trick his way through life: that people want to be fooled, as Simplicissimus learns. In some ways, the picaresque is really an elaborate expansion in a variety of styles of the old saying that "a really honest man can't be swindled" (or in the words W. C. Fields is supposed to have said, "You can't cheat an honest man"). This theme is given especially solid and unusual treatment in Melville's *The Confidence-Man*.

MOTIFS

A motif is a minimal thematic unity that recurs in support of a larger theme.

Unusual Birth or Childhood

The circumstances surrounding the picaro's entrance into the world are often unusual. They parody the romance hero's genealogy. But within the picaresque, they first establish the picaro's singularity. Even his birth is a departure from normalcy. Second, they foreshadow his later "birth" or rebirth into a chaotic picaresque world. Lazarillo is born on the river. Simplicissimus does not know the circumstances of his birth until much later in life, and in early childhood he is witness to a horrible assault on his family. Guzmán de Alfarache in telling about his birth enters into prenatal details, like Oskar in *The Tin Drum*, and, like Oskar, he claims to have two fathers. Lizardi's Periquillo (*The Itching Parrot*) blames a succession of nurses for his bad character. Roderick Random's mother has a strange dream before giving birth. The boy in *The Painted Bird* experiences a childhood other children do not see even in nightmares. The unusual birth and childhood motifs reinforce the theme of solitude by making alienation or separation or outsiderdom part of the condition of the picaro's birth rather than a psychologically or philosophically motivated act later in life.

The Trick

Tricks in their infinitely variable forms play an important role in the picaro's relationship with his landscape; to some extent, they constitute that relationship. Their execution provides the internal rhythm of picaresque narrative. Their ingenuity (as well as their familiarity) probably generated much of the initial pleasure readers had in the picaresque. Tricks tend to serve as initiation rites to the world of chaos (the picaro is always tricked first by the landscape), but what begins as initiation is soon converted by the picaro into initiative. After Lazarillo gets his head banged against the stone bull by the blind man, he soon "sees" and learns how to pay him back in kind. As the tricks become more active rather than reactive, they support the picaresque theme of gullibility.

Role Playing

Metamorphoses and changing roles are part of the picaro's survival kit; as the world is in flux, so he can change roles to face it. Picaresque existence is a constant change of masks on the world-as-stage. For Guzmán, fortune is "like a Sphericall Figure, in a plaine body. That, which she gives to day, she takes away to morrow: she is the flowing of the Sea, tossing and tumbling us to and fro, till she leaves us at last upon drie land, on Deaths shore, from which she never returnes to recover us; And while we live, injoyning us (like Players) to con over our parts, and to learne daily new toyes and devices, to present them upon the stage of this World" (One, II, 7). Quevedo's Pablos plays roles constantly and at one point even "impersonates" himself. Simplicissimus begins his career as a jester; like Pablos, he too becomes an actor, and his adventures in Paris as "Beau Alman" prefigure the more sophisticated role playing of his descendant Felix Krull. Grimmelshausen's Courage poses as a boy, Smollett's Ferdinand as a count, Lizardi's Periquillo and Lesage's Gil Blas as doctors, Meriton Latroon as a girl in a boarding school. In his ability to play roles, the picaro is as illusory and illusive (and elusive) as the very illusory world he confronts. One of his necessary tools in that world is role playing, part of what Stuart Miller calls his "protean form": "There is no part the picaro will not play. . . . He assumes whatever appearance the world forces on him, and this a-personality is typical of the picaresque world, in which appearance and reality constantly mingle, making definition and order disappear. . . . The picaro is every man he has to be, and therefore no man" (*The Picaresque Novel*, 70–71). The very ability of the picaro to perform in as many jobs as he does and to play as many tricks as he can resides in this large repertoire of masks. He is not only the servant of many masters but the master of many masks. Estebanillo González in his prologue claims to have played eighty-three roles during his life. Beyond its function as a survival tactic, role playing supports the themes of vanity and gullibility.

The Grotesque or Horrible Incident

Picaresque fiction may often compress the blackness and horror of the debased world into one specific and very particularized incident. The meat pie episode in *El Buscón* is an example, when we are shocked into the realization that the pie being eaten is probably filled with the flesh of Pablos's recently executed father. In *La pícara Justina*, the picara's mother dies by choking on an enormous black sausage. In Cela's *The Family of Pascual Duarte*, Pascual's little brother has his ears bitten off by a hog and later dies by falling into an oil vat, an image that suggests some grotesque fetus, birth, and death all in one. In Grimmelshausen's *Runagate Courage*, a dead man's frozen legs are chopped off in order to steal the pants. Pito Pérez lives with a human skeleton and sleeps with it as his wife. Periquillo digs up the body of a woman so he can rob it of its jewels.

The blind man shoves his long and pointed nose down Lazarillo's throat until he vomits. Any incident in *The Tin Drum* would do, as would most of the boy's adventures in *The Painted Bird*. A primary function of grotesque motifs in picaresque fiction is to arouse a shocked response from us, to pummel us into an awareness and reaction to the nightmare world of chaos, a decidedly blacker world than the worlds of history and comedy on the spectrum of fictional modes, and in its way more disturbing than even the more radically distorted world of satire because in picaresque this world is portrayed as existentially valid human experience (it is experienced by a picaro who is narrating to us) while in formal satire the stylization and artifice are buffers between audience and shocking content. Grotesque motifs tend to emphasize the unpredictable tendency of the apparently normal to shift suddenly into abnormalcy and horror. As such they resemble the world upside down or world inside out topos that was a convention in literature before the picaresque (Randall, *The Golden Tapestry*, 217), and they support the fictional world rendered by picaresque.

Ejection

Lazarillo is ejected from home. Eichendorff's Good-for-Nothing is simply turned loose by his family. Moll Flanders is, "as it were, turned out of Door to the wide world" at the age of fourteen. Kafka's Karl Rossmann is "simply turned out . . . by his parents, just as you turn a cat out of the house when it annoys you" (ch. 1). Guzmán cannot believe, on first entering it, that the world cannot be encompassed in a single glance, just as Simplicissimus is ejected into the world as a totally blank slate. Periquillo is aware, on facing the world for the first time, that he has left the asylum of innocence behind him. Ejection is the picaro's second "birth"—it comes usually immediately before the world's first trick on him and is thus a kind of initiation shock. Kosinski's little boy in *The Painted Bird* is doubly ejected: first from his parents' home and then from his caretaker's. Ejection repeats itself in less radical ways forever after in the picaro's life as he leaves or is left by one master after another or has to flee circumstances. It energizes the external rhythm, the Sisyphus rhythm, and supports the theme of solitude. In Guillén's conception of the picaro as a new Adam, the first and most radical ejection would recapitulate humanity's expulsion from the Garden of Eden, and the resulting wandering journey is thus an attempt, filled with many ejections from lesser substitute gardens, to complete (in Parker's phrase) the "circle of existence," to reenter the Garden, to find home.

Thus our hypothetical fiction P.

We are now in the thick of the works themselves, and the discriminations of genre study demand that characteristics such as these be refined and tested until they describe a specific body of works that are enough like one another to be called the picaresque genre, which in turn will help us respond appropriately to those works and others like them. Genre theory exists not for its own sake but to help us shape our encounters with texts into intertextual and contextual orders that will guide us in our responses to individual texts that were themselves created in awareness of literary orders. Such encounters will be the business of part II.

Basic Studies in Picaresque Narrative/ Works Cited

This list is restricted to works that deal with aspects of picaresque narrative: problems of definition, genre considerations, type characteristics, themes, comparative and influence studies, historical surveys, contemporary variations, formal problems, narrative traditions, narrative technique, and related narrative forms. Focused studies of individual picaresque fictions are excluded here and given instead under the appropriate entry for that fiction in part II unless such studies also concern themselves with picaresque narrative in general.

BIBLIOGRAPHIES

Laurenti, Joseph L. *Bibliografía de la literatura picaresca: desde sus orígenes hasta el presente/A Bibliography of Picaresque Literature: From Its Origins to the Present.* Metuchen, N.J.: Scarecrow, 1973. Rpt. New York: AMS Press, 1973.
———. *Supplement.* New York: AMS Press, 1981.
Ricapito, Joseph V. *Bibliografía razonada y anotada de las obras maestras de la picaresca española.* Madrid: Castalia, 1980.

CRITICAL ANTHOLOGIES AND COLLECTIONS

Criado de Val, Manuel, ed. *La picaresca: orígenes, textos, y estructuras.* Actas del I Congreso Internacional sobre la Picaresca organizado por el Patronato "Arcipreste de Hita." Madrid: Fundación Universitaria Española, 1979.
Gaunt, J. L., John P. Kent, and Bernard Oldsey, eds. *The Picaresque Tradition.* Spec. issue of *College Literature* 6, no. 3 (1979): 165-270.
Heidenreich, Helmut, ed. *Pikarische Welt: Schriften zum europäischen Schelmenroman.* Darmstadt: Wissenschaftliche Buchgesellschaft, 1969.
Pellón, Gustavo, and Julio Rodríguez-Luis, eds. *Upstarts, Wanderers or Swindlers: Anatomy of the Picaro, A Critical Anthology.* Amsterdam: Rodopi, 1986.
Picaresque espagnole: Actes du 1re. table ronde internationale du C.N.R.S. organizée

en nov. 1974. Montpellier: Université Paul Valéry, Centre d'études sociocritiques, 1976.

Vaíllo, Carlos, ed. *La novela picaresca y otras formas narrativas*. In *Siglos de Oro: Barroco*. Edited by Bruce W. Wardropper. Vol. 3 of *Historia y crítica de la literatura española*, edited by Francisco Rico. 8 vols. Barcelona: Editorial Crítica, 1983.

Whitbourn, Christine J., ed. *Knaves and Swindlers: Essays on the Picaresque Novel in Europe*. University of Hull Publications. London: Oxford University Press, 1974.

BOOKS AND ARTICLES

Albérès, R. M. "Renaissance du roman picaresque." *Revue de Paris* 75 (1968): 46–53.

Alewyn, Richard. "Der Roman des Barock." *Formkräfte der deutschen Dichtung vom Barock bis zur Gegenwart*. Göttingen: Vandenhoeck and Ruprecht, 1963. (In Heidenreich, above; pp. 397–411.)

Alfaro, Gustavo A. *La estructura de la novela picaresca*. Serie "La Granada Entreabierta," 16. Bogotá: Instituto Caro y Cuervo, 1977.

———. "El cuento intercalado en la novela picaresca." *Hispanófila* 40 (1970): 1–8.

———. "El despertar del pícaro." *Romanische Forschungen* 80 (1968): 44–52.

Allen, H. Warner. "The Picaresque Novel, An Essay in Comparative Literature." 1908. In Fernando de Rojas, *Celestina or The Tragi-Comedy of Calisto and Melibea*. London: Routledge, 1923.

Alonso, Amado. "Lo picaresco de la picaresca." *Verbum* 22 (1929): 321–38. (In German as "Das Pikareske des Schelmenromans" in Heidenreich, above; pp. 79–100.)

Alonso, Dámaso. "The Spanish Contribution to the Modern European Novel." *Journal of World History* 6 (1960–1961): 878–97.

Alter, Robert. *Rogue's Progress: Studies in the Picaresque Novel*. Cambridge, Mass.: Harvard University Press, 1964.

Alvarez, G. E. *El amor en la novela picaresca española*. The Hague: Van Goor Zonen, 1958.

———. *Le Thème de la femme dans la picaresque espagnole*. Groningen: Wolters, 1955.

Antkowiak, A. "Schelm und Schelmenroman: Zu einer Form plebjischer Tradition in der Literatur." *Aufbau* 14 (1958): 68–77.

Aribau, Buenaventura Carlos. "Novela picaresca." In *Novelistas anteriores a Cervantes*. Vol. 3 of the *Biblioteca de autores españoles*. Madrid, 1846.

Atkinson, William. "Studies in Literary Decadence: The Picaresque Novel." *Bulletin of Hispanic Studies* 4 (1927): 19–27.

Aubrun, Charles V. "Picaresques: A Propos de cinq ouvrages recents." *Romanic Review* 59 (1968): 106–21.

———. "La gueuserie aux XVIe et XVIIe siècles en Espagne et le roman picaresque." In *Littérature et société: Problèmes de methodologie en sociologie de la littérature*, pp. 137–50. Eds. Lucien Goldmann, Michel Bernard, and Roger Lallemand. Colloque organisé conjointement par l'Institut de sociologie de l'université libre de Bruxelles et l'Ecole pratique des hautes études (6e section) de Paris du 21 mai au 23 mai 1964. Brussels: Université libre de Bruxelles, Editions de l'Institut de sociologie, 1967.

Ayala, Francisco. "Formación del género 'novela picaresca': El *Lazarillo*" and "El

Guzmán de Alfarache: Consolidación del género picaresco." In *Experiencia e invención (Ensayos sobre el escritor y su mundo)*, 127–57. Madrid: Taurus, 1960.

Babcock, Barbara A. " 'Liberty's a Whore': Inversions, Marginalia, and Picaresque Narrative." In *The Reversible World: Symbolic Inversion in Art and Society*, 95–116. Ed. Barbara A. Babcock. Ithaca, N.Y.: Cornell University Press, 1978.

Barine, Arvède. "Les gueux d'Espagne." *Revue des deux mondes*, 15 April 1888, 870–904.

Bataillon, Marcel. *Pícaros y picaresca*. Trans. Francisco R. Vadillo. Madrid: Taurus, 1969.

Baumanns, Peter. "Der *Lazarillo de Tormes* eine Travestie der Augustinischen *Confessiones?*" *Romanistiches Jahrbuch* 10 (1959): 285–91.

Beberfall, Lester. "The Pícaro in Context." *Hispania* 37 (1954): 288–92.

Beck, Werner. *Die Anfänge des deutschen Schelmenromans: Studien zur frühbarocken Erzählung*. Zurich: Juris-Verlag, 1957.

Bělič, Oldřich. "La novela picaresca como orden artístico." *Romanistica Pragensia* 3 (1963): 5–36. (Also in *Universidad de la Habana* 27 [September–October 1963]: 7–30.)

———. "La novela picaresca española y el realismo." *Romanistica Pragensia* 2 (1961): 5–15.

Benítez Claros, Rafael. *Existencialismo y picaresca*. Colleción "O crece o muere." Madrid: Ateneo, 1958.

Bermejo, José M. "Lección de pícaros." *Cuadernos Hispanoamericanos* 273 (1973): 611–16.

Bertrand, J.-J. A. "L. Tieck et le roman picaresque." *Revue germanique* 10 (1914): 443–61.

Bjornson, Richard. *The Picaresque Hero in European Fiction*. Madison: University of Wisconsin Press, 1977.

Blackburn, Alexander. *The Myth of the Picaro: Continuity and Transformation of the Picaresque Novel, 1554–1954*. Chapel Hill: University of North Carolina Press, 1979.

Blanco Aguinaga, Carlos. "Cervantes y la picaresca. Notas sobre dos tipos de realismo." *Nueva Revista de Filología Hispánica* 11 (1957): 313–42. (Trans. and abr. as "Cervantes and the Picaresque Mode" in *Cervantes: A Collection of Critical Essays*, ed. Lowry Nelson, Jr. Englewood Cliffs, N.J.: Prentice-Hall, 1969.)

Borgers, Oscar. "Le Roman picaresque. Réalisme et fiction." *Les Lettres romanes* 14 (1960): 295–305; 15 (1961): 23–38, 135–48.

Braidotti, Erminio. "Genealogiá y licitud de la designación 'novela picaresca.' " *Cuadernos Hispanoamericanos* 346 (1979): 97–119.

Broich, Ulrich. "Tradition und Rebellion: Zur Renaissance des pikaresken Romans in der englischen Literatur der Gegenwart." *Poetika: Zeitschrift für Sprach und Literaturwissenschaft* 1, no. 2 (1970): 214–29.

Brun, Félix. "Pour une interpretation sociologique du roman picaresque." In *Littérature et société* (see Aubrun, above), 174–80. Trans. and abr. in Pellón and Rodríguez-Luis, above.

Cabrera, Rosa M. "El pícaro en las literaturas hispánicas." In *Actas del tercer Congreso Internacional de Hispanistas*, 163–73. Ed. Carlos H. Magis. Mexico City: El Colegio de México por la Asociación Internacional de Hispanistas, 1970.

Campusano, Elizabeth. "Ciertos aspectos de la novela picaresca." *Hispania* 32 (1949): 190–97.

Cañedo, Jesús. "Tres pícaros, el amor y la mujer." *Ibero-romania* 1 (1969): 193–227.

———. "El *curriculum vitae* del pícaro." *Revista de Filología Española* 49 (1966): 125–80.

———. "La 'naturaleza' en la novela picaresca." *Revista de Literatura* 30 (1966): 5–38.

Caneva, R. "Picaresca: anticaballería y realismo." *Universidad de Antioquia* (Medellín, Colombia) 110 (1953): 373–89.

Carrillo, Francisco. *Semiolingüística de la novela picaresca.* Madrid: Ediciones Cátedra, 1982.

Casas de Faunce, María. *La novela picaresca latinoamericana.* Planeta/Universidad de Puerto Rico. Madrid: Cupsa Editorial, 1977.

Castro, Américo. Introduction to *La vida de Lazarillo de Tormes,* v–xii. Ed. Everett W. Hesse and Harry F. Williams. Rev. ed. Madison: University of Wisconsin Press, 1961.

———. "Perspectiva de la novela picaresca." 1935. In *Hacia Cervantes,* 118–42. 3d ed. Madrid: Taurus, 1967. (In German as "Perspektive des Schelmenromans" in Heidenreich, above; pp. 119–46.)

———. "Lo picaresco." 1925. In *El pensamiento de Cervantes,* 228–44. New edition amplified by Julio Rodríguez-Puértolas. Barcelona-Madrid: Editorial Noguer, 1973.

Chandler, Frank Wadleigh. *Romances of Roguery, An Episode in the History of the Novel. Part I, The Picaresque Novel in Spain.* New York: Columbia University Press, 1899. Rpt. New York: Burt Franklin, 1961.

———. *The Literature of Roguery.* 2 vols. Boston: Houghton Mifflin, 1907. Rpt. New York: Burt Franklin, 1958.

Chesterton, G. K. "The Romance of a Rascal." In *The Common Man,* 42–49. London: Scheed and Ward, 1950.

Childers, J. Wesley. *Tales from Spanish Picaresque Novels: A Motif-Index.* Albany: State University of New York Press, 1977.

Clarke, Henry Butler. "The Spanish Rogue-Story (Novela de Pícaros)." In *Studies in European Literature: Taylorian Lectures 1889–1899,* 313–49. S. Mallarmé, W. Pater, E. Dowden, W. M. Rossetti et al. Oxford: Clarendon Press, 1900.

Corominas, Joan. "Pícaro." In *Diccionario crítico etimológico de la lengua castellana,* vol. 3, 768–71. Madrid: Gredos, 1954–1957. (In German as "Das Wort 'pícaro,' " in Heidenreich, above; pp. 255–66.)

Crawford, J. P. Wickersham. "The Pícaro in the Spanish Drama of the Sixteenth Century." In *Schelling Anniversary Papers by His Former Students,* 107–16. New York: Century, 1923.

Cros, Edmond. *Protée et le gueux: Recherches sur les origines et la nature du récit picaresque dans "Guzman de Alfarache."* Paris: Didier, 1967.

Daghistany, Ann. "The Picara Nature." *Women's Studies* 4 (1977): 51–60.

Delay, Florence. "Vies picaresques." *Nouvelle revue française* 17 (1969): 441–47.

Dooley, D. J. "Some Uses and Mutations of the Picaresque." *Dalhousie Review* 37 (1957–1958): 363–77.

Dunn, Peter N. *The Spanish Picaresque Novel.* Boston: Twayne, 1979.

Eisenberg, Daniel. "Does the Picaresque Novel Exist?" *Kentucky Romance Quarterly* 26 (1979): 203–19.

Eoff, Sherman. "*Oliver Twist* and the Spanish Picaresque Novel." *Studies in Philology* 54 (1957): 440–47.

———. "A Galdosian Version of Picaresque Psychology." *Modern Language Forum* 38 (1953): 1–12.

Escarpit, Robert. "Le Roman picaresque." *Bulletin du Centre d'études et discussions de littérature générale* (Bordeaux) 1, no. 3 (1951–1952): 2–3, 1–18.

Feldman, Joel I. "First-Person Narrative Technique in the Picaresque Novel." In *Studies in Hispanic History and Literature*, 160–73. Ed. on behalf of the Department of Spanish and Latin American Studies by B. Jozef. Vol. 26, *Scripta Hierosolymitana*, Publications of the Hebrew University. Jerusalem: Magnes Press, 1974.

Fitzmaurice-Kelly, James. Review of F. W. Chandler's *Romances of Roguery* and Fonger de Haan's *An Outline History of the Novela Picaresca*. *Revue hispanique* 10 (1903): 296–301.

Ford, Jeremiah Denis Matthias. "Possible Foreign Sources of the Spanish Novel of Roguery." In *Anniversary Papers by Colleagues and Pupils of George Lyman Kittredge*, 289–93. Boston and London: Ginn, 1913.

Fowler, Alastair. "The Confidence Man." *The Listener*, 4 May 1961, 781, 784.

Francis, Alán. *Picaresca, Decadencia, Historia: Aproximación a una realidad histórico-literaria*. Biblioteca Románica Hispánica. Madrid: Gredos, 1978.

Frank, Waldo. "The First Rogue." *Saturday Review of Literature*, 13 February 1926, 561.

Friedman, Edward H. *The Antiheroine's Voice: Narrative Discourse and Transformations of the Picaresque*. Columbia: University of Missouri Press, 1987.

Frohock, Wilbur M. "The Failing Center: Recent Fiction and the Picaresque Tradition." *Novel: A Forum on Fiction* 3 (1969): 62–69. (See also Gerber, below.)

———. "The Idea of the Picaresque." *Yearbook of Comparative and General Literature* 16 (1967): 43–52.

———. "The 'Picaresque' in France before *Gil Blas*." *Yale French Studies* 38 (1967): 222–29. (Abr. in Pellón and Rodríguez-Luis, above; pp. 279–84.)

Frutos Gómez de las Cortinas, J. "El antiheroe y su actitud vital (Sentido de la novela picaresca)." *Cuadernos de Literatura* 7 (1950): 97–143.

Galloway, David D. "A Picaresque Apprenticeship: Nathanael West's *The Dream Life of Balso Snell* and *A Cool Million*." *Wisconsin Studies in Contemporary Literature* 5 (1964): 110–26.

———. "The Absurd Man as Picaro: The Novels of Saul Bellow." *Texas Studies in Literature and Language* 6 (1964): 226–54.

García Blanco, Manuel. *Mateo Alemán y la novela picaresca alemana*. Madrid: Blass, 1928.

García Mercadal, José. "Inclinación picaresca" and "Pícaros y hampones." In *Estudiantes, sopistas, y pícaros*, 153–68, 169–86. 1934. Buenos Aires: Espasa-Calpe, 1954.

Garriga, Francisco Javier. "Estudio de la novela picaresca española." *Revista contemporanea* 16 (1890): 561–75; 17 (1891): 135–46, 283–89. Rpt. Madrid: Hernandez, 1891.

Gauchat, Louis. "*Lazarillo de Tormes* und die Anfänge des Schelmenromans." *Archiv für das Studium der neueren Sprachen und Literaturen* 129 (1912): 430–44.

Gerber, Philip L., and Robert J. Gemmett. "Picaresque and Modern Literature: A Conversation with W. M. Frohock." *Genre* 3 (1970): 187–97.

Giddings, Robert L. *The Tradition of Smollett*. London: Methuen, 1967.

Gili Gaya, Samuel. "La novela picaresca en el siglo XVI," "Apogeo y destintegración de la novela picaresca," and "Evolución histórica de la novela picaresca." Vol. 3 of *Historia general de las literaturas hispánicas*, 79–103, iii–xxv. Ed. Guillermo Díaz-Plaja. Barcelona: Barna, 1953.

Gillespie, Gerald. "Estebanillo and Simplex: Two Baroque Views of the Role-Playing Rogue in War, Crime, and Art (with an Excursus on Krull's Forebears)." *Canadian Review of Comparative Literature* 9 (1982): 157–71. (Abr. in Pellón and Rodríguez-Luis, above; pp. 285–95.)

———. "Rogues, Fools, and Satyrs: Ironic Ghosts in American Fiction." In *Proceedings of the Comparative Literature Symposium, Vol. 5: Modern American Fiction. Insights and Foreign Lights. January 27 and 28, 1972*, 89–106. Ed. Wolodymir T. Zyla and Wendell M. Aycock. Lubbock: Texas Tech University, 1972.

Gómez Lance, Betty Rita. *La actitud picaresca en la novela española del siglo XX*. Kalamazoo, Mich.: Kalamazoo College, 1968.

Gómez-Moriana, Antonio. "Intertextualidad, Interdiscursividad y parodia: Sobre los orígenes de la forma narrativa en la novela picaresca." *Dispositio* 8 (1983): 123–44.

González Palencia, Angel. *Del "Lazarillo" a Quevedo*. Madrid: CSIC, 1946.

Grass, Roland. "Morality in the Picaresque Novel." *Hispania* 42 (1959): 192–98.

Greifelt, R. "Die Ubersetzungen des spanischen Schelmenromans in Frankreich." *Romanische Forschungen* 50 (1936): 51–84.

Guedj, Aime. "Structure du monde picaresque." *La Nouvelle critique*. Special issue (1968): 82–87.

Günther, Helmut. "Der ewige Simplizissimus. Gestalt und Wandlungen des deutschen Schelmenromans." *Welt und Wort* 10 (1955): 1–5.

Guillén, Claudio. "Genre and Countergenre: The Discovery of the Picaresque." In *Literature as System: Essays toward the Theory of Literary History*, 135–58. Princeton, N.J.: Princeton University Press, 1971. Translation and expansion of "Luis Sánchez, Ginés de Pasamonte y los inventores del género picaresco," in *Homenaje a Rodríguez-Moñino: Estudios de erudición que le ofrecen sus amigos o discípulos hispanistas norteamericanos*, vol. 1, 221–31. Madrid: Castalia, 1966.

———. "Toward a Definition of the Picaresque." In *Proceedings of the IIIrd Congress of the International Comparative Literature Association*, 252–66. Ed. W. A. P. Smit. The Hague: Mouton, 1962. Rpt. in his *Literature as System*, 71–106.

———. "La disposición temporal del *Lazarillo de Tormes*." *Hispanic Review* 25 (1957): 264–79.

———. *The Anatomies of Roguery: A Comparative Study in the Origins and the Nature of Picaresque Literature*. Ph.D. dissertation, Harvard University, 1953. New York: Garland, 1987.

Guise, R. "La Fortune de *Lazarillo de Tormès* en France, au XIXe siècle." *Revue de Littérature Comparée* 39 (1965): 337–57.

Haan, Fonger de. *An Outline of the History of the Novela Picaresca in Spain*. Ph.D. dissertation, Johns Hopkins, 1895. The Hague and New York: Martinus Nijhoff, 1903.

———. "Pícaro y ganapanes." In *Homenaje a Menéndez y Pelayo*, vol. 2, 149–90. Madrid: Juarez, 1899.

Habel, Ursula. *Die Nachwirkung des picaresken Romans in England (von Nash bis Fielding und Smollett)*. Breslau: Pribatsch, 1930.

Haley, George. *Vicente Espinel and "Marcos de Obregón": A Life and Its Literary Representation*. Providence, R.I.: Brown University Press, 1959.

Hall, James. "The Unconfident Confidence Man." In *The Tragic Comedians: Seven Modern British Novelists*, 99–110. Bloomington: Indiana University Press, 1963.

Hanrahan, Thomas, S. J. *La mujer en la novela picaresca española*. 2 vols. Madrid: José Porrúa Turanzas, 1967.

Hassan, Ihab H. "The Anti-Hero in Modern British and American Fiction." In *Comparative Literature: Proceedings of the Second Congress of the International Comparative Literature Association*, vol. 1, 309–23. Chapel Hill: University of North Carolina Press, 1959.

Hatfield, T. M. "Some German Picaras of the Eighteenth Century." *Journal of English and Germanic Philology* 31 (1932): 509–29.

Heilman, Robert B. "Variations on Picaresque (*Felix Krull*)." *The Sewanee Review* 66 (1958): 547–77.

Herrero, Miguel. "Nueva interpretación de la novela picaresca." *Revista de Filología Española* 24 (1937): 343–62.

Ife, B. W. *Reading and Fiction in Golden-Age Spain: A Platonist Critique and Some Picaresque Replies*. Cambridge: Cambridge University Press, 1985.

Jacobs, Jürgen. *Der deutsche Schelmenroman*. Artemis Einführungen 5. Munich and Zurich: Artemis, 1983.

Jauss, Hans Robert. "Ursprung and Bedeutung der Ich-Form im *Lazarillo de Tormes*." *Romanistisches Jahrbuch* 8 (1957): 290–311.

Jenisch, Erich. "Vom Abenteuer- zum Bildungsroman." *Germanisch-Romanische Monatsschrift* 14 (1926): 339–51.

Jolles, André. "Die literarischen Travestien: Ritter–Hirt–Schelm." Trans. Otto Gerner, in Heidenreich (see above), pp. 101–18. Orig. in *Blätter für deutsche Philosophie* 6 (1932–1933): 281–94.

Jørgensen, Kathrine Sørenson Ravn. "Pour une Nouvelle approche du roman picaresque." *Revue romane* 21 (1986): 77–95.

Jung, C. G. "On the Psychology of the Trickster-Figure." In *The Collected Works of C. G. Jung*, vol. 9 (part I), 255–72. Ed. Sir Herbert Read, Michael Fordham, and Gerhard Adler. London: Routledge and Kegan Paul, 1959. Trans. R. F. C. Hull. Orig. in Paul Radin, *The Trickster* (see below), 195–211.

Karl, Frederick R. "Picaresque and the American Experience." *Yale Review* 57 (1968): 196–212.

Katona, Anna. "Picaresque Satires in Modern American Fiction." *Acta Litteraria Academiae Scientarium Hungaricae* (Budapest) 12 (1970): 105–20.

Kearful, Frank J. "Spanish Rogues and English Foundlings: On the Disintegration of Picaresque." *Genre* 4 (1971): 376–91.

Kent, John P., and J. L. Gaunt. "Picaresque Fiction: A Bibliographic Essay." *College Literature* 6 (1979): 245–70.

Kerényi, Karl. "The Trickster in Relation to Greek Mythology." Trans. R. F. C. Hull. In Paul Radin, *The Trickster* (see below), pp. 171–91.

Kirkpatrick, F. A. "The First Picaresque Romance." *Bulletin of Hispanic Studies* 5 (1928): 147–54.

Klüppelholz, Heinz. "Le Roman picaresque espagnol: Evolution et caractéristiques du genre." *Les Lettres romanes* 33 (1979): 127–61.

Kuhlmann, Susan. *Knave, Fool, and Genius: The Confidence Man as He Appears in Nineteenth-Century American Fiction.* Chapel Hill: University of North Carolina Press, 1973.

Laurenti, Joseph L. *Los prólogos en las novelas picarescas españolas.* Madrid: Castalia, 1971.

————. *Estudios sobre la novela picaresca española.* Madrid: CSIC, 1970.

Lázaro Carreter, Fernando. "Glosas críticas a *Los pícaros en la literatura* de Alexander A. Parker." *Hispanic Review* 41 (1973): 469–97.

————. *"Lazarillo de Tormes" en la picaresca.* Barcelona: Ariel, 1972.

Lewis, R. W. B. *The Picaresque Saint: Representative Figures in Contemporary Fiction.* Philadelphia: Lippincott, 1959.

Lindberg, Gary. *The Confidence Man in American Literature.* New York: Oxford University Press, 1982.

Lovett, Gabriel H. *"Lazarillo de Tormes* in Russia." *Modern Language Journal* 36 (1952): 166–74.

Mähl, Hans-Joachim. "Narr und Picaro: Zum Wandel der Narrenmotivik im Roman des 17. Jahrhunderts." In *Studien zur deutschen Literatur: Festschrift für Adolf Beck zum siebzigsten Geburtstag,* 18–40. Ed. Ulrich Fülleborn and Johannes Krogoll. Probleme der Dichtung 16. Heidelberg: Winter, 1979.

Mancing, Howard. "The Picaresque Novel: A Protean Form." *College Literature* 6 (1979): 182–204.

Mancini, G. "Classicismo e *novela picaresca." Annali della Facoltà di Lettere e Filosofia dell' Università di Cagliari* 8 (1950): 161–220.

Maravall, José A. *La picaresca desde la historia social.* Madrid: Taurus, 1988.

————. "Relaciones de dependencia e integración social: criados, graciosos y pícaros." *Ideologies and Literature* 1 (1977): 3–32.

————. "La aspiración de 'medro' en la novela picaresca." *Cuadernos Hispanoamericanos* 312 (1976): 590–625.

May, T. E. " 'Pícaro': A Suggestion." *Romanic Review* 43 (1952): 27–33.

Mesa, Carlos E. "Divagaciones sobre la literatura picaresca." *Thesaurus* 26 (1971): 559–617.

Miller, Stuart. *The Picaresque Novel.* Cleveland: Case Western Reserve University Press, 1967.

Moldenhauer, Gerhard. "Spanische Zensur und Schelmenroman." In *Estudios eruditos in memoriam de Adolfo Bonilla y San Martín (1875–1926),* vol. 1, 223–39. Madrid: Viuda e Hijos de Jaime Ratés, 1927.

Molho, Maurice. "El Pícaro de Nuevo." *Modern Language Notes* 100, no. 2 (1985): 199–222.

————. *Introducción al pensamiento picaresco.* Trans. Augusto Gálvez-Cañero y Pidal. Salamanca: Anaya, 1972. Orig. the introduction to *Romans picaresques espagnols* (Paris: Bibliothèque de la Pléiade, 1968).

Monte, Alberto del. *Itinerario de la novela picaresca espanola.* Barcelona: Editorial Lumen, 1971. (Trans. and rev. of *Itinerario del romanzo picaresco spagnolo.* Florence: Sansoni, 1957.)

Monteser, Frederick. *The Picaresque Element in Western Literature.* Studies in the Humanities No. 5. University: University of Alabama Press, 1975.

Montesinos, José F. "Gracián o la picaresca pura." In *Estudios y ensayos de literatura española*, 132–45. Mexico City: Ediciones de Andrea, 1959. Orig. in *Cruz y Raya* (Madrid) 4 (1933): 37–63. (Trans. and abr. as "Gracian or the Pure Picaresque" in Pellón and Rodríguez-Luis, above; pp. 188–97.)

Montolíu, Manuel de. "El alma picaresca." In *El alma de España y sus reflejos en la literatura del siglo de oro*, 253–354. Barcelona: Clarosó, 1942.

Moreno Báez, Enrique. *Lección y sentido del "Guzmán de Alfarache."* Madrid: CSIC, 1948.

Nagy, Edward. "El pícaro y la envoltura picaresca." *Hispania* 45 (1962): 57–61.

Nemoianu, Virgil. "Picaresque Retreat: From Xenophon's *Anabasis* to Defoe's *Singleton*." *Comparative Literature Studies* 23 (1986): 91–102.

Nykl, A. R. "Pícaro." *Revue hispanique* 77 (1929): 172–86.

Ortega y Gasset, José. "La picardía original de la novela picaresca." In *Obras completas*, vol. 2, 121–25. Madrid: Rev. de Occidente, 1957–1962. Orig. part of "Una primera vista sobre Baroja," in *La Lectura* (1915), 337–79. In German as "Die originelle Schelmerei des Schelmenromans" in Heidenreich, above; pp. 8–14.

Parker, Alexander A. *Literature and the Delinquent: The Picaresque Novel in Spain and Europe, 1599–1753*. Edinburgh: University Press, 1967.

Paulson, Ronald. "Picaresque Narrative: The Servant-Master Relation" and "Swiftean Picaresque: *Gulliver's Travels*." In *The Fictions of Satire*, 58–73, 162–85. Baltimore: Johns Hopkins University Press, 1967.

Pereda Valdés, Ildefonso. *La novela picaresca y el pícaro en España y América*. Montevideo, 1950.

Pérez Minik, Domingo. "Sentido vigente de la novela picaresca," "El *Lazarillo de Tormes* y su impresionismo," and "Actualidad de *Guzmán de Alfarache*." In *Novelistas españoles de los siglos XIX y XX*, 9–55. Madrid: Guadarrama, 1957.

Petriconi, Helmut. "Zur Chronologie und Verbreitung des spanischen Schelmenromans." *Volkstum und Kultur der Romanen* 1 (1928): 324–42. In Heidenreich, above; pp. 61–78.

———. "Abenteuer und kein Ende." *Romanisches Jahrbuch* 14 (1963): 27–44; 15 (1964): 160–71.

Pfandl, Ludwig. "Der Ritter als Schelm oder die novela picaresca." In *Geschichte der spanischen Nationalliteratur in ihrer Blütezeit*, 262–89. Freiburg: Herder, 1929. In Spanish as "El caballero como pícaro," in *Historia de la literatura nacional española en la edad de oro*, 291–321. Trans. Jorge Rubió Balaguer. Barcelona: Gili, 1933.

"Picaresco Romances." *The Southern Review* 2 (July 1867): 146–71.

Polaino Ortega, Lorenzo. *La delincuencia en la picaresca*. Seville, 1964.

Praag, Jonas Andries van. "Des Problèmes du roman picaresque espagnol." *Revue de l'université de Bruxelles* 10 (1957–58): 303–20.

———. "La Pícara en la literatura española." *Spanish Review* 3 (1936): 63–74.

Praag-Chantraine, Jacqueline. "El pícaro en la novela española moderna." *Revista Hispánica Moderna* 29 (1963): 23–31.

———. "Chronique des lettres espagnoles: Actualité du roman picaresque." *Synthèses* 14 (1959): 121–33.

Radin, Paul. *The Trickster: A Study in American Indian Mythology*. 1956. Orig. *Der göttliche Schelm* (Zurich, 1954). Commentaries by Jung and Kerenyi (see above). New York: Schocken, 1972.

Randall, Dale B. J. *The Golden Tapestry: A Critical Survey of Non-Chivalric Spanish*

Fiction in English Translation (1543–1657). Durham, N.C.: Duke University Press, 1963.

Rauhut, Franz. "Vom Einfluss des spanischen Schelmenromans auf das italienische Schrifttum." *Romanische Forschungen* 54 (1940): 382–89.

———. "Influencia de la picaresca española en la literatura alemana." *Revista de Filología Hispánica* 1 (1939): 237–56.

Rausse, Hubert. "Zur Geschichte des spanischen Schelmenromans in Deutschland." *Münstersche Beiträge zur neueren Literaturgeschichte* 8 (1908): 33–39.

———. "*La novela picaresca* und die Gegenreformation." *Euphorion* 16 (1909): 6–10.

Reed, Helen H. *The Reader in the Picaresque Novel*. London: Tamesis, 1984.

Reed, Walter L. *An Exemplary History of the Novel: The Quixotic versus the Picaresque*. Chicago: University of Chicago Press, 1981.

Rexach, Rosario. "El hombre nuevo en la novela picaresca española." *Cuadernos Hispanoamericanos* 275 (1973): 367–77.

Rey, Alfonso. "La novela picaresca y el narrador fidedigno." *Hispanic Review* 47 (1979): 55–75.

Ricapito, Joseph V. "Societé et ambiance historique dans la critique du roman picaresque espagnol." In *Picaresque espagnole*, above; vol. 1, 9–36.

———. "From Bocaccio to Mateo Alemán: An Essay on Literary Sources and Adaptations." *Romanic Review* 6 (1969): 83–95.

Rico, Francisco. *The Spanish Picaresque Novel and the Point of View*. Trans. Charles Davis, with Harry Sieber. Cambridge: Cambridge University Press, 1984. Orig. *La novela picaresca y el punto de vista*. Barcelona: Editorial Seix Barral, 1970.

Riggan, William. *Pícaros, Madmen, Naïfs, and Clowns: The Unreliable First-Person Narrator*. Norman: University of Oklahoma Press, 1981.

Rodríguez-Luis, Julio. "*Pícaras*: The Modal Approach to the Picaresque." *Comparative Literature* 31 (1979): 32–46.

Rojas Carrasco, Guillermo. *La novela picaresca en la literatura española*. Santiago: Instituto Pedagógico de la Universidad de Santiago de Chile, 1919.

Roland, A. "La psicología de la novela picaresca." *Hispania* 36 (1953): 423–26.

Ronquillo, Pablo J. *Retrato de la pícara: La protagonista de la picaresca española del XVII*. Madrid: Playor, 1980.

Rötzer, Hans Gerd. " 'Novela picaresca' und 'Schelmenroman': Ein Vergleich." In *Literatur und Gesellschaft im deutschen Barock*, 30–76. Ed. Conrad Wiedemann. *Germanisch-Romanische Monatsschrift*, supp. 1. Heidelberg, 1979.

———. *Picaro—Landstörtzer—Simplicius: Studien zum niederen Roman in Spanien und Deutschland*. Darmstadt: Wissenschaftliche Buchgesellschaft, 1972.

Sacy, S. de. "Le Miroir sur la grande route: Les romans de Stendhal et le roman picaresque." *Mercure de France* 306 (1949): 64–80.

Saldana, Quintiliano. "El pícaro en la literatura y en la vida española." *Nuestro Tiempo* 26 (1926): 193–218.

Salillas, Rafael. *El delincuente español. Hampa. Antropología picaresca*. Madrid, 1898.

Salinas, Pedro. "El 'héro' literario y la novela picaresca española. Semántica e historia literaria." *Revista de la Universidad de Buenos Aires* 4 (1946): Also in *Ensayos de literatura hispánica* (Madrid, 1961), 57–72. In German as "Der literarische 'Held' und der spanische Schelmenroman: Bedeutungswandel und Literaturgeschichte," in Heidenreich, above; pp. 192–211.

Schleussner, Bruno. *Der neopikareske Roman: Pikareske Elemente in der Struktur mod-*

erner englischer Romane 1950–1960. Abhandlungen zur Kunst-, Musik- und Literaturwissenschaft 61. Bonn: H. Bouvier, 1969.

Scholes, Robert. "Fabulation and Picaresque." In *The Fabulators*, 59–94. New York: Oxford University Press, 1967.

Schultheiss, Albert. *Der Schelmenroman der Spanier und seine Nachbildungen*. Sammlung gemeinverständlicher wissenschaftlicher Vorträge. Hamburg, 1893.

Schumann, Willy. "Wiederkehr der Schelme." *PMLA* 81 (1966): 467–74.

Seidlin, Oskar. "Picaresque Elements in Thomas Mann's Work." *Modern Language Quarterly* 12 (1951): 183–200.

Seifert, Walter. "Die pikareske Tradition im deutschen Roman der Gegenwart." In *Die deutsche Literatur der Gegenwart: Aspekte und Tendenzen*, 192–210. Ed. Manfred Durzak. Stuttgart: Reclam, 1971.

Selig, Karl L. "Concerning Gogol's *Dead Souls* and *Lazarillo de Tormes*." *Symposium* 8 (1954): 138–30.

Shaw, Patrick W. "Old Genre, New Breed: The Postwar American Picaro." *Genre* 7 (1974): 205–11.

Sieber, Harry. *The Picaresque*. The Critical Idiom 33. London: Methuen, 1977.

Simpson, Lesley Bird. "A Precursor of the Picaresque Novel in Spain: *El libro de la vida y costumbres de Don Alonso Enríquez, Caballero, noble, desbaratado*." *Hispania* First Special Issue (1934): 53–62.

Smith, Paul Julian. *Writing in the Margin: Spanish Literature of the Golden Age*. New York: Oxford University Press, 1988.

Sobejano, Gonzalo. "Un perfil de la picaresca: El pícaro hablador." In *Studia Hispánica in Honorem R. Lapesa*, vol. 3, 467–85. Cátedra-Seminario Menéndez Pidal. Madrid: Gredos, 1975.

Souiller, Didier. *Le roman picaresque*. Que Sais-Je? Paris: Presses universitaires de France, 1980.

Spitzer, Leo. "Pícaro." *Revista de Filología Española* 17 (1930): 181–82.

Stamm, James R. "The Use and Types of Humor in the Picaresque Novel." *Hispania* 42 (1959): 482–87.

Stoll, Andreas. "Wege zur einer Soziologie des pikaresken Romans." In *Spanische Literatur im goldenen Zeitalter: Fritz Schalk zum 70. Geburtstag*, 461–518. Ed. Horst Baader and Erich Loos. Frankfurt: Klostermann, 1973.

Striedter, Jurij. *Der Schelmenroman in Russland: Ein Beitrag zur Geschichte des russischen Romans vor Gogol*. Veröffentlichungen der Abteilung für slavische Sprachen und Literaturen des Osteuropa-Instituts an der Freien Universität Berlin, 21. Berlin, 1961.

Suarez, Mireya. *La novela picaresca y el pícaro en la literatura española*. Madrid: Imprenta Latina, 1923.

Talens, Jenario. *Novela picaresca y práctica de la transgresión*. Madrid: Júcar, 1975.

Tierno Galván, Enrique. "Sobre la novela picaresca." In *La novela picaresca y otros escritos*, 9–135. Madrid: Tecnos, 1974.

Toda Oliva, E. "Amanecer de la picaresca española." *Atenea* (Concepción, Chile) 32 (1955): 309–23.

Todesco, V. "A proposito di una nuova interpretazione del romanzo picaresca." *Convivium* 14 (1942): 152–61.

Vasquez de Prada, André. "La Moralité dans le roman picaresque." *La Table ronde* 191 (1963): 65–81.

Verdevoye, P. "La novela picaresca en Francia." *Clavileño* 6 (1955): 30–37.

Villanueva, Darío. "Narratario y lectores implícitos en la evolución formal de la novela picaresca." In *Estudios en honor a Ricardo Gullón*, 343–67. Ed. Luis T. González-del-Valle and Darío Villanueva. Lincoln, Neb.: Society of Spanish and Spanish-American Studies, 1984.

Wadlington, Warwick. *The Confidence Game in American Literature*. Princeton, N.J.: Princeton University Press, 1975.

Walter, Monika. "Der spanische Schelmenroman." In *Realismus in der Renaissance: Aneignung der Welt in der erzählenden Prosa*, 522–621. Ed. Robert Weimann. Berlin: Aufbau, 1977.

Wasmuth, Hans Werner. "La novela picaresca y de aventuras en la literatura alemana contemporánea." *Boletín de Estudios Germánicos* (Universidad Nacional de Cuyo, Mendoza, Argentina) 6 (1960): 76–84.

Watts, Henry Edward. "Quevedo and His Works, with an Essay on the Picaresque Novel." In his edition of *Pablo de Segovia, The Spanish Sharper*. London, 1927.

Weil, H. H. "The Conception of the Adventurer in German Baroque Literature." *German Life and Letters* 6 (1953): 285–91.

Weinstein, Arnold. *Fictions of the Self: 1550–1800*. Princeton, N.J.: Princeton University Press, 1981.

Weisgerber, Jean. "A la Recherche de l'espace romanesque: *Lazarillo de Tormes*, *Les Adventures de Simplicius Simplicissimus*, et *Moll Flanders*." *Neohelicon* 3 (1975): 209–27.

Welles, Marcia L. "The *Pícara*: Towards Female Autonomy, or the Vanity of Virtue." *Romance Quarterly* 33 (1986): 63–70.

Weston, Harold. "Picaresque Form." In *Form in Literature: A Theory of Technique and Construction*, 263–95. 1934. Rpt. London: Folcroft, 1970.

Wicks, Ulrich. "Narrative Distance in Picaresque Fiction." *College Literature* 6 (1979): 165–81.

———. "The Romance of the Picaresque." *Genre* 11 (1978): 29–44.

———. "Onlyman." *Mosaic* 8 (1975): 21–47.

———. "The Nature of Picaresque Narrative: A Modal Approach." *PMLA* 89 (1974): 240–49.

———. "Picaro, Picaresque: The Picaresque in Literary Scholarship." *Genre* 5 (1972): 153–92.

———. "A Picaresque Bibliography." *Genre* 5 (1972): 193–216.

———. "More Picaresque." Review essay of Helmut Heidenreich's *Pikarische Welt* and Bruno Schuleussner's *Der neopikareske Roman*. *Novel: A Forum on Fiction* 5 (1971): 71–74.

Will, Wilfried van der. *Pikaro heute: Metamorphosen des Schelms bei Thomas Mann, Döblin, Brecht, Grass*. Stuttgart: W. Kohlhammer, 1967.

Wilson, William E. "The Picaro Discusses Work and Charity." *Bulletin of Spanish Studies* 16 (1939): 37–42.

Zalazar, Daniel E. "Libertad y determinismo en la novela picaresca española." *Cuadernos Hispanoamericanos* 301 (1975): 47–68.

Zamora Vicente, Alonso. *Qué es la novela picaresca*. 1962. 2d ed. Buenos Aires: Columba, 1970.

GENRE THEORY, NARRATIVE TECHNIQUE, LITERARY HISTORY, AND OTHER RELATED STUDIES

Allen, Walter. *The English Novel: A Short Critical History.* 1954. New York: E. P. Dutton, n.d.

Alter, Robert. *Partial Magic: The Novel as a Self-Conscious Genre.* Berkeley: University of California Press, 1975.

Auerbach, Erich. *Mimesis: The Representation of Reality in Western Literature.* 1946. Trans. Willard R. Trask. Princeton, N.J.: Princeton University Press, 1968.

Bakhtin, M. M. *The Dialogic Imagination: Four Essays.* 1975. Ed. Michael Holquist. Trans. Caryl Emerson Michael Holquist. Austin: University of Texas Press, 1981.

Booth, Wayne C. *The Rhetoric of Fiction.* 1961. 2d ed. Chicago: University of Chicago Press, 1983.

Brenan, Gerald. *The Literature of the Spanish People: From Roman Times to the Present Day.* 1951. 2d ed. 1953. Cleveland, Ohio: World, 1957.

Chatman, Seymour. *Story and Discourse: Narrative Structure in Fiction and Film.* Ithaca, N.Y.: Cornell University Press, 1978.

Colie, Rosalie L. *The Resources of Kind: Genre-Theory in the Renaissance.* Ed. Barbara K. Lewalski. Berkeley: University of California Press, 1973.

Culler, Jonathan. *Structuralist Poetics: Structuralism, Linguistics and the Study of Literature.* Ithaca, N.Y.: Cornell University Press, 1975.

Davis, Robert Murray. "Defining Genre in Fiction." *Genre* 2 (1969): 341–53.

Druff, James H., Jr. "Genre and Mode: The Formal Dynamics of Doubt." *Genre* 14 (1981): 295–307.

Dubrow, Heather. *Genre.* The Critical Idiom 42. London: Methuen, 1982.

Eakin, Paul John. *Fictions in Autobiography: Studies in the Art of Self-Invention.* Princeton, N.J.: Princeton University Press, 1985.

Eliot, T. S. "Tradition and the Individual Talent." 1917. In *The Sacred Wood: Essays on Poetry and Criticism*, 47–59. 1928. University Paperbacks. New York: Barnes and Noble, 1960.

Fitzmaurice-Kelly, James. *A History of Spanish Literature.* New York, 1898.

Fowler, Alastair. *Kinds of Literature: An Introduction to the Theory of Genres and Modes.* Cambridge, Mass.: Harvard University Press, 1982.

———. "Genre and the Literary Canon." *New Literary History* 11 (1979): 97–119.

Freedman, Ralph. "The Possibility of a Theory of the Novel." In *The Disciplines of Criticism: Essays in Literary Theory, Interpretation, and History*, 57–77. Ed. Peter Demetz, Thomas Greene, and Lowry Nelson, Jr. New Haven, Conn.: Yale University Press, 1968.

Friedman, Norman. "Point of View in Fiction: The Development of a Critical Concept." *PMLA* 70 (1955): 1160–84.

Frye, Northrop. *The Educated Imagination.* Bloomington: Indiana University Press, 1964.

———. *The Anatomy of Criticism: Four Essays.* Princeton, N.J.: Princeton University Press, 1957.

Genette, Gerard. *Narrative Discourse.* 1972. Trans. Jane E. Lewin. Oxford: Basil Blackwell, 1980.

Goffman, Erving. *The Presentation of Self in Everyday Life.* Woodstock, N.Y.: Overlook, 1973.

Green, Otis H. *Spain and the Western Tradition*. 4 vols. Madison: University of Wisconsin Press, 1963–1965.

Hernadi, Paul. *Beyond Genre: New Directions in Literary Classification*. Ithaca, N.Y.: Cornell University Press, 1972.

Hirsch, E. D., Jr. *Validity in Interpretation*. New Haven, Conn.: Yale University Press, 1967.

Huizinga, Johan. *Homo Ludens: A Study of the Play-Element in Culture*. 1938. Trans. R. F. C. Hull. Boston: Beacon, 1955.

Hume, Martin. *Spanish Influence on English Literature*. 1905. New York: Haskell House, 1964.

Iser, Wolfgang. *The Act of Reading: A Theory of Aesthetic Response*. 1976. Baltimore, Md.: Johns Hopkins University Press, 1978.

———. *The Implied Reader: Patterns of Communication in Prose Fiction from Bunyan to Beckett*. 1972. Baltimore, Md.: Johns Hopkins University Press, 1974.

Jauss, Hans Robert. *Toward an Aesthetic of Reception*. Trans. Timothy Bahti. Minneapolis: University of Minnesota Press, 1982.

Jolles, André. *Einfache Formen: Legende, Sage, Mythe, Rätsel, Spruch, Kasus, Memorabile, Märchen, Witz*. 1930. 2d rev. ed. Halle: M. Niemeyer, 1956.

Jusserand, Jean J. *The English Novel in the Time of Shakespeare*. Trans. Elizabeth Lee. Rev. ed. London, 1890.

Kent, Thomas. *Interpretation and Genre: The Role of Generic Perception in the Study of Narrative Texts*. Lewisburg, Pa.: Bucknell University Press, 1986.

Kern, Edith. "The Romance of Novel/Novella." In *The Disciplines of Criticism: Essays in Literary Theory, Interpretation, and History*, 511–30. Ed. Peter Demetz, Thomas Greene, and Lowry Nelson, Jr. New Haven, Conn.: Yale University Press, 1968.

Levin, Harry. "The Example of Cervantes." 1955. In *Contexts of Criticism*, 79–96. 1957. New York: Atheneum, 1963.

Lifton, Robert Jay. "Protean Man." *Partisan Review* 35 (1968): 13–27.

Lotman, Jurij. *The Structure of the Artistic Text*. 1971. Trans. Gail Lenhoff and Ronal Vroon. Ann Arbor: Michigan Slavic Contributions, 1977.

McKeon, Michael. *The Origins of the English Novel, 1600–1740*. Baltimore, Md.: Johns Hopkins University Press, 1987.

Maldonado de Guevara, Francisco. "La teoría de los géneros literarios y la constitución de la novela moderna." In *Estudios dedicados a Menéndez Pidal*, vol. 3, 299–320. Madrid: CSIC, 1952.

Martin, Wallace. *Recent Theories of Narrative*. Ithaca, N.Y.: Cornell University Press, 1986.

Mayer, Hans. *Outsiders: A Study in Life and Letters*. 1975. Trans. Denis M. Sweet. Cambridge, Mass.: MIT Press, 1982.

Morgan, Charlotte E. *The Rise of the Novel of Manners: A Study of English Prose Fiction between 1600 and 1740*. 1911. Rpt. New York: Russell and Russell, 1963.

Morrissette, Bruce. "The Alienated 'I.' " In *Novel and Film: Essays in Two Genres*, 95–107. Chicago: University of Chicago Press, 1985. Orig. "The Alienated 'I' in Fiction." *Southern Review* 10 (1974): 15–30.

Novel vs. Fiction: The Contemporary Reformation. Ed. Jackson I. Cope and Geoffrey Green. Genre Special Topics 6. *Genre* 14 (1981).

Packard, Vance. *A Nation of Strangers.* 1972. New York: Pocket Books, 1974.

Pavel, Thomas G. *Fictional Worlds.* Cambridge: Harvard University Press, 1986.

Pérez Firmat, Gustavo. "The Novel as Genres." *Genre* 12 (1979): 269–92.

Rabinowitz, Peter J. *Before Reading: Narrative Conventions and the Politics of Interpretation.* Ithaca, N.Y.: Cornell University Press, 1987.

Reynier, Gustave. *Le Roman réaliste au XVIIe siècle.* Paris, 1914.

Richetti, John J. *Popular Fiction before Richardson: Narrative Patterns, 1700–1739.* Oxford: Clarendon Press, 1969.

Romberg, Bertil. *Studies in the Narrative Technique of the First-Person Novel.* Trans. Michael Taylor and Harold H. Borland. Stockholm: Almqvist and Wiksell, 1962.

Ryan, Marie-Laurie. "Toward a Competence Theory of Genre." *Poetics* 8 (1979): 72–91.

Schlauch, Margaret. *Antecedents of the English Novel 1400–1600 (From Chaucer to Deloney).* Warsaw and London: PWN–Polish Scientific Publishers, 1963.

Scholes, Robert. *Structuralism in Literature: An Introduction.* New Haven, Conn.: Yale University Press, 1974.

————. "Towards a Poetics of Fiction: An Approach through Genre." *Novel: A Forum on Fiction* 2 (1969): 101–11. (Incorporated into *Structuralism in Literature*, 129–38.)

————, and Robert Kellogg. *The Nature of Narrative.* New York: Oxford University Press, 1966.

Stam, Robert. *Reflexivity in Film and Literature: From Don Quixote to Jean-Luc Godard.* Studies in Cinema 31. Ann Arbor, Mich.: UMI Research Press, 1985.

Stanzel, F. K. *A Theory of Narrative.* Orig. *Theorie des Erzählens* (Göttingen: Vandenhoeck and Ruprecht, 1979; rev. ed. 1982). Trans. Charlotte Goedsche. Cambridge: Cambridge University Press, 1984.

————. *Narrative Situations in the Novel: Tom Jones, Moby-Dick, The Ambassadors, Ulysses.* Orig. *Die typischen Erzählsituationen im Roman* (Vienna: Wilhelm Braumüller, 1955). Trans. James P. Cusack. Bloomington: Indiana University Press, 1971.

Stonequist, Everett V. *The Marginal Man: A Study in Personality and Culture Conflict.* New York: Charles Scribner's Sons, 1937.

Ticknor, George. *History of Spanish Literature.* 6th ed. 3 vols. Boston, 1891.

Tilley, E. Allen. "The Modes of Fiction: A Plot Morphology." *College English* 39 (1978): 692–706.

Tillyard, E. M. W. *The Epic Strain in the English Novel.* 1958. London: Chatto and Windus, 1967.

Todorov, Tzvetan. *The Poetics of Prose.* Orig. *La Poétique de la prose* (Paris: Editions du Seuil, 1971). Trans. Richard Howard. Ithaca, N.Y.: Cornell University Press, 1977.

————. *The Fantastic: A Structural Approach to a Literary Genre.* Orig. *Introduction à la littérature fantastique* (Paris: Seuil, 1970). Trans. Richard Howard. Ithaca, N.Y.: Cornell University Press, 1975.

Torrance, Robert M. *The Comic Hero.* Cambridge: Harvard University Press, 1978.

Uspensky, Boris. *A Poetics of Composition: The Structure of the Artistic Text and Typology of a Compositional Form.* 1970. Trans. Valentina Zavarin and Susan Wittig. Berkeley: University of California Press, 1973.

Visser, N. W. "The Generic Identity of the Novel." *Novel: A Forum on Fiction* 11 (1978): 101–14.

Warren, Frederick M. *A History of the Novel Previous to the Seventeenth Century*. New York, 1895.

Watt, Ian. *The Rise of the Novel: Studies in Defoe, Richardson and Fielding*. 1957. Berkeley: University of California Press, 1964.

Wellek, René. "Genre Theory, the Lyric, and *Erlebnis*." In *Discriminations: Further Concepts of Criticism*, 225–52. New Haven, Conn.: Yale University Press, 1970. Orig. in *Festschrift für Richard Alewyn*. Ed. H. Singer and Benno von Wiese. Cologne: Böhlau, 1967.

————, and Austin Warren. *Theory of Literature*. 1948. Rev. ed. New York: Harcourt, 1956.

West, Paul. *The Modern Novel*. 1963. 2 vols. 2d ed. London: Hutchinson, 1965.

Williams, Stanley T. *The Spanish Background of American Literature*. 2 vols. New Haven, Conn.: Yale University Press, 1955.

Wilson, W. Daniel. "Readers in Texts." *PMLA* 96 (1981): 848–63.

PART II

A GUIDE TO BASIC PICARESQUE FICTIONS

INTRODUCTION

This guide is not intended to be encyclopedic; no single volume could even list, much less describe, the many thousands of works that have been called picaresque over the years. Nor does this guide make any claim to comprehensiveness within each listing. Some of these works have a formidable body of critical commentary behind them, while others have been studied little or not at all in the context of the picaresque. In these entries, I have tried to be informational first and analytical or interpretive second, and in both cases I have tried to avoid the reductiveness or valorizing inflation that can easily become the fallacy of the generic approach. I hope I have not wrung any swans or pumped up any sparrows to pigeonhole size.

The length of an entry does not constitute in any systematic way a value judgment or correspond directly to an estimation of that work's importance to the picaresque narrative tradition. Some works are given more attention than might be expected because they demonstrate particularly well a specific feature of picaresque narrative or illustrate a significant variation within the tradition; others are discussed less fully than the reader might want because so much has already been written about them or because they have long been considered part of the historically defined genre of *la novela picaresca* within the picaresque mode, though they may be little read today (an inattention that is the cause of much misunderstanding about the term, especially among non-Hispanists). It should be emphasized that the bibliographies following most entries are minimal suggestions for further reading. The editions and translations given, when choice is possible, are those the reader is likely to find most accessible. Finally, this guide excludes those works a reader might anticipate finding here but are only incidentally or peripherally picaresque, such as Voltaire's *Candide*, West's *A Cool Million*, or even *Don Quixote*. Many of these fictions are touched on in part I insofar as they help to clarify the nature of picaresque narrative proper.

The fictions described in this guide constitute the major reference points in the development of mainstream picaresque as the mode has evolved and meta-morphosed among the forms of Western narrative from Greek mythology to our own day. In direct proportion to the ortho- or heterodoxy of their own generic and modal concepts, some readers will object to the inclusion of certain works, while another group of readers will protest the exclusion of others. I think it only fair, therefore, to explain my own guidelines for preparing this guide.

In considering these (and a good many other) fictions, I asked myself a series of questions: How, and how fully, does a given work explore its picaresque potentialities according to the modal and generic features discussed in part I—themselves derived from the thick of the phenomena, a collective consideration of the works themselves? ("Vicious circularity" is a Sisyphian frustration inherent in the generic approach; see part I.) Does it illuminate the work at hand to explore it in the context of the picaresque narrative tradition? And, conversely, does it illuminate, expand, or enrich our concept of the picaresque narrative tradition to refract a given work through it? My steady purpose in proceeding this way has been to add a little bit to literary understanding—of a given work and of a specific narrative mode, of how one illuminates the other in mutual refraction, and of their metamorphosing reciprocity in practice, whether self-conscious or naive. *Formas halló y mudanzas más que luna / Mi peregrinación y mi ejercicio*, says one of the dedicatory verses to part I of *Guzmán de Alfarache* (q.v.): "My Travels, and my Studies found est-soone / More Forms, and Changes, then are in the Moone."

Entries for the works are alphabetically arranged according to the most commonly abbreviated form of the title—for example, *Moll Flanders* rather than *The Fortunes and Misfortunes of the Famous Moll Flanders*; *Huckleberry Finn* rather than *The Adventures of Huckleberry Finn*. The full formal title is given at the beginning of each entry. Non-English works are listed according to their translated title, except when no translation exists or, as in the case of *El Buscón*, when no single translation is standardly accepted. The cross-referencing within entries follows the same pattern. Except as noted, quotations from primary texts are cited by page number to the edition given at the end of each entry; quotations from other sources are cited by author's last name and page number from the works listed in the selected bibliography following each entry.

ALONSO, MOZO DE MUCHOS AMOS

(*Alonso, Servant of Many Masters*, 1624, 1626)

Jerónimo de Alcalá Yáñez y Rivera

Known after its 1804 edition as *El donado hablador* (The Talkative Lay-brother), this work is narratively notable for its use of the dialogue form, which Cervantes had used in "The Dogs' Colloquy" (q.v.) and which Jose Rubén Romero was to give interesting picaresque shape in *The Futile Life of Pito Pérez* (q.v.). In the first part (1624), Alonso tells his life story to the vicar of the convent where he is employed; in the second part (1626), he is a hermit and tells his story to the curate of San Zoles, who is given more dialogue (much of it moralizing) than was the vicar in the first part. It turns out that Alonso was dismissed from the convent for gossiping and interfering—thus the epithet that became the title in 1804.

Chandler found it transitional between the first, or crude, stage of the picaresque and the more developed fictions that were to come. "Both parts of this novel were exceedingly discursive," he wrote, and Alonso "was less a picaro than his brothers, and often only an adventurer passing through society with eyes wide open" (269). Parker, though recognizing *Alonso*'s religious focus as an attempt to continue the major theme of *Guzmán de Alfarache* (q.v.), finds that the narrating vantage point from which the story is presented—first a convent and then a hermitage—reduces the tension we experience in the narrative dualism of *Guzmán*: "This non-involvement and sense of security from first to last robs the story of any tension, of any suffering or anguish" (56). From his focus of exploring how picaresque fiction comes to grips with delinquency in all its forms, Parker finds *Alonso* "an evasion of the issue."

Bjornson, on the other hand, groups it with *Marcos de Obregón* (q.v.) as a work that retains "the morally serious tone, encyclopedic tendency, and auto-biographical perspective of *Guzmán*" (70). Alonso is basically a good person without evil inclinations, but he constantly finds that the inconstant world mistreats him. His retreat to a hermitage, Bjornson suggests, is a declaration of "psychological independence from earthly vanities (subject to the arbitrariness of fortune) and social approbation (subject to the caprices of others)" in "a place where he can act according to his nature without being punished for doing so" (86). But the necessity of such a retreat raises perhaps the most problematic of all the questions repeatedly raised by picaresques: the irreconcilability of world-view with world experience. What Parker calls an evasion of the issue, Bjornson explains as follows: "Essentially a conformist caught in the inherent contradiction between a stereotyped world view and his own experience in an arbitrary, unjust society, Alonso represses the dilemma of the submissive subordinate by simply reaffirming the justice of the existing order" (87).

However well intentioned and serious it may be—and it certainly does not smack of the hack writer's trying to cash in on the popularity of the picaresque—*Alonso* is a relatively minor work in the Spanish tradition. It is too tame to grapple dynamically with its potential themes. Perhaps the most incisive comment on *Alonso* comes from Dunn, who sees its essential problem in the narrative technique itself. The great innovation of *Lazarillo de Tormes* (q.v.) and *Guzmán*, Dunn feels, was their narrating posture against an unknown reader, creating a dynamic reader-narrator relationship. "Since both Lazarillo and Guzmán write for a reader whose motive in reading they are unsure of, there is a continuous play of doubts and uncertainty between what [the I-narrator] says and what he might have said, but which we shall never know" (98). In *Alonso* the complexities of the confessional situation are lacking: "Since we as readers no longer occupy the position of the person addressed, we are not involved in the Process of the novel, by which the I-as-object becomes the I-as-subject, the narrated becomes the narrator'' (99). Finally, *Alonso* leaves out the most important device of verisimilitude, not just for picaresque but for all autobiographical fiction: the simple, obvious need to disclose the reason for the act of writing—or at least the editorial means of transmission. But neither of Alonso's listeners records the storytelling.

In not inventing an occasion for narration and in statically portraying the occasion of narration, Alcalá Yáñez keeps the reader who has interacted with Lazarillo and Guzmán at an off-putting remove. The anticipated full-dimensional potentiality of narrative distance is barely used, much less explored. *Alonso, mozo de muchos amos* is likely to strike the reader fresh from *Lazarillo* or *Guzmán* as a dress rehearsal of picaresque conventions, waiting for a performance that never takes place.

EDITION

No known English translation exists. The original text is available in any of the editions of Angel Valbuena Prat's 1943 anthology *La novela picaresca española*; in the 6th edition (Madrid: Aguilar, 1968), pp. 1197–1339.

SELECT BIBLIOGRAPHY

Richard Bjornson, *The Picaresque Hero in European Fiction* (Madison: University of Wisconsin Press, 1977); Fidel F. Cea, *Función del refrán en la novela "El donado hablador" de Gerónimo de Alcalá Yáñez y Ribera* (Quito: Casa de la Cultura Ecuatoriana, 1986); Frank Wadleigh Chandler, *Romances of Roguery* [1899] (New York: Burt Franklin, 1961); Peter N. Dunn, *The Spanish Picaresque Novel* (Boston: Twayne, 1979); Alexander A. Parker, *Literature and the Delinquent: The Picaresque Novel in Spain and Europe, 1599–1753* (Edinburgh: University Press, 1967); Florencio Sevilla, "Sobre el desarollo dialogístico de *Alonso, mozo de muchos amos*," *Edad de Oro* 3 (1984): 257–74.

AMERIKA

(1913, 1927)

Franz Kafka

The least read of Kafka's three longer works, *Amerika*, was acutally the first of what Max Brod, in 1927, in a note to the first published edition of 1913, called a *Trilogie der Einsamkeit* ("a trilogy of loneliness") in which the fundamental theme is "estrangement [*Fremdheit*], radical separation [*Isoliertheit*] in the midst of human beings." The first chapter was published during Kafka's lifetime as "The Stoker," the title by which he referred to this work in progress until he suddenly stopped working on it with no explanation, but, according to Pascal and others, the intended full title was to be *Der Verschollene* ("The One Who Disappeared" or "Lost without Trace"). According to Brod again, Kafka worked on the manuscript with eager pleasure and delighted in reading sections of the last chapter aloud. Kafka never traveled farther than France and northern Italy, and so the landscape in *Amerika* is entirely the work of his imagination, aided most likely by his readings in travel books and memoirs, which he enjoyed. Brod says Benjamin Franklin's *Autobiography* was one of Kafka's favorite books, from which he used to read aloud, and that there existed in him a "yearning for freedom and distant lands."

Like *The Metamorphosis*, *The Trial*, and *The Castle*, *Amerika* opens with a radical alteration in the protagonist's world (in a passage deleted from *The Trial*, Kafka had Joseph K. say that "the moment of waking up was the riskiest moment of the day"):

As Karl Rossmann, a poor boy of sixteen who had been packed off to America by his parents because a servant girl had seduced him and got herself a child by him, stood on the liner slowly entering the harbour of New York, a sudden burst of sunshine seemed to illumine the Statue of Liberty, so that he saw it in a new light, although he had sighted it long before. The arm with the sword rose up as if newly stretched aloft, and round the figure blew the free winds of heaven. (3)

We are well past that final sentence before we stop and ask ourselves exactly what it is the Statue of Liberty does hold aloft, and once this sneaky adjustment to the dial of reality registers, we orient ourselves toward a fictional world in which Karl will be on continuous trial, in which he will have to negotiate labyrinthine paths armed with wielders of power, as foreshadowed by the episode with the stoker in the bowels of the ship. And yet, though the statue does not carry an illuminating torch, for Karl it itself is illumined by "a sudden burst of sunshine," with the "free winds of heaven" blowing around it. Having been ejected from the Old World for his transgression, Karl will traverse the New World with his burden in hopes of finding freedom, perhaps even insight. Until the open air of the last chapter, however, his journey is through a succession of mazes, beginning with the ship, where

he had painfully to find his way down endlessly recurring stairs, through corridors with countless turnings, through an empty room with a deserted writing-table, until in the end, since he had taken this route no more than once or twice and always among a crowd of other people, he lost himself completely (4)

and continuing through the many secret compartments of his uncle's writing desk (41) and the house, Mr. Pollunder's country house (74), the restaurant buffet where "nothing remained for Karl but to find another point of vantage and start all over again" (119), the hotel elevators, of which there are thirty (146), the dormitory (148–49), the lobby (203), the apartment house (222), and even the theater itself. The entire landscape, even outside New York City proper, is teeming with cars:

Karl was soon in the open air, but had still to keep along the front of the hotel, for an unbroken line of cars was slowly moving past the entrance and he could not reach the road. These cars, in their eagerness to get to their owners as quickly as possible, were actually touching each other, nosing each other forward. A pedestrian here and there, in a particular hurry to cross the road, would climb through the nearest car as if it were a public passage, not caring at all whether there was only a chaffeur in it and a couple of servants, or the most fashionable company. (203–4)

New York's skyscrapers "stared at Karl with their hundred thousand eyes" (12), and Karl in turn perceives the world in nightmarish perspective:

From morning to evening and far into the dreaming night that street was the channel for a constant stream of traffic which, seen from above, looked like an inextricable confusion, for ever newly improvised, of foreshortened human figures and the roofs of all kinds of vehicles, sending into the upper air another confusion, more riotous and complicated, of noises, dust and smells, all of it enveloped and penetrated by a flood of light which the multitudinous objects in the street scattered, carried off and again busily brought back, with an effect as palpable to the dazzled eye as if a glass roof stretched over the street were being violently smashed into fragments at every moment. (39)

This traffic changes its direction every minute, "as if caught up in a whirlwind and roaring like some strange element quite unconnected with humanity" (53), "as if a certain number of them were always being despatched from some distant place and the same number were being awaited in another place equally distant" (117).

Onto this seething chaos Karl is ejected, "simply . . . turned out by his parents, just as you turn a cat out of the house when it annoys you" (26), in the words of his Uncle Jacob, who at first might provide a home for Karl but who in turn ejects him again: "I must . . . expressly send you away from me" (94). Uncle Jacob had told him that "the first days of a European in America might be likened to a re-birth, and though Karl was not to worry about it unduly, since one got used to things here more quickly than an infant coming into the world from the other side, yet he must keep in mind that first judgments were always unreliable and that one should not let them prejudice the future judgments which would eventually shape one's life in America" (39). Karl himself realized that "he no longer had a home. In this country, sympathy was something you could not hope for; in that respect America resembled what Karl had read about it" (38). So, just as he had descended the ship's rope ladder (36), itself an echo of his descent to meet the stoker (4), Karl now will descend in the social hierarchy from the world of his rich and powerful uncle to the vagrant world of Robinson and Delamarche. His job as an elevator boy, like Felix Krull's (*Felix Krull*, q.v.), quite literally takes him up and down and makes him part of "the community of the lift-boys" (159), the lowest member of "the stupendous hierarchy of the hotel staff" (165). Along the way, Karl marvels at the vastness of the world. He "was amazed at the extent of the ship's organisation" (11) and the hotel, which at one point has five floors (124) and at another, seven (163), teems with five thousand guests (173)—in which he sees potential for self-betterment: "Now I must really attend to every word," he says (25), putting himself on the alert in much the way Lazarillo does with the blind man (*Lazarillo de Tormes*, q.v.), and keeping to a goal of improvement: "It was right and needful for him to begin as a lift-boy, but equally needful for him to advance with extra rapidity" (143). He feels unprepared for life, blames "bad luck" (81), and, after his ejection by Uncle Jacob, "chose a chance direction and set out on his way" (98), which leads him to Rameses, and eventually the hotel, from which in the end he is ejected into the world a third time, his job as a lift-boy not proving, "as he had hoped, a step to something higher," but rather pushing him "farther down" (202).

He takes up again with Delamarche and Robinson, who claim to have "picked him up when he was down and out" when he had "just come from Europe, where they had no use for him either" and thinking to "make a decent human being out of him" (216). This claim is ironic, since Delamarche and Robinson are low-life rogues who belong in the landscape, in contrast to the picaro figure who always stands to a large degree against it. Such secondary picaros recur in mainstream picaresque fictions from the beginnings up to such characters as O'Keefe in *The Ginger Man* (q.v.), Rinehart in *Invisible Man* (q.v.), and another Robinson in *Journey to the End of the Night* (q.v.). Although he aspires to get away from their world, Karl cannot help but sympathize with their plight and the plight of others like them. A strong social theme emerges in *Amerika*, the only work of Kafka's to explore what Pascal calls "the humane social outlook of its author." Karl sees his uncle as a representative capitalist and therefore an exploiter of the downtrodden. Karl thinks Pollunder's mansion "an incredible squandering of space," which makes him think in turn "of the east end of New York . . . where it was said that several families lived in one little room and the home of a whole family consisted of one corner where the children clustered round their parents. And here so many rooms stood empty and seemed to exist merely to make a hollow sound when you knocked on the door" (74). The grotesquely fat and wealthy Brunelda, whom Delamarche serves as constantly humiliated lover and to whom Robinson clings in hopes of the leftovers, comes to be a symbol of tyranny over the proletariat. When Karl wants to reject Delamarche's offer that Karl become his servant in turn, the student who lives next door makes Karl realize that every job is a moral compromise: "If all servants were as fastidious in their choice of masters as you are!" (266). This uncharacteristically Kafkaesque emphasis on the dehumanizing effects of big business (as represented by Uncle Jacob, Mr. Pollunder, the hotel staff, and Brunelda) provides the sociocritical dimension that is inherent in the picaresque vision. The very landscape teems with striking workers (53) and politicial demonstrations (248ff). Although Karl has trouble understanding what is going on, he senses nevertheless that this strange land in some ways lends itself to action that will have predictable consequences (which is not true of the less accessible worlds of *The Trial* and *The Castle*). At the end of the penultimate chapter of *Amerika*, Karl falls asleep with visions of success that reflect the Old World's stereotypical dream of the land of opportunity:

As he shut his eyes he was comforted by the reflection that he was still young and that some day or other he was bound to get away from Delamarche; this household certainly did not look as if it were established for all eternity. . . . He would think only of the interests of the firm he had to serve, and undertake any work that offered, even work which the other clerks rejected as beneath them. Good intentions thronged into his head, as if his future employer were standing before the couch and could read them from his face. (270–71)

Karl falls asleep, disturbed only once by Brunelda, "who was apparently troubled by bad dreams and twisted and turned on her bed" (271).

Like the internal immigration of blacks from south to north reflected in El-lison's *Invisible Man*, the great waves of immigration from the Old World to the New are reflected in picaresque fiction in general—at the end of *El Buscón* (q.v.), for example, and in *Moll Flanders* (q.v.) and *Journey to the End of the Night*. The picaro arrives expecting to find the new Eden, Paradise regained, but discovers instead a dehumanizing gigantism, whether expressed in Céline's vision of a Detroit factory or Kafka's immense Hotel Occidental or Ellison's Harlem. Céline's Ferdinand and Defoe's Moll return to the Old World in the end, but Karl Rossmann finds "The Nature Theatre of Oklahoma," the last chapter of *Amerika* as Max Brod put the book together after Kafka's death and which he claimed Kafka had intended to be the concluding chapter, which "should end on a note of reconciliation." Brod says Kafka used to hint that within this "almost limitless" theater, "his young hero was going to find again a profession, a stand-by, his freedom, even his old home and his parents, as if by some celestial witchery" (299). In this chapter, "the immensity of America is now benign" (Ruland, 114). Karl first becomes aware of the theater from a placard: "Today only and never again! If you miss your chance now you miss it for ever! . . . Everyone is welcome! If you want to be an artist, join our company! Our Theatre can find employment for everyone, a place for everyone!" (272). Karl joins up, drawn particularly by the invitation that "everyone is welcome"—"Everyone, that meant Karl too" (273). As labyrinthine in its complexity as the ship, his uncle's desk, and the hotel, the Nature Theatre nevertheless opens doors of opportunity, with a category for every profession. Karl will be an engineer after all. "It's the biggest theatre in the world," Fanny says, "there are almost no limits to it" (279). The theater even has a box reserved for the president of the United States. Karl notices "what destitute, disreputable characters were here assembled, and yet how well they had been received and cared for!" (296). As all the new members leave, they had never known "such a carefree journey in America" (297):

The first day they travelled through a high range of mountains. Masses of blue-black rock rose in sheer wedges to the railway line; even craning one's neck out of the window, one could not see their summits . . . (297–98)

This extraordinary vision concludes *Amerika*. Is it indeed the home Karl has been yearning for from the beginning, when he felt "so much at home" in the stoker's bunk (8), the home he knows he has lost as he contemplates a photograph of his mother and father (103–4), evoking in himself a version of the homesickness Hesse's Knulp (*Knulp*, q.v.) suffers from? Brod says that Kafka intended it to be, and Klaus Mann in his introduction to the American edition reaffirms this, though Pascal cites evidence to the contrary from Kafka's journal that Karl was to suffer the penalty of death. And the image of the Nature Theatre is an ambiguous one. On the one hand it is (in Klaus Mann's phrase) a "gigantic WPA project" and utopia, a state of being in which every outsider can belong to a collective creative effort of gargantuan magnitude—perhaps even an image of salvation, as suggested by the "angels in white robes with great wings on their shoulders . . . blowing on long trumpets that glittered like gold" (274). But it is also a place of illusion and disillusionment: it is a theater and thus a place of show, of appearances; and it is also like a court, and thus a place of trial, where the Statue of Liberty's sword may finally come down on him. Karl is particularly nervous as he is shunted from bureau to bureau in front of a succession of "judges" until he finds the one that is appropriate to his situation, "the bureau for European intermediate pupils," "a booth on the outer verge of the course, not only smaller but also humbler than all the others" (285). In his attempt to find a place for himself, the Nature Theatre becomes for Karl a place of continuous testing (Karl lies about his name, giving them a nickname he has picked up, "Negro"). And the angels are replaced every two hours by devils: "Half of them blow, the other half beat on drums" (279). But despite its troublesome ambiguity and even taking Brod's comments about Kafka's intentions with a grain of salt, the final vision of *Amerika* remains unique among Kafka's works. Karl will eventually die, of course, but the suggestion is strong that it will be a reconciled death like those of Simplicius (*Simplicius Simplicissimus*, q.v.) and Knulp. Kafka's version of the picaresque circle of existence is in *Amerika* integrated into the larger myth of the journey from the Old World to the New; compromise, accommodation to the "show" of the theater, is perhaps all even the New World has to offer.

In an early essay, Austin Warren called Kafka's three longer fictions "novels of the spiritual picaresque" because they render a world in which the innocent "I" is "pushed about, pursued, regimented by potencies veiled of visage—in which one is forever being orally examined by dignitaries who forever flunk one." In the juxtaposed opposition between self and world, "if one is not being pursued by the world or carried off by the world, one is running after it" (124). It is a world of hierarchy, providing "for deferment of responsibility or infinite regress. One's complaint always reaches the wrong office"; shunted from office to office, the protagonist moves up the scale of delegated authority "only to find that the proper official to handle the complaint is out of town, or the necessary documents are lost, or by delay one's claim is outlawed." A similar characterization of Kafka's fictional world by Barrett is worth quoting in full:

A man wants to ring up somebody whose number he does not know; the telephone is unaccountably missing, and he searches in vain for it in all the cubicles of the enormous office; he will try Switchboard; she gives him the Central Operator, who tells him to ask Information; he does not have Information's number, but Operator has already rung off and he has lost the connection with Switchboard; he will have to try again; but Switchboard is busy and he will have to wait; when he gets her and tries to explain she immediately gives him Operator again, and a fresh voice, unaware of what he has already gone through, tells him he will find the number in his telephone book. Repeat several times with variations. He hangs up. Downstairs there is a drugstore with a telephone booth and its book that he has in fact sometimes used to make calls which he did not want Switchboard to overhear; this is not such an occasion, which makes the present confusion more absurd. Waiting for the elevator, slow descent of seventeen floors, frequent stops for people getting on and off. Down at last; but something has happened to the drugstore in the last week: the telephone booth has been removed, and the book with it, to make space for a display of greeting cards. He could send one of the cards instead of telephoning, but decides not to. He gives up—but . . . only for the time being. (214–15)

But to suggest that this is what Kafka is all about—these "tedious and banal comedies of frustration, these baffled failures to make connections in the midst of a society too intricately organized"—is perhaps to trivialize his thematic fictional quest. But "he must strike some deep and uneasy chord in our being for his name [in the form "Kafkaesque"] to be pressed into this common coinage," while it is just as significant of something in our civilization "that in speading his name it must also dilute his meaning" (215).

And yet this meaning of "Kafkaesque" is but another form of the Sisyphus rhythm (q.v.) common to picaresque narrative, and, unlike either *The Trial* or *The Castle*, *Amerika* functions according to this rhythm in a morally rendered concrete social milieu (most of the action in the other two books takes place inside, both literally and psychologically, though such a rhythm dominates their narrative structures as well). That Kafka himself might have approved of such a common coinage (the problem of dilution aside) is evident from his own apparent sense of humor—especially of the kind we call gallows humor and for a time referred to as black humor (according to Brod, Kafka is supposed to have laughed uproariously while reading *The Metamorphosis* aloud). And Kafka liked Dickens, who can often be overly sentimental. (He had Dickens's *David Copperfield* specifically in mind while writing "The Stoker" chapter, his intention being "to write a Dickens novel" because he admired his "naive, sweeping power.") His personal vision of the Dickensian combined with an Old World image of the New World landscape to produce a picaresque blend of an unjust society that is often comically Kafkaesque in the way it bounces the innocent but nevertheless tainted picaro around (Kafka makes it clear that Karl was passive in his transgression: he was seduced by the servant girl; we are not told whether the servant girl is made to suffer, which is the common stereotype from the masculine point of view—in any case, Karl carries the burden of guilt). The long episode with the police (208–21) shows Karl as the innocent bystander who nevertheless feels guilt in the face of authority as the policeman questions his identity. Karl is, after all, the immigrant, a stranger in the land. The encounter soon attracts a crowd, who look on in interest. Karl is confused, even exasperated: "So in America too it was the habit of authorities to ask questions about what they could see for themselves. (How exasperated his father had been over the pointless inquiries of the officials when he was getting Karl's passport!) Karl felt like running and hiding himself somewhere, if only to escape answering more questions'' (214). The encounter ends in a mad chase, with policemen blowing their whistles ''ready to spring out on [Karl] at the right moment'' (219–20). But Karl is suddenly yanked into a doorway by Delamarche, while ''the two policemen were really running past, their feet ringing in the empty street like the striking of steel against stone'' (220). This is the very American landscape of the Keystone Cops.

The comparison of Kafka's *Amerika* landscape with that of the Mack Sennett comedies, particularly those starring Charlie Chaplin, was made originally by Max Brod, then picked up by Klaus Mann and Roy Pascal, and elaborated on by Parker Tyler. Brod, in making the comparison, admits that these Chaplin films had not even been made at the time Kafka was beginning work on *Amerika*, but he suggests that Kafka's episodes foreshadow them. In fact, Chaplin had just come to the United States with his vaudeville act around that time; he quickly attracted Hollywood attention and was making comedies for Mack Sennett by 1913. (Kafka has left us few observations, mostly negative, about the nature of the film medium.) Pascal uses the comparison to explore the relative immaturity of *Amerika* in relation to the later novels, in which ''we shall not have heroes who are the typical 'little men,' the innocent Charlie Chaplins, knocked about by the evil men of power, but maintaining their goodness to the end, and even finding in the end a haven'' (224). Klaus Mann says that every detail of Kafka's description of American life is inaccurate, though the picture as a whole has poetical truth: ''The hyper-modern desk which the generous uncle puts at his nephew's disposal looks like a grotesque piece of furniture in a Charlie Chaplin film: it is an alarming object with innumerable technical tricks—secret drawers that pop open when one touches a hidden button, little trapdoors, complicated locks'' (vx). But it is Tyler who explores the comparison fully. Although there is no question of derivation or influence in either direction, it is the parallelism that is significant: the emergence of two distinct characters (Karl and the Tramp) who are ''heroes of the identical international myth: the great adventure of the young foreigner coming head-on to the United States to start a new life and hoping to rise to a level beyond any available to him in his native land'' (301). Aside from specific similarities of origins (disreputable), wardrobe (Karl's box, the Tramp's bundle), down-and-out situations, rich villains, comic encounters with an alien landscape, and so on, the two artists created visions of America that are largely theatrical: Kafka visualizing it ''much as a spectator might,'' with the Nature Theatre of Oklahoma becoming ''the metaphoric figure for all America as visually anticipated by those naive ones still separated from it by an ocean: the Land of Opportunity as a stage setting presided over by 'female' angels raised high above the ground'' (304); while ''the *commedia dell' arte* vein of Chaplin's farces gave an artificial feeling to whatever was identifiably American in his films.'' In sum, ''Kafka's 'Amerika' is reciprocally telescoped by Chaplin's'' (304). This is most apparent in Chaplin's 1917 film *The Immigrant*. Tyler concludes:

In whatever moral or physical stance we may leave the Chaplinesque or the Kafkan hero, we sense around him the strange, by no means reassuring, atmosphere of a ''World's Fair,'' an often shocking polyglot of art and reality, a ''theater of action'' containing castles and courtrooms, nature and machines, love and murder, jobs and joblessness, the innocent inextricably fused with the guilty, and youth making its way; in other words: a fantasy ''Amerika'' that we find difficult to keep separate from the real one. (311)

This comparison of the picaro figure to Charlie Chaplin's Tramp figure was originally made, in direct reference to the Spanish picaresque, by Gerald Brenan: ''Guzmán [*Guzmán de Alfarache*, q.v.] is Charlie Chaplin viewed by a sixteenth-century Calvinist minister. At every moment he is falling into some disgrace or humiliation, which the commentary then explains, no doubt correctly enough, as an inevitable consequence of our sinful human nature. We watch him stumbling and rising, rising and stumbling, through sixty chapters—but we are not allowed to rejoice in his buoyancy'' (172). Karl Rossmann and the Tramp exist in no less hostile or brutal a world, but the moral framework in which their stumblings and risings take place is much less judgmental and more problematical.

Among the critics who have written extensively on the picaresque, Claudio Guillén stands almost alone in pointing attention toward *Amerika*, ''perhaps the first important picaresque novel of our time'' (262) in the broader sense of his definition (that is, not adhering rigidly to the original Spanish pattern but nevertheless exhibiting most of the major characteristics of the genre). For Guillén, *Amerika* ''employs in its own way the solitude of the young boy away from home, his horizontal pilgrimage in a strange land, his exile from reality, his search for a new native city, a New World.'' But it lacks ''both the first-person form and a sufficient amount of picaresque behavior'' (263). It can be argued, however, that in its Old World vision of the New, *Amerika* integrates the circle of existence pattern with the land of opportunity myth into a grand-scale picaresque vision that is perhaps the most ambitious in all of mainstream picaresque fiction. Although Karl is not a typical rogue or trickster, he schemes all the time in his own mind, dissembling right up to the end in the Nature Theatre. As for the absence of the first-person form, Kafka's narrative technique in all his fictions is to use a voice that is almost exclusively limited to the protagonist, so that we have the sense of perceiving everything only through the eyes and the sensibility of Karl Rossmann alone. This method of writing from within the mind of the hero (as Warren puts it) reinforces the solitude of the character in his world—''man alone, man hunted and haunted, man confronted with powers which elude him . . . , man prosecuted and persecuted'' (131). And Pascal singles this out as the original and fascinating characteristic of *Amerika*: ''We are not told that the world is hostile and bewildering; we experience it as such with the hero. We learn only what is available to this young stranger'' (225). Henry James would call Kafka's Karl a ''center of consciousness.'' But the lack of the purely autobiographical voice does away with the dimensions of narrative distance and thus with the picaro's traditional evaluative introspection and retrospection (Karl makes observations, even moral judgments, all the time, but these are of the moment, not outside it temporally, psychologically, morally, or aesthetically). And yet the limitation of this rigidly located (almost imprisoned) narrative voice is singularly appropriate in its circumscription to the world rendered in *Amerika*, where no answers are given, no reasons explained, no meanings offered. *Amerika*'s America is the experiential realm pure and simple; its vastness and open-endedness, like the valleys that "lost themselves" in the book's final image, mean nothing to the picaro. Whatever "home" the Oklahoma *gran teatro del mundo* may offer, no omniscient voice emerges to make possible the kind of dialogue that ends *Knulp* or the inner dialogue that concludes *Simplicissimus*. In Kafka's vision, the picaro is so alone that he cannot even engage in a dialogue with himself.

TRANSLATION

Willa and Edwin Muir [1938] (New York: Schocken Books, 1962), with Klaus Mann's preface [1940]. The afterword by Max Brod is only partially translated in this edition and is available in full in the Fischer edition of the German text (Frankfurt and Hamburg, 1956), 233–35.

SELECT BIBLIOGRAPHY

William Barrett, *Time of Need: Forms of Imagination in the Twentieth Century* (New York: Harper & Row, 1972); Gerald Brenan, *The Literature of the Spanish People from Roman Times to the Present* [1951, 1953] (Cleveland, Ohio, and New York: World Publishing Company, 1957); Claudio Guillén, "Toward a Definition of the Picaresque," *Proceedings of the IIIrd Congress of the International Comparative Literature Association* (The Hague: Mouton, 1962), 252–66 (rpt. in his *Literature as System: Essays toward the Theory of Literary History* [Princeton, N.J.: Princeton University Press, 1971], 71–106); Richard R. Malmsheimer, "Kafka's 'Nature Theatre of Oklahoma': The End of Karl Rossmann's Journey to Maturity," *Modern Fiction Studies* 13 (1967): 493–501; Roy Pascal, *The German Novel* (Manchester: Manchester University Press, 1956); Richard Ruland, *America in Modern European Literature: From Image to Metaphor* (New York: New York University Press, 1976); E. W. Tedlock, "Kafka's Imitation of *David Copperfield*," *Comparative Literature* 7 (1955): 52–62; Parker Tyler, "Kafka's and Chaplin's 'Amerika,' " *The Sewanee Review* 58 (1950): 299–311; Austin Warren, "Franz Kafka," in his *Rage for Order* [1948], rpt. *Kafka: A Collection of Critical Essays*, ed. Ronald Grey (Englewood Cliffs, N.J.: Prentice-Hall, 1965), 123–32.

AVENTURAS DEL BACHILLER TRAPAZA, QUINTA ESENCIA DE EMBUSTEROS Y MAESTRO DE EMBELECADORES

(*Adventures of the Bachelor Trapaza, Quintessence of Liars and Master of Imposters*, 1637)

Alonso de Castillo Solórzano

Although Chandler admired Castillo Solórzano's softening of the picaresque as a recovery from the "excess of realism into which by a recoil from pure idealism

it plunged'' and so considered his fictions the ''high-water mark'' of the picaresque in Spain (324), subsequent critics tend to see the works of this entertaining
writer as indications of the deterioration of serious picaresque in Spanish literature. Trapaza—his name means ''deceit'' or ''fraud'' and is a composite of the
names of his mother Tramoya (''intrigue'') and father Trampa (''trap'')—is a
resourceful con man whose exploits end with his being sent to the galleys through
the contrivance of his mistress Estefanía, who shortly bears a daughter, who
will become the picara in a sequel of sorts, *La garduña de Sevilla* (q.v.).

Like the fictional world of Salas Barbadillo (*La hija de Celestina*, q.v.), the
rendered world of Castillo barely resembles the existentially anguished world of
Guzmán de Alfarache (q.v.). The moralizing has become conventional lip-service; the picaro is seen merely as a social-climbing upstart who will use any
means to reach his goals; and, except for *La niña de los embustes* (q.v.), the
narration is not the picaro's or picara's. This is purely formulaic picaresque, and
of a most superficial kind.

Nevertheless, Castillo's fiction does tell something about the taste of audiences
who were familiar with the picaresque narrative tradition. As Bjornson points
out,

Because Castillo's picaresque adventurers are imaginary people in a fictional world without
ultimate consequences or tragic potential, upper-class readers could momentarily suspend
disbelief and take pleasure in the outwitting of uncongenial victims by handsome and
talented rogues. When kept on the level of harmless stage entities, these clever and
audacious picaresque heroes proved highly entertaining to members of Spain's privileged
classes. (96)

Dunn, too (in *The Spanish Picaresque Novel*), notes the appeal Castillo's plush
world had for his readers, ''but the picaresque cannot survive transformation
into a novel of manners'' 104).

The works of Castillo Solórzano are exercises in escapist fantasy for readers
excluded from aristocratic realms and amusing self-congratulations for readers
who already have a place there.

EDITION

The original text is accessible in one of the editions of Angel Valbuena Prat's *La novela
picaresca española*; in the 6th edition (Madrid: Aguilar, 1968), it is on pp. 1425–1525.

SELECT BIBLIOGRAPHY

Richard Bjornson, *The Picaresque Hero in European Fiction* (Madison: University of
Wisconsin Press, 1977); Frank Wadleigh Chandler, *Romances of Roguery* [1899] (New
York: Burt Franklin, 1961); Peter N. Dunn, *Castillo Solórzano and the Decline of the
Spanish Novel* (Oxford: Basil Blackwell, 1952) and *The Spanish Picaresque Novel* (Bos-
ton: Twayne, 1979).

BARRY LYNDON

(1844, 1856)

William Makepeace Thackeray

While it is fairly common to encounter the unexamined labeling of *Vanity Fair* as a picaresque and of Becky Sharp as a picara, *Barry Lyndon* receives relatively scant attention as a picaresque in historical surveys of the English novel, despite Chandler's having praised it early on as "altogether the most powerful in the range of picaresque fiction" (462). Serialized in *Fraser's Magazine* under the title *The Luck of Barry Lyndon, a Romance of the Last Century*, it was presented to the public through one of the masks Thackeray was using at the time (1844), a certain "George Savage Fitz-Boodle." Except for a pirated New York edition in 1852, its first appearance in book form was in the third volume of Thackeray's *Miscellanies* in 1856, when its title was changed to *The Memoirs of Barry Lyndon, Esq., Written by Himself*. Thackeray made a number of revisions, dropping Fitz-Boodle as editor of and commentator on Lyndon's memoirs, excising several long passages, and converting the chapter headings into autobiographical form (Fitz-Boodle had used titles referring to Barry in the third person).

The story was, however, rejected by *Fraser's Magazine* readers in 1844, the explanation for which has been that they did not read the book ironically and instead took the self-praise of a megalomaniac at face value—despite the moralizing intrusions of Fitz-Boodle and the editorial temper of *Fraser's Magazine* against the popular "Newgate Novels" for their sentimentalizing of rogues and criminals. Thackeray had expressed his attitude toward them in both direct condemnation and such precursors to *Barry Lyndon* as *The Memoirs of Mr. C. J. Yellowplush, Sometime Footman in Many Genteel Families* (1837–1838) and *Catherine* (1839–1840). The inability, or refusal, of contemporary readers to respond to the work has been attributed to Victorian expectation of "easy moral instruction and obvious humor": "But in the nineteenth century the average English magazine reader regarded it as a scandalous—almost indecent— book, and was obliged to reject it" (Morris, xiii, xxiii). Nevertheless, when Thackeray came to revise it (after securing his fame with *Vanity Fair*), he removed most of the overtly didactic framing narrative, leaving only five short footnotes and an eight-paragraph, morally neutral conclusion by an anonymous and objective compiler who has put Barry's papers together. And although Trollope at the end of the century singled out Thackeray's control of irony in *Barry Lyndon* as without equal, the fear of misreading still persisted well into this century. Charles Elbert Rhodes, introducing a 1920 edition of the work, felt compelled to emphasize that "in *Barry Lyndon* Thackeray abandoned for a time his usual satire and attempted a stupendous feat in pure irony. . . . To represent Thackeray as lauding a rogue is to confess a woeful failure to understand him; to see him let a conceited rogue condemn himself out of his own mouth while he boasts and brags, wholly oblivious of his real character, is to get the real point of the book. This is the key to *Barry Lyndon*: *Remember that it is pure irony''* (Morris, xx).

In its reception as an unsavory book, *Barry Lyndon* thus shares with many others picaresques that air of disrepute, even scandal, that is the result of both the upstart nature of picaresque narrative as such and the resentment that comes from having been conned (for surely those early readers must have come to realize their misreadings sooner or later). Such resentment intensifies in the face of the realization that Barry Lyndon, whose voice we hear for all but a handful of paragraphs, has no sense of irony; Thackeray cannot be faulted for this scrupulously accurate portrayal of an unscrupulous egotist. Barry is simply being true to himself; there is no overt or covert attempt to trick the reader. And with the footnotes and conclusion providing an objectively neutral frame of reference outside Barry's own narrative, there is no narrative confidence game being played through the anonymous editor either. Thus, to be misled by *Barry Lyndon* is simply to misread Barry Lyndon as a character, and to fall into such a trap strikes more deeply than would our failure to grasp purely verbal or presentational irony. With the latter our wit has failed, but with the former our moral perceptions have malfunctioned. To read *Barry Lyndon* as though Barry Lyndon were to be taken as a justifiable character is to fail at both wit and moral perspicacity. The centripetal and centrifugal forces that operate as part of narrative distance must be properly responded to in picaresque narrative, or the act of reading goes awry.

The first paragraph of *Barry Lyndon*, before any editorial apparatus appears, should alone serve as a dial of adjustment for the reader's relationship to the fiction:

Since the days of Adam, there has been hardly a mischief done in this world but a woman has been at the bottom of it. Ever since ours was a family (and that must be very *near* Adam's time,—so old, noble, and illustrious are the Barrys, as everybody knows) women have played a mighty part with the destinies of our race. (3)

The unfocused misanthropy that is a major characteristic of the picaro's attitude here becomes a preposterous misogyny. The original sin that, as Guzmán suggests (*Guzmán de Alfarache*, q.v.), we all inherit from our original parents through our mothers and fathers and that governs the general conditions of our existence is here particularized by being feminized. That first sentence functions centrifugally and centripetally by being simultaneously a lure (against our better judgment) and a warning (to maintain our distance). Followed by the parenthetical swagger of the next sentence, the provocative outrageousness of this first paragraph makes us sit up and pay attention while at the same time alerting us to put up our guard. The appropriate response here is neither sympathy nor revulsion but rather fascination.

Barry Lyndon does not toy ironically with the reader, though he is quite conscious of narrative distance:

Were these memoirs not characterised by truth, and did I deign to utter a single word for which my own personal experience did not give me the fullest authority, I might easily make myself the hero of some strange and popular adventures, and, after the fashion of novel-writers, introduce my reader to the great characters of this remarkable time. These persons (I mean the romance-writers), if they take a drummer or a dustman for a hero, somehow manage to bring him into contact with the greatest lords and most notorious personages of the empire; and I warrant me there's not one of them but, in describing the battle of Minden, would manage to bring Prince Ferdinand, and my Lord George Sackville, and my Lord Granby, into presence. It would have been easy for me to have *said* I was present when the orders were brought to Lord George to charge with the calvalry and finish the rout of the Frenchmen, and when he refused to do so, and thereby spoiled the great victory. But the fact is, I was two miles off from the cavalry when his Lordship's fatal hesitation took place. (72)

I am not going to entertain my readers with an account of my professional career as a gamester, any more than I did with anecdotes of my life as a military man. I might fill volumes with tales of this kind were I so minded; but at this rate, my recital would not be brought to a conclusion for years, and who knows how soon I may be called upon to stop? I have gout, rheumatism, gravel, and a disordered liver. I have two or three wounds in my body, which break out every now and then, and give me intolerable pain, and a hundred more signs of breaking up. Such are the effects of time, illness, and free-living, upon one of the strongest constitutions and finest forms the world ever saw. Ah! I suffered from none of these ills in the year '66, when there was no man in Europe more gay in spirits, more splendid in personal accomplishments, than young Redmond Barry. (143)

I do not intend to make a history of battles in the Prussian any more than in the English service. I did my duty in them as well as another, and by the time that my moustache had grown to a decent length, which it did when I was twenty years of age, there was not a braver, cleverer, handsomer, and I must own, wickeder soldier in the Prussian army. I had formed myself to the condition of the proper fighting beast; on a day of action I was savage and happy; out of the field I took all the pleasure I could get, and was by no means delicate as to its quality or the manner of procuring it. (108)

Such passages acknowledge narrative distance but show no inclination to play ironically with it. From Fleet Prison in 1814, when he is around seventy years old, Barry Lyndon straightforwardly tells his story with a narrative spirit that matches the experiential vigor. There are no regrets, except for the loss of his son Bryan. There is no repentance, no conversion. Although he blames fate and universal corruption—"If the world were not composed of a race of ungrateful scoundrels" (301)—as much as does any other picaro, he does not try to manipulate our sympathies. He really believes everything he says about himself. And it is for this uncompromising sincerity that, ironically, we muster up some grudging admiration to blend with our fascination. The boasting scoundrel who believes in himself is no boasting scoundrel from his own point of view. He knows exactly who he is and who he wants to be. He accepts his identities as well as his conditions and thus does not suffer any instabilities from picaresque apersonality. His identity coexists with the sheer drive of his protean adaptability. He is almost like a force on the landscape, reflected in the pure narrative energy with which he tells his *vida*. Perhaps Victorian readers did not misread him so much as deny him; even to condescend to pay attention to him would be subversive.

Thackeray modeled *Barry Lyndon* after Fielding's *The Life of Mr. Jonathan Wild the Great* (1743), a satire based on the life of an actual criminal, whose activities had already been chronicled by Defoe in his *True and Genuine Account of the Life and Actions of the Late Jonathan Wild* (1725). To early-eighteenth-century readers, such criminal biographies had the same appeal that stories about such figures as Al Capone and Bonnie and Clyde—indeed, any underworld crime lord—have had for readers in this century. (The real-life Wild presided over a community of rogues more tightly structured than the law-abiding society around it; he made his way as Peachum into John Gay's *Beggar's Opera* [1728], and in turn into Brecht's *Three-Penny Opera* [1928].) Fielding's *Jonathan Wild* is sometimes considered a picaresque, but it shares only superficial and incidental similarities with the picaresque. Wild functions for Fielding as a symbol of pure evil, and the carefully controlled third-person attack on "greatness," targeted against contemporary politics, reveals all the characteristics of formal satire.

In the years just before *Barry Lyndon*, Thackeray had been studying what he called the " 'greatness' of Fielding's antihero" (Morris, xx), and there is little doubt that Lyndon grew out of this interest in *Jonathan Wild*. In addition, Thackeray worked into his characterization details from the lives of several rogues of reality, as Chandler points out (457), as well as attributing to Lyndon aspects of his own darker side (his compulsive gambling, for example). Thackeray's foray into picaresque has also been explained as growing out of "certain underground connections" he had "with an older, picaresque ethic": "Thackeray sees in the earlier period an age when life was dangerous and challenging, not humdrum, when daring skill, not base mercantile values, enabled a man to excel" (Alter, 114, 115). But in the middle of the nineteenth century, "for a writer and a reading public that hold sacred some strict ideal of social conformity and propriety, the picaresque novel is no longer a real possibility" (Alter, 114). In this view, Thackeray's portrait of Barry Lyndon is a kind of nostalgic wish fulfillment that eventually must yield to the socially dutiful moralist-novelist who reluctantly makes Barry exchange "the costume of the vagabond rogue for that of the villain of nineteenth-century melodrama, stalking around his ill-gotten estate, his fierce mustaches bristling, a whiskey bottle in each pocket and a horsewhip in his hand" (Alter, 117). Thus, the would-be dissident Thackeray produced, Alter concludes, "fifteen chapters of sparkling picaresque narrative before he foundered on the rock of his Victorian solid moral purpose" (117). Such an approach, however, relies on questionable assumptions about the nature of the picaresque; and the moral duty that Alter sees so specifically asserting itself in the fifteenth chapter is hardly easy to detect in the 1856 version, which Alter quotes from (baldly moralizing notes are more prominent in the 1844 version, though they seem not to have carried any weight for readers, who turned away from the book anyway). Actually Barry is no more and no less detestable at the end than he is at any other point in his narrative, his Fleet Prison narrating voice remaining constant throughout.

Blackburn, on the other hand, reproaches Barry Lyndon on his own terms:

Barry does not develop or reveal that kind of honesty with himself that might permit him to escape convention. He *is*. Thackeray presents Barry's insatiable craving for wealth and title, not as the plausible outgrowth of a false ideal in the mind of an unwanted child, but as a ruling passion. Barry's dishonorable actions originate, not in the picaro's frustrated attempt to gain a recognized social standing, but in his own belief that he is, in fact, honorable. And thus, unlike the picaro in symbolic deceptiveness, Barry, believing in his own pretensions, never seriously passes himself off as other than he thinks he is. He is one of the possessed. (143)

Finally, Blackburn adds, *Barry Lyndon* does not have the "double plane of the picaresque novel whereby both picaro and society disintegrate," and thus Thackeray makes it clear that Barry Lyndon "could be integrated into the good were he not, by nature, evil." Yet, as Chandler had pointed out long before, there is little, if any, good in the rendered world of *Barry Lyndon*: "Even those victims who appeal to the reader's sympathy are far from admirable" (458), though such measurements of value are oversimplifications if they do not (as Chandler rarely does) take narrative distance and discourse into account. Such characters, after all, are being rendered by Barry, whose vision of humanity is really a reflection of himself.

In the vision of reality portrayed by *Barry Lyndon*, Barry's rogueries stand out for their intensity, not for their rarity in the landscape he renders. Barry is, in fact, very well integrated into his world. He is an upstart not because he is more of a scoundrel than anyone else but because he is undissembling about his own nature and that of the world he sees around him. Even when his own behavior corroborates a moral flaw he criticizes in others, he does not try to cover up the contradiction or try to rationalize his actions (except, on occasion, to blame it on drink). This is the way he is, and this is the way he sees the world. Barry Lyndon's self-concept coincides exactly with his being.

He ends his days, after nineteen years in prison, "falling into a state of almost imbecility," being "tended by his tough old parent as a baby almost," who "would cry if deprived of his necessary glass of brandy" (331). This image of a return to the womb, of a filling out of the circle of existence, recalls the picture of Simplicius on his deserted island, where he ends his days as a hermit in a cave, as he had begun his life with his hermit father (*Simplicius Simplicissimus*, q.v.). But Barry Lyndon neither repents his actions nor renounces the world. His end, which is related by the anonymous editor with a matter-of-fact objectivity that resembles the transcriber's final report of the death of Pascual in *The Family of Pascual Duarte* (q.v.), is more twentieth century than Victorian, just as the unrepentant picaro is more of a twentieth-century creation. Thackeray was conscious of the kind of character he was creating, as the one remaining full discursive editor's footnote in the 1856 revision suggests:

Mr. Barry Lyndon is not, we repeat, a hero of the common pattern; but let the reader look around, and ask himself, Do not as many rogues succeed in life as honest men? more fools than men of talent? And is it not just that the lives of this class should be described by the student of human nature as well as the actions of those fairy-tale princes, those perfect impossible heroes, whom our writers love to describe? There is something *naïve* and simple in that time-honoured style of novel-writing by which Prince Prettyman, at the end of his adventures, is put in possession of every worldly prosperity, as he has been endowed with every mental and bodily excellence previously. The novelist thinks that he can do no more for his darling hero than make him a lord. Is it not a poor standard that, of the *summum bonum*? The greatest good in life is not to be a lord; perhaps not even to be happy. Poverty, illness, a humpback, may be rewards and conditions of good, as well as that bodily prosperity which all of us unconsciously set up for worship. But this is a subject for an essay, not a note; and it is best to allow Mr. Lyndon to resume the candid and ingenious narrative of his virtues and defects. (265–66)

If Thackeray is here speaking through his editor's mask, his own ideas about the purpose of fiction run as counter to the prevailing expectations of readers as does Barry Lyndon's behavior. This is no socially dutiful author changing course in midstream; Thackeray is going against the stream.

There is no explaining Barry Lyndon away with irony. Even after his death, when the calm, nonjudgmental voice of the editor briefly ties up some loose narrative threads, an assertive energy lingers on, reverberating the defiance of Fielding's Jonathan Wild when he says, "I had rather stand on the summit of a dunghill than at the bottom of a hill in Paradise." (bk. I, ch. 5), words that echo those of the Christian trickster archetype himself, Satan, in Milton's *Paradise Lost*: "Better to reign in Hell than serve in Heaven" (bk. I, l. 263). Wherever and whenever it appears, the picaresque challenges the operative social, moral, and aesthetic norms. The *Fraser's Magazine* audience that stopped reading *Barry Lyndon* did not need a Fitz-Boodle to tell them Lyndon was really a scoundrel (he does that very well himself); nor did they need a lecture on irony. Perhaps they were not misreading it at all. It is possible that they rejected the book because they did not want to read it; they refused to confront the book's disturbing vision. Thackeray's excision of all the moralizing apparatus twelve years later would thus be his acknowledgment that sugarcoating was unnecessary, perhaps even condescending. His readers knew what they were about. They were not misreading, they were avoiding. (This makes Trollope the misreader.) Upstart literature must wait for another age before it finds readers. Thackeray's excursion into picaresque dangerously rocked his readers' boat.

EDITION

The Memoirs of Barry Lyndon, Esq., ed. Robert L. Morris (Lincoln: University of Nebraska Press, 1962).

SELECTED BIBLIOGRAPHY

Robert Alter, *Rogue's Progress: Studies in the Picaresque Novel* (Cambridge: Harvard University Press, 1964); Alexander Blackburn, *The Myth of the Picaro: Continuity and*

Transformation of the Picaresque Novel, 1554–1954 (Chapel Hill: University of North Carolina Press, 1979); Frank Wadleigh Chandler, *The Literature of Roguery* [1907] (New York: Burt Franklin, 1958).

BRIGHT LIGHTS, BIG CITY

(1984)

Jay McInerney

This first novel resembles Donleavy's *The Ginger Man* (q.v.), to which reviewers occasionally compared it. McInerney's protagonist is a budding writer employed, incongruously, as a fact checker at an unnamed magazine that resembles *The New Yorker*, a job he performs so ineptly that he gets himself fired by Department of Factual Verification head Clara Tillinghast. He pines for his estranged wife and sorrows over the death of his mother a year before. His nights, and much of his days, are spent drifting through nightclubs, bars, and private parties that for their crush of bodies might as well be public. The geographical panorama is limited to Manhattan, and the temporal expanse is confined to roughly a week, though flashbacks to childhood, early marriage, and the death of his mother expand the horizon in both time and space, as do the drugs that the unnamed character is dependent on.

This aimless skimming over the surfaces of life is depicted by McInerney in recognizably picaresque fashion by way of a gallery of human types, chance encounters, comic mishaps, reversals of fortune, and elaborate tricks that resemble those of Donleavy's Sebastian Dangerfield in Dublin. He also resembles another picaro on the run, Ellison's unnamed protagonist (*Invisible Man*, q.v.). Although they exist in different parts of Manhattan and are of different races, they inhabit the same realm of exile, from which they are seeking a home. McInerney's protagonist comes to realize this slowly as his memories of his mother's death spark the awareness that his values really are those of the home he has been exiled from:

The candor was infectious. It spread back to the beginning of your life. You tried to tell her, as well as you could, what it was like being you. You described the feeling you'd always had of being misplaced, of always standing to one side of yourself, of watching yourself in the world even as you were being in the world, and wondering if this was how everyone felt. (166–67)

The full awareness comes early one morning after another night of drug-drenched partying, when he smells bread baking. He begs some from the baker's delivery man as he is loading his truck:

You get down on your knees and tear open the bag. The smell of warm dough envelops you. The first bite sticks in your throat and you almost gag. You will have to go slowly. You will have to learn everything all over again. (182)

A conversion, a return to innocence in the circle of existence, is germinating here like the yeast in the bread of life.

McInerney's narrative technique is noteworthy. He tells his story in what, for lack of more precise terminology, can only be called "second person," a relatively infrequent narrating stance that has the effect of objectifying the "I" of autobiographical narration but without losing the immediacy of the confessional presence. Thus the alienated self and the more conscious narrating self are simultaneously present at every point in the very act of narration itself. This is a refinement on narrative distance, and it is similar to Grass's "I/He" technique in *The Tin Drum* (q.v.) and Donleavy's less sustained mixture of first and third person in *The Ginger Man*. Lazarillo (*Lazarillo de Tormes*, q.v.) addresses a narrative "you," but that "you" is another person, not the picaro himself. It is curious that this relatively rare narrative method should be considered experimental whenever it is encountered because the subtitution of "you" for "I" in personal anecdotes in every possible variation of everyday discourse is so common as to be almost unnoteworthy. This narrating technique is particularly appropriate to the picaresque mode because it builds the multiple selves of the picaro—traditionally rendered by way of the temporal perspectives inherent in narrative distance—into the narrating act itself, creating a sense of simultaneity (in space and time) and immediacy (in space and time) without sacrificing psychological, emotional, or philosophical distance. In sustaining this technique, *Bright Lights, Big City* is unique among mainstream picaresque fictions.

EDITION

New York: Vintage Contemporaries, 1984.

SELECT BIBLIOGRAPHY

Bruce Morrissette, "Narrative 'You,' " in his *Novel and Film: Essays in Two Genres* (Chicago and London: University of Chicago Press, 1985), 108–40.

EL BUSCÓN

(*Historia de la vida del buscón, llamado don Pablos, ejemplo vagamundo y espejo de tacaños*, 1626)

Francisco de Quevedo y Villegas

The full title of the Saragossa edition might be translated as *History of the Life of the Swindler Called Don Pablos, Model of Vagabonds and Mirror of Cunning*, but in its several English versions it is invariably abbreviated, even retitled, with *buscón* rendered variously as "cheat," "sharper," "scavenger," and "swindler," and the earliest English translator (Davies in 1657) even using it as Pablos's proper name. Begun perhaps as early as 1604 and long circulating in different manuscript versions before its eventual publication (which Quevedo himself did not authorize), *El Buscón* is a typically Quevedesque work by the author who would become internationally famous for his acclaimed *Sueños*, which have been called the verbal equivalent to the paintings of Bosch and which in turn influenced Goya. But the typically Quevedesque and the typically picaresque mix as uneasily as oil and water, and as a result *El Buscón* has had a controversial time of it in the context of the picaresque narrative tradition. While few deny its significance in the development of the Spanish picaresque, many heavily qualify its generic status as a picaresque fiction.

The generic status of *El Buscón* as a major picaresque is virtually impossible to refute, for if it was indeed conceived (if not entirely composed) in 1604— immediately in the unprecedented wake of the best-selling *Guzmán de Alfarache* (q.v.) and the renewed popularity of *Lazarillo de Tormes* (q.v.)—then it is, a year before *La pícara Justina* (q.v.), the first fully self-conscious Spanish picaresque, aware of itself as a picaresque in ways that *Lazarillo* and *Guzmán* could not be. Ludwig Pfandl in his *Geschichte der spanischen Nationalliteratur in ihrer Blütezeit* (1929) called it the purest type of picaresque ("der reinste Typus der *novela picaresca*") in intent, content, and form because it gives clear and unadulterated expression to the truest meaning that this narrative form is capable of ("weil sie den tiefsten Sinn, den diese Erzählungsform haben konnte, klar und unverfälscht zum Ausdruck bringt" [279]). This view of *El Buscón* as consumate work fulfilling the true potential of the picaresque narrative form was reasserted almost forty years later by Parker, who argued that it be considered "the masterpiece of the picaresque tradition," the "zenith to which *Guzmán* marked the rise" (*Literature and the Delinquent*, 72). But its generic self-consciousness can also be turned against it. Calling it simultaneously a "work of genius" and a "very bad picaresque novel," Rico faults Quevedo for not understanding the function of autobiographical narration in *Lazarillo* and *Guzmán* and thus producing a work that merely imitates because it was not conceived as an artistically unified whole: "It is difficult to avoid suspecting him of plagiarism" (75, 79, 81).

Its severely reductive value judgment aside, Rico's assessment is representative of one major line of approach to *El Buscón* that has its roots in Spitzer's 1927 essay, "Zur Kunst Quevedos in seinem *Buscón*," which explores what Spitzer calls the "Baroque tension" (*barocke Spannung*) between *Weltsucht* ("seeking the worldly") and *Weltflucht* ("fleeing the worldly"). But while this theme of *desengaño* serves as the book's organizing principle, there is little of the unifying self-revelation of the protagonist that makes *Simplicius Simplicissimus* (q.v.), for example, transcend the merely clever and entertaining. For Spitzer, Pablos emerges as a kind of "*sobre-pícaro*" (576), a marionetteer who reduces the world around him to fragments of a puppet play, which he sets in motion at his whim (580). Adherents of this approach focus on Quevedo as a satirist who makes use of picaresque conventions to display his brilliant wit through clever word play and caricature. Lázaro Carreter, whose work is central to this view of *El Buscón*, considers the book to be, as it must surely have been for its seventeenth-century readers, primarily a brilliant, sparkling entertainment, a *libro de ingenio*. It would thus go against its own grain to look for any kind of novelistic unity based on structure, character, or consistent moral vision.

Another view, almost diametrically opposed, finds *El Buscón* to be a unified, coherent work according to novelistic criteria. This approach sees it as a carefully structured, psychologically plausible, morally serious treatment of the delinquent individual in a corrupt society. First put forth by Parker in 1947 and integrated twenty years later as a prime argument for his thesis in *Literature and the Delinquent*, this line of interpretation has also been followed by May, Morris, and Dunn (1950), although in his *The Spanish Picaresque Novel* (1979), Dunn partially withdraws his support of this approach (150). For Parker, Quevedo's work is "a novel rich in human truth, one that gives us a psychological study of a delinquent that is far in advance of its time, an analysis of the relationship between character and environment that reaches through the pressure of external circumstances into the heart of the conflict between the individual and society, and probes the inner, deep-seated motives that make a delinquent choose that manner of life rather than another" (62). In "attempting to compensate himself for his sense of guilty inferiority," Pablos had "pitched his aims inordinately high and is, as a result, plunged into the depths of social disgrace. Because of a moral weakness that had begun as the fruit of ingrained fear and that had grown through indulgence in self-conceit into the pride of unscrupulous over-confidence, he attempts to impose himself upon a hostile society by cunning and fraud, and becomes a socially unadapted person, a moral reprobate" (*Literature and the Delinquent*, 69–70). Parker's reading makes Pablos almost a tragic hero; and T. E. May, whose interpretation Parker incorporates, examines Pablos as a Christ figure suffering for all fallen humanity but refusing to take up his cross.

It is perhaps because it is so much more outrageous than either of its two predecessors that *El Buscón* has evoked such controversial critical debate. Lazarillo and Guzmán are both upstarts in relationship to their rendered social worlds, and in their presumptuous (though nevertheless plausibly motivated) acts of narration, they are both asserting their upstart natures while simultaneously seeking to justify them. Pablos is more usurper than upstart, and in the sometimes almost demonic gratuitousness of his tricks—he apparently helps murder two policemen just before the end—there is more than a little of the archetypal trickster (q.v.) in him. Moreover, the specific occasion for his narrative act is not at all clear; it appears that he is neither being asked to tell his story, as Lazarillo is, nor is he narratively driven, as Guzmán is, by the confessional impulse. (In some versions, there is a prefatory passage setting up a narrating situation similar to that in *Lazarillo*, but it is not certain that it is by Quevedo.) There is, however, a directly addressed *señor* in his opening sentence—"Yo, señor, soy de Segovia" ("I, sir, come from Segovia")—as well as a *vuesa merced* in his closing one—"Y fuéme peor, como vuesa merced verá en la segunda parte, pues nunca mejora su estado quien muda solamente de lugar, y no de vida y costumbres" ("And things went worse for me, as Your Honor will see in the second part, for he will never improve his lot who simply changes location without changing his life and ways'')—both of which Alpert omits in his translation, along with the allusion to a second part (which occurs in a manuscript version of Quevedo's text but was dropped when the work was printed in two parts). With no further delineation of a particular narrating situation and with no narrative purpose other than the vaguely moralistic (and insincerely perfunctory) one hinted at in that final sentence, even Pablos's telling of his story seems gratuitous. There is, finally, very little self-reflective and almost no self-reflexive exploitation of the various dimensions of narrative distance between the narrating self and the narrated self. For all of its self-awareness as a picaresque in content, character, structure, and form, *El Buscón* surprises in its narrating unself-consciousness.

Randall quotes two passages expressing strong antipathy toward the book. The first is from David Hannay's *The Later Renaissance* (1898):

If you can gloat over starvation—if the hangman expatiating joyfully over halters and lashes seems a pleasant spectacle to you—if blows, falls, disease, hunger, dirt, and every form of suffering, told with a loud callous laugh, and utterly unrelieved, seem to you worth reading about,—then *Pablo de Segovia* is much at your service. (Randall, 209)

The other is from James Fitzmaurice-Kelly's "*La vida del Buscón*" (*Revue hispanique* 43 [1918]):

There are few characters so odious, so uniformly base, so devoid of any pleasing, redeeming vice. Quevedo writes the epic of famished roguery, sparing no detail however loathsome and defiling. Swift himself does not dwell more fondly on the obscene squalor of existence, and Quevedo has an individual love of the ghastly which holds him still further aloof from common humanity. (Randall, 209–10)

Randall rejects such naively literal readings by commenting, ''It is almost as if one should denounce Defoe for wanting to hang all dissenters, or damn Swift for wanting to cook Irish babies'' (210), having earlier pointed out that *El Buscón* is, after all, a youthful work: ''Written by a young man, it sometimes has, not surprisingly, the harsh and smutty qualities of collegiate humor'' (208). Nevertheless, Quevedo's rendered world is startlingly ugly, even to the reader who has already traversed the unrelentingly hostile and vicious worlds of *Lazarillo* and *Guzmán*. Pablos's childhood is among the most sordid in all of picaresque narrative until Pascual's in *The Family of Pascual Duarte* (q.v.). His mother is a whore and a witch who is suspected of having Moorish or Jewish blood; his brother is a pickpocket who at age seven was ''caught in the act and the little angel died from a few lashes they gave him in prison'' (85); and his father is a drunken barber who robs his customers and is later hanged (by Pablos's uncle), with his remains buried alongside the road and his flesh probably dug up by the town pastry cook as filling for the pies that are served to Pablos when he returns home to claim the little money he has been left. If the picaro's family origins recapitulate in symbolic form humanity's original sin and expulsion from the garden, then Quevedo's indictment of the family of humanity is among the darkest in picaresque fiction. "The world of *Buscón* is totally damned, totally chaotic" (Blackburn, 84).

But despite this childhood shame, which wounds him deeply (and which critics like Parker see as the key to opening up his psychology), and despite the viciousness with which the world continues to assault him—all of which ought to make us feel sorry for him—we never really like Pablos, no matter how much he suffers physically and emotionally as he is being publicly dumped in excrement one minute, or spat upon until he is dripping wet another, or being humiliated for his artistocratic pretense by his former friend don Diego—whose own purity of blood is, to the knowing contemporary reader, questionable (see Johnson). The smug, cocksure attitude of Pablos as he perpetrates his own tricks on the world cancels out whatever sympathy he wins from being victim. Nor do we like him any more as narrating Pablos, despite the immediate identification between reader and character that is automatically established by the inherent intimacy of the autobiographical narrative stance. In *El Buscón*, the tone of the narrating voice is as insolent as the tricks are repulsive.

This tone is established in the "Al lector" ("To the Reader") preface that precedes the narrative proper. (Lázaro Carreter claims this is not by Quevedo. However, it is read by every reader. Ife calls it an ironic "curtain-raiser.") Unlike similar addresses to the reader by Lazarillo and Guzmán in their own voices, this one creates a speaking persona who is neither Quevedo nor Pablos:

Dear Reader or Listener (for the blind cannot read) I can just imagine how much you want to read about my delightful Don Pablos, Prince of the Roving Life.

Here you will find all the tricks of the low life or those which I think most people enjoy reading about: craftiness, deceit, subterfuge and swindles, born of laziness to enable you to live on lies; and if you attend to the lesson you will get quite a lot of benefit from it. And even if you don't, study the sermons, for I doubt if anyone buys a book as coarse as this in order to avoid the inclinations of his own depraved nature. Let it serve you as you like; praise it, for it certainly deserves applause, and praise the genius of its author who has enough common sense to know it is a lot more amusing to read about low life when the story is written with spirit, than about other more serious topics. (83)

At first, the snidely ironic tone seems recognizably that of Pablos as he later interjects similar ironic narrative shrugs into his story, such as calling his brother a "little angel," or concluding the sordid details of his family life with, "I was left by myself thanking God for having given me parents who were so clever and concerned about my welfare" (87). But when we remember that Quevedo probably expected his reader to have just emerged from a reading of *Lazarillo* and *Guzmán* and to be picking up *El Buscón* precisely because of a taste for more of the same, we see a controlling narrative voice that subsumes that of Pablos. The parenthetical reference to the blind is not only a double entendre (listeners are not necessarily blind—they could be illiterate—and readers can be blind too if they fail to perceive), it is also an allusion to *Lazarillo de Tormes* and a similar reversal of meaning in the significance to Lazarillo's education of his first master, the blind man. The admonition in the middle of the second paragraph to "study the sermons" is ironic (there being none), and it is also an allusion to *Guzmán de Alfarache*, which is full of them. The narrative voice here is fully aware of situating the reader not only intertextually by acknowledging specific generic expectations but intratextually by warning that these same expectations will be undercut and undermined for satirical purposes if the reader is not too "blind" to see this. The voice situates the reader extratextually by cutting through all moral pretense to the real motivation for picking up a book like *El Buscón*: "I doubt if anyone buys a book as coarse as this in order to avoid the inclinations of his own depraved nature." The reader's deepest cravings for the lurid and depraved—the need to let go of all normal restraint—are simultaneously uncovered and covered up, as though the voice were to say, "You and I know why we're really here, so let's beat around the bush anyway, heh heh." It is offputting in its insolence but not enough to keep the reader from plunging ahead anyway—as though to prove (can we detect Quevedo smirking?) the narrative voice absolutely correct, thus plunging to the very core of the picaresque's appeal for the reader, which is at direct odds with its ostensible purpose. The picaresque is being used to unmask itself. And the reader, too, is stripped of any masks he or she might have brought to a reading of the book— and then given another mask to wear. The reader proceeds uneasily, given apparent freedom to roam but suspecting all the time that he or she is being maneuvered, for the narrative voice of the prefatory address to the reader has unmasked itself just enough to reveal the face of that master narrative puppeteer, the formal satirist.

In *Guzmán* and *Simplicissimus*, there is modal tension between picaresque and romance as these two opposing fictional modes attract and repel one another like magnets, energizing the narrative. In *El Buscón* there is modal tension between satire and picaresque, which are neighbors on the spectrum of fictional modes. One line of approach to Quevedo's work emphasizes the satire and trivializes the picaresque; the other plays down the satire and focuses on the picaresque as a prenovelistic form. A third line of approach might reconcile how Quevedo himself integrates the two and to what ends. The prefatory note to the reader, as we have seen, certainly signals the legitimacy of such an attempt; it prepares us for a satirical treatment of the picaresque by parodying it.

As *Memoirs of a Good-for-Nothing* (q.v.), for example, will later create mutual parodying of romance and picaresque through modal tension, so *El Buscón* sees in the newly emerging picaresque genre both a popular means of expression and an immediately satirizable form. New genres generate their own parodies even as they evolve. Taking just such an approach is Bjornson, who continues a line of interpretation that Serrano Poncela was among the first to explore. Bjornson's subtitle for his chapter on *El Buscón* is "Quevedo's Annihilation of the Picaresque," and he sees the book as a serious indictment of the picaresque vision:

As an aristocrat who decried the loss of traditional values, the disintegration of a divinely ordained social hierarchy, and the presumptuousness of the lower classes, [Quevedo] attributed the material and social aspirations of conversos and commoners to an unwarranted dissatisfaction with their proper places in society. For this reason, he started with a character like Guzmán, but rather than treating his pícaro seriously, he exaggerated Pablos' dominant characteristics and reduced him to a one-dimensional, static figure whose ridiculous behavior stands for the psychological reality of a particular type of moral blindness—that of a buscón or pícaro. (110)

Writing for readers who share his assumptions about the social hierarchy, Quevedo "exposes the inherent absurdity of all vulgar but ambitious conversos like Guzmán" (111). Rejecting the portrayal, in *Lazarillo* and *Guzmán*, of the picaro as the victim of circumstances caused by society, Quevedo by "parodying the structures and basic assumptions of these novels . . . was implicitly defending his own traditionalist, elitist opinions and providing upper-class readers with a palatable alternative to earlier portrayals of the pícaro's dilemma in a corrupt society" (126). Thus Bjornson finds unity precisely in those disparate elements that lead others to consider *El Buscón* as satire rather than picaresque and in the characterization of Pablos that leads still others to find unity in psychological verisimilitude:

In parodying the morally serious pseudoautobiographical perspective and the idea of character as process, [Quevedo] projected his own world view into the picaresque myth, and it was this world view which molded the novel's isolated anecdotes and ingenious repartee into an artistically unified, intellectually provocative commentary upon pícaros and the picaresque life. (126)

Such a reading is not as accessible to today's reader, whose sympathies are much more likely to be with the underdog and whose experiences of social structures are vastly different from those of Quevedo's aristocratic contemporaries. But Bjornson's interpretation does not rely exclusively on historical and biographical contexts; he tries to demonstrate that the text signals this very reading. In fact, if we now take Bjornson's analysis back with us to the address to the reader, we find that the reference to blindness now has another possible meaning: the blindness of Pablos himself, which in turn should make us see.

Parody means, literally, "beside the song" and in explicitly and implicitly juxtaposing *El Buscón* with its two immediate picaresque predecessors, Quevedo builds into the Spanish picaresque genre a savage self-critique. But it seems doubtful that a satirist of Quevedo's range and talent would be satisfied with parody alone, which is only one of the satirist's potent formal weapons and is directed at a specific literary work or form. Although the parodist can confine himself within a literary frame of reference, the satirist always has at least an implicit, if not explicit, corrective vision of society as such. Bjornson suggests as much by saying that Quevedo's worldview molded *El Buscón* into a commentary on picaros and the picaresque way of life. But when we move beyond literary parody into such a larger social vision, we run into a major problem. The world that is depicted in *El Buscón* is so black and so bleak—there does not seem to be a single admirable character in it or any redeeming qualities of any kind—that it could not possibly be used to demonstrate Quevedo's support of the social status quo without raising serious questions about the satirist's moral values. Ife confronts this problem and suggests that in *El Buscón* Quevedo is "busy knocking down upstarts in books when he is powerless to do anything about them in real life." The laughter elicited by Pablos's destruction at the end "may in fact be the nervous giggle of a class busy putting out more flags to stave off an unthinkable defeat." In order to debase Pablos, Quevedo has to unmask Diego; in doing so, he is pulling down the very ideal of respectability to which the lowly Pablos aspires. To fend off upstart intruders like Pablos, those on the inside find that "the only way they can effectively deny him entry is by denying that there is anything to enter." Despite his victory over Pablos, "the world Quevedo portrays in the *Buscón* is one in which the pícaros have taken over, one where all values have been eroded away. There is nowhere for Quevedo's own class to take refuge in all this, and nowhere for us, as readers, to retreat to if we do not like what we see" (171). Ife's reading makes *El Buscón* the book as bleak as the world rendered in it. It turns Quevedo into something of an irate apologist, making a desperate last stand for a social order he knows is lost. A truly satirical vision would break through such class xenophobia into larger considerations of the human condition.

The verbal pryotechnics that make the book almost untranslatable in parts and the grotesque distortions and caricatures that convulse the world into nightmare must have bigger game in mind than parody of a popular literary form, or defense of the rightfulness of a particular social order. Perhaps the intended satirical victims of *El Buscón* are those very readers with whom Quevedo is supposedly allied—those near the top of the social hierarchy who take pleasure in the humiliation of the already humiliated. These implied readers (they are not technically narratees) may think they are being indulged, justified, and entertained; in reality, the joke is on them. They may gleefully watch over the destruction of Pablos, but in that glee is their own impending destruction as well. This glee is, in fact, a telltale symptom of their own end. And while they are occupied with righteous laughter at the eradication of an obnoxious picaro, the real picaro of *El Buscón*—Quevedo—has conned them after all.

TRANSLATIONS AND EDITIONS

Quotations are from Michael Alpert's translation *The Swindler* in *Two Spanish Picaresque Novels* (Baltimore, Md.: Penguin, 1969). *El Buscón* was first translated into English from La Geneste's 1633 French version as *The Life and Adventures of Buscon the Witty Spaniard* in 1657 by a "Person of Honour," identified by Randall (see below) as John Davies of Kidwelly. An abridged translation appeared in 1683. *The Life of Paul the Spanish Sharper* by Captain John Stevens in *The Comical Works of Don Francisco de Quevedo* was published in 1707 (reprinted in 1709 and 1942); in 1743 Pedro Pineda used it as the basis for his translation, as did subsequent versions issued in 1798, 1832, 1841, and 1892. More recent renderings include those by Charles Duff, *History of the Life of the Great Rascal Paul, An Exemplary Vagabond and Ideal Sharper*, in *Quevedo: The Choice Humorous and Satirical Works* (London: Routledge; New York: Dutton, 1926); "divers hands'' revised and edited by Mack Hendricks Singleton, *The Life and Adventures of Don Pablos the Sharper*, in *Masterpieces of the Spanish Golden Age*, ed. Angel Flores (New York: Holt, Rinehart and Winston, 1957); Frank Mugglestone (under the pseudonym Francisco Villamiquel y Hardin), *The Life and Adventures of Don Pablos the Sharper* (Leicester: Anglo-Spanish Library, 1928); and Hugh A. Harter, *The Scavenger* (New York: Las Americas, 1962).

There are major textual problems with *El Buscón*. These are presented in the critical edition by Fernando Lázaro Carreter, *La vida del buscón llamado don Pablos* (Salamanca: Clásicos Hispánicos, 1965), which has become the standard edition for scholarly studies. Lázaro Carreter states that Robert Duport, a Saragossa bookseller who published *El Buscón* without Quevedo's permission, must have written the "Al lector" ("To the Reader"), pretending that Quevedo wrote it, in order to "authorize" the edition; thus this prefatory note should be more appropriately titled, *El Librero, al lector* ("The Bookseller to the Reader") (p. xv). In his concluding remarks, Lázaro Carreter states again that this preface is not by Quevedo (p. lxxviii). Another accessible edition—designed for nonnative readers as a class text—is by B. W. Ife, *La Vida del Buscón Llamado Don Pablos* (Oxford: Pergamon Press, 1977). Ife follows Lázaro Carreter's edition and notes in his preliminary discussion of the text that the "Carta Dedicatoria" (the note establishing the narrating situation) "may be by Quevedo; the *Al Lector* is almost certainly by Duport, but it has been included here since its irony has made it a traditional—and highly appropriate—curtain-raiser for Quevedo's work" (33).

SELECT BIBLIOGRAPHY

Victorio G. Agüera, "Dislocación de elementos picarescos en el *Buscón*," in *Estudios literarios de hispanistas norteamericanos dedicados a Helmut Hatzfeld con motivo de su 80 aniversario*, ed. Joseph M. Sola-Solé, Alessandro Crisfaulli, and Bruno Damiani (Barcelona: Hispam, 1974), 357–67, "Nueva interpretación del episodio 'Rey de Gallos' del *Buscón*," *Hispanófila* 49 (1973): 33–40, and "Notas sobre las burlas de Alcalá de *La Vida del Buscón* llamado Pablos," *Romance Notes* 13 (1972): 503–6; Richard Bjornson, *The Picaresque Hero in European Fiction* (Madison: University of Wisconsin Press, 1977); Alexander Blackburn, *The Myth of the Picaro: Continuity and Transformation of the Picaresque Novel, 1554–1954* (Chapel Hill: University of North Carolina Press, 1979); Frank Wadleigh Chandler, *Romances of Roguery* [1899] (New York: Burt Franklin, 1961); Joseph Chorpenning, "Classical Satire and *La vida del Buscón*," *Neophilologus* 61 (1977): 212–19; Edmond Cros, *L'Aristocrate et le carnaval des gueux: Etude sur le Buscón de Quevedo* (Montpellier: Etudes sociocritiques, Université Paul Valéry, 1975); Gonzalo Díaz Migoyo, *Estructura de la novela: anatomía de "El Buscón"* (Madrid: Fundamentos, 1978); Peter N. Dunn, "Problems of a Model for the Picaresque and the Case of Quevedo's *Buscón*," *Bulletin of Hispanic Studies* 59 (1982): 95–105, *The Spanish Picaresque Novel* (Boston: Twayne, 1979), and "El individuo y la sociedad en *La vida del Buscón*," *Bulletin Hispanique* 52 (1950): 375–96; Sherman Eoff, "The Tragedy of the Unwanted Person in Three Versions: Pablos de Segovia, Pito Pérez, Pascual Duarte," *Hispania* 39 (1956): 190–96; W. M. Frohock, "*The Buscón* and Current Criticism," in *Homenaje a William L. Fichter: Estudios sobre el teatro antiguo y otros ensayos*, ed. A. David Kossoff and José Amor y Vásquez (Madrid: Castalia, 1971), 223–27; Hugh A. Harter, "Language and Mask: The Problem of Reality in Quevedo's *Buscón*," *Kentucky Foreign Language Quarterly* 9 (1962), 205–9; James Iffland, "Pablos's Voice: His

Master's?'' *Romanische Forschungen* 91 (1979): 215–43; Carroll B. Johnson, "*El Buscón*: D. Pablos, D. Diego y D. Francisco," *Hispanófila* 51 (1974): 1–26; Fernando Lázaro Carreter, "Originalidad del *Buscón*," in *Studia Philologica: Homenaje ofrecido a Damaso Alonso por sus amigos y discípulos con ocasión de su 60 aniversario* (Madrid: Gredos, 1960–1963), II, 319–38; Raimundo Lida, "Pablos de Segovia y su agudeza: Notas sobre la lengua del *Buscón*," in *Homenaje a Casalduero* (Madrid: Gredos, 1972), 285–98, and "Sobre el arte verbal del *Buscón*," *Philological Quarterly* 51 (1972): 255–69; T. E. May, "Good and Evil in the *Buscón*: A Survey," *Modern Language Review* 45 (1950): 319–35; Stuart Miller, *The Picaresque Novel* (Cleveland: Case Western Reserve University Press, 1967); Maurice Molho, "Cinco lecciones sobre el *Buscón*," in *Semántica y poética* (Barcelona: Crítica, 1977); Cyril B. Morris, *The Unity and Structure of Quevedo's "Buscón"* (Hull: University of Hull, 1965); Alexander A. Parker, *Literature and the Delinquent: The Picaresque Novel in Spain and Europe, 1599–1753* (Edinburgh: University Press, 1967), and "The Psychology of the 'Pícaro' in 'El Buscón,' " *Modern Language Review* 42 (1947): 58–69; Dale B. J. Randall, *The Golden Tapestry: A Critical Survey of Non-Chivalric Spanish Fiction in English Translation (1543–1657)* (Durham, N.C.: Duke University Press, 1963); Joseph V. Ricapito, "Quevedo's *Buscón*—'Libro de entretenimiento' or "Libro de desengaño': An Overview," *Kentucky Romance Quarterly* 32 (1985): 153–64; Francisco Rico, *The Spanish Picaresque Novel and the Point of View* [1970], trans. Charles Davis with Harry Sieber (Cambridge: Cambridge University Press, 1984); William Riggan, *Pícaros, Madmen, Naïfs, and Clowns: The Unreliable First-Person Narrator* (Norman: University of Oklahoma Press, 1981); Fritz Schalk, "Uber Quevedo und seinem *Buscón*," *Romanische Forschungen* 74 (1962): 11–30; Segundo Serrano Poncela, "¿El *Buscón*—Parodía picaresca?" *Insula* 12, no. 154 (1959): 1, 10; Harry Sieber, *The Picaresque* (London: Methuen, 1977) and "Apostrophes in the *Buscón*: An Approach to Quevedo's Narrative Technique," *Modern Language Notes* 83 (1968): 178–211; Leo Spitzer, "Zur Kunst Quevedos in seinem *Buscón*," *Archivum Romanicum* 11 (1927): 511–80 (rpt. in his *Romanische Stil- und Literaturuntersuchungen* [Marburg a. Lahn: N. G. Elwertsche Verlagsbuchhandlung, 1931], II, 48–125); Henry Thomas, "The English Translations of Quevedo's *La Vida del Buscón*," *Revue hispanique* 81 (1933): 282–99; Henry Edward Watts, "Quevedo and His Works, with an Essay on the Picaresque Novel," in his edition of *Pablo de Segovia, The Spanish Sharper* (London, 1927); Arnold Weinstein, *Fictions of the Self: 1550–1800* (Princeton: Princeton University Press, 1981); Edwin Williamson, "The Conflict between Author and Protagonist in Quevedo's *Buscón*," *Journal of Hispanic Philology* 2 (1977): 45–60.

A CLOCKWORK ORANGE

(1962)

Anthony Burgess

Futuristic or speculative fiction (sf) projects distorted and exaggerated aspects of the present landscape into a future vision from which we can perceive the present more clearly. It distances us temporally so that we can orient ourselves spatially to the immanent dangers in the world around us; it distorts so that we may look and see; it alienates in one sense in order to make us familiar in another; it estranges in order to bring us closer. Scholes has given the name *structural fabulation* to this kind of fiction, which he traces back in the evolution of narrative forms to didactic romance (as opposed to what he calls "pure romance," which is sublimation with minimal cognition, and as opposed as well to what he calls "dogmatic fabulation," which works out of a closed, antispeculative system of belief). "When romance returns deliberately to confront reality it produces the various forms of didactic romance or fabulation that we usually call allegory, satire, fable, parable, and so on—to indicate our recognition that reality is being addressed indirectly through a patently fictional device " (*Structural Fabulation*, 29). Elsewhere Scholes has discussed picaresque as a strand of fabulation, with its "traditional cruelty and violence modified [in Hawkes] by its passage from a proto-realistic form to a surrealistic one," and Céline's (*Journey to the End of the Night*, q.v.) recognition of its "natural tendency . . . toward a grotesque exaggeration of misfortunes: an intensification of everyday troubles into an ironic vision of a distorted cosmos, where a poetic injustice reigns, which destroys all who do not learn to accommodate themselves to it" (*The Fabulators*, 60–61).

In the spectrum of fictional modes, picaresque has a direct affinity for satire and often looks toward its opposite, pure romance. The blending of these into the specific genre of sf has rarely, if ever, been noted, despite the obviously episodic nature of much sf, with its journeys and galleries of cosmic types and, especially, its frequent rendering of planetary homelessness. In its equally frequent depictions of a rigidly hierarchical social order, sf occasionally brings in trickster (q.v.), as in, for example, Harlan Ellison's " 'Repent, Harlequin!' Said the Ticktockman" and Kurt Vonnegut's "Harrison Bergeron." In *A Clockwork Orange* Alex is not only a version of trickster; he is also on a journey through the circle of existence; and through Alex, Burgess explores a fundamental picaresque theme: the paradoxical nature of freedom, a theme struck in Alex's opening words to all three parts of the book: "What's it going to be then, eh?"

The landscape of Alex's world is, to use one of Burgess's clever coinages, "bezoomny" [mad]. This totalitarian state is polluted and full of random violence. The newspapers and entertainment industries are state owned. The jails are full to bursting. The teenage argot is Nadsat, a mixture of Russian and English, and a popular singer is called Johnny Zhivago. It is an ominous world of personal anarchy and repressive totalitarianism. In part I Alex narrates the various forays he and his gang of droogs make in this landscape, inflicting violence as they feel like it. Betrayed by his fellow droogs, Alex is captured by the police and sentenced to prison. Part II is about his rehabilitation through the Ludovico technique, a kind of lobotomizing through drugs and aversion therapy, which leaves Alex "ready to turn the other cheek" when he is victimized. In part III he describes the attempts of the government to use him as an example of the kind of beneficial behavioral engineering that this technique can achieve; he is taken in by a dissenting writer named F. Alexander, who wants to use him as an example of the government's robotizing of human beings. Feeling that "not one chelloveck in the whole horrid world was for me" (194), Alex tries to kill himself by jumping out the window. Sensitive to the resulting negative publicity, the state reverses the Ludovico procedure while Alex is recuperating from the fall.

Throughout Alex is seen in a dual perspective. On the one hand, he is a kind of satiric victim, the character who in formal satire is the object of satiric attack; as such, he does not elicit compassion because of the violence he inflicts on his environment. The anarchic impulses he acts out make him unsympathetic—a self-characterization reinforced by the estrangement caused by the language he uses. Given his unwillingness to straighten out, we tend to sympathize with the forces of order who are at a loss as to what to do with him, as society did not know what to do with Pascual Duarte (*The Family of Pascual Duarte*, q.v.). But at the same time, narrative distance is manipulated in such a way as to make Alex also a kind of engaging villain—and, to some extent, even a tragic victim. There is no doubt that he is despicable; yet he is superior to all the other people in his world, except perhaps the prison chaplain (the charlie). He is quite open about acting out the sinister and dark urges within all of us; this is his trickster function. He takes a genuine interest in other people; he takes a stand against hard drugs; he honestly *likes* being bad:

But, brothers, this biting of their toe-nails over what is the *cause* of badness is what turns me into a fine laughing malchick. They don't go into what is the cause of *goodness*, so why of the other shop? If lewdies are good, that's because they like it, and I wouldn't ever interfere with their pleasures, and so of the other shop. And I was patronizing the other shop. More, badness is of the self, the one, the you or me on our oddy knockies, and that self is made by old Bog or God and is his great pride and radosty. But the not-self cannot have the bad, meaning they of the government and the judges and the schools cannot allow the bad because they cannot allow the self. And is not our modern history, my brothers, the story of brave malenky selves fighting these big machines? I am serious with you, brothers, over this. But what I do I do because I like to do. (46–47)

His moral code is one of amorality, of premorality in the spirit of trickster. That it does not fit in with a repressive regime is made clear time and again when Alex is victimized by the world around him and in ways that narrow our emotional distance from him. When Alex emerges from prison he finds that the landscape around him has institutionalized, indeed normalized, the very tactics of brutality that Alex has just been serving time for: the droog who betrayed him is now a policeman; the old man in the library whom he beat up now beats him up; and the writer (whose wife he had raped, from the after-effects of which she died) and his associates use him as so much fodder for their own brand of agitprop journalism. Like the traditional picaro, Alex is as much victim as he is victimizer in a hostile and morally unpredictable world.

The paradoxical duality of Alex's character is reflected in the paradoxical nature of freedom, which is the book's major theme. As Burgess explores it in the situation of Alex, it might be expressed as follows: Is all self-expression to be valued absolutely even if one chooses to use one's freedom to commit atrocities? Is the will to perpetrate evil better than no will at all? Two characters address the issue directly. The first is the chaplain, who tells Alex, ''Goodness comes from within, 6655321. Goodness is something chosen. When a man cannot choose he ceases to be a man" (95–96), and "What does God want? Does God want goodness or the choice of goodness? Is a man who chooses the bad perhaps in some ways better than a man who has the good imposed upon him?" (110), and finally, "He ceases to be a wrongdoer. He ceases also to be a creature capable of moral choice" (145). In the end, the chaplain rejects the Ludovico method of rehabilitation, leaves his prison job, and goes around preaching on the subject of moral choice. The other character who addresses the issue is the writer, F. Alexander, in whom Alex recognizes an image of himself ("Good Bog . . . another Alex" [183]). "They have turned you into something other than a human being. You have no power of choice any longer. You are committed to socially acceptable acts, a little machine capable only of good," he tells Alex, and then echoes the chaplain: "But the essential intention is the real sin. A man who cannot choose ceases to be a man" (180). But Alex soon realizes that the writer's idea of liberty is an abstraction; for the sake of his political rhetoric, he dehumanizes Alex by making him a mere tool in the service of a concept, and in this he is as repressive toward the individual as the government has been in using the Ludovico technique. Alex's recurring question begins to resonate with the thorny issue: "What's it going to be then, eh?" Re-rehabilitated, Alex ends the sixth chapter of part III with the words, "I was cured all right" (205).

The tight symmetry of *A Clockwork Orange* reflects the picaresque dance pattern: in part I, Alex is the inflicter of violence; in part II, he is programmed penitent; and in part III, he is the victim as most of the characters he has done wrong to in part I exact their revenge on him, including the writer, who finally comes to realize who Alex really is and who plays the music that drives Alex to suicide. The symmetry also recapitulates the picaresque circle of existence: alienated from his own parents, who are meek and uncaring cogs in their repressive society, Alex sees a sign saying HOME outside the cottage of the writer whose wife he rapes; he stumbles here again in part III, having been beaten up by the police. "Home, home, home, it was home I was wanting, and it was HOME I came to, brothers" (175). The writer, unaware of who his visitor is, shelters him. Alex sees again the manuscript the writer had been working on during his first visit here: *A Clockwork Orange*. Alex's later realization ("another Alex") adds a self-reflexive dimension to the book as we realize that the book we are reading is by Alex and is called *A Clockwork Orange*: the circle of existence becomes a vicious circle and suggests an eternal journey of recurrence in which the individual's passage from unbridled youth toward adulthood and maturity recapitulates the stages of civilization or a collective mythic image of the emergence of the race from a premoral, undifferentiated mode of being. Alex himself will come to write this book.

The ending of the version published in the United States destroys the symmetry (there are only six chapters in the third part, as compared to seven each in the first two parts) and will not really support such a reading, however. The book as published, in fact, suggested a different cycle—that the violence was going to begin all over again and that Alex has learned nothing. As Burgess himself explains it, his New York publisher (Norton) felt the ending was too sentimental, and so the twenty-first chapter was omitted: "When they were going to publish it in America, they said, 'we're tougher over here' and thought the ending too soft for their readers. If it was me now, faced with the decision I'd say no. I still believe in my ending" (Rabinovitz, 538). Only in 1987, after an entire generation of readers was misled, did Norton bring out the full twenty-one-chapter version in the United States.

In commenting on the theme of the book, Burgess has said:

Catholics of my kind don't become disappointed, because we *expect* evil. . . . We're *surprised* at his capacity for good. Look at history, and you'll see that man has survived only because of his odd flashes of goodness. . . . As a lapsed Catholic, I find my sense of good and evil is quite simple, really: I don't think of God as being good in the sense of giving money to the poor and meek, who definitely have *not* inherited the earth. God is good when He gives us a grilled steak. There's good when we make love or eat an apple or watch a sunset. Evil certainly exists too; it is undoubtedly evil to fart during Beethoven's *Ninth*. But choice is all. To *impose* good, whether through force or through some technique like aversion therapy, is evil; to act evil is better than to have good imposed. (70)

What little free will man possesses is too precious to encroach on, whatever good intentions the encroacher may have.

The final chapter begins, like the first, "What's it going to be then, eh?" Alex has a new gang of droogs. They hang out at the Korova Milkbar, go out and beat up an old man, wander to the Duke of New York where the old ladies greet them with the same "God bless you, boys," and so on, but Alex is reluctant to shell out money to buy drinks. His droogs pump him for the reason, and one of them discovers a picture of a baby in Alex's pocket: "It was of a baby gurgling goo goo with all like moloko dribbling from its rot and looking up and like smecking at everybody, and it was all nagoy and its flesh was like in all folds with being a very fat baby" (210). Alex leaves the gang and goes home, unexcited about the violence they were supposed to have that and the following night: "It was like something soft getting into me and I could not pony why. What I wanted these days I did not know" (212). His taste in music is even running toward the sentimental: "I got a sudden like picture of me sitting before a bolshy fire in an armchair peeting away at this chai, and what was funny and very very strange was that I seemed to have turned into a very starry chelloveck, about seventy years old, because I could viddy my own voloss, which was very grey, and I also had whiskers, and these were very grey too. I could viddy myself as an old man, sitting by a fire, and then the like picture vanished" (213). He goes into a restaurant and observes a couple engaged in pleasant conversation. The man turns out to be his old droog Pete. The pretty girl is his wife. Pete now works for an insurance company and no longer talks Alex's Nadsat. Pete, it turns out, is almost twenty, and Alex is just eighteen. Alex has a vision of himself coming home to a hot dinner, a wife, and a baby: "Yes yes yes, there it was. Youth must go, ah yes. But youth is only being in a way like it might be an animal. No, it is not just like being an animal so much as being like one of these malenky toys you viddy being sold in the streets, like little chellovecks made out of tin and with a spring inside and then a winding handle on the outside and you wind it up grr grr grr and off it itties, like walking, O my brothers. But it itties in a straight line and bangs straight into things bang bang bang and it cannot help what it is doing. Being young is like being like one of these malenky machines'' (217). Alex then thinks he will tell this truth to his future son, even though his son may go out and do all the things Alex has done. ''And so it would itty on to like the end of the world, round and round and round, like some bolshy gigantic like chelloveck, like Old Bog himself (by courtesy of Korova Milkbar) turning and turning and turning a vonny grahzny orange in his gigantic rookers'' (218). Now on the lookout for a wife, Alex answers his own earlier question. The last two paragraphs of the final chapter are:

That's what it's going to be then, brothers, as I come to the like end of this tale. You have been everywhere with your little droog Alex, suffering with him, and you have viddied some of the most grahzny bratchnies old Bog ever made, all on to your old droog Alex. And all it was was that I was young. But now as I end this story, brothers, I am not young, not no longer, oh no. Alex like groweth up, oh yes.

But where I itty now, O my brothers, is all on my oddy knocky, where you cannot go. Tomorrow is all like sweet flowers and the turning vonny earth and the stars and the old Luna up there and your old droog Alex all on his oddy knocky seeling like a mate. And all that cal. A terrible grahzny vonny world, really, O my brothers. And so farewell from your little droog. And to all others in this story profound shooms of lip-music brrrrr. And they can kiss my sharries. But you, O my brothers, remember sometimes thy little Alex that was. Amen. And all that cal. (218–219)

What Alex chooses here is what Lazarillo chooses (*Lazarillo de Tormes*, q.v.): the domesticated coziness of home—though whether Alex will achieve it is left as ambiguous as the problem of Lazarillo's apparent self-deception at the end. Both have made a moral choice, however, in trying to satisfy their desire for a home in this world. And in becoming writers, they have both come home in another sense: they are reflectors of their own meanings.

EDITION

Page references are to the revised Ballantine edition (New York, 1988).

SELECT BIBLIOGRAPHY

Rubin Rabinovitz, ''Mechanism vs. Organism: Anthony Burgess' *A Clockwork Orange*,'' *Modern Fiction Studies* 24 (1978): 538–41; Robert Scholes, *The Fabulators* (New York: Oxford University Press, 1967) and *Structural Fabulation: An Essay on Fiction of the Future* (Notre Dame and London: University of Notre Dame Press, 1975); Darko Suvin, ''On the Poetics of the Science Fiction Genre,'' *College English* (December 1972): 372–82. Burgess's own comments are from an extensive interview in *Playboy* (September 1974): 69–86.

COLONEL JACK

(1722)

Daniel Defoe

In its third part, this work superficially resembles Defoe's more purely adventurous *Captain Singleton* (1720), and its full title reinforces such an impression: *The History and Remarkable Life of the Truly Honourable Col. Jacque, Commonly Call'd Col. Jack, Who Was Born a Gentleman, Put 'Prentice to a Pick-Pocket, Was Six and Twenty Years a Thief, and Then Kidnapp'd to Virginia. Came Back a Merchant, Was Five Times Married to Four Whores; Went into the Wars, Behav'd Bravely, Got Preferment, Was Made Colonel of a Regiment, Came Over, and Fled with the Chevalier, and Is Now Abroad Compleating a Life of Wonders, and Resolves to Dye a General.* But in its first two thirds, it ranks with *Moll Flanders* and *Roxana* (q.q.v.) as a major picaresque in eighteenth-century English literature. What distinguishes *Colonel Jack* from Defoe's other two variations in the picaresque tradition is its sustained and detailed depiction, in the first third, of a life of thievery bred by necessity and its thoughtful exploration, in the middle third, of the New World as a place of moral as well as economic rebirth (in *Moll Flanders* the New World becomes a place of horror when Moll discovers she has unwittingly committed a primal sin). In its portrayal of the criminal life, *Colonel Jack* links directly with the community of rogues motif that recurs in the picaresque from *El Buscón*, *Guzmán de Alfarache*, and "Rinconete and Cortadillo" (q.q.v.) on. And in its Virginia plantation scenes, it develops a New World motif that is only a germ at the end of *El Buscón* and finds fuller expression in later picaresques.

Colonel Jack begins with an editorial preface that is exemplary of the ostensible didactic aim of early picaresque; it could stand at the front of *Guzmán*:

Every wicked Reader will here be encouraged to a Change, and it will appear that the best and only good End of a wicked mispent Life is Repentence; that in this, there is Comfort, Peace, and often times Hope, and that the Penitent shall be return'd like the Prodigal, *and his latter End be better than his Beginning.* (2)

In the first sentence, Jack calls his life "a Chequer Work of Nature" (3), explaining how he has been told that, though born out of wedlock, he is the son of a "Man of Quality" and a "Gentlewoman," and that explains his having been turned over to a nurse to be raised. When she dies, his thieving days begin. But Defoe makes it clear that Jack is an involuntary thief who leads the life of a criminal only to survive. About to make restitution to an old woman he had robbed a year earlier, he reproaches himself for "the Villainy" he had committed: "O! that I had some Trade to live by, I would never rob no more, for sure 'tis a wicked abominable Thing. Here indeed I felt the loss of what just Parents do, and ought to do by all their Children; I mean being bred to some Trade or Employment, and I wept many times, that I knew not what to do, or what to turn my Hand to, tho' I resolved to leave off the wicked Course I was in" (83).

When he is tricked and sold as a slave to a plantation owner in Virginia, he

believes he is being punished for his wicked ways. His humanitarian treatment
of the slaves soon earns him the owner's respect, and he is eventually rewarded
with his freedom and some land of his own. Materially prosperous now, he
contemplates his fortunes. Typical of Defoe, itemization of worldly goods leads
to moral stock-taking as well:

Every *Newgate* wretch, every Desperate forlorn Creature; the most Despicable ruin'd
Man in the World, has here [in the New World] a fair Opportunity put into his Hands
to begin the World again, and that upon a Foot of certain Gain, and in a Method exactly
Honest; with a Reputation, that nothing past will have any Effect upon; and innumerable
People have thus rais'd themselves from the worst Circumstance in the World; Namely,
from the *Condemn'd-Hole* in *Newgate*. (153)

His words here echo Guzmán's *volver de nuevo*. Now thirty years old, he begins
to reflect on "the Foundation of my new Life" (157), with the help of an
indentured servant, transported as a felon, whom he calls his tutor and who is
himself an impoverished scholar who has learned the reality of Moll's impossible
situation: give me not poverty lest I steal. The tutor says much the same thing:
"To be reduc'd to Necessity is to be wicked; for Necessity is not only the
Temptation, but is such a Temptation as human Nature is not empower'd to
resist" (161), and he cites the same prayer (163), which is from Proverbs 30:9.
When Jack returns to his plantation after years of adventures in Europe, the
picaresque dance pattern also emerges strongly as he discovers his first wife
among his own indentured servants.

But *Colonel Jack* also manifests a major transformation in the picresque mode
from its earlier Spanish generic prototypes. Like such later eighteenth-century
works as *Roderick Random* and *Gil Blas* (q.q.v.), *Colonel Jack* is modally mixed.
Jack, like the other eighteenth-century versions of the picaro, is not really of
low birth. Though illegitimate, he has been told—and strongly believes—that
he is of good blood. Although experientially he shares the picaro's essential
condition of exclusion, psychologically he knows that he belongs; this in fact
helps guide him through his days of thievery: "I had something in me, by what
secret Influence I knew not, kept me from the other degrees of Raking and Vice,
and in short, from the general Wickedness of the rest of my Companions . . . I
had a strange original Notion, as I have mentioned in its Place, of my being a
Gentleman" (60). Even in his Virginian prosperity he feels he "might still be
born for greater things than these" (157). Though Defoe never goes on to tie
up the loose ends of Jack's parentage, Jack is the first in a line of picaros who
are ultimately heroes of a comic romance. The world Defoe depicts in *Colonel
Jack* is apparently picaresque but ultimately providentially ordered. "In collecting the various Changes, and Turns of my Affairs," Jack concludes, "I saw
clearer than ever I had done before, how an invisible over-ruling Power, a Hand
influenced from above, Governs all our Actions of every Kind, limits all our
Designs, and orders the Events of every Thing relating to us" (307–8). *Colonel
Jack* can even "be seen as an adumbration of the *Bildungsroman*" (Monk, xvi).

Chandler dismissed the work as insignificant next to *Moll Flanders,* and Parker does not find it to be a serious psychological or moral study of delinquency: "Delinquency is treated by Defoe with a certain superficial optimism, which is a note alien to the Spanish picaresque tradition even in its decline" (110). Blackburn considers Defoe's works nonpicaresque because they "never question the validity of experience" (122), because their "rudimentary pattern of Christian redemption . . . is diametrically opposed to the disintegration pattern of the picaresque," and because Defoe argues that his protagonists' crimes are morally justified by necessity (124).

EDITION

London: Oxford University Press, 1965; edited, with an introduction, by Samuel Holt Monk.

SELECT BIBLIOGRAPHY

Alexander Blackburn, *The Myth of the Picaro: Continuity and Transformation of the Picaresque Novel, 1554–1954* (Chapel Hill: University of North Carolina Press, 1979); F. W. Chandler, *The Literature of Roguery* [1907] (New York: Burt Franklin, 1958); A. A. Parker, *Literature and the Delinquent: The Picaresque Novel in Spain and Europe, 1599–1753* (Edinburgh: University of Edinburgh Press, 1967).

THE CONFIDENCE-MAN: HIS MASQUERADE

(1857)

Herman Melville

The protean, shape-shifting title character of this singular fiction has been described as "an amalgam of America's popular comic figures: the sly, dupe-bilking Yankee and the frontier sharper. Indeed, the riverboat swindler himself was by 1856 a standard addition to the rogues' gallery of American picaresque lore" (Hoffman, 128). And the book's mid-nineteenth-century Mississippi River setting has been portrayed, by H. Bruce Franklin, in a historical context that in its social instability resembles the pictures such early scholars as F. W. Chandler (in his *Romances of Roguery*) and Fonger de Haan (in *An Outline History of the Novela Picaresca in Spain*) painted of the sixteenth- and seventeenth-century Spanish socioeconomic conditions, which, in their view, produced an abundance of rogues and consequently a literature about them and their rogueries. In its startlingly similar evocation of a landscape that some thirty years later would also become the setting for the great American picaresque, *Huckleberry Finn* (q.v.), Franklin's summary of life along America's vital artery is worth quoting at some length:

America in the 1850's was a jungle in which all kinds of hunters pursued their quarry: slaves, factory workers, buffalo, Indians, Mexicans, Mormons, Catholics, Protestants, gold, land, and suckers. American troops had just seized almost half of Mexico, were

now busy exterminating Indians from Florida to Oregon, and were preparing to attack
the Mormons in Utah. Slavery had already caused much blood to flow, and the nation
was on the brink of civil war. Bands of killers roamed almost at will on both sides of
the Mississippi and far to the west, undaunted by meeting the heads of other killers stuck
on poles. Violence came from the Gold Rush, land claims, competing settlements, economic catastrophes, obscure feuds, racism, and plain blood lusts. This is the immediate
world of *The Confidence-Man,* which refers again and again to the violent events of this
world and presents many kinds of men who had their being in these events. (xv–xvi)

From this "symbolic center of America," the story's violence extends historically back to the beginnings of time, and geographically beyond the banks of
the river, through Melville's numerous allusions. "Only one physical blow is
struck on board the riverboat Fidèle, but its decks are slippery with the blood
of history." Moreover,

All the varieties of fraud and swindling are also here. On board the Fidèle are American
representatives of herbdoctors, land agents, counterfeiters, imposters, charity agents, card
sharps, divines, transcendental philosophers, con men of all kinds. They and their victims
discuss, quote, and reenact the roles of other con men of history, such as Plato, Pontius
Pilate, Seneca, Augustine, Machiavelli, Bacon, Rochefoucauld, Chesterfield, and P. T.
Barnum.
   Many American types and American figures are passengers on the Fidèle. While we
are on this ornate riverboat we are floating down the Mississippi River in the middle of
nineteenth-century America, surrounded by local forms, local customs, local language,
local characters. But just as black turns out to be an appearance of white, this West is
also the East, and this time conjoins past with future. (Franklin, xv–xvi)

Even after we compensate for its somewhat exuberant exaggeration, this summary captures the essence of Melville's rendered world in *The Confidence-Man:*
the twenty-four hours of All Fools' Day on board a ship of fools gliding down
the Mississippi—a fictional world whose primary characteristic is metamorphosis
in motion, a seething confusion extending even into the relationship between
narrator and reader, as a result of which nothing seems to be what it appears to
be, including *The Confidence-Man* itself as a work of fiction.
   Thematically and generically, *The Confidence-Man* proved as elusive as its
title character behind his masks. When it was first published, the American
reviewers for the most part wrote little more than notices; the British critics were
more thorough in their puzzlement. The reviewer in the *Literary Gazette* felt
"an uncomfortable sensation of dizziness in the head" and did not think that a
series of conversations "conducted by personages who might pass for the errata
of creation" constituted a novel (quoted in Hoffman, 129). Like Melville's own
thirty-year silence as a writer of fiction after its publication, *The Confidence-
Man* more or less dozed among Melville's works until it was prodded to critical
life again almost a century later. In the extensive introduction to her landmark
1954 edition, Elizabeth Foster too speculated on its literary ancestry, calling it,
among other things, "a modern *Candide*" (xiv) and suggesting that

even the inchoate form of the external story has a certain traditional appropriateness. For the external novel is a picaresque tale, and merely conforms to type when it strings roguish episodes loosely on the thread of a single character. It is also like the picaresque romances in its social satire and in making use of some of the stock characters who are traditional objects of satire and ridicule in rogue fiction—the barber, the miser, the quack doctor. Melville's long-continued interest of this genre shows in his reading and also in his appropriation of the idiom from time to time, most fundamentally in *Omoo, Israel Potter,* and *The Confidence-Man.* In the last two, roguery has become a symbol of larger evil. Reminiscences of the form and content of the romances of roguery increase the understatement of Melville's allegory of the cosmic *pícaro.* (xcii)

We know, too, that long before William Dean Howells made his oft-quoted suggestion to American writers about the picaresque in *My Literary Passions* (1895), Melville had taken an avid interest in Spanish fiction. His copy of *Don Quixote,* with his own penciled marginalia, survives. In 1849, he had bought a copy of *Guzmán de Alfarache* (q.v.), and a year later he borrowed a copy of *Lazarillo de Tormes* (q.v.), having "previously demonstrated his thorough acquaintance with Smollett and other English masters of the picaresque" (Levin, 101; Williams, 224, 395). The suggestion that *The Confidence-Man* "demands comparison with those great picaresque satiric romances whose scope is as ambitious as its own: not only *Gulliver's Travels,* but *Don Quixote, Gargantua and Pantagruel,* and *Candide*" (Hoffman, 142) is obviously less thoroughly grounded in orthodox picaresque than Melville's own knowledge through his reading of the two (very different) prototypes, *Guzmán* and *Lazarillo.*

Among other suggestions for the book's literary ancestry have been Plato's dialogues, *The Pilgrim's Progress, Paradise Lost,* the plays of Shakespeare, and Jonsonian satire and masque (Hartman). Melville may well have been writing in conscious continuation of a tradition of criticism of the national character, whose most famous previous example had been Cooper's *Homeward Bound* (Wright). Certainly Melville had in mind Sebastian Brant's *The Ship of Fools (Das Narrenschiff,* 1494), which he knew directly or through allusions to it in Burton's *Anatomy of Melancholy* (Rosenberry). There is a direct allusion in chapter 3:

"You fools!" cried he with the wooden leg, writhing himself loose and inflamedly turning upon the throng; "you flock of fools, under this captain of fools, in this ship of fools!" (15)

But the immedite source for the title character and his mode of operation seems to have been an actual historical swindler whose arrest was reported in the *New York Herald* of July 8, 1849:

For the last few months a man has been travelling about the city, known as the "Confidence Man:" that is, he would go up to a perfect stranger in the street, and being a man of genteel appearance, would easily command an interview. Upon this interview, he would say, after some little conversation, "have you confidence in me to trust me with your watch until to-morrow;" the stranger, at this novel request, supposing him to be some old acquaintance, not at the moment recollected, allows him to take the watch, thus placing "confidence" in the honesty of the stranger, who walks off laughing, and the other, supposing it to be a joke, allows him so to do. In this way many have been duped. (Bergmann, 561).

This is the first known appearance of the term *confidence man,* though the figure it describes is as old as trickster (q.v.). The satirical implictions of this coinage were expanded upon immediately when, on July 11, the *Herald* published an essay that shifted the perspective on confidence tricks:

His genius has been employed on a small scale in Broadway. Theirs has been employed in Wall street. That's all the difference. He has obtained half a dozen watches. They have pocketed millions of dollars. He is a swindler. They are exemplars of honesty. He is a rogue. They are financiers. He is collared by the police. They are cherished by society. He eats the fare of a prison. They enjoy the luxuries of a palace. He is a mean, beggarly, timid, narrow-minded wretch, who has not a sou above a chronometer. They are respectable, princely, bold, high-soaring "operators," who are to be satisfied only with the plunder of a whole community. . . . Long life to the real "Confidence Man!"— the "Confidence Man" of Wall street—the "Confidence Man" of the palace uptown— the "Confidence Man" who battens and fattens on the plunder coming from the poor man and the man of moderate means! As for the "Confidence Man" of "the Tombs," he is a cheat, a humbug, a delusion, a sham, a mockery! Let him rot! (Bergmann, 563– 65)

The topsy-turvydom of this point of view is typical of the satirical dimension of picaresque because "society as a whole is seen to be corrupt, divided into fools and knaves" (Bergmann, 565). A month later, the periodical *Literary World* found a positive side to confidence games: "It is a good thing, and speaks well for human nature, that, at this late day, in spite of all the hardening of civilization, and all the warning of newspapers, men *can be swindled"* (Bergmann, 566). This very vulnerability, of course, is what makes mass swindling of the kind satirized by the *Herald* possible. Subsequent and continuing public fascination with confidence men of all kinds extends the relationship one further step, from *can be swindled* to *want to be swindled,* for what makes the trickster-victim relationship a reciprocal process of conscious game playing is the need of the swindler and his victim to gratify each other. Such a realization is at the core of the picaro-victim relationship, as expressed in *Simplicius Simplicissimus* (q.v.) when the pastor tells young Simplicius: "The foolish world wants to be fooled" (Bk. II, ch. 8), a truth fully explored by Mann in *Felix Krull* (q.v.), the only other major picaresque to use the term *confidence man* as part of its title.

Melville could not have remained unaware of this immediate metaphorical extension of an actual occurrence in the world around him, for his title could not have come to him any other way. He recognized the immense possibilities of the confidence game as an analogy for fiction making, and he realized its potential for a philosophical examination of a cross-section of society. He there-fore blended the archetypal trickster who embodies two antithetical, nonrational experiences of man with the natural world, his society, and his own psyche: on the one hand, a force of treacherous disorder that outrages and disrupts, and on the other hand, an unanticipated, usually unintentional benevolence in which trickery is at the expense of inimical forces and for the benefit of mankind (Wadlington, 15)

with a gallery of human types through the microcosmic device of the ship of fools, which, "generically considered, is one of the great images of world literature, along with the metaphoric utopia and the philosophic voyage" (Rosenberry, 608) into an exploration of the game of confidence mirroring and mirrored in the art of fiction, in which both (game and art)

depend on an internally consistent representation of reality which sustains belief, even if it does not mirror actuality. Furthermore, since the "game" is generated by and predicated upon the known weaknesses of the victim, the confidence man's operations serve the turn of the satirist, the moralist, the critic of society. There is also a latent symbolism in the nature of any "con game," for it is a systematic and overt expression of a venerable theme—the confusion between appearance and reality. Indeed it even has an inherent philosophical bias; it suggests a comic-pessimistic view of the universe in which man is manipulated and victimized without gaining in stature. The fact that both the "game" and the "art" support an illusion by the control of rhetoric makes the relationship between the con-man character and his artistic creator particularly sensitive and self-revealing. (Kuhlmann, 7)

The result is an unusual variation on picaresque—and one of the most extraordinary fictions in American literature. *The Confidence-Man* develops basic picaresque conventions in unexpected directions, even turning some of them inside out.

The difficulties of reading *The Confidence-Man* are at first more daunting than challenging, even for the reader familiar with metafictional narrative trickery. It is, first of all, the most heavily interextual picaresque before *The Tin Drum* (q.v.). Even the most rudimentary narrative line of action, or plot, is hard to find. The number of guises (seven, eight, ten?) assumed by the Confidence Man—or even if there is a single character behind a set of masks—cannot be definitely established. And with the occasional direct intrusion of an authorial narrative voice, the book itself as a work of fiction becomes slippery, almost palpably eluding our analytical grasp. Since its critical revival in the middle of this century, all of the annotation and interpretation aimed at demystifying *The Confidence-Man* have helped us to understand why we do not understand the book; but they have added little more than elaborately specific detail to the general impression felt by the first reviewer in the *Literary Gazette,* whose reaction still rings true for today's reader:

To describe [Melville's] book, one had need to be a Höllen-Brueghel; to understand its purport, one should be something of a Sphinx. It may be a *bonâ fide* eulogy on the blessedness of reposing "confidence"—but we are not at all confident of this. Perhaps it is a hoax on the public—an emulation of Barnum. Perhaps the mild man in mourning, who goes about requesting everybody to put confidence in him, is an emblem of Mr.

Melville himself, imploring toleration for three hundred and fifty-three pages of rambling, on the speculation of there being something to the purpose in the three hundred and fifty-fourth; which, by the way, there is not, unless the oracular announcement that "something further may follow of this masquerade," is to be regarded in that light. (Quoted in Hayford et al., 325)

Such a reading experience corroborates the Missourian's words in chapter 21— "I have confidence in distrust" (108)—a paradoxically positive negative attitude that is at the heart of the picaresque view of the world.

   In a sustained discussion of *The Confidence-Man* within the entire picaresque narrative tradition, Blackburn calls it "a picaresque novel in a nonautobiographical symbolic form" (176). He lists seven characteristics that link it directly with the central picaresque tradition: (1) it "parodies heroic and epic literature," (2) it presents life "as a series of encounters between the picaro and society," (3) it makes the picaro and society "mutually reflective aspects of the same reality," (4) it shows reality "functioning as an illusion," (5) it reveals "disintegration into chaos and spiritual death," (6) it makes the world's lack of love "desperately apparent," and (7) it has a picaro for a protagonist, taking the title character to be both a failed identity and a half-outsider, another invisible man: "He has a kind of character as a stranger who seeks by means of imposture to enter in to the human community" (176–77). Moreover, he finds a suggestive kinship between what might be Melville's composite recollection of Lazarillo and Guzmán in the figure of the ragged peddler boy in the last chapter, who is described as "disclosing leopard-like teeth, like those of Murillo's wild beggar-boy's" (244). Blackburn calls the title character a "cosmic picaro" (172, 274)—a term first used by Foster (xcii)—by which he means the devil as an imposter, a usurper of identity.

   In *The Confidence-Man* Melville both adopts and adapts picaresque conventions, playing freely within a fictional mode in which he finds just the fluidity and flexibility he needs for his weighty ruminations. Like such early picaresques as *Guzmán* and *Simplicissimus*, *The Confidence-Man* is ultimately a philosophical speculation in fictional guise. In dissolving the picaro into a succession of masks, Melville cuts to the heart of the great picaresque theme of illusion making gratified. The role-playing agility of the picaro is distilled to the repertory of pure roles, which in turn are mirrored by all members of society, who shape themselves accordingly aboard a stagelike boat gliding, on April Fools' Day, through the heart of—and yet slightly apart from—a still unformed social order. The picaro as a manifestation of trickster does not exist in *The Confidence-Man*; in Melville's rendered world, trickster animates all human behavior, and thus the single point of view provided by one manifestation (the picaro) would be narratively inappropriate. Instead, multiple confessional perspectives are provided through constant dialogue as the characters reveal themselves, tell stories, and make observations.

"Tell me, sir, do you really think that a white could look the negro so? For one, I should call it pretty good acting."

"Not much better than any other man acts."

"How? Does all the world act? Am *I*, for instance, an actor? Is my reverend friend here, too, a performer?"

"Yes, don't you both perform acts? To do, is to act; so all doers are actors." (31)

This is echoed at the end of chapter 41:

With these words and a grand scorn the cosmopolitan turned on his heel, leaving his companion at a loss to determine where exactly the fictitious character had been dropped, and the real one, if any, resumed. If any, because, with pointed meaning, there occurred to him, as he gazed after the cosmopolitan, these familiar lines:

> "All the world's a stage,
> And all the men and women merely players,
> Who have their exits and their entrances,
> And one man in his time plays many parts."
> (224)

The geographical and temporal expanses of the conventional picaresque are condensed into twenty-four hours aboard a microcosmic stage-as-world. At the beginning of chapter 1, the placard announcing a reward for the capture of an imposter is perused by the crowds "as if it had been a theatre-bill" (3). At the end of the second chapter, the *Fidèle* is described as a place of estrangement:

Though her voyage of twelve hundred miles extends from apple to orange, from clime to clime, yet, like any small ferry-boat, to right and left, at every landing, the huge Fidele still receives additional passengers in exchange for those that disembark; so that, though always full of strangers, she continually, in some degree, adds to, or replaces them with strangers still more strange. (8)

"As among Chaucer's Canterbury pilgrims," the passengers form a congress "of all kinds of the multiform pilgrim species, man," creating a "sort of pagan abondment and assurance," which the Mississippi, "uniting the streams of the most distant and opposite zones," drives along "helter-skelter, in one cosmopolitan and confident tide" (9). What the picaresque normally achieves by accretion, Melville accomplishes through the manipulated landscape of the ship of fools device, which proves as tricky as the tricksters inhabiting it. It suggests in its "gigantic miniaturism" (the term is Mann's) a cosmos presided over by a trickster god.

But this cosmos and its trickster god are created by yet another trickster, the fiction maker himself. In the three excuruses on the nature of fiction (chapters 14, 33, and 44), the narrator expands on a phenomenon inherent in the picaresque narrative situation itself: the narrating picaro is always a masker and unmasker of his recreated selves, as in experience he influenced the masks that others wore in his presence, and in his role as shaper of his past he wears the mask of the creator. The disturbing theme of *The Confidence-Man* is that no human being sustains a stable personality for very long, that masks are put on and exchanged with every encounter, and that ultimately we exist only as masks. The supreme fiction is thus life itself. "What are you? What am I?" asks the Confidence-

Man-as-the-Cosmopolitan: "Nobody knows who anybody is. The data which life furnishes, towards forming a true estimate of any being, are as insufficient to that end as in geometry one side given would be to determine the triangle" (193). To write a fiction is therefore a perfectly logical and natural consequence of life, for, rather than reflecting or refracting life, it extends it. In the cosmic masquerade that is human existence; there is no difference in kind between con men and victims. There is only a changing difference in degree as each can become the other in a continuing game of mutually gratifying deception. And the fiction maker who writes about this is simply acknowledging that, in Alter's words, he "knows he cannot escape his location deep within the recesses of the Platonic cave, intimating with the shadows of shadows the incandescent nature of the reality outside" (137).

At the end of *The Confidence-Man,* the light is quite literally extinguished, and "in the darkness which ensued, the cosmopolitan kindly led the old man away" (251). The abrupt next sentence—the last in the book—is troublesome: "Something further may follow of this Masquerade." In the context of the picaresque, this could be interpreted as a variant of the overtly didactic claim the picaro conventionally makes in presenting his *vida* as a morally instructive foray into realms beyond strictures and structures. Having depicted the creating and erasing of selves that is daily existence in this universal masquerade, Melville may be saying that we will have more insight into the trickiness of getting along in life. But the tentative phrasing suggests that the masquerade will merely continue, with little hope of finding a real face behind the masks. Thus, the "total effect of *The Confidence-Man,* in form and content, is painful: human reality seems to hang very precariously near the abyss, as it did in the Spanish picaresque novels" (Blackburn, 162).

Such a reading—almost nihilistic—is often defended in part by pointing to Melville's more than thirty-year silence as a writer of fictions after the publication of *The Confidence-Man.* In this view, to create a verbal fiction is to be an accomplice to the given game of masks that is our human lot and thus to be enslaved to the very masquerade we want to unmask. It may well be that, having written this book, Melville felt he had nothing more to say. *The Confidence-Man* implicates all of his previous fictions as it implicates the human condition itself. To stop writing is at least a partial unmasking, even if it has no measurable effect on that condition. The "something further" could, ironically, be the not-making fictions. When the Confidence Man makes his initial appearance—and there is nothing to disprove that he is not the "man in cream-colors"—we are told:

He had neither trunk, valise, carpet-bag, nor parcel. No porter followed him. He was unaccompanied by friends. From the shrugged shoulders, titters, whispers, wonderings of the crowd, it was plain that he was, in the extremest sense of the word, a stranger. (3)

This opening chapter has all the ingredients of a quiet conclusion, as the stranger settles down to sleep. "Though he might not have a long way to go, yet he seemed already to have come from a very long distance" (6). He is a deaf-mute. Is this the author-picaro, creating the final chapter of his journey in art and life? As the crowd jeers and jostles (their epithets continue in chapter 2), the "lamb-like figure relaxed," and he lies motionless, "as some sugar-snow in March . . . softly stealing down over night." This character is alien yet "not entirely ignorant of his place," a stranger from regions far away yet at home, a being at once "gentle and jaded." Long "without the solace of a bed," he sits down, his aspect "increasing in tired abstraction and dreaminess." The final word of chapter 1 is *daybreak,* contrasting with the darkness at the end of the last chapter. Otherwise mute and deaf to the verbal hostilities of the crowd, the confidence-man-as-writer sinks into the "white placidity" of a late-winter snow. It is as though the crowd itself, in the incantatory beginning of chapter 2, conjures up the subsequent beings of the book through its evocations: "Humbug!" "Moon-calf." "Beware of him." "Escaped convict." "Meantime, like some enchanted man in his grave, happily oblivious of all gossip, whether chiseled or chatted, the deaf and dumb stranger still tranquilly slept, while now the boat started on her voyage" (7–8). It is as though Melville has already fallen silent and is letting life itself be fiction. Many years before the nouveau roman and other developments, Melville was anticipating the literature of exhaustion, of self-erasure, of silence.

EDITIONS

Quotations are from the CEAA-approved text ed. Harrison Hayford, Hershel Parker, and G. Thomas Tanselle (Evanston and Chicago: Northwestern University Press and the Newberry Library, 1984), with extensive historical background by Watson Branch, Parker, Hayford, and Alma A. MacDougall. Another well-annotated edition besides Elizabeth Foster's (see below) is H. Bruce Franklin's (Indianapolis and New York: Bobbs-Merrill, 1967). Franklin emphasizes in his copious notes the intertextuality of Melville's book: "By reference, allusion, parody, and quotation, it appropriates and incorporates whole works into itself: many of Shakespeare's plays, many books of the Bible, Ovid's *Metamorphoses,* the *Aeneid, Paradise Lost,* and numerous other works are as integral to *The Confidence-Man* as the little stories told by its own characters. Furthermore, some of these characters are caricatures of historical personages (such as Diogenes, Cooper, Socrates, Emerson, Timon, Thoreau, Poe), and others represent mythic figures (such as Manco Capac, Christ, Orpheus, Satan, Vishnu, Buddha)" (xvi–xvii).

SELECT BIBLIOGRAPHY

Robert Alter, *Partial Magic: The Novel as a Self-Conscious Genre* (Berkeley and Los Angeles: University of California Press, 1975); Johannes Dietrich Bergmann, "The Original Confidence Man," *American Quarterly* 21 (1969): 560–77; Alexander Blackburn, *The Myth of the Picaro: Continuity and Transformation of the Picaresque Novel, 1554–1954* (Chapel Hill: University of North Carolina Press, 1979); Elizabeth S. Foster, Introduction to her edition of *The Confidence-Man: His Masquerade* (New York: Hendricks House, 1954), xiii–xcv; Alastair Fowler, "The Confidence Man," *The Listener,* May 4, 1961, 781, 784; Jay H. Hartman, *"Volpone* as a Possible Source for Melville's *The Confidence Man,"* *Susquehanna University Studies* 7 (1965): 247–60; Daniel G. Hoffman,

"The Confidence-Man: His Masquerade," in *Melville: A Collection of Critical Essays,* ed. Richard Chase (Englewood Cliffs, N.J.: Prentice-Hall, 1962), 125–43 (originally in Hoffman's *Form and Fable in American Fiction* [New York: Oxford University Press, 1961]); Susan Kuhlmann, *Knave, Fool, and Genius: The Confidence Man as He Appears in Nineteenth-Century American Fiction* (Chapel Hill: University of North Carolina Press, 1973); Harry Levin, *"Don Quixote* and *Moby-Dick"* [1947], in his *Contexts of Criticism* (New York: Atheneum, 1963), 97–109; Gary Lindberg, *The Confidence Man in American Literature* (New York and Oxford: Oxford University Press, 1982); Tom Quirk, *Melville's Confidence Man: From Knave to Knight* (Columbia and London: University of Missouri Press, 1982); Edward H. Rosenberry, "Melville's Ship of Fools," *PMLA* 75 (1960): 604–8; John Seelye, *Melville: The Ironic Diagram* (Evanston, Ill.: Northwestern University Press, 1970); Warwick Wadlington, *The Confidence Game in American Literature* (Princeton, N.J.: Princeton University Press, 1975); Stanley T. Williams, *The Spanish Background of American Literature* (New Haven, Conn.: Yale University Press, 1955), I, 224–36; Nathalia Wright, "The Confidence Men of Melville and Cooper: An American Indictment," *American Quarterly* 4 (1952): 266–68.

DEATH ON THE INSTALLMENT PLAN

(*Mort à crédit,* 1936)

Louis-Ferdinand Céline

See JOURNEY TO THE END OF THE NIGHT

LA DESORDENADA CODICIA DE LOS BIENES AJENOS: ANTIGUEDAD Y NOBLEZA DE LOS LADRONES

(*The Disordering Covetousness of Other People's Property: Antiquity and Nobility of Thieves,* 1619)

Carlos García

Published in Paris by an exiled converso, this long short story is, like *Alonso, mozo de muchos amos* (q.v.), another variation on picaresque narrative technique. It begins with an anonymous narrator, called simply "el autor," making an elaborate comparison between prison and hell, which develops into a thinly veiled discourse on the loss of freedom in a tone that probably reflects García's own situation. Bjornson sees it, along with the second part of *Lazarillo de Tormes* (q.v.) by Juan de Luna, another Spanish exile in France, as representing a strain of socially critical picaresque fictions in the wake of *Guzmán de Alfarache* (q.v.), whose vision of a corrupt society these works adopt. *Las desordenada codicia* was in fact placed on the Index and was never published in Spain until the middle of the nineteenth century. The prison, according to Bjornson, resembles the "hell" of real-life Spain dominated by the Inquisition, where many innocent people lost their freedom (97).

Beginning in the second chapter of *La desordenada codicia,* the narrator strikes up a conversation with a prisoner named Andrés, whose picaresque life dominates the rest of the story, interspersed with the narrator's brief observations. In telling his *vida,* Andrés takes digressive turns, elaborating on the history of thieves and discoursing on thievery as a fundamental mode of existence that turns upside down conventional meanings of "honesty" and "thievery," concluding finally with a description of the hierarchical organization of thieves ("De los estatutos y leyes de los ladrones"), which harks back to the *Liber Vagatorum* (q.v.) tradition. This recurrent "community of rogues" motif in the picaresque functions here, as elsewhere, to mock the existing social order by positing a countersociety that apes it but on the opposite side of the law.

In its world upside down inversions—for example, Andrés's argument that a thief who owns up to his thievery is a more honest and admirable man than the doctor, lawyer, or clergyman who must cover up his innate and inescapable thievery, which he shares with every other human being born in sin—*La desordenada codicia,* as its title implies, indicts a cosmic order built on stealing in which the honest (those who steal openly) are unjustly condemned by the dishonest (those who manage to conceal their thefts).

García's work had more impact and influence in France and England than it did in Spain, where, if it was read at all, it had to be circulated surreptitiously. The several reprintings of the English translation, all under different titles—two of which capitalized on the popularity of Mabbe's translation of *Guzmán*—left their mark on the evolution of rogue literature in England, as Chandler pointed out: "It came closer than any other Spanish work to following the course suggested in the rogue-pamphlets of Harman, Greene, and Dekker, and but for its humor and satire was not unlike its contemporaries there, the *Essayes and Characters of a Prison and Prisoners* by Geffray Mynshul of 1618, or more nearly still, *The Compter's Commonwealth* by William Fennor in 1617, reprinted in 1619 as *The Miseries of a Jaile"* (264). Several episodes from the life of Andrés found their way into *The English Rogue* (q.v.) as well.

TRANSLATION/EDITION

One English version is known to exist: *The Sonne of the Rogue, or the Politick Theefe; With the Antiquitie of Theeves,* translated by W. M. (thought to be William Melvin, about whom little else is known) and printed in London in 1638. It was translated from D'Audiguier's 1621 French rendering, *L'Antiquité des larrons.* In 1650 it was reissued under the title *Lavernae, or The Spanish Gipsy.* Like a picaro changing masks, it appeared again in 1657, with the title *Guzman, Hinde and Hannam Outstript,* linking it not only with Mabbe's version of *Guzmán de Alfarache* but also with two notorious real-life criminals, James Hind and Richard Hainam. It made a fourth appearance in 1659 under the title *A Scourge for a Den of Thieves.* The original Spanish text is available in one of the editions of Angel Valbuena Prat's 1943 anthology, *La novela picaresca española;* in the 6th edition (Madrid: Aguilar, 1968), it is on pp. 1156–1195.

SELECT BIBLIOGRAPHY

Richard Bjornson, *The Picaresque Hero in European Fiction* (Madison: University of Wisconsin Press, 1977); Alfredo Carballo Picazo, "El doctor Carlos García, novelista español de siglo XVII," *Revista Bibliográfica y Documental* 5 (1951): 5–46; Frank Wadleigh Chandler, *Romances of Roguery* [1899] (New York: Burt Franklin, 1961); Dale B. J. Randall, *The Golden Tapestry: A Critical Survey of Non-chivalric Spanish Fiction in English Translation (1543–1657)* (Durham, NC: Duke University Press, 1963).

"THE DOGS' COLLOQUY"

("El Coloquio de los perros," 1613)

Miguel de Cervantes Saavedra

By the time Cervantes published the first part of *Don Quixote* in 1605, *Guzmán de Alfarache* (q.v.) had appeared in two parts (1599–1604) and become an unprecedented best-seller, reviving interest in *Lazarillo de Tormes* (q.v.). Though he never tried his hand at a full-fledged picaresque narrative, Cervantes kept a keen eye on this emergent genre of fiction that rivaled, if it did not exceed, the popularity of his own remarkable new work. In Ginés de Pasamonte, a galley slave like Guzmán, Cervantes created a genuine picaro figure who is already contemplating writing his life in the manner of *Lazarillo* and "everything in that style that has ever been written" (pt. I, ch. 22) and who will dart in and out of *Don Quixote,* later stealing Sancho's ass and reappearing in disguise as Master Pedro the puppeteer in the second part. Among the twelve stories published as the *Novelas ejemplares* in 1613 are three miniature picaresques—this one and "The Illustrious Kitchen-Maid" and "Rinconete and Cortadillo" (q.q.v.)—each of which is a distinct variation of the mode and which together with the figure of Ginés de Pasamonte reveal Cervantes's ambivalent attitudes toward the popular new genre.

In "The Dogs' Colloquy," two old hospital dogs named Berganza and Scipio acquire the power of speech one night and decide to tell each other's life stories. Berganza goes first, relating his service with a succession of masters, beginning with a slaughterer in one of the most lawless parts of Seville and ending with the "good Christian Mahudes" (247), who takes him on in this hospital. Like the picaro retiring from life to become the teller of it, Berganza is a highly self-conscious narrator, aware especially of the reflective dimension of narrative distance:

Brother Scipio, God give you all you desire if you will let me philosophize a bit without getting annoyed; because if I didn't tell you straight away the things that happened to me then and which have come into my mind at this moment, I don't think my story would be complete or of any value at all. (211)

Like Lazarillo, Berganza sprinkles his *vida* with proverbs, eliciting Scipio's observation that, as is true of all picaresques in which sins become virtues in the telling, Berganza would be considered a hypocrite if he were a human being for covering his acts with "the cloak of virtue" just to "win praise" (214). When Berganza makes a typically picaresque appeal to fortune, Scipio responds:

That's the way of the world, and there's no reason why you should start exaggerating the swings of fortune, as if there were much to choose between serving a butcher and a constable. I haven't the patience to put up with listening to the complaints which some men make about fortune, when the best fortune they ever had was the hope of becoming a squire. What curses they hurl at her! How they abuse her! And only so that those who listen to them might think they have known better days and fallen on hard times. (216)

This is perhaps a veiled allusion to Guzmán's narrative, and it, like the explicit allusion to *The Golden Ass* (q.v.) in a mischievous context (231), reveals Cervantes's somewhat ironic attitude toward the picaresque as a mode of narrative.

In using the colloquy form, Cervantes preserves the immediacy of autobiographical narration while building another voice into the narrative situation, the critical commentary of Scipio (who never gets to tell his own story), which serves as ironic reflector for the picaro's already self-reflecting storytelling. Though not a major characteristic of picaresque narrative technique, the dialogue form has been used in various ways throughout the centuries of the picaresque tradition (e.g., *La desordenada codicia, La hija de Celestina, The Futile Life of Pito Pérez*, q.q.v.)

Moreover, "The Dogs' Colloquy" is narratively telescoped inside the previous story, "The Deceitful Marriage" ("El Casamiento engañoso"), in which an ensign tells a licentiate about his marriage and how he, intending to deceive his bride to be about his wealth, was in turn tricked by her. Now confined to the hospital for treatment of a venereal disease, the ensign has overheard the dogs one night, just before his last "sweat treatment"; he wrote down their colloquy and now asks the licentiate to read it, though the latter scoffs at the absurdity: "Good heavens . . . we're back to the time of Methuselah, when pumpkins talked; or Aesop's days when the cock conversed with the fox and animals talked to each other" (192). "The Dogs' Colloquy" thus exists as an act of reading inside another story in which it may be the result of a feverish dream.

The reflective and self-reflective narratives of Berganza and Scipio thus become also self-reflexive, an embryonic variation of the complex telescoping that was to greet readers of the second part of *Don Quixote* two years later when Don Quixote and Sancho discover that the people they meet have read the first part of the very book in which they are fictional characters. "The Dogs' Colloquy" is quite literally an extraordinary shaggy dog story, anticipating the anecdote about the difficulty of blowing up dogs in the prologue to part II of *Don Quixote*. But in its equally extraordinary narrative trickery, Cervantes builds into the emerging picaresque tradition a playfully critical skepticism that shakes up its very conventions from the start. The story is not so much reflective of Cervantes's negative attitude toward the picaresque (as it has sometimes been interpreted to be) as it is another mischievous exploration, through narrative experimentation, of the reality-illusion problem that is profoundly both technique and subject matter in *Don Quixote*. As Forcione points out, this story represents a complex process of "hybridization of narrative forms" in its assimilation and refashioning of traditional genres—"including the picaresque novel, the Lucianic satire, the philosophical dialogue, the miracle narrative, the devotional and consolatory treatise, the sermon, the fable, the aphorism, and the anecdote . . . with the result that a kind of literary experimentalism and doctrinal instability pervade the text" in a way that evokes *Don Quixote* more than it does any of the other novellas (17). In its very narrative act, "The Dogs' Colloquy" explores the fundamental picaresque situation of seeking stability from past and present disorientation and deception through the narrating process: "that is, how the process of narration creates the past and is at the same time created out of the past" (El Saffar, 80).

Cervantes's narrative experimentation attracted the attention of the German romantics, who made use of his fictions for their concept of romantic irony. Among these was E. T. A. Hoffmann, who embellished on "The Dogs' Colloquy" with a continuation of sorts in his "Nachricht von den neuesten Schicksalen des Hundes Berganza" (News of the latest fortunes of the dog Berganza), published in *Phantasiestücke in Callots Manier* (1814). Of more than casual comparative interest, too, is Kafka's "Investigations of a Dog."

TRANSLATION

C. A. Jones, in *Exemplary Stories* (New York: Penguin, 1972).

SELECT BIBLIOGRAPHY

Carlos Blanco Aguinaga, "Cervantes y la picaresca. Notas sobre dos tipos de realismo," *Nueva Revista de Filología Hispánica* 11 (1957): 313–42 (translated and abbreviated as "Cervantes and the Picaresque Mode" in *Cervantes: A Collection of Critical Essays,* ed. Lowry Nelson, Jr. [Englewood Cliffs, N.J.: Prentice-Hall, 1969]); F. W. Chandler, *Romances of Roguery* [1899] (New York: Burt Franklin, 1961); Peter N. Dunn, "Cervantes De/Re-Constructs the Picaresque," *Cervantes* 2 (1982): 1909–31; Ruth El Saffar, *Novel to Romance: A Study of Cervantes's* Novelas ejemplares (Baltimore and London: Johns Hopkins University Press, 1974); Alban K. Forcione, *Cervantes and the Mystery of Lawlessness: A Study of* El casamiento engañoso y El coloquio de los perros (Princeton, N.J.: Princeton University Press, 1984), and "El *Coloquio de los perros* en la picaresca y otros apuntes," *Hispanic Review* 43 (1975): 25–41; Harry Sieber, *The Picaresque* (London: Methuen, 1977).

EL DONADO HABLADOR

See ALONSO, MOZO DE MUCHOS AMOS

DOWN AND OUT IN PARIS AND LONDON: A NOVEL

(1933)

George Orwell

In some of the attempts at formal definition of the picaresque, a sharp distinction has been made between the *Liber Vagatorum* (q.v.) and beggar-book tradition on the one hand and the genuine picaresque on the other, paralleling a similar distinction between jest books like *Till Eulenspiegel* (q.v.) and the picaresque. Chandler called the beggar books "anatomies of roguery" and included them, along with picaresque novels proper and criminal biographies, within a larger category he called "literature of roguery," which he defined as "determined by subject matter rather than form, and depending upon observed actuality rather than ideals," and presenting "low life in lieu of heroic, and manners rather than conscience and emotion" (1). An anatomy of roguery is "an essay descriptive of the grades, cheats, or manners of professional criminals," and it includes beggar books, coney-catching pamphlets, prison tracts, and "modern sociological studies of crime" (87). In critical practice, however, the distinction has been problematic, with some mutually contradictory criteria applied to exclude a given work from the picaresque because its protagonist is a hardened criminal and at the same time excluding another book because the protagonist is not criminal enough.

A problem of this sort arises when we consider Orwell's book in a picaresque context. It has a strong essayistic and sociological tendency, and yet it proclaims itself a novel. Its narrator is a beggar and tramp apparently by choice. Orwell's disclaimer in the conclusion reads: "It is a fairly trivial story, and I can only hope that it has been interesting in the same way as a travel diary is interesting" (213). Using these criteria, Sieber puts it in the tradition of the beggar book and then goes on to say that Orwell's "real purpose, of course, is far more subtle and serious. The narrator shows the wastefulness and stupidity of a system which condemns men to the useless expending of energy," a strong indication of the social conscience that finds powerful expression in Orwell's later works (66–67). And yet, remembering one of Chandler's basic characteristics—"the spirit of the story of the anti-hero was necessarily satirical and corrective" (*Romances*, 16–17)—wouldn't it be muddling our already muddled definitions to reject a book as picaresque precisely because of its sociocritical dimension? The appropriate question is, Does it help us understand and appreciate *Down and Out in Paris and London* to explore it as a variation on picaresque? Does it illuminate our conception of the picaresque mode to consider *Down and Out in Paris and London* within it?

Although we do not know anything about the origins of the anonymous narrator, we do know that he becomes penniless unexpectedly and by chance and that his subsequent hunger is both excruciating in experience and vivid in the telling:

Hunger reduces one to an utterly spineless, brainless condition, more like the after-effects of influenza than anything else. It is as though one had been turned into a jellyfish, or as though all one's blood had been pumped out and luke-warm water substituted. Complete inertia is my chief memory of hunger; that, and being obliged to spit very frequently, and the spittle being curiously white and flocculent, like cuckoo-spit. (38)

Poverty, with its successive humiliations in pawnshops and its increasingly futile efforts to find even menial work, quickly becomes an ironic kind of comfort:

You discover boredom and mean complications and the beginnings of hunger, but you also discover the great redeeming feature of poverty: the fact that it annihilates the future. Within certain limits, it is actually true that the less money you have, the less you worry. . . . A bread and margarine diet does, to some extent, provide its own anodyne.

And there is another feeling that is a great consolation in poverty. I believe everyone who has been hard up has experienced it. It is a feeling of relief, almost of pleasure, at knowing yourself at last genuinely down and out. You have talked so often of going to the dogs—and well, here are the dogs, and you have reached them, and you can stand it. It takes off a lot of anxiety. (20–21)

His job as a *plongeur* in the subterranean filth of a luxury hotel in Paris exposes the seamy behind-the-scenes activities that we never see in the hotel environment of *Felix Krull* (q.v.) and get only a glimpse of in the labyrinthine hotel in Kafka's *Amerika* (q.v.): "Everywhere in the service quarters dirt festered—a secret vein of dirt, running through the great garish hotel like the intestines through a man's body"(81). Swindling customers by overcharging for inferior food and services is the norm, as are trickery and thievery among the service staff. Disorder itself becomes a kind of order:

Anyone coming into the basement for the first time would have thought himself in a den of maniacs. It was only later, when I understood the working of a hotel, that I saw order in all this chaos. (65)

Even a murder on the street below his window is no excuse for wasting sleep:

For nothing could be simpler than the life of a *plongeur*. He lives in a rhythm between work and sleep, without time to think, hardly conscious of the exterior world; his Paris has shrunk to the hotel, the Metro, a few *bistros* and his bed. (91)

Paris is the landscape for roughly the first half of the book, and Orwell provides a panoramic rogues' gallery of a particular section of the city; anachronistic details aside, it could easily come from Guzmán's or Pablos's accounts of their experiences as beggars (*Guzmán de Alfarache, El Buscón*, q.q.v.), complete with tricks, proverbs, and the ingenious efforts that go into maintaining that sense of honor that even poverty will not eradicate. Along the way, Orwell's narrator is ridiculed, duped, laid low by fortune, and made aware that honesty is not the best policy in this world. Promised another job, he thinks it only fair to give notice, for which he is rebuked by his vagrant friend Boris, who makes him get his job back by lying—"my first lession in *plongeur* morality. Later I realised how foolish it had been to have any scruples, for the big hotels are quite merciless towards their employees" (60).

The second half of the book takes place in England, which at first "seemed to me a sort of Paradise" (126) in comparison to Paris. But he is soon even worse off here, having to pawn his clothes for a cheaper used set in which he at first does not recognize himself as the tramp reflected in a shop window: "The dirt was plastering my face already. Dirt is a great respecter of persons; it lets you alone when you are well dressed, but as soon as your collar is gone it flies toward you from all directions" (129). With its description of begging techniques and types of tramps and beggars, the London episodes indeed resemble the *Liber Vagatorum* tradition, but even here Orwell makes sensitive social observations:

And as a social type a beggar compares well with scores of others. He is honest compared with the sellers of most patent medicines, high-minded compared with a Sunday newspaper proprietor, amiable compared with a hire-purchase tout—in short, a parasite, but a fairly harmless parasite. He seldom extracts more than a bare living from the community, and, what should justify him according to our ethical ideas, he pays for it over and over in suffering. I do not think there is anything about a beggar that sets him in a different class from other people, or gives most modern men the right to despise him. (173)

As Orwell's narrative point of view is from inside out in the experience and from outside in through the telling, so his narrator's justifications of beggars and tramps turn conventional points of view about the social order inside out and outside in:

I have even read in a book of criminology that the tramp is an atavism, a throw-back to the nomadic stage of humanity. And meanwhile the quite obvious cause of vagrancy is staring one in the face. Of course a tramp is not a nomadic atavism—one might as well say that a commercial traveller is an atavism. A tramp tramps, not because he likes it, but for the same reason as a car keeps to the left; because there happens to be a law compelling him to do so. . . . He is a vagrant because, in the state of the law, it is that or starve. (291)

In his observant and sensitive dissection of low life in Paris and London, Orwell puts in the foreground those communities of rogues that were a conventional part of the landscape in early picaresques and that recur in picaresque fictions throughout their history—for example, the Dusters in *The Tin Drum* (q.v.). In concentrating on this aspect of the picaresque, Orwell has not produced only a twentieth-century beggar book, or simply a sociological tract, or merely a voluntary foray into low life as travel literature. *Down and Out in Paris and London* renders lived, felt, and reflected experience with a recognizably picaresque world vision that turns our received values topsy-turvy as it asks us to examine a social structure we take for granted. In chapter 22, Orwell asks some touchy questions about the life of a *plongeur* who, in his view, is "one of the slaves of the modern world" (116). But why, Orwell asks, does this slavery continue? Is a *plongeur's* work really necessary to civilization?

[A *plongeur*] is the slave of a hotel or restaurant, and his slavery is more or less useless. For, after all, where is the *real* need of big hotels and smart restaurants? They are supposed to provide luxury, but in reality they provide only a cheap, shoddy imitation of it. . . . No doubt hotels and restaurants must exist, but there is no need that they should enslave hundreds of people. . . . Essentially, a "smart" hotel is a place where a hundred people toil like devils in order that two hundred may pay through the nose for things they do not really want. If the nonsense were cut out of hotels and restaurants, and the work done with simple efficiency, *plongeurs* might work six or eight hours a day instead of ten or fifteen. (118)

The instinct to perpetuate useless work is, "at bottom, simply fear of the mob," based on the idea that there is "some mysterious, fundamental difference between rich and poor, as though they were two different races, like negroes and white men" (119–20). But the only difference is one of income, "and the average millionaire is only the average dishwasher dressed in a new suit. Change places, and handy dandy, which is the justice, which is the thief?" (120).

Orwell's final paragraph is a repentance of sorts as he describes how he will not be judging society anymore with the class-conscious blinders he wore before his experience. In its modesty, the "conversion" strikes us as sincere. But that apparent disclaimer about his "fairly trivial story" that might prove interesting the way a "travel diary" does, which occurs in the penultimate paragraph, is heavy with irony. The deceptive rhetoric muffles outrage. The reader who would take that statement at face value becomes the victim of a rhetorical trick, which Orwell must feel he deserves.

EDITION

New York: Harcourt, Brace, 1961.

SELECT BIBLIOGRAPHY

F. W. Chandler, *The Literature of Roguery* [1907] (New York: Burt Franklin, 1958) and *Romances of Roguery: An Episode in the History of the Novel* [1899] (New York: Burt Franklin, 1961); Harry Sieber, *The Picaresque* (London: Methuen, 1977).

THE ENGLISH ROGUE

(1665)

Richard Head with Francis Kirkman

Its full title is *The English Rogue: Described in the Life of Meriton Latroon, a Witty Extravagant. Being a Compleat History of the Most Eminent Cheats of Both Sexes,* and it was such a popular success that the bookseller Francis Kirkman urged Head to write a continuation. When Head refused, Kirkman wrote a second part himself (1668, though the earliest extant edition is 1671), which also includes a third and fourth part written by Kirkman and Head together. A uniform edition was published in 1680, the year in which Bunyan's *Life and Death of Mr. Badman* (q.v.) also appeared. A commendatory verse titled "On the English Rogue" by one "N.D." prefaces Head's original first part:

> What others writ, was ta'en upon the Score;
> Thou art in *Re,* what they but *feign'd* before.
> They did but *lisp, or worse,* speak through the Nose:
> Thou hast pronounc't, and liv'st in *Verse* and *Prose.*
> *Guzman, Lazaro, Buscon,* [q.q.v.], and *Francion*
> Till thou appear'dst did shine as at high Noon.
> Thy Book's now extant; those that judge of Wit,
> Say, They and *Rablais* too fall short of it.

This wishful literary pedigree has done nothing for Head's reputation in the histories of literature, in which he is noteworthy primarily for being a shameful hack who wrote a pandering best-seller for his time. Chandler's assessment of *The English Rogue* and its authors is representative:

Lacking in art and feeling, never finished, yet of bewildering extent, it is less a novel than a chaotic collection of all the picaresque tricks on record at the moment of its publication. It knows no unity; it attempts no study of character or manners; it imitates but one phase of the Spanish romances of roguery, and neglects everything that made them a link in the development of the modern novel.

Head and Kirkman were poor-devil hacks who set pens to paper for hire alone. . . . Neither possessed talent or even skill. While Head may have been only half disreputable, Kirkman was beneath contempt. (211)

Rather than perpetuating its literary heritage, *The English Rogue* plagiarized it. Chandler lists entire incidents borrowed from or in direct imitation of *La desordenda codicia*, *Lazarillo de Tormes*, *El Buscón*, *Estebanillo González*, *Marcos de Obregón*, *Alonso, mozo de muchos amos*, *Simplicius Simplicissimus* (q.q.v.), the *Francion*, among others, including Boccaccio's *Decameron*—this, despite Head's own "Epistle to the Reader," which begins: "It hath been too much the humour of late, for men rather to adventure on the Forreign crazy stilts of other mens inventions, then securely walk on the ground-work of their own home-spun fancies. What I here present ye with, is an original in your own Mother-tongue," insists that "I have here given an accompt of my readings, not in Books, but Men," and concludes by claiming that this is not a "spurious issue" but rather "a legitimate off-spring," which was "begot by one singly and soly" (x–xi).

But literary opinion has been kinder when considering Head's original first part on its own. Even Chandler calls it "the first and best part" (212), and Bjornson gives it an objective assessment for the way it "introduced literary conventions and ideological assumptions which were not present in the earlier picaresque or comic novels" (164). The most important of these is the rationalization of the portrayal of criminal activity "on the basis of its value as a negative moral example," which—as it will in Defoe's *Moll Flanders* (q.v.)— reveals a disturbing incongruity between its "overt condemnation of illicit behavior and the morality implied in the narrative—the morality which allows a rogue both to repent and retain the profits of his former dishonest enterprises." In *The English Rogue*, Bjornson says, "the social world is a battlefield where everyone is competing against everyone else." It is morally good—even a duty— to acquire wealth, and though stealing is condemned, it is a dog-eat-dog world: "Just as others betray Meriton, he has no qualms about betraying them." In this emerging capitalist world, "acquisitiveness and mask-wearing are the natural concomitants of his and every person's struggle for survival and success." Meriton Latroon's acceptance of the resulting solitude and universal distrust, even once he himself is comfortably off, represents a socializing process through character change: "thus, the idea of character as process (evident in both *Lazarillo* and *Guzmán*) would be reinvented for lower- and middle-class English Protestant audiences" (165). This harsh view of life in purely economic terms makes of Meriton Latroon "a sort of Hobbesian hero," his "*modus vivendi* being governed solely by self-interest and self-gratification" (Shinagel, ix). Such a world vision puts it directly in the mainstream picaresque tradition.

In structure, subject matter, and narrative technique, *The English Rogue* is almost formulaically picaresque, including its pretense toward moral edification through indulgence in immoral behavior, expressed in the repentant narrative voice, first in the prefatory epistle to the reader—"And how shall any be able to do this [avoid evil], unless they make an introspection into Vice? which they may do with little danger; for it is possible to injoy the Theorick, without making use of the Practick" (x)—and at the end of Head's original work: "Nothing jars the world's harmony more than men that break their ranks. . . . Experience giveth us to understand, that he which first disorders himself, troubles all the company. Would every man keep his own life, what concord in music would every family be!" (263). Along the way he makes such observations as, "You see I know the difference between good and evil, because I talk so well, though I act so ill" (159).

As for other picaros, the world Meriton Latroon is born into is a landscape ravaged by war (his father is killed during the Irish rebellion in 1641), and this disorder foreshadows the moral and social chaos of the landscape he is consequently displaced onto for a lifetime of wandering. In telling his story, Meriton blends into his narrative most of the popular narrative conventions of rogue literature, including jest books, beggar books, coney-catching pamphlets, canting catalogs, criminal biographies, and prison pamphlets and recantations. It is thus of interest as a document reflecting popular taste in Head's time. But as Shinagle points out, it is also interesting for "its social significance, for the panoramic sweep of 17th century low life it affords" (v). Its popularity, moreover, was mostly due to its reflecting—as did the original Spanish picaresques—the very life its lower-class audience was actually living, something that the epic, the romance, and the pastoral did not do. And it is part of the flood of rogue fictions that followed in the wake of Mabbe's translation of *Guzmán*, known in English as *The Rogue*. Among these were *The Sonne of the Rogue* (1638), *Guzman, Hind and Hannam Outstript* (1657) (actually a translation of *La desordenada codicia*), George Fidge's *English Gusman* (1652), *The French Rogue* (1672), *The Dutch Rogue, or Guzman of Amsterdam* (1683), and *Teague O'Divelly, or The Irish Rogue* (1690), as well as a number of rogue plays (Randall, 183). Sieber adds that *Don Tomaso, or the Juvenile Rambles of Thomas Dangerfield* (1680) contains a passage that emphasizes an essential difference between the Spanish picaro and the English rogue figures: that the latter always have mercantile interests in the forefront, while the former have to survive in a rigidly hierarchical society in which lineage is all important, and the picaro's lack of "blood" allows him no recourse to commerce as a means of survival (52). This emphasis on the dynamic interaction between the economic individual and an emerging capitalist society in English picaresques will find fuller expression in the next century in Defoe's *Moll Flanders*. And Chandler suggests that *The English Rogue* influenced American literature as well when he comments that Mark Twain's *The Prince and the Pauper* (1882) "draws most of its low-life direct from *The English Rogue*" (487).

EDITIONS

A reprint of Head's original first part is published by New Frontiers Press (Boston, 1961), with an introduction by Michael Shinagel. The full Head and Kirkman work is in four volumes (London: Pearson, 1874).

SELECT BIBLIOGRAPHY

Richard Bjornson, *The Picaresque Hero in European Fiction* (Madison: University of Wisconsin Press, 1977); Frank Wadleigh Chandler, *The Literature of Roguery* [1907] (New York: Burt Franklin, 1958); W. Kollmann, "Nashe's 'Unfortunate Traveller' und Head's 'English Rogue,' die beiden Hauptvertreter des englischen Schelmenromans," *Anglia* 22 (1899): 81–140; Alexander A. Parker, *Literature and the Delinquent: The Picaresque Novel in Spain and Europe, 1599–1753* (Edinburgh: University of Edinburgh Press, 1967); Dale B. J. Randall, *The Golden Tapestry: A Critical Survey of Non-chivalric Spanish Fiction in English Translation (1543–1657)* (Durham, N.C.: Duke University Press, 1963); Harry Sieber, *The Picaresque* (London: Methuen, 1977).

ESTEBANILLO GONZÁLEZ

(La vida y hechos de Estebanillo González, hombre de buen humor. Compuesto por él mismo, 1646)

If evidence were needed of the generic self-consciousness of a narrative genre by then approaching the century mark, it can be found in the "Al lector" of this work, in which Estebanillo claims that his *vida* is neither "la fingida de Guzmán de Alfarache" (*Guzmán de Alfarache*, q.v.) nor "la fabulosa de Lazarillo de Tormes" (*Lazarillo de Tormes*, q.v.) but rather "una relación verdadera" (Valbuena Prat, 1721). The anonymous author of this book published in Antwerp thus has his dramatized narrator ostensibly refute the very form of fiction he is drawing intertextual strength from. In setting up an antithesis between "feigned" or "fabulous" and "true account," he is employing a narrative sleight of hand not unlike that of Cervantes in *Don Quixote*, in which the story of Quixote and Sancho takes on more and more the illusion of an *historia* the more the story itself (part I) is denied within the story (part II). Like the frontispiece to *La pícara Justina* (q.v.), the prefatory "To the Reader" of *Estebanillo González* assumes a knowing reader whose narrative frame of reference will coincide with that of the author. Also like *Justina*, and *El Buscón* (q.v.), it is thought (by Bataillon) to have been written especially for a closed circle of readers. It is dedicated to the powerful Duke Piccolomini, and it must have provided comic in-house entertainment for an elite readership in the Spanish-occupied Low Countries.

Estebanillo's adventures as barber's apprentice, card sharp, robber, soldier, sailor, camp follower, and so on, cover the geographic expanse of much of Europe during the time of the Thirty Years' War. He finally becomes a jester and as such has connections with people of high importance all over Europe. At the time of his narration, he is planning to settle down by running a combination bordello and gambling den in Naples. The story is told hurriedly, with incident after incident piling up to create a verbal onslaught of tricks that resembles a jest book more than it does a picaresque fiction. Chandler, in fact, judged it as "distinctly below" other picaresques:

This strange and hurried account, with its quips and satirical turns, its absolute lack of plan or development, was unique in some respects among the romances of roguery. Rude and merciless, it was succession of practical jokes of a low order, perpetrated without malice and also without pity. True comedy never appeared, but coarse and ironic, with a devotion to fact not always entertaining, the narrative rattled on devoid of self-consciousness, meaning, or moral. The range of journeys undertaken was the largest in Spanish picaresque fiction. . . . But tricks, not observation, were always uppermost in the jesting anti-hero's mind. . . . The tradition of the service of master Estevanillo preserved, but his pace was so rapid that he failed to secure the full benefit of the scheme. (248–49)

Parker, who acknowledges that *Estebanillo González* is the one Spanish picaresque that "unfolds its story, from beginning to end, in the setting of historical and not imaginary warfare" and who does not deny its value as a social document in expressing what must have been the common soldier's cynicism at the time, finds it a work whose only significance is "the significance of decadent literature." Unlike *Simplicius Simplicissimus* (q.v.) a few years later, *Estabanillo González* does not show "the slightest realization of [war's] horror and its suffering." Estebanillo "is completely devoid of any human feeling, of any sense of compassion, jesting about his drunkenness while men are slaughtered and cities burn around him. It is a completely heartless book; there is nothing, not even his own soul, that he can take seriously" (76–77).

But this apparent heartlessness can also be seen as the buffoon's facade, the comic mask of the clown hiding the unstable self whose very survival depends on his self-humiliation through jesting. Bjornson, who has penetrated this mask, says, "While bartering his self-respect for the good will and money of his audiences, [Estebanillo] is not merely an entertainer; he is also a human being who suffers pain and humiliation. It is perhaps a truism to assert that beneath the comic gestures of a clown lie intimations of sadness and anxiety, but this truism has seldom been more poignantly illustrated than in the pathetic story of Estebanillo González" (*The Picaresque Hero,* 133). Nonetheless, his means of survival in a corrupt and unstable world is his role-playing ability, no matter how self-debasing this becomes psychologically. He needs to do it for mere physical sustenance, and his constant drunkenness is his means of keeping shame—and thus psychological self-destruction—at a distance. Even his narrative act is a final performance as clown: to finance his casino in Naples, he needs money, and thus his dedication to Piccolomini and "everything in his autobiography is calculated to justify his appeal for sponsorship and money" (136). Behind this mask, though, and perhaps most daring of all in the Spanish picaresque tradition, is Bjornson's contention that the book mocks the very readers it is nuzzling up to:

Estebanillo González also appears to reaffirm ideological assumptions of the dominant classes in Spanish society, but beneath the surface of an allegedly "true account" of his adventures, Estebanillo reveals how society perpetuates and institutionalizes one form of self-degradation, and his unabashed renunciation of stereotyped heroic poses allows him to expose the pseudovalues, idealistic myths, and appalling cruelty of the very people for whom he was ostensibly writing. (128)

Spadaccini, who also emphasizes the buffoon's mask, sees Estebanillo as "one of the most self-conscious narrators in the Spanish picaresque tradition" ("Estebanillo González," 212). In telling his life, Estebanillo has not moved to a different moral or spiritual plane; his narrational act is simply one more trick or performance to extract money from his audience. "In the midst of a European war that was to bring about the secularization of politics and the defeat of the notion of a united Christendom, with traditional social patterns and institutions going through a process of accelerated disintegration, the pícaro-buffoon's worm's-eye view of life is consistently materialistic and empirical. . . . Honor, whether social or spiritual is, in Estebanillo's materialistic philosophy, an exchangeable commodity" (219). Estebanillo González thus provides a critique of earlier picaresque fictions like Guzmán, and it looks forward to the kind of picaresque we will see in Moll Flanders (q.v.).

TRANSLATION/EDITION

The only known English version is in The Spanish Libertines or the Lives of Justina, the Country Jilt; Celistina the Bawd of Madrid, and Estevanillo Gonzales, The Most Arch and Witty of Scoundrels. To Which Is Added a Play, an Evenings Adventures. All Four Written by Eminent Spanish Authors and Now First Made English by Captain John Stevens (London: Samuel Bunchley, 1707). The original Spanish text is most accessible in one of the editions of Angel Valbuena Prat's 1943 anthology, La novela picaresca española; in the 6th edition (Madrid: Aguilar, 1968), Estebanillo González is on pp. 1797–1848.

SELECT BIBLIOGRAPHY

Marcel Bataillon, "Estebanillo González, buffon 'pour rire,' " in Studies in Spanish Literature of the Golden Age Presented to Edward M. Wilson, ed. R. O. Jones (London: Tamesis, 1973), 25–44; Arthur Bates, "Historical Characters in Estebanillo González," Hispanic Review 8 (1940): 63–66; Richard Bjornson, "Estebanillo González: The Clown's Other Face," Hispania 60 (1977): 436–42, and The Picaresque Hero in European Fiction (Madison: University of Wisconsin Press, 1977); Amancio Bolaño e Isla, Estudio comparativo entre el Estebanillo González y el Periquillo Sarniento (Mexico City: Universidad Nacional Autónoma de México, 1971); Frank Wadleigh Chandler, Romances of Roguery

[1899] (New York: Burt Franklin, 1961); Idalia Cordero de Bobonis, *"La vida y hechos de Estebanillo González:* Estudio sobre su visión del mundo y actitud ante la vida," *Archivum* 15 (1965): 168–89; Peter N. Dunn, *The Spanish Picaresque Novel* (Boston: Twayne, 1979); Gerald Gillespie, "Estebanillo and Simplex: Two Baroque Views of the Role-Playing Rogue in War, Crime, and Art (with an Excursus on Krull's Forebears)," *Canadian Review of Comparative Literature* 9 (1982): 157:71 (rpt. in *Upstarts, Wanderers or Swindlers: Anatomy of the Picaro, A Critical Anthology,* ed. Gustavo Pellón and Julio Rodríguez-Luis [Amsterdam: Rodopi, 1986], 285–95); Ernest Moore, "Estebanillo González's Travels in Southern Europe," *Hispanic Review* 8 (1940): 24–45; Alexander A. Parker, *Literature and the Delinquent: The Picaresque Novel in Spain and Europe, 1599–1753* (Edinburgh: University Press, 1967); Nicholas Spadaccini, *"Estebanillo González* and the Nature of Picaresque 'Lives,' " *Comparative Literature* 30 (1978): 209–22, and "History and Fiction: The Thirty Years War in *Estebanillo González,"* *Kentucky Romance Quarterly* 24 (1977): 373–87.

THE FAMILY OF PASCUAL DUARTE

(La familia de Pascual Duarte, 1942)

Camilo José Cela

From the prison cell where he awaits execution, Pascual Duarte—the "most murderous picaro" in "the continuing picaresque of Spain" (Kerrigan, 141)— narrates a brutal *vida* that in sheer horror, though not in graphic detail, approaches that of *The Painted Bird* (q.v.). His youth and young manhood are spent among the grotesque members of his "family"—a thieving animalistic father who dies a rabid death; a slovenly alcoholic mother; a syphilitic sister who lives with a pimp; a retarded baby brother who has his ears bitten off by a hog and later drowns in an oil vat, face down in the sediment like some preserved fetus; a first wife, Lola, whom Pascual deflowers on his brother's fresh grave and who dies bearing another man's child; and a second wife, Esperanza, who, along with his mother, drives him to his final extreme act of matricide. It is this final crime that he is about to narrate when he pauses to observe:

I wanted to put ground between my shadow and myself, between my name and me, between the memory of my name and the rest of me, between my flesh and me myself, that me myself who, without shadow and name and memory and flesh would be almost nothing. (121–22)

The details of Pascual's life seem so absurdly extreme that they become ludicrous in summarizing, and the chaos-world in Cela's book is probably one of the blackest worlds in picaresque fiction, a world so dark that it can be dealt with only by a sick laughter of roughly the same hue. The cruel irony of the title is obvious—"Life in our house went down the same drains as always" (34)—and the irony darkens when we consider that Pascual's life is spent entirely with his family rather than on the road, and yet it is one of the loneliest lives of any picaro figure. Pascual himself sees the cold-blooded hilarity of it all:

The birth of poor Mario—for such we were to call our new brother—was more of an accidental and bothersome affair than anything else. For, as if the scandal caused by my mother's giving birth were not enough, and by way of last straw, the whole thing coincided with the death of my father. Looked at in cold blood—and except for the tragic side of it—it would make anyone laugh. (34)

Or he can accept a sick joke about the similarity of his diet to that of an aristocrtic and richer member of the family of mankind. Behind his house runs a stream, "always dirty and stinking like a troop of gypsies," where

sometimes when I wanted to kill an afternoon, I'd catch some fine eels there. My wife used to say, and despite everything, what she said was humorous enough, that the eels were so fat because they ate the same as Don Jesus—only a day later. (18)

For the most part Pascual's life is a constant struggle with primeval forces of violence and destruction, both within himself and within the world he must survive in. He is in prison, we discover, because he has killed his mother and murdered Don Jesus—to whose friend, Don Joaquín Barrera Lopez, he sends his manuscript before his execution. Pascual's narrative act is in many ways the traditional picaresque attempt at reintegration. Having lived a life of extremes, he analyzes his role as onlyman and tries to justify himself in some way to everyman. His self-conscious narrative is a constant attempt to see if the memory can interpret the act. It is an attempt to reconcile the rationalized what-might-and-should-have-been with the totally incomprehensible what-was. His memoir moves not chronologically but randomly and episodically back and forth between the events of his life and the more meditative reconsiderations he now makes. (His narrative is more episodic than his life has been.) It is a dualism pointed out also in his character. He is a mixture of animal spontaneity and moral sensibility—the first, on the whole, is himself in the active past within society, and the second is himself in the passive present outside that society. But even in his past life, he was apart from it, an exile whom the priest calls "a rose on a dunghill" (36). And in the narrative present, he retains some of the self-indulgent and uncontrollable animality that he purports to criticize because he revels narratively in the sensational detail. Thus the distinction between what he was in life and what he is now is not as clear-cut as a simple dualism would suggest. His self-perception is not altogether new, nor was it won entirely through misfortune; and the peculiar temperament that precipitated his nightmarish life has not left him entirely. Pascual is constantly and undeniably aware that he is one of those whose life (as he says himself) takes the thorny rather than the flowery path to death (14). He is repeatedly aware of himself as victim of his environment and heredity, yet he is simultaneously aware that he is not entirely without guilt, not entirely without fault in his reactions to the onslaught of his world. When his wife miscarries, he brutally slaughters the mare that threw her; when he is the butt of a tavern joke, he starts an almost fatal brawl; when his newborn son dies, he blames it on a *mal aire*. Then he escapes to Madrid and lives a vagabond life, yet—and the irony gets darker—this traditionally picaresque existence proves to be the one relatively stable episode in his life. His retreat from picaresque life is a reentry into exile. At his homecoming, he finds his wife pregnant and dying. "It's just that blood seems to be a kind of fertilizer in your life," she tells him as he threatens the father of the child (98). He kills him, ends up in prison, and begins to take stock. But, ironically again, his release from prison is only his reimprisonment in exile, in the squalor of his family life. The one good turn society does him leads to disaster. "They opened the gates, and turned me out, without defenses, into the very midst of Evil" (107). He wants to shout that he is a "free man" but thinks better of it. He goes home again, to an indifferent mother whom he despises, to a new wife, and to new misfortune. The two women come to be poisonous shadows to his paranoic mind, and, in a final violent outburst, he kills the woman he blames for causing his wretchedness, his mother. His narrative ends here.

A sensible man in an animal world, Pascual is nevertheless actively subject to that world as he intellectually rejects it. His narrative is an exploration of a past that was almost entirely spontaneous action. It could have been written by a strange and humorous combination of Sancho Panza and Lazarillo (*Lazarillo de Tormes,* q.v.), who, in addressing the superior to whom he is telling his *vida,* intersperses apologetic *vuestra mercedes* and *refranes* throughout, as does Sancho when he talks. It becomes a habit for Pascual to say *con perdón* with each sordid detail of his life, as though all this were offensive to the ears of the social being (someone "who matters") to whom he is writing, and often his observations are tagged with some homey refrain. Yet he is at the same time a bottom-of-the-barrel Quixote, trying to idealize the life that should have been. If as Lionel Trilling suggested, all prose fiction is a variation on the theme of *Don Quixote*—that is, an exploration of the problem of reality and appearance—then the problem of reality and appearance (and how to know them) that Pascual has is the reverse of Quixote's. Pascual, who has had the stark reality before he was aware of its appearance, is engaged in his narrative in a kind of search for some meaningful "appearance." The question he might well ask is not "What is reality?" but "What is appearance?" and thus he makes his final ironical twist on picaresque life, which has always in fiction kept this problem in central focus.

Pascual's narrative is the symmetrical center of the book. Cela has taken great pains to add psychological, emotional, and moral distance to the narrative distance inherent in the autobiographical form. Pascual's story is found in a pharmacy in 1939 by the *transcriptor*. In its original form, the manuscript was almost unreadable, "for the writing was rough and the pages were unnumbered and in no consecutive order" (7). There is also a letter to the Don Joaquín to whom Pascual addressed the narrative, along with a will from the former condemning the book to be burned for its immorality and portrayal of evil manners. The transcriber's own prefatory note sets the didactic aim: he is publishing the book as an example of bad conduct, a conventional disclaimer in the picaresque narrative tradition. At the end he reproduces two letters, one from a priest, one from a warden, both of whom were present at Pascual's execution. The priest sees him as a near-saint, a "lamb at bottom" (like the paschal lamb implied by his name), lured inevitably to his fate. The warden sees him as mentally ill, an unstable man who lost his composure as death crept near and had to be dragged violently to his execution.

There is in this game of perspectives an attempt by Cela to manipulate our points of view, to distance Pascual toward a cooler objectivity than would be possible if we had only Pascual's own narrative unmediated. Cela's narrative layering puts a frame around the unrelieved chaos and violence of Pascual's life. Although this self-conscious attempt to distance the fiction at times makes the book's bones protrude, it was necessary not only to provide a corrective lens for Pascual's own perceptions but also to protect the book from censorship, a recurrent problem with picaresque fictions (after its second edition in November 1943, *La familia de Pascual Duarte* was indeed suppressed).

At the same time this *Rahmentechnik* is also used for opposite effect. The transcriber says in the preface that he has pruned the "repugnant intimacies" from the manuscript. The horrors of Pascual's life are thus made all the more horrible because they are said to be censored. If this is what has passed the censor, how much worse, we are asked to consider, must the rest have been. Cela "puts in" by creating the illusion that he has taken out. Moreover, the device of the found manuscript imbues the tale with an air of mystery and supernatural qualities.

Much has been made of Cela's *tremendismo,* a technique that as its name implies, is a heightening of a described event into its extreme possibilities to achieve some devastating effect. It is really a kind of sensationalism, and it focuses on the ugly, the cruel, and the violent. The description of the short life and grotesque death of Pascual's brother Mario serves as a good illustration (36–39). This shocking passage exemplifies Cela's own definition of *tremendismo:* "We understand by 'tremendismo' the bloody caricature of reality—not the gory portrait, monstrous and deformed, of an absurd reality." Though shockers like this are perhaps in danger of satisfying what Trilling has called "the pleasure in cruelty licensed by moral indignation," they are Cela's way of rendering a chaos-world that is not portrayable through traditional techniques of realism. Cruelty has always been part of picaresque existence, even in its comic forms, and *tremendismo,* whatever its merits as an actual technique, is a short-cut for Cela in the portrayal of a landscape whose actual extremes demand narrative extremes. For a man who has been at the limits of human and bestial experience, *tremendismo* is the appropriate way to render what has been a tremendous life. The fury of this book has its visual equivalent in Picasso's *Guernica.*

Eoff writes that Piscual Duarte is "a soul gone astray, alone and drifting, but drifting more in cosmic than in earthly realms" (195). Cosmic exile is an attribute of other contemporary picaro figures, and Pascual is an exile in the etymological sense of the word ("to wander about"). He is also a *wretch,* a word related to an older word meaning "exile," "adventurer," and—curiously, in the light of the picaro's emergence as an antitype to the romance hero—"knight-errant."

Pascual calls himself a wretch in prison (107). Though he lives a more structured social life than the typical picaro, Pascual is most exiled cosmically. He cannot in the end understand his exclusion, despite his final role as shaper of his life through the narrative act. He has been unable all his life to join the family of mankind, and he is a misfit even in a picaresque landscape—the picaro in extremis. At the end, society gets rid of Pascual, just as it does Pito Pérez *(The Futile Life of Pito Pérez,* q.v.). As Cela has said, "We killed Pascual Durte because it would have been too inconvenient to keep him alive; the truth is, we did not know what to do with him."

TRANSLATION

Anthony Kerrigan (New York: Avon, 1964). A text edition of the original, ed. Harold L. Boudreau and John W. Kronik (New York: Appleton-Century-Crofts, 1961), includes "Palabras ocasionales," a short essay by Cela from which his own words in this entry are quoted.

SELECT BIBLIOGRAPHY

Sherman Eoff, "Tragedy of the Unwanted Person, in Three Versions: Pablos de Segovia, Pito Pérez, and Pascual Duarte," *Hispania* 39 (1956): 190–96; Hortensia Viñes, "Notas para una interpretación de *Pascual Duarte*—La novela virtual," in *La Picaresca: Orígenes, Textos, y Estructuras,* ed. Manuel Criado de Val (Madrid: Fundación Universitaria Española, 1979), 929–34; Ulrich Wicks, "Onlyman," *Mosaic* 8 (1975): 21–47. Lionel Trilling's observations are from "Manners, Morals, and the Novel" (1947) in his *The Liberal Imagination* (Garden City, N.Y.: Doubleday [n.d.]).

FANNY: BEING THE TRUE HISTORY OF THE ADVENTURES OF FANNY HACKABOUT-JONES, A NOVEL

(1980)

Erica Jong

In his enthusiastic review of *Fanny*, Anthony Burgess wrote that Jong had "contrived an authentic picaresque novel with a female protagonist" (54) and thus "she may be said to have filled a gap in the great tradition of the picaresque novel" (55). Both claims—that it is an authentic picaresque, and that a female rogue, or picara, fills a gap in the picaresque tradition—are valid, however, only insofar as we conceive of *picaresque* in the heavily qualified sense of its eighteenth-century transformations in *Gil Blas* and, especially, *Roderick Random* (q.q.v.), and insofar as we recognize that *Fanny* is hardly the first fiction to depict a picara, although it is surely unique in being by a woman.

Fanny grows up a foundling, raised by Lord and Lady Bellars at their country estate, Lymeworth. Her passion is to be a writer, despite her awareness of the unlikelihood of ever reaching that goal. "Orphan'd, female, and a secret Scribbler—what worse might the Fates bestow?" (32). At age seventeen, she is raped by Bellars, whereupon she disguises herself as a man and runs away to London. On the road, she meets Isobel White, who initiates her into witchcraft but who is apparently murdered when the coven of witches is ravaged by a gang. Next she becomes the victim of a band of robbers, whose leader is Lancelot Robinson, a latter-day Robin Hood who calls his gang the Merry Men. He gives Fanny her name: "But yerself, Madam, I christen Fanny Hackabout—because ye have, in truth, been cruelly hackt about by Fate"; the surname Jones will teach her modesty, "because yer too vain of yer Beauty already!" (128). Lancelot's band resembles the brotherhoods or communities of rogues we see in many picaresque fictions, and Lancelot himself has a philosophy of thievery that evokes similar views in such Spanish works as *La desordenada codicia* (q.v.): "Now, Stealin' is the most honourable Occupation ye can name. Why e'en the Good Lord stole Adam from the Earth an' Eve from his Rib!" (147). "Honour amongst Thieves was all his Creed" (215), and the code called the law " 'tis naught but an Excuse to kill the Poor, whilst the Rich may steal an' go free!" (250). The robbers are apprehended, as a result of which Lancelot ends up in Newgate prison, while Fanny is lured to work in a brothel. She endures this degrading profession only to survive, and above all to earn money to ease the prison life of Lancelot, with whom she has fallen in love despite his avowed homosexuality and misogyny. Among her customers in the brothel are Dean Swift and William Hogarth, as well as John Cleland, who "was later to exploit my History so callously in his *Memoirs of a Woman of Pleasure*" (237), otherwise known as *Fanny Hill* (1748–49). Meanwhile, Fanny has discovered that she is pregnant with Bellars' child and, after a harrowing attempt at abortion, chances to meet Bellars, who falls passionately in love with her not knowing who she actually is because she is masked. With financial support from Bellars—and sustaining her disguise—Fanny eventually gives birth to her daughter Belinda, in a then-illegal Caesarean delivery performed by a midwife who turns out to be Isobel White. A wet nurse steals the infant and heads for the New World. Fanny pursues her, embarking on a horrifying sea adventure from which she is eventually rescued by Lancelot, who has in the meantime escaped from Newgate and become a pirate. Eventually, with the help of pirate Anne Bonny (who will remain a role model for Fanny until the end), Belinda is recovered, and they all return to Lymeworth. At this point, Fanny sums up her history: "Witch, Whore, Stow-away, Slaver, Amanuensis, Pyrate—I knew the Things a Woman could be forced to do for Want of Bread, for Want of Freedom, for Want of Strength, for Want of Manhood. Ne'er again would I condemn a Sister for her Luck" (503).

Up to this point, all the coincidence and chance encounters resemble the typically picaresque dance pattern of recurring characters in a chaotic landscape. But now the eighteenth-century romance machinery quickly descends onto the stage, as Fanny discovers to her simultaneous horror and joy that she is the daughter of Isobel White—by Lord Bellars, who has just died in full penitential knowledge of his incestuous sin and left Fanny his vast fortune along with the estate of Lymeworth. Home again in the place she had once called Eden (36),

Fanny turns to writing, while Lancelot tends the estate, a prosperous but nevertheless *Candide*-like garden in comparison to the utopian country of Libertalia he had hoped to found in the New World. It is here that Fanny decides to write her memoirs, addressed specifically to Belinda, "so that the Inheritor of this Testament shall learn how to avoid Wickedness or indeed transform it into Goodness" (17). Having discovered that she was not really an orphan after all, although having suffered the experience of being one, Fanny now philosophizes in recognizably picaresque fashion: "Thus, do we all feel like Orphans (or e'en like Changelings), whilst we grow apace 'neath our Parents' Roofs. In truth, the Accident of Birth is most capricious—for *all* of us, incestuous or no!" (518).

While much of the plot and action of *Fanny* depends, in a deliberately intertextual way, on eighteenth-century conventions of fiction, the character of the female rogue goes back to the Spanish tradition—to *La pícara Justina* (q.v.), whose narrator is as self-consciously a writer as Fanny is; to *La hija de Celestina* (q.v.), whose heroine shares ingenuity and beauty with Fanny; and to *La niña de los embustes* and *La garduña de Sevilla* (q.q.v.), whose heroines (Teresa and Rufina, respectively) exist in a landscape of improbable adventure which is more *novela cortesana* than picaresque and which resembles the wild adventures Jong has conjured up for Fanny. But despite their travels, these picaras never traverse the range of experience that is accorded to picaros, due almost entirely to a society that relegated women to static roles such as mother, wife, and nurturer. In this early seventeenth-century world, Dunn says, the picaro "plays out a drama of tensions between freedom and entrapment, responsibility and determinism, high aspirations and sordid accommodations. It is difficult to see how a picara could have faced similar tensions without exposing the unexposable, the traditionally venerated roles of womanhood, wife and mother" (132). Thus, through the picaresque female, this fiction "turns into a literature of crude entertainment, displaying jokers and swindlers of a criminal or near-criminal sort, who commit only such acts of violence as accord with the prejudices of the readers" (133). As Hanrahan points out, given what the picaresque sought to express and given woman's status in society, a genuine picara was an impossibility in Spanish fiction at this time (II, 237–38). And Rodríguez-Luis asserts that Spanish picaras "never become serious characters" (42).

Fanny's true predecessors in the relatively small gallery of picaras are Courage (*The Runagate Courage*, q.v.), whose self-assertion and bawdiness Fanny shares; Moll (*Moll Flanders*, q.v.), whose self-reliance and determination (although not her disregard for offspring) Fanny has inherited; Roxana (*Roxana*, q.v.), whose profession Fanny must practice for a while; and, in a curious time-warp invited by Jong herself in writing an eighteenth-century novel in 1980, Sara Monday (*Herself Surprised*, q.v.), whose relationship to Gulley Jimson is not unlike that of Fanny's to Lancelot. This last comparison also highlights something that sets *Fanny* apart from other picaresques, male or female: it is, in the conventional sense of the term, a historical novel as well. Picaresques are usually contemporaneous with the society in which they are created, a condition demanded by the picaresque's affinity for satire. The longest chronological distance between the picaro's or picara's time of writing and the time of presentation is in *Moll Flanders*, where some fifty years have passed since Moll penned her memoirs. In *Fanny*, this historical distance is almost two and a half centuries, as the title page inside the narrative makes clear: *The True History of the Adventures of Fanny Hackabout-Jones. In Three Books. Comprising her Life at Lymeworth, her Initiation as a Witch, her Travels with the Merry Men, her Life in the Brothel, her London High Life, her Slaving Voyage, her Life as a Female Pyrate, her eventual Unravelling of her Destiny, et cetera. Printed for G. Fenton in the Strand. MDCCLI.*

This subtitle titillates in the same manner as does the subtitle to *Moll Flanders*, and both promise a taste of moral abandonment in the service of an eventually victorious moral sense, a typical picaresque lure. The 1980 reader may be more honest with himself about his motivations for reading such a book than we surmise the reader of 1751 to have been, but the lessons to be learned are equally powerful. For Jong's singular achievement in *Fanny* is to use this old picaresque narrative trick to indeed provide moral improvement, but not of the conventional morality that the picaresque traditionally pays lip service to. While indulging in violence and sex more graphically depicted than in any other picaresque fiction with the exception of *The Painted Bird* (q.v.), the reader gradually assents to a feminist worldview that is all the more persuasive because of the book's apparent innocence: its dislocation in a distant time, its exotic adventures, its melodramatic situations, its stereotypical characters (truly villainous villains and villainesses, a dashing hero and voluptuous heroines), and its superficially teasing narrative style, intertextually arousing the reader with expectations of *Fanny Hill*–type erotica. *Fanny* delivers on all its teases, but in thus gratifying the reader it also accomplishes its real task, which is nothing short of calling into question our whole gender-based structure of existence (and thus of meaning) in the world.

Fanny's impulse to narrate is fourfold. First, she wants to give moral guidance to Belinda, the narratee who is directly addressed throughout. Second, she wants to make her mark as a writer—a profession she has been praised for until it was discovered that under her pseudonyms she was a woman. Third, she is, like Courage spiting Simplicissimus, writing to spite John Cleland, by whose *Memoirs of a Woman of Pleasure* she is outraged and whom she manages to demolish even as she builds her own narrative out of his:

That the Book was written by a credulous Man, not a canny Woman, may easily be seen by the excessive Attention Mr. Cleland pays to the Description of the Masculine Organ, for which he hath more Terms than Lancelot Robinson hath Names for the Corresponding female one! Only a Man (and an indiff'rently-endow'd one at that) would dwell so interminably upon the Size and Endurance of sundry Peewees, Pillicocks, and Pricks—for a Woman hath better Things to do with her Reason and her Wit. (186–87)

And, finally, moving more and more away from confiding in her specific narratee toward addressing the reading public at large, Fanny uses her history to question, and often to scold about, the role of woman in the world. In her most agonizing moments of picaresque solitude—"I'm so alone," she tells Lancelot, "I'm an Orphan. No one cares for me" (142)—her condition seems almost more hopeless than that of the picaro, because she is a woman. While the picaro may feel isolated in being low-born, Fanny is doubly estranged because she is (or rather, at this point feels she is) both low- and female-born in a world in which well-born males hold all privilege and power. This consciousness pervades every encounter, and it rules the narrational stance of the re-membering Fanny. Even as she writes she has declined to marry Lancelot (a decision with which he agrees) because the law would force her to hand over all her possessions to him, which echoes a similar incident in Defoe's *Roxana*.

Her rejection of social codes, combined with her defiance of the literary establishment, energizes her act of narration. "For tho' 'tis no easy Thing to be born a Man in this Vale of Tears, 'tis more difficult still to be born a Woman," she tells Belinda in her second paragraph (17). Fanny thus extends the typically picaresque motivation for narrating, expressed first in Lazarillo's prologue (*Lazarillo de Tormes*, q.v.), to include the condition of gender as well. This expansion, which makes *Fanny* unique among picaresques and which makes this book a major achievement in the evolution of picaresque narrative, is itself fundamentally picaresque in spirit. In a patriarchal society, any woman who asks the questions Fanny asks is an upstart; in questioning male-dominated social structures and in spiting masculine literary structures, Fanny Hackabout-Jones is a genuine picara by virtue of her very acts of rebellion. As she writes, she discovers that she is an orphan in a literary sense as well as a social one: she has no truly feminine literary genealogy to give her a sense of identity in the context of a continuing literary legacy. Courage, Moll, and Roxana, driven as they may seem to realize their female selves, are masculine creations. Thus Fanny, almost a recluse on her estate, is truly alone in many ways. Her most audaciously rebellious act, therefore, is to create such a legacy for Belinda, in spite of whatever child-rearing codes may be violated. And behind the narrating Fanny within the eighteenth-century historical framework there is the implied author discoursing to us in the twentieth century. By projecting a contemporary female sensibility backward in time, she is creating an irony that eventually jolts us into awareness that the anachronism we had so smugly decided to humor actually is an anachronism in reverse: eighteenth-century attitudes toward woman are anachronistically alive here and now. *Fanny*, singular in being a historical picaresque, is most truly contemporary.

EDITION

Quotations are from the Signet paperback edition (New York: New American Library, 1981).

SELECT BIBLIOGRAPHY

Anthony Burgess, "Jong in Triumph," *The Saturday Review* August 1980: 54–55; Ann Daghistany, "The Picara Nature," *Women's Studies* 4 (1977): 51–60; Peter N. Dunn,

"The *Pícara*: The Rogue Female" in his *The Spanish Picaresque Novel* (Boston: Twayne, 1979), pp. 113–33; Edward H. Friedman, "The Precocious Narrator: *Fanny* and Discursive Counterpoint" in his *The Antiheroine's Voice: Narrative Discourse and Transformations of the Picaresque* (Columbia: University of Missouri Press, 1987), pp. 203–19; Thomas Hanrahan, *La mujer en la novela picaresca española* (Madrid: José Porrúa Turanzas, 1967); Julio Rodríguez-Luis, "*Pícaras*: The Modal Approach to the Picaresque," *Comparative Literature* 31 (1979): 32–46; Pablo J. Ronquillo, *Retrato de la pícara: La protagonista de la picaresca española del XVII* (Madrid: Playor, 1980); Marcia L. Welles, "The *Pícara*: Towards Female Autonomy, or the Vanity of Virtue," *Romance Quarterly* 33 (1986): 63–70.

FELIX KRULL
CONFESSIONS OF FELIX KRULL, CONFIDENCE MAN

(Bekenntnisse des Hochstaplers Felix Krull: Der Memoiren erster Teil, 1911, 1954)

Thomas Mann

Mann began this work as a young man and published a portion in 1911. He then laid it aside to write *Death in Venice,* worked on it in the 1930s, and finally continued it at the end of his life, starting again on the very page he had stopped on. Like John Hawkes, who has discussed his conscious use of the picaresque, Mann was deliberately working in the picaresque mode, aware not only of the tradition itself but also of the clever variation he was making. In one of his later essays, Mann noted that *Felix Krull* was a fragment and would probably remain so even if he were given the time and inclination to extend it. Because the form allowed continuation, one could, he said, "fabulate further." For him, the picaresque provided a scaffolding on which any number of possible things could be hung, a narrative realm *(epischer Raum)* in which everything imagined and everything contributed by life could be accommodated. The most interesting aspect of picaresque narrative is that it can "break off" or "stop" but never be "finished," as he put it. *Felix Krull,* he goes on to say, belongs to this picaresque tradition, whose German prototype is *Simplicius Simplicissimus* (q.v.). "A young writer began it. An old one continues it." Its original idea was "the parodistic transference of artistic power *[Künstlertum]* into a deceptive-criminal realm," though the work gained in inner breadth and experience and grew into a multifaceted humoristic-parodistic Bildungsroman, a particularly German form of fiction that Mann repeatedly imitated and parodied throughout his career, especially in *The Magic Mountain. Felix Krull* was also influenced by the memoirs of Georges Manolescu, which appeared in 1905 and in which Mann took a deep interest. He is, moreover, having fun with the confessional form itself, an inherent characteristic of picaresque narrative. And finally, Mann is playing with an imitation of Goethe, which runs throughout all his works. As Heilman has pointed out, in *Felix Krull* are Mann's own "fantastically jocular *Dichtung und Warheit* and *Wilhelm Meister* (Wilhelm's son, incidentally, was named Felix)" (111).

George Steiner has noted the direct affinities of the work to Grimmelshausen's *Simplicissimus:* "At times Mann insinuates a direct quote into his own fiction. Simplex and Felix are brothers under the skin; their very names echo" (323).

We have in *Felix Krull* a picaresque variation by a writer whose self-consciousness about his models and their traditions results in a complex and intricate fiction that is learned in the best sense. We get the impression that, as Felix performs in life and then performs that performance for us narratively, so Mann is performing here and knows it. His is a virtuoso fiction about a virtuoso picaro. Felix is the picaro as actor *ludens* on the world-as-stage.

He shares with earlier picaros a difficult birth, made unusual by his being aware of the moment of being born: he shows "no eagerness to enter the world" and is reluctant "to exchange the darkness of the womb for the light of day" (9). His early childhood, though physically comfortable, is lonely; soon he learns to trick his way out of going to school, and he learns to steal. Then his father's business of making cheap champagne fails, and, as Seidlin points out, "he goes bankrupt, as thoroughly bankrupt as the father of Guzmán de Alfarache whose economic position was about as sound as Engelbert Krull's" (185). After his father's suicide, Felix feels himself particularly alone in the world, with "the tendency to misanthropy and withdrawal from the world which had always been a part of my character." When his mother moves the family to Frankfurt and opens a tiny pension, Felix earns "many a welcome coin" by hailing carriages in front of theater lobbies. Like Lazarillo and Guzmán *(Lazarillo de Tormes, Guzmán de Alfarache,* q.q.v.), Felix finds himself ejected into a world wider than any he had dreamed existed:

Now observe this youth in ragged clothes, alone, friendless, and lost in the crowd, wandering through this bright and alien world. He has no money with which to take any real part in the joys of civilization. . . . But his senses are lively, his mind attentive and alert; he sees, he enjoys, he assimilates; and if at first the rush of noise and faces confuses this son of a sleepy country town, bewilders him, frightens him indeed, nevertheless he possesses mother wit and strength of mind enough slowly to become master of his inner turmoil and turn it to good purpose for his education, his enthusiastic researches. (62)

The picaro's retrospective self-pity is a minor tone in the narratives of Lazarillo, Guzmán, and Simplicius, though it never becomes unpalatably self-indulgent. Felix, on the other hand, looks outward at the world all the time and prepares himself for it without much woebegone commentary about his bad lot in life or the adversities of fate. For Felix, the world is both "alien" and "bright," a place where he can make "researches" with his "mother wit" as help. Although he is at first bewildered, he aims at being master of himself and his relationship to the world.

In Frankfurt, Felix detaches himself from his mother and sister and is on his own for good. He tricks the military and avoids induction, becomes a pimp, and goes to Paris, where he steals (or rather lets himself become the thief of—the distinction is important) some jewels and where, for almost the last time, he is aware of his poverty:

It thus seems wisest to society simply to avert her eyes from this damaged product of her order. "Poverty," it is said, "is no sin," but that is just talk. To its possessor it is highly sinister—half defect, half undefined reproach; it is in every way extremely repulsive, and any association with it may lead to unpleasant consequences. (102)

He works at a series of jobs (elevator boy, dishwasher, waiter) in Paris. Although he will remain a "damaged product" of the social order in another sense, poverty will be an obstacle no longer; with the money from the stolen jewels, he begins to live a double life that will ultimately lead to his role as impersonator and confidence man, and, as we note from occasional hints in his narrative, he will see much of prisons. This is the basic outline of Felix's situation in the world: alone, clever, portable, unstable in both place and role.

But it is his special ability to make positives out of negatives that forms the basis of Felix's relationship to that world. He masters to perfection one of the picaro's traditional tricks: role playing, or the deceit of the mask. His whole life, or what he tells of it, is a continuing empirical try-out on the world-as-stage. Rarely in much danger of not surviving physically and experientially, Felix devotes his energies to shaping experience artistically. He began his role playing early in life: "When I was still in dresses I liked to pretend I was the Kaiser" (10). He practices extraordinary physical control of himself in front of mirrors and is soon posing in various get-ups for his painter godfather Schimmelpriester: "I seemed not only able to put on whatever social rank or personal characteristics I chose, but could actually adapt myself to any given period or century" (20). The episode in the theater with the actor Müller-Rosé, who is hideous and repulsive without his makeup, teaches Felix a crucial lesson about the world and how to manipulate it: "What unanimity [between audience and actor] in agreeing to let oneself be deceived! Here quite clearly there is in operation a general human need, implanted by God himself in human nature, which Müller-Rosé's abilities are created to satisfy" (26). In learning the lesson Simpliccissimus is taught by the pastor—"The foolish world wants to be fooled"—Felix realizes the essence of his role as actor *ludens*: the deceiver and the deceived gratify each other in a willingly reciprocal process of illusion and delusion. "He who really loves the world shapes himself to please it" (53) observes the older Felix in what could stand as his motto.

He puts this perception to practical use. Hating school, "that malignant institution," he only wants to be in conditions "that leave my spirit and imagination completely free," and so he deceives everyone, even the family doctor, into believing that he is genuinely sick. His awareness of his role—and his role playing—grows:

I had improved upon nature, realized a dream; and only he who has succeeded in creating a compelling and effective reality out of nothing, out of sheer inward knowledge and contemplation—in short, out of nothing more than imagination and the daring exploitation of his own body—he alone understands the strange and dreamlike satisfaction with which I rested from my creative task. (32)

The supreme achievement of his early career—one of the most hilarious and satirical tricks ever played by any picaro on the very symbol of authority and order—is his trick on the military to avoid induction. As he had reacted against school because it limited his freedom, so this is an even more vital challenge to his picaresque-artistic freedom. Like Guzmán begging as a cripple, fake sores and all, in Rome, Felix hones an old picaresque trick and stages an epileptic attack in front of the examiners. What Guzmán does for bare survival (though the element of putting one over on the world is not absent either) Felix lifts to a higher plane: his survival depends on absolute freedom, on the picaresque right to encounter multifaceted life experientially and on his own artistic right to shape the world (and himself) through the art of role playing. Felix rejects the rule of society without actively setting out to destroy it or even undermine it. He can "be" a soldier without literally having to become one: "If it is permissible to describe and define intellectually an emotional treasure as noble as freedom, then it may be said that to live like a soldier but not as a soldier, figuratively but not literally, to be allowed in short to live symbolically, spells true freedom" (87).

Krull's fine sense of audience is also revealed in this episode. He reinforces the examiner's doubts by denying his "malady"; by negating the illusion and appearance, he actually exploits them and, as far as his audience goes, converts appearance into reality itself. Later Krull transfers this sense of audience to the world at large. On the train to Paris, he sees that role playing is part of life. He sees the conductor and himself as marionettes, acting out their roles on the stage of life. Once in Paris, he performs his jobs in the hotel with all the self-conscious staging of the actor-poseur he cultivates himself to be. And the bustling hotel itself, with its gallery of human types, becomes for Krull the wide wide world, and the adventures he has there mount up in varied and frantic succession. Mann's twist on the panoramic road novel is to let Felix Krull's elevator cage become for several episodes the vantage point from which he sees the world and encounters it, in the microcosm of the hotel. Like Karl Rossman in Kafka's *America* (q.v.), also an elevator boy in a hotel, Felix does not at first move much horizontally and geographically in the world panorama; he moves up and down in one place, a vertical movement that is an ironic parallel to his later ability to move vertically in the social hierarchy of the world by virtue of his roles. In the hotel Felix refines his ability to see life as stage and himself one of the star players.

There was a certain charm in playing this role against a background of secret wealth. . . . My secret wealth . . . transformed my uniform and my job into a role, a simple extension of my talent for "dressing up." Although later on I achieved dazzling successes in passing myself off for less, and it is an open question which deception gave me the greater inner amusement, the greater delight in this fairy-tale magic. (152)

From what had been earlier an expedient masquerade (to avoid a distasteful imprisonment) Krull turns his attention fully and lovingly to the art (not always

the necessity) of being someone else. Soon he feels confined and bored by one
role, and he longs to be among the people, in the thick of things. He becomes
a dishboy and waiter, all the time continuing his double life. He is thus outside
society because he refuses to play a fixed role in the continuum of things, and
he is able to participate in that society at will through his own kind of tricks.
He

inwardly withdrew from the crowd, which was only the passive victim of entertainment,
revelling in self-forgetfulness, and repudiated any idea that I was one of them. They
merely enjoyed, and enjoyment is a passive condition that will never satisfy one who
feels himself born to act and to achieve. (161)

He becomes thoroughly aware of his position inside-outside the social continuum
and of his role-playing relationship to it. He cannot even be a member of the
audience, literally and figuratively. He sees all life as a series of roles, and as
far as he is concerned even being in the audience is to play a role:

Thus I masqueraded in both capacities, and the undisguised reality behind the two appearances, the real I, could not be identified because it actually did not exist. Nor am I
willing to say that I gave my role as a man of distinction any definite preference over
the other. I was too good and successful a waiter to feel appreciably happier when I was
the one who was waited on—a part, by the way, that requires as much natural talent as
the other. (189)

The real "I" is fragmented into the apersonality of multiple "I's." He refers
to his "silent game of exchanging roles" and even sees this art as socially useful:
"Sympathetic reader! I was very happy. In my own eyes I was priceless, and I
loved myself—in the way that is really socially useful, self-love turned outward
as amiability" (209). It is as a master of disguise, thoroughly in love with
himself, his profession, the world, that Felix finds his relationship to that world.
In his roles he holds the dreary and fragmentary world together in the temporary
relationships based on illusion of picaro to victim, of willing deceiver to willing-
to-be-tricked victim.

Mastery of his art—and by extension the mastery of the world that art deludes—makes Krull an ironical exaggeration of the picaro and simultaneously a
kind of negation of the picaro figure. It is almost as though the picaro has
mastered himself too well; as the traditional picaro was often the servant of many
masters, Felix, in contrast and exaggeration, becomes something of a comical
master-servant combination. His picaresque apersonality is at the service of his
artistic mastery. Krull is a double not only literally because he actually impersonates other people but also, more significantly, because he carries within
"himselves" both the servant-picaro and the master-artist. At one point he even
sees masters and servants in interchangeable roles:

My basic attitude toward the world and society can only be called inconsistent. For all
my eagerness to be on affectionate terms with them, I was frequently aware of a considerable coolness, a tendency to critical reflection, which astonished me. There was, for
example, an idea that occasionally preoccupied me when for a few leisure moments I
stood in the lobby or dining-hall . . . watching the hotel guests being waited and fawned

upon. . . . It was the idea of *interchangeability*. With a change of clothes and make-up, the servitors might often just as well have been the masters, and many of those who lounged in the deep wicker chairs, smoking their cigarettes, might have played the waiter. It was pure accident that the reverse was the fact, an accident of wealth; for the aristocracy of money is an accidental and interchangeable aristocracy. (184)

This is in the tradition of the picaro speculating about fortune and accident in life. And it is a convention for the picaro to aspire to masterhood. But Felix Krull's attained mastery, not only of his roles but of his all-encompassing world-view, goes beyond that of the traditional picaro. His artistry enables him to attain remarkable shaping powers over himself and thus over the world fragments he traverses. In all these ways, Mann's version of the picaro is the consummation and the negation of the picaro figure—the picaro's role-playing talent so well perfected that the picaro can be obliterated by the picaresque artist who resides in his very being. Furthermore, the world, though it rejects Krull's integration into it, and though he rejects it in turn, is sporadically accommodating to this picaro. Diane Philibert, from whom he had stolen the jewels, actually makes him steal again. Earlier the candy store had been conveniently empty to accommodate his first thefts. And Lord Strathbogie is willing to make the picaro a generous arrangement. Felix's role is so undefined that he excites both men and women sexually. Finally, the marquis de Venosta gives Krull the chance for the biggest role of his career (as far as he narrates it). This accommodation of the world is the secret Felix learned early in life when he visited Müller-Rosé's dressing room: that the world needs a picaro to play tricks on it, an imposter to deceive it, an artist to lie to it.

Heilman in his perceptive essay has examined especially this aspect of the picaro's relationship to his world. Krull combines, he says, a "racketeering toughness with a constant aesthetic awareness" (116), and in this picaro-artist combination "Felix does not merely use others; he gratifies them" (118). "Like the confidence man in real life and the picaro in fiction, the artist must win assent or confidence" (123). There is thus an analogy between the picaro-victim and the artist-audience, and in the background a third, analogous to these: deity and humanity. Felix, as he makes clear throughout his narrative, is hypersensitively aware of the world's need for a picaro, and, to use Heilman's analogy, of reality's need to be deceived. Although he would not be accepted into society (and he would not accept any acceptance), Krull is well aware that here he performs an acceptable function in society by approaching it from without. More than any other picaro in fiction, Felix Krull has perceived the real meaning—has gone behind the scenes, as it were—of the trickster-victim relationship. This relationship is essential to the picaresque. While many other picaros function within it and on both ends of the relationship, Felix has seen through it to the meaning beyond, capitalizing on it as a less perceptive picaro capitalized on everything that came his way, and made it into the very stuff of his life in the world and into the theme of the art he makes of his life by narrating it.

Mann's fiction of Krull's narrative is, trickily, a fiction about fictions in the way Mann has Krull use the potential for irony that is built into the narrative distance of the confessional form. By the time he narrates, Felix is old and has served time in prison. The act of narrating his life thus becomes his final performance, his final confidence game, his last role on the world-as-stage, a role that subsumes all of his other roles because it contains them. Called Hermes (q.v.), the trickster god, by both Diane Philibert and Professor Kukuck, Felix takes on the godlike powers of illusion that art permits. The shape-shifting trickster Felix (Trickster Archetype, q.v.) shapes himself to please the world as he now, in narrating that series of gratifications, shapes the "dear reader" relationship to please us, who are equally willing to let ourselves be deceived. Every picaro, because he exists only through the masks created by his narrative act, is as elusive and illusive as the deceiving and willing-to-be-deceived world he must make his way in. In exploiting this mutual awareness between reader and narrator, which is inherent in all autobiographical forms of narrative, Thomas Mann's variation in the narrative tradition of the *Schelmenroman* exemplifies picaresque metafiction.

TRANSLATION

Denver Lindley, *Confessions of Felix Krull, Confidence Man* (New York: Signet Classics, 1957); page references are to this edition. A later edition (New York: Vintage Books, 1969) does not contain George Steiner's excellent afterword.

SELECT BIBLIOGRAPHY

Mann's own comments on *Felix Krull* are in his *Nachlese, Prosa, 1951–1955* (Berlin and Frankfurt, 1967). Some thorough discussions of picaresque aspects are Robert Alter, *Rogue's Progress: Studies in the Picaresque Novel* (Cambridge: Harvard University Press, 1964); Alexander Blackburn, *The Myth of the Picaro: Continuity and Transformation of the Picaresque Novel, 1554–1954* (Chapel Hill: University of North Carolina Press, 1979); Robert B. Heilman, "Felix Krull: Variations on Picaresque." *The Sewanee Review* 66 (1958): 547–77 (cited from rpt. in *Perspectives on Fiction*, edited by James L. Calderwood and Harold E. Toliver [New York, 1968], pp. 101–25); Klaus Hermsdorf, *Thomas Manns Schelme: Figuren und Strukturen des Komischen* (Berlin: Rutten und Loening, 1968); Werner Hollmann, "Thomas Mann's *Felix Krull* and *Lazarillo de Tormes*," *Modern Language Notes* 66 (1951). 445–51; Donald F. Nelson, *Portrait of the Artist as Hermes: A Study of Myth and Psychology in Thomas Mann's "Felix Krull"* (Chapel Hill: University of North Carolina Press, 1971); Oskar Seidlin, "Picaresque Elements in Thomas Mann's Work," *Modern Language Quarterly* 12 (1951): 183–200. See also Helmut Günther, "Der ewige Simplicissimus. Gestalt und Wandlung des deutschen Schelmenromans," *Welt und Wort* 10 (1955): 3; and Wilfried van der Will, *Pikaro heute: Metamorphosen des Schelms bei Thomas Mann, Döblin, Brecht, Grass* (Stuttgart: Kohlhammer, 1967).

THE FUTILE LIFE OF PITO PEREZ

(La Vida inútil de Pito Pérez, 1938)

José Rubén Romero

This Mexican fiction is technically a first-person narrative but not the picaro's. Here an anonymous narrator, a poet, tells the story of Pito's life, and he does so primarily by letting Pito talk. Thus the book is also a dialogue, a method that accomplishes two goals: it retains the traditional fictional ''I'' of the picaro, and at the same time it removes the actual process of narrating from the picaro, making it one of the episodes in his life. The result is a picaro who is completely contained within the fiction; he is not the projecting ''I'' that creates the fiction itself. The effect is that of a simpler, more clear-cut portrait, relatively uncomplicated by narrative distance. The picaro is usually both in his fiction and outside it, bridging the narrative distance between himself as narrator of his life and as character within the fictional world he creates. What Romero has done is to experiment with picaresque narrative technique, for which there are precedents in seventeenth-century picaresque: in Salas Barbadillo's third-person *La hija de Celestina* (q.v.), where the picara tells her own life story within the narrative, and Garcia's *La desordenada codicia* (q.v.) where the picaro tells his story to the first-person narrator, and in Cervantes's ''The Dogs' Colloquy'' (q.v.), in which dialogue produces an ironic undermining voice.

Romero tends to distance the mad, unstructured, anecdotal bursts of Pito Pérez. Here we have a picaro who is not seen entirely in his dual role, the narrating role that is often contradictory to the picaro's role in life. The verisimilitude of picaresque narrative is often strained by the disparity beteen the picaro-in-life, who does not strike us as being the kind of person who will be able (or care) to narrate that life, and the picaro-as-narrator, who seems to have become a different person. But we accept these widely differing roles as part of the picaro's protean character, his ability to shift roles. By intermediating the primary narrator, Romero has kept his focus on the picaro within the fiction. As he is portrayed, Pito Pérez would be incapable of the poet's narrative role; his life is too much with him. Actually Romero has split the picaro into two parts—the experiencer of life and the narrator of it within the life. Thus the dialogue form creates a picaresque narrative in which the picaro's life is almost simultaneous with the telling of it.

''Come on over,'' says the poet-narrator. ''Sit down. Let's talk as if we were old friends.'' Pito answers, ''Suits me. Our converstion could be titled: *Dialogue between a Poet and a Madman*.'' Then:

We sat down on the outside edge of the tower with our legs dangling down. My new shoes, next to Pito's, were well polished and they shone with that foolish pride of the rich. In fact, they had such a shine that Pito looked at them very scornfully and I felt the full impact of his stare. Our feet epitomized our entire social world filled with its injustices and inequalities. (6)

Here, in one of the few descriptive pasages in the book, the narrator points out the extreme distance that separates the two socially, just as Romero has distanced the picaro from direct confrontation with us by providing a surrogate picaro (who lives Pito's life vicariously) whose more objective stance modulates our attitude toward Pito. Romero's picture is, in a sense, the Ferdinand of Céline

(Journey to the End of the Night, q.v.) as he might appear if he did not do his own narrating.

After the preliminary conversation with the narrator, Pito tells the story of his life: "The narration which you asked for and which I believe is completely useless." He begins, like all other picaros, with his birth, which in Pito's case had the unusual circumstances that are a traditional motif in picaresque fiction:

And the day I was born, there was another child in the neighborhood who had been left without a mother so mine gave him her full breasts. This stranger grew strong and robust and I was left weak and sickly because there wasn't enough milk for the two of us. This was the first of the misfortunes which have been repeatedly my lot throughout all of my life. (13)

With Pito, as with Lazarillo *(Lazarillo de Tormes,* q.v.), the misfortunes of life begin with being born. As he grows up, his life follows a typical picaresque pattern. He learns to steal by robbing the church poor box but gets cheated in turn by his accomplice. He receives the nickname *Pito* (meaning "a small flute") because of a bamboo whistle he plays interminably. He steals again, this time sugar from a candy store, and he rationalizes the theft with picaresque sleight of mind:

That was no theft! To the contrary! It was a loan, obtained with God's permission! I never lay my hands on anything which belongs to someone else without first offering a mental request to the Supreme Creator of all things Who is, therefore, absolute owner and master of all that exists. If the Lord agrees to my request, He permits me to take what I need. If He doesn't agree, He alerts the temporary owner. (27)

But this picaresque amorality is coupled with the necessary and more important picaresque awareness that no such rationalization works in a crazy picaresque landscape: "I don't have too much confidence in my system because I know full well that what life gives with one hand, it takes away with the other" (27).

He roams the countryside and works in a drugstore. Here the almost obligatory episode involving the medical profession provides, as usual, the strongest satire (which priests receive in almost equivalent doses in picaresque fiction). The corrupt pharmacist substitutes cheap, harmless preparations for the prescribed drugs he is supposed to dispense and rationalizes this switch as being a benefit to humanity "since, by altering the prescription, we kill fewer people" (31). It is a picaresque world, Pito finds out, and he has to adapt himself to it. His initiation into sex comes with the pharmacist's lecherous wife. It ends badly, of course, and as this episode in his adventures closes, Pito observes with the picaro's characteristic inclination toward proverbs: "That night, travelling my lonesome way, I thought sadly: 'How short are the pleasures of this world and how easily we let ourselves be overcome by temptations.' Again homeless and penniless, I was on the adventure trail all because I had forgotten the story of Potiphar's wife" (36).

He wanders through "flea-bitten small towns" telling stories to simple folk who are "spellbound with my lies" (40). He works for some time for a priest, learns to love the bottle, has bad love affairs, works in his uncle's store (where he gives everything away) and gets to know many jails firsthand: "I have spent a lot of time in them" (80). Between parts I and II of the book, ten years pass. When the narrator and Pito again meet, the latter has become an itinerant peddler covered with bells, each of which is the sounding memory of towns he has been in. "I listen to them as they talk among themselves, as they tell of what they have seen or of the lives they have lived" (107). When the narrator tells Pito that he has left his *vida* unfinished, Pito replies, "To go on living it, my friend, and to have something to talk about. That whirlwind, the Revolution, came down from the north and those of us without roots were sent flying" (105).

More cynical now, his life ravaged by revolutionary chaos, thoroughly addicted to alcohol, Pito Pérez has become the total outsider: he has stepped completely away from the social order. Always sympathetic to the poor, always outraged at the rich and the privileged, he has now stepped away even from the reality of the poor. Content earlier to disrupt the social order since he could not participate within its structure, he has now left even that behind:

"And now that you are telling these things, Pito Pérez, wouldn't we be correct in thinking that you have gotten a little out of touch with reality?"

"But, can you tell me which is my reality and which is my dream? I am certain that everything I see exists and that Death has loaned me her eyes so that I can see with supernatural powers and thus amuse myself with the landscapes of other worlds." (120)

Pito Pérez has learned, like Céline's Ferdinand, to see life "from the other side."

Pito Pérez has been studied (by Sherman Eoff) as an example of the "unwanted or excluded person" suffering from the picaro's "sensitiveness to an inferior position in society" (191). Pito's bitter social criticism is "the castigatory reaction of one who wanted to belong and could not" and thus like Quevedo's Pablos (*El Buscón,* q.v.) and Cela's Pascual (*The Family of Pascual Duarte,* q.v.) he is outside, alienated. Yet Pito is not as pathetically swallowed up by his bitterness as Eoff's analysis suggests. Pito's life as it builds up and explodes in its final outburst is not only the key to his psychology (Eoff: "an effort of the ignored child to attract attention"); it is also the self-consciously assertive act of onlyman against a society from which he has been irrevocably exiled and which he no longer wants to belong to, as even Lazarillo and Pablos still do. In his exile he has perceived too much and, though he does not like it, he turns his bitterness into a positive, assertive act against the world of everyman.

This tendency toward total alienation had been building all along. Long ago he had learned to stop taking even his pain seriously:

And do you think . . . that my life is a mosaic of witty remarks? or a little music box that plays only happy tunes? My life is a sad one, like that of all cheats. But, I have seen people laugh so often at my sorrow that I have ended up laughing at it myself, thinking that my pain will not be so bitter since it affords some pleasure to others. (10–11)

At other moments he sees things differently, suspects the world (represented in part by the narrator) of being superficially and condescendingly interested in him, and sees himself as pathetic victim—yet aware of his picaresque condition to the extent that he affirms his outsider status:

Who has ever taken a real interest in me? You yourself, the very person to whom I am telling my life story, have you ever really tried to know me, to study me with any real serious intent? No! You want me to tell you stories that will make you laugh: my adventures as a knave-like Periquillo; my tricks as a wandering rascal, like Gil Blas. But, have you ever noticed that my tricks are not funny ones? . . . I will be rotten to the core until the very end. (61)

In his fluctuation between bitter alienation and reconciliation with his outsiderdom, he can sympathize with the poor and tell them to obey the law, but he can also tell them "to piss on its representatives" (59). He can see the need for the idea of an ordered world, but he speaks more strongly for chaos, so much so that he identifies with the devil himself:

Oh, the poor Devil. How sorry I am for him! He has never heard a single word of compassion or of love. . . .

I am not aware that Faust thanked the Devil for the youthful life, for the money, or for the love which the Devil gave him.

The Devil moves about in shadowy circles, struggling continuously against hatred and envy, a stranger who is denied all affection, all expression of tenderness. (63)

He has attacks of delirium tremens and is transported to "regions undreamed of by the rest of mankind." Toward the end of his life, he is living with "the most faithful love I have had in all my life," the skeleton of an old woman:

"Aren't you afraid to go to bed with a skeleton?"

"Afraid? Why should I be? Aren't we even more repugnant skeletons covered as we are with rotted flesh? And still knowing all of this, we look for contact with women. My woman has no bodily functions to worry about. She does not have body odor. Neither does she demand anything in the way of clothes or jewelry. She is not a coquette, or a chatterbox, or a religious fanatic. Nor is she capricious. Quite the contrary, she is the model of all virtue. How lucky I was to meet up with her!" (127)

The paradox here is that he finds normalcy and dullness of routine only in an extremely grotesque relationship such as this. And it is not only grotesque; it is hilarious as well since the obvious analogy of the ventriloquist and his dummy suggests itself. Death has attached itself to him before figuratively, but now it literally accompanies him on a weird, horrible travesty of marriage, one of the basic social institutions. Literally and figuratively, grotesquely and comically, now he can talk through the mouth of death.

Pito's withdrawal as onlyman culminates with his death when, in a blazing outcry of condemnation, he removes himself from the world literally, bequeathing to it all he has learned on the other side, in exile from it. His body, appropriately, is found in a pile of garbage. He has appeared throughout the book always as an emerging or disappearing thing in the landscape; at the beginnings of both parts I and II, Pito is seen coming from a distance, slowly taking shape as a thing distinct from the landscape around him. He disappears the same way: "Pito Pérez disappeared down the spiral stairway of the tower, like a dirty penny disappears into the slot of the collection box" (11). In death he joins a part of the landscape set apart, as he had always been apart in life. He leaves a last will and testament:

To Humanity, I bequeath the entire lot of my bitterness. To the rich, hungry for gold, I leave the excrement of my life.

To the poor, because they are so cowardly, I will my contempt. . . .

Humanity, I know you! I have been one of your victims.

. . . People gathered around me, as if I were a clown, so that I could make them laugh with the stories of my adventures. But never, never did anyone dry a single one of my tears!

Humanity, I stole some money from you; I made fun of you; my vices ridiculed you. I do not repent! And at the very moment of my death, I wish I had the strength to spit all of my scorn into your face (130–31)

In his onlyness, Pito Pérez breaks a typical picaresque pattern. In mainstream picaresque fiction, the picaro's act of narration is a movement toward integration, expressing a yearning for order that is being satisfied through the act of telling about his disordered life. Pito does not engage in such a process; he moves ever more outward, away from integration, into a kind of cosmic exile. He finally excludes the world that has excluded him. His very extremity in life makes him incapable of the poet's reflective act of self-creation through narration. He is exiled even from art.

TRANSLATION

William O. Cord (Englewood Cliffs, N.J.: Prentice-Hall, 1966).

SELECT BIBLIOGRAPHY

Maria Casas de Faunce, *La novela picaresca latinoamericana* (Madrid: Cupsa Editorial, 1977); Raymond L. Corro, "La vida inútil de Pito Pérez," in *La Picaresca: Orígenes, Textos, Estructuras,* ed. Manuel Criado de Val (Madrid: Fundación Universitaria Española, 1979), 1055–62; Sherman Eoff, "Tragedy of the Unwanted Person, in Three Versions: Pablos de Segovia, Pito Pérez, Pascual Duarte," *Hispania* 39 (1956): 190–96; Ulrich Wicks, "Onlyman," *Mosaic* 8 (1975): 21–47.

LA GARDUÑA DE SEVILLA Y ANZUELO DE LAS BOLSAS

(*The Marten of Seville and Angler of Purses,* 1642)

Alonso de Castillo Solórzano

A sequel to *Aventuras del bachiller Trapaza* (q.v.), this work portrays the adventures of Trapaza's daughter Rufina, whose beauty allows her to succeed in playing elaborate confidence games that take her through the worlds of the rich and also beyond the law as she gets involved with and finally triumphs over a band of robbers. In the end she settles down to run a shop (though in one of the English translations, she and her lover were hanged at the end). This is another of Castillo Solórzano's escapist picaresques, not very different in atmosphere and mechanical use of formulaic convention from his other works, including *La niña de los embustes* (q.v.), and an earlier work occasionally mentioned in picaresque contexts, *Las harpías en Madrid y coche de las estafas* (The harpies in Madrid and coach of swindles, 1631).

Both Chandler and Fonger de Haan thought highly of the works of Castillo, the former considering them the high-water mark of the romances of roguery and the latter thinking them underappreciated in their time. Nevertheless, to consider *La garduña de Sevilla* as a picaresque requires considerable qualifying of a degree that severely compromises the integrity and usefulness of a generic definition. Castillo Solórzano's works are perhaps best described as picaresque-like, or as peripheral picarsques, for they are really, as Dunn points out in *The Spanish Picaresque Novel,* moving well "in the direction of the *novela cortesana* . . . Castillo was himself an accomplished practitioner of the *novela cortesana;* he knew the formulas, and which ones could be applied to his hybrid picaresque narratives" (127). For Bjornson, Castillo transforms picaresque adventurers "into vaguely outlined actors in stereotyped scenes on a stage manipulated by the author" (96). And Rico, for whom only form is capable of identifying a literary species, finds the abandonment of autobiographical narration in *La garduña*—"this desertion of the first person"—cause for placing it in "a separate sub-group within the category of 'narratives with a *pícaro.*' The numerous interpolations become so prominent that they swamp the character, and it is no longer possible to regard them as dependent on a single first-person consciousness that would serve as the common denominator of the multifarious contents" (86). It might even be argued that Rico's subgroup is inadequate. There is little of Lazarillo or Guzmán *(Lazarillo de Tormes, Guzmán de Alfarache,* q.q.v.) in Rufina.

TRANSLATION/EDITION

La garduña de Sevilla was "render'd into English, with some Alterations and Additions" by John Davies of Kidwelly as *La Picara, or The Triumphs of Female Subtilty, Display'd in the Artifices and Impostures of a Beautiful Woman, Who Trappan'd the Most Experienced Rogues, and Made All Those Unhappy Who Thought Her Handsome* (London, 1665). Around 1700 an abridged edition with a changed ending, "done into English by the ingenious Mr. E. W.," was published as *The Life of Donna Rosina, A Novel.* In 1717, it reappeared as *The Spanish Pole-Cat: or, the Adventures of Seniora Rufina,* "Begun to be translated by Sir Roger L'Estrange; And Finish'd, By Mr. Ozell"; this was reprinted in 1727 as *Spanish Amusements: Or, the Adventures of the Celebrated Courtezan Seniora Rufina Call'd The Pole-Cat of Seville.* The three stories, or *novelas,* within *La garduña de Sevilla* were published separately in 1712, although not in the order in which they appear in the original, as *Three Ingenious Spanish Novels: Namely, I. The Loving Revenge: Or, Wit in a Woman. II. The Lucky Escape: Or, the Jilt Detected. III. The Witty Extravagant: Or, the Fortunate Lover.* The original Spanish text is accessible in one of the editions of Angel Valbuena Prat's *La novela picaresca española;* in the sixth edition (Madrid: Aguilar, 1968), it is on pp. 1526–1618.

SELECT BIBLIOGRAPHY

Richard Bjornson, *The Picaresque Hero in European Fiction* (Madison: University of Wisconsin Press, 1977); Frank Wadleigh Chandler, *Romances of Roguery* [1899] (New York: Burt Franklin, 1961); Peter N. Dunn, *Castillo Solórzano and the Decline of the Spanish Novel* (Oxford: Basil Blackwell, 1952) and *The Spanish Picaresque Novel* (Boston: Twayne, 1979); Mireya Pérez-Erdelyi, *La pícara y la dama: la imagen de las mujeres en las novelas picaresco-cortesanas de María de Zayas y Sotomayor y Alonso de Castillo Solórzano* (Miami, Fla.: Ediciones Universal, 1979); Francisco Rico, *The Spanish Picaresque Novel and the Point of View* [1970], trans. Charles Davis with Harry Sieber (Cambridge: Cambridge University Press, 1984); Julio Rodríguez-Luis, "*Pícaras:* The Modal Approach to the Picaresque," *Comparative Literature* 31 (1979): 32–46.

GIL BLAS
(THE ADVENTURES OF GIL BLAS OF SANTILLANE)

(Histoire de Gil Blas de Santillane, 1715, 1724, 1735)

Alain-René Lesage

Three-quarters of a century after Smollett translated *Gil Blas* and acknowledged his debt to it in *Roderick Random* (q.v.), Sir Walter Scott was still singing the praises of Lesage in *The Lives of the Novelists* (1822, 1827). After discussing *Le Diable Boiteux* (1707, 1726), Lesage's enormously popular "celebrated moral satire," at some length, he fairly gushes with admiration for *Gil Blas*:

Few have ever read this charming book without remembering, as one of the most delightful occupations of their life, the time which they first employed in the perusal; and there are few also who do not occsionally turn back to its pages with all the vivacity which attends the recollection of early love. . . . If there is any thing like truth in [Thomas] Gray's opinion, that to lie upon a coach and read new novels was no bad idea of Paradise, how would that beatitude be enhanced, could human genius afford us another *Gil Blas*! (124)

Lesage's admiration for Spanish literature, in particular for the Spanish picaresque—in 1732 and 1734, respectively, he published translations of *Guzmán de Alfarache* and *Estebanillo González* (q.q.v.), and *Gil Blas* is specifically influenced by *Marcos de Obregón* (q.v.)—resulted in a curious case study for the literary historian whose task it is to distinguish among influence, imitation, translation—and even plagiarism, with which Lesage was in fact charged by his contemporaries. Scott dismisses this charge as "a favourite theme of laborious dulness . . . to reduce genius of the higher order to the usual standard of humanity, and, of course, to bring the author nearer a level with his critics" (124). He compares the situation to that of a clay pit whose proprietor demands equal credit with the artist for the sculpture that is created: "The question is in both cases the same—not so much from whom the original rude substance came, as to

whom it owes that which constitutes its real merit and excellence'' (124). Scott
is so taken with Lesage that he does not bother to examine his own dubious
analogy; instead, he goes on to make the Spanish picaresque a mere handmaiden
in the service of Lesage's narrative triumph in *Gil Blas*:

It is therefore no disparagement to Le Sage, that long before his time there existed in
other countries, and particularly in Spain, that species of fiction to which *Gil Blas* may
be in some respects said to belong. There arises in every country a species of low or
comic romance, bearing somewhat the same proportion to the grave or heroic romance,
which farce bears to tragedy. We . . . acknowledge ourselves interested in the tale, because
we are *men* and the events are *human*. (124–25)

While admitting the specific resemblances to certain parts of *Guzmán de Alfarache*—and disagreeing with the suggestion that *Gil Blas* had predecessors and
prototypes in such French works as Sorel's *Francion* (1623–1633) and Scarron's
Roman comique (1651–1657)—Scott defends Lesage's borrowings: "The whole
concoction of *Gil Blas* appears to me as original, in that which constitutes the
essence of a composition, as it is inexpressibly delightful.'' As proof of Lesage's
genius, he cites the Spanish translator's vaunt that rendering Lesage's works
into Spanish had "restored them to the language in which they were originally
written.'' Because of Lesage's "wonderful observation of costume, and national
manners,'' the Spanish translator was able to reclaim the work "as the original
property of Spain'' (126).

This territorial claim, which Scott unquestioningly accepts as demonstration
of Lesage's powers of observation and imagination, is undermined by an examination of Lesage's apparent readings of the Spanish picaresque works as
revealed through his translations. His version of *Guzmán de Alfarache* (the fourth
known French translation) omits so much that the work is radically altered,
according to Parker:

[Lesage's] version reduces the novel to the bare bones of the narrative by omitting not
only the "moralities'' but all reference to religious feelings as well. . . . For Lesage,
Guzmán is a cynical cad to the very end. The meaning of the work is thus completely
altered and Lesage does not warn his readers that this has happened. There is nothing
underhand in this procedure; it is simply that the necessity for this "improvement'' was
taken for granted, the probable reason being that religion was a subject to be treated
"seriously'' and its association with the low world of the "comic'' was contrary to
established taste. The dissociation was, of course, helped by the age's dislike of religious
"enthusiasm'' and by a general weakening of the sense of sin. (116)

Not only did French readers who failed to consult the original thus receive a
gross distortion of Alemán's work, but the problem spread to England as well
when English translations from Lesage's translation began to appear in 1821.
They had been preceded by a translation of another French version (Brémond's,
1695), which had also removed many of Alemán's digressions. "Thus, for the
whole of the eighteenth century and for most of the nineteenth, in both England
and France, *Guzmán de Alfarache* appeared divorced from the moral-theological

setting that alone gave meaning to the study of the delinquent's life" (Parker, 117). By the time Lesage did his translations, as Bjornson points out, he had published most of *Gil Blas,* the success of which "had already established the popularity of the narrative formulas which he later imposed upon [the original Spanish works]. Precisely for that reason, his modifications of the Spanish texts clearly reveal the principles according to which he composed his own picaresque fiction and the reasons why his versions surpassed the originals in popularity" (208). His "translation" of *Guzmán* went through some thirty editions between 1732 and 1883. Lesage thus occupies a singular place in the narrative evolution of the picaresque mode. It appears that he reshaped the generic conventions of his narrative heritage to conform to the works he himself was creating. His and subsequent readers were therefore reading *Gil Blas* in the context of a picaresque narrative tradition that Lesage himself had defined for them through his renderings of Spanish picaresques. Generic awareness always results in reciprocal illumination; while our sense of kind helps us understand the specific literaturary work, that work simultaneously alters our sense of kind. It is a continuing process of refinement and adjustment in which the experience of each new work of literature catalyzes a reshaping of our entire literary frame of reference. But Lesage manipulates, and ultimately controls, our generic awareness by creating the very genre within which he wants his work contextually perceived.

This phenomenon might be singled out as a mere curiosity of literary genetics were it not for its distorting impact on subsequent concepts of picaresque fiction. Almost all definitions of the picaresque by non-Hispanists use as prime (and often as only) examples just two works—*Lazarillo de Tormes* (q.v.) and *Gil Blas.* The first is not universally accepted as a full-fledged picaresque and is sometimes relegated to the status of a precursor, and the latter is radically different from the first, as well as from *Guzmán, El Buscón* (q.v.), *Simplicius Simplicissimus* (q.v.), and other widely agreed-upon picaresques. For the resulting muddle, perpetuated even now in handbooks, and literary surveys, Lesage seems to be the cause, however innocent he may have been of the consequences. Nevertheless, Lesage's apparently serious perception of his narrative heritage is a fact of literary history and must be taken into account in any consideration of the generic development of the picaresque mode.

However diligently Lesage modeled his fiction on Spanish originals, he created in *Gil Blas* a work that is almost universally regarded as very different from the Spanish picaresque works (with the notable exception of *Marcos de Obregon,* itself quite different from other Spanish picaresques). With *Gil Blas,* qualifiers have to be summoned, and so we read of its "aristocratization" of the picaresque (Parker, 121) and of the "picturesque" picaresque (Kearful, 386); the 1724 sequel has been described as "post-picaresque" (Alter, 33); and Gil Blas is seen as a "lucky" and "fulfilled" picaro (Longhurst, 136), while still others put the work into a picaresque context only to yank the label out from under it (Miller, 118; Blackburn, 118) in the end. However we qualify or otherwise situate *Gil*

Blas in the picaresque narrative tradition, we have to come to terms with its contradictory status within that tradition. There is no disputing the fact that it is one of the most deliberately conscious imitations of the Spanish genre; yet it is markedly different from those Spanish picarsques in setting, tone, worldview, and character, preserving from them for the most part only rudimentary elements of plot and pattern. Evidence—both extraliterary and internal—for the former abounds. The latter has been attributed to major differences in social conditions and literary taste, of which the following summaries serve as representative examples:

Rather than an attempt to tone down the less acceptable aspects of Spanish picaresque novels, the innovations in *Gil Blas* are the product of the positive philosophy of optimism and happy fate that was beginning to emerge in eighteenth-century France. This roseate view pervades the whole work: not only the life of the protagonist, but also the life of other characters, so that we are shown by and large only the brighter side of things and events, and there is less interest in the life of the underdog. From this optimistic philosophy there springs directly the author's attitude to his protagonist. The Spanish picaresque author disapproved of his hero, was opposed to his every aspiration and therefore condemned him to failure in all spheres. In *Gil Blas,* Lesage feels sympathy both for the protagonist and for his aims, and therefore allows him to succeed, to rise socially, morally, and materially. (Longhurst, 136)

While *Gil Blas* is not the tale of a shameless and cynical swindler from a morally sordid background like the *picaro* Guzman, it is nonetheless a novel within the picaresque tradition, adapted by Lesage to the portrayal of the social reality of Regency France. Similarly it can be argued that *Le Paysan parvenu* is a further adaptation, this time of the Lesagian picaresque, required by the introduction of a psychological reality which is not prominent in *Gil Blas*. The reason why Lesage and Marivaux could write novels which bear a marked similarity with the Spanish originals is that the social reality which they sought to convey in them had much in common with the setting in which the Spanish *picaros* lived out their adventures. Both French and Spanish novels can be seen to portray feudal society at critical stages in its disintegration. But whereas in the Spanish novel the perspective is bleakly pessimistic since there is nothing to replace the decaying feudalism of agrarian seventeenth-century Spain, in the French novel of the beginning of the eighteenth century the outlook is essentially optimistic, for the portrayal of feudal decadence is set within the perspective of the ascension of the bourgeois in the persons of Gil Blas and Jacob. It can therefore be seen that the picaresque form and the picaresque hero provided a malleable literaturary convention within which the emergent conflict between middle-class and feudal values in eighteenth-century France could be posed in artistic terms. (Strugnell, 95)

The troublesome question of literary taste also arises, for which the following passage may well be exemplary. It is from an anonymous review of a French translation of Fielding's *Jonathan Wild,* which has—primarily because of its subject matter and specific allusion to *Guzmán*—sometimes been considered a picaresque; the review appeared in *L'Année littéraire* (February 23, 1763):

The new work that has just been translated is well below those works of this author just mentioned. Little action, many reflections, above all a general tincture of bad baste and detestable pleasantries. . . . I do not speak of the main character who may be odious only to us French. We do not like to follow for two volumes a hero of roguish and wicked actions who ends on the gallows. The *Vie de Cartouche,* no matter now much art is put into its presentation, will be a disgusting book and will fall from our hands. But these pictures are less revolting to the English, who love nature wherever they find it. (Paulson and Lockwood, 435)

Just a few years earlier, Smollett, holding Lesage up as a model, had had to argue in his preface to *Roderick Random* that English fiction should have the same right to depict the sordid side of life, a right that English readers granted to, and praised in, foreign novels but criticized in their own—and a right that, if this review is representative, French readers already assumed for English fiction and the tastes of English readers. In any case, eighteenth-century French literary taste may well explain why "in Lesage, we are offered an amusing glimpse of Spanish low-life, as if seen from the safe perspective of an eighteenth-century French drawing room" (Kearful, 385; he is referring specifically to Lesage's translation of *Guzmán*). While on the one hand "Lesage simultaneously flattered bourgeois aspirations for upward social mobility and reinforced aristocratic assumptions about inherent nature and the hierarchical ordering of society," he was forced on the other to metamorphose his inherited fictional conventions in order to depict an "artificial reality" that "resembles an enormous comic stage, where all the characters are playing roles in a kaleidoscopic sequence of scenes which reconcile the audience's sentimental expectations of poetic justice with its demands for verisimilitude" (Bjornson, 225). Moreover, "Lesage's classical prose, pure, flexible, unhurried, is perfectly adapted to a narrative intended to convey the general truth of human life. Whereas the reality-destroying style of the picaresque novelists has a pictorial complement in El Greco's haunted luminosity or in Goya's savage line, the style of an eighteenth-century French rationalist conveys the insulated calm of a Watteau" (Blackburn, 114). There is even a chauvinistic reading of *Gil Blas,* as Alter points out, that explains Gil Blas's ability to resist the corruption of the world around him: "Gil Blas was thought up by a Frenchman, a fact which in itself is enough to make him more moral than any picaro conceived by a scurrilous Spaniard. The line of critics who have adopted this position runs from Ferdinand Brunetière to Maurice Bardon, but it reached its apogee . . . in Gustave Lanson, who went so far as to assert that anything artistically bad or morally reprehensible in *Gil Blas* was Spanish, while anything in the novel morally or artistically admirable had a French source" (13).

From the moment in the first chapter when Gil Blas describes his leaving home, we realize that the world this character is going to traverse will hardly ruffle, and certainly not disorient, his sense of stability or decency. His departure is by no means an ejection, a rebirth into a morally and physically chaotic universe:

When the time of my departure arrived, affecting the most lively sorrow on leaving an uncle, to whom I owed so many obligations, the honest man was melted, and gave me more money than he would have done, could he have seen to the bottom of my heart. Before I set out, I went to take leave of my father and mother, who enriched me with advice, exhorted me to pray to God for my uncle, to live inoffensively, to eschew evil, and by all means to refrain from stealing. After they had held forth a good while, they made me a present of their blessing, which was all I expected from them; and I, mounting my mule, bade adieu to Oviedo. (7)

Later, comfortably ensconced in an inn, he ponders his lot and decides: "I will turn gentleman, and endeavour to make my fortune in the world" (62). This in itself is a typical picaresque aspiration, and one of the major tensions in picaresque narrative results from the unbridgeable gap between the determination with which the picaro affirms it and the fierceness with which the world resists its fulfillment. While Gil Blas has his ups and downs and is vulnerable to temptation, the rhythm that governs his narrative is not Sisyphean; it is providential. He must learn to mask himself in a world of guise, and his protean adaptability serves him as it does any other picaro, but he is not subject to that instability of being that Stuart Miller calls apersonality; he is basically the *honnête homme* about whom and to whom the French moralists were writing. When Gil Blas has had enough of the disorders of theatrical life, he searches his soul and decides to move on:

A remnant of honour and religion, which I did not fail to preserve amidst such corruption of morals, made me resolve not only to leave Arsenia, but also to break off all correspondence with Laura, whom, however, I could not help loving, though I was sensible of her flagrant infidelity. Happy is he who can thus profit by those moments of reflection that interrupt the pleasures which engross his attention! Early one morning . . . I quitted the house where I had breathed nothing but the air of debauchery; and I had no sooner performed such a good action than Heaven rewarded me for it, by throwing me in the way of the steward of Don Matthias, my late master. Having saluted him, he knew me, and stopped to inquire if I was in any service: to which I answered, that I had been about a minute or two out of place; for that, after having lived about a month with Arsenia, whose behavior I did not like, I had left her of my own accord, in order to preserve my innocence. The steward, as if he had been scrupulously religious, approved of my delicacy, and told me that, since I was a young man of such honour, he would make it his business to settle me in an advantageous place. (212–13)

This passage, in which Gil Blas is the calm reflector of his reflections not only on the plane of narration, but on the plane of action itself, was immediately preceded (in the twelfth chapter of book III) by his waking up to the realization that would lead to his action. Having given himself up "to all manner of debauchery" but "frequently seized with sentiments of remorse that proceeded from my education, and embittered all my enjoyments," Gil Blas morally masters himself:

Vice could not get the better of these warnings, which augmented in proportion as I became more debauched; and, by the effect of a happy disposition, I began to abhor the disorders of a theatrical life. "Ah, wretch!" said I to myself, "is it thus thou fulfillest the expectation of they family? Was it not enough to cheat it by choosing another employment than that of a tutor? Does thy servile condition hinder thee from living like an honest man [*honnête homme*]? or does it become thee to live among such sinners? some of whom are possessed by envy, rage, and avarice; whilst others have banished all sense of shame? These are abandoned by intemperance and sloth; and those indulge their pride even to an excess of insolence. I am resolved, and will no longer dwell with the seven deadly sins." (211)

While such reflections can be found in Guzmán's narrative, they come only retrospectively. Gil Blas is not digressing in the act of telling, however; his moral discourse is integrated into his line of action and is presented as being simultaneous with it. With his moral rudder always keeping him upright—and with good fortune coming immediately in a direct cause-and-effect relationship— Gil Blas never experiences the intensity of radical outsiderdom, the *solo soy* of Lazarillo, or the constancy of inconstancy of Simplicissimus. His life appears to have been experienced in much the same calm and rational manner with which he narrates it. There is little narrative distance of any kind except the temporal; psychologically and morally, *Gil Blas* offers little tension of the kind we find in *Guzmán* or *Simplicissimus*.

When he does step out of bounds and serves a prison sentence for it—in the middle books—he falls sick, and, "by the greatest good luck in the world, a perfect tranquility of mind was the fruit of my disease. I then had no need of consolation: I entertained for riches and honour all the contempt which the opinion of approaching death had made me conceive: and now restored as it were, to myself, blessed my misfortune" (570–71). He resolves never to return to court and proposes instead to buy a cottage and "live in it like a philosopher." At this point, Blackburn comments, the "quest-for-reason pattern supersedes the search-for-credit pattern," and the final books work out a compromise between the two patterns. "Unlike the picaro, Gil Blas is so integrated into society that he emerges as its representative type, the *honnête homme*" (117–18). "We get no sense of a real subjectivity disturbed by the world's chaos and telling about it" (Miller, 118).

Alter suggests that in the end, *Gil Blas* is less a picaresque than it is a Bildungsroman and that it looks forward to Stendhal in its use of "prison confinement as a symbolic womb for the hero's rebirth" (32). This linking of picaresque and Bildungsroman is frequently made but often without an adequate concept of the latter (which has been problematical in critical usage as well). The integrative vision of the classic Bildungsroman puts it squarely within the romance mode; and while *Gil Blas* may not share some of the finer characteristics of the Bildungsroman, Lesage's world is romance-like in its makeup. When Gil Blas can write at the end,

I have for three years, gentle reader, led a delicious life with people whom I love so much; and to crown my felicity, Heaven has blessed me with two children, whom I piously believe to be my own, and whose education shall be the amusement of my old age (758),

he is comfortably inhabiting a world in which he has always been at home. The affirmation of his children's paternity may raise an eyebrow or two, but there is none of the dismay we feel at the end of Lazarillo's story when we realize what compromises he has had to make for the comforts of home. While every picaresque contains within it an implicit romance, *Gil Blas* is a romance that contains within it only an implicit picaresque, yet one that has "tricked" subsequent readers into taking it for the norm.

TRANSLATION

Trans. Tobias Smollett [1749] (New York: D. Appleton and Co., 1854).

SELECT BIBLIOGRAPHY

Robert Alter, *Rogue's Progress: Studies in the Picaresque Novel* (Cambridge: Harvard University Press, 1964); Richard Bjornson, *The Picaresque Hero in European Fiction* (Madison: University of Wisconsin Press, 1977); Alexander Blackburn, *The Myth of the Picaro: Continuity and Transformation of the Picaresque Novel, 1554–1954* (Chapel Hill: University of North Carolina Press, 1979); Glen Campbell, "The Search for Equality of Lesage's Picaresque Heroes," in *L'Egalité,* ed. Leon Ingber (Brussels: Bruylant, 1984), 136–43; Frank Wadleigh Chandler, *The Literature of Roguery* [1907] (New York: Burt Franklin, 1958); W. M. Frohock, "The 'Picaresque' in France before *Gil Blas,*" *Yale French Studies* 38 (1967): 222–29; Hendrik van Gorp, "Translation and Literary Genre: The European Picaresque Novel in the 17th and 118th Centuries," in *The Manipulation of Literature: Studies in Literary Translation,* ed. Theo Hermans (New York: St. Martin's Press, 1985), 136–48; Rolf Greifelt, "Die Übersetzungen des spanischen Schelmenromans in Frankreich im 17. Jahrhundert," *Romanische Forschungen* 50 (1936): 51–84; Frank J. Kearful, "Spanish Rogues and English Foundlings: On the Disintegration of Picaresque," *Genre* 4 (1971): 376–89; Ronald D. LeBlanc, *The Russianization of Gil Blas: A Study in Literary Appropriation* (Columbus, Ohio: Slavica Publishers, 1987); Jennifer Longhurst, "Lesage and the Spanish Tradition: *Gil Blas* as a Picaresque Novel," in *Studies in Eighteenth-Century French Literature Presented to Robert Niklaus,* ed. J. H. Fox, M. H. Waddicor, and D. A. Watts (Exeter: University of Exeter, 1975), 123–37; Stuart Miller, *The Picaresque Novel* (Cleveland, Ohio: Case Western Reserve University Press, 1967); Vivienne G. Mylne, "Structure and Symbolism in *Gil Blas,*" *French Studies* 15 (1961): 134–45, and "A *Pícara* in *Candide:* Paquette," *College Literature* 6 (1979): 205–10; Alexander A. Parker, *Literature and the Delinquent: The Picaresque Novel in Spain and Europe, 1599–1753* (Edinburgh: University Press, 1967); Ronald Paulson and Thomas Lockwood, eds., *Henry Fielding: The Critical Heritage* (New York: Barnes and Noble, 1969); Sir Walter Scott, *On Novelists and Fiction,* ed. Joan Williams (New York: Barnes and Noble, 1968); English Showalter, Jr., *The Evolution of the French Novel, 1641–1782* (Princeton, N.J.: Princeton University Press, 1972); A. R. Strugnell, "Diderot's *Neveu de Rameau:* Portrait of a Rogue in the French Enlightenment," in *Knaves and Swindlers: Essays on the Picaresque Novel in Europe,* ed. Christine J. Whitbourn (London, New York, Toronto: Oxford University Press, 1974), 93–111.

THE GINGER MAN

(1955, 1963 rev. ed.)

J. P. Donleavy

"Dear Mr. Skully," writes Sebastian Dangerfield to his landlord, whom he owes rent and whose house he has partially wrecked, "I have caught my neck in a mangle and will be indisposed for eternity. Yours in death, S. D.'' (190). The letter serves at once as an expression of Dangerfield's farcical sense of existence and as an image of his mangled life, in which he is forever being indisposed or indisposing others. In its simple, innocent tone and in its mischievous sense of play, the letter is a trick, a joke played on the exploiting landlords of the world by a picaro in an Eulenspiegel mood (*Till Eulenspiegel*, q.v.). In its format and in its polite language, the letter-joke shows the picaro's concession to the social proprieties: the picaro's resourcefulness allows him to mimic the social world while giving it the shaft. But underneath the surface mimicry and the causal joke, there is the sense of something unfunny and all too true. The juxtaposition of the polite *indisposed* (a temporary thing) with *eternity* (an absolute) is funny because of the incongruity, but it is actually true of Sebastian Dangerfield, who is unwilling to be (and incapable of being) healthy in the world's concept of health. Similarly, the ''neck in a mangle'' image shifts from the surface joke into the seriousness beneath, and the equation could read: neck = me, mangle = life.

In Donleavy's variation on, and episode in, the picaresque, the picaro races through a mad, frenzied, helter-skelter life full of pratfalls, intoxication, and free-for-all in a world that tries to be order itself but which he perceives from the vantage point of chaos. He is an American in Ireland, a law student at Trinity College in Dublin, and there is an absurd incongruity in the distance between the life he leads and the representative of order he seeks in vain to become. Domestically he is bound to a proper English wife, Marion, whom he alternately fights with bitterly and makes passionate love to. Marion is the constant nagging reminder of the middle-class conventional coziness that Dangerfield is just as constantly preventing her from having. Sebastian's proper element is not home and family but rather the realm of intoxication—Dublin's pubs—and the world of poverty, filth, and deformity. In this he resembles some of his ancestors (for example, Pito Pérez in *The Futile Life of Pito Pérez*, q.v.), at least one direct descendant (the protagonist of *Bright Lights, Big City*, q.v.), and a distant cousin (Hans Schnier in Böll's *The Clown*). Dangerfield's contacts with the world around him are kaleidoscopic, fleeting: after Marion, a succession of mistresses (Chris, Miss Frost, Mary); a fragmentary relationship with the one-eyed red-haired pervert Kenneth O'Keefe, another picaro in the landscape; and a change of scene to London, interspersed with flashbacks to his earlier days in the United States. ''I've got a cloacal grip on life,'' he says. ''Lots of people have said that. Nor am I going to let go. If there is illusion, live it with a flourish'' (174). And he does, except that life just as often has a cloacal grip on him. His existence is in fact a tug of war between the debt-haunting Skullys of the world, the ''gombeen men'' as he calls them, the proper Marions on the one hand, and the Dangerfield life of boundless episodes that scorns the artificial code books of the social world and demands (and gets) no more than the fragmentary moment:

Sometimes I feel fifty three. Seldom, but at times, I feel twenty. Like the days. Ever feel a Saturday on a Tuesday? Or a week of one Friday after another? Recently I've been seventy. But I remember thirty four as a fine age. (200)

Though he is desperate for money, and though he is halfheartedly preparing himself for smooth integration into the social continuum, and though he is not averse to having Marion ask her father for financial help, Dangerfield is hopelessly floundering in his seething world because he has no commitment to anything, no sense of order, no stability that goes beyond the exuberant desires and the madcap actions that define his self. He has the picaro's internal gyroscope— the balancing mechanism that keeps his head up in a world that chaotically swirls around him. He forages in life:

I stoop to menial things. But there just hasn't been enough money. However, in the flux. Keep one's eyes wide and never know when or what might come up. Live off the environment. Take fruit from my trees. Fine shirts from counters and charge them. Ton of turf from my fuel merchant and bill me later. (248)

Like Felix Krull (*Felix Krull*, q.v.), Sebastian is something of an actor. In shops, on the street, over the telephone, in letters, and in pubs, he can carry on the roles of those in the world around him by adapting himself to the conversational topics and styles appropriate to the situation. With Miss Frost he can be perfectly proper, and with O'Keefe he can even be a mentor of sorts. But he is also an unpredictable reactor who, like a madman, impulsively lashes out at the world: he tries to smother his child with a pillow (ch. 4), starts a fight in a tavern (ch. 12), and fights in public with Mary (ch. 30). At times he is the unwitting butt of unmotivated tricks as the landscape around him humiliates him: a mere flush of the toilet sends excrement cascading on his wife in the kitchen below (ch. 6); a ride on the train, with his fly open and his member out, results in a hilarious comic scene in which he, unaware of the cause of the consternation in his fellow passengers, suspects them of obscene behavior (ch. 10); and a meal in a cafeteria turns into a mess:

But it is such a very pleasant experience to go into this dining hall on a Dublin cold day and say, how do, to the lovely woman at the door taking gowns and move along in the academic line with a tin tray. . . . I went through the line gathering all the food, arranging it with care. And my head was hard and thick from thinking and tired eyes. My tray skidded from my fingers and fell on the floor. My orange jelly mixed with broken glass on this day when I bought a glass of milk to have with my Chelsea bun. They told me I was clumsy and asked why did I do it. And at times in my heart there is a music that plays for me. Tuneless threnody. They called me names. I was so afraid of them. And they could never look inside me and see a whole world of tenderness or leave me alone because I was so sad and suffering. Why did you do it. And hearts. And why was love so round. (119–20)

The outer chaos of action and the inner sadness of thought are blended here into a Chaplinesque image. (Gerald Brenan in *The Literature of the Spanish People* describes Guzmán de Alfarache [*Guzmán de Alfarache*, q.v.] as "Charlie Chaplin viewed by a sixteenth-century Calvinist minister.") As his last name suggests, Dangerfield lives in a landscape that is constantly setting traps for him, a recurring escape from and running to in a field of danger. The social continuum, represented most strongly by Skully and Marion, victimizes him, as Sebastian was martyred.

At other times and from other perspectives, he is a danger to that landscape, as he enacts his trickster (q.v.) function. His epithet, too, enlarges the mixture of images: *ginger* is pungent, spicy, and by extension has the meaning of "piquant" or "animated." Yet *gingerly* suggests extreme caution, hesitation. And he is a wild, fantastic gingerbread man cavorting across the landscape. (The gingerbread man comes from a tale with roots in Norwegian, Danish, German, Lithuanian, and Russian folklore; in the end, he is eaten by the fox.)

Donleavy's fiction has been called "comic anarchy," an attitude and response toward life that Dangerfield embodies because "he chooses isolation as a life-style, denies all authority, and uses laughter as his strategic response to the chaos of the external world" (Sherman, 216). Conversely, Dangerfield has been interpreted as the hostile figure in an otherwise neutral world: "It is he who is hostile, not society. . . . [He] is an imbalanced hero, carried along by the doubling and oscillating fantasies of his life which constitute his status as an outsider even to himself" (Sieber, 71–72). This composite Charlie Chaplin, Hermes (q.v.), and Dionysus (and we should remember that Hermes helped at Dionysus's birth) constantly changes shape, an almost primeval force in the straitlaced world he alternately smacks on its behind and shyly retreats from.

Narratively, the normal "I" perspective of the picaresque shifts shape as well through Donleavy's use of randomly alternating first- and third-person points of view, like Grass's technique in *The Tin Drum* (q.v.). The picaro's "I" is a stabilizing perspective, projected backward from the present over the instabilities of the episodic past. But Dangerfield's narrative reflects the instability of his personality, as well as of the world around him. Moreover, he narrates simultaneously with the action; there is no temporal narrative distance. The effect, as in Gulley Jimson's similar compression of temporal distance (*The Horse's Mouth*, q.v.), is one of immediacy as Sebastian Dangerfield renders his experiences with rapidly gathered sentence fragments, phrases, words, abrupt shifts of thought, sensation, or perception. (There is even a remarkable similarity of incident, as when Gulley tells Nosy he himself is not there [ch. 6] and when Dangerfield denies his existence to Skully [ch. 14].) The rapid shifts in I-He narration resemble lens changes, from close-up to telescopic and back again, a technique that one moment allows us to be inside Dangerfield looking out and at another moment allows us to be outside Dangerfield looking at. Dangerfield's volatility is such that purely "I" narration—with its one-to-one correspondence between the narrative act and the action narrated—could become incoherent in its subjectivity. In his trickster function, he is almost preconscious; he acts—and thinks later. And even then his thoughts, in their kaleidoscopic whirl, seem like actions. The "He" narration keeps him anchored as object by distancing us emotionally and psychologically. And it lets us see that the hostile landscape he inhabits is not his own projection. In this landscape he is at the end "a straight dark figure and stranger" (347) who, like Knulp (*Knulp*, q.v.), needs divine sanction:

> God's mercy
> On the wild
> Ginger Man.

EDITIONS

Page references are to the Penguin Books edition (New York, 1968). Other editions are New York: Berkley Medallion, 1959; New York: Dell, 1973 (Laurel edition), and a Delta edition (n.d.).

SELECT BIBLIOGRAPHY

Dean Cohen, "The Evolution of Donleavy's Hero," *Critique: Studies in Modern Fiction* 12 (1971): 95–109; William David Sherman, "J. P. Donleavy: Anarchic Man as Dying Dionysian," *Twentieth Century Literature* 13 (1968): 216–28; Harry Sieber, *The Picaresque* (London: Methuen, 1977), 70–73.

GOING PLACES

(*Les Valseuses*, 1974)

Directed by Bertrand Blier

This film, written by Blier with Philippe Dumarcay and based on Blier's novel of the same title (a slang term for testicles, roughly equivalent to "balls"), is one of the few movies that should be called picaresque (the term is as ubiquitous among film critics as it is among book reviewers, and just as often loosely used). When it was released in the United States, it caused something of a sensation and a few years later was even yanked from showing on cable television. It was called "sordid," "disgusting," and "a grotesque exercise in sadism." One reviewer claimed to have felt "molested" by it.

And yet the film had its defenders. "This careening picaresque French film" is "one of the most mordant satires ever made about rebellious youth" (Schjeldahl). "Blier writes psychological picaresques," wrote Pauline Kael, "he begins with a group of characters and a certain tone, and then he may veer off and go wherever his subconscious takes him." The disturbing effect of the film is explained, if not lessened, by recognizing its picaresque nature. Like the vision it renders, picaresque narrative as a fictional mode has always had to contend with a disreputable literary reputation, a ranking as low in the literary hierarchy as its vision from below and from outside.

Going Places portrays two young men, Jean-Claude and Pierrot, on the road, going everywhere and yet nowhere, from one end of France to the other. Along the way they rob, rape, terrorize, and destroy. At the beginning of the film, they pay an innocent young mother on a train some money to suckle her breast; momentarily terrorized, she lets them, emerging from the encounter with a satisfied smile on her face. At the end, they are on the road with another innocent—a young teenage girl whom they have liberated sexually, socially, and physically from her straitlaced, stultifying parents. Most of their antisocial, indeed criminal, activities seem to give their victims pleasure. In their gratification of others' not always conscious needs, they function as trickster figures (q.v.). Their often infantile behavior, their obsession with sex, even their bisexuality, emphasize their reinvigorating function in a dead landscape. Their crude energy is almost like a natural force, one that they apparently cannot help expending. If they are yearning for anything, that object is symbolized by the tunnel they are entering at the end, which, like their Priapian hunger for sex, suggests the desire to return to the womb, a variation on the picaro's yearning for home.

Our uneasiness with the film comes from not separating the moral vision of the film from the apparent moral vision in the film, a disturbing confusion that results directly from the film medium's inability to narrate in the first person (except intermittently). The moral dimension that the retrospective narrating picaro makes overt is in this film indirectly conveyed. The film's rhetoric does not ask us to admire these two men; it asks us to acknowledge them as necessary forces in revitalizing a dying and deadening society. In such a rigidly ordered world, these two picaros have to stir up disorder. In chaos they thrive, and in their thriving, others find a kind of fulfillment.

SELECT BIBLIOGRAPHY

Vincent Canby, review, *The New York Times*, May 14, 1974, 31; Pauline Kael, "Bertrand Blier," *The New Yorker*, October 16, 1978, 96–109; Peter Schjeldahl, "Why Does the French Film *Going Places* Infuriate So Many of Its Critics?" *The New York Times*, June 2, 1974, B:11.

THE GOLDEN ASS

(second century A.D.)

Lucius Apuleius

Actually titled *Metamorphoses* but popularized as *The Golden Ass*, this has been called the "sole Latin novel that survives entire," and it, along with *The Satyricon* (q.v.), is considered a precursor of picaresque narrative. Chandler, while pointing out that the main character, Lucius, is no rogue but rather the victim of unhappy chance and his own curiosity, maintains that Apuleius's work "bore a closer analogy to the picaro and his vicissitudes than any other classical type" (*Romances*, 4). Not only were many of its incidents incorporated into the Spanish and subsequent picaresque fictions, *The Golden Ass* provided the essential form of picaresque narrative: "The essential idea of describing society through the narrative of one in servitude whose passage from master to master should afford opportunities for observation and satire" (4–5). Moreover, Apuleius's fiction "receives honorable mention" in the course of most of the Spanish novels, "and the *Pícara Justina* [q.v.] expressly proposes it among others as a pattern" (*Romances*, 5). In a 1619 French translation of *Guzmán de Alfarache* (q.v.), Jean Chapelain calls Alemán's work "une satyre bien formée sur les pas de Luciá et d'Apulee en leur Asne d'or" ("it is believed that Apuleius, like his contemporary Lucian, who wrote a satire called *Lucius, or, The Ass*, drew from a common source, a story by Lucius of Patrae, now lost").

The Golden Ass was translated and reprinted several times during the early sixteenth century, and its relative popularity, along with that of the *The Satyricon*, makes direct influence very likely, especially in the comic and satiric uses of the pseudo-autobiographical perspective. Apuleius's work had been translated into German around 1480 and was translated into French and English during the middle of the sixteenth century. Chandler's assessment, which gives little recognition to the subject matter, tone, and characterization of the central character, survives to our own day: "What happens to Lucius when he is turned into an ass is implausible; what happens to Lazarillo is something of which psychological analysis might take account" (Blackburn, 28).

And yet a closer look at Apuleius's narrative warrants a more considered judgment. Its narrative stance is not unlike Lazarillo's (*Lazarillo de Tormes*, q.v.). "*Lector, intende; laetaberis,*" begins Lucius: "Gentle reader, if thou attend and give ear, thou shalt be well contented withal." Like Lazarillo, Apuleius's narrator apologizes for his lack of polish: "I first crave and beg your pardon, lest I should happen to displease or offend any of you by the rude and rustic utterance of this strange and foreign language," his first language being Greek. Lazarillo, too, apologizes for his "childish little story" and hopes readers will enjoy it even "if it *is* written in a crude way." Throughout his account, Lazarillo interjects beg-your-pardons for the low-life material he is presenting. In his self-awareness, too, the narrator of *The Golden Ass* echoes the outsiderdom felt by Lazarillo and other picaros: "My evil fortune, which was ever so cruel against me, whom I, by travel of so many countries, could in no wise escape nor appease the envy thereof by all the woes I had undergone, did more and more cast its blind and evil eyes upon me, with invention and new means to afflict my poor body, in giving me another master very fit for my hard fate" (ch. 36). Unidentified, this passage could easily have come from Lazarillo or Guzmán or Simplicius (*Simplicius Simplicissimus*, q.v.). Apuleius's narrator is also self-conscious about the narrative situation and plays with its inherent narrative distance: "But peradventure some scrupulous reader may demand me a question, how I, being an ass, and tied always within the walls of the millhouse, could be so clever as to know the secrets of these women: learn then, I answer, notwithstanding my shape of an ass, yet having the sense and knowledge of a man, how I did curiously find out and know out such injuries as were done to my master" (ch. 41).

Like other picaresques, *The Golden Ass* contains within itself both an explicit and an implicit romance. The famous story of Cupid and Psyche is interpolated in much the same way—and with similar thematic juxtaposing—as the Mummelsee episode in *Simplicissimus* and the story of Daraxa and Ozmin in *Guzmán de Alfarache*. And the implicit romance of the picaresque, the yearning for a spiritual "home" often achieved by a religious conversion, finds expression in *The Golden Ass* through the narrator's conversion at the end, when he becomes a priest and executes "mine office in great joy" (ch. 48).

TRANSLATION

William Adlington [1556], *Lucius Apuleius: The Golden Ass*, ed. Harry C. Schnur (New York: Collier, 1962). In his introduction, Schnur calls it "a picaresque novel, the same genre as the only other Latin novel we have (and that one, unfortunately, only a torso), the much more original and rightly celebrated *Satyricon*" (9).

SELECT BIBLIOGRAPHY

Angelo Armendariz, "Petronius and Apuleius in the Spanish Picaresque Novel," *Fu Jen Studies* (Republic of China) 3 (1970): 37–61; Alexander Blackburn, *The Myth of the Picaro: Continuity and Transformation of the Picaresque Novel, 1554–1954* (Chapel Hill: University of North Carolina Press, 1979); Fernando Lázaro Carreter, *"Lazarillo de Tormes" en la picaresca* (Barcelona: Ariel, 1972); Frank Wadleigh Chandler, *Romances of Roguery* [1899] (New York: Burt Franklin, 1961); Jean Molino, "Lazarillo de Tormes et les Métamorphoses d'Apulée," *Bulletin hispanique* 67 (1965): 332–33; A. Scobie, "Petronius, Apuleius, and the Spanish Picaresque Romances," in *Words: Wai-Te-Ata Studies in Literature*, ed. P. T. Hoffmann, D. F. McKenzie, and Peter Robb (Wellington, New Zealand: Wai-Te-Ata Press, 1966), 92–100; P. G. Walsh, " 'Nachleben': The Roman Novel and the Rebirth of the Picaresque," in his *The Roman Novel: The "Satyricon" of Petronius and the "Metamorphoses" of Apuleius* (Cambridge: Cambridge University Press, 1970), 224–43.

GUZMAN DE ALFARACHE

(*Primera parte de Guzmán de Alfarache*, 1599; *Segunda parte de la vida de Guzmán de Alfarache, atalaya de la vida humana, por Mateo Alemán, su verdadero autor*, 1604)

Mateo Alemán

"What workes can ye instance in, that in so short a time, have had so many Impressions?" asks Luis de Valdés in a dedicatory eulogy to Part Two, claiming to know about twenty-six printings totaling more than 50,000 copies of Part One during the five years between its publication and the appearance of the authentic sequel he is here introducing. That it went through sixteen of these reprintings during the two years immediately after publication is evidence of an extraordinary success. Yet Alemán profited little; most of the editions were pirated ones. Capitalizing on this unprecedented popularity, a man identified by Alemán as Juan Martí in 1602 had produced an apocryphal continuation under the pseudonym Mateo Luján de Saavedra; it saw four editions in its first year and ten the next, most of these pirated as well. So widely known had the first part become, not only in Spain but also in Italy, France, Flanders, and Germany, that Valdés "never heard his [Alemán's] name mentioned, but with the addition of some honourable Epithite, even to the giving of him this noble Attribute, *El español divino*, The divine Spaniard" (Pt. Two, Elogio; Mabbe, vol. III, p. 10).

Guzmán de Alfarache had been immediately translated into French in 1600, followed by an Italian translation six years later. In 1615 Albertinus rendered it into German, providing Grimmelshausen with the prototype for *Simplicius Simplicissimus* (q.v.). *Guzmán* was a genuine blockbuster of its day, a European best-seller whose instant popularity surpassed even that which *Don Quixote* (1605, 1615) would soon have. Alemán's work quickly became known familiarly as simply *El pícaro*. This near-antonomasia is directly alluded to by Cervantes in "The Illustrious Kitchen-Maid" (q.v.) when Carriazo is described as one who "fared so well with the occupation of a *pícaro* that he could have lectured from a chair in the faculty to the famous Alfarache" (34). But Alemán through Guzmán lamented this synonymousness of his character with the type and insisted on emphasizing the reflective dimension of his work. Aware of the popularity of his first part, Guzmán in an aside in the sixth chapter of the first book of Part Two sees this generic expansion of his individuality as in fact a humiliating reduction of self, yet another misfortune in his life:

Let him indure the title of a badde name, that desires to have it dye quickly. For, with the more violence wee seeke to shake it off, so much the closer it cleaveth unto us. Insomuch, that it continueth many times to the fifth generation; and then those, which succeed them, doe glory and boast themselves thereof, and blazon that for their Armes, which their Ancestors held for an affront. The like hath befalne this my poor booke, which I having intituled with the name of *Atalaya de la vida humana*, The Watch-Tower of mans life, they have put the nickname of *Picaro* thereupon, and now it is knowne by no other name.

Although Alemán seems to have referred to his work as the *atalaya de la vida humana*, he did not explicitly make "the watchtower of human life" part of the title until Part Two.

The epithet was so well established by the time James Mabbe began to translate the work into English in 1622 that he simply titled his rendering *The Rogue*. The encomiastic verses to the translator in Part Two make clear, however, that the morally reflective part of Guzmán's character was significant and that he was indeed to be read as a symbolic "watchtower on human life," though Mabbe chose not to use that phrase in his English title. One such verse, by Edward Burton, reads in part:

> Would any man see Proteus? Would hee see
> Proteus againe, and say; That this is hee?
> Or see the Moone? And when she waxes light,
> Know her to be the same, at second sight?
> In this same Optick-Art, who strives to thrive,
> Let him use Guzman as a Perspective.
> Guzman is all the World; know him alone,
> And then yee know a Multitude in One.
> (III, 19)

Another, signed only "E. B.," praises Mabbe's version in the larger context of Guzmán's universality:

Loe, what Art hath done.
Here the Reflection's brighter then the Sunne.
One Language is too narrow to containe
The boundlesse-rascall-froath of Guzmans braine.

(III, 18)

Other "reflections" continued in the wake of its initial success. In 1615, the second part had been translated into Italian (the version from which Mabbe seems to have translated), and in 1619 it had been retranslated into French as *Le Gueux, ou la Vie de Guzman d'Alfarache. Image de la vie humaine*, which by 1689 went through ten editions. Even a Latin version, also emphasizing Alemán's watchtower image and adding a character named Lazarillo de Tormes (*Lazarillo de Tormes*, q.v.), appeared in 1623, 1624, and 1652 as *Vitae humanae proscenium*. Two Dutch translations came out in 1655. Another French translation, by Brémond, was published in Amsterdam (and later in Paris) in 1695. In 1732, Lesage produced the fourth French translation, which in its subtitle reads *"purgée des moralités superflues."* As late as the nineteenth century, *Guzmán* was still being translated—into Hungarian in 1822–1824 and into Portuguese in 1848. Chandler sums up the impact *Guzmán* had: "No other Spanish picaresque novel ever attained the same general celebrity or exercised so broad an influence as this one" (233).

But in the eighteenth century, this reflection "brighter then the Sunne" was eventually eclipsed, not only by *Don Quixote* but by the radically distorted image of *Guzmán de Alfarache* transmitted through Lesage's translation-expurgation and by his own *Gil Blas* (q.v.). Writing on Defoe in 1827, Sir Walter Scott looked down his nose at the Spanish picaresque fictions as a "coarse species of amusement" unsuitable for most readers (*Moll Flanders*, q.v.), while in another essay five years earlier, he had praised Lesage's *Gil Blas* as a product of human genius. In 1898 Henry Butler Clarke considered Guzmán's morally reflective narrating stance a flaw: "This spoils the book from an artistic point of view, and Guzmán is at times little better than a weakling and a sneak. Only here and there does the author slacken his moral rein and give himself up to the genuine fun of his subject" (329). Even Chandler, writing a year later, gets irritated: "In style, Alemán had been so discursive as to try the patience of the most indulgent reader, and his moralizings unnecessary and out of place" (222). This dichotomizing of Alemán's narrative method has, until relatively recently, been a major obstacle to full consideration of Alemán's original text. Lesage's severely excised version supplanted Mabbe's in England for almost two centuries; even in Spain itself, as McGrady and Dunn point out, shortened editions were produced. A dominant attitude among nineteenth-century critics was that Alemán's moralizing passages were created to prevent the censure and censorship that had befallen *Lazarillo de Tormes*. Thus, even when Alemán's full text was studied, its moral and religious dimensions were not taken seriously. This was an unfortunate literary fate for a work whose stupendous international success revived interest in *Lazarillo* and probably did more to hasten the demise of books of chivalry than did *Don Quixote*. From the beginning of the eighteenth century until the middle of the twentieth, Alemán's true text was little known and even less read outside of Spain.

This mutation in the history of literary genetics has more than anything else been responsible for the muddle in defining the picaresque. Among those who have sought to restore *Guzmán de Alfarache* to its rightful place in a European context, the most assertive is A. A. Parker, whose *Literature and the Delinquent* seeks not only to refocus *Guzmán de Alfarache* as the prototype of picaresque fictions but also to provide a new perspective on the entire picaresque tradition in the context of emerging European realism and the development of the modern novel. The accomplishments of the two major picaresques, *Guzmán* and *El Buscón* (q.v.), Parker says, "cannot rightly be excluded from the history of the conquest of reality in European literature" (27); accordingly, "the history of the modern European novel should be rewritten with a truer perspective" (137). Subsequent studies in comparative contexts by Miller, Bjornson, Sieber, Blackburn, Riggan, and others have helped bring the significance of *Guzmán* into the perspective Parker calls for, as well as clarifying for a wider, non-Hispanist readership a more accurate conception of picaresque narrative than one based on eighteenth-century English and French models. *Guzmán de Alfarache* is, from almost every narrative characteristic we choose to look at, a paradigmatic picaresque. There is universal agreement among Hispanists that it is the prototypical picaresque; some even consider it as great a narrative achievement as *Don Quixote*. No truly accurate concept of the picaresque could fail to take it into account, yet many do not, inadvertently perpetuating the most serious distortion about the nature of picaresque narrative.

Like Lazarillo, Guzmán writes to justify himself, and he shares Lazarillo's less than reputable birth, thus exemplifying the picaresque motif of unusual birth or childhood. In telling of his sordid origins, Guzmán, like Oskar Matzerath (*The Tin Drum*, q.v.), enters into prenatal details; he also, like Oskar, claims to have two fathers because he cannot be absolutely certain given his mother's promiscuity: "For it were great indiscretion and unadvisednesse in me, to affirme, which of these two did beget mee, or whether I were the sonne of a third" (One, I, 2; I, 84). His father Alfarache is a usurer, swindler, womanizer, *converso*, and possibly homosexual; his mother, daughter of a whore, is almost a common prostitute herself. Not only does this inherited depravity prefigure the kind of world he will grow up into, it also symbolizes the sinful condition of all fallen humanity. Like Simplicius, whose paradisiacal childhood forest is repeatedly ravaged by the war, and like Ellison's picaro (*Invisible Man*, q.v.) whose edenic college campus erupts into the disorder that starts him running, Guzmán sees in his individual existence a specific recapitulation of the collective misery of the human race. He describes his father's home—and the place of his conception—as a "Paradise upon earth" (One, I, 2; I, 69), but it is also the birthplace of sin and corruption:

All whatsoever, either hath bin, is, or shall be, is still one and the self-same thing. Our first Father was credulous and light of beliefe; our first mother a Lyer, and false of her word; The first sonne that was borne into the world, a thiefe and a Fratricide, one that killed his owne and only brother. (One, III, 1; II, 130).

Guzmán's tainted stock is an individual instance of the original sin of the entire race, just as war represents in *Simplicissimus* a fallen humanity that has lost its way. In *Guzmán*, "there is all the time a non-narrative background against which much of the realism of the narrative can take on symbolic value," with Guzmán's wanderings in the world becoming "symbolical of mankind's spiritual odyssey" (Parker, 40).

Ejecting himself from home, Guzmán faces a hostile world, which immediately jolts him into awareness of the *solo soy* condition Lazarillo soon discovered. As he leaves the city gate, "two great Rivers (like an over-flowing Nilus) did breake out from forth mine eyes, watring my face in great abundance, till it was bathed all over with teares. What with this, and the nights comming on (for it grew darke) I could not discerne any light of heaven; nor perceive so much as a hands-breadth of earth as I went along" (One, I, 3; I, 93–94). This all-important moment in picaresque narrative is here rendered through an image of radical solitude: he is simultaneously estranged from his roots in the earth (the home he comes from) and as yet alienated from the lights of heaven (the home toward which he is heading). This suspension between two havens—one in which he could not stay and another he cannot get to—is the picaro's essential condition in the world. Very real pangs of hunger soon intrude on this solitude, reminding the picaro of the nature of this condition, in which the basic survival needs of food, shelter, and clothing become matters of life and death. ("It is good," he will later say, "to have a father, it is good to have a mother; but to have meat to put in a mans mouth, is better then them both" [One, II, 1; I, 235].) He is sitting, significantly, on the steps leading to San Lázaro when his empty stomach prompts another image of his condition: "I found my selfe betwixt feares and hopes; a steepe downefall before mine eyes, and ravening Wolves ready to devoure me at my backe. My thoughts began as fast to waver, as my feet did to wander: at length I was willing to put my selfe into God's hands" (I, 95). Here he sees himself as food for other creatures, which expands Javier Garriga's nineteenth-century appellation of the picaresque as the "epic of hunger" to take on a double meaning: the picaro is as much being consumed by the world as he is going hungry in it.

But the wavering thoughts try to stay in tune with the wandering feet, and Guzmán adapts himself to his momentary adversity by going to sleep on the steps of a church. Devouring and being devoured come to be but one of many synonymous images to express the conditions of the picaro's journey between homes. Another is the sheer size of the world and its plenitude of misfortune. "Good God, who would thinke, that the world were so large and so long as it is? I had scene it in some Maps, and me thought it was all plaine and smooth, and huddled (as it seemed there to be) all together, without any great either difference, or distance. I did not imagine, there could have been so many troubles, and so many miseries in it'' (One, I, 7; I, 154). This first perception of the immensity of the world's chaos is a shocking initiation into the world of discontinuity, and it is incorporated into the larger cosmic frame of reference by being almost immediately followed by yet another edenic allusion: ''But I did like a simple Youth, (as I was) having neither wit nor government in me; and therefore I was justly punished, for that living so at ease as I did; and being as it were in Paradise, I would goe abroad into the world; and like my first forefathers, could not see when I was well'' (I, 155).

As it portrays an often starving outsider in a predatory world, picaresque fiction becomes an epic of hunger in a third sense: Guzmán is spiritually hungry. That hunger is eventually satisfied, first by the conversion he undergoes, and second, by his act of narrating. From the perspective of his postconversion remembering self, he can articulate in a more discursive way what he claims to have felt and sensed in rudimentary ways as his younger experiencing self. The lack of spiritual sustenance slowly emerges into consciousness and conscience until the conversion. Its development is caused by Guzmán's increasing awareness of earthly vanities (then felt, now analyzed), which becomes in the narrating process the controlling theme of his *vida* (both as lived and as now reperceived). ''Vanity of Vanities,'' he writes, ''and nothing but Vanity'' (One, II, 4; II, 16). This is the quintessential baroque theme, which will also control *Simplicissimus*; as such, it is very much of its period and its Counter-Reformational concerns. But in a secularized form, it transcends its time and becomes, in different shapes and variations, the dominant theme of all picaresque.

For Guzmán, the world is a tricky place; it is out to get the picaro in many different ways. At times Guzmán focuses on its predatory nature:

All goes topsie-turvy; all Kim, Kam; all, is tricks and devices; all Riddles and unknowne Mysteries; you shall not finde man, with man; we all live in ambush, lying in wait one for another, as the Cat, for the Mouse, or the Spider for the Fly; who roming carelessly up and downe, suffers her selfe to be taken by a slender thread, whilest that venemous vermine, seazing on her head, holds her fast, never leaving her, till shee hath kill'd her with her poison. (One, II, 4; 19–20)

In an image that will literally as well as metaphorically reflect the actual situations of Simplicissimus and a number of twentieth-century picaros, Guzmán sees the world in a constant state of war:

Mans life is a warre-fare upon earth, there is no certainty therein; so settled assurance, no estate that is permanent; no pleasure that is perfect; no content that is true; but all is counterfeit and vaine. (One, I, 7; I, 147)

Three and a half centuries later, the grandfather of the picaro in Ellison's *Invisible Man* will echo these words precisely.

The constant inconstancy (to adapt a phrase that Simplicius will use) of this world is condensed in the image of fickle fortune, who is

brittle, unstable, restlesse, *Tanquam Figura sphaerica in corporo plano*; like a Sphericall Figure, in a plaine body. That, which she gives to day, she takes away to morrow: she is the flowing of the Sea, tossing and tumbling us to and fro, till she leave us at last upon drie land, on Deaths shore, from which she never returnes to recover us; And while we live, injoyning us (like Players) to con over our parts, and to learne daily new toyes and devices, to present them upon the stage of this World. (One, II, 7; II, 61–62)

Picaresque life requires a constant change of masks on the world-as-stage presided over by fortune's flux.

Guzmán's condition in the world and his vision of the world are merged into a striking image that reflects the essential thematic and structural characteristics of all picaresque. After years of study, about to receive his degree, Guzmán abandons everything for what he calls the disease of love:

And being come now to the height of all my labours and paines-taking, and when I was to have received the reward of them, and to take mine ease after all this toyle, the stone rolled downe, and I was forced like Sisiphus, to beginne the world anew, and to fall afresh to my worke. (Two, III, 4; IV, 220)

Although Camus has, for the time being, appropriated the figure of Sisyphus (q.v.) into the context of the absurd, it has always had universal appeal as an expression of the human condition. It is particularly appropriate to the picaresque because it exemplifies both the life rhythm and the narrative rhythm of picaresque fictions: "to beginne the world anew" and to "fall afresh" to the task of survival in the landscape of the discontinuous is the picaro's inescapable situation in life, and it is expressed in a narrative structure that is episodic and Sisyphus-like in its rhythm. For Guzmán, this rhythm is monotonously repetitive until the moment of conversion, when it becomes cumulative and resolves itself into a harmony in which both the life and the narration of it soon come to an end:

And as I was thinking and considering on these things, I said one night with my selfe; Guzman, thou seest heere the top of that Mountain of miseries, where-unto thy filthy sensualitie hath brought thee: now art thou come to the highest part of it, and must either make a speedy leape downe to the bottomlesse pit of hell, or which thou mayst more easily doe, by lifting up thy armes, take hold on Heaven. (Two, III, 8; IV, 327–28)

"Returne home unto thy selfe," he tells himself shortly after, and next morning he awakes to find "my selfe another manner of man then I was before" (IV, 329). When this is happening to him, he is, significantly, serving a sentence as a galley slave, a punishment that in the repetitiveness of the forced task resembles in essence the eternal punishment of Sisyphus.

Guzmán's conversion is the culmination of his life as picaro and the genesis of his existence as narrator. As a key moment, simultaneously justifying and engendering the narrative, it has drawn a great deal of attention. The result has been a continuing critical debate rooted in that unavoidable contradiction of picaresque fictions: the apparent irreconcilability between their moralizing aim and the relish with which they portray the seamy side of existence. In *Guzmán de Alfarache*, after the attempts to do away with the moralizing dimension altogether, this debate has focused specifically on its accuracy in portraying

Counter-Reformational orthodoxy and on the sincerity of that portrayed stance. Enrique Moreno Báez started off the debate, and many other critics have pursued it (Parker summarizes it well in his book). But Dunn points out that it is as much of a mistake to focus exclusively on the moral dimensions of the work as it is to ignore them completely: "The vision of the world which the book contains is, then, no less important artistically than the destiny of Guzmán and his displacement of success by the chance of salvation. If the world is a battleground or an arena and if, as Guzmán continually reminds us, we are in his shoes, then whatever we learn from his picaresque life is as important as what we learn from his chastened words. Each serves the other" (56).

What is even more important, however, is to recognize that each exists only through the other and that mechanically separating them—either by expurgation or by labeling them "digressions"—violates the work. The degree of Alemán's doctrinal orthodoxy and the (still not absolutely proved) supposition that he was writing as an outsider who wanted to be in because his ancestry was Jewish both matter, certainly, in all sorts of period contexts and considerations. But accusations against Guzmán's sincerity do not automatically impugn Alemán's, since the depiction of an unreliable narrator is hardly an act of insincerity on the part of the author; the picaro is in fact much more likely than most other narrators to be untrustworthy at times, as *Lazarillo, Moll Flanders* (q.v.), and *Barry Lyndon* (q.v.), for example, demonstrate disturbingly well. What is crucial for understanding the nature of picaresque narrative—and for which *Guzmán* much more than *Lazarillo* is the paradigm—is narration itself as such.

From Guzmán's first words in the first chapter of the first book of the first part, we are in the hands of a controlling narrator who knows exactly what he is doing:

Curious Reader, The desire which I had to recount my life unto thee, made me make great haste to ingulfe my selfe therein, without first preparing some things fit to be related, which (serving as an induction and entrance to the matter) had beene very needfull for the better informing of thy understanding: (for beeing essentiall to this Discourse) they would likewise have given thee no small content. But through too much haste, I forgat to shut the doore after mee, and so unawares have left a way of entrance open, for every wrangling Sophister, and smatterer in Logicke, to taxe me of ignorance, and to lay it as a fault o my charge, that I did not proceed *a definitione ad definitum*, from the definition to the thing defined. (I, 37–38)

His eager desire to get going establishes some intimacy with us; his candor in revealing himself to be an amateur gains our sympathy; and his anticipated vulnerability to the critics makes us feel protective (and perhaps a bit superior). What begins as an overt confession of Guzmán's narrating inadequacy shrewdly becomes a covert bond that establishes narrative credibility. It is a narrative confidence trick fundamental to picaresque narration.

At the beginning of Part Two, his desire becomes the reader's:

I am now imbark't, I have set foot a Ship-boord, and I cannot goe backe. The Dice are throwne; my promise is past, and I cannot recall it. I have begun, and I must goe on.

The Subject is meane and base; the beginning small; But that which I intend to treat of, if like the Oxe, thou wilt ruminate thereupon, and chew the Cud, suffring it to passe from thy stomacke to thy mouth, it may prove important, grave, and great. I will doe all that I can to satisfie thy desire; knowing, that I should have rather given thee trouble, then content, in unfolding one part of my life, and hyding the other from thee. (III, 28–29)

Throughout the telling, Guzmán sustains our narrative confidence by recurrently expressing his desire to be listened to. In Part Two, he assumes the reader's desire to listen (the success of the first part being built, as it is in *Don Quixote*, into the narrative of the second). His final words are, "And heere (gentle Reader) doe I put a full point to these my mis-fortunes. I have given thee a large account of my lewd life; it is truly summ'd up unto thee," followed by a promise of a third part (which Alemán never wrote). The narrative strategies of hesitation that opened the story have long since been replaced by a more authoritative stance; they were used to establish the narrative confidence necessary for gratifying both Guzmán's and the reader's desires.

The picaro's quest for home takes the form of striving for material and social success in *Lazarillo*; achieving social integration and respectability in *El Buscón*; and attaining spiritual union with God in *Simplicissimus* and *Guzmán de Alfarache*. But it also often takes the form of verbal recreation of the self through the narrative act. *Guzmán*, even more than *Simplicissimus*, is the exemplary text for this in the picaresque narrative tradition. It might be said in literary terminology that the picaro's essential condition is to be suspended between two romances: an edenic world of pure harmony and a wished-for paradise regained. The impulse to shape his life in words reflects the picaro's yearning for a home; the actual narrating process allows him to impose aesthetic and moral order on the chaotic past, which can now be re-membered as a structure, a home of sorts. What justifies Guzmán's *vida* may well be its overt moral usefulness. But what satisfies him in the telling of it is the form-completion it brings to life. After the conversion—during which he tells himself, "Returne home unto thy selfe" (Mabbe's embellishment of Alemán's simple *vuelve*)—and before the exchange of "this transitorie [life], for one that is eternall" (*antes de la eterna que todos esperamos*, as he says at the very end)—the only attainable home is the one achieved through verbal creation.

TRANSLATION

The only English translation is James Mabbe's *The Rogue, or The Life of Guzman de Alfarache* [1622] (London: Constable & Co., 1924; rpt. New York: AMS Press, 1967), 4 vols. (Tudor Translations, Second Series, vols. 2–5), with an informative introduction (1923) by James Fitzmaurice-Kelly. Citations are by part, book, and chapter, followed by the volume and page numbers of the AMS edition.

SELECT BIBLIOGRAPHY

Victorio G. Agüera, "La salvación del cristiano nuevo en *Guzmán de Alfarache*," *Hispania* 66 (1974): 23–30; Joan Arias, *Guzmán de Alfarache: The Unrepentant Narrator*

(London: Tamesis, 1977); Richard Bjornson, *The Picaresque Hero in European Fiction* (Madison: University of Wisconsin Press, 1977); Alexander Blackburn, *The Myth of the Picaro: Continuity and Transformation of the Picaresque Novel, 1554–1954* (Chapel Hill: University of North Carolina Press, 1979); Gerald Brenan, *The Literature of the Spanish People: From Roman Times to the Present* [1951] (Cleveland and New York: World, 1957); Michel Cavillac, *Gueux et marchands dans le "Guzmán de Alfarache" (1599–1604): Roman picaresque et mentalité bourgeoise dans l'Espagne du Siècle d'Or* (Bordeaux: Institut d' études ibériques et ibéro-américaines de l'Université de Bordeaux, 1983); Frank Wadleigh Chandler, *Romances of Roguery* [1899] (New York: Burt Franklin, 1961); Henry Butler Clarke, "The Spanish Rogue-Story (Novela de Pícaros)" [1898] in *Studies in European Literature, Being the Taylorian Lectures, 1889–1899* (Oxford: Clarendon Press, 1900), 313–49; Edmond Cros, *Protée et le gueux: Recherches sur les origines et la nature du récit picaresque dans "Guzmán de Alfarache"* (Paris: Didier, 1967) and *Mateo Alemán: Introducción a su vida y a su obra* (Salamanca: Anaya, 1971); Barbara Davis, "The Style of Mateo Alemán's *Guzmán de Alfarache*," *Romantic Review* 66 (1975): 199–213; Peter N. Dunn, *The Spanish Picaresque Novel* (Boston: Twayne, 1979); Sherman Eoff, "The Picaresque Psychology of *Guzmán de Alfarache*," *Hispanic Review* 21 (1953): 107–19; C. Espinoza Rodríguez, *La novela picaresca y el Guzmán de Alfarache* (Havana: O. Echevarría, 1935); Alan Francis, *Picaresca, decadencia, historia: Aproximación a una realidad histórico-literaria* (Madrid: Gredos, 1978); Malcolm Jerome Gray, *An Index to "Guzmán de Alfarache," Including Proper Names and Notable Matters* (New Brunswick, N.J.: Rutgers University Press, 1948); B. W. Ife, *Reading and Fiction in Golden-Age Spain: A Platonist Critique and Some Picaresque Replies* (Cambridge: Cambridge University Press, 1985); Carroll B. Johnson, *Inside "Guzmán de Alfarache"* (Berkeley and Los Angeles: University of California Press, 1978); J. A. Jones, "The Duality and Complexity of *Guzmán de Alfarache*: Some Thoughts on the Structure and Interpretation of Alemán's Novel," in *Knaves and Swindlers: Essays on the Picaresque Novel in Europe*, ed. Christine J. Whitbourn (London: Oxford University Press, 1974), 25–47; Donald McGrady, *Mateo Alemán* (New York: Twayne, 1968); Alberto del Monte, *Itinerario de la novela picaresca española* [1957] (Barcelona: Lumen, 1971); Enrique Moreno Báez, *Lección y sentido del "Guzmán de Alfarache"* (Madrid: CSIC, 1948); M. N. Norval, "Original Sin and the 'Conversion' in the *Guzmán de Alfarache*," *Bulletin of Hispanic Studies* 51 (1974): 346–64; R. J. Oakley, "The Problematic Unity of *Guzmán de Alfarache*," in *Hispanic Studies in Honour of Joseph Manson*, ed. D. M. Atkinson and A. H. Clarke (Oxford: Oxford University Press, 1972), 185–206; A. A. Parker, *Literature and the Delinquent: The Picaresque Novel in Spain and Europe, 1599–1753* (Edinburgh: University Press, 1967); Helmut Petriconi, "Zur Chronologie und Verbreitung des spanischen Schelmenromans," *Volkstum und Kultur der Romanen* 1 (1928): 324–42 (also in *Pikarische Welt: Schriften zum europäischen Schelmenroman*, ed. Helmut Heidenreich [Darmstadt: Wissenschaftliche Buchgesellschaft, 1969], 61–78); R. A. del Piero, "The Picaresque Philosophy in *Guzmán de Alfarache*," *Modern Language Forum* 42 (1957): 152–56; Dale B. J. Randall, *The Golden Tapestry: A Critical Survey of Non-Chivalric Spanish Fiction in English Translation (1543–1657)* (Durham, N.C.: Duke University Press, 1963); J. V. Ricapito, "Love and Marriage in *Guzmán de Alfarache*: An Essay on Literary and Artistic Unity," *Kentucky Romance Quarterly* 15 (1968): 123–35; Francisco Rico, *The Spanish Picaresque Novel and the Point of View* [1970], trans. Charles Davis with Harry Sieber (Cambridge: Cambridge University Press, 1984); William Riggan, *Pícaros, Madmen, Naïfs, and Clowns: The Unreliable First-Person Narrator*

(Norman: University of Oklahoma Press, 1981); Carlos Antonio Rodríguez Matos, *El narrador pícaro: Guzmán de Alfarache* (Madison: Wis.: Hispanic Seminary of Medieval Studies, 1985); Bertil Romberg, *Studies in the Narrative Technique of the First-Person Novel*, trans. Michael Taylor and Harold H. Borland (Stockholm: Almqvist & Wiksell, 1962); Hans Gerd Rötzer, *Picaro—Landstörtzer—Simplicius: Studien zum niederen Roman in Spanien und Deutschland* (Darmstadt: Wissenschaftliche Buchgesellschaft, 1972); Angel San Miguel, *Sentido y estructura del "Guzmán de Alfarache" de Mateo Alemán* (Madrid: Gredos, 1971); Harry Sieber, *The Picaresque* (London: Methuen, 1977); Gonzalo Sobejano, "De la intención y valor del *Guzmán de Alfarache*," in *Estudios dedicados a Menéndez Pidal* (Madrid: CSIC, 1954), V., 283–306; Christine J. Whitbourn, "Moral Ambiguity in the Spanish Picaresque Tradition," in her *Knaves and Swindlers* (see Jones, above), 1–24; Judith A. Whitenack, *The Impenitent Confession of Guzmán de Alfarache* (Madison: Wis.: Hispanic Seminary of Medieval Studies, 1985); M. J. Woods, "The Teasing Opening of *Guzmán de Alfarache*," *Bulletin of Hispanic Studies* 57 (1980): 213–18.

HERMES MYTH

As a character, Hermes (Mercury in Roman mythology) is one of the youngest gods, though in origin he is one of the oldest and most nearly primitive. Among the etymologies that have been proposed for his name is a Greek word that conveys the idea of movement. He appears more often in the tales of mythology than any other god, and his roles are as varied as his presence is ubiquitous. He was the god of travelers, conductor of souls to the underworld, messenger of Zeus, god of commerce, god of profit (lawful and unlawful), god of games of chance, and presider over athletic contests (thus his representation in art as an athlete-god). He was above all a Trickster (q.v.) who on the day he was born displayed his mischievousness by stealing the cattle belonging to Apollo, his half-brother. Apollo found out; Hermes denied any knowledge of the theft. Zeus, to whom Apollo carried Hermes for judgment, made him give the cattle back, but not without admiring Hermes's cunning. In reconciliation, Hermes made the lyre from a tortoise shell and gave it to Apollo, who, in turn, presented Hermes with a whip or golden wand, which later became the caduceus. Apollo became the god of music, and Hermes assumed one of his many roles: protector of flocks and herds. From this point on, the two gods remained good friends. In the many stories in which he appears, Hermes is often a secondary character, darting in and out behind the scenes but with crucial functional roles. He taught Pandora to lie, had to bring Sisyphus (q.v.) forcefully back to the underworld, helped save the life of Dionysus from Hera's wrath, and fathered (with Aphrodite) Hermaphroditus. He was liked by the other gods despite his trickeries; in fact, his ingenuity made him a valued ally, especially for Zeus. In Crete, Hermes is associated with a ritual resembling the Saturnalia, in which the world is turned topsy-turvy and presided over by a mock king or lord of misrule, with masters and servants changing roles.

According to Campbell, Hermes is not only the messenger of the gods and the guide of souls to the underworld (in which role he is known as Psychopompus), he "also brings souls to be born again and so is regarded as the generator both of new lives and of the New Life." Carrying his caduceus, with its entwined serpents, he is characterized as the generative force of nature. Not only did he invent the lyre and the art of making fire, he is "the archetypal trickster god of the ancient world" (416–17). Kerényi makes a distinction between the trickster hero and the trickster god when he states that the latter always contains the former: Hermes is the "hoverer-between-worlds who dwells in a world of his own" and his staff "a symbol of those *divine* qualities which transcend mere trickery" (189). All trickster figures in specific myths are thus variations of Hermes, who contains them all; they operate in the lower world, while Hermes alone mediates between the divine and the earthly (and the underworld) yet belongs wholly to the Olympian realm.

In mainstream picaresque fiction, Hermes is often implied and sometimes explicitly alluded to. Felix Krull *(Felix Krull,* q.v.) is called Hermes by both Diane Philibert and Professor Kukuck, and to the marquis de Venosta, the only mythological figure he claims to know is Hermes: "Aside from him I know very little" (bk. III, ch. 3). And Simplicissimus *(Simplicius Simplicissimus,* q.v.), with whom Mann explicitly linked Felix, is called a Mercury (bk. V, ch. 5).

SELECT BIBLIOGRAPHY

Joseph Campbell, *The Masks of God: Primitive Mythology* [1959] (New York: Penguin, 1976); Karl Kerényi, "The Trickster in Relation to Greek Mythology," trans. R. F. C. Hull, in Paul Radin, *The Trickster: A Study in American Indian Mythology* [1956] (New York: Schocken, 1972), 171–91; Donald F. Nelson, *Portrait of the Artist as Hermes: A Study of Myth and Psychology in Thomas Mann's "Felix Krull"* (Chapel Hill: University of North Carolina Press, 1971).

HERSELF SURPRISED

(1941)

Joyce Cary

Part of a trilogy that also includes *To Be a Pilgrim* (1942) and *The Horse's Mouth* (q.v.), this story is told by Sara Monday in a style and pace similar to those of *Moll Flanders* (q.v.): "But as for my robberies, that was another thing and I still wonder at myself. For at this very time, when I was helping Mr. W. [Wilcher, who narrates *To Be a Pilgrim*] to economize, and cutting down even his own dinners, I was still cheating him. How I came into this double way of life, I cannot tell, except that I got used to my pickings" (225).

Among the men in her life is Gulley Jimson, who narrates his own and Sara's last days in *The Horse's Mouth* and who matches her roguery trick for trick. "Now I come to the time of my meeting with Gulley Jimson, who was the turning point in my downfall, and, I dare say it, the instrument of Providence, to punish my prosperity and forgetfulness" (41). From Gulley's narrative, we get the sense that Sara is a picara, and *Herself Surprised* confirms it. She is a recognizable descendant of such picaras as Moll, Justina (*La pícara Justina*, q.v.), and Courage (*The Runagate Courage*, q.v.).

The tripartite narration allows Cary to provide perspective on the same general subject matter through three different sensibilities, though the chronologies of the three narratives do not exactly coincide. Grimmelshausen provided a similar multiple view for Courage, and Defoe hinted in his preface to *Moll Flanders* that there would be two other narratives, one from the point of view of Moll's last husband, another from the perspective of her governess, but these were never written.

EDITION

New York: Harper & Brothers, 1941.

LA HIJA DE CELESTINA

(*Celestina's Daughter*, 1612)

Alonso Jerónimo de Salas Barbadillo

Republished in 1614 in a slightly expanded version called *La ingeniosa Elena* (The ingenious Helen), this work trades in title only on Fernando de Rojas's *La Celestina* (1499) and perhaps Francisco Delicado's *La lozana andaluza* (1528). Chandler thought it "possessing unusual unity" and in subject matter "a frank romance of roguery," Salas Barbadillo's "best picaresque novel" (288). Bjornson considers it representative of one type of picaresque in the wake of the popularity of *Guzmán de Alfarache* (q.v.): the picaresque adventure story, which catered "to a public fascinated by the cleverness and apparent freedom of rogues" but a public that was not willing to grant "fully dimensioned human existence . . . to vulgar characters," and so Salas Barbadillo, like Castillo Solórzano (*La niña de los embustes*, *Aventuras del bachiller Trapaza*, and *La garduña de Sevilla*, q.q.v.), portrayed his picaresque adventurers "not as tragic victims in a corrupt society, but as corrupt excrescences upon a fundamentally sane social order" (91). As a character, Elena is, except in outward trappings and behavior, far removed from Lazarillo (*Lazarillo de Tormes*, q.v.) and Guzmán—even from *La pícara Justina* (q.v.), her immediate ancestor in the picara tradition. Although the narrator comments moralistically on Elena's own moral blindness as she plays her confidence tricks, she herself gets to narrate only a small portion of the story, when she tells of her earlier life. At the end, after ruthlessly poisoning her lover, she is hanged.

Parker sees little to admire in this work's "slickness of style and technique," "pseudo-sophisticated tone," and superficial gaiety: "There is no attempt to probe delinquency, no explanation sought for the protagonist's behaviour other than the sparkle of her eyes. Her death on the gallows is only a conventional ending: there is no sense of guilt, or of tragedy, or of compassion. The work is, in short, at the very opposite pole from *Guzmán de Alfarache*, and this must be attributed directly to the influence of *La pícara Justina*" (51). Rodríguez-Luis, in his survey of the picara figures in the picaresque tradition, sees Elena as another of the frivolous picaras who "lead the picaresque novel away from the depth of characterization and philosophical preoccupation attained by Alemán's Guzmán" (34). For him, the reason is as much social as it is literary: a seventeenth-century woman with the same ambition as a picaro simply had no path toward attaining it except prostitution, which did not provide a sufficiently panoramic canvas for a full portrait of external customs and internal ruminations on the meanings of life.

Rico dismisses *La hija de Celestina* for not being genuinely picaresque. He considers the autobiographical form fundamental and essential to picaresque narrative:

Our *pícaro* (not to be confused, as we know by now, with the *pícaro* of real life) first appeared in conjunction with a certain narrative pattern, and this synthesis had the ability to organize many types of material, which had previously existed only as unconnected episodic fragments, into a unified structure. Salas Barbadillo and Carlos García [*Le desordenada codicia*, q.v.] reverse the process that led to the birth of the genre: they squeeze the original pattern down to one episode and insert it into a structure drawn from the very tradition which the very first picaresque novels were aiming to transcend. (83)

These works might be called narratives with a picaro, Rico adds, "but they run directly counter to the principles of composition which created the original design of the picaresque" (83).

Other fictions by Salas Barbadillo occasionally considered in a picaresque context but generally written off as superficial and impure narrative mixtures are *El necio bien afortunado* (1621), which was translated into English by Philip Ayres as *The Fortunate Fool* in 1670 (and reissued in 1760 as *The Lucky Idiot: or, Fools Have Fortune*), and *El sutil cordobés Pedro de Urdemalas* (1620), which Rico includes in his subcategory of "narratives with a picaro."

TRANSLATION/EDITION

The only known English version is *The Hypocrites*, translated around 1660 by John Davies of Kidwelly from the French version (*Les Hypocrites*) by Scarron, and published together with two stories (*The Innocent Adultery* and *The Fruitless Precaution*) by María de Zayas y Sotomayor. The Spanish text of *La hija de Celestina* is accessible in one of the editions of Angel Valbuena Prat's 1943 anthology, *La novela picaresca española*; in the 6th edition (Madrid: Aguilar, 1968), it is on pp. 887–919.

SELECT BIBLIOGRAPHY

Richard Bjornson, *The Picaresque Hero in European Fiction* (Madison: University of Wisconsin Press, 1977); Leonard Brownstein, *Salas Barbadillo and the New Novel of Rogues and Courtiers* (Madrid: Playor, 1974); Francisco A. Cauz, *La narrativa de Salas Barbadillo* (Santa Fe, Argentina: Ediciones Colmegna, 1977); Frank Wadleigh Chandler, *Romances of Roguery* [1899] (New York: Burt Franklin, 1961); Peter N. Dunn, *The Spanish Picaresque Novel* (Boston: Twayne, 1979); Alexander A. Parker, *Literature and the Delinquent: The Picaresque Novel in Spain and Europe, 1599–1753* (Edinburgh: University Press, 1967); Myron Peyton, *Alonso Jerónimo de Salas Barbadillo* (New York: Twayne, 1973); Edwin B. Place, "Salas Barbadillo, Satirist," *Romanic Review* 17 (1926): 230–42; Dale B. J. Randall, *The Golden Tapestry: A Critical Survey of Non-Chivalric Spanish Fiction in English Translation (1543–1657)* (Durham, N.C.: Duke University Press, 1963); Francisco Rico, *The Spanish Picaresque Novel and the Point of View* [1970], trans. Charles Davis with Harry Sieber (Cambridge: Cambridge University Press, 1984); Julio Rodríguez-Luis, "*Pícaras*: The Modal Approach to the Picaresque," *Comparative Literature* 31 (1979): 32–46; Harry Sieber, *The Picaresque* (London: Methuen, 1977).

THE HORSE'S MOUTH

(1944)

Joyce Cary

Gulley Jimson, the scruffy artist who is protagonist and narrator of this variation on picaresque, lives up to the implications of his name by being both gull and trickster in a world that is both gullible and tricky in turn. He is quite literally an obsessed artist:

> I knocked my can on the wood; respectfully.
> "No, I won't serve you any more," said Coker. "You've had enough." "But this is my birthday." "Yesterday was your birthday too, and you had too much. Every day seems to be your birthday." "Yes, every day's my birthday. Often twice a day. Due to art." "Art has a lot to answer for, all right, all right," said Bert. "Yes, and it doesn't answer. It only keeps on." "Keeps on? Keeps on what?" "Keeping on." (278)

In this quick exchange, Gulley expresses at once his constantly fresh relationship to life and the source of that relationship, art. In contrast to Felix Krull (*Felix Krull*, q.v.), for whom we might say life is fulfilled through art that heightens and deludes life, Gulley Jimson is the man for whom art comes before anything else. For Felix, art is a confidence game with life. For Gulley, life threatens to deceive and betray art. Felix is the unorthodox artist, the *actor ludens*, who uses his vision of art (however sincere and profound his view of the world as illusion prone may be) to put one over on life; he is the artist qua con man, who is audience oriented. For Gulley, on the other hand, art is the very core of his being, and life, picaresque life, is always threatening to fragment what is the only potential order and equilibrium in his chopped-up life. Gulley uses life for art's sake. Felix Krull and Gulley Jimson are mirror images of each other at opposite ends of a spectrum, the latter seeing art as being continually conceived and the former seeing it in terms of its end result. Felix overcomes the fragmentation of picaresque life through the unifying effect of his vision (though his life becomes no less episodic for all that). Gulley, in contrast, begins with art, and it is the life-chaos that threatens at every turn of his jagged life to annihilate it.

In *Felix Krull*, the romance mode, however parodistically used by Mann, imposes a kind of order on the picaresque. In *The Horse's Mouth*, the picaresque experience threatens the potential romance of art, of beauty and order. In the traditional sense, then, *The Horse's Mouth* is "more" picaresque than *Felix Krull*. Cary shows us the world-chaos tearing away at Gulley Jimson's gyroscope, his artistic creation. Alter (in *Rogue's Progress*) makes the important distinction that Felix is an elaboration on the artistic side of the rogue's personality, while Gulley is an inversion of this—an exploration of the roguish side of the artist:

If the rogue borrows from the artist something of his professional method, the artist assumes much the same peculiar social standing as the rogue. The artist—ideally, at any rate—is, like the picaresque hero, an individual of unusual worth who can never seriously hope to be properly acknowledged by society. Like the picaroon, the artist cannot be set down as an out-and-out criminal, yet the activity in which he engages remains profoundly suspect in the eyes of the respectable world. (129)

And indeed, compared to a refined picaro-aesthete like Felix, Gulley Jimson is the very essence of the rogue, the bum, the bohemian, for whom life is a free-for-all where the old picaro's toughness counts for everything: "We all know what the world is. Free for all. And the winner is the chap who gets knocked out first and comes to while the others are still asleep" (103). Unlike the extremely and exquisitely sensitive artists of the *Künstlerroman* (a tradition of which Novalis's *Heinrich von Ofterdingen*, Mann's *Tonio Kröger*, and Jens Peter Jacobsen's *Niels Lyhne* are representative), or any of the artistic heroes in literature (Goethe's Werther, Mackenzie's Man of Feeling, Mann's Aschenbach, and others), who often seem like elaborately antennaed insects about to be crushed by the world's cloddy foot, Gulley Jimson has the robust bounce-back resiliency of the traditional rogue. He lives on his Blakean vision of art, and his relationship to what he calls the "boorjay" world is based on defending his very being (art) against the world's hostility—and at the same time making some demands of his own, which he will accomplish by hook or by crook.

When his narrative opens, Gulley has just emerged from prison (not for the first time). By the time his story is over, he has been in prison again, endured a hospital stay after being beaten up, and is on the way to the hospital again when he ends his story. In between, he traverses a landscape that Cary has compressed as full of human types as any much more voluminous picaresque fiction of the past: Nosy, Coker, Sara Monday, Sir William and Lady Beeders, Mr. Plant, Mr. Hickson, Professor Alabaster—high and low, rich and poor, rogues and uprights, all of them making up a world in a small part of London that seems much more panoramic and full than the brief temporal and narrow geographical expanse of Gulley's rendered world would seem to allow. His narrative covers only about a year of his life (though there are flashbacks), and he is, as both narrator and as character, an old man. Cary makes little attempt at a memoir perspective, and as a result of the action's being almost simultaneous with the narration, the various dimensions of narrative distance are exploited.

Gulley narrates in choppy, fragmented, half-done sentences and phrases that make all action appear immediate and reflect the disorder and lack of coherence in the world, as well as the distortions of Gulley's own acts of perception. Cary's narrative style is as different from the style of *Felix Krull* as Gulley is different in his personality from Felix.

Still the incorrigible rogue at sixty-seven, with no intention of retiring from life, Gulley tricks his way through life and art. He steals, breaks windows, pawns other people's furniture, lies, deceives, and plays tricks. Society and the rules of the norm mean nothing to him, and as the world thwarts him at every turn, he tricks back.

Like Felix Krull—and here they are fundamentally alike—Gulley Jimson needs freedom, which Cary defined as "freedom to create." In order to create, which for him means to survive, Gulley needs absolute independence from the demands of society, though not from its handouts, and his life is thus a constant struggle of remaining outside society so that he can trick it out of what he needs to live. This freedom, this ability to exist both inside and outside, is typical for the picaro, and it is absolutely necessary for the artist. As a combination of both, Gulley has a particularly penetrating and satirical view of the inside, from the outside. It is his paradoxical inside-outside situation, his freedom from and yet dependence on society, his flaunting of the law and yet his running afoul of it, that define Gulley's picaresque status in life. He is free this minute and in jail or in the hospital the next. He can go on with his art one minute, and the next he is scrounging for money. His freedom to live, paradoxically, is bound by the limits of society, since society will put him away when he steps beyond its bounds. Even his freedom to create is bound by the availability of paints and canvases and other people's walls. His real freedom resides more properly in his refusal to take society, life, art—even his freedom itself—too seriously.

Toward society his attitude is cynical. He tells Nosy:

If you want to get that scholarship and go to Oxford and get into the Civil Service and be a great man and have two thousand pounds a year and a nice clean wife with hot and cold and a kid with real eyes that open and close and a garage for two cars and a savings' book, you'll have to work in your dinner-time. All the good boys around here work in their dinner-time. (5)

And the only good government for Gulley is "a bad one in the hell of a fright; yes, what you want to do with government is to put a bomb under it every ten minutes and blow its whiskers off—I mean its sub-committees" (209). His attitude toward art is similarly deprecatory. When Nosy tells him that he wants to be an artist, Gulley replies, "Everybody does once. But they get over it, thank God, like the measles and the chicken-pox. Go home and go to bed and take some hot lemonade and put on three blankets and sweat it out" (14). When Nosy insists that there "must be artists," Gulley says:

Yes, and lunatics and lepers, but why go and live in an asylum before you're sent for? If you find life a bit dull at home . . . and want to amuse yourself, put a stick of dynamite in the kitchen fire, or shoot a policeman. Volunteer for a test pilot, or drive off the Tower Bridge with five bob's worth of roman candles in each pocket. You'd get twice the fun at about one-tenth of the risk. (14)

He himself, he says, was once happy living an ordinary life as a "nice happy respectable young man" with a wife, a nice little baby, and a bank account. He had never meant to be an artist until one day "I dropped a blot on an envelope" (51). For Gulley art is like a mosquito "biting a big public behind." "If you left the world to itself," he says, "it would die of fatty degeneration in about six weeks" (207).

As a picaro who tricks society and as an artist who stings it, Gulley is suspicious of anything that comes his way. He suspects a joke—"somebody is pulling my leg"—when Alabaster proposes a book on "The Life and Works of Gulley Jimson" (105), which, a footnote tells us, was published posthumously—an editorial intrusion that adds a narrative level to Gulley's own version. This is perhaps the "big" joke: that a man who lived his art at society's expense should have his art live after he dies. When he finds an irresistible wall for his new mural, his first reaction is, "It's another joke. They're having me on. I can hear them getting ready with the big big laugh" (233). But at the same time, Gulley has fortified himself against the world by picking fruits from the tree of adversity. "My stomach," he says, "has had two kicks a day for sixty years. . . . It can take anything. And eat its own hay. And organize its own kicks. And save up a bite that will take the bloody pants off the seat of government" (105).

He is constantly on guard against the world as the world is wary of him. To take anything too seriously at first glance—a mistake in a deceptive world—is to be less than picaresque-wise. And for the world to take him seriously would be for Gulley Jimson a "joke," part of the "big big laugh." It is this comical give-and-take between Gulley and the world that allows him to live in and out of it and that allows it to let him live around it. It is, in fact, by fabricating Gulley's narrative around a succession of comical incidents in society that Cary reaches back to something essential in the picaresque tradition: to the farce and the slapstick. While *Felix Krull* is comical in a subtler way, through its clever parodies and Krull's inflated yet sincere attitude toward himself, *The Horse's Mouth* is comical in the low style of the picaresque. Stuart Miller, whose view of the picaresque is primarily existential, excludes *Felix Krull* because it is comic, and he would presumably exclude *The Horse's Mouth* as well, though to ignore the comic element in picaresque fiction is to misunderstand the essential picaresque vision. The four picaresque works whose characteristics define the essential picaresque form and worldview—*Lazarillo de Tormes*, *Guzmán de Alfarache*, *El Buscón*, and *Simplicius Simplicissimus* (q.q.v.)—are full of comic episodes, however unpalatable and gruesome the modern reader may find the baser human instincts around which such episodes revolve.

Not only is Gulley's life a series of slapstick episodes, he has a robust sense of the comic in his own attitude toward the world and himself. He can see through to the hilarity within, because he has freedom, which, as he says, "is nothing but THE INSIDE OF THE OUTSIDE" (94). It allows him to see literally what goes on under the skin and thus to picture the hilarious incongruity between what goes on there and the external appearance. When he tells a lawyer about his relationship with Sara Monday, he observes:

There was a short pause while this news filtered through the loopholes of the blockhouse to Mr. W. within. Who then stood on one leg, put his finger in his ear and gave a loud halloo, followed by uproarious and uncontrollable laughter; that is to say, he wanted to do so; but being a respectable blackcoat, he could only place his hands together, press them hard so they cracked, and remark, "Indeed. Ahem." (175–76)

Both his visualizing talent and a keen sense of humor allow him this observation, as well as another that follows a few lines later:

At this Mr. W. sprang clean through the ceiling, turned several somersaults in mid air, sang a short psalm of praise and thanksgiving out of the Song of Solomon, accompanied on the shawm, and returned through the letter-box draped in celestial light. That is to say, he raised his right toe slightly from the carpet, said "in-deed" in mi-fa, and relaxed his ceremonial smile into an expression of tolerance. "In-deed," he repeated, this time in me-do, "an impediment." (176)

In giving us this picture of what Mr. W. might really want to do, Gulley is revealing his rebellion against any and all inhibition. The observing picaro-outsider and the freely imagining artist-visualizer are cleverly combined in a style that is the verbal pantomime of the observing and imagining act it renders.

Although his art means more to Gulley than anything else, it does not mean enough to destroy his essentially comic attitude toward himself. As he can see into Mr. W., so he can see himself and his art without taking either very seriously. In fact, Gulley Jimson never finishes a painting during the period that he narrates his life, though we know he has, both from *The Horse's Mouth* and from the other two works that make up a trilogy—*Herself Surprised* (q.v.), narrated by the roguish Sara Monday, and *To Be a Pilgrim* (1942), narrated by Wilcher (Mr. W.). Like the wide-open landscape in which life is touch and go, the blank canvas is something to daub at, to start on, but not to complete with the dedication that commitment demands. "I love starting," he says, "but I don't like going on" (161). The artist's relationship to his art is much like the picaro's relationship to life, to experience: constantly new, fresh, unstable, and unstructured.

In mixing the artist figure with the picaro figure, Cary creates a character who can never entirely become one. On occasion art pulls Gulley toward a stable center in the picaresque world, and picaresque life pulls him away again, scattering his half-done canvases behind him across the landscape. Only his perfect awareness of himself, his robust sense of humor, makes it all bearable. "How you don't enjoy life, mother," he tells the nun in the ambulance that is speeding him to a hospital at the end. "I should laugh all around my neck at this minute if my shirt wasn't a bit on the tight side." "It would be better for you to pray." "Same thing, mother" (289). Gulley Jimson is perhaps the one picaro who, paradoxically again, manages to be on good (laughing) terms with the world at the same time that he is at odds with it. And he can laugh-pray in a picaresque world because he is a *pictor ludens* who is ultimately on the best of terms with himself:

"They can give you all that, Mr. Jimson," said Walter, who was upset. "It wouldn't be right. What would they give you seven years for?"

"Being Gulley Jimson," I said, "and getting away with it." (49)

EDITIONS

The Horse's Mouth (New York: Universal Library, 1957); all page references are to this edition. The Perennial Library edition (New York: Harper & Row, 1965) has an afterword by Andrew Wright, who collaborated with Cary in revising the 1944 edition.

SELECT BIBLIOGRAPHY

Robert Alter, *Rogue's Progress: Studies in the Picaresque Novel* (Cambridge: Harvard University Press, 1964); Alexander Blackburn, *The Myth of the Picaro: Continuity and Transformation of the Picaresque Novel, 1554–1954* (Chapel Hill: University of North Carolina Press, 1979), who argues that Cary's novel is not picaresque and cites additional sources debating the issue; Stuart Miller, *The Picaresque Novel* (Cleveland, Ohio: Case Western Reserve University Press, 1967).

HUCKLEBERRY FINN
(THE ADVENTURES OF HUCKLEBERRY FINN)

(1885)

Samuel Langhorne Clemens (Mark Twain)

William Dean Howells learned Spanish so that he could someday write a life of Cervantes (though he never got around to it). In the course of developing his reading knowledge, he ran into *Lazarillo de Tormes* (q.v.). His "rapturous delight" in and fondness for this book stayed with him; even years later, as he reminisced about his formative readings, he thought of it as "an old personal friend whom I had known in the flesh." Reading *Lazarillo*, he wrote in *My Literary Passions* in 1895, "brought back the atmosphere of Don Quixote, and all the landscape of that dear wonder-world of Spain, where I had lived so much." He then went on to suggest to budding writers that the picaresque could provide a quintessentially American form of fiction:

I am sure that the intending author of American fiction would do well to study the Spanish picaresque novels; for in their simplicity of design he will find one of the best forms for an American story. The intrigue of close texture will never suit our conditions, which are so loose and open and variable; each man's life among us is a romance of the Spanish model, if it is the life of a man who has risen, as we nearly all have, with many ups and downs. (143)

Years later, in *My Mark Twain* (1910), Howells saw *The Adventures of Huckleberry Finn* in this context, though with qualifications that make his conception of the picaresque suspect (but hardly unrepresentative of his time):

Even now I think [Mark Twain] should rather be called a romancer, though such a book as *Huckleberry Finn* takes itself out of the order of romance and places itself with the great things in picaresque fiction. Still, it is more poetic than picaresque, and of a deeper psychology. (173)

Several years before (1905), a book about Spanish influence on English literature had concluded a chapter called "The Picaresque and Peripatetic Novels in England" with the following comparison to *Lazarillo* and *Guzmán de Alfarache* (q.v.):

One sees in Mark Twain's *Huckleberry Finn* a transparent intention to experiment with an American picaro, as near as circumstances could make him to Lazarillo, Guzman de Alfarache, and the rest of the goodly company of sharp-witted youngsters with pockets as light as their hearts, who sprang from the Spanish genius as a reaction from the wandering knights of chivalry. (Hume, 183)

Half a century later, in an introduction to an edition of *Huckleberry Finn* (later reprinted in *The Liberal Imagination*), Lionel Trilling would write:

The form of the book is based on the simplest of all novel-forms, the so-called picaresque novel, or novel of the road, which strings its incidents on the line of the hero's travels. But, as Pascal says, "rivers are roads that move," and the movement of the road in its own mysterious life transmutes the primitive simplicity of the form: the road itself is the greatest character in this novel of the road, and the hero's departures from the river and his returns to it compose a subtle and significant pattern. The linear simplicity of the picaresque novel is further modified by the story's having a clear dramatic organization: it has a beginning, a middle, and an end, and a mounting suspense of interest. (111)

Writing at about the same time, Harry Levin referred to Cervantes's "Rinconete and Cortadillo" (q.v.) as "a tale endearing to American readers as a Sevillian adumbration of *Tom Sawyer* and *Huckleberry Finn*" (87).

And a quarter of a century later, we find a couple of dubious footnotes in the second edition of the Norton Critical Edition of *Huckleberry Finn*. One explains an allusion Tom Sawyer makes in chapter 3: "The ancient *Arabian Nights' Entertainments* (first English translation, 1838–41) and the 'hero' of Cervantes's picaresque narrative (1605) are the chief romance authorities Tom garbles here" (16). Another annotates a passage from Hooper's *Some Adventures of Captain Simon Suggs*, a book Twain knew in his youth that may well have influenced him: "Hooper's book imposed the picaresque tradition of Cervantes upon frontier life in the old American Southwest, a region which produced a roguish literature of oral anecdote" (253).

This overview of nearly a century's worth of commentary on the picaresque in America reveals a generic and modal confusion similar to what we find when we look at eighteenth-century English picaresque (*Roderick Random*, q.v.) and the ways in which the Spanish works were metamorphosed in French literature (*Gil Blas*, q.v.). Twain himself had mentioned *Gil Blas* as a model for the narrative technique he might have used in *The Adventures of Tom Sawyer*: "I have finished [*Tom Sawyer*] & didn't take the chap beyond boyhood. I believe it would be fatal to do it in any shape but autobiographically—like Gil Blas. I perhaps made a mistake in not writing it in the first person" (Norton Critical, 282). Like Smollett and Lesage himself, Twain is conscious of genre, but his generic conception of the picaresque mixes the Cervantine of *Don Quixote* (*not* of "Rinconete and Cortadillo" or "The Illustrious Kitchen-Maid," q.q.v.) with transmitted versions of the picaresque (by way of *Gil Blas*) into an image of a "dear wonder-world" (as Howells put it) that obscures the specific makeup of the works generally agreed upon as forming the original *novela picaresca* of Spain.

Howells's suggestion that writers study Spanish fiction contains within it the implied assertion that the picaresque may well prove to be the American form of fiction. But this does not seem to be an accurate assessment of American fiction before 1900, nor did it turn out to be prophetic for the fiction of the twentieth century. Before *Huckleberry Finn*, the major fiction often cited in this context is Brackenridge's *Modern Chivalry* (1792–1805): "Like *Don Quixote*, Sterne's *Tristram Shandy*, and Fielding's *Tom Jones*, all of which must often have been in Brackenridge's mind as he wrote, *Modern Chivalry* is a tale of adventuring, episodic and repetitive—what is generally known, perhaps with not too much discrimination, as a picaresque novel" (Leary, 15). Aldridge has suggested Cooper's *Autobiography of a Pocket-Handkerchief* (1843) as showing a direct generic link with the picaresque tradition of Alemán (*Guzmán de Alfarache*) and Quevedo (*El Buscón*, q.v.), even as it mixes in the minor genre of the personified object. And Melville's *The Confidence-Man* (q.v.) is a special case. Picaresque-like fictions abound, of course, especially in the twentieth century (examples are *The Adventures of Augie March*, *A Cool Million*, *The Magic Christian*, *Malcolm* and *V.*), but they depend for their perceptions as picaresques on misperceptions about the picaresque. American literature does not seem to have any more genuine picaresques than do the literatures of other countries. If Howells proved prophetic, he did so only in a heavily qualified sense: he perpetuated (however unintentionally) a distorted meaning of a generic term whose ubiquity among subsequent critics and reviewers far exceeds the number of fictions to which it ought accurately to apply. Having tried to tell American writers what kind of fiction might best suit American material, Howells succeeded instead in getting American critics to find it everywhere. (His own confusion is further demonstrated toward the beginning of *My Literary Passions* when he calls the design of *Don Quixote* "the supreme form of fiction" and speculates that "if we ever have a great American novel it must be built up on some such large and noble lines.")

But Howells's statement that *Huckleberry Finn* belongs "with the great things in picaresque fiction" rings true, even if it does not carry the resounding impact of Hemingway's assertion that all of modern American literature comes from this single book by Mark Twain. Whatever else it may be, *Huckleberry Finn* is the exemplary American picaresque, and not only in the limited sense of Trilling's conception of the picaresque. In situation and narrative voice, it links directly with *Lazarillo de Tormes*: "One of the reasons that *Huckleberry Finn* is a closer approach to the picaresque than most novels of its time or ours is that it deals with boyhood" (Alter, 121), a characteristic often overlooked in considerations of the picaresque—and especially important in examining narrative distance. The boy's perspective, complicated by the retrospective narrating adult, forces revisions in our automatic conceptions of childhood and adulthood. Just as Lazarillo is often psychologically more adult than the chronological adults around him— particularly true with the *hidalgo* in the third chapter—so Huck portrays Jim as naively childlike and himself as almost paternalistic. This typically picaresque topsy-turvydom of the child-as-adult and the adult-as-child, which functions strongly in *The Painted Bird* (q.v.) and in the early childhood chapters of many other picaresques, relies on a connotative shift in our attitudes toward "child" and "adult," from the strongly positive in "child-as-adult" to the negative in "adult-as-child." Childhood is admirable when it makes room for the supposedly mature observations we associate with adulthood; but that same adulthood is contemptible, or at best pathetic, when it perceives the world with the naiveté we associate with childhood—that same childhood that can be so adult in its perceptions and observations. This almost paradoxical reversal is complicated even further in *Huckleberry Finn* by racial attitudes, as Ralph Ellison has quietly pointed out. Although Jim's dignity and human capacity do emerge from behind the stereotype mask of the minstrel tradition into which Twain fitted him, Ellison says, Twain was "not so free of the white dictum that Negro males must be treated either as boys or 'uncles'—never as men. Jim's friendship for Huck comes across as that of a boy for another boy rather than as the friendship of an adult for a junior; thus there is implicit in it not only a violation of the manners sanctioned by society for relations between Negroes and whites, there is a violation of our conception of adult maleness" (51).

In the serious social, moral, and religious complexity it raises through the picaresque perspective on the relationship between the individual and society, *Huckleberry Finn* also links directly with such fundamental picaresques as *Guzmán de Alfarache* and *Simplicius Simplicissimus* (q.v.), particularly in exploring the full range of that perspective beginning with childhood awareness of racial or class outsiderdom and culminating in visions of irreconcilability. Although Twain's actual consciousness of picaresque fiction may have been limited to Lesage's variation on it, his work rejects the eighteenth-century romance machinery that constructs compromises. "The truth is that *Huckleberry Finn* has neither real freedom nor lasting love for our comfort. It is almost a nihilistic book. It is certainly a very sad book" (Blackburn, 187). In this, Twain's work anticipates an exemplary twentieth-century American picaresque, *Invisible Man* (q.v.). It is hardly the piece of sunlit nostalgia many readers wish it were, including, much to his discredit, Chandler: "Few books in the range of picaresque literature can equal this in pure fun, and it is deserving of praise for its fidelity to boyhood and to a phase of American life now passed away" (489). Such a reading dismisses the seriousness of the child's view of the world and is, in essence, antipicaresque.

Huckleberry Finn begins metafictionally with an intertextual self-reference: "You don't know about me, without you have a read a book by the name of 'The Adventures of Tom Sawyer,' but that ain't no matter. That book was made by Mr. Mark Twain, and he told the truth, mainly. There was things which he stretched, but mainly he told the truth" (7). But Huck's is only one of the voices speaking to us throughout this narrative. Preceding this opening of the first chapter are three reader-addressing items. The first foreshadows the intertextual beginning of the autobiography proper by identifying the title character as "Tom Sawyer's comrade" and setting the scene as the Mississippi, forty to fifty years before. The second is a bordered "NOTICE": "Persons attempting to find a motive in this narrative will be prosecuted; persons attempting to find a moral in it will be banished; persons attempting to find a plot in it will be shot" (2). And the third is an explanatory note, also from "the author," about the various dialects used in the text. The first of these is both intertextual and extratextual, linking the book to a previous fiction and to an actual geographical place and historical time. The other two are primarily intratextual: they are self-reflexive of this text itself, and they are also self-deprecating in the ironic manner typical of other prefatory disclaimers in the picaresque (for example, *Lazarillo de Tormes* and *El Buscón*). As such, they create other narrative voices that will be speaking to the reader alongside the dramatized voice of Huck himself. There is not much chronological spread of narrative distance between the time of action and Huck's narration of it, and so Twain has to create these voices to provide indirectly the more mature, reflective perspective that traditionally comes from the re-membering picaro toward the end of his life. Author and reader are not only implied; they are implicated in the text itself, directly and indirectly, seriously and ironically. This playful author-reader collaboration, established extratextually, is sustained throughout the narrative by constant allusion to fiction making—directly to specific fictions (*The Adventures of Tom Sawyer*, *Don Quixote*, the romances of Sir Walter Scott, and others) and indirectly through the fictions characters create for and about themselves, and for and about others (Tom's elaborate book-bred escape plans in chapter 35, for example, which are doubly inventive because Jim, being already a freed slave, does not need to be set free; the equally elaborate confidence games of the "duke" and "king"; and even Huck's own invented past in chapter 20, a stock survival tactic for the picaro, for whom lying is the mother of invention when expediency is at stake; Huck also invents through role playing, when he disguises himself as first a girl and then another boy in chapter 11 and in his impersonation of Tom—and Tom's of Sid—in the last part of the book.) *Huckleberry Finn* is above all a fiction about fictions. "I never seen anybody but lied, one time or another," Huck says in the first paragraph (7).

Both the metafictional front-framing and Huck's own voice in the first paragraph create a narrative presentation that is a curious mixture of generic unself-consciousness, ingenuous allusiveness, and parodistic and satirical literariness. Coming after the three prefatory notes, Huck's first paragraph might easily be judged precious were it not for the naturalness with which Twain creates Huck creating himself out of another book. Paradoxically, it is because of his known book existence that Huck can take shape as credibly as he does, his autonomous voice emerging from the third-person objectification of *The Adventures of Tom Sawyer*. Just as Cervantes in part II of *Don Quixote* takes Quixote and Sancho out of a previous book (part I) and gives their book existence a magical credibility by putting them into a world in which a book exists about them, with the result that they are simultaneously both inside and outside the fiction, so Twain uses a similar stroke of fiction—a magic wand almost—to conjure up a Huck Finn who, in stepping out of a book, becomes more lifelike than fictional characters normally do. The ingenuousness with which Twain pulls off this ingenious trick rivals that of Cervantes; in both books the trick goes almost unnoticed until we begin to probe the precise nature of the fictional worlds the authors have created. In *Huckleberry Finn* Twain is rewriting *Tom Sawyer* from the inside out, just as Cervantes seems to have realized the full fictional dimensions of *Don Quixote* only when he began the second part. And just as Cervantes played parodistically and satirically with chivalric romances and their influence, so Twain has Tom Sawyer use Don Quixote for similar ends.

But beyond their common metafictionality and their parody of romance, specific resemblance between the two books fades. Huck Finn is no Sancho Panza, to whom he is often compared. He is, rather, a radical outsider who has tried to integrate himself into the prevailing social structure but cannot feel at home in it. He cannot make the compromise or accommodation necessary for life with the Widow Douglas and Miss Watson. In the midst of all the comforts of more or less conventional home, Huck feels exiled: "I felt so lonesome I most wished I was dead" (9). The meandering great river is his chosen mode of existence: "We said there warn't no home like a raft, after all. Other places do seem so cramped up and smothery, but a raft don't. You feel mighty free and easy on a raft" (96). And after he thinks he has eluded the king and duke, he says, "So, in two seconds, away we went, a sliding down the river, and it *did* seem so good to be free again and all by ourselves on the big river and nobody to bother us" (162). After his first crisis of conscience, he mulls over his condition:

They went off, and I got aboard the raft, feeling bad and low, because I know very well I had done wrong, I see it warn't no use for me to try to learn to do right; a body that don't get *started* right when he's little, ain't got no show—when the pinch comes there ain't nothing to back him up and keep him to his work, and so he gets beat. Then I thought a minute, and says to myself, hold on,—s'pose you'd a done right and give Jim up; would you felt better than what you do now? No, says I, I'd feel bad—I'd feel just the same way I do now. Well, then, says I, what's the use you learning to do right, when it's troublesome to do right and ain't no trouble to do wrong, and the wages is just the same? I was stuck. I couldn't answer that. So I reckoned I wouldn't bother no more about it, but after this always do whichever come handiest at the time. (76)

A kind of resolution to a genuine dilemma is arrived at by an appeal to the experiential self, not to prevailing codes of moral and social behavior. A typically picaresque reperspectivizing of right and wrong calls into question the whole social, even cosmic, structure and the individual's relationship to it. Huck rejects society but is burdened by its strictures, even as its structure seems to break down in a succession of duplicities and senseless acts of violence. The king and duke are con men duping the willing to be deceived, but when a crowd, equally willing to undeceive, tars and feathers them, Huck feels guilty because the punishment strikes him as disproportionate for the crime. "Human beings *can* be awful cruel to one another," he observes (182). Like the duke and king, he is himself on the fringes of society, yet he can feel the remorse they do not feel; they are, in fact, objects of his sympathy. From society's point of view, the crowd is justified in putting an end to deception, but Huck does not identify with the crowd in its attempt to restore proper rhythm to a social order that has been momentarily disrupted. Despite his alienation from the social order, Huck actually manages to connect more intimately with the vital moral issues at the core of such acts of restoration. He feels to blame, somehow, "—though *I* hadn't done nothing. But that's always the way; it don't make no difference whether you do right or wrong, a person's conscience ain't got no sense, and just goes for him *anyway*. . . . It takes up more room than all the rest of a person's insides, and yet ain't no good, nohow" (183). While observing society's attempt to restore order, Huck has to preserve himself against a potentially disruptive internal moral disorder. Lazarillo, finding himself at the end of his third chapter in the singular situation of being a servant deserted by his master rather than the other way around, sinks into a similarly helpless mood as he perceives (though he cannot yet fully articulate) the futility of behavior that is governed too strictly by codes: "Now I was convinced of my tragic destiny and saw that everything was against me. All I did was upside down." His sympathy for the unyieldingly proud *hidalgo*, like Huck's for the con artists, leads to a typically picaresque paradox: the more closely the picaro perceives and feels the heart of the matter, the more distanced and exiled he becomes.

Huck's second crisis of conscience is imbued with religious considerations that immediately evoke *Guzmán de Alfarache*, as Huck tries to reconcile human emotion with social, moral, and religious codes that have been pounded into him. But Huck's conversion is the opposite of that of Guzmán and Simplicissimus. Agonizing over the social and moral disgrace he will suffer for sheltering a slave, Huck finds himself feeling more and more "wicked and low-down and ornery" and finally realizes that he cannot hide completely, no matter how far he escapes from the immediate situation:

And at last, when it hit me all of a sudden that here was the plain hand of Providence slapping me in the face and letting me know my wickedness was being watched all the time from up there in heaven, whilst I was stealing a poor old woman's nigger that hadn't ever done me no harm, and now was showing me there's One that's always on the lookout, and ain't agoing to allow no such miserable doings to go only just so fur and no further, I most dropped in my tracks I was so scared. Well, I tried the best I could to kinder soften it up somehow for myself, by saying I was brung up wicked, and so I warn't so much to blame; but something inside of me kept saying, "There was the Sunday school, you could a gone to it; and if you'd a done it they'd a learnt you, there, that people that acts as I'd been acting about that nigger goes to everlasting fire." (168)

He kneels down and tries to pray, but the words will not come because "I was playing double. I was letting *on* to give up sin, but away inside of me I was holding on to the biggest one of all." He realizes that there are two beings he cannot deceive: himself and God. "I was trying to make my mouth *say* I would do the right thing and the clean thing, and go and write to that nigger's owner and tell where he was; but deep down in me I knowed it was a lie—and He knowed it. You can't pray a lie—I found that out" (169). He writes a letter to Miss Watson and feels "all washed clean of sin." But memories intrude, and all moral, legal, social, and religious obligations crumble in the face of a more powerful bond:

It was a close place. I took [the letter] up, and held it in my hand. I was a trembling, because I'd got to decide, forever, betwixt two things, and I knowed it. I studied a minute, sort of holding my breath, and then says to myself:
   "All right, then, I'll *go* to to hell"—and tore it up.
   It was awful thoughts, and awful words, but they was said. And I let them stay said; and never thought no more about reforming. I shoved the whole thing out of my head; and said I would take up wickedness again, which was in my line, being brung up to it, and the other warn't. (169–70)

This inversion of the traditional conversion jumbles the conventional concepts of right and wrong. In the end, Huck's decision loses some of its radical rebelliousness when he learns that Jim had been freed by Miss Watson, but at the time he is making his difficult choice he does not know this. The consequence of his decision is a willed perpetual outsiderdom.

One immediate manifestation of this outsiderdom is Huck's identity shift for much of the remainder of the book. At the Phelps's plantation, Huck is automatically given an identity, which makes him uneasy and eager to "find out who I was" (175). When he realizes they are mistaking him for Tom Sawyer, he is relieved: "for it was like being born again, I was so glad to find out who I was" (177). By the last two chapters, Huck knows who he is not: he loses his identity as Tom, learns that Jim is already free, and finds out that his father is dead. This triple unmasking of assumed identities strips Huck bare, though he curiously makes no direct comment on himself as a being who knows only who he is not. He is free to be no one, free to "light out for the Territory ahead of the rest, because Aunt Sally she's going to adopt me and sivilize me and I can't stand it. I been there before" (229). What has been called the negative, even nihilistic, vision of the book has its source in the problematic freedom evoked in the last paragraph of Huck's account: he wants to be free to escape from identity, not to quest for it. Like Pablos heading for the Americas in *El Buscón*, this ending is typically picaresque in its final vision of irreconcilability.

Even the potentially integrative act of constructing his *vida* gives Huck little satisfaction. "There ain't nothing more to write about, and I am rotten glad of it, because I'd knowed what a trouble it was to make a book I wouldn't a tackled it and ain't agoing to no more" (229). Tom Sawyer's book-bred fantasies have lured Huck into participating in a cruel fictionalization of actuality in which Jim is not an entirely innocent victim, having himself withheld the truth about Huck's father. *Huckleberry Finn* "is finally more persuasive as a document of enslavement, of the variety of imprisonments within verbal styles and fictions than as a testimony to freedom" (Trachtenberg, 971). Thus the autobiographical act is as full of traps and lures, of accommodations and compromises, as experiencing "sivilized" life itself.

In the end, Huck realizes he can do little better in the matter of truth telling than did the book "made by Mr. Mark Twain" from which his narrative emerges and against which he implicitly asks us to measure his own story: "There was things which he stretched, but mainly he told the truth" (7). There will now be an end to stretching in fiction: "THE END. YOURS TRULY, HUCK FINN" (229). There will also be an end to the stretching required in life by the tension between the individual conscience and society's expectations. In ending his narrative, Huck also seeks to end his social existence by lighting out for the territory. The dark irony here is that in ending his verbal effort with an assertion of silence, he is simultaneously constructing a gigantic fiction about life.

EDITION

The second Norton Critical Edition, ed. Sculley Bradley, Richmond Croom Beatty, E. Hudson Long, and Thomas Cooley (New York: W. W. Norton, 1977).

SELECT BIBLIOGRAPHY

A. Owen Aldridge, "Fenimore Cooper and the Picaresque Tradition," *Nineteenth-Century Fiction* 27 (1972): 283–92; Robert Alter, *Rogue's Progress: Studies in the Picaresque Novel* (Cambridge: Harvard University Press, 1964); Louise K. Barnett, "Huck Finn: Picaro as Linguistic Outsider," *College Literature* 6 (1979): 221–31; Harold Beaver, *Huckleberry Finn* (Winchester, Mass.: Allen and Unwin, 1987); Alexander Blackburn, *The Myth of the Picaro: Continuity and Transformation of the Picaresque Novel, 1554–1954* (Chapel Hill: University of North Carolina Press, 1979); Frank Wadleigh Chandler, *The Literature of Roguery* [1907] (New York: Burt Franklin, 1958); Ralph Ellison, "Change the Joke and Slip the Yoke," in his *Shadow and Act* (New York: Vintage Books, 1972) [originally published in 1958 in *Partisan Review* as a debate with Stanley Edgar Hyman: "The Negro Writer in America: An Exchange"]; Janet A. Gabler-Hover, "Sympathy Not Empathy: The Intent of Narration in *Huckleberry Finn*," *Journal of Narrative Technique* 17 (1987): 67–75; William Dean Howells, *My Literary Passions*

[1895] (New York: Greenwood Press, 1969), and *My Mark Twain* (New York and London: Harper and Brothers, 1910); Martin Hume, *Spanish Influence on English Literature* (London: Eveleigh Nash, 1905); Susan Kuhlmann, *Knave, Fool, and Genius: The Confidence Man as He Appears in Nineteenth-Century American Fiction* (Chapel Hill: University of North Carolina Press, 1973); Lewis Leary, Introduction to Hugh Henry Brackenridge, *Modern Chivalry* (New Haven, Conn.: College and University Press, 1965); Harry Levin, "The Example of Cervantes" [1956] in his *Contexts of Criticism* (New York: Atheneum, 1963), 79–96; Gary Lindberg, *The Confidence Man in American Literature* (New York: Oxford University Press, 1982); Charles R. Metzger, "The Adventures of Huckleberry Finn as Picaresque," *The Midwest Quarterly* (Spring 1964): 249–56; Lyall Powers, "Mark Twain and the Future of Picaresque," in *Mark Twain: A Sumptuous Variety*, ed. Robert Giddings (Totowa, N.J.: Barnes and Noble Books, 1985), 155–75; William Riggan, *Pícaros, Madmen, Naïfs, and Clowns: The Unreliable First-Person Narrator* (Norman: University of Oklahoma Press, 1981); Joseph Sawicki, "Authority/Author-ity: Representation and Fictionality in *Huckleberry Finn*," *Modern Fiction Studies* 31 (1985): 691–702; Alan Trachtenberg, "The Form of Freedom in *Adventures of Huckleberry Finn*," *The Southern Review* 6 (1970): 954–71; Lionel Trilling, "Huckleberry Finn" [1948], in his *The Liberal Imagination: Essays on Literature and Society* (Garden City, N.Y.: Doubleday Anchor, [n.d.]), 100–113; Warwick Wadlington, *The Confidence Game in American Literature* (Princeton, N.J.: Princeton University Press, 1975); Stanley T. Williams, *The Spanish Background of American Literature* (New Haven, Conn.: Yale University Press, 1955), II, 240–67.

"THE ILLUSTRIOUS KITCHEN-MAID"

("La Illustre fregona," 1613)

Miguel de Cervantes Saavedra

This is one of the three *Novelas ejemplares* often called picaresque, the other two being "The Dogs' Colloquy" and "Rinconete and Cortadillo" (q.q.v.). Of the three it is the most self-conscious in its use of picaresque material. Cervantes several times uses the terms *pícaro* and *picaresca*, and he alludes directly to *Guzmán de Alfarache* (q.v.) and indirectly to *Lazarillo de Tormes* (q.v.), having one of the characters spend part of his vagabondage in the "tunny fishery of Zahara, which is the *finibus-terre* of the roguish fraternity" (35; *finibusterre de la picaresca* in the original), which refers to Lazarillo's adventures among the fish in the anonymous 1555 continuation.

Carriazo, whose real name is Don Diego de Carriazo, is well born but restless, and he decides to break the confines of his well-to-do existence. At age thirteen,

solely from a vagabond inclination, without receiving from his parents any ill-treatment to force him to the step, but simply for his own pleasure and fancy, he played truant, as children say, from his father's house, and went forth through the world, so satisfied with an untrammelled life, that, in the midst of the hardships and miseries it brings with it, he did not miss the abundance of his home, nor did trudging on foot weary him, nor cold injure him, nor heat tire him. (34)

He does so well in his "occupation of a *pícaro* that he could have lectured from a chair in the faculty to the famous Alfarache." In him, "the world beheld a virtuous rogue, clean, well-bred, and more than moderately shrewd," passing through "all the grades of *pícaro*" and taking "a master's degree at the tunny fishery."

Oh *pícaros* of the kitchen, dirty, fat and sleek, feigning poverty, sham cripples, misers of Zocodover and of the square of Madrid, who pray to be seen praying, carriers of baskets at Seville, panders to the bully, with all the interminable crowd who is massed together under the name of *pícaro*, lower your ostentation, abate your swagger, do not call yourselves *pícaros*, if you have not attended two courses in the academy at the tunny fishery. There, there is at its height labour combined with indolence; there are unadulterated nastiness, plump corpulence, hunger imminent, abundant satiety, vice without disguise, constant gambling, quarrels every instant, death at any moment, foul language at every step, dances as at weddings, scraps of song as in print, inflated ballads, poetry without action. In this spot there is confessing, in that there is denying. Yonder there is quarrelling, this way there is gaming, everywhere there is thieving. Here liberty is conspicuous, and labour shines out. Here come or send many fathers of quality to seek their sons, and they find them, and the latter feel as much their removal from this life as if their fathers were carrying them off to put them to death. Yet all this sweetness which I have described has an acrid juice which embitters it; and it is the inability to sleep a secure sleep, without dread of being in an instant transported from Zahara to Barbary. (35)

Carriazo spends three summers here, in "those barren sands, which to him appeared more fresh and green than the Elysian fields." After the last, he washes off his rogue's role, rehabilitates himself, and goes home, telling everybody "a thousand magnificent and lengthy lies regarding things that had happened to him during the three years of his absence" (36). He convinces his friend Avendaño to return there with him, under pretense of going off to college together. On the way, they hear of a beautiful kitchen maid in service at an inn. Avendaño falls in love, and the two stay there, the former becoming "an hostler under the name of Tomas Pedro" and "Carriazo under the style of Lope the Asturian, turned water-carrier" (47). Although the story portrays low life in and around the inn, "The Illustrious Kitchen-Maid" slowly turns into a romance, as improbable coincidences reveal still further coincidences leading to the revelation that the kitchen maid is the illegitimate daughter of Carriazo's father, and ending finally with a triple marriage: "In this way all were contented, cheerful, and satisfied" (79).

As in the other two exemplary stories, Cervantes's attitude toward the picaresque is here problematic again. There is much ironic playfulness in the description of picaresque existence in the opening pages, and Carriazo's life as a picaro is itself a kind of dressing up, a play, as are the lies with which he tells his story afterward—a self-reflecting that is not within Cervantes's narrative vision to explore. Américo Castro has said that "what the picaro thinks does not interest Cervantes" (235). Moreover, as Blanco Aguinaga points out, Cer-

vantes is "a presentational novelist" who "depicts reality as someone who sees
it in all its complexity, from the outside, without aspiring to know it absolutely
and from within, like the picaresque character-novelist," and thus "the so-called
picaresque novels of Cervantes have nothing in common with the picaresque
novel whose formal and thematic culmination is *Guzmán de Alfarache*: they are
in opposition to it" (150–51).

But it is nevertheless crucial to an understanding of the picaresque that Cervantes's three exemplary tales be taken into consideration. Along with the Ginés
de Pasamonte episode in part I of *Don Quixote*, they constitute a kind of antipicaresque that is developing side by side with the developing Spanish picaresque
narrative tradition. Cervantes had claimed in his prologue to the *Novelas ejemplares* that "I am the first to essay novels in the Castilian tongue, for the many
novels which go about in print in Spanish are all translated from foreign languages, while these are mine own, neither imitated nor stolen" (6). In trying
out the *novela*, the "new," Cervantes had to experiment with the newly emerging
picaresque. In doing so mostly ironically, he perspectivized the picaresque within
larger narrative frameworks, thus building into the tradition near its beginning
a self-consciously critical dimension. "All [Cervantes's] best fiction is intergeneric, and we as readers have to begin by deconstructing that nineteenth-
century invention, the picaresque, and the criticism that has kept it in place"
(Dunn, 131).

TRANSLATIONS

Quotations are from N. Maccoll, *Exemplary Novels*, 2 vols. (Glasgow: Gowans & Gary,
1902), vols. 7 and 8 of *The Complete Works of Miguel de Cervantes Saavedra*; see also
Harriet de Onís, trans., *Six Exemplary Novels* (Great Neck, N.Y.: Barron's Educational
Series, 1961).

SELECT BIBLIOGRAPHY

Carlos Blanco Aguinaga, "Cervantes y la picaresca. Notas sobre dos tipos de realismo,"
Nueva Revista de Filología Hispánica 11 (1957): 313–42 (translated and abbreviated as
"Cervantes and the Picaresque Mode: Notes on Two Kinds of Realism" in *Cervantes:
A Collection of Critical Essays*, ed. Lowry Nelson, Jr. [Englewood Cliffs, N.J.: Prentice-
Hall, 1969]); Américo Castro, *El pensamiento de Cervantes* (Barcelona and Madrid:
Editorial Noguer, 1973); Peter N. Dunn, "Cervantes De/Re-Constructs the Picaresque,"
Cervantes 2 (1982): 110–31; Fernando G. Salinero, "Dos arquetipos de la picaresca
cervantina: el esportillero y el rufián," in *Proceedings: Pacific Northwest Conference on
Foreign Languages*, ed. Walter C. Kraft (Corvallis: Oregon State University, 1973),
115–18.

INVISIBLE MAN

(1952)

Ralph Ellison

This is the only contemporary work Stuart Miller includes in *The Picaresque
Novel* because it is, as he says, "picaresque in the traditional sense" and in

nearly every respect "it conforms to the old patterns" by being in character and structure expressive "of a certain essential and unending chaos in life" (134–35).

With its headline contemporaneity, *Invisible Man* speaks powerfully and immediately to us, rendering a social milieu that blends with an actuality that we can say is "real" in the world around us. In this Ellison reemphasizes the sociocritical aspect of the picaresque.

Ellison's man narrates from his self-imposed exile outside the order (or disorder) of things. Burrowed in his hole under the surface, cut off from the world, he narratively spans the temporal and spatial gap to contemplate his participation in that world. His life up to the moment of narration has followed a typical picaresque course. He has had many masters (Dr. Bledsoe, the college president; Mr. Kimbro and Brockway at the paint factory; the leaders of the Brotherhood; white man in general), played many roles (boxer, student, chauffeur, factory worker, speechmaker, political activist, and now narrator of his life), and has wandered the landscape (the South, New York-Harlem). Although his actual geographical travels are rather limited, Harlem comes to be a microcosm of the picaresque world-chaos. "I would have to take Harlem a little at a time," he says (143). For the transplanted southern black, Harlem is exile, a crazy place where he loses his sense of being "at home in the world," as Ellison has written in the essay "Harlem Is Nowhere."

The world lifts Ellison's man up and drops him in turn. His grandfather on his deathbed had given the "younguns" a warning that it took Guzmán (*Guzmán de Alfarache*, q.v.) years of experience to discover and that the Invisible Man will find corroborated by experience: "our life is a war" (19). Ellison's man finds out early; the speech he has to give at a men's club turns into a humiliating boxing match and riot where he grovels for coins on an electrified rug (ch. 1). An innocent drive in the country with a college supporter leads to his expulsion from school (ch. 2). He has the typically picaresque unfamiliarity with the world when he is cast into it after being expelled from college—an expulsion from paradise by the "coal-black daddy of whom we were afraid" (105). After having eaten breakfast at a white café, he is made aware of his picaresque condition, which in this case is the condition of being black in a world that does not practice civil rights: "I took out another dime, thinking, Is it an insult when one of us tips one of them?" (153). In making racial issues central to his picaresque vision, Ellison connects with tradition; if we accept Américo Castro's thesis that the picaresque was born out of the outsiderdom experienced by the Spanish *converso* (converted Jew), the problem of racial exile can be considered essential to the picaresque condition of existence from the beginnings of the mainstream tradition. Job seeking turns out to be an aimless and futile affair for the Invisible Man when he discovers that he has been the butt of a trick: a letter of recommendation turns out to be a condemnatory note. When he discovers life's trick on him, he says, "I sat on the bed and laughed. They'd sent me to the rookery all right" (171). As a picaro he can laugh at the trick of which he has been the victim, and he continues to see the world and himself in a trick–being tricked way. A job in a paint factory totally mystifies him: "I had a feeling that something had gone wrong, something more important than the paint; that either I had played a trick on Kimbro or he, like the trustees and Bledsoe, was playing one on me" (180). An explosion in that factory ends up with a lobotomy in a nightmarish hospital room, a rebirth of sorts, similar to the "new Ferdinand" who emerges from the assembly lines of mechanized Detroit in Céline's *Journey to the End of the Night* (q.v.). His work with the Brotherhood ends disastrously and violently in a riot, though not disastrously for the Brotherhood, which has been using him for a "trick" of its own. And finally, Ellison's man is an outsider among outsiders, situated somewhere between his own black world and that of the whites who control and manipulate the Brotherhood. Even the simple act of trying to get rid of a package in an alley garbage can may arouse the hostility of his world (284–85). Obeying the most commonplace social rules wins him the snarling accusation that he "is making trouble."

Ellison's man several times reshapes himself in order to play the game in a world that seems always to be playing with him. "Who was I, how had I come to be?" he wonders after the lobotomy, which is itself a kind of transformation through the machine, a rebirth even (shock treatments, "umbilical" electrical nodes tied to his stomach). When he later makes a spur-of-the-moment speech for an evicted couple, he is approached by someone from the Brotherhood to speak for them. "Well, I had a new name and new problems" (274). He feels himself transformed and sees the Brotherhood as a pattern and a world to cling to:

Still, I liked my work during those days of certainty. I kept my eyes wide and ears alert. The Brotherhood was a world within a world and I was determined to discover all its secrets. . . .

The organization had given the world a new shape, and me a vital role. We recognized no loose ends, everything could be controlled by our science. Life was all pattern and discipline; and the beauty of discipline is when it works. And it was working very well. (330–31)

The Brotherhood resembles that community of rogues in the traditional pica-resque, such as we find it in *Guzmán de Alfarache*, "Rinconete y Cortadillo," *La desordenada codicia*, *The English Rogue* (q.q.v.), and *Jonathan Wild*, not to mention *El Buscón* and a variation of it such as the Dusters in *The Tin Drum* (q.q.v.). These brotherhoods of thieves, like the one in Brecht's *Threepenny Opera*, serve as a parody of the social order, with their elaborate hierarchies devoted to theft and extortion; paradoxically, these brotherhoods are much more ordered and structured than the social order that they both mime and undermine. Although Ellison's Brotherhood is not a real community of rogues, it is an ironic brotherhood because it turns out to be the betrayer not only of the black society it is supposed to improve but of the Invisible Man himself. "It was all a swindle, an obscene swindle!" he says (438).

Until his final break with the Brotherhood, Ellison's man had been a typical picaresque man of action: "I believe in nothing if not in action" (16) When he begins to doubt the Brotherhood, he also begins to perceive the full consequences of his role in a picaresque world. First of all there is the fanatical Ras (race?), the antiwhite militant who does by violence what the Brotherhood is trying to do through more organized and subtle (and deceptive) means. Then there is Rinehart, whom he comes to know about as a result of a chance encounter with a woman who mistakes him for Rinehart. Rinehart is

a broad man, a man of parts who got around. Rinehart the rounder. It was true as I was true. His world was possibility and he knew it. He was years ahead of me and I was a fool. I must have been crazy and blind. The world in which we lived was without boundaries. A vast seething, hot world of fluidity, and Rine the rascal was at home. Perhaps *only* Rine the rascal was at home in it. . . .
. . . I caught a brief glimpse of the possibilities posed by Rinehart's multiple personalities and turned away. It was too vast and confusing to contemplate. (430–31)

Ras and Rinehart each represent extremes—the one a fanatical attempt at self-assertion (stability through violent disorder), the other a constantly changing attempt at survival through disguises (stability through shifting identities and roles). "Ellison has said that he took Rinehart's name from the 'suggestion of inner and outer,' seeming and being, and that he is an emblem of chaos—'He has lived so long with chaos that he knows how to manipulate it.' So Rinehart and Ras both represent chaos, two versions of disorder" (Schafer, 88). But while Rinehart epitomizes the picaro figure, he is also, from the Invisible Man's perspective, a superpicaro, in the sense that he has subsumed the picaresque world-chaos by learning to manipulate it so well that he is no longer subject to it. Although Ellison has given his specific reasons for choosing the name Rinehart, the allusion to Reynard the Fox (*Reynard the Fox*, q.v.), that tricky ancestor of the picaro, is implicit. Ellison's man is attracted to Rinehart because he represents the spectrum of possible roles in a picaresque world. It is his realization that in this boomerang world he often has to "do a Rinehart" that makes his picaresque awareness complete:

My God, what possibilities existed! And that spiral business, that progress *goo*! Who knew all the secrets; hadn't I changed my name and never been challenged even once? And that lie that success was a rising *upward*. What a crummy lie they kept us dominated by. Not only could you travel upward toward success but you could travel downward as well; up *and* down, in retreat as well as in advance, crabways and crossways and around in a circle, meeting your old selves coming and going and perhaps all at the same time. (441)

A world of "fluidity," "multiple personalities," "old selves"—a world in which only Rinehart is at home and in which Rinehart makes him aware that if he is no one, he is potentially everyone. The trickster Rinehart—who is ironically the really invisible man in *Invisible Man* because we never see him—exists as a succession of masks, a possibility for the Invisible Man to con himself into a series of potential identities.

Yet Rinehart's technique fails him. Consciously playing the roles he had previously played unwittingly for the Brotherhood, the Invisible Man still plays into the hands of betrayal. In the climactic confrontation with Ras, just before he kills him, Ellison's man confirms his invisibility, saying in effect that no role is the same as many roles because in both cases one is "invisible":

I stood there, knowing that by dying, that by being hanged by Ras on this street in this destructive night I would perhaps move them one fraction of a bloody step closer to a definition of who they were and of what I was and had been. But the definition would have been too narrow; I was invisible, and hanging would not bring me to visibility, even to their eyes, since they wanted my death not for myself alone, but for the chase I'd been on all my life; because of the way I'd run, been run, chased, operated, purged— although to a great extent I could have done nothing else, given their blindness (didn't they tolerate both Rinehart and Bledsoe?) and my invisibility. And that I, a little black man with an assumed name should die because a big black man in his hatred and confusion over the nature of a reality that seemed controlled solely by white men whom I knew to be as blind as he, was just too much, too outrageously absurd. And I knew that it was better to live out one's own absurdity than to die for that of others. (483–84)

He kills Ras and heads underground, burning one by one all of the certificates of his existence (high school diploma, his Brotherhood name, and so on). In doing so, he actually "does a Rinehart" in reverse: he strips himself down to invisibility, the man with no roles as opposed to the man who can play all roles. This is, paradoxically, the biggest Rinehart of all: stepping totally out of things invisibly as opposed to stepping over them visibly through multiple roles. "And now I realized that I couldn't return to Mary's, or to any part of my old life. I could approach it only from the outside" (494). He makes himself invisible in a blind world, a double negation.

Both the prologue and the epilogue take place in the narrative present. The whole story of his life is compressed between them, and the state of his invisibility casts its light on that life. For it is an illumination of sorts. His dark hole is actually bright (lit with 1,369 bulbs), and it is actually warm ("Mine is a warm hole"), a refuge resembling Simplicius's cave (*Simplicius Simplicissimus*, q.v.). Here we see the pattern that A. A. Parker calls the "circle of existence," in which the picaro moves from a state of innocence (Simplicius in his forest, the Invisible Man at college, which he calls "this Eden" [101]), through the world and the hell of experience, and finally the yearned-for edenic home (Simplicius's island, the Invisible Man's womblike hole). Now the act of narration illuminates that process. He sees himself as an object in the past; he has removed himself from himself, and his invisible narrating "I" lets him see the visible "I's" of his past. "Time was as I was, but neither that time nor that 'I' are any more" (38). He has learned his picaresque lessons:

That . . . is how the world moves: Not like an arrow, but a boomerang. (Beware of those who speak of the *spiral* of history; they are preparing a boomerang. Keep a steel helmet handy.) I know; I have been boomeranged across my head so much that I now can see the darkness of lightness. (10)

Like the "twice two makes five" perverseness of Dostoevsky's Underground Man, the "darkness of lightness" and the lightness of darkness keep Ellison's man in a perpetual tension between onlyness and togetherness. It is his condition of onlyness that now is bright, warm, stable, and whole in comparison to his boomerang past, "for all life seen from the hole of invisibility is absurd" (501).

Ellison's Invisible Man is a creature of exile in exile (and the word *exile* is etymologically related to a word meaning "to wander about"). In his hole, in narrating what Guzmán de Alfarache calls the "warre-fare" of life, the Invisible Man sees his singularity, his onlyness; he is not everyman but rather onlyman: "I've come a long way from those days when full of illusion, I lived a public life and attempted to function under the assumption that the world was solid and all the relationships therein. Now I know men are different and that all life is divided and that only in division is there true health" (498–99). It is time to emerge: "Now that I've tried to put it all down the old fascination with playing a role returns, and I'm drawn upward again" (501). Unlike Pascual Duarte and Pito Pérez (*The Family of Pascual Duarte*, *The Futile Life of Pito Pérez*, q.q.v.), who are destroyed in their extremity, the Invisible Man has a way back. "I must shake off the old skin and come up for breath," he says. "I'm coming out, no less visible without it, but coming out nevertheless. And I suppose it's damn well time. Even hibernation can be overdone, come to think of it" (503). And his way back is in fact the old picaresque way—where the end promises a new beginning, a continuation: a small triumph over chaos-life by daring to reenter it with the possibility of new roles.

EDITIONS

New York: Random House, 1952; New York: Signet Classics, n.d. (page numbers refer to this edition); New York: Vintage Books, 1972.

SELECT BIBLIOGRAPHY

Ellison's "Harlem Is Nowhere" is in his *Shadow and Act* (New York: Vintage Books, 1972); see also Susan L. Blake, "Ritual and Rationalization: Black Folklore in the Works of Ralph Ellison," *PMLA* 94 (1979): 121–36; Stuart Miller, *The Picaresque Novel* (Cleveland: Case Western Reserve University Press, 1967); Charles H. Nichols, "The Slave Narrators and the Picaresque Mode: Archetypes for Modern Black Personae," in *The Slave's Narrative*, ed. Charles T. Davis and Henry Louis Gates, Jr. (Oxford: Oxford University Press, 1985), 283–98; Alexander A. Parker, *Literature and the Delinquent: The Picaresque Novel in Spain and Europe, 1599–1753* (Edinburgh: Edinburgh University Press, 1967); John M. Reilly, ed., *Twentieth Century Interpretations of "Invisible Man"* (Englewood Cliffs, N.J.: Prentice-Hall, 1970); William J. Schafer, "Ralph Ellison and the Birth of the Anti-Hero," *Critique: Studies in Modern Fiction* 10 (1968): 81–93; Raney Stanford, "The Return of the Trickster: When a Not-a-Hero Is a Hero," *Journal of Popular Culture* 1 (1967): 228–42; Ulrich Wicks, "Onlyman," *Mosaic* 8 (1975): 21–47. For a vivid depiction of Harlem in the 1940s and early 1950s, see Claude Brown,

Manchild in the Promised Land (New York: Macmillan, 1965): "We accepted this as the ways of life. Everybody was stealing from everybody else" (21).

THE ITCHING PARROT

(*El Periquillo Sarniento*, 1816, 1830)

José Joaquín Fernández de Lizardi

Like its twentieth-century descendant *The Futile Life of Pito Pérez* (q.v.), which has a direct allusion to its ancestor, *El Periquillo Sarniento* emerged from a period of revolutionary fervor in Mexico. Lizardi was a prolific political pamphleteer who, at the time when Mexico was fighting for independence from Spain, wrote in the spirit of the Enlightenment philosophy at the back of the American and French revolutions. Among the periodicals he established as outlets for his ideas were *The Mexican Thinker* (which also came to be his epithet) and *The Lightning Conductor*, which got him into constant trouble—and into prison. *El Periquillo Sarniento* began to appear in bits and pieces in 1816 but was not fully published until three years after Lizardi's death. On his deathbed, Lizardi composed his "Testament and Farewell of the Mexican Thinker," the bitterness of which is echoed by Pito Pérez in his "Last Will and Testament." In the final version of *El Periquillo*, Lizardi padded the narrative with many of the political pamphlets he had written throughout his life. By 1885, there had been nine editions. Translator Katherine Anne Porter calls it "without dispute The Novel of the past century, not only for Mexico but for all Spanish-speaking countries" (until the civil war, a Barcelona press reprinted it at the rate of more than a million copies a year) and remembers: "In Mexico I used to see it at every smallest sidewalk book stall; in the larger shops there were always a good number of copies in hand, selling steadily. It was given to the young to read as an aid to manners and morals, and for a great while it must have been the one source of a liberal education for the great mass of people, the only ethical and moral instruction they could have, for Lizardi's ideas of modern education got no foothold in Mexico for nearly a century after him" (xxxvi).

Evoking an earlier picaresque, *Periquillo, el de las gallineras* (q.v.), Lizardi's *El Periquillo* is narratively framed in a conventional picaresque way. The primary narrator is The Mexican Thinker himself, who in an epilogue describes receiving the manuscript just before the writer's death. Inside this frame is the autobiographical account itself, which begins with a deathbed prologue in which don Pedro (he receives his nickname at school as a result of his outfit—green jacket and yellow breeches—the diminutive of his name—Pedrillo—and the fact that he has caught the itch) addresses himself directly to his children:

I desire that by reading this you learn to avoid many errors here confessed, by me and by others, and that, warned by my example, you may not expose yourselves to such ill-treatment as I have suffered through my own fault. Be assured it is better to profit by other men's disillusions than by your own. Especially I beg you be not scandalized at the disorders of my youth, which I shall recount without hiding anything and with shame enough; for, since you are exposed to the same dangers, my desire is to instruct you and save you from the reefs whereon my youth was shattered so many times.

. . . Take warning from my mad errors; do not let yourselves be deceived by the falseness of men; observe the maxims I teach, remembering I learned them at cost of very painful experiences. (1–3)

With this typically picaresque admonition—a conventional disclaimer that rationalizes the lure of the forbidden with the guise of the morally edifying and that had already become ironic in the preface to *El Buscón* (q.v.)—don Pedro launches his *vida*.

He blames his lot in life on his upbringing (parents who spoiled and neglected him, nursemaids with strange habits, a wet-nurse's "cursed nature") and on having to change schools, and thus masters: "How unstable is fortune in this life! Grudgingly she shows us a smiling face for a single day and then frowns upon us for many months. God, how I realized this truth when I changed my school! In a moment I found I had passed from heaven to hell, and from the care of an angel into that of a tormenting devil. The world was turned upside down for me" (15). He is picked on, becoming "the *ne plus ultra* of buffoons and jesters" (21). After his father's death, he enjoys an indolent playboy period, followed by his becoming a gambler. Finally he is induced to become involved in thievery and is soon in prison, "poor, naked, dying of hunger, without any means of getting a cent" (131). He becomes the servant of many masters, sets himself up as a doctor until he is exposed, and eventually ends up shipwrecked after a stint in Manila (part of an eight-year sentence to serve in the king's troops as a result of gambling away public monies, among other deceits). At one of his lowest points, he attempts suicide, fails, and joins a band of robbers. Attacked by another gang, he survives, flees, and on the road sees his friend Januario hanging from a tree. This is the beginning of his conversion. In the last chapters, he encounters a number of people from his earlier days, a pattern of coincidence that resembles the picaresque dance pattern. He inherits his last master's estate, settles down, and compensates for his wicked ways by subjecting himself to "a life of strict reason and the wise principles of sane morality" (285).

In its horizontal and vertical panorama of society and in its heavy morality, *El Periquillo Sarniento* is directly in the picaresque tradition represented by *Guzmán de Alfarache* and *Simplicius Simplicissimus* (q.q.v.). Representative of its picaresque narrative technique is chapter 23, "How Poll Became a Sacristan, His Adventure with a Corpse, His Entry into the Brotherhood of Beggars, and Other Little Things as True as They Are Curious"; it begins:

If all men would write the history of their lives simply and truthfully as I do, a multitude of Polls would be revealed in this world, whose ups and downs of fortune are now kept secret because every man attempts to conceal his own mistakes. The events of my life already related and those I have yet to write contain nothing rare or fictitious, my children. They are true, commonplace, and natural enough. They have happened not only to me, but many of them happen daily to other humiliated, furtive Polls. I beg of you only what

I have already asked: not to read my life as simple pastime, but to try to benefit by the solid moral maxims that are sown among these my misdeeds, ridiculous incidents, digressions, and comic interludes: imitate virtue where you recognize it, shun vice, and take warning for yourselves from seeing how evil is punished. Thus you will learn to separate the grain from the chaff; and you will not only read with pleasure but gather fruit from these chapters. (197)

The gallows humor of the attempt to strip a corpse of its jewels and the episode with the community of rogues (during which he poses as a blind man)—whom he betrays in order to advance himself—are purely picaresque in their vision of a world of disorder in which chance and accident mirror the moral chaos of an unstable personality beset by homelessness and hunger.

One of the ambiguities of picaresque narrative results from the manner in which the picaro's conversion is presented: how much we take seriously the work's moral dimension depends in direct proportion on our perception of the degree of sincerity conveyed in the depiction of that moment. In *El Periquillo*, that moment itself seems genuine enough, though it is motivated in part by considerations of economic well-being. But the moral overlay that is insistently hammered from the temporally immediate level of the narrating process is often overpowered by the *fictor's* obvious relish in his life as lived, not as reflected. In Lizardi, the picaro's moral impulse, however genuine, often rings false in comparison to the fictive energy that brings the trickeries to narrative life. As a result, as Porter suggests is true of all picaresques, "the reader has uneasy moments of wondering whether it is the hero or the author who is deficient in moral sensibility" (xxxviii). There is no doubt that Lizardi was entirely committed to social justice and abhorred injustice in any form; but in the creation of his picaro, he has imperfectly integrated the various dimensions of narrative distance, leaving us with a work that is genuinely picaresque precisely because its vision is stronger than its rhetoric. In this perhaps unintentional contradiction—or unconscious revelation of a despairing view of human nature, which must be masked by moral guise—*El Periquillo Sarniento* has direct affinities in the picaresque narrative tradition with *Moll Flanders* (q.v.).

TRANSLATION

Katherine Anne Porter, *The Itching Parrot* (Garden City, N.Y.: Doubleday, 1942) (an abridged translation: "at last the story has been stripped of its immense accumulation of political pamphlets and moral disquisitions, which served their purpose once, let us hope, as the author meant them to. What remains, I believe, is a typical picaresque novel, almost the last of its kind" [Porter, vii]).

SELECT BIBLIOGRAPHY

Amancio Bolaño e Isla, *Estudio comparativo entre el Estebanillo González y el Periquillo Sarniento* (Mexico City: Universidad Nacional Autónoma de México, 1971); Maria Casas de Faunce, *La novela picaresca latinoamericana* (Madrid: Cupsa Editorial, 1977); Carlos Lozano, "*El Periquillo Sarniento* y la *Histoire de Gil Blas de Santillane*," *Revista Iberoamericana* 20 (1955): 263–74; Jacqueline van Praag-Chantraine, "*El Periquillo*

Sarniento: Un Pícaro Criollo," in *La Picaresca: Orígenes, Textos, Estructuras*, ed. Manuel Criado de Val (Madrid: Fundación Universitaria Española, 1979), 1047–54; Nancy Vogeley, "Defining the 'Colonial Reader': *El Periquillo Sarniento*," *PMLA* 102 (1987): 784–800.

JOURNEY TO THE END OF THE NIGHT

(*Voyage au bout de la nuit*, 1932)

Louis-Ferdinand Céline

Allen Ginsberg has called this book "the first genius international beat XX century picaresque novel written in modern classical personal comedy prose by the funniest & most intelligent of mad Doctors whose least tenderness is an immortal moment" (Steiner, 109). Wayne Booth, on the other hand, says that Céline in *Journey* creates a "seductive point of view" that leads the reader to "succumb morally as well as visually" to the verbal onslaught: "Taken seriously, the book would make life itself meaningless, except as a series of self-centered forays into the lives of others" (383–84). By their very nature, picaresque fictions deal with the night side of life in often radically unsettling terms. But even within the darker visions of the picaresque modal spectrum, Céline's stands out for its extremity. In both *Journey* and *Death on the Installment Plan* (*Mort à crédit*, 1936), which is narrated by Ferdinand and thus forms a kind of contin-uation (though chronologically it takes us back to Ferdinand's childhood), Céline produces a fiction for which words like *explosive* and *incendiary* seem inadequate, as they are for such other radical picaresques as *The Painted Bird*, *The Futile Life of Pito Pérez*, and *The Family of Pascual Duarte* (q.q.v.). In the development of modern picaresque,

Céline is a crucial figure and his *Journey to the End of the Night* a crucial book. This work is so important because in it Céline seemed to recognize, more deeply than anyone before him, a natural tendency in picaresque toward a grotesque exaggeration of mis-fortunes: an intensification of everyday troubles into an ironic vision of a distorted cosmos, where a poetic injustice reigns, which destroys all who do not learn to accommodate themselves to it. Céline's surrealism gets to the black heart of the picaresque tradition and finds there an existential despair of the human condition. (Scholes, 60–61)

Moreover, Céline's vision links directly to *Guzmán de Alfarache* (q.v.), which is

saturated through and through with a belief in the utter corruption of human nature. But its pessimism goes beyond that. Alemán is obsessed not only by the wickedness of man, but by the squalor and ugliness of life. Like Swift, he has a scatalogical mind. If in conduct the groundwork is sin, in tangible things it is excreta. And what goes into the body can be as disgusting as what comes out of it: his neurosis about food blossoms in a chapter of horrors, when an innkeeper serves to his guests horse-meat instead of calf. There are also his irrational hatreds. His hero hates the poor, though he is poor himself, because they are coarse, brutal and envious. He hates women and regards them as bitches and liars whose only thought is how to get money out of men for nothing: his own dealings with them always end in his discomfiture. Hatred and disgust for life well up so automatically that we end by being reminded of a modern book—Céline's *Voyage au bout de la nuit*. But Alemén is saved from Céline's complete despair, which made him a Fascist, by his Catholic faith. (Brenan, 172)

Ferdinand Bardamu's journey begins, like Simplicissimus's (*Simplicius Simplicissimus*, q.v.), in war: "So there was no mistake? So there was no law against people shooting at people they couldn't even see! It was one of the things you could do without anybody reading you the riot act. In fact, it was recognized and probably encouraged by upstanding citizens, like the draft, or marriage, or hunting! . . . No two ways about it. I was suddenly on the most intimate terms with war. I'd lost my virginity" (10). Recuperating from a wound, he stays in various hospitals; then, with his "brains . . . scrambled for good" (94), he decides to make his fortune in Africa, in an episode that evokes *Heart of Darkness*. On board ship, he sees the true nature of his fellow human beings:

From that moment on we saw, rising to the surface, the terrifying nature of white men, exasperated, freed from constraint, absolutely unbuttoned, their true nature, same as in the war. That tropical steam bath called forth instincts as August breeds toads and snakes on the fissured walls of prisons. In the European cold, under gray, puritanical northern skies, we seldom get to see our brothers' festering cruelty except in times of carnage, but when roused by the foul fevers of the tropics, their rottenness rises to the surface. That's when the frantic unbuttoning sets in, when filth triumphs and covers us entirely. It's a biological confession. Once work and cold weather cease to constrain us, once they relax their grip, the white man shows you the same spectacle as a beautiful beach when the tide goes out: the truth, fetid pools, crabs, carrion, and turds. (95–96)

After his jungle experience, he is tricked into becoming a galley slave and lands in the United States, where, in a New World portrait as surrealistic as Kakfa's (*Amerika*, q.v.), he works for a time catching and classifying fleas on arriving immigrants at Ellis Island and makes his way to Detroit to work for Ford, where "I became, little by little, a different man . . . a new Ferdinand" (195) by becoming like a machine on an assembly line. He becomes a doctor back in France and practices in a slum neighborhood near Paris. Finally, he works in an insane asylum. He ends *Journey* with the death of Robinson, a secondary picaro (again echoing Kafka's *Amerika*) who has been darting in and out of Ferdinand's life since the war and the galleys episode.

Céline renders the night side of life by way of a verbally delirious style that retrospectively churns Ferdinand's experienced reality into the nightmare visions of the totally excluded being he has become when he narrates. "The world only knows how to do one thing, to roll over and kill you, as a sleeper kills his fleas," he says: "That would be a stupid way to die . . . to let myself be crushed like everybody else. To put your trust in men is to get yourself killed a little" (152). In *Death on the Installment Plan*, Ferdinand sets himself apart from the world, screaming at it from his dark paranoic vantage point: "Life begins again. When I get to see God in his place, I'll blast his ear, the inner ear, I've studied those things. I wonder how he'll like that. I'm the Devil's stationmaster. The day I go, wait and see how the train jumps the track'' (40). The withdrawal into the night-side of life is, paradoxically, also an immensely assertive act. It is the picaro's way of fighting back at mad life with his own madness, which itself has tremendous force. The prose is full of shifts and changes of direction and strange verbal gestures; it poses questions that seem to be made in the present and yet apply to the past the narrator is rendering. In its discontinuity, this verbal energy heightens the distorted world it renders:

... Ah, it's an awful thing ... and being young doesn't help any ... when you notice for the first time ... the way you lose people as you go along ... buddies you'll never see again ... never again ... when you notice that they've disappeared like dreams ... that it's all over ... finished ... that you too will get lost someday ... a long way off but inevitably ... in the awful torrent of things and people ... of the days and shapes ... that pass ... that never stop ... (*Death*, 392)

Those ubiquitous three dots function less as ellipses than as emphatic connectors creating a continuous outburst of discontinuity that collapses narrative distance and reduces all that is rendered into the constant immediacy of the act of narration itself. Given without chapter divisions, *Death on the Installment Plan* has the effect of one stutter-like yet continuous burst of language rendering the installments on death. In its unrelieved pounding, it conveys the very onslaught of the chaos-world itself. *Death* begins as though chopped off from some previous thing:

Here we are, alone again. It's all so slow, so heavy, so sad ... I'll be old soon. Then at least it will be over. So many people have come into my room. They've talked. They haven't said much. They've gone away. They've grown old, wretched, sluggish, each in some corner of the world. (15)

And it ends, or rather stops, the same way. This burst of narrative comes from a characteristic basic to Céline's art: immense verbal energy. "Logorrhea," Steiner says, "is the very condition of Céline's achievement and limitation" (112); in his "true heirs—Grass [*The Tin Drum*, q.v.], Burroughs, Kerouac [*On the Road*, q.v.]—something of the same frantic loquacity prevails. Often the language is animate with energies that exceed the novelty or intelligence of what is being said" (113). Céline's version of the picaro is first of all thoroughly energetic—a picaro whose tactic in asserting himself against the world, in order to survive outside it, is to use his picaresque energy verbally. The compressing of narrative distance compacts this energy into what has been called a "delirium":

This consistent narrative polarity established by the narrator's static present and the picaro protagonist's chaotic past points to Céline's view of temporality as a form of *délire*. The picaro, Ferdinand, is engaged, usually catastrophically engaged, in the temporal duration that is, in effect, time past for the older narrator. Yet the sense of duration and the sense of insane destruction worked through time are preserved in the novels. Ferdinand's acts and outcries are not fixed by the passing of time in a series of historical moments. His perception is fluid, deliriously confronted with an ever unfolding present time. (Thiher, 206)

Where the more traditional picaro exists in a world full of bits of chaos, Céline's Ferdinand exists in a chaos full of little bits of world. He hopes, in moments of despair, to turn it into some sort of stability:

> . . . All these assholes, these pests . . . you'll never see them again . . . soon they'll be gone . . . all these harmless people parading along the shop fronts . . . I wanted to jump out on them . . . to plant myself in front of them . . . and make them stop where they were . . . Grab them by their coats . . . a dumb idea . . . and make them stop . . . and not move anymore . . . stay where they were, once and for all . . . and not see them going away anymore. (392)

But the very force and energy of his own narrative act negate any stability, even of narrative order. Whatever the world out there may be like, Céline's Ferdinand converts it into a constantly moving, constantly shifting, constantly pulsating thing. He compresses onto every page (indeed, into every verbal gesture) the panoramic sense of movement and teeming life that other picaresques convey only in much larger narrative segments. He exhausts the reader through his delirious acts of perception themselves, which it is often difficult, by any normative means of measuring narrative distance, to distinguish from reperceptions. The result, as Hayman points out, "is a vehicle capable of carrying everything, a tidal wave—or, to use Céline's own tongue-in-cheek expression, a 'métro émotif' (emotive subway) sucking the outer world into its dark maw and spewing it out again reconstituted" (13). This world of Ferdinand, "the picaro and pariah caught in the unbearable immediacy of constantly unfolding madness," is one of "absolute flux, of chaos and violent upheaval"; its narrative rendering constitutes "one of the most naked revelations of the tormented self in modern literature" (Thiher, 211–12). With its timeless and universal situations of war, illness, death, lunacy—even the dehumanizing assembly lines of Detroit—Ferdinand's narrative can be seen as "a morality play with Bardamu an Everyman for whom everything always comes up tails" (Ruland, 81, 85). But Ferdinand sets himself so far apart—from his world, from us as readers—that we hover precariously between being victims of his onslaught and feeling superior to him because he sees himself as the victim. He is the bitter clown, with a squirt gun that shoots fouler stuff than water. Ferdinand is really like some wild-funny-sad-mad clown, daring to act as though he were the only man by existing totally outside the continuum of things. From there, Guzmán's *atalaya* or "watchtower" of human life becomes not so much a vantage point of observation as it does a projector; it offers not perceptions but rather nightmare visions. In that realm of darkness, Ferdinand is both corrupted victim and corrupting victimizer—and his own judge as well. He is a surrogate for our darkest selves, a heightened version of the picaro's routine vicarious enactment of our disruptive desires. In becoming a kind of radical onlyman, Ferdinand does the dirty work for us in the circus of life.

TRANSLATIONS

Ralph Manheim, *Journey to the End of the Night* (New York: New Directions, 1983) and *Death on the Installment Plan* (New York: Signet, 1966); quotations are from these editions. *Death* is also available from New Directions. Previous translations were by John P. Marks: *Journey* (Boston: Little, Brown, 1934; rpt. New York: New Directions, 1960) and *Death* (Boston: Little, Brown, 1938; rpt. New York: New Directions, 1947).

SELECT BIBLIOGRAPHY

Wayne C. Booth, *The Rhetoric of Fiction* [1961], 2d ed. (Chicago: University of Chicago Press, 1983); Gerald Brenan, *The Literature of the Spanish People from Roman Times to the Present* [1951] (Cleveland, Ohio, and New York: World, 1957); Jane Carson, "Céline: The Fire in the Night," *Symposium* 35 (1981): 117–30; David Hayman, *Louis-Ferdinand Céline* (New York: Columbia University Press, 1965); Richard Ruland, *America in Modern European Literature: From Image to Metaphor* (New York: New York University Press, 1976); Robert Scholes, *The Fabulators* (New York: Oxford University Press, 1967), rpt. *Fabulation and Metafiction* (Urbana: University of Illinois Press, 1979); George Steiner, "Cry Havoc," *The New Yorker*, January 20, 1968, 106–15; Allen Thiher, *Céline: The Novel as Delirium* (New Brunswick, N.J.: Rutgers University Press, 1972); Ulrich Wicks, "Onlyman," *Mosaic* 8 (1975): 21–47.

KNULP: THREE TALES FROM THE LIFE OF KNULP

(Knulp: Drei Geschichten aus dem Leben Knulps, 1915)

Hermann Hesse

The blending of picaresque with romance patterns as in Eichendorff's *Memoirs of a Good-for-Nothing* (q.v.) is also at work in this book, which, though eclipsed today by his later works, was Hesse's most popular book before *Demian*. Each of the tales is an episode in Knulp's wandering life. The first, "Early Spring," is told by a kind of communal narrative voice that substitutes for the traditional self-narration of the picaro: "our friend Knulp" (3). He is a familiar figure on the landscape: "He had always had plenty of friends, he would have met with a friendly reception in almost every town in the region" (3). Discharged from a hospital, Knulp spends some time with a tanner, and during the course of the stay we learn about his vagabond life. He is a man of "many arts" (18) who knows "the language of every trade and the signs by which its practitioners recognize one another" (14). Variously referred to as a "vagrant" (26), "tramp" (39), and "dusty wayfarer" (79), Knulp is rootless, reflected in his roadbook:

In its dazzling perfection, his roadbook was a delightful fiction, a poem. Each of the officially accredited entries bore witness to a glorious station in an honest, laborious life. The only seemingly discordant feature was his restlessness, attested by frequent changes of residence. The life certified by this official passport was a product of Knulp's invention, and with infinite art he spun out the fragile thread of this pseudo-career. (9)

At the end of the first story, he is gone once again.

The second story, "My Recollections of Knulp," is narrated by a fellow wanderer and takes place in midsummer. It consists mostly of a dialogue with Knulp about the meaning of life, which is as elusive as a stable existence: "But every day you find some piece of wisdom, and the next day you give it up" (67), the narrator tells him. The third story, "The End," takes place in autumn and concludes with Knulp's apparent death. Before his "desire to sleep" overcomes all other desires, Knulp has a talk with God, in which he learns the value of his own existence in the scheme of things. God tells him:

Can't you see what it all means? Can't you see that you had to be a gadabout and a vagabond to bring people a bit of child's folly and child's laughter wherever you went? To make all sorts of people love you a little and tease you a little and be a little grateful to you? (112)

His divinely sanctioned role has been that of trickster (q.v.), to reinvigorate life-denying dullness and routine:

You were a wanderer in my name and wherever you went you brought the settled folk a little homesickness for freedom. In my name, you did silly things and people scoffed at you; I myself was scoffed at in you and love in you. You are my child and my brother and a part of me. There is nothing you have enjoyed and suffered that I have not enjoyed and suffered with you. (113)

As trickster, his divinely sanctioned activities are also socially sanctioned by the community, thus explaining his gallery of friends and the interest expressed in him by all inhabitants of the landscape. He is the communal vagabond who vicariously enacts the freedom that "the more settled members of the population" (30) lack. But in this role he feels at times painfully alone: "Now it was my turn to taste the loneliness which in Knulp's opinion was the lot of every man and which I had never really believed in. It was bitter" (74), says the friend-narrator of the second story. Moreover, he also suffers from a homesickness of his own, bred by and nurtured by his loneliness. "But time and time again a strange anxiety and homesickness had driven this migrant, who was always on the move and could never settle down" (12). Returning, in the third story, to the scenes of his earlier life, the "homecomer" savors the "appeasing feeling of being at home," and "with his whole being the wanderer drank in the enchantment of home, of recognition, of memory, of comradeship with every street corner and every curbstone" (99). His very integrative function as trickster paradoxically alienates him from the landscape he enlivens. At the end, however, he is indeed finally home in a sense that transcends the yearned-for paradise in the picaresque circle of existence as exemplified, say, by Simplicius's tropical island (*Simplicius Simplicissimus*, q.v.).

The wandering picaro has always been the fictional expression of homelessness; his is the prototype of a human condition with which our literature has become increasingly concerned. Barrett writes that the progress of [the last] three centuries has produced today a world in which, both in philosophical theory and in social fact, man feels himself homeless. The most searching philosopher of the period, Heidegger, in analyzing human existence has declared that man's fundamental Being in the world is a "not being at home" in it. (272)

Loren Eisley calls man a "cosmic orphan" wandering somewhere between "uncertain beginnings and an indefinite ending." Picaresque fictions have always, with varying degrees of emphasis, rendered such a vision of existence, and the picaro figure, metamorphosed as he often is in modern fiction, embodies this very homelessness. He is the archetype of "not being at home" in the world, and Hesse's *Knulp* is an exploration of this archetype, as is Kafka's *Amerika* (q.v.) in which Karl Rossmann finds a home in "The Nature Theatre of Oklahoma," a transcendence of the earth-bound that fulfills the circle of existence. Both Knulp and Karl are cosmic exiles whose search for and ultimate possession of home goes beyond the merely social and geographical to the spiritual and the aesthetic.

This exploration of homelessness and homesickness emphasizes the picaro as reflector, as onlooker, as a contemplative, who has "learned to enjoy life as a spectator" (34) and "wanted nothing of life but to look on" (23). Knulp "had lived as an outsider, an idler and onlooker, well liked in his young manhood, alone in his illness and advancing years" (104). Hesse thus focuses on the reflective and reflecting role that the picaro traditionally takes on at the end of his life in the course of narrating that life. This kind of picaresque has been called (by Freedman) "vagabond picaresque," "romantic picaresque," and even "allegorical picaresque," as Hesse fuses the traditional picaresque with German romantic narrative forms. In this variety of lyrical fiction, external experiences are emphasized in their inward absorption by the self.

Again we have an example of a picaresque fiction that is not narrated by the picaro but nevertheless maintains a picaresque voice in its method of narration. The communal narrator of the first story is complemented by a close friend in the second; the first focuses on Knulp in his communal function as trickster, while the second explores his loneliness, mostly through a dialogue in which Knulp speaks directly. The effect is similar to that achieved by the dialogue technique Romero uses in *The Futile Life of Pito Pérez* (q.v.). Hesse's third story is omnisciently and anonymously narrated, but the point of view is so close to Knulp that it, like Kafka's similar focus through Karl in *Amerika*, simulates the first-person point of view. As the seasons move from spring through summer to autumn, the narrative voice moves from a group voice, to an individual voice, to a divine vindication. The absent fourth story would, of course, take place in winter. But our last image of Knulp is of him being covered by snow, his "desire to sleep" having grown "stronger than any other desire" (114). In the divine scheme of things, trickster hibernates until spring begins the circle yet again. In *Knulp*, romance indeed triumphs over picaresque.

TRANSLATION

Ralph Manheim (New York: Farrar, Straus and Giroux, 1971).

SELECT BIBLIOGRAPHY

William Barrett, *Time of Need: Forms of Imagination in the Twentieth Century* (New York: Harper & Row, 1972); Loren Eisley, "The Cosmic Orphan," *Saturday Review/ World*, February 23, 1974, 16–19; Ralph Freedman, *The Lyrical Novel: Studies in Hermann Hesse, André Gide, and Virginia Woolf* (Princeton, N.J.: Princeton University Press, 1963); Ulrich Wicks, "Onlyman," *Mosaic* 8 (1975): 21–47.

LAZARILLO DE TORMES

(La vida de Lazarillo de Tormes y de sus fortunas y adversidades,
1554)

In her incisive 1919 essay on Defoe, occasioned by the bicentennial of the publication of *Robinson Crusoe* and reprinted in *The Common Reader: First Series* (1925), Virginia Woolf wrote of *Crusoe* that

it resembles one of the anonymous productions of the race itself rather than the efforts of a single mind; and as for celebrating its centenary we should as soon think of celebrating the centenaries of Stonehenge itself. Something of this we may attribute to the fact that we have all had *Robinson Crusoe* read aloud to us as children, and were thus much in the same state of mind towards Defoe and his story that the Greeks were in towards Homer. It never occurred to us that there was such a person as Defoe, and to have been told that *Robinson Crusoe* was the work of a man with a pen in his hand would either have disturbed us unpleasantly or meant nothing at all. The impressions of childhood are those that last longest and cut deepest. It still seems that the name of Daniel Defoe has no right to appear upon the title-page of *Robinson Crusoe*, and if we celebrate the bicentenary of the book we are making a slightly unnecessary allusion to the fact that, like Stonehenge, it is still in existence. (89–90)

The same might be said, perhaps even more incisively and appropriately, of the deliberately anonymous *Lazarillo de Tormes*, which three and a half decades later was having its quadricentennial. Of the major Spanish Golden Age picaresques, *Lazarillo* is the only one to have achieved some kind of stature in world literature, though it has—inexplicably—never made its way into the anthologies of world masterpieces. This at first glance unassuming little book is a remarkable achievement, not only in the specific context of the historically identifiable genre of which it is the progenitor but also—both directly and by way of the genre it engendered—in the whole evolution of Western narrative forms.

In some ways, *Lazarillo* still relies heavily on received conventions and traditional stories, popular associations, even jests. Its borrowings from folklore have been traced, and the image of a blind man paired with a crafty guide boy (illustrated on the title page of the Alcalá de Henares edition) evoked for contemporary audiences a stock relationship going back as early as the fourteenth century. Its gallery of human types is not as large and diverse as the ones in later picaresques and still reflects a medieval worldview: Lazarillo's first three masters (the blind man, the priest, and the squire) represent the three estates of the medieval social structure (respectively, commoners, the clergy, and the nobility). The literary allusions in the prologue are obligatory, and the use of proverbs is formulaic. Many of the tricks Lazarillo plays on his masters were widely known from other sources. Even the evocation of the two biblical Lazaruses, the beggar in Luke 16 and the resurrected dead man in John 11, must have seemed natural and appropriate for this constantly starving, death-obsessed, homeless urchin who with God's help overcomes abject poverty and grows up into a new life. With its reworking of familiar materials, *Lazarillo de Tormes* must have been in its day a highly accessible book. After more than four centuries, some of that intimacy of the immediately recognizable has gotten lost.

But *Lazarillo* is also a daring and innovative book whose originalities stand out in bolder relief as time passes. Although low life had been treated seriously in *La Celestina* (1499, 1502), which Chandler called a "dialogued novel" (185), and although autobiographical forms were familiar from such earlier works as *El libro de buen amor* by the fourteenth-century Juan Ruiz (Archpriest of Hita), St. Augustine's *Confessions* (397–401), and Apuleius's *The Golden Ass* (q.v.), *Lazarillo* struck new ground in its rendering of a child growing up told from the adult's point of view through the voice of the younger self. A narrative technique traditionally reserved for personages of importance telling of accomplishments of some import is here used to tell the life of a nobody from nowhere striving to be somebody somewhere. Dunn, summarizing the work of such scholars as Castro, Bataillon, and Lázaro Carreter on *Lazarillo's* autobiographical precedents, says: "The novelty of the unknown author in creating the autobiography of a character who commands no admiration, enjoys no social preeminence, and has no profound thoughts to deliver, was absolute" (32–33). The effrontery of this narrative situation must have been startlingly attention grabbing, and this narrative presumptiveness has become one of the indispensable characteristics of mainstream picaresque narrative. In the last few decades, most of the abundant criticism on *Lazarillo* has focused particularly on a specific aspect of that narrative impudence: its clever strategies of manipulating the reader in various relationships to the text.

While the self-portrayal of an insignificant person may have been a boldly unanticipated use of established narrative convention, the rendered situation of *Lazarillo* is so universal that it might have, as Woolf implies of *Crusoe*, emerged unauthored directly from the collective unconscious. Lazarillo's is a human condition so archetypal that it strikes deep chords in the being of readers whose experiential frame of reference hardly coincides with Lazarillo's but whose residual childhood fears of abandonment or loss are here given exemplary fictional form. "In the history of narrative forms," says Claudio Guillén, "*Lazarillo de Tormes* represents the first significant appearance of the myth of the orphan." This orphaned condition is total: abandoned by family, by society, and, to all appearances, even by God, the boy is unmitigatedly alone. Guillén adds that "all values must be rediscovered by him anew, as if by a godless Adam" ("Toward a Definition," 79). Lazarillo is a major literary incarnation of what

Loren Eisley has called the "cosmic orphan." He is the prototype for what the picaro figure represents in mythic terms:

There is something so elemental, so primordial, about that solitary, loveless ego called Lazarillo that he impinges on a reader's consciousness as a mythical being more remote even than Lear's "bare, forked animal, unaccommodated man," not only detached from human society but, parodistically, the precondition and creator of himself. Shorn of traditionally meaningful spiritual existence, he—through the author's painterlike awareness of reduction to a vanishing point—has come to symbolize the timeless, undifferentiated natural being within every individual. His origins are indeed past finding out! Lacking even physical appearance (unlike Sancho Panza, for example), he seems to exist no only without roots but also without boundaries. (Blackburn, 12–13)

At the same time, this archetypal figure is rendered with a psychological particularity that astonishes even now, when child-narrators and -protagonists have become commonplace in fiction. R. O. Jones says in *A Literary History of Spain* that "no previous narrative offers what this one does: a portrait of a child in the process of becoming a man, an account of how he is moulded imperceptibly by the example of others, so that when we realize with a shock that his childish innocence has gone for good we cannot decide when and where the change took place" (quoted in Sieber, *The Picaresque*, 14).

Lazarillo de Tormes appeared simultaneously in three editions (at Burgos, Antwerp, and Alcalá de Henares). Much scholarship has gone into studying these editions, with a variety of speculations about the identity of the author, about the existence of a *princeps* edition or circulating manuscript as early as the 1520s, and about the specific chronology of Lazarillo's life. Arguments have been put forth that the author was a heterodox humanist, an Erasmian, even a *converso*. Although its anticlericalism (five of Lazarillo's nine masters are connected with the church, and they are not admirable) is squarely in the medieval tradition, *Lazarillo* was among the first books to be put on the Index, or *Catalog of Prohibited Books*, in 1559. After the ban was lifted some dozen years later, it was republished five times before the end of the century. But between 1599 and 1603—coinciding precisely with the unprecedented popularity of *Guzmán de Alfarache* (q.v.)—at least nine editions of *Lazarillo* were published, sparking what Guillén calls "a double acceptance, a convergence, from which there arose, during the years immediately following the publication of *Guzmán* (1599), the idea of a *género picaresco*" ("Genre and Countergenre," 144), and so "the picaresque novel as a genre emerges . . . out of the confluence of the *Lazarillo* and of the autobiography of a criminal [Guzmán]" (Sieber, *The Picaresque*, 24). In chapter 22 of part I of *Don Quixote* (1605) Cervantes saw this emerging narrative form as a distinct fictional type when he has Ginés de Pasamonte claim, with a boast precisely in the spirit of the effrontery that characterizes the picaro's narrational dare: "It's so good," he says, "that *Lazarillo de Tormes* will have to look out, and so will everything in that style [*de aquel género*] that has ever been written or ever will be." Ginés is a galley slave, like Guzmán, and in this double allusion—one direct, the other indirect—Cervantes is acknowledging the nascent picaresque genre. (In "The Illustrious Kitchen-Maid" [q.v.] he also acknowledges the picaresque as an established type, this time reversing the double allusion by referring directly to *Guzmán* and indirectly to *Lazarillo*.) For almost fifty years, Lazarillo seems to have existed sui generis; and, as Cervantes's distinctly generic references along with the renewed popularity of *Lazarillo* after 1599 demonstrate, it is through its basic narrative similarities with *Guzmán de Alfarache*—despite major differences—that *Lazarillo* comes to be perceived in generic terms. "It was the combined popularity and publication of the *Lazarillo* and the *Guzmán* that generated imitations, emulations, and parodies of the new genre" (Sieber, *The Picaresque*, 24). Through a curiously ironic kind of narrative back-formation, the literary child (*Guzmán*) in a sense becomes "father to the man," the child (*Lazarillo*) who engendered him.

Before this development, however, *Lazarillo* was dogged by false continuations (which would later also plague *Guzmán* and *Don Quixote*, although both Alemán and Cervantes in their own second parts were able to take delicious revenge on their hack imitators). A *Second Part of Lazarillo de Tormes* was published anonymously in Antwerp in 1555 (reprinted in Milan in 1587 and 1615). It is more in the tradition of the fantastic journey, depicting Lazarillo's metamorphosis into a tuna fish. "Although the *Second Part* alludes to Lázaro's previous life and continues the themes of fortune and adversity, it is more in the satirical tradition of the *Golden Ass* and the tales of Lucian than the picaresque genre" (Fiore, 16). This spurious continuation in turn gave cause for another, written—like Courage's sequel (*The Runagate Courage*, q.v.) to spite Simplicius (*Simplicius Simplicissimus*, q.v.)—deliberately to refute the truth and credibility of the earlier one. The second *Second Part of Lazarillo de Tormes* was published in Paris in 1620 and written by Juan de Luna, a native of Toledo who had been persecuted by the Inquisition. A third sequel, *Lazarillo de Manzanares* by Juan Cortés de Tolosa, was published in Madrid in 1620; it ends with Lazarillo on board a ship sailing for the New World.

Meanwhile, the original *Lazarillo* became widely disseminated and firmly established in world literature as the first translations began to appear in French (1560), English (in David Rowland's still popular version of 1568, followed by others in 1576, 1586, 1596, 1624, and 1631), Dutch (1579), Italian (1608), German (1617), and even Latin (1623). Shakespeare took an English audience's familiarity with at least the first chapter for granted, when Benedick says to Claudio in *Much Ado about Nothing*: "Ho! now you strike like the blind man: 'twas the boy that stole your meat, and you'll beat the post" (act II, scene I). *Lazarillo* is the only one of the original Spanish picaresques that is still widely read today. And it even continues to be continued. In 1944, Camilo José Cela portrayed Lazarillo in twentieth-century Spain in *Nuevas andanzas y desventuras de Lazarillo de Tormes* (q.v.). At the turn of this century, William Dean Howells thought that *Lazarillo* and Spanish picaresque fiction provided the most appropriate pattern for American fiction (*Huckleberry Finn*, q.v.). Like the apparently stock image of blindman-guide that it originally incorporated, *Lazarillo* has in turn produced a stock character of its own: through anatonomasia, Lazarillo's name in lower case has come to mean "blind person's guide" in the Spanish language. In the light of what Lazarillo does to the blind man, this reflects not a little lexical mischief.

Despite its wide impact, *Lazarillo de Tormes* is not unanimously accepted as the prototypal picaresque or even as a full-fledged picaresque work. Chandler, though he acknowledges that its claim "to be the first romance of roguery and the originator of a literary species is unshaken" (191), nevertheless treats the book in a chapter called "Crude Forms of the Picaresque Novel," where he classes it with *Guzmán* and *La pícara Justine* (q.v.) as works of a "primitive order," belonging to "the first stage of picaresque fiction" (243). Marcel Bataillon has also resisted its full inclusion, while at the same time emphasizing its absolute originality as a work of fiction. And Parker prefers to consider it as the precursor and *Guzmán* as the prototype, mostly because *Lazarillo* does not explore delinquency in its moral and socioeconomic dimensions as fully as later picaresques, especially *El Buscón* (q.v.), will. Such generic refinements, of course, depend heavily on each critic's genre concept, although much is often made of the nearly half a century that passed before *Lazarillo* had a successor in *Guzmán* (the first work to use the word *pícaro*). Guillén has explored this generic isolation, as well as the formal and thematic differences between *Lazarillo* and later picaresques. Building on Bataillon's assertion in his introduction to the anthology *Le roman picaresque* (1931) that *Lazarillo* was "un commencement absolu," Guillén claims that the position of *Lazarillo* in its day "was truly singular" and that the failure to understand or assimilate a genuine original is a fairly ordinary occurrence in the history of the arts. The appearance of *Guzmán* in 1599 ended the isolation of *Lazarillo*:

On a certain level, *Guzmán de Alfarache* (a didactic and dogmatic monolith) and *Lazarillo de Tormes* (compassionate and pluralistic) seem nearly antithetical. But the seventeenth-century reader very probably had his eye on another level, where the two works converged. The result of this convergence was a common *género picaresco*, which did not come into being until 1599, of course—just as the heroic couplet did not exist until Chaucer had enough admirers and imitators. (142)

The successes of *Lazarillo* and *Guzmán* were secondary; the main development was the recognition by Alemán's readers of generic similarities between the two: "the surge of popularity of the model, the pattern, the genre, which they [*Lazarillo* and *Guzmán*] sustained not singly but conjointly" (143). By the time he was writing the Ginés de Pasamonte episode of *Don Quixote* only a few years later, Cervantes could assume a generic conception of the picaresque as a common frame of reference among his readers.

But while the debate about *Lazarillo's* generic purity and plenitude persists, there is no denying that all of the major characteristics we might single out as being indispensable to the picaresque genre can be found in it, even if only in embryonic form: a panoramic structure that covers some horizontal (geographical) breadth as well as vertical (socially hierarchical) depth through a gallery of human types; the external (Sisyphus) and internal rhythms of episodic narration; major themes such as hunger, vanity, disillusionment, moral compromise, freedom, fortune, and social climbing; basic motifs such as the unusual birth and disreputable childhood, the grotesque or horrible incident, ejection, role playing, and the meticulous execution of crude and familiar tricks; and the essential picaro-landscape relationship, with its radical solitude resulting in social, moral, and psychological instability. Even the moralizing repentance that will motivate such subsequent picaresques as *Guzmán*, *Simplicissimus*, and *Moll Flanders* (q.v.) exists in *Lazarillo* in kernel form in Lazarillo's habit of interjecting proverbs into his narration, as Sancho Panza will do in talking to Don Quixote. Although *Lazarillo* is not self-consciously picaresque (as many later works will be), it is aware of itself as different from conventional fictions (expressed with appropriate cheekiness in the prologue); in its subject matter and tone, it implicitly parodies romance forms (George Tyler Northup says in his *An Introduction to Spanish Literature* that *"Lazarillo de Tormes* killed the [romance of chivalry] quite as much as did *Don Quixote"*). Its exploitation of the inherent trickiness of autobiographical narrative technique, employing fully all the dimensions of narrative distance, is among the most sophisticated in all of the picaresque narrative tradition. (These characteristics are illustrated in concrete detail, using *Lazarillo* as a prime example, in chapter 4.)

One of the technical achievements of *Lazarillo de Tormes* is the way it modulates point of view and voice in order to manipulate reader relationships to the text. In picaresque narrative, we are always aware of vertical and horizontal distances in the narration. We are looking down with the narrator toward his past self; we are looking up from the past self to the present self (sometimes forgetting, in the mutually agreed-upon suspension of disbelief that comprises the contract between audience and work, that the past self is entirely the creation of the present self); and we are looking across to the total narrating and narrated self in its psychological, moral, and intellectual proximity to or distance from us (and so is he in relation to us). A passage from the third chapter demonstrates this complex narrating reciprocity. Lazarillo is with his third master, an impoverished *hidalgo* (translated as "gentleman" or "squire," the lowest rank of nobility) who is too proud to admit his condition. The roles of master and servant are ironically reversed in this episode, as the gentleman, who would rather starve than stoop below what his absolute code of honor dictates, comes to depend for basic survival on the reality-oriented, resourceful picaro. The irony culminates in a world-upside-down image at the end of the chapter, when the *hidalgo* absconds, leaving Lazarillo facing a landlord demanding the rent: "Now I was convinced of my tragic destiny and saw that everything was against me. All I did was upside-down because masters are usually left by their servants but with me it was the opposite: he left me, in fact he deserted me" (65). This chapter has been much admired for its sensitive portrayal of two individuals from opposite ends of the social hierarchy. At the end of their first day together, the two had gone to bed hungry, with the gentleman claiming it was too late and too far to the market, and he had been eating out, and besides, "there's only one way to a ripe old age and that's to eat little." Lazarillo says to himself, "Well, if that's true, I'll never die."

When morning came we got up and he began to brush and dab away at his breeches, his doublet, his coat and his cloak. I acted as his valet. He dressed very slowly and solemnly. I poured water over his hands; he combed his hair and put his sword into his belt. As he did this he said to me:

"You don't realize, lad, what a fine weapon this is! I wouldn't sell it for its weight in gold. Of all the swords that the famous Antonio of Toledo made there isn't one as well-tempered as this one."

And he took it out of the scabbard and tested it with his finger and said:

"See this? I bet I could cut straight through a ball of wool with it."

"I could bite through a whole loaf," I said to myself, "and my teeth aren't made of steel." (53)

There is a double perspective here that only the older narrator (Lázaro) could render. The gentleman's sword represents honor (an abstract luxury), while the picaro's teeth represent hunger (a physical misery); the one stands for illusion, appearances, hollowness, the other for the reality of physical survival; the *hidalgo* upholds a social ideal, while Lazarillo is concerned only with the physical self. Both are ultimately antisocial—the one above society, the other below it. The analogy Lazarillo makes is one he perhaps felt at the time, but it is one only the older Lázaro of the narration can articulate.

While the gentleman prances around keeping up appearances, Lazarillo manages to beg some tripe and bread. At home later, when Lazarillo sits down to finish eating, there is at first a valiant attempt on both their parts to wear their respective masks. Lazarillo hesitates to ask him to share because he thinks the gentleman will refuse, claiming to have had lunch. But the gentleman's hunger is obvious beneath the mask. An unspoken communion of compatible desires begins, with Lazarillo hoping "God takes as much pity on me as I did on him, because I felt for his suffering as I had often endured it and still endured it most days" (56). Finally,

God granted my wish and his own, I think, because when I began to eat and he began to walk up and down, he came up to me suddenly and said:

"You know, Lázaro, it's a real pleasure to watch the way you eat. Anybody watching you can't help feeling hungry even if he isn't really."

"Why don't you come out straight with it?" I said to myself. "You're starving."

Still, I thought I ought to help him. He was helping me and showing me the way to invite him, so I said:

"Sir, they say that good tools make a good workman. This bread is really very tasty and the cow's foot is very well cooked and seasoned. Anybody's mouth would water at its smell."

"Cow's foot, is it?"

"Yes, sir."

"You know, that's the tastiest thing I know. I'd rather have that than pheasant any day."

"Well, have a piece, sir, and you'll see how good it is."

I put the cow's paw into his and three or four pieces of the whitest bread and he sat down beside me and began to eat as if he meant it, gnawing every little bone like a dog.

"This exquisite dish," he said, "has been made with garlic sauce."

"You've got more sauce than the meat has," I said to myself.

"God, it tastes so good that I feel I haven't eaten anything else today."

"I hope I drop dead right here if you have," I said to myself. (57)

Within the normal dimensions of autobiographical narrative distance, which by nature involves at least two voices (here, those of Lázaro the narrating self and Lazarillo the narrated self), *Lazarillo de Tormes* creates dual levels of spoken and unspoken communication that are presented as part of the recreated self's experience but need the narrating self's perception for their articulation. The narrative distance is obvious between Lazarillo and Lázaro, between the *hidalgo* and both Lázaro and Lazarillo, and between the reader and the *hidalgo*. The narrative strategy of temporal and intellectual distancing manipulates the reader's attitude toward the *hidalgo* as a pathetically ludicrous creature. But at the same time, the narrational strategy is to bring us to very close psychological proximity to Lazarillo (and thus to Lázaro, who "ventriloquizes" this), with the result that a potentially stock satirical victim is sensitively humanized through the self-rendered humanitarianism of Lazarillo. Perceptual and conceptual points of view and a carefully controlled narrating voice function together to create a portrait of Lazarillo as a universally likable character and of Lázaro as an admirable narrator. As a result, emotional proximity gets in the way of adequate distancing in the reader-text relationship. Have we been narratively tricked? Or is this in fact what narrative by its very nature seeks to accomplish?

These questions arise when we get to the seventh and final chapter of *Lazarillo*, in which the temporal distance between Lazarillo and Lázaro is reduced to a minimum. We remember from the prologue that *Lazarillo* has a very specifically delineated narrating situation: now a town crier, married to a servant girl whom he is said to share sexually with the archpriest, Lázaro has been asked to tell his story to a certain *Vuestra Merced* ("Your Honor"), an unnamed authority figure who is apparently investigating the scandal of this ménage à trois. Lazaro's "case" thus motivates his every narrational move. Once we are stunned into realizing what compromises Lázaro seems to be making, we distance ourselves in all ways from him and from Lazarillo. We feel we have been tricked, through the manipulation of narrative distancing, into learning to like a narrated self created primarily for the justification of the spiritually corrupt narrating self.

But we have to examine this much-explicated final chapter further. As Woodward reminds us, there are four people involved in the narration: the real author, *Vuestra Merced*, Lázaro, and the reader (43). We also have to remember that Lázaro is on trial in this situation and that the narrative is his defense. One of his strategies is to set up alliances—between reader and recreated self (Lazarillo) on the one hand and between Lázaro and *Vuestra Merced* on the other. But "the reader's relationship of empathy with the younger man becomes overlaid with one of complicity with the older man, and Lázaro and V. M. [*Vuestra Merced*]— first and second persons singular—find themselves allies—first persons plural— in league with each other, with Lazarillo the ironic victim. The result of this technique is a literary equivalent of the Necker cube, in which the reader sees the events of the narrative from opposing points of view almost, but not quite, simultaneously. Either he stands with Lazarillo or with Lázaro, in which case he sees his former engagement with detachment" (Ife, 99). Lázaro as narrator tries to ingratiate himself with *Vuestra Merced* by making him feel superior in recognizing the false values and deceiving appearances that permeate the society through which the boy Lazarillo has had to struggle to become Lázaro the man.

But at the end, Lázaro turns defiant, almost insolent, in his insistence on keeping up present appearances as far as he and his wife and the archpriest are concerned. As Ife says, Lázaro has maneuvered *Vuestra Merced* into an untenable position by pointing out, in effect, as though he were defending himself in court: "I argued earlier, and you agreed, that the world is a hostile theatre of illusion peopled by hypocrites; nothing in the world is what it appears to be. And now you judge me by appearances . . . you pay heed to the lowest kind of gossip and ignore everything that I have been trying to tell you. . . . You have learned nothing from what I have been saying. How can you dare to sit in judgment on me and expect me to accept your verdict?" (115). Lázaro's defense thus is turned into an accusation.

But what about the other two of the four persons in the narrating situation, the author and reader (and their shadows, the implied author and implied reader)? Here is where much of the contemporary criticism on *Lazarillo* is focused. Their verdict is still up in the air, with some coming down self-righteously against the moral accommodation Lázaro has made and others seeing the author as portraying the necessity of surviving in a corrupt world in which the picaro is, in Bjornson's phrase, always in a "no-exit situation" (21).

The narrative—and thus interpretive—problematics of *Lazarillo de Tormes* are not unique to it. All picaresque fictions are narrationally disturbing, and not their least upsetting aspect is the virtuosity with which the picaro-become-artist can pull off the telling of his life. In this accomplishment, Lázaro is indeed an admirable figure at the end, to both his author and the reader. By his very act of narration, the picaro always ends up a superior being aesthetically. If he were not, he could not interest us in his former self. His rise in commerce and in art accompanied by a fall in common decency and morality is not in itself cause for outrage. He is adapting himself to his world, not unlike Candide settling in, and for, his garden. The anger of Lazarillo's anonymous author, like that of Voltaire, can be sensed in this ending. But the anger is not directed at Lázaro, any more than Voltaire shakes his fist, as it were, at Candide.

When Lazarillo had his eyes opened by the blind man—"though he was blind he revealed things to me and made me see what life was about" (28)—he was only at the first stage of perception; by the time he narrates, he has perfect vision. He has become the blind person's guide that his name is synonymous with, and he is leading us. In our righteous eagerness to condemn him for that, we forget what is happening at the end to *Vuestra Merced*: Lazarillo is leading him rhetorically by the nose, and his very last words show total control: "I will inform Your Honour of my future in due course" (79). The triumph of the real author is in opening our eyes to that.

TRANSLATIONS / EDITION

Quotations are from the translation by Michael Alpert in *Two Spanish Picaresque Novels* (Baltimore: Penguin, 1969). Other accessible English versions include those by J. Gerald Markley, *The Life of Lazarillo de Tormes* (New York: Bobbs-Merrill, 1954); Mack Hendricks Singleton, *Lazarillo de Tormes*, in *Masterpieces of the Spanish Golden Age*, ed. Angel Flores (New York: Holt, Rinehart and Winston, 1957); Harriet de Onís, *The Life of Lazarillo de Tormes* (Woodbury, N.Y.: Barron, 1959); W. S. Merwin, *The Life of Lazarillo de Tormes: His Fortunes and Adversities* (Garden City, N.Y.: Doubleday Anchor, 1962 (rpt. Magnolia, Mass.: Peter Smith; and in Merwin's *From the Spanish Morning* [New York: Atheneum, 1985]); Robert S. Rudder, *The Life of Lazarillo de Tormes: His Fortunes and Misfortunes as Told by Himself, with a Sequel by Juan de Luna* (New York: Ungar, 1973). There are many editions of the original text; the most readily available in the United States has been *La vida de Lazarillo de Tormes y de sus fortunas y adversidades*, ed. Everett W. Hesse and Harry F. Williams, with an introduction by Américo Castro (Madison: University of Wisconsin Press, 1948; rev. 1961).

SELECT BIBLIOGRAPHY

Margit Frenk Alatorre, "Tiempo y narrador en el *Lazarillo* (episodio del ciego)," *Nueva revista de filología hispánica* 24 (1975): 195–218; Gustav A. Alfaro, "El despertar del pícaro," *Romanische Forschungen* 80 (1968): 44–52; Robert Alter, *Rogue's Progress: Studies in the Picaresque Novel* (Cambridge: Harvard University Press, 1964); Robert Archer, "The Fictional Context of *Lazarillo de Tormes*," *Modern Language Review* 80 (1985): 340–50; Francisco Ayala, *"El Lazarillo": Nuevo examen de algunos aspectos* (Madrid: Taurus, 1971); Horst Baader, "Noch einmal zur Ich-Form im *Lazarillo de Tormes*," *Romanische Forschungen* 76 (1964): 437–46; Marcel Bataillon, *Novedad y fecundidad del "Lazarillo de Tormes*," trans. Luis Cortés Vázquez (New York: Las Americas, 1968); Peter Baumanns, "Der *Lazarillo de Tormes* eine Travestie der Augustinsichen *Confessiones*?" *Romanistisches Jahrbuch* 10 (1959): 285–91; Aubrey Bell, "The Rhetoric of Self-Defense of 'Lázaro de Tormes,' " *Modern Language Review* 68 (1973): 84–93; Richard Bjornson, *The Picaresque Hero in European Fiction* (Madison: University of Wisconsin Press, 1977); Alexander Blackburn, *The Myth of the Picaro: Continuity and Transformation of the Picaresque Novel, 1554–1954* (Chapel Hill: University of North Carolina Press, 1979); Marina Scordilis Brownlee, "Generic Expansion and Generic Subversion: The Two Continuations of *Lazarillo de Tormes*," *Philological Quarterly* 61 (1982): 317–27; Douglas M. Carey, *"Lazarillo de Tormes* and the Quest for Authority," *PMLA* 94 (1979): 36–46, and "Asides and Interiority in *Lazarillo de Tormes*," *Studies in Philology* 66 (1969): 119–34; F. W. Chandler, *Romances of Roguery* [1899] (New York: Burt Franklin, 1961); Edmond Cros, "Le Folklore dans le *Lazarillo de Tormes*: Nouvel examen, problèmes méthodologiques," *Actes picaresques européenne* (Montpelier: Centre d'études sociocritiques, Université Paul Valéry, 1976), rpt. with

"Lecture idéologique du lien épistolaire" in *Co-textes*, no. 8 (1984): 5–20, 105–15, respectively; Beverly J. DeLong-Tonelli, "La ambigüedad narrativa en el *Lazarillo de Tormes*," *Revista de estudios Hispánicos* 10 (1976): 378–89; Alan D. Deyermond, *"Lazarillo de Tormes": A Critical Guide* (London: Grant and Cutler, 1975); Peter N. Dunn, *The Spanish Picaresque Novel* (Boston: G. K. Hall, 1979); Frank Durand, "The Author and Lazaro: Levels of Comic Meaning," *Bulletin of Hispanic Studies* 45 (1968): 89–101; Robert L. Fiore, *Lazarillo de Tormes* (Boston: G. K. Hall, 1984); Stephen Gilman, "The Death of Lazarillo de Tormes," *PMLA* 81 (1966): 149–66; Eduardo Godoy Gallardo, "Funciones de las formas lingüísticas de primer persona plural en el plano temático de *Lazarillo de Tormes*," *Boletín de Filología* (Montevideo) 27 (1976): 135–49; Antonio Gómez-Moriana, "La subversión del discurso ritual: Una lectura intertextual del *Lazarillo de Tormes*" and "Autobiografía y discurso ritual: Problemática de la confesión autobiográfica destinada al tribunal inquisitorial" in *Co-textes*, no. 8 (1984): 21–79, 81–103; Claudio Guillén, "La disposición temporal del *Lazarillo de Tormes*," *Hispanic Review* 25 (1957): 264–79, and "Toward a Definition of the Picaresque" and "Genre and Countergenre: The Discovery of the Picaresque" in his *Literature as System: Essays toward the Theory of Literary History* (Princeton, N.J.: Princeton University Press, 1971), 71–106, 135–58; Javier Herrero, "The Great Icons of the *Lazarillo*: The Bull, the Wine, the Sausage and the Turnip," *Ideologies and Literature* 1 (1978): 3–18, "The Ending of *Lazarillo*: The *Wine* against the *Water*," *Modern Language Notes* 93 (1978): 313–19, and "Renaissance Poverty and Lazarillo's Family: The Birth of the Picaresque Genre," *PMLA* 94 (1979): 876–86; Norma Louise Hutman, "Universality and Unity in the *Lazarillo de Tormes*," *PMLA* 76 (1961): 469–73; B. W. Ife, *Reading and Fiction in Golden-Age Spain: A Platonist Critique and Some Picaresque Replies* (Cambridge: Cambridge University Press, 1985); Didier T. Jaén, "La ambigüedad moral del *Lazarillo de Tormes*," *PMLA* 83 (1968): 130–34; Hans Robert Jauss, "Ursprung und Bedeutung der Ich-Form im *Lazarillo de Tormes*," *Romanistisches Jahrbuch* 8 (1957): 300–11; Margot Kruse, "Die parodistischen Elemente im *Lazarillo de Tormes*," *Romanistisches Jahrbuch* 10 (1959): 292–304; Fernando Lázaro Carreter, *"Lazarillo de Tormes" en la picaresca* (Barcelona: Ariel, 1972); Howard Mancing, "The Deceptiveness of *Lazarillo de Tormes*," *PMLA* 90 (1975): 426–32; Stuart Miller, *The Picaresque Novel* (Cleveland, Ohio: Case Western Reserve University Press, 1967); Maurice Molho, *Introducción al pensamiento picaresco* [1968], trans. Augusto Gálvez-Cañero y Pidal (Salamanca: Anaya, 1972); Charles H. Nichols, "The Slave Narrators and the Picaresque Mode: Archetypes for Modern Black Personae," in *The Slave's Narrative*, ed. Charles T. Davis and Henry Louis Gates, Jr. (Oxford and New York: Oxford University Press, 1985), 283–98; Alexander A. Parker, *Literature and the Delinquent: The Picaresque Novel in Spain and Europe, 1599–1753* (Edinburgh: University Press, 1967); T. Anthony Perry, "Biblical Symbolism in the *Lazarillo de Tormes*," *Studies in Philology* 67 (1970): 139–46; Anson Piper, "The 'Breadly Paradise' of *Lazarillo de Tormes*," *Hispania* 44 (1961): 269–71; Marguerite C. Rand, "Lazarillo de Tormes, Classic and Contemporary," *Hispania* 44 (1961): 222–29; Dale B. J. Randall, *The Golden Tapestry: A Critical Survey of Non-chivalric Spanish Fiction in English Translation (1543–1657)* (Durham, N.C.: Duke University Press, 1963); Walter L. Reed, *An Exemplary History of the Novel: The Quixotic versus the Picaresque* (Chicago: University of Chicago Press, 1981); Antonio Rey Hazas, "Poética comprometida de la 'novela picaresca,' " *Nuevo Hispanismo* 1 (1982): 55–76; Francisco Rico, *The Spanish Picaresque Novel and the Point of View* [1970], trans.

Charles Davis with Harry Sieber (Cambridge: Cambridge University Press, 1984), and "Puntos de vista: Posdata a unos ensayos sobre la novela picaresca," *Edad de Oro* 3 (1984): 227–40; William Riggan, *Pícaros, Madmen, Naïfs, and Clowns: The Unreliable First-Person Narrator* (Norman: University of Oklahoma Press, 1981); Hans Gerd Rötzer, *Picaro—Landstörtzer—Simplicius* (Darmstadt: Wissenschaftliche Buchgesellschaft, 1972); Sylvia Roubaud, "Cartas son cartas: Apuntes sobre la carta fuera del género epistolar," *Criticón* 30 (1985): 103–25; George A. Shipley, "The Critic as Witness for the Prosecution: Making the Case against Lázaro de Tormes," *PMLA* 97 (1982): 179–94, and "A Case of Functional Obscurity: The Master Tambourine-Painter of *Lazarillo, Tratado* VI," *Modern Language Notes* 97 (1982): 225–53; Harry Sieber, *Language and Society in "La vida de Lazarillo de Tormes"* (Baltimore: Johns Hopkins University Press, 1978) and *The Picaresque* (London: Methuen, 1977); F. Courtney Tarr, "Literary and Artistic Unity in *Lazarillo de Tormes*," *PMLA* 42 (1927): 404–21; R. W. Truman, "*Lazarillo de Tormes*, Petrarch's *De remediis fortunae*, and Erasmus's *Praise of Folly*," *Bulletin of Hispanic Studies* 52 (1975): 33–53, "Lázaro de Tormes and the *Homo Novus* Tradition," *Modern Language Review* 64 (1969): 62–67, and "Parody and Irony in the Self-Portrayal of Lazaro de Tormes," *Modern Language Review* 63 (1968): 600–605; Bruce W. Wardropper, "El trastorno de la moral en el *Lazarillo*," *Nueva Revista de Filología Hispánica* 15 (1961), 441–47, and "The Strange Case of Lázaro Gonzáles Pérez," *Modern Language Notes* 92 (1977): 202–12; Arnold Weinstein, *Fictions of the Self: 1550–1800* (Princeton, N.J.: Princeton University Press, 1981); Ulrich Wicks, "Narrative Distance in Picaresque Fiction," *College Literature* 6 (1979): 165–81; Raymond Willis, "Lazarillo and the Pardoner: The Artistic Necessity of the Fifth Tractado," *Hispanic Review* 27 (1959): 267–79; M. J. Woods, "Pitfalls for the Moralizer in *Lazarillo de Tormes*," *Modern Language Review* 74 (1979): 580–98; L. J. Woodward, "Author-Reader Relationships in the *Lazarillo de Tormes*," *Forum for Modern Language Studies* 1 (1965): 43–53.

LIBER VAGATORUM

(c. 1509)

The earliest extant editions were titled *Liber vagatorum: der Betler Orden* (literally, "Book of Vagrants: The Orders of Beggars"), by a pseudonymous "Expertus in Truffis" that is, "expert in roguery"), who has not been identified, though surmises about authorship exist. Part I consists of twenty-eight chapters describing different mendicant types and the tricks they use; this section is thought to have been based on the city archives of Basel, where the authorities between 1411 and 1479 provided the first detailed accounts of the types of beggars and the deceits common to each type. Part II, *Notabilia*, gives additional tips on how to beware of being tricked. And part III is a *Vocabularius* of *Rotwelsch*, the argot or rogues' cant used to describe the various confidence tricks. At least eighteen editions of the book—including a rhyming version by Pamphilus Gengenbach (Basel, 1515)—appeared by the time Martin Luther wrote a preface for a 1528 edition, which carried the title *Von der falschen Betler Büeberey* (literally, "Of the Knavish Tricks of Deceitful Beggars").

To read the *Liber Vagatorum* today is not unlike reading a current consumer manual on how to avoid being taken in by false charities. In its graphically precise descriptions and admonitory tone, it must have been an indispensable how-to book for the comfortable, well-ordered fifteenth- and sixteenth-century household wanting to protect itself from being fleeced and at the same time salving its Christian conscience to give charity where it is legitimately due. According to Thomas, such protection had become necessary as the preceding centuries saw vagrancy become an increasingly disruptive socioeconomic force:

> By 1250 Vagabondage was organized on a large scale [in Europe]. . . . By 1400 Vagabondage had become a regular business east of the Rhine. . . . In 1342–3 certain classes of [vagabonds] had become such a nuisance at Augsburg that they were publicly proscribed and forbidden the city. . . . The fifteenth century saw Vagabondage firmly established as an integral part of social structure. Municipal action was taken against this pest in Vienna (1443), Cologne (1446), Nuremberg (1478), and at Breslau a little later (1512). . . . The decay of feudalism, the growth of the burgher classes, and the Reformation together produced an attitude of mind which could no longer tolerate the imposture of the idle. (5–11)

Complicating the situation was the establishment of the mendicant orders (the Franciscans in 1209 and the Dominicans in 1220), whose brotherhoods, along with wandering scholars, came into substantial disrepute and confused the charitable about whom to give alms to. By the time Luther wrote his preface, "*Der Betlerorden*—'the Mendicant Brotherhood' was . . . a name applicable equally to the Mendicant Religious or to the scum of society. The innuendo is unmistakeable. The Protestant sense of individuality reaffirmed what the legal logic of a byegone age had been impotent to enforce. Luther's preface marks the real starting point of the systematic measures directed against vagrancy in Germany. The anonymous author showed the vagabond up in his true colours; and Luther imprinted the seal of his approbation" (13).

In his short preface Luther wrote:

> I have thought it a good thing that such a book should not only be printed, but that it should become known everywhere, in order that men may see and understand how mightily the Devil rules in this world; and I have also thought how such a book may help mankind to be wise, and on the look out for him, viz. the Devil. Truly, such Beggars Cant has come from the Jews, for many Hebrew words occur in the Vocabulary, as any one who understands that language may perceive.
>
> But the right understanding and true meaning of the book is, after all, this, viz. that princes, lords, counsellors of state, and everybody should be prudent, and cautious in dealing with beggars, and learn that, whereas people will not give and help honest paupers and needy neighbors, as ordained by God, they give, by the persuasion of the devil, and contrary to God's judgment, ten times as much to Vagabonds and desperate rogues—in like manner as we have hitherto done to monasteries, cloisters, churches, chapels, and mendicant friars, forsaking all the time the truly poor.
>
> For this reason every town and village should know their own paupers, as written down in the Register, and assist them. But as to outlandish and strange beggars they ought not to be borne with, unless they have proper licenses and passports; for all the great rogueries

mentioned in this book are done by these. If each town would only keep an eye upon their paupers, such knaveries would soon be at an end. I have myself of late years been cheated and befooled by such tramps and liars more than I wish to confess. Therefore, whosoever hear these words let him be warned, and do good to his neighbor in all Christian charity, according to the teaching of the commandment.
SO HELP US GOD! AMEN. (63–65)

The harsh anti-Catholic and -Semitic tone combines with down-to-earth personal experience to warn about the men and women of the streets. The frequency of subsequent editions with Luther's preface attests to the widespread necessity of the book, which makes it a telling document of the social, moral, economic, and religious climate of its time.

In the history of picaresque fiction, the *Liber Vagatorum* is significant, in Chandler's words, as "the first pure example of German rogue realism" (*Literature of Roguery,* 27) and as representative of the beggar books whose "curious catalogues of the orders of rascals and their cheats, preceding or contemporary with the appearance of picaresque fiction, were its invaluable adjuncts, and the collectors for it of raw material (*Romances,* 12). The *Liber Vagatorum* inspired *Il Vagabondo* (1627) by Giacinto Nobili, an Italian compendium of thirty-four classes of fraudulent beggars. "No Spanish picaresque novel reveals anything like the range and ingenuity of confidence tricks listed for Germany and Italy by these two books" (Parker, 11). Both the *Liber Vagatorum* and *Il Vagabondo* were soon translated into other languages, including Dutch and French. Although an English translation of the *Liber Vagatorum* did not appear until 1860, England saw the first of many such books in John Awdeley's *The Fraternity of Vagabonds* (1561) and Thomas Harman's *A Caveat for Common Cursitors* (1566), and two that give detailed accounts of the underworld of London: Dekker's *The Bellman of London* (1608) and *Lantern and Candlelight* (1608).

But Chandler makes important distinctions between the picaresque proper and these parallel or peripheral developments of rogue literature, which he subdivides into specific categories such as the jest book, whose prototype is *Till Eulenspiegel* (q.v.) or *Reynard the Fox* (q.v.). The *Liber Vagatorum* belongs to the beggar book tradition, which is a subcategory of the anatomy of roguery, defined as "an essay descriptive of the grades, cheats, or manners of professional criminals" (*Literature,* 87). Implicit in Chandler's taxonomy is a major distinction between the primarily invented fictional quality of the picaresque proper and the essayistic or discursive characteristics of the anatomies, though the fundamental picaresque narrative situation is always to some extent essayistic. The distinction Chandler seems to have in mind is best illustrated by comparing an episode from a picaresque fiction—say, Lazarillo's experiences with the blind man, his first master (*Lazarillo de Tormes,* q.v.)—with the following complete chapter from the *Liber Vagatorum*:

The xith chapter is of the *Zickisches,* or *Blind Beggars.* Mark: there are three kinds of blind men who wander about. Some are called *Blocharts* or blind men—made blind by the power of God. They go on a pilgrimage, and when they come into a town they hide their round hats, and say to the people they have been stolen from them, or lost at the places where they had sheltered themselves, and one of them often collects ten or twenty caps, and then sells them. Some are called blind who have lost their sight by evil-doings and wickednesses. They wander about in the country and carry with them pictures of devils, and repair to the churches, and pretend they had been at Rome, to Saint James, and other distant places, and speak of great signs and wonders that had taken place, but it is all lies and deception. Some of the blind men are called *Broken Wanderers*. These are such as have been blinded ten years or more; they take cotton, and make the cotton bloody, and then with a kerchief tie this over their eyes, and say that they have been mercers or peddlers, and were blinded by wicked men in a forest, that they were tied fast to a tree and so remained three or four days, and, but for a merciful passer-by, they would have miserably perished;—and this is called *broken wandering*.

   Conclusion: Know them well before thou givest to them; my advice is only give to those thou knowest. (102–3)

Lazarillo's rendering of his firsthand encounter has the vividness of lived experience, discernibly the product of a *fictor*, while the *Liber Vagatorum* is just as clearly the product of a *histor* with an overpowering voice of the preacher. All picaresques reveal an explicit or implicit essayistic-sermonizing impulse, but in the *liber vagatorum* tradition, this impulse is dominant. Nonetheless, it is important to note that the beggar book tradition and the picaresque tradition frequently converge, as when almost purely *liber vagatorum* forms are fully integrated into picaresques in the recurrent community of rogues motifs, which we find, for example, in such works as *El Buscón, Guzmán de Alfarache,* "Rinconete y Cortadillo," *La desordenada codicia,* and, more recently, in *Down and Out in Paris and London, Invisible Man,* and *The Tin Drum* (q.q.v.).

   The protean swindler in his many guises is an archetype of human behavior first given narrative forms in the myths about trickster (q.v.). When you disregard the particulars that specifically fix the *Liber Vagatorum* historically and socially, you are left with essential situations that resemble those of the myths. Nor would Luther have any problem orienting himself in a study done almost five centuries after his own preface—Maurer's *The American Confidence Man* (1974). Though the term *confidence man* is relatively recent (*The Confidence-Man,* q.v.) and though Maurer studies confidence games of the twentieth century, the principles underlying these tricks "are very ancient, going back through the history of Europe to the Near East, where their origins are lost in the haze of antiquity" (vii). Whether it is one of Luther's "blind" men or one of Maurer's slick operators, trickster himself is the single reality behind their appearances. And the audience is in essence unchanged as well, controlled by the contradictory impulses of repulsion and attraction, of suspicion and collaboration, which are but outward actions governed by a fundamental behavioral truth that fuels trickster's very reason for being: people want to be fooled, or as Simplicius soon learns, "the foolish world wants to be fooled" (*Simplicius Simplicissimus,* q.v.). Indeed, given his own self-confessed gullibility, Luther might well take pause at Maurer's observation that "a confidence man prospers only because of the fundamental dishonesty of his victim":

> Because of their high intelligence, their solid organization, the wide-spread connivance of the law, and the fact that the victim must virtually admit criminal intentions himself if he wishes to prosecute, society has been neither willing nor able to avenge itself effectively. Relatively few good con men are ever brought to trial; of those who are tried, few are convicted; of those who are convicted, even fewer ever serve out their full sentences. (3)

EDITION/TRANSLATION

J. C. Hotten's 1860 translation (on facing pages with the original German) is in *The Book of Vagabonds and Beggars, with a Vocabulary of Their Language and a Preface by Martin Luther*, ed. D. B. Thomas (London: Penguin, 1932).

SELECT BIBLIOGRAPHY

Frank Wadleigh Chandler, *Romances of Roguery* [1899] (New York: Burt Franklin, 1961) and *The Literature of Roguery* [1907] (New York: Burt Franklin, 1958); David W. Maurer, *The American Confidence Man* (Springfield, Ill.: Charles C. Thomas, 1974); A. A. Parker, *Literature and the Delinquent: The Picaresque Novel in Spain and Europe, 1599–1753* (Edinburgh: University Press, 1967). C. J. Ribton-Turner's *A History of Vagrants and Vagrancy and Beggars and Begging* (London: Chapman & Hall, 1887) provides a panoramic picture of vagrancy in all of Europe.

THE LIFE AND DEATH OF MR. BADMAN

(1680)

John Bunyan

"Despite the dialogue form, the allegory, and the absence of humor, Bunyan has here subscribed to the picaresque scheme in setting up an anti-hero as antithesis to the hero of *The Pilgrim's Progress*," wrote Chandler in his comprehensive study of picaresque literature, emphasizing that in this "Puritan romance of roguery" Bunyan's preface "strikes the same chord as Alemán's preface to *Guzmán de Alfarache* [q.v.]" (225–26). Although subsequent historians of the English novel, among them Ernest Baker in *The History of the English Novel* (1929), rejected this classification, Parker followed up on Chandler's observation by comparing *Guzmán* with *Mr. Badman* in some detail: Bunyan's work has a dualistic structure similar to Alemán's; the latter's grew out of the Counter-Reformation's condemnation of secular literature, just as Bunyan reflects the Puritan's opposition to wordly writings. Furthermore, "both books start with an emphasis on Original Sin. . . . Both [protagonists] are married twice; the first time both marry for money; the second time both wives turn out to be dissolute. Both embark on business careers and both go bankrupt. Near the end of one novel, Guzmán feigns sanctity in order to exploit the charity of the pious; near the end of the other novel Mr. Badman feigns repentance'' (101–2). These similarities do not prove any direct influence, though there is a possibility that Bunyan may have known of Mabbe's translation of *Guzmán* or of Head's *The English Rogue* (q.v.). What is clear, however, is that both books are "literary products of movements of religious reform," and both are "religous treatments of the theme of delinquency. *Mr. Badman* should be classed with *Simplicissimus* [q.v.] as a picaresque novel of the type exemplified by *Guzmán de Alfarache''* (102). Blackburn, on the other hand, dismisses the issue: Bunyan's work "presents neither a trickster nor a novelistic kind of society. Mr. Badman is a generic portrait of a sinner, a vile body depicted from on high," whose sources are the Bible and morality plays (99). As the history of picaresque criticism shows, however, a novel-centered approach to the picaresque can lead to major distortions of the generic and modal nature of picaresque fiction, as exemplified by Walter Allen's calling (though with qualifications) not *Mr. Badman* but *The Pilgrim's Progress* a picaresque novel in his *The English Novel* (1954).

Bunyan's work, however, should receive serious consideration in the context of the picaresque, if only to reinforce the strongly didactic dimension that is so neglected by non-Hispanist critics when they consider the picaresque narrative tradition. Bunyan's "The Author to the Reader" makes clear the moralistic aim:

Yes, I do trace him in his Life, from his Childhood to his Death; that thou mayest, as in a Glass, behold with thine own eyes, the steps that take hold of Hell; and also discern, while thou art reading of Mr. *Badmans* Death, whether thou thy self art treading in his path thereto.

And let me entreat thee to forbear Quirking and Mocking, for that I say Mr. *Badman* is dead; but rather gravely enquire concerning thy self by the Word, whether thou art one of his Linage or no: For Mr. *Badman* has left many of his Relations behind him; yea, the very World is overspread with his Kindred. True, some of his Relations, as he, are gone to their place, and long home, but thousands of thousands are left behind. (4)

He has used the dialogue form, he says, "that I might with more ease to my self, and pleasure to the Reader, perform the work," yet he has not let that method distance him from "mine own observation of things," all of which "have been acted upon the stage of this World, even many times before mine eyes" (3). His purpose, as he later reemphasizes, is to make all English people aware of wickedness, "this deadly plague," which "like a flood is like to drown our English world" (13). The dialogue takes place between Mr. Wiseman and Mr. Attentive, who talk about the recently deceased Mr. Badman. In the course of their dialogue, a vivid picture of a rogue's existence emerges. Commenting on Mr. Badman's death, which was quiet and without fear ("Mr. *Badman* died like a lamb"), Mr. Wiseman describes the otherworldly fate of the unrepentant wicked: "They goe *as an Ox to the slaughter,* and *as a fool to the correction of the Stocks;* that is, both sencelessly and securely. O! but being come at the gates of Hell! . . . O! but when they see that that is their home, and that they must go in thither, then their peace and quietness flies away for ever: Then they roar like Lions, yell like Dragons, howl like Dogs, and tremble at their Judgment, as do the Devils themselves'' (274).

Mr. Badman is picaresque in its subject matter, tone, and attitude, but narratively it is on the periphery of the picaresque mode. The dialogue technique is not absent from the tradition (for example, ''The Dogs' Colloquy,'' *The Futile Life of Pito Pérez, La desordenada codicia,* q.q.v.), but in *Mr. Badman* the picaro himself does not participate in the dialogue—in fact, he is already dead. The lack of a strong first-person narrative voice from the picaro himself prevents the work from being fully picaresque. Nonetheless, it is an important book in the development of English picaresques leading toward Defoe's *Moll Flanders* (q.v.).

EDITIONS

The World's Classics series (London: Oxford University Press, 1929). Oxford published the first critical edition (ed. James F. Forrest and Roger Sharrock) in 1988.

SELECT BIBLIOGRAPHY

Alexander Blackburn, *The Myth of the Picaro: Continuity and Transformation of the Picaresque Novel, 1554–1954* (Chapel Hill: University of North Carolina Press, 1979); F. W. Chandler, *The Literature of Roguery* [1907] (New York: Burt Franklin, 1958); A. A. Parker, *Literature and the Delinquent: The Picaresque Novel in Spain and Europe, 1599–1753* (Edinburgh: University Press, 1967); J. B. Wharey, ''Bunyan's Mr. Badman and the Picaresque Novel,'' *Texas Studies in English* 4 (1924): 49–61.

LITTLE BIG MAN

(1964)

Thomas Berger

Incorporating characteristics of the indigenously American tall tale, which in turn echoes the European tradition of the braggart romance (such as Reuter's *Schelmuffsky* [1696–1697], Raspe's *Baron Münchausen* [1785]), this picaresque fills in part of the vast canvas of the American landscape, for the narrative rendering of which William Dean Howells suggested the Spanish picaresque as the most appropriate fictional form (*The Confidence-Man, Huckleberry Finn,* q.q.v.). The narrator is Jack Crabb, whose very name and age—he is 111 years old at the time of narration in 1952—suggest his ability to move backward, forward, and sideways in the temporal and geographical American landscape. Crabb is also ''little big man,'' an epithet given him by Old Lodge Skins, a Cheyenne chief who raised him from the age of ten, when Crabb's father, an illiterate itinerant preacher, is killed by the Indians and the rest of his family dispersed (though in a typically picaresque dance pattern, Crabb will reencounter by chance both his sister and brother several times). He does not regret losing his ''family'': ''No, my Ma was well-meaning but ignorant. My Pa was crazy and my brother was a traitor. Then there was Caroline. They weren't much of a family, I guess, but then I was not with them long'' (42–43).

Among the Cheyenne, he becomes a Human Being, their term for themselves to distinguish them both from whites and from other tribes. His boyhood among the Indians is as innocent in some ways as Simplicius's with his "second father" in the forest (*Simplicius Simplicissimus,* q.v.). He learns the ways of the tribe, including their cosmogeny, and is initiated into manhood by his second father: "He is himself little in body and he is now a man. But his heart is big. Therefore his name from now on shall be: Little Big Man" (93).

So I, Jack Crabb, was a Cheyenne warrior. Had made my kill with bow and arrow. Been scalped and healed with hocus-pocus. Had an ancient savage who couldn't talk English for my Pa, and a fat brown woman for my Ma, and for a brother a fellow whose face I hardly ever saw for clay or paint. Lived in a skin tent and ate puppy dog. God, it was strange. (95)

Up to his mid-thirties, which is as far as he tells his *vida,* his experiences alternate between Indian tribal life and white frontier society. He establishes first an Indian family (killed by cavalry) and then a white family (dispersed in an Indian attack). He is simultaneously an outsider and insider to both realms, and he observes each from the perspective of the other. Superimposing the two perspectives results in satirical visions that emphasize the essential incompatibility of the two worlds in the picaresque topsy-turvydom of the American West. Old Lodge Skins insists that:

whatever else you can say about the white man, it must be admitted that *you cannot get rid of him.* He is in never-ending supply. There has always been only a limited number of Human Beings, because we are intended to be special and superior. Obviously not everybody can be a Human Being. To make this so, there must be a great many inferior people. To my mind, this is the function of white men in the world. Therefore we must survive, because without us the world would not make sense. (181–82)

But Crabb sees the Indian mode of life coming to an end and observes:

Maybe white men was more natural than Indians! was what I had got to thinking. Even prairie dogs had fixed villages. . . . Now I know that every living thing is neither more nor less of Nature than the next, but I was young then and them distinctions bothered me, what with the conflicting claims: Indians believing they was more "natural" than white men, and the latter insisting they themselves was more "human." (182–83)

Jack Crabb's adventures back and forth between two mutually exclusive world visions take place in a post–Civil War landscape that is seething with moral, social, and racial instability:

There was considerable Army deserters in the eastern Nations, along with freed slaves who now didn't have no work, and former Reb soldiers in a similar situation, and Indians what had gone bad, also fugitives from justice back in the States, bullyboys, cutthroats, and just plain rotten fellows. There was in addition every sort of breed in them parts: some being part white, Negro, and Indian all at the same time, with the worst traits of each. (283)

His fortunes fluctuate wildly in this chaos as he falls from relative wealth and comfort to vagrancy in St. Louis and bankruptcy in Denver. He becomes a buffoon, and for a time he teams up with a con man who teaches him a truth that all picaros learn: "That in any swindle there was two crooks, both victim and victimizer, and that you couldn't never work a confidence scheme on a square man" (332–33). Such lessons allow him to stand back as the picaresque philosophizer who, like Lazarillo (*Lazarillo de Tormes,* q.v.), fits in appropriate proverbs from the temporally immediate plane of narrative distance: "If you want to really relax sometime, just fall to rock bottom and you'll be a happy man. Most all troubles come from having standards" (164). Along the way, he has a showdown with Wild Bill Hickok, whom he outwits, and observes his sister brawling with Calamity Jane. The culmination of his experiences—and of the narrative he relates—is his participation in Custer's Last Stand, of which he claims (his italics) to be "*the only man what survived out of them 200-odd who rode down Medicine Tail Coulee towards the ford of the Little Bighorn River*" (405). Not only is this battle climactic in Jack Crabb's life and memoirs, it is also climactic in the history of the American West, since the Indians' victory soon yields to defeat as they surrender more and more to reservation life. Whether civilization triumphed over savagery or vice-versa is an irony that has all along been part of Jack Crabb's double exposure in a landscape undergoing radical transformation: "God knows I thought enough about it and kept telling myself I was basically an Indian, just as when among Indians I kept seeing how I was really white to the core" (160). The last words of his memoirs are "fading light" (445).

Crabb's narrative is presented to us by "a man of letters" named Ralph Fielding Snell, who reveals himself to be an effete aesthete with a vicarious involvement in the Old West by way of artifacts and books. Because of an intervening nervous breakdown, it takes him a decade to transcribe the tapes Jack Crabb had dictated to him in the nursing home Snell found him in. "You're a sissy, ain't you, son?" Jack Crabb says on first meeting him (19). When Snell disassociates himself from Crabb's apparent approval of violence, he states, "I am after all a white man, and believe that reason must eventually prevail, the lion *will* lie down with the lamb," to which Jack Crabb replies, "That's O.K., son, so long as you add fresh lambs now and again" (446). Snell's temperament is the polar opposite of Crabb's, and, given the instability of Snell's constitution, it is not out of line to suspect that these memoirs emerged as a wish-fulfillment fantasy out of Ralph Fielding Snell's impressionable imagination—a possibility he tries to circumvent by including in his epilogue a disclaimer about Jack Crabb's reliability while simultaneously insisting on the integrity of the antique dealer who sold Snell Crazy Horse's war bonnet, which Crabb insists Crazy Horse had not been wearing during the battle but which Snell accepts as authentic. We thus have the storytelling situation of a primary narrator (Snell) who is all too credulous about his questionable feather headdress but who is incredulous toward the detailed account of his secondary narrator (Crabb): a tall tale enclosing a tall tale, perhaps? "So, as I take my departure, dear reader, I leave the choice in your capable hands. Jack Crabb was either the most neglected hero in the history of this country or a liar of insane proportions," concludes Snell (447). This typically picaresque narrative con game brings to mind Jack Crabb's observation about victims and victimizers, and readers who make it to the final playful paragraph of the epilogue realize they have been had, not without their own participation, by a real bunco artist: Thomas Berger himself.

EDITION

New York: Laurel/Seymour Lawrence, 1985.

SELECT BIBLIOGRAPHY

Fred M. Fetrow, "The Function of the External Narrator in Thomas Berger's *Little Big Man*," *Journal of Narrative Technique* 5 (1975): 57–65; Jay Gurian, "Style in the Literary Desert: *Little Big Man*," *Western American Literature* 3 (1968): 285–96; L. L. Lee, "American, Western, Picaresque: Thomas Berger's *Little Big Man*," *The South Dakota Review* 4 (1965): 35–42; John W. Turner, "*Little Big Man*, the Novel and the Film: A Study of Narrative Structure," *Literature/Film Quarterly* 5 (1977): 154–63.

MARCOS DE OBREGON

(Relaciones de la vida del escudero Marcos de Obregón, 1618)

   Vicente Espinel

Already a celebrated poet who had invented a verse form that came to be named after him (the *espinela*), Espinel in 1599 obliged Alemán by writing a dedicatory epigram in Latin for the first part of *Guzmán de Alfarache* (q.v.). He was friends with Quevedo, in whose *El Buscón* (q.v.) the sacristan (bk. II, ch. 3) mentions having had dinner several times with Espinel. When Marcos begins telling his life story to the hermit (bk. I, ch. 8), he echoes the first words of Pablos de Segovia by saying, "Yo, senor . . . soy de Ronda." But despite Espinel's insider status in the literary establishment and despite his self-conscious use of picaresque materials, *Marcos de Obregón* has been for quite some time a work whose status as a picaresque is heavily qualified, even denied. Clarke said it occupied "a halfway position between the rogue-story, pure and simple, and the ordinary novel of adventures" and that its chief pleasure is in taking us back to "one of the most picturesque societies that ever existed. Rags and finery jostle one another, villainy and heroism go hand in hand. We pass from the dim garret of the starving student at Salamanca to an assembly of *virtuosos* in an Italian saloon, from a thieves' kitchen in Seville to a palace in Algiers. And the whole story is told by a shabby old serving-gentleman to his friend the hermit while sheltering from a downpour of rain on the outskirts of Madrid" (342–43). Chandler thought Marcos "less a picaro than almost any other member of the Spanish rogues' gallery" (304), and Parker points out that in using picaresque conventions to fulfill his own Horatian aim "to tune the right note between the too tightly stretched string of doctrine and the too loosely stretched string of entertainment,"

Espinel produced a subdued, genteel form of fiction in the course of which he in fact "destroyed the special significance of the *genre*. Instead of a psychological, spiritual, and social tension between good and evil, he produced an agreeable enough, but rather commonplace, balance that points directly to the neoclassical world of Lesage" (54–55).

Marcos de Obregón achieved much of its fame on the rebound, through *Gil Blas* (q.v.), when Voltaire in 1775 accused Lesage of having plagiarized Espinel, setting off a furious literary dispute that went on until well into the nineteenth century and in which Sir Walter Scott also took part. Thus Espinel's work is of historical import in the development of picaresque narrative because it, more than *Lazarillo de Tormes* (q.v.), *Guzmán,* or *El Buscón,* provided the paradigm for eighteenth-century picaresque in France, which in turn directly influenced the concept of picaresque in the developing English novel—with still lingering consequences in contemporary usage of the term *picaresque.*

The world Espinel portrays in *Marcos de Obregón* is fundamentally good, and the ideological assumption in the worldview presented by it is that one should know one's place in such a world and strive to fulfill one's purpose within that established order. For Marcos, says Bjornson, "life is filled with direct manifestations of God's will. Rather than distrusting that which his senses register as beautiful, he seems to refine and sharpen his senses to become more intensely aware of the perfection in the universe" (*Picaresque Hero,* 74). While such a rendered world brings us extremely close to romance as a given in the fictional world (rather than wished for, as in *Guzmán*) and thus to a negation of picaresque, its consciously picaresque origins cannot be overlooked. As Dunn points out, it is not so much a matter of dismissing *Marcos de Obregón* as nonpicaresque as it is of recognizing that early seventeenth-century Spanish writers did not regard picaresque fiction "as a genre, whose integrity had to be preserved" but rather as "a bundle of possibilities, which could be taken apart and exploited separately. Espinel is one writer who responded to the genre by experimenting in his own way with autobiographical narrative, flashback, and an episodic life taken as a cumulative experience" (94).

And it is indeed Espinel's curious handling of autobiographical narration that is likely to intrigue contemporary readers sophisticated in narrative technique. Although at first criticized for being inconsistent and even implausible, Espinel's narrating situation in *Marcos de Obregón* tells us much about the function of narration in picaresque—and in pseudo-autobiographical narration in general. The almost Cervantine narrative trick of having Marcos orally tell his *vida* within the written *vida* we are reading, and thus creating two narrating voices, one of which is also the narrated voice of the other, has been compared to Velázquez's *Las meninas.* This narrative dimension, which prefigures such later developments in Western fiction as Proust's, Unamuno's, and Gide's, has been thoroughly studied by Haley, who summarizes Espinel's accomplishments:

On one hand, the novel is an ironic game of identifications in which the author's purpose is to reveal himself at the same time he continues to be masked behind his literary projection. On the other hand, Espinel sometimes loses himself in the labyrinth of his own construction, and Marcos de Obregón consequently achieves a certain degree of illusory independence from the author he represents in the work. The fluctuation of the first-person narrative between author and alter ego uncovers the mechanics of fictional creation, and Marcos de Obregón is revealed for what he is: the author's persona in an incomplete state of objectification. (181)

Quoting Ortega's description of *Las meninas* as a work that presents the spectacle of "a portraitist portrayed portraying," Haley concludes that Espinel "has created a *doble espejismo* [double mirroring] in which the artist, like Velázquez in *Las meninas,* is at once the eye and part of the view, the creator inverted into his own creation" (183).

When we consider the narrative complexities of the apparently simple and straightforward *Lazarillo* and when we consider the narrative games played in some twentieth-century picaresques (for example, *Felix Krull,* q.v.), it is possible to see *Marcos de Obregón* as genuinely picaresque for reasons that have nothing to do with the elements of structure, content, and ideology that eighteenth-century imitators saw in it. Marcos is playing with masks. Through narrative prestidigitation, he is exercising the picaro's fundamentally protean being. Our interest in *Marcos de Obregón* today is more likely to focus on its picaresque self-reflexiveness than on its reflection of the emerging genre at the beginning of the seventeenth century. Espinel's interest is in the picaro's final role as artist.

TRANSLATION/EDITION

The only known English translation is *The History of the Life of the Squire Marcos de Obregon* by Algernon Langton (London: John Booth, 1816). The original Spanish text is accessible in one of the many editions of Angel Valbuena Prat's anthology, *La novela picaresca española* (1943); in the sixth edition (Madrid: Aguilar, 1968), it is on pp. 921–1087.

SELECT BIBLIOGRAPHY

Ignacio B. Anzoategui, "La picaresca y Vicente Espinel," *Cuadernos hispáno-americanos* 31 (1957): 54–65; Richard Bjornson, *The Picaresque Hero in European Fiction* (Madison: University of Wisconsin Press, 1977) and "Social Conformity and Justice in *Marcos de Obregón,*" *Revista de estudios hispánicos* 9 (1975): 285–307; Frank Wadleigh Chandler, *Romances of Roguery* [1899] (New York: Burt Franklin, 1961); H. Butler Clarke, "The Spanish Rogue-Story (Novela de Pícaros)" in *Studies in European Literature, Being the Taylorian Lectures 1889–1899* (Oxford: Clarendon Press, 1900), 313–49; Peter N. Dunn, *The Spanish Picaresque Novel* (Boston: Twayne, 1979); George Haley, *Vicente Espinel and "Marcos de Obregón": A Life and Its Literary Representation* (Providence, R.I.: Brown University Press, 1959); Adrian G. Montoro, " 'Liberated cristiana': Relectura de Marcos de Obregon," *Modern Language Notes* 91 (1976): 213–30; Alexander A. Parker, *Literature and the Delinquent: The Picaresque Novel in Spain and Europe 1599–1753* (Edinburgh: University Press, 1967).

MEMOIRS OF A GOOD-FOR-NOTHING

(*Aus dem Leben eines Taugenichts*, 1826)

Joseph Freiherr von Eichendorff

The tendency of picaresque to mix with its modal opposite, romance, is most apparent in this work, in which Eichendorff takes the picaro's protean form, makes an artist of him, and sends him on a physical and spiritual journey through the social and moral panorama of the Bildungsroman. In this new role, the prototypal low-life figure wanders into what seems an unlikely episode: the symbolic and lyrical dream world of romanticism and the morally ordered ideal world of the apprenticeship novel. But nothing, in the literary long run, is unlikely for the protean picaro, and to understand this particular metamorphosis of the picaresque, we need to summarize briefly the significant influence of *siglo de oro* Spanish literature on other European literatures, in this case on German romanticism in particular.

Cervantes is the filter through which Spanish fiction entered the romantic mainstream, and his full mixture of realism and idealism, of picaresque and romance, of illusion creating and destroying (mirrored in an elegant narrative self-reflexiveness) had great impact on German narrative fiction. Ludwig Tieck translated not only *Don Quixote* but Espinel's *Marcos de Obregón* (q.v.) as well: *Leben and Begebenheiten des Escudero Marcos de Obregón* (1827). E. T. A. Hoffman continued in his own vein Cervantes's "The Dogs' Colloquy" (q.v.) in *Nachricht von den neuesten Schicksalen des Hundes Berganza* in his *Phantasiestücke* (1814). Sometimes the influence comes by way of France, as in the 1822 *Der deutsche Gil Blas*, so titled and introduced by Goethe.

One characteristic feature of some of the German fiction of this time is the blending of picaresque and romance modes, playing with the modal tension operative in the picaresque from its beginnings—in *Guzmán de Alfarache* (q.v.) and *Simplicius Simplicissimus* (q.v.), for example, the unresolved tension between experience-as-experienced in chaos (the picaresque world) and experience-as-reflected in moral order (the romance world). The Bildungsroman has been called the distinctive type of German narrative in its depiction of the formation of a character up to the moment when he ceases to be self-centered and becomes society centered, thus beginning to shape his true self (Pascal, 11, 23–24). In Bildungsromane such as Tieck's *Franz Sternbalds Wanderungen* (1798), Novalis's *Heinrich von Ofterdingen* (1802), and Goethe's *Wilhelm Meister* (1796, 1829), an artist-hero, himself a malleable entity, confronts experience as a plastic substance to be absorbed inwardly and then to be projected out again as a new way of looking at the world, a new order of things between the individual and the world out there. Life for Franz Sternbald, for example, is a continuing quest during which he constantly questions his own state of wholeness and being: "I no longer know what I am," to which the narrator comments, "Thus Franz

Sternbald was at this time . . . I don't know whether to call him a matured child or a child-like adult'' (I, ch. 6). Wilhelm Meister says, ''The cultivation of my individual self, as I am here, has been from youth my hazy wish and purpose (*Lehrjahre*, V, ch. 3). Wilhelm's episodic life is a continuous *werden* or coming-to-be—a quest for ultimate integration into a social, moral, and aesthetic whole. The picaro usually does not achieve such a goal (if he is even aware of it as a goal) until the act of memory engages in narration. The disorder, chance, and freedom of mobility in the Bildungsroman are revealed at the end to have been only apparent: the Society of the Tower shaped much of Wilhelm's life, and thus the old picaresque theme of reality versus illusion dissolves into the apparent triumph of moral order, the victory of the romance world. Such a victory is only partially glimpsed, and barely grasped, by Simplicius on his island or Guzmán in his last role as narrator. Morally and spiritually, they may be integrated into a higher order, but physically and socially, they are even more alienated. For the Bildungsroman hero, integration is whole; for the picaro, it is in the end still a yearning. In this expressed desired, the picaresque often has an eye on romance, just as romance, as particularized in the Bildungsroman form, often has a wary eye on the disorder expressed through picaresque.

Eichendorff's *Good-for-Nothing* is neither a Bildungsroman nor a picaresque fiction in the strictly orthodox sense of the terms. But in its mixture of picaresque and romance modes, it illustrates the inadequacy of our catch-all term *novel* even to begin to cope with the complexly evolving forms of Western narrative in the nineteenth and twentieth centuries. It illuminates Eichendorff's work, as it also helps us understand the nature of picaresque narrative, to look at *Good-for-Nothing* in the context of the picaresque. At first glance this work seems to be antipicaresque, thought not unpicaresque, in its celebration of nature and the lyric voice. And yet it embodies essential picaresque characteristics: in the personality of the protagonist, his situation in the world, the episodes, the freedom of reckless vagabondage, the self-conscious aloneness of the narrator and his awareness of outsiderdom socially, and finally in the deceptive world that tricks him. In combining these picaresque elements with an intricate plot, Eichendorff creates a mixture that reveals an interesting metamorphosis of the picaro and his tale.

The metamorphosis of the picaro-in-society into a wanderer-in-nature who mirrors life musically results in a figure who retains the picaresque qualities while at the same time becoming an active kind of artist, one who becomes a poet not only through the telling process alone. This active artist-picaro figure will appear in later picaresque in characters such as Felix Krull (*Felix Krull*, q.v.) and Gulley Jimson (*The Horse's Mouth*, q.v.). Eichendorff's variation on the picaro-artist is rendered through a blend of narrative and lyrical forms of presentation. The conventional *Ich-Erzählung* of picaresque narrative is mixed with a lyrical voice though which the wanderer absorbs his loneliness in the landscape and projects it again outward in an effort at integration. In moments of solitude, he quite literally sings to himself. These songs fuse his *solo soy* condition with his perceived loneliness of the landscape, just as the picaro's rendering of his experienced world is inescapably colored by the psychological chaos of his own mind.

On the level of encounter and adventure, Eichendorff's story follows the typical picaresque patterns. The narrative begins with ejection as the narrator, content in his lazy existence at this father's mill, is suddenly confronted by his father who in a single gesture both releases him from his social identity and throws him out of home and hearth: "You good-for-nothing! . . . I can't feed you here any longer. Spring is at hand: go out into the world for once and earn your own living" (1). Accepting his epithet (he will never tell us his name), the good-for-nothing decides to "go out into the world and make my fortune"; he takes his violin and leaves, observing his friends at work on his way out of the village:

I was secretly filled with delight, seeing all my old acquaintances and companions going out to right and left, digging and ploughing, just the same as all other days, while I was free to rove out into the world. (2)

He becomes an innocent, childlike vagabond, feeling, as he puts it, as if there were "an endless Sunday" within him. Shortly after he converts the identity shift into song:

The dullards in their houses lying
Are not refreshed by morning's red:
They only know of babies crying,
Of burdens, cares, and daily bread. (2)

The social experience of rejection and ejection is turned into an artistic one of self-contentment through the lyricization of experience. Eichendorff turns the picaro loose and exploits the expectations of the picaresque: the would-be La-zarillo (*Lazarillo de Tormes*, q.v.) or Simplicissimus, cast into a cold world, becomes the poet Lazarillo or Simplicissimus who converts experience into song and lets us see him doing it.

The Taugenichts submits naively to God's power and to what he assumes is an ordered world. But hardly out of town, he looks around and sees a coach containing two elegant ladies listening to his song. They ask him where he is going, and on the spur of the moment he answers Vienna, which is where they happen to live. In this way, he serves his first masters. Later, when he gets the chance to work as a gardener's helper at the estate where these women live, he reflects on his empty pockets, quickly says yes, and listens to the gardener's sermon on the senselessness of wandering aimlessly through life. But the Tau-genichts has not yet had his head banged against the stone bull, and he shrugs it off:

There were some more very pretty, well-phrased, and useful teachings, but the trouble is that since then I have forgotten most of them. And anyway I really haven't any idea how this had come about, for I merely kept saying "Yes" to everything. I felt just like a bird whose wings have been watered. And so, praise God, here I was a breadwinner! (5)

Later, in a lonelier mood, he thinks about isolation, uttering commonplaces about life in the tradition of the reminiscing narrator-picaro:

There is no cradlesong that predicts the infant's future; sometimes a blind hen finds a grain of corn; he who laughs last laughs best; it's often the unexpected that happens; man proposes and God disposes. In such fashion I was meditating the next day, again sitting in the garden with my pipe, and, looking attentively down at my person, almost feeling as if I were nothing but a ragamuffin. (7)

He is constantly aware of his ejected state. When everyone else is having fun in the Sunday sun,

I was sitting like a bittern among the reeds of a solitary pond in the park, rocking in a skiff that was tied up there, while the vesper bells rang out from the city across the garden, and the swans floated slowly back and forth on the water around me. I felt sad enough to die. (9)

But just as Guzmán or Lazarillo would overcome a setback by plunging immediately into new things, so the Taugenichts counteracts the vicissitudes of life with his special kind of survival tactic: he sings.

In love with a woman whose social position is far above his, he ponders the distinction:

All at once it came over me so clearly, how that she is so lovely and I so poor and despised and forsaken by the world—and when they had all disappeared behind the bushes, I could restrain myself no longer, but flung myself down in the grass and wept bitterly. (12)

He does not have the wit or the initiative to woo the lady, though he goes so far as to make a resolution to settle down, "to save up money like the others." But after reconsidering his condition he tells himself:

Everybody is so merry, and nobody cares about you. And that is my lot always and everywhere. Each one has his plot of ground staked out, has his warm stove, his cup of coffee, his wife, his glass of wine in the evening, and is thoroughly content; even the hall porter feels quite happy inside his tall body. For me there's no happiness anywhere. It's as if I had always come just too late, as if the entire world had not counted me in at all. (22)

Convinced later that he is a fool in a love affair that appears to be completely one-sided, he learns his lesson in picaresque self-awareness and ejects himself out into the world again. "Our kingdom is not of this world," he tells his violin. He forgets the actual woman, idealizes her, and converts his love from a subjective social despair into an aesthetically objective image.

Leaving the estate, he starts a journey that takes him, more by chance than by design, to Italy. Along the way the incidents of the fellow travelers Guido and Leonhart, the intrigue at a castle, the incident at an inn, and the visit to Rome become external events through which he wanders innocently and, so it appears to the reader, haphazardly. During his wanderings, he contemplates the wide world and is, like Guzmán and his German relative Schelmuffsky (*Schel-muffsky's Veritable Curious and Very Dangerous Travel Account by Sea and Land* [1696], by Christian Reuter), shocked by the vastness of the world:

> The world all at once seemed to me so horribly big and wide, and I so utterly alone in it, that I could have wept from the bottom of my heart. (37)

But soon he begins to value experience for its own sake: "What all can't a man experience, if once he quits hearth and home!" (46).

But with the episode involving Guido and Leonhart (chs. 3 and 4), we begin to suspect that the landscape here is not exactly like that of other picaros, who live chaotically at the whims of chance and fortune. The good-for-nothing only appears to be living life at random. The mysterious events at the castle (ch. 6) and the strange appearance of his lady in Rome (chs. 7 and 8) confirm the suspicion that some kind of elaborate plot is at work. Ostensibly free, ostensibly wandering aimlessly and haphazardly, the Taugenichts has actually had his ad-ventures manipulated for him. This is all unraveled in the last chapter when the Taugenichts returns from Rome to the castle that had been the scene of his first adventure and where he had fallen in love. As it turns out, all the mysteries and strange coincidences of his wanderings had been designed and manufactured by the count in order to pursue a love affair of his own. The good-for-nothing had been an innocent and unsuspecting part of a plot all along. As everything is quickly explained in the last chapter, we learn that nothing had been what it appeared to be: Guido was not a man but a woman in disguise, Leonhart was not who he claimed to be but the count himself, and the lady the Taugenichts loved—and then despaired of loving, first because he thought she was a countess, and second because he thought she was betrothed to someone else—is not really a countess at all but an orphan who had been brought up at the castle, and so on. Everything in the Taugenichts's experience had been set up. It was not the picaresque world of chance and disorder after all, though it appeared to be. "I suppose you have never read a romance?" the count asks. The Taugenichts says no. "Well, then you have helped to play one." The apparent picaresque world of disorder is revealed to be the world of order, of romance:

> "And now," said Mr. Leonhart, "we must quickly enter the castle, for everybody is waiting for us. And so in concusion, as is of course obvious and becoming to a well-trained romance: discovery, repentance, reconciliation, we are all once more gaily united, and the wedding day is day after tomorrow!" (116)

Memoirs of a Good-for-Nothing has been dismissed as a charming and in-genious but ultimately senseless work, a parody of romanticism itself. And yet this little picaresque romance—and here Chandler's term "romance of roguery" seems particularly apt—follows in miniature a pattern that emerged in eighteenth-century picaresque variations such as *Gil Blas* and *Roderick Random* (q.q.v.): the pattern of recurring characters and connected events. Gils Blas, for example, is forever picking up the bits and pieces of old incidents, and Smollett's Roderick

Random has more coincidences in his adventures than seems possible in a world of disorder and chance. Stuart Miller has called this pattern the "dance pattern":

> The dance pattern . . . is of course similar to the pattern of romance. The difference is that while in the romance a coincidence leads to some momentous conclusion, in the dance pattern [of the picaresque] it may lead to nothing more than a recitation of adventures or a job for the picaro. . . . The dance pattern thus stands between the typical picaresque and romance plots, giving a greater feeling of order in action than does the picaresque but less order than does the tightly fated design of the romance. (17–18)

Miller does not talk about *Memoirs of a Good-for-Nothing,* but his method of exploring picaresque fiction by constant comparison to romance patterns is an appropriate way to look at Eichendorff's work, which functions within and between the fictional modes of romance and picaresque. Helmut Günther, in a brief consideration of Eichendorff's work as picaresque (it is rarely so considered), notes that the good-for-nothing stands, like the traditional picaro, at the edge of society, but he does not stand against it. The theme of the work, Günther feels, is freedom, which he defines as a state of not being bound to anything, a romantic absence of confines; but the freedom enjoyed by the good-for-nothing is not achieved actively by himself but through the will of God, to whose hand he repeatedly commits himself.

The enclosure of the picaresque world by a romance pattern of order through a comic ending adds a parodistic dimension to *Memoirs of a Good-for-Nothing* that is appropriate to the German romantic notion of romantic irony, which was derived in large part from Cervantes's narrative technique. In Eichendorff, romance is mocking picaresque. The picaro has been the butt of a joke played on him by the world of romance (the count's elaborately designed plot); this comic reversal in turn neutralizes the experiential realm for the picaro; he can live happily ever after. But in this ending, there is an ambiguity that echoes (though only faintly) the heavily ironic self-deception of the morally impoverished Lazarillo as he accomodates himself to society's corrupt terms of existence. The good-for-nothing lets himself be absorbed into the puppet-stringed life that has been set up for him. His final words—"and all was right with the world!"— may also be spoken through a self-constructed mask. And if we thus are not entirely convinced of the sincerity of the good-for-nothing's conclusion (as we certainly are not of Lazarillo's), then perhaps this is in turn the picaresque's mockery of romance. The object of desire in the picaresque world is romance order; but it is attainable only through compromise, accommodation, and self-deception. Perhaps the picaresque encloses the romance after all.

TRANSLATION

Bayard Quincy Morgan (New York: Frederick Ungar, 1955).

SELECT BIBLIOGRAPHY

J.-J. A. Bertrand, "L. Tieck et le roman picaresque," *Revue Germanique* 10 (1914): 443–61; Helmut Günther, "Der ewige Simplizissimus. Gestalt und Wandlungen des deutschen Schelmenromans,'' *Welt und Wort* 10 (1955): 1–5; Stuart Miller, *The Pica-resque Novel* (Cleveland, Ohio: Case Western Reserve University Press, 1967). For a good discussion of the Bildungsroman, see Roy Pascal, *The German Novel* (Manchester University Press, 1956).

METAMORPHOSES

See THE GOLDEN ASS

MIDNIGHT COWBOY

(1969)

Directed by John Schlesinger

Two bus trips across the American landscape frame this film, written by Waldo Salt (from a novel by James Leo Herlihy). The first shows Joe Buck leaving his small Texas home town and heading to New York, where he hopes to be a male prostitute. Through flashbacks, we learn that he is the son and grandson of prostitutes and that a traumatic sexual incident alienated him radically from normal connection to other human beings. The second shows Buck with his friend Ratso, a thieving, crippled son of an illiterate hunchback, on their way to Miami Beach, Ratso's longed-for Garden of Eden. Ratso dies before the bus reaches its destination. In between these points of the circle of existence, the film shows in episodic fashion a variety of deceits, disillusionments, and reversals of fortune in which Joe the hustler ends up being hustled (even, at first, by Ratso). Much of the action takes place in the sleazy underside of big city life. "Like the tawdry environment they inhabit, [Joe and Ratso] are the products of a ceaselessly, carelessly exploitative society. Controlled and consoled by the viciously moronic ideas it has implanted in them, they are on a lifelong bad trip and unable to end it'' (Schickel). Their very outsiderdom becomes the tie that binds them, until, in the end, they are composite parts of a single picaro figure seeking home.

As with *O Lucky Man!* (q.v.), the film's rhetoric was almost consistently criticized by reviewers. "*Midnight Cowboy* is just a little too knowing, pert and pat,'' John Simon wrote, going on to point out the film's dishonesties:

Worse yet is the glib exploitation of America the all-purpose bogey as the causes of Joe's downfall: the mass-media with their mendacious siren songs; the suspiciousness and lovelessness rampant in the land; the cruel socio-economic gap between haves and have-nots; the maniacal, dehumanizing pursuit of money and success; etc., etc. But aside from the fact that these are commonplaces and remain so in the film, no matter how gussied up with superficial cleverness, there is not clear demonstration of how the society affects Joe Buck, of how his individual guilt is begotten by the community. (72)

Simon finds its "contrived, manipulative technique, adroit though it may be,'' offensive. Schlesinger too was irritated by the film's "dissolution of linear narration into a whirl of images'' (78). Without the highly critical and often distorting perspective of the picaro himself, however, cinematic narration compensates for the absence of autobiographical narration and discourse by generating the appropriate rhetoric through such techniques as the juxtaposing and counterpointing of images and sounds in the tradition of Sergei Eisenstein's concept of *montage*. Such distortive manipulation for the purposes of powerful statement is no more heavy-handed than, say, Quevedo's portrait of the schoolmaster Cabra in *El Buscón* (q.v.) or Voltaire's verbally puppeteered horrors and improbabilities in *Candide*. These are the stock-in-trade of the formal satirist, and the picaresque mode has always had direct affinities with the mode of satire.

What does jar slightly in Schlesinger's picaresque vision is what the other reviewers mostly praised: the tender relationship that develops between Joe and Ratso. Such a relationship is virtually absent in picaresque fictions except as another setup for further disillusionment—which, in the end, it is in *Midnight Cowboy,* if we interpret the final scene to represent Joe's awakening to the realization that this is a radically hostile world that rejects even its otherwise sanctioned trickster figures (q.v.). Joe and Ratso are halves of a composite picaro figure, with Ratso the trickster and Joe the psychologically and socially estranged wanderer who together search for a final home. But the melodrama serves the satire, and the heightened poignancy of the relationship is used to make the world all the more cruel, by way of the reaction shots of the other passengers on the bus.

In his concise analysis of the film as picaresque, Fiore does not make such objections or qualifications. His careful application of Guillén's and Parker's concepts to the characters of Joe and Ratso, and his use of such models as *Lazarillo de Tormes* and *Guzmán de Alfarache* (q.q.v.), make for a convincing treatment. He stops short of exploring the problematics of medium-specific manner of presentation, however, except to acknowledge that such a difference exists: "In the film Joe Buck and Ratso Rizzo are *pícaros,* but in this case it is the eye of the camera which provides the narration, with its various points of view, its sound track of words, music, noise and silence'' (270). In that difference, though, lie the significant characteristics that help us distinguish between the few fully picaresque films and the many superficially picaresque movies. As in *O Lucky Man!* the cinematic equivalent to picaresque autobiographical narration is self-reflexiveness. In *Midnight Cowboy,* the whole narrational framework, and the audience's relationship to it, is given at the beginning when the camera pulls back from a white screen to reveal that it is indeed a white movie screen (literally, a drive-in movie screen in daylight). From that moment on, our point of view is consciously—and not, as is more often the case in conventional film narrative, unconsciously—with the camera in its rhetorically manipulative function, just as in verbal picaresques we are consciously with the narrating picaro, always aware of the manner of telling.

SELECT BIBLIOGRAPHY

Robert L. Fiore, ''The Picaresque Tradition in *Midnight Cowboy,''* *Literature/Film Quarterly* 3 (1975): 270–76, and *''Lazarillo de Tormes* and *Midnight Cowboy:* The Picaresque

Model and Mode," in *Studies in Honor of Everett W. Hesse,* ed. William C. McCrary and José A. Madrigal (Lincoln, Neb.: Society of Spanish and Spanish American Studies, 1981), 81–97; Richard Schickel [review in *Life*], Arthur Schlesinger [review in *Vogue*], and John Simon [review in *The New Leader*], all in *Film 69/70: An Anthology by the National Society of Film Critics,* ed. Joseph Morgenstern and Stefan Kanfer (New York: Simon & Schuster, 1970), 69–70, 77–78, 71–75, respectively.

MOLL FLANDERS
(THE FORTUNES AND MISFORTUNES OF THE FAMOUS
MOLL FLANDERS)

(1722)

Daniel Defoe

Although his contemporary readers would have had immediate associations of criminality with the title character's name, with its echo of "Moll Cutpurse," a notorious seventeenth-century female thief, and its association with contraband Flemish lace—both alluded to directly in the text (197, 204, 208)—Defoe increased the titillation in the manner (if not the length) of a supermarket-tabloid headline writer of today by extending his title: *Who Was Born in Newgate, and during a Life of Continu'd Variety for Threescore Years, besides Her Childhood, Was Twelve Year a Whore, Fives Times a Wife (Whereof Once to Her Own Brother) Twelve Year a Thief, Eight Year a Transported Felon in Virginia, at Last Grew Rich, Liv'd Honest, and Died a Penitent. Written from Her Own Memorandums.* This subtitle also gave Defoe's audience a recognizable generic context by explicitly placing the work within then popular and familiar traditions: the criminal biography, the dying speech, the coney-catching pamphlet, providence literature, the repentance, and the other variations on criminal life described by Chandler in chapters 3 and 4 of the first volume of *The Literature of Roguery* (1907). *Moll Flanders* went through five editions within two years (the third was abbreviated); almost immediately, in 1723, a German translation appeared, and that same year J. Read published a pirated abridgement that cut the text in half, divided it into chapters, gave Moll a name (Laetitia Atkins), and appended an account of her death. But by the end of the century, both the popularity and the reputation of *Moll Flanders* had waned, not to be revived until the early twentieth century.

The nineteenth-century distaste for *Moll Flanders* was representatively expressed early in the century by Sir Walter Scott in his essay on Defoe (1827). Although Scott was among the first to place some of Defoe's works within the picaresque tradition, he did so with a sniffing condescension that contradicts the warm praise he had lavished on Lesage's picaresque fiction a few years earlier (*Gil Blas,* q.v.). Defoe, says Scott, applied his first-hand knowledge of low life to works of fiction "in the style termed by the Spaniards *Gusto Picaresco,* of which no man was ever a greater master." Nevertheless,

This class of the fictitious narrative may be termed the Romance of Roguery, the subjects being the adventures of thieves, rogues, vagabonds, and swindlers, including viragoes and courtezans. The improved taste of the present age has justly rejected this coarse species of amusement, which is, besides, calculated to do an infinite deal of mischief among the lower classes, as it presents in a comic, or even heroic shape, the very crimes and vices to which they are otherwise most likely to be tempted. (166)

He then compares Defoe's "strange and blackguard scenes" to Murillo's depictions of gypsy boys (Melville later also alluded to the painter in *The Confidence-Man,* q.v.). He mentions not only *Moll Flanders* but *Roxana* and *Colonel Jack* (q.q.v.) as containing "strong marks of genius" but

from the coarseness of the narrative, and the vice and vulgarity of the actors, the reader feels as a well-principled young man may do, when seduced by some entertaining and dissolute libertine into scenes of debauchery, that, though he may be amused, he must be not a little ashamed of that which furnishes the entertainment. So that, though we could select from these *picaresque* romances a good deal that is not a little amusing, we let them pass by, as we would persons, however otherwise interesting, who may not be in character and manners entirely fit for good society. (167)

Among those rescuing Defoe's reputation from an exclusive dependence on *Robinson Crusoe* were Virginia Woolf and E. M. Forster. In her 1919 essay on Defoe, Woolf's assessment of Moll Flanders as a character is actually closer to the essence of the picaresque (though she does not use the term) than is Scott's (though Scott was familiar with the tradition, at least as it was perpetuated by Lesage):

From the outset the burden of proving her right to exist is laid upon her. She has to depend entirely upon her own wits and judgment, and to deal with each emergency as it arises by a rule-of-thumb morality which she has forged in her own head. The briskness of the story is due partly to the fact that having transgressed the accepted laws at a very early age she has henceforth the freedom of the outcast. The one impossible event is that she should settle down in comfort and security. (92)

Woolf here cuts to the quick of the picara's problematic freedom, an existential condition at the core of the total situation in which the picaro finds himself, and which picaresque narrative explores in many of its paradoxical ramifications; for an outcast is in many significant ways hardly free, and the one impossibility (to settle down comfortably and securely) in her life is in fact the goal toward which all of Moll's considerable energies are expended. And Forster's discussion of *Moll Flanders* as a "novel of character" in *Aspects of the Novel* (1927) helped to bring this work out of the shadows of Victorian moralism. Forster shows a trust in his fellow readers that Scott did not.

Among the issues that subsequent twentieth-century criticism on *Moll Flanders* has dealt with is the question of whether it is a picaresque. Chandler may have given Defoe something of a backhanded compliment when he said that "Defoe at a blow changed a comic and satirical fiction to one, in some sense, of character. He showed the decline of a soul from innocence to knowledge, temptation, and sin, and then its rise, by virtue of repentance, from distress through honesty to prosperity and calm'' (289). As Parker has shown, Chandler seriously misread Spanish picaresque fiction as a primarily comic form. For Parker, *Moll Flanders* shares with the works of Alemán (*Guzmán de Alfarache*, q.v.) Quevedo (*El Buscón*, q.v.), and Grimmelshausen (*Simplicius Simplicissimus*, q.v.) a serious exploration of delinquency, but it also serves as a watershed dividing ''the complex, ultimately pessimistic, response of the seventeenth century to the human condition, and the simple, ultimately optimistic, response of the eighteenth.'' Moreover, Defoe's attitude ''is much more humanitarian than that of his predecessors, and . . . there is in him a sociological interest that is foreshadowing an economically and socially less cruel world'' (107). Alter, perpetuating Chandler's readings, claims that ''there is a perceptible relaxation of existential seriousness in the picaresque novels: here, one feels, is life as it could be lived, with difficulties to overcome, but without crushing responsibilities to bear. In the world of *Moll Flanders*, however, the individual must carry the weight of a single unending responsibility which necessarily converts the conduct of his life into an austere discipline'' (57). And Ian Watt rejects it as a picaresque on similar grounds: although the picaro, Watt says, has a real historical basis in the breakdown of the feudal order, this is not the point of his adventures. His function is ''as a literary convention for the presentation of a variety of satiric observations and comic episodes,'' whereas Defoe presents his rogues ''as ordinary people who are normal products of their environment, victims of circumstances which anyone might have experienced and which provoke exactly the same moral conflicts between means and ends as those faced by other members of society.'' ''The *picaro* enjoys that charmed immunity from the deeper stings of pain and death which is accorded to all those fortunate enough to inhabit the world of comedy.'' And finally, the difference between *Moll Flanders* and the picaresque ''is also the result of a specific social change closely related to the rise of individualism, a change whereby one of the characteristic institutions of modern urban civilization had come into existence by the early eighteenth century: a well-defined criminal class and a complex system for handling it, with law-courts, informers, and even crime reporters like Defoe'' (94–95). Yet the criminal element had been a problem of major proportions in Europe since long before (*Liber Vagatorum*, q.v.), and hierarchical communities of rogues are a constant feature of picaresques at least as far back as the first part of *Guzmán*.

Michie sees *Moll Flanders* as outwardly a success story, though ''inwardly it is an imaginative demonstration of the way in which sin leads to more sin, and of how evil can diminish the freedom to do good. Hardened by success, [Moll's] will has become enslaved'' (88–89). The book is thus concerned with ''the difficulties of reconciling social aspirations and the life of the spirit'' (91), a concern that for Blackburn ''must recall the process of spiritual disintegration in *Lazarillo de Tormes* [q.v.]'' (100) but with the difference that the considerable moral ambiguity in *Moll Flanders* leaves open the possibility of social integration. Bjornson carefully explores this ambiguity, though he sees *Lazarillo* and *Moll*

Flanders offering contrasting visions, with the former being "an implicit condemnation of the dehumanized value system which [the socializing] process
conditions people to accept" and the latter reflecting "the assumption that it is
a perfectly natural phenomenon which perpetuates the necessary techniques of
survival" (188). The disjunction between Lazarillo's attitudes and the worldview
implicit in *Lazarillo* is clear, "whereas Moll's ideas frequently overlap with the
standards according to which she is presumably judged. In this difference and
in the diametrically opposed endings of the two novels are reflected both the
rise of bourgeois society and the ambiguity of bourgeois attitudes toward success" (206).

Translations of *El Buscón* and *Guzmán* and most of the other Spanish picaresques were popular in the first three decades of the eighteenth century, and it
has generally been assumed that Defoe could not have avoided being influenced
by these even as he relied heavily on such indigenous narrative forms as the
criminal biography. Spadaccini has explored what little external evidence exists:
Defoe mentions *Lazarillo* in his other writings, and he owned a copy of *La
pícara Justina* (q.v.) in the original Spanish (12). This latter fact is especially
significant, not only because it opens up the possibility that Defoe had primary
(not just secondary and tertiary) access to the Spanish picaresque but because
Justina is the prototype for picaras, thus giving Defoe the idea for a female
rogue. (If this is true, it would mean mild qualifications in feminist approaches
to *Moll Flanders* as, for example, "unique among pre-twentieth-century heroines
in resisting reduction to the literary alternatives of marriage or death" [Chaber,
213].) *La pícara Justina* has also been called "an implicit satire on the aims
and structures of *Guzmán de Alfarache*" (Parker, 50), which leads Spadaccini
to a close analysis of Defoe's preface to *Moll Flanders*, revealing allusions to
Guzmán (as well as to Ginés de Pasamonte in *Don Quixote*), and finally to a
direct comparison with *El Buscón* to examine Defoe's "fully conscious" changes
in his inherited narrative tradition through his "constant dialogue with the genre's
conventions" (23).

Another major critical concern with *Moll Flanders*—related to but often discussed apart from generic considerations—is the matter of irony. Ian Watt, in
a much-quoted conclusion to a thorough exploration of the tendency to read the
book ironically, says that "*Moll Flanders* is undoubtedly an ironic object, but
it is not a work of irony" (130). Defoe, Watt claims, was serious about his
material: "He was not ashamed to make economic self-interest his major premise
about human life; he did not think such a premise conflicted either with social
or religious values; and nor did his age" (127). Ironigenic attitudes toward *Moll
Flanders* are thus reader responses coming after more than two hundred years
of social, moral, and cultural change—including the rise of the novel itself as
an ever-more refined narrative instrument for examining social, moral, and spiritual complexities.

One alternative in avoiding an ironic reading of *Moll Flanders* is to come to
Mark Schorer's conclusion that it is "the true allegory of an impoverished soul—

the author's'' (67). Lacking adequate resources of technique to separate himself
from his material, with the point of view of Moll being "indistinguishable from
the point of view of her creator," Defoe presented, according to Schorer, "our
classic revelation of the mercantile mind: the morality of measurement, which
[he] has completely neglected to measure." But Schorer turns innocence or
primitivism of early-eighteenth-century narrative technique into a twentieth-century moral condemnation of the author himself, which seems an unsatisfying,
aesthetically unsound way to resolve an issue that in Defoe's other major picaresques (*Colonel Jack, Roxana,* q.q.v.) has generated little debate. Although
both Watt's and Schorer's arguments have been persuasively refuted (among
others, by Novak), the debate is likely to continue. A part of us wants to take
Moll at face value as Defoe's face-value narrative portrait; our own moral superiority diminishes her and thus comforts us. Another part of us resists literal
readings and tries to put Moll in a context that makes her "represent" (the
condition of women in a patriarchy, the individual in a capitalist economic
structure, self-interest triumphant over self-knowledge, and so on). And still
another part of us is afraid of being conned by Moll if we do not poke around
in Defoe's rhetoric.

These are precisely the reader responses at work when we read picaresque
fiction, and all three operating simultaneously have one thing in common: to
keep the picaro from coming too close for comfort. It thus does not really matter
how we approach *Moll Flanders* so long as we satisfy our instinct to protect
ourselves—not from what she might mean but rather from what she is. What
she might mean, in fact, disguises her from what she is, and pursuit of such
meanings is equivalent to forcing masks on a character who, in recounting her
life (if not in living it), refuses to wear any.

Like most other picaresques, *Moll Flanders* is dually narrated, with a voice
in a preface enclosing, or framing, the voice of the picara, which is further
divided between the narrating self and the narrated self. But what is too often
overlooked is that we are not reading Moll's own words—a narrative situation
simply and directly signaled to us right in the long third-person title, which
concludes, "written from her own memorandums," and not "written by her
own hand." In effect, Moll's account is "ghost-written," as the preface makes
clear:

> It is true that the original of this story is put into new words, and the style of the
> famous lady we here speak of is a little altered; particularly she is made to tell her own
> tale in modester words than she told it at first, the copy which came first to hand having
> been written in language more like one still in Newgate than one grown penitent and
> humble, as she afterwards pretends to be.
>
> The pen employed in finishing her story, and making it what you now see it to be,
> has had no little difficulty to put it into a dress fit to be seen, and to make it speak
> language fit to be read. When a woman debauched from her youth, nay, even being the
> offspring of debauchery and vice, comes to give an account of all her vicious practices,
> and even to descend to the particular occasions and circumstances by which she first
> became wicked, and of all the progression of crime which she ran through in threescore

years, an author must be hard put to it to wrap it up so clean as not to give room, especially for vicious readers, to turn it to his disadvantage.

All possible care, however, has been taken to give no lewd ideas, no immodest turns in the new dressing up of this story; no, not to the worst parts of her expressions. To this purpose some of the vicious part of her life, which could not be modestly told, is quite left out, and several other parts are very much shortened. What is left 'tis hoped will not offend the chastest reader or the modestest hearer; and as the best use is made even of the worst story, the moral 'tis hoped will keep the reader serious, even where the story might incline him to be otherwise. To give the history of a wicked life repented of, necessarily requires that the wicked part should be made as wicked as the real history of it will bear, to illustrate and give a beauty to the penitent part, which is certainly the best and brightest, if related with equal spirit and life. (28–29)

This editor or narrator (who is not Defoe, the real author, or Schorer's "impoverished soul," the implied author) is here providing a fairly conventional picaresque disclaimer that, from *Lazarillo* on, has been used to sanction reader indulgence in the experientially forbidden for the sake of moral self-improvement. This narrator knows his readers' tastes and goes on to state straightforwardly that the "penitent parts" do not really have the appeal that the wicked parts do; but he also trusts the intelligence of his readers, pointing out that all of them "will have something of instruction, if he pleases to make use of it" (30). The reader is thus placed in a relationship to the text that is also dual, lured into it by the promise of forbidden fruit and simultaneously saddled with the heavy responsibility of keeping that fruit at a moral distance.

The title page and the preface to *Moll Flanders*, then, establish a balanced narrating-reading relationship between text and audience that keeps two narrative voices constantly interacting with two reader responses. The narrator of the preface is fully aware of what he is doing with conventions of narrative technique. "The author is here supposed to be writing her own history," he says in the second paragraph (28), making overt right from the beginning that he is using the device of the dramatized or feigned ("supposed to be") narrator. And immediately in the first paragraph, he acknowledges the participatory role of the reader: "to leave the reader to pass his own opinion upon the ensuing sheets, and take it just as he pleases." This is a narrator rhetorically in control of his material, hardly the naive, primitive prenovelist, deficient in technique, which he is sometimes made out to be. He also makes use of the picaresque narrative trick of "putting in" by "taking out": "the whole relation is carefully garbled of all the levity and looseness that was in it" (30). When Moll then begins to narrate, she may be speaking for herself, but she is not herself speaking; hers is really the second voice of the ventriloquist-narrator of the preface. Given this carefully constructed narrating situation, the issue of intentional versus unintentional irony becomes moot; a dual-voiced narrative has irony built into it.

The temporal narrative distance between the self at the time of action and the self at the time of narration makes further demands on the reader's rhetorical alertness. It has been said that "Defoe is not much interested in the time-span and the changes wrought by time; he is never keenly conscious of the double point of view involved when a character is talking about his own past" (McKillop, 31). Yet this is precisely what the narrator of the preface emphasizes when he insists that this is a story told by a penitent, a story he has taken considerable pains to prune and revise both in the "wicked part" and in the "penitent part." When Moll relates her stealing of a necklace from an innocent child, she does so in the context of an attempted repentance that she realized was not sincere. Repeatedly she blames her behavior on two causes: an "evil counsellor within," or "the devil" (191); and poverty, which "hardened my heart" (190, 191), echoing the proverb that functions as her motto: "Give me not poverty, lest I steal" (188). What has been considered problematic is the manner in which Moll rationalizes the theft:

My own necessities made me regardless of anything. The last affair left no great concern upon me, for as I did the poor child no harm, I only said to myself, I had given the parents a just reproof for their negligence in leaving the poor little lamb to come home by itself, and it would teach them to take more care of it another time. (191–92)

She then adds a couple of additional reproaches based on hypothesis: "perhaps the vanity of the mother, to have her child look fine at the dancing school, had made her let the child wear [the necklace]"; and the "careless jade" of a maid no doubt sent to take care of the child "was taken up perhaps with some fellow that had met her by the way" (192). These rationalizations ring psychologically true in the immediacy of the act, for Moll is quite naturally denying the true nature of what she has done. We are not supposed to take her reproaches as serious moral judgments because Moll is in the heat of the moment using a self-justifying protective device that echoes familiarly to many readers in lesser situations. Behind the narrated self's emotional attempt to justify her actions is the narrating self, who puts the whole incident in the larger moral, social, and psychological contexts provided through temporal distancing: poverty, the devil, and fear. And behind them both is the voice of the narrator of the preface, who has made this rhetorical arrangement. Irony does not become an issue because we are not meant to take Moll's admonitions seriously as reflections; they belong to the immediacy of the moment and as such have only emotional, not moral or sociological, validity.

More crucial than irony is the issue of Moll's sincerity. In the following passage, there is some confusion of narrative distance:

Then it occurred to me, "What an abominable creature am I! and how is this innocent gentlemen going to be abused by me! How little does he think, that having divorced a whore, he is throwing himself into the arms of another! that he is going to marry one that has lain with two brothers, and has had three children by her own brother! one that was born in Newgate, whose mother was a whore, and is now a transported thief! one that has lain with thirteen men, and has had a child since he saw me! Poor gentleman!" said I, "what is he going to do?" After this reproaching myself was over, it followed thus: "Well, if I must be his wife, if it pleases God to give me grace, I'll be a true wife to him, and love him suitably to the strange excess of his passion for me; I will make him amends if possible, by what he shall see, for the cheats and abuses I put upon him, which he does not see." (181)

It is difficult to believe that these are the thoughts of the younger Moll at the time of experience. Although they are narrated as such through direct quotation, they really belong to the older Moll who is not entirely unproud of the sensational variety in her catalog of sins. That the narrating self puts these words into the mind of the narrated self does not go unnoticed; in fact, it is a blatant manipulation of moralizing rhetoric that, in being inappropriate to the moment being dramatized, actually works against itself. The same is true when Moll moralizes directly:

On the other hand, every branch of my story, if duly considered, may be useful to honest people, and afford a due caution to people of some sort or other to guard against the like surprises, and to have their eyes about them when they have to do with strangers of any kind, for 'tis very seldom that some snare or other is not in their way. The moral, indeed, of all my history is left to be gathered by the senses and judgment of the reader; I am not qualified to preach to them. Let the experience of one creature completely wicked, and completely miserable, be a storehouse of useful warning to those that read. (254)

This sounds hollow because it lacks conviction. The narrating Moll is perfunctorily doing her duty as a narrator here. Her obligatory lip-service to morality is undermined by her admitted lack of qualification as a preacher while simultaneously indulging in preaching. The narrating Moll knows that the reader's interest is in the narrated Moll; it is the narrator behind the narrating Moll who feels that duty must be done.

This narrator, who had said in the preface that the penitent parts can never be as interesting as the wicked parts, prepared us for an insincere Moll by also telling us that toward the end of her life, Moll "was not so extraordinary a pentient as she was at first" (32). He also, like Moll herself in the passage above, tells us that the moral in Moll's story is to alert us to the snares that the Molls of the world lay out for us: "All the exploits of this lady of fame . . . stand as so many warnings to honest people to beware of them, intimating to them by what methods innocent people are drawn in, plundered, and robbed, and by consequence how to avoid them" (30). The moral instruction has little to do with the reformation, through penitence, of characters like Moll; rather, the burden is put upon us to stay out of their way. Moll never achieves genuine self-knowledge because she is incapable of it. She seems most authentic when she sinks her narrative teeth into lived experience; she seems least sincere when her ventriloquist makes her moralize. She thrives in her being, not in self-reflection about being. Once the narrator lets her speak, after the preface, she bursts forth with a typographically continuous narrative unrelieved by chapter pauses. Her sheer narrative energy creates "a remarkably persuasive mimetic structure" (Stevick, 177).

Among picaresques, *Moll Flanders* most resembles *Barry Lyndon* (q.v.) in the responses of earlier readers and in the subsequent attempts to justify ironies. And, as with Thackeray's picaresque, the Victorian repulsion from Defoe's work may reflect a more honest reading than the latter-day ironic dressing up reflects. Moll is a subversive character who bursts all boundaries as she takes narrative form, drawing her life from the ventriloquist-narrator who by the end is quite forgotten as a distinct narrative voice. Ultimately *Moll Flanders* transcends any questions about narrative technique and irony. We are afraid of her, as we are of Barry Lyndon. But we yield to our simultaneous attraction toward her by safely approaching her with layers of self-protective irony or condescending compensations for Defoe's poverty of technique. Her danger to us is that she is pure drive; she has no self-knowledge because she is incapable of it. She is an aspect of undifferentiated trickster (q.v.), descended through the Widow of Ephesus (*The Satyricon,* q.v.) and Chaucer's Wife of Bath, by way of Courage (*The Runagate Courage*, q.v.), and prefiguring Erica Jong's *Fanny* (q.v.). What startles, even shocks, in *Moll Flanders* is the vibrancy with which Defoe has made her simply *be*: a force of nature, the incarnation of an archetype best described by Dorothy Van Ghent:

The immense and seminal reality of an Earth Mother, progenetrix of the wasteland, sower of our harvests of technological skills, bombs, gadgets, and the platitudes and stereotypes and absurdities of a morality suitable to a wasteland world. (43)

EDITIONS

Quotations are from the Penguin English Library edition, ed. Juliet Mitchell (New York, 1978). Two critical editions, with backgrounds, sources, and criticism, exist: The Crowell Critical Library Edition, ed. J. Paul Hunter (New York: Crowell, 1970), and the Norton Critical Edition, ed. Edward Kelly (New York: Norton, 1973).

SELECT BIBLIOGRAPHY

Robert Alter, *Rogue's Progress: Studies in the Picaresque Novel* (Cambridge: Harvard University Press, 1964); A. Bellesort, "Les Romans picaresques de Daniel Defoe," *Revue bleue* 58 (1920): 442–45; Richard Bjornson, *The Picaresque Hero in European Fiction* (Madison: University of Wisconsin Press, 1977); Alexander Blackburn, *The Myth of the Picaro: Continuity and Transformation of the Picaresque Novel, 1554–1954* (Chapel Hill: University of North Carolina Press, 1979); Lois A. Chaber, "Matriarchal Mirror: Women and Capital in *Moll Flanders*" *PMLA* 97 (1982): 212–26; Frank Wadleigh Chandler, *The Literature of Roguery* [1907] (New York: Burt Franklin, 1958); E. M. Forster, *Aspects of the Novel* (New York: Harcourt, Brace, 1927); Edward H. Friedman, "The Enlightened Narrator: *Moll Flanders* and the Social Imperative," in his *The Antiheroine's Voice: Narrative Discourse and Transformations of the Picaresque* (Columbia: University of Missouri Press, 1987), 121–47; Frank J. Kearful, "Spanish Rogues and English Foundlings: On the Disintegration of Picaresque," *Genre* 4 (1971): 376–89; John P. Kent and J. L. Gaunt, "Picaresque Fiction: A Bibliographic Essay," *College Literature* 6 (1979): 245–70; Arnold Kettle, *An Introduction to the English Novel,* vol. 1 (London: Hutchinson University Library, 1951); Bruce McCullough, *Representative English Nov-*

elists: Defoe to Conrad (New York: Harper & Row, 1946); Alan Dugald McKillop, *The Early Masters of English Fiction* (Lawrence: University of Kansas Press, 1956); J. A. Michie, "The Unity of *Moll Flanders*," in *Knaves and Swindlers: Essays on the Picaresque Novel in Europe*, ed. Christine J. Whitbourn (London: Oxford University Press, 1974), 75–92; Stuart Miller, *The Picaresque Novel* (Cleveland, Ohio: Case Western Reserve University Press, 1967); Maximillian E. Novak, "Conscious Irony in *Moll Flanders:* Facts and Problems," *College English* 26 (1964): 198–204; A. A. Parker, *Literature and the Delinquent: The Picaresque Novel in Spain and Europe, 1599–1753* (Edinburgh: University Press, 1969); John J. Richetti, "Rogues and Whores: Heroes and Anti-Heroes," in his *Popular Fiction before Richardson: Narrative Patterns, 1700–1739* (Oxford: Clarendon Press, 1969), 23–59; Julio Rodríguez-Luis, "*Pícaras:* The Modal Approach to the Picaresque," *Comparative Literature* 31 (1979): 32–46; Mark Schorer, "Technique as Discovery" [1948], in *Discussions of the Novel*, ed. Roger Sale (Boston: D.C. Heath, 1960), 65–76; Sir Walter Scott, *On Novelists and Fiction*, ed. Ioan Williams (New York: Barnes and Noble, 1968); Harry Sieber, *The Picaresque* (London: Methuen, 1977); Nicholas Spadaccini, "Daniel Defoe and the Spanish Picaresque Tradition: The Case of *Moll Flanders*," *Ideologies and Literature* 2 (1978): 10–26; Philip Stevick, "The Theory of Fictional Chapters," in *The Theory of the Novel*, ed. Philip Stevick (New York: Free Press, 1967); Alain Thomas, "Essai d'analyse socio-critique d'un passage de *Moll Flanders*," *Actes picaresques européenne*, ed. Edmond Cros (Montpelier: Centre d'études sociocritiques, Université Paul Valery, 1976), 181–211; Dorothy Van Ghent, *The English Novel: Form and Function* [1953] (New York: Harper & Row, 1961), 33–43; Ian Watt, *The Rise of the Novel: Studies in Defoe, Richardson and Fielding* [1957] (Berkeley and Los Angeles: University of California Press, 1964); Ulrich Wicks, "Narrative Distance in Picaresque Fiction," *College Literature* 6 (1979): 165–81; Virginia Woolf, "Defoe" [1919] in her *The Common Reader, First Series* (New York: Harcourt, Brace, and World, 1925), 89–97.

LA NIÑA DE LOS EMBUSTES, TERESA DE MANZANARES

(The Trickster Girl, Teresa de Manzanares, 1632)

Alonso de Castillo Solórzano

Fonger de Haan thought this book was worth careful study, "for nowhere else in Spanish literature do we find a more lifelike and unvarnished account of the circumstances in which the actresses lived at this epoch" (46), and Chandler judged it "well and swiftly told in the same satirical vein as the *Hija de Celestina* [q.v.], although fuller of incident and less detailed" (314). But on the whole, *La niña de los embustes* is another variation in Castillo Solórzano's hybridization of the picaresque into a blend of escapist adventure-picaresque in which a male or female rogue aspires toward material comforts and security. Teresa is, for much of her story, appropriately enough an actress, and she ultimately acquires her fortune through confidence tricks for which she is never held morally accountable: "Her marriage demonstrates that a picara could achieve upward social mobility and escape the poetic justice meted out to Salas' Elena [in *La hija de Celestina*], who dies on the gallows after poisoning her lover" (Bjornson, 94).

This is the only one of Castillo's escapist picaresques (*Aventuras del bachiller Trapaza, La garduña de Sevilla,* q.q.v.) in which the pseudo-autobiographical narrative technique essential to picaresque is sustained, but Rico finds it deficient: "Here the use of autobiography is so gratuitous that the author, who was after all an intelligent literary craftsman, switched over much more happily to the conventional third person" in his other works (86). And Dunn adds, "The autobiographical narration is nonfunctional; it achieves nothing which the third-person narration could not achieve. No reason is given for her addressing the reader, or for Castillo's adopting an inconsistent third-person address in his prologue" (*The Spanish Picaresque Novel,* 126).

Even more frustrating than the watering down of the essential picaresque technical devices has been Castillo's portrait of the picara. Although he is hardly original in depicting a female picaro (*La pícara Justina,* q.q.v.), one looks in vain among his female characterizations for even a small amount of the psychological depth and serious self-exploration of identity with which earlier picaros such as Lazarillo, Guzmán, and even Pablos (*Lazarillo de Tormes, Guzmán de Alfarache, El Buscón,* q.q.v.) are depicted or of the sheer life force of such driven picaras to come as Courage and Moll (*The Runagate Courage, Moll Flanders,* q.q.v.). Dunn, in his *Castillo Solórzano and the Decline of the Spanish Novel,* has said that in fictions about picaras, it is not the prospect of starvation that leads the character to a life of roguery; rather, the female rogue's beauty, wit, and ingenuity make picaresque existence attractive in itself: "There is neither that necessity which we find in the *Lazarillo* nor that sense of guilt which dominates the *Guzmán*" (115). Rodríguez-Luis in his study of the inadequacy of fictions about picaras before *Moll Flanders* summarizes as follows:

Pícaras, as opposed to mere whores, were in fact implausible in a society which placed such heavy constraints on the social mobility of the common woman. Consequently, those picaresque novels which concern themselves with *pícaras* lack the characteristic depth of the novels which treat their male counterparts. This depth results from the tension between ambition and means, a tension which, if it is to be creative or artistically valid, must be based on a realistic hope. Yet what in fact occurs in *pícara* novels is a suspension of the internal verisimilitude of the work, something which can only be fatal to a novel based on the imitation of reality. . . . Consequently, the narrative space which constitutes the substance of picaresque fiction merely becomes a void to be filled with a caricature of society and the greed of the heroine. (40–41)

In his chapter on picaras in his *The Spanish Picaresque Novel,* Dunn comes to similar conclusions. Fictions with picaros portray women in traditional roles (wife, mother, innkeeper, seamstress) or the lawless world of prostitutes, procuresses, and camp followers. In a severely hierarchical and stratified world, even the picaro's mobility was constrained by rigid limitations bred of fear that social mobility would threaten disorder and the breakdown of authority and obedience. In such a society, the female was even more imprisoned: "Female roles were static: wife, mother, provider. Even inns, which dissolved social boundaries and put people in tempting proximity to one another, could be a gate into that unruly outer world where freedom was a synonym for licentiousness" (132). Although the emergence of the picara "seems to promise the most interesting stroke of originality in a series of novels which are outstanding for their continual innovations" (132), the realities of seventeenth-century social structures imposed either of two absolute extremes: an honest woman whose life would be much too narrowly confined for any kind of picaresque experience, or a femme fatale so far beyond normalcy that she could not be taken as a serious depiction of human personality. Because social reality denied women a middle ground, the literary picara on the model of Lazarillo or Guzmán was an impossibility. Dunn concludes, "Whereas *Lazarillo de Tormes* and *Guzmán de Alfarache* sharpen consciousness, [novels with picaras] dull it. The ingenuity is superficial, the moral vision confused" (133).

There was one female writer in the seventeenth century who occasionally wrote stories with picaresque themes: Doña María de Zayas y Sotomayor, whose story "El castigo de la miseria" (The Chastisement of Misery, 1637) is included in Angel Valbuena Prat's *La novela picaresca española* (1619–1635). Bjornson points out that her "picaresquelike stories show the failure of ruses played by female rogues and the success of ones played by men" (266), in contrast to the deceits of picaras in the works of Salas Barbadillo and Castillo Solórzano.

EDITION

No English translation is known to exist. The original text is accessible in one of the editions of Angel Valbuena Prat's 1943 anthology *La novela picaresca española;* in the 6th edition (Madrid: Aguilar, 1968), it is on pp. 1342–1424.

SELECT BIBLIOGRAPHY

Richard Bjornson, *The Picaresque Hero in European Fiction* (Madison: University of Wisconsin Press, 1977); Frank Wadleigh Chandler, *Romances of Roguery* [1899] (New York: Burt Franklin, 1961); Peter N. Dunn, *Castillo Solórzano and the Decline of the Spanish Novel* (Oxford: Basil Blackwell, 1952) and *The Spanish Picaresque Novel* (Boston: Twayne, 1979); Fonger de Haan, *An Outline of the History of the Novela Picaresca in Spain* [1895] (The Hague and New York: Martinus Nijhoff, 1903); Mireya Pérez-Erdelyi, *La pícara y la dama: la imagen de las mujeres en las novelas picaresco-cortesanas de María de Zayas y Sotomayor y Alonso de Castillo Solórzano* (Miami, Fla.: Ediciones Universal, 1979); Edwin B. Place, "María de Zayas, An Outstanding Woman Short-story Writer of Seventeenth Century Spain," *University of Colorado Studies* 13 (1923): 1–56; Francisco Rico, *The Spanish Picaresque Novel and the Point of View* [1970], trans. Charles Davis with Harry Sieber (Cambridge: Cambridge University Press, 1984); Julio Rodríguez-Luis, "*Pícaras*: The Modal Approach to the Picaresque," *Comparative Literature* 31 (1979): 32–46.

NUEVAS ANDANZAS Y DESVENTURAS DE LAZARILLO DE TORMES

(New Fortunes and Misfortunes of Lazarillo de Tormes, 1944)

Camilo José Cela

In the prologue to one of his later works, Cela mentions having been attracted to one of the oldest and illustrious myths of Spanish literature, that of the rogue servant with many masters who lives by miracle and by chance. This work is in a long tradition of "continuations" of *Lazarillo de Tormes* (q.v.) and makes explicit its variation on picaresque in a way that *The Family of Pascual Duarte* (q.v.) does not. Cela's twentieth-century Lazarillo finds the original book among the papers of Don Roque, an apothecary, whom he serves in an episode described at length in a later chapter. Cela's Lazarillo is happy to find the book, which, he thinks, must have been written by his grandfather. That Lazarillo elsewhere tells us he did not learn to read and write until later in life, during his army service, is a major slip on Cela's part, unless it is deliberately intended to establish the kind of narrative unreliability that makes the original *Lazarillo* resonate so problematically. In any case, it is not this Lazarillo's reliability that we pay attention to so much as we regret his inability to capture us emotionally. Despite his narrative sleight-of-hand in the last chapter—or perhaps because of it—the original Lazarillo communicated his alienation, paradoxically, with a sincerity that engages us, while Cela's Lazarillo seems psychologically distanced from us, a narrative tonality that is nevertheless appropriate to the more radically alienated twentieth-century picaro—though Cela's Lazarillo is not the total outsider Pascual Duarte is.

Divided into nine *tratados* or chapters, *Nuevas andanzas* tells of Lazarillo's birth, abandonment, and subsequent service to a variety of masters (shepherds, musicians, a penitent, a circus acrobat and his troupe, a pharmacist, and a witch-like woman named Tia Librada, who has been compared to Celestina). "When he changes masters, it is not because of hunger or poor accommodations, but because of disgust and disillusionment with them as human beings" (Foster, 57). The landscape this picaro traverses is "a fusion of the external world about him with the fantasies of his subconscious and the absurdities of his dreams," in which "fact and fantasy blend into a kind of superreality" (Rand, 225). In the last chapter, Lazarillo calls these episodes up until his enlistment "the first part" of his life; in a short epilogue, he says that "if these pages seem bitter at times, remember that they were written by an old man, without recourse" (my trans., p. 518). A final note by the "editor" (which did not appear in the first edition) relates the primary narrator's visit to old Lazarillo in a Madrid hospital to ask him if he had written the second part. Lazarillo replies that second parts are never any good.

In a foreword written in 1960, Cela in assessing his career called *Nuevas andanzas* "un libro crítico," a book that marked a period of crisis. He felt he had to try his art in "the shady grove of the classics," and "the anonymous and illustrious *Lazarillo* which served me as a model is a marvel of grace and artlessness" (360). Although now he looks at his version of the story "with gratitude and with love," he had earlier worried about the dangers of producing merely a pastiche. Cela's *Nuevas andanzas* shares with other twentieth-century picaresques a self-concious awareness of the narrative tradition he is working in, but it is unique among those fictions in actually using the prototype itself, a narrative gesture that dares comparison with one of the landmark works of world literature. "Cela's novel is intimately concerned with whether or not a picaresque novel is possible in our age" (Foster, 49).

EDITION

Obra completa de Camilo José Cela, vol. 1 (*Las tres primeras novelas*) (Barcelona: Ediciones Destino, 1962), 355–520.

SELECT BIBLIOGRAPHY

David W. Foster, "*Nuevas andanzas y desventuras de Lazarillo de Tormes:* The Revitalization of a Prototype" in his *Forms of the Novel in the Work of Camilo José Cela* (Columbia: University of Missouri Press, 1967), 49–60; Jacqueline Praag-Chantraine, "Chronique des lettres espagnoles: actualité du Roman picaresque," *Synthéses* 14 (1959): 121–33; Marguerite C. Rand, "Lazarillo de Tormes, Classic and Contemporary," *Hispania* 44 (1961): 222–29.

O LUCKY MAN!

(1973)

        Directed by Lindsay Anderson

With a screenplay by David Sherwin (from an idea by Malcolm McDowell), this film depicts episodes in the life of Mick Travis, who begins as a trainee-salesman at the Imperial Coffee Company and makes his way through various fortunes both good and bad. The film opens with a black and white prologue (silent) in which a peasant (apparently a plantation worker in one of the British Empire colonies), played by the same actor who plays Travis, has his hands cut off for an unspecified crime. The word *Now* flashes like a title card, and we are into the first of the adventures of Mick's life, each of which proves in some satirical way that now is no different from then. As he journeys horizontally through present-day Britain and aims vertically to make his way to the top, we are exposed to a corrupt society in which such concepts as success, justice, and propriety are repeatedly double-exposed, in the conventional manner of picaresque narrative, to call into question the mere appearances of reality. Travis is tricked by almost everyone he meets, jailed for wanting to succeed, and beaten up by a band of vagrants. In the makeup of his character, he is more closely related to Candide than to the conventional picaro—until the final episode when, all hope abandoned, he finds a film company having a cast party and joins up, as Karl did in "The Nature Theatre of Oklahoma" in *Amerika* (q.v.). But Anderson's ending is self-reflexive: the film that is about to be made, and in which Mick Travis will play the lead, is *O Lucky Man!* Unlike Candide, who grudingly accommodates himself to the pitifully pale imitation Eden and more or less throws up his hands, Travis seizes his *desengaño* and, in an ambiguous gesture that could be interpreted as defiance as well as resignation, actively joins the world of appearances. Having been one of the deluded in life, he will now become one of the deluders in art. The ending is as problematic in its way as the ending of *Lazarillo de Tormes* (q.v.).

O Lucky Man! elicited mixed reviews when it was first released. These may have been due to the film's narrative technique, which is unconventional in its fragmentary juxtaposition of Alan Price's combo recording the film's soundtrack in a studio with the various episodes in the fortunes and misfortunes of Mick Travis. "Their unchanging choric presence," wrote Penelope Gilliatt in a sensitive, positive review, "is oddly consoling in the splintered form of the picture, which deliberately has a random and pushed-around character" (80). Either directly rendered or heard as voice-overs in counterpoint to the action, Price's songs create a narrative "voice" that conveys the film's moral point of view. "The score exhibits real irony about the ghastly indecencies that [screenwriter] Sherwin so ponderously tries to ridicule," wrote Canby, who, though praising the performances, the cinematography (by Miroslav Ondricek), and the music, came down hard on the screenplay, which he felt did not meet up to the ambition of its intention: "The wit is too small, too perfunctory, for the grand plan of the film and the quality of the production itself." He distinguishes Travis from such figures as Candide and Paul Pennyfeather (in Evelyn Waugh's *Decline and Fall*) by suggesting that Mick "would hardly qualify for citizenship in any but the most haphazardly administered state of grace"—which may be an indirect way of saying that he is more of a picaro than they are. Canby wanted a purer hero than Anderson portrays: "Mick wants to succeed and he is willing to try just about anything to do it. His completely unfounded belief that he can succeed, that he will overcome all obstacles, becomes the badge that certifies his innocence. It is a second-rate sort of badge, like something out of a cereal box, and a second-rate sort of innocence, quite in keeping with the second-rate morality of the times we live in" (review, p. 58). But this is in fact the picaresque situation. And Alterman, too, came down hard on the film as "an adolescent hodge-podge of fumbling black comedy and simple-minded anti-establishment propaganda" whose message is "that no matter what we do, or even think we can do to get ahead in life . . . it's all a matter of luck whether we end up on the top or the bottom of the heap." It is typical for genuinely picaresque narratives to elicit strong responses, as can be seen in the history of picaresque narrative from *Lazarillo* to *Going Places* (q.v.), another film that put viewers and reviewers off. *O Lucky Man!* is criticized (mostly unwittingly) for being effectively what it is.

Anderson said he had a didactic aim, claiming that everything in the film "is real, a reflection of the real dangers of the world we live in. We have taken poetic liberties, of course, to give the film the element of surprise, so that it will challenge and stimulate and suggest." It is chancy to take at face value the statement of so ironic an artist as Anderson, but his point about poetic liberties and surprise needs to be heeded. The self-reflexive ending, which simultaneously absorbs the film narrative into itself and opens up the multilayered discourse of the film's rhetoric, was mostly ignored by reviewers—even by Gilliatt, though she does discuss the film's Brechtian technique in making this Anderson's "most complex, irascible, and contenting feature so far" (83). In becoming an actor in the very film we are watching, Travis becomes the master of illusion other picaros become when they turn writers. The film comes full circle but with the added dimension of narrative distance of the kind we expect in picaresque narration. Like the dance pattern that recurs by having the same actors play different roles throughout, Travis's reenactment of his role (and of his role in Anderson's earlier film *If . . .* , whose protagonist was also called Mick Travis) is the cinematic analogue of the picaro's living his life again through his verbal effort.

SCREENPLAY

David Sherwin and Lindsay Anderson (London: Plexus, 1973).

SELECT BIBLIOGRAPHY

Loraine Alterman, "A Good Rock Score Can Sometimes Save a Bad Movie," *The New York Times,* July 8, 1973; Vincent Canby, [review], *The New York Times,* June 14, 1973, 58, and "*O Lucky Man!* Ran Out of Luck," *The New York Times,* June 24, 1973, B1; Frank R. Cunningham, "Lindsay Anderson's *O Lucky Man!* and the Romantic Tradition," *Literature/Film Quarterly* 2 (1974): 256–61; Guy Flatley, [interview with Anderson], *The New York Times,* July 1, 1973, B1; Penelope Gilliatt, [review], *The New Yorker,* June 16, 1973, 80–83; David L. Lavery, "*O Lucky Man!* and the Movie as Koan," *Literature/Film Quarterly* 8 (1980): 35–40.

ON THE ROAD

(1957)

Jack Kerouac

Picaresque fiction is often simplistically equated with a vague concept called "the road novel," a term that serves no generic function and provides only a general hint about the content of a particular work. Something like this is probably what William Dean Howells had in mind when in his 1895 *My Literary Passions* he proposed the Spanish picaresque novel as "one of the best forms for an American story" (*Huckleberry Finn,* q.v.). And certainly the sheer geographic immensity of the United States provided the landscape for a major body of fictions in which movement itself becomes the focus of interest, only some of which (for example, *Little Big Man,* q.v.) are genuinely picaresque. *On the*

Road has become the prototype of fictions that explore the open-endedness of the American landscape as a limitless realm for the development of the self, and as such it has become, with a great deal of misunderstanding, the prototype of American picaresques as well.

Although not literally born into his lot, Kerouac's narrator, Sal, is reborn after a marital split-up and subsequent serious illness and "my feeling that everything was dead" (5). In this same first paragraph, though, it becomes clear that the picaro figure in this book is not Sal but Dean Moriarty: "Dean is the perfect guy for the road because he actually was born on the road, when his parents were passing through Salt Lake City in 1926, in a jalopy, on their way to Los Angeles." Like Hannes's identification with Siggy in Irving's *Setting Free the Bears* (q.v.), Sal's attachment is strong even before he actually meets him: "We understood each other on other levels of madness" (7). "He was conning me and I knew it . . . and he knew I knew (this has been the basis of our relationship)" (8). Sal's infatuation with such a mode of existence motivates him to uproot himself, put aside his literary efforts, and take to the wide open spaces, "the whole mad swirl of everything that was to come" (8).

I shambled after as I've been doing all my life after people who interest me, because the only people for me are the mad ones, the ones who are mad to live, mad to talk, mad to be saved, desirous of everything at the same time, the ones who never yawn or say a commonplace thing, but burn, burn, burn like fabulous yellow roman candles exploding like spiders across the stars. (9)

His first day out is, in typical picaresque fashion, a disaster, and when he wakes up some days later in Des Moines, he has momentarily lost his identity: "That was the one distinct time in life, the strangest moment of all, when I didn't know who I was. . . . I was just somebody else, some stranger, and my whole life was a haunted life, the life of a ghost" (16). His wild journeys back and forth, up and down, culminate in Mexico, "the magic land at the end of the road" (225), where he falls seriously ill again, and which does not turn out to be a "home" of any kind. At the end of his narrative, Sal is still seeking Dean Moriarty, "the father we never found" (254).

On the Road has also come to stand for the attitudes of a whole generation, variously described as "beat," "hip," and "drop-out." Although an exception can be made for Dean Moriarty, as it can be for Siggy in *Setting Free the Bears*, the Sals of this worldview are primarily outsiders by choice—an important distinction: "The modern American picaresque novel is thus the literature of voluntary alienation. The contemporary picaro is a conscious rebel, not a rebel or an outsider by birth, providence, or circumstance" (Shaw, 208).

On the Road plays with the typical inside and outside perspectives of the picaresque. Sal is a would-be picaro who can only enact picaresque being through vicarious experience and the narrative recapitulation of it; he cannot be a picaro, and thus there is a certain wistful hero worship to Sal's tone that is atypical of the picaro. "On a deeper level Sal is responding to Dean not only as a modern

American con man but as an archaic trickster [q.v.] whose primal energy crashes through all cultural bounds'' (Lindberg, 269). Moriarty is a genuine picaro in the traditional sense, and Sal's adulation of him is tinged with adolescent infatuation. And his yearning to be (or be like) the outsider Moriarty is itself a condition of outsiderdom, but it is an exclusion that leaves him neither inside nor outside. *On the Road* is more of a variation with, rather than a variation in, the picaresque narrative tradition. As such, it portrays the interestingly paradoxical figure of the insider who wants to be out.

EDITION

New York: New American Library, n.d.

SELECT BIBLIOGRAPHY

Gary Lindberg, *The Confidence Man in American Literature* (New York and Oxford: Oxford University Press, 1982); Patrick W. Shaw, ''Old Genre, New Breed: The Postwar American Picaro,'' *Genre* 7 (1974): 205–11.

THE PAINTED BIRD

(1965)

Jerzy Kosinski

This is perhaps the most disturbing book in a fictional mode that thrives on reader disturbance. In impact and controversy, it ranks with such unsettling picaresques as *Journey to the End of the Night* and *The Family of Pascual Duarte* (q.q.v.). Some readers cannot finish the book; others refuse to. Those who have read it are likely to express themselves somewhere along a spectrum of reactions ranging from angry denial, a refusal to have our noses rubbed in one of the darknesses of twentieth-century existence, to an outraged realization of what Kurtz in Conrad's *Heart of Darkness* must have been trying to express in his ''The horror! The horror!'' Somewhere between these two extremes, the reader longs for a surrogate like Conrad's Marlow to mediate the vision. But unlike Conrad's narrative technique in *Heart of Darkness,* Kosinski's *The Painted Bird* is presented in an almost purely monotonal form of picaresque narration, with a minimum of narrative discourse. We are uneasy, finally, with the narrative technique itself for not giving us a secure point of view.

There is no editorial framing that would position us in relation to the book, like Quevedo's ''To the Reader'' in *El Buscón* (q.v.): ''Study the sermons, for I doubt if anyone buys a book as coarse as this in order to avoid the inclinations of his own depraved nature.'' Such a preface (or parody of prefaces) would make room for degrees of ironic distance (there are no sermons in Quevedo's picaresque, and acknowledgment of our unmasked motivation for reading such books makes explicit the narrative confidence game that is implicit in the picaresque narrative situation). Nor does it help much to analyze our motives in the light of Lionel Trilling's observation that pleasure in cruelty can be "protected and licensed by moral indignation" and that at times moral indignation "may be in itself an exquisite pleasure" (213). These are implied in Quevedo's ironic statement. But for Trilling, who believes that "for our time the most effective agent of the moral imagination has been the novel of the last two hundred years," these are of secondary importance anyway:

> Is it not of the first importance that we be given a direct and immediate report on the reality that is daily being brought to dreadful birth? The novels that have done this have effected much practical good, bringing to consciousness the latent feelings of many people, making it harder for them to be unaware or indifferent, creating an atmosphere in which injustice finds it harder to thrive. . . . Life presses us so hard, time is so short, the suffering of the world is so huge, simple, unendurable—anything that complicates our moral fervor in dealing with reality as we immediately see it and wish to drive headlong upon it must be regarded with some impatience. (213–15)

The Painted Bird certainly gives us a "direct and immediate report" on a reality "brought to dreadful birth," but it is precisely this fictive power that in turn "complicates our moral fervor" as we try to flee from the book in various masks of indignation. In doing this, the book almost undermines its own reason for being.

Kosinski has said, in an afterword written some dozen years after publication, that *The Painted Bird* was to be the first in a five-book cycle that would present "archetypal aspects of the individual's relationship to society" and that this first book was to deal with "the most universally accessible of these societal metaphors":

> Man would be portrayed in his most vulnerable state, as a child, and society in its most deadly form, in a state of war. I hoped the confrontation between the defenseless individual and overpowering society, between the child and war, would represent the essential anti-human condition. (256–57)

In the wake of such powerfully representative and universally influential twentieth-century works as Conrad's *Heart of Darkness,* Malraux's *Man's Fate* (*La Condition humaine* is its original title), and Camus's *The Plague,* it seems almost redundant to speak of the antihuman condition. Kosinski complicates our responses by his decision to set his work "in a mythic domain, in the timeless fictive present, unrestrained by geography or history" (257), thus diverting attention toward questions of authenticity and historical accuracy and even inviting speculation about Kosinski's own childhood in wartime Poland. He has been accused of "watering down historical truth" and has said that events were even far more brutal than the most bizarre fantasies—a not uncommon picaresque disclaimer in which, by creating the illusion of self-censorship, the narrator intensifies the already graphic material even more by encouraging the reader to embellish on the "inclinations of his own depraved nature." In the end, having finished *The Painted Bird,* and refusing either of the extremes of righteous indignation, we are perhaps most disturbed at not knowing how to respond at all.

The boy's narrative voice dominates the book. The only other voice we hear is that of a distanced, anonymous narrator-editor who in a ten-paragraph italicized headnote to chapter 1 gives a few details to provide context: a six-year old "olive-skinned, dark-haired, and black-eyed" boy, speaking "a language of the educated class," is sent by his parents (who have to go into hiding because of the prewar anti-Nazi activities of the father) from "a large city in Eastern Europe" to be placed in foster care. Because of the "confusion of war and occupation, with continuous transfers of population," the parents lose contact. When his foster mother dies after two months, the boy is "left alone to wander from one village to another" in "the most backward parts of Eastern Europe," populated by "ignorant and brutal" people "united only by their extreme superstition and the innumerable diseases plaguing men and animals alike" and forced to bend to the severe demands of the occupying Germans on the one hand and the partisans on the other. Among these people, the boy "was considered a Gypsy or Jewish stray," the sheltering of whom could mean "the harshest of penalities at the hands of the Germans." Then begins the boy's narrative itself: "I lived in Marta's hut, expecting my parents to come for me any day, any hour. Crying did not help, and Marta paid no attention to my sniveling."

No other modern picaresque links so directly, in situation, plot, and narrative voice, with the first five chapters of *Lazarillo de Tormes* (q.v.), not even Cela's *Nuevas andanzas y desventuras de Lazarillo de Tormes* (q.v.). And though it is almost a constant of the picaresque mode that the landscape be one of war (actual or metaphorical), no other modern picaresque links so directly, in its graphic depiction of the horrors of war in everyday life, with Grimmelshausen's rendering of the Thirty Years' War in *Simplicius Simplicissimus* (q.v.). The landscape of *The Painted Bird* is, ultimately, the Holocaust itself, as the boy's individually witnessed and experienced barbarities accumulate to form a collective image of unspeakable cruelty and chaos, giving the lie to whatever remnants of meaning *civilization* may have left after World War II. The little boy is Kurtz himself, and we are Marlows (not Marlow's listeners), following close on his heels.

What is especially frightening about *The Painted Bird* is that much of the savagery takes place outside and beyond the specific cause-and-effect influence of the war raging in the world around these isolated villages. Through the boy's eyes, these seem to be normative conditions of human existence, to which the plunders of the partisans or the punishments of the occupying forces contribute but which they do not cause. The horrible irony is that an already disordered landscape easily integrates into itself the disorders of war. As perceived by the boy, this disorder-as-order is an extreme version of picaresque topsy-turvydom as expressed centuries before by Guzmán (*Guzmán de Alfarache*, q.v.): "Man's life is a warre-fare upon the earth, there is no certainty therein; no settled assurance, no estate that is permanent," and echoed by the Invisible Man's grandfather as "our life is a war" (*Invisible Man,* q.v.). The first of these statements comes from the pen of a *converso* and the second from a black man, linking their works directly with the racial outsiderdom that is part of the boy's situation in *The Painted Bird* and that emphasizes the otherness that is always a characteristic of the picaro. Although we are not told for sure whether the boy is indeed a gypsy (this seems unlikely because of his origins) or a Jew, he is nevertheless perceived as such because of his complexion and coloring among people who are predominantly blond. "Historically, of course, the Jew is the archetypal outsider" (Barrett, 218). In a landscape that seems to have been ravaged for eternity and that at the moment is suffering the additional ravagements of war, the little boy has no place. War itself is more at home than he.

"No one wanted to keep me," he says, "there was no room for me."

Weeks went by and the village left me alone. Some of the boys said occasionally that I should be delivered to the German headquarters, or that the soldiers should be told about the Gypsy bastard in the village. Women avoided me on the road, carefully turning away the heads of their children. The men looked me over in silence, and casually spat in my direction. (84–85)

This exemplifies his essential condition in the world, no matter where he wanders. Acts of kindness are few and far between and may come from unexpected sources, as in the case of the German soldier who, ordered to kill him, sets him free. From a priest's oversimplified sermon on indulgences, he deduces some sense in the universe:

Suddenly the ruling pattern of the world was revealed to me with beautiful clarity. I understood why some people were strong and others weak, some free and others enslaved, some rich and others poor, some well and others sick. The former had simply been the first to see the need for prayer and for collecting the maximum number of days of indulgence. Somewhere, far above, all these prayers coming from earth were properly classified, so that every person had his bin where the days of indulgence were stored. (131–32)

When he is beaten by his master at the time for all his praying, he summarizes: "Thus my life was spent alternately praying and being beaten" (133).

He comes to believe that the "real rules of this world" reside in the Evil Ones, versions of the devil who picked "only those who had already displayed a sufficient supply of inner hatred and maliciousness" (159) and who "turned somersaults over my head and could send me anywhere at their whim" (165). When the peasants fear that the advancing Soviets will nationalize everything "right down to wives and children," the boy sees a romance vision before him:

If it was true that women and children might become communal property, then every child would have many fathers and mothers, innumerable brothers and sisters. It seemed to be too much to hope for. To belong to everyone! Wherever I might go, many fathers would stroke my head with warm, reassuring hands, many mothers would hug me to their bosoms, and many older brothers would defend me against dogs. (183)

But during a savage pillaging by Kalmuks, the boy again feels his outsiderdom, blaming all his previous sufferings on his resemblance to them: "My hair and eyes were as black as these Kalmuks'. Evidently I belonged with them in another world. There could be no mercy for such as me. Some dreadful Devil had sentenced me to have black hair and eyes in common with this horde of savages" (188). When the Russians arrive first, the boy is taught to read and is indoctrinated by Mitka, whose teachings the boy takes with him to the orphanage he is finally placed in. Here there is a kind of community of rogues, demanding a behavioral pattern based on what he has learned in his wanderings and from Mitka's teachings: "A person should take revenge for every wrong or humiliation. There were far too many injustices in the world to have them all weighed and judged. A man should consider every wrong he had suffered and decide on the appropriate revenge" (227). Taken in by a couple who appear to be his parents (though this is left somewhat ambiguous), the boy continues his battles at night: "In daytime the world was at peace. The war continued at night" (246). Finally his parents remove him from this nocturnal delinquency and send him off to live in the mountains with an old ski instructor, with whom he spends his days mostly in silence (the boy had become mute after being tortured and thrown into a manure pit to drown). His narrative ends when, recuperating in a hospital after a skiing accident, the telephone rings and he finds himself regaining his voice: "I spoke loudly and incessantly . . . convincing myself again and again and again that speech was now mine and that it did not intend to escape through the door which opened onto the balcony" (251). The anonymous voice of the opening headnote does not reappear.

Although the narrating must be taking place at some point after this final episode (which is itself taking place at some undetermined time, perhaps when the boy is about thirteen or fourteen), there is little conscious exploitation of narrative distance in *The Painted Bird*. The voice we hear is that of the narrated self perceiving his world as he was then. Only infrequently does the narrating self call attention to itself, and then with either sledgehammer irony or a blunt aside. When some shepherds want to burn his feet, he resists, observing: "I had no intention of being burned in such an ordinary campfire when others were incinerated in special and elaborate furnaces built by the Germans and equipped with engines more powerful than those of the largest locomotives" (100). Although the boy may have experienced such a feeling at the time, the ironic effect comes from the more mature reflecting self who is now experientially distanced and narratively manipulative of that experience.

When he contemplates the body of a child thrown from a train heading for one of the extermination camps, he identifies momentarily with the child's situation:

I tried to think what he had thought before dying. When he was tossed out of the train his parents or his friends no doubt assured him that he would find human help which would save him from a horrible death in the great furnace. He probably felt cheated, deceived. He would have preferred to cling to the warm bodies of his father and mother in the packed car, to feel the pressure and smell the hot tart odors, the presence of other people, knowing that he was not alone, told by everyone that the journey was only a misunderstanding. (102–103)

But his momentary identification with another outsider almost immediately turns to rejection as his own savage survival instinct reasserts itself. He is glad the boy is dead because discovery of him would jeopardize his own safety. When a German officer approaches him later, he is full of envy:

In a world of men with harrowed faces, with smashed eyes, bloody, bruised and disfigured limbs, among the fetid, broken human bodies, he seemed an example of neat perfection that could not be sullied: the smooth, polished skin of his face, the bright golden hair showing under his peaked cap, his pure metal eyes. Every movement of his body seemed propelled by some tremendous internal force. The granite sound of his language was ideally suited to order the death of inferior, forlorn creatures. I was stung by a twinge of envy I had never experienced before, and I admired the glittering death's-head and crossbones that embellished his tall cap. I thought how good it would be to have such a gleaming and hairless skull instead of my Gypsy face which was feared and disliked by decent people. (119)

And, finally, with the ski instructor he presents what has come to be his outlook on life:

It mattered little if one was mute; people did not understand one another anyway. They collided with or charmed one another, hugged or trampled one another, but everyone knew only himself. (249)

The articulation of such feelings in this way could not occur at that point in the boy's chronological age, which is early adolescence. Narrative distance becomes most strongly apparent in this final chapter and creates a cynicism that resembles the attitude of Céline's Ferdinand, perhaps even that of Lazarillo himself in his last chapter.

In outlook and behavior, the boy has become cold and cruel, an emotional outsider certainly, and in action a delinquent of the type A. A. Parker finds central to the picaresque. Now that people are willing to help him, he treats them in ways similar to the treatments he received during his wanderings. Having learned from experience, he is just as much an outsider in the world of relative order as he had been in the disorder of war. In this changed landscape, his survival instincts are no longer necessary—are indeed disruptions. We even distance ourselves from him somewhat just as we do when Lazarillo makes a moral compromise at the end of his story. The last paragraph of *The Painted Bird* suggests that he will use his regained voice to produce this account that we are reading, though we do not know when, where, how, or specifically why. Everything about him at the end makes it hard to believe that he would care to narrate his story, despite what he says in the final sentences. All along he has had trouble communicating, first because of the different peasant dialects of the regions he traverses and then because of his muteness. His radical outsiderdom would seem to preempt any attempt at communication, much as he has abandoned attempts at communion with his fellow beings. He is like the painted bird of the title, which comes from an episode in chapter 5 in which a bird seller paints birds exotic colors, releases them, and, as they try to rejoin flocks of their own kind, watches as the other birds kill them. In chapter 19, when the boy is presented to his parents, he tells us he felt like the painted birds of this episode. Thus the title is yet another sign of the narrative distance between the experiencing self and the reflecting self and of the boy's inability ever to rejoin his fellow beings either through communion or through communication. Who is creating this discursive level of meaning? Is it the anonymous front-framing "editor"? Is it the boy himself in his role as narrator? Does it refer to his narrative effort, as well as to his situation in the world?

The ending to the book has been interpreted positively: "If Lázaro's *Vida* is the story of the growth of an artist in words, it is also the story of a liar, and the presentation of his autobiography is essentially an act of moral cowardice. To write the autobiography which constitutes *The Painted Bird*, on the other hand, is an act of moral courage, and it is in this respect that the work makes its most original contribution to the picaresque tradition" (Meszaros, 240). Instead of the alternatives available to the picaro—"immoral complicity with the world" (*Lazarillo*) or "moral isolation from it" (*Simplicissimus*)—the protagonist of *The Painted Bird* finds a different resolution: "Neither rejoining the world nor continuing to isolate himself from it, the protagonist survives to witness, to testify to the world's evil, including his own" (242). And this is indeed suggested by the image of the boy's being enraptured by the sounds of his own voice. Thus the boy becomes something of a hero for bearing witness.

But the difficult ambiguity of the final image lingers. Significantly the book stops "speaking" just when the boy regains his voice; it falls silent narratively and discursively just as he experientially tests his powers of speech. He does not intend to let his voice escape out the balcony door—like the painted bird that flies away in a doomed effort to rejoin its flock. In this last paragraph, the boy is quite literally speaking only to himself. And given his belief that "everyone thought only of himself," the boy-become-narrator may well also believe that *The Painted Bird* will be like the painted bird, rejected by its flock, just as his exotic features made him an outcast and a victim among his fellow human beings. Yet *The Painted Bird* is not at all "painted" in a rhetorical sense; whatever discursive levels we detect are muted in favor of the pure simplicity of direct narration. But the power that results from the immediacy of this narration is so strong that the book seems like something that does not belong in our world, and we make every effort to reject it through outrage, righteous indignation, or stunned silence. Not knowing how to respond, we try not to. In thus silencing its own voice, *The Painted Bird* is the darkest of the often dark picaresques. In his muted simplicity, the boy speaks so well that we wish we were deaf.

EDITION

The revised 1978 edition that includes Kosinski's afterword is published by Bantam Books.

SELECT BIBLIOGRAPHY

William Barrett, *Time of Need: Forms of Imagination in the Twentieth Century* (New York: Harper & Row, 1972); Patricia K. Meszaros, "Hero with a Thousand Faces, Child with No Name: Kosinski's *The Painted Bird*," *College Literature* 6 (1979): 232–44; Alexander A. Parker, *Literature and the Delinquent: The Picaresque Novel in Spain and Europe, 1599–1753* (Edinburgh: University Press, 1967); Lionel Trilling, "Manners, Morals, and the Novel" [1947] in his *The Liberal Imagination: Essays on Literature and Society* (Garden City, N.Y.: Doubleday [n.d.]).

PERIQUILLO, EL DE LAS GALLINERAS

(Periquillo of the Poultry Yard, 1668)

Francisco Santos

Valbuena Prat includes this as the penultimate work in his 1943 anthology, *La novela picaresca española*. Although the anthology established something of a picaresque canon, not all the works in it are universally accepted as picaresque. Chandler thought Santos the end of the already declining picaresque tradition. Periquillo was clearly, in his cynicism, "heir to the picaros of old, but rather tedious than amusing. He went through the same viscissitudes as they but only mechanically. All the vitality was gone out of him, for in Spain the romance of roguery had lived its day and fulfilled its mission" (394). Parker does not even consider it, dimissing it as a picaresque because it has a saintly hero (167). For Rico, "The abandonment of autobiography [in *Periquillo*] is consistent with the conversion of the hero into a character who scarcely retains any features of the literary picaro (and instead conforms entirely to the tradition of the mendicant philosopher: Apollonius, Diogenes, Aesop)" (128).

The work is self-consciously picaresque. In the fifth chapter, or *discurso,* Periquillo briefly serves a blind man, having consciously chosen the life of a picaro, but he is persuaded to leave "la guía de un ciego a lazarillos y alfaraches [*Lazarillo de Tormes, Guzmán de Alafrache,* q.q.v.]" (1870). And his name, Periquillo, is revived by Mexican writer José Joaquín Fernández de Lizardi (*The Itching Parrot,* q.v.) and in turn alluded to by José Rubén Romero in *The Futile Life of Pito Pérez* (q.v.).

EDITION

Angel Valbuena Prat, *La novela picaresca española,* 6th ed. (Madrid: Aguilar, 1968), 1849–1916.

SELECT BIBLIOGRAPHY

Frank Wadleigh Chandler, *Romances of Roguery* [1899] (New York: Burt Franklin, 1961); Alexander A. Parker, *Literature and the Delinquent: The Picaresque Novel in Spain and Europe, 1599–1753* (Edinburgh: University Press, 1967); Francisco Rico, *The Spanish Picaresque Novel and the Point of View* [1970], trans. Charles Davis with Harry Sieber (Cambridge: Cambrdige University Press, 1984).

PERIQUILLO SARNIENTO, EL

See THE ITCHING PARROT

LA PICARA JUSTINA

(*Libro de entretenimiento de la pícara Justina, en el cual debajo de graciosos discursos se encierran provechosos avisos*, 1605)

Francisco López de Ubeda

The generic self-consciousness of Spanish picaresque fiction is evident in this work, which was composed before the second part of *Guzmán de Alfarache* (q.v.) was published and while *El Buscón* (q.v.) was probably still being written. In addition to indirect allusions to *Lazarillo de Tormes* (q.v.) and *Guzmán*, Justina refers to her servant as "mi lazarillo" and calls herself "la Guzmana de Alfarache," and she coins new variations on the word *pícaro*, such as *pícaral*, *picardía*, *picaresco*, and *apicarada*. At the time of her writing, she claims to be married to Guzmán himself and promises to fill readers in on this part of her life in a continuation (which never appeared). The prologue alludes to *Lazarillo*, *Celestina*, and *The Golden Ass* (q.v.), among other literary predecessors, and makes the presumptuous claim that not only does *La pícara Justina* surpass all these works but "there is no good thing in ballad, play, or Spanish poet, but that its cream and quintessence is herein contained." The full title translates "Book of Entertainment of the Picara Justina, in Which, under Witty Discourses, Are Hidden Profitable Morals," and it continues on the original title page: "At the end of each chapter you will find an explanation showing how you may profit by the book to flee from the deceits which are common in our days. It is also an Art of Poetry containing fifty-one kinds of verse never till now set forth" (Clarke, 332). At the beginning of the evolution of the picaresque genre in Spain, Aleman's serious first part of *Guzmán* had engendered in *La pícara Justina* an immediate parody.

The book's self-announced intertextuality demands a reader who will bring the appropriate narrative contexts to the reading. This generic self-consciousness was heightened in the first edition by a frontispiece that appears in Valbuena Prat's anthology *La novela picaresca española* and has been much reproduced since. It depicts a ship, "La nave de la vida picaresca," sailing on the Rio del olvido ("river of forgetfulness"). It is being steered by Time toward the port of Death, represented by a skeleton holding a mirror-like object labeled *desengaño* ("disillusion"). On board the ship, besides Time, are Guzmán, wearing a satchel labeled "poor and content"; Justina, holding an open book, and standing amidships; and Celestina, in front of Justina, holding a wine bottle. Bacchus sits on the masthead, and Venus, Cupid, and Ceres are pictured on the sails. In a rowboat next to the ship is Lazarillo, apparently towing the larger vessel. In the boat with him is the bull of Salamanca (against which the blind man had smashed him); behind him is an object labeled *oliste* ("you smelt"), alluding to Lazarillo's revenge on the blind man when he makes the latter smash into a stone post. Surrounding this scene are twenty-four pictures of objects, each with a letter, ultimately forming the phrase *el axuar de la vida picaresca* ("the equipment of the picaresque life"). For Parker, this frontispiece supports his contention that *Lazarillo* is really a precursor of the picaresque genre proper (149); for Bjornson, the picture reaffirms the ideological assumptions of Ubeda's readers, who, though they may well find the depicted life of frivolity vicariously appealing,

> would of course never abandon the perquisites of their respectable positions to experience the actual hardships of lower-class existence, and Ubeda's implicit pejorative judgment of picaresque insouciance served to reassure them that their own "serious" concerns were more valid than the "trivial" pursuits of pícaros. As a poor but ingenious and happy-go-lucky rogue who wastes his life upon sensual pleasures, the pícaro appealed to readers who felt morally and socially superior to him because he offered them entertainment without either engaging their sympathy for his sufferings or questioning society's responsibility for his corrupt behavior. (70)

The ship of picaresque life is dominated by a sleeping figure labeled *ociosidad,* or "idleness," whose languor—Bjornson's reading notwithstanding—lures as much as Death distances. Our relationship to the illustration is as problematic as our relationship to picaresque narrative; we enter in with darker motives than those of moral and social superiority. Our ostensible masks of propriety cover up a foray into recklessness that we pretend not to face directly. The picture lures as much as it warns.

Among Hispanists at the turn of this century, *La pícara Justina* was not highly ranked, either as a picaresque or as a work of literature. Fonger de Haan wrote in his survey, "The work is pretentious from the very Preface, and is a monument of Spanish literature mainly for the reason that it is the earliest important specimen of the wretched taste that was soon to prevail" (19–20). Chandler thought John Stevens's severely abridged English version "a vast improvement" (242–43). And Clarke wrote, "For digression, laboured wit, and indecency the *Pícara Justina* may be compared with *Tristram Shandy*, but it is *Tristram Shandy* without trace of the charming scenes and characters that illuminate and redeem that monument of perversity. It has moreover the unenviable distinction of being cited by the learned Gregorio Mayans y Siscar as the first example of the corrupt Spanish prose of the seventeenth century. Its pages are crowded with strained conceits and witless plays upon words, making it quite untranslatable, were anybody found rash enough to undertake the thankless task" (333). Even Menéndez Pelayo called it "extravagant, obscure, tedious" and a "monument of bad taste" (quoted in Parker, 46).

But Chandler did acknowledge that its major innovation—the creation of a female picaro—influenced the picaresque narrative tradition for the better. By replacing the picaro with a picara, Chandler says, the element of the service of many masters was eliminated, for women were not in those days admitted to

most trades. As a result, the portrait of the picara was much more personal:
"The picara thus secured inevitably greater freedom of movement than the picaro,
and through her was to come the evolution of the rogue novel to a higher stage,
where the theme was not so much the classes in society as individual adventures
and aspects of life" (239). Thus in a curiously ironic way, social oppression in
the real world gives rise in a literary form to more freedom of expression in the
portrayal of private experience, opening the way for the more subjective characterization and the serious treatment of everyday life that will come to be the
primary domain of the literary form we have come to call the novel. It will take
a while, as Justina first becomes the model for such subsequent picaras as those
in *La hija de Celestina, La niña de los embustes, La garduña de Sevilla* (q.q.v.),
and, later, *The Runagate Courage* (q.q.v.), whose picara emerges from another
book (*Simplicius Simplicissimus,* q.v.) in a more concrete and credible way than
Justina emerges from *Guzmán,* and finally toward the more recognizably novelistic in *Moll Flanders* and *Roxana* (q.q.v.).

It has been pointed out, too, that the narrating Justina's self-reflexiveness in
this self-conscious work may have had a directly positive influence on the metafictional concerns of Sterne in *Tristram Shandy.* Throughout her first three
chapters, Justina addresses her pen, which has a hair on it, thus spoiling her
writing and causing a free flow of associations on all the possible meanings of
the word *hair,* just as Tristram, who at the end is telling just a "cock and bull"
story, spends most of his narrating time telling the reader how impossible it is
to render narrated time.

In more recent criticism, *La pícara Justina* has been given more balanced
assessments as it is restored to its appropriate social and literary context. Marcel
Bataillon especially has done a great deal of research that has decoded the work
in a way that was not accessible to later readers like Chandler and Clarke. *La
pícara Justina* is, says Parker "a treasure-house of the language of burlesque,
a riot of verbosity in which popular speech is given an exuberant ornamentation
by being overladen with the language of polite literature" (46). The work seems
to be something on the order of an elaborate roman à clef, with allusions to
events, persons, and places that only the contemporary knowing in-crowd reader
could unlock. Bjorson, who sees *Justina* as being representative of one type
of variation on the *Lazarillo-Guzmán* model—the parodic reduction of the picaro
through one-dimensional caricature—points out that Ubeda's work "lacks many
of the most important elements of the picaresque myth. Justina never undergoes
a process of initiation and social conditioning" (88). Moreover, "the primary
level of communication in *Justina* exists between an author witty enough to
'contrive' a 'statue of free living' and socially elite readers capable of appreciating
his wit and sanctioning his assumption that lower-class characters are best portrayed as caricatures or comic figures" (89–90).

Ironically, whatever brilliance *Justina* may have had as a *libro de entretenimiento* for its contemporary readers was also the primary cause for its lack of
readers in subsequent ages. As Dunn puts it, this "vaudeville script written for

an attentive and sharp-witted audience . . . has suffered the fate of all such literature that is relevant to its moment and to a particular public: it is almost meaningless to another audience and another time without the aid of an interpreter'' (119). In spite of these reassessments, *La pícara Justina* is still not considered much of a picaresque, even by critics willing to give it due credit for its achievements in the specific context in and for which it was written. As a parody, it uses picaresque conventions in all the worst senses of that word. The equally parodistic (and elite) but much more serious *El Buscón*, on the other hand, sets up and then tries to deflate picaresque conventions for ultimately satirical ends that raise problematical questions. While *El Buscón* in forcing us to examine the ideological and aesthetic premises of picaresque has something of a constructive "counterpicaresque" about it, *La pícara Justina* in its glib literary destructiveness has something of what we might call antipicaresque about it; its parody demolishes utterly, leaving only rubble, including its own witty inside jokes, which neither translate geographically nor transcend temporally. In its parodic destructiveness, it also destroys itself.

Still, it retains some interest as an antipicaresque for its demonstration of how a newly emerging genre can be immediately cannibalized by a supposedly superior audience engaging in privileged discourse but lacking its own original form for that discourse. If most of what *Justina* was intended to do and almost all of what it accomplished escape us today, what does not escape us is the ludicrous irony of using a narrative archetype of outsiderdom for the purposes of exchanging coded wit through exclusive discourse within a closed circle of insiders. The only picaro in *La pícara Justina* is the excluded reader.

TRANSLATION/EDITION

The only known English version is *Justina, the Country Jilt*, a much abbreviated rendering by John Stevens, published in the collection *The Spanish Libertines or the Lives of Justina, the Country Jilt; Celestina, the Bawd of Madrid, and Estevanillo Gonzales, The Most Arch and Witty of Scoundrels. To Which Is Added a Play, an Evenings Adventures. All Four Written by Eminent Spanish Authors and Now First Made English by Captain John Stevens* (London: Samuel Bunchley, 1707; rpt. London, 1889). The preface states in part that this is "not a translation, but rather an extract of all that is diverting and good in the original, which is swelled up with so much cant and reflection, as really renders it tedious and unpleasant; for which reason all that unsavory part is omitted, and only so much rendered into English as may be diverting and instructing." The original text is available in any of the many issues of *La novela picaresca española*, edited by Angel Valbuena Prat, first published in Madrid by Aguilar in 1943. In the 6th edition (1968), *Justina* is on pages 703–885.

SELECT BIBLIOGRAPHY

Marcel Bataillon, *Pícaros y picaresca: "La pícara Justina"* (Madrid: Taurus, 1969); Richard Bjornson, *The Picaresque Hero in European Fiction* (Madison: University of Wisconsin Press, 1977); Frank Wadleigh Chandler, *Romances of Roguery* [1899] (New York: Burt Franklin, 1961); H. Butler Clarke, "The Spanish Rogue-Story" in *Studies in European Literature, Being the Taylorian Lectures 1889–1899* (Oxford: Clarendon Press, 1900), 313–49; Fonger de Haan, *An Outline of the History of the Novela Picaresca in Spain* [1895] (The Hague and New York: Martinus Nijhoff, 1903); Peter N. Dunn, *The Spanish Picaresque Novel* (Boston: Twayne, 1979); Alexander A. Parker, *Literature and the Delinquent: The Picaresque Novel in Spain and Europe, 1599–1753)* (Edinburgh: University Press, 1967); Antonio Rēy Hazas, "Parodía de la retórica y visión crítica del mundo en *La pícara Justina*," *Edad de Oro* 3 (1984): 201–25; Francisco Rico, *The Spanish Picaresque Novel and the Point of View* [1970], trans. Charles Davis with Harry Sieber (Cambridge: Cambridge University Press, 1984); Julio Rodríguez-Luis, "*Pícaras:* The Modal Approach to the Picaresque," *Comparative Literature* 31 (1979): 32–46; Jonas Andries van Praag, "La pícara en la literatura española," *The Spanish Review* 3 (1936): 63–74 (also in German as "Die Schelmin in der spanischen Literatur," trans. Gottlieb Blumenstock, in *Pikarische Welt: Schriften zum europäischen Schelmenroman,* ed. Helmut Heidenreich [Darmstadt: Wissenchaftliche Buchgesellschaft, 1969], 147–64).

REYNARD THE FOX

(*Le Roman de Renart,* twelfth century)

The character of Reynard the Fox emerges from a series of tales (called *branches*) written in Old French between 1174 and 1205. These stories soon made their way into other vernaculars and into English (from Dutch) in 1481 by William Caxton. Chandler gives much credit to the influence of the *Roman de Renart,* which,

with its masquerade and bold parody, and its rogue hero, the fox, went a long way toward preparing for the advent of the picaro. Those animals, Renart, Ysengrin, Tibert, and the rest, were individualized characters, operated by human motives, and holding up the glass to human folly; nor was Renart the only rogue among them, but rather the most astute. Fraud and deceit were glorified ironically; no class in society was exempted from attack, and the spirit of chivalry already found a foe. Inexhaustible in gayety and indiscriminating in satire, the *Roman de Renart,* which would spare the *villain* no more than the *chatelain,* was marked by its sympathy with the anti-hero, and from it to the picaresque novel descended perhaps the latter's best inheritance in its example of consistent roguery. (6)

Unlike the beast fables of Aesop or LaFontaine (or even Orwell's *Animal Farm*), *Reynard the Fox* did not orginally have an overt moral aim; yet its transference of human behaviors to the animal realm for essentially satirical purposes developed easily into didacticism. The Dutch version from which Caxton is believed to have worked had as its explicit purpose the moral improvement of the reader. "Caxton translated these moral exhortations and no doubt read the book in the light of the prologue and epilogue. His translation was popular and it was constantly reprinted with the moral nature of the work becoming continually more explicit. In the early seventeenth century the morals for each chapter were printed in the margin so that no one could be in any doubt as to the intepretation of individual passages. Finally these morals were incorporated into the text''; thus, ''although the story of Reynard was originally a humorous parody with satirical overtones, it quickly developed into a moral fable in which the satire is mordant and heavily didactic: the parody becomes allegory'' (Blake, li). This trend was well established in all versions of the story by the time Caxton made his translation.

The aspect of the beast epic that is particularly crucial to the nature of picaresque narrative is the reader-character relationship, which is paradoxically both alienating and empathizing. When animals act human roles, we feel superior, like gods; we are simultaneously distanced yet identifying with these actors and their actions. By looking down at them, we are also looking down on ourselves yet without the self-humiliation or self-debasement that a more direct confrontation would cause. This is a moral stretching, which the picaresque relies on. Lazarillo (*Lazarillo de Tormes,* q.v.) makes just such an acknowledgment when he says in his prologue: ''I'd . . . like people who are proud of being high born to realize how little this really means, as Fortune has smiled on them, and how much more worthy are those who have endured misfortune but have triumphed by dint of hard work and determination.'' The picaro is most an upstart in the daring of his narrative conditions, as though to say, ''A lowly figure like me really has no right to create an autobiography that anyone should be expected to pay attention to, but if you'll deign to listen . . . '' The morally and socially superior reader is asked to make concessions for the sake of a disreputable being who insists on being heard. Such a narrative situation allows the real reader to disassociate himself from the narratee here and condescend to the level of experience and perception so cheekily being requested by the narrator. The effrontery of the picaro's narrative demand is thus sidetracked by an implied narrative reassurance of the reader's superiority despite the accommodation being made to allow the picaro to speak. Our relationship to the picaresque experiential situation always depends on a moral and social distancing that parallels the narrative distancing of the narrating situation; from *Lazarillo* to *Moll Flanders* (q.v.) to *Felix Krull* (q.v.), the reader is constantly aware of this double movement of moral condescension toward dared identification on the one hand and the simultaneous reassurance of a stable superiority on the other. That this superiority is in fact a smug illusion is the prime satirical target here, though it is invariably covert, part of the discourse between implied author and implied reader. The reader's role in the narrative discourse of the beast fable or epic is much the same.

In Caxton's *Reynard the Fox,* readers are reassured at the end that the moral lessons do not apply to them specifically:

that who that wyl rede this mater / though it be of iapes and bourdes / yet may he fynde therein many a good wysedom and lernynges / By which he may come to vertue and worship. There is no good man blamed herin / hit is spoken generally / Late euery man take his owne part as it belongeth and behoueth / and he that fyndeth hym gylty in ony dele or part thereof / late hym bettre and amende hym And he that is veryly good / I pray god kepe hym therein And yf only thyng be said or wreton herin / that may greue or dysplease ony man / blame not me / but the foxe / for they be his wordes and not myne. (112)

In Branch VIII Reynard ends his days with a hermit, foreshadowing Simplicius (*Simplicius Simplicissimus,* q.v.), so that through the instruction of a pious man, he can win forgiveness for his life of sin. In the end, he abandons his pilgrimage and returns home. Like many picaros, Reynard wants the constancy, peace, and security of home; whatever forms this home may take, its yearned-for harmony is always part of the implied romance of picaresque fiction.

In Branch XVII, Reynard is buried, only to spring from the grave and begin his tricks all over. "If the raw material of these animal legends is primitive and universal, the poems are at the same time, however, intensely contemporary and local. The hero of the *Roman de Renart,* whatever his genesis, is not the undifferentiated Trickster of folklore but a rebel within and against the society of his own place and time who gives birth to a new awareness by reincarnating age-old traditions" (Torrance, 102). In his adventures, as in the relationship between reader and narrator, the parody of feudal society in these stories reflects the resentment of a disenfranchised group that can have no voice except through acceptably masked and distanced fictions of this kind. Reynard is the "vicarious comic hero of a class without the self-confidence to evolve their own heroes; a class at once defiant and different toward *seigneurs* whose authority they alternately acknowledged and flouted"; the animal fable allows just enough sanctioned distance to permit vicarious expression without consequential disruption: "For all his impudent defiance of feudal institutions Reynard . . . affirms the necessity of an order that he harasses by repeated outrages but never . . . calls into serious question. Neither transformation nor transcendence is accessible to him. . . . Having defiantely emancipated himself from his world he discovers that he knows no other and lingers on around its fringes, neither wholly belonging nor entirely apart: a pest and, by the same token, parasite" (Torrance, 104, 109–110).

Like *Till Eulenspiegel* (q.v.), *Reynard the Fox* represents a development of the trickster archetype (q.v.), whose Greek embodiment is Hermes (q.v.) and who exists in a variety of different trickster-figures in many myths. "Our stories of Brer Rabbit or Reynard the Fox preserve the essentials of the Trickster myth" (Henderson, 104). As Kerényi has pointed out, whether he appears in human form or as a cunning animal, the trickster is "the prototype of Reynard the Fox, whose equivalent for some tribes was the coyote, for others the raven, but who in all his manifestations was a primordial being of the same order as the gods and heroes of mythology" (175). In modern picaresque fictions, Reynard is explicitly embodied in Reinhart, the character in *Invisible Man* (q.v.) who actually is invisible but with whom the narrator is, ironically, more closely involved than any other character because he is a mirror self, a "man of many parts" who "gets around" and who is both mind and heart in a world of flux. Among the writers who have worked with the material is Goethe, in *Reineke Fuchs* (1794).

TRANSLATION

William Caxton [1481], *The History of Reynard the Fox,* ed. with an introduction by N. F. Blake (London: Oxford University Press, 1970); Patricia Terry, *Renard the Fox* (Boston: Northeastern University Press, 1983).

SELECT BIBLIOGRAPHY

Frank Wadleigh Chandler, *Romances of Roguery* [1899] (New York: Burt Franklin, 1961); Joseph L. Henderson, "Ancient Myths and Modern Man," in *Man and His Symbols,* ed. Carl G. Jung and M.-L. von Franz (New York: Dell, 1964), 95–156; Karl Kerényi, "The Trickster in Relation to Greek Mythology," in Paul Radin, *The Trickster: A Study in American Indian Mythology* (New York: Schocken, 1972), 171–91; Donald B. Sands, "Reynard the Fox as *Pícaro* and *Reinaerts Historie* as Picaresque Fiction," *Journal of Narrative Technique* 1 (1971): 137–45; Robert M. Torrance, "Renegade Vassal," in his *The Comic Hero* (Cambridge: Harvard University Press, 1978), 83–110.

"RINCONETE AND CORTADILLO"

("Rinconete y Cortadillo," 1613)

Miguel de Cervantes Saavedra

This story, together with "The Dogs' Colloquy" and "The Illustrious Kitchen-Maid" (q.q.v.), is one of the miniature picaresques in the *Novelas ejemplares* (1613). Superficially it is the most conventionally picaresque of the three in its depiction of the Seville underworld. Although we learn much about the two rogues' lives by way of a dialogue they have with each other in the first part of the story, the tale itself is presented in the third person. While calling it "the most picaresque" of the twelve exemplary stories, Chandler nevertheless treats it in a chapter entitled "Imperfect and Allied Forms" (351–52).

Two boys meet by chance in front of an inn. The older one (Rinconete) asks the younger (Cortadillo) where he is from. "I don't know," he replies, "where I came from, or where I am going either. . . . All I have . . . is a father who doesn't treat me as his son and a stepmother who treats me in the way stepchildren are usually treated. I am going where chance directs, and I shall stop wherever I find someone who will give me the wherewithal to get through this wretched life" (85–86). They tell each other their stories. Rinconete is the son of a pardoner who has made off with a bag of money, and Cortadillo is the son of a tailor who "taught me his trade, and having started cutting with shears, my natural talent soon taught me to cut purses" (88). Having discovered their mutual roguery, they go off to Seville, where they eventually join a brotherhood of thieves. Cervantes's depiction of this milieu is one of the most interesting of all the renderings of rogue communities in picaresque fictions from *El Buscón* to *The Tin Drum* (q.q.v.). This elaborate hierarchy of thieves, beggars, prostitutes, and assorted social riffraff, under the leadership of Monipodio, perversely mirrors the social order. These gangsters, though they in effect undermine the social and moral orders, operate with strict law and order among themselves, even rationalizing their activities as being "in the service of God and all good folk" (95). The two boys observe all this, though at some moral distance. Rinconete especially is "shocked by the slackness of the law in that famous city of Seville, where such pernicious and perverted people could live almost openly; and he made up his mind to advise his companion that they should not spend much time in that evil and abandoned way of life, so uncertain, lawless, and dissolute" (119). Through lack of resolve caused by inexperience and youth, he nevertheless spends some months with the community. Then Cervantes stops the story, leaving further accounts "for another occasion," and concludes with a traditionally picaresque moral disclaimer that "the other events which took place in that infamous academy [are] all worth consideration and capable of serving as an example and warning to those who may read them" (120).

Despite its vision of disorder, however, in this story "the depiction of villainy is stylized for humorous effects, and the rapidity of its condensed, conventional action and gesture, the exaggerated comedy of situation, and the processional caricature endow the entire work with the playful tonality and the highly contrived character of a puppet show rather than with the seriousness of a philosophical tale" (Forcione, 62). Parker finds it lacking in serious treatment of delinquency:

For Cervantes shows only one aspect of delinquency—the most naive and humorous aspect—and shows it as a self-subsisting world, already formed and static; it is a limited manifestation of delinquent psychology rather than an exploration of it. His thieves are caught in the trap and are happy in it; he does not try or want to tell us either how they came to be ensnared or how they could struggle to escape. (30–31)

TRANSLATION

C. A. Jones, in *Exemplary Stories* (New York: Penguin, 1972).

SELECT BIBLIOGRAPHY

Carlos Blanco Aguinaga, "Cervantes y la picaresca. Notas sobre dos tipos de realismo," *Nueva Revista de Filología Hispánica* 11 (1957): 313–42 (translated and abbreviated as "Cervantes and the Picaresque Mode" in *Cervantes: A Collection of Critical Essays,* ed. Lowry Nelson, Jr. [Englewood Cliffs, N.J.: Prentice-Hall, 1969]); F. W. Chandler, *Romances of Roguery* [1899] (New York: Burt Franklin, 1961); Peter N. Dunn, "Cervantes De/Re-Constructs the Picaresque," *Cervantes* 2 (1982): 110–31; Alban K. Forcione, *Cervantes and the Mystery of Lawlessness: A Study of* El casamiento engañoso y El coloquio de los perros (Princeton, N.J.: Princeton University Press, 1984); A. A. Parker, *Literature and the Delinquent: The Picaresque Novel in Spain and Europe 1599–1753* (Edinburgh: Edinburgh University Press, 1967).

RODERICK RANDOM
(THE ADVENTURES OF RODERICK RANDOM)

(1748)

Tobias Smollett

In the context of eighteenth-century fiction, the use of the term *picaresque* becomes even more problematical than usual. Except perhaps for Defoe, there is no denying the impact of Spanish fiction on the developing English novel. But much of this influence is by way of Cervantes, causing a confusion about the nature of the picaresque that persists to this day in the popular misconception that *Don Quixote* is a picaresque fiction. Smollett himself exemplifies this confusion of ancestry in his preface to *Roderick Random,* in which he gives a capsule history of fictional types beginning with "the heathen mythology, which is no other than a collection of extravagant Romances" (xliii). A second age of romance developed in the Middle Ages: "When the minds of men were debauched by the imposition of priest-craft to the most absurd pitch of credulity; the authors of romance arose, and losing sight of probability, filled their performances with the most monstrous hyperboles" (xliv). When the world actually began to "be infected with the spirit of knight-errantry," Cervantes came along and, by "an inimitable piece of ridicule, reformed the taste of mankind, representing chivalry in the right point of view, and converting romance to purposes far more useful and entertaining, by making it assume the sock, and point out the follies of ordinary life." He then goes on:

The same method has been practised by other Spanish and French authors, and by none more successfully than by Monsieur Le Sage, who in his adventures of Gil Blas, has described the knavery and foibles of life, with infinite humour and sagacity.—The following sheets I have modelled on his plan, taking the liberty, however, to differ from him in the execution, where I thought his particular situations were uncommon, extravagant, or peculiar to the country in which the scene is laid.—The disgraces of Gil Blas, are for the most part, such as rather excite mirth than compassion; he himself laughs at them; and his transitions from distress to happiness, or at least ease, are so sudden, that neither the reader has time to pity him, nor himself to be acquainted with affliction.— This conduct, in my opinion, not only deviates from probability, but prevents that generous indignation, which ought to animate the reader, against the sordid and vicious disposition of the world. (xliv–xlv)

Smollett, who published his own translation of *Gil Blas* (q.v.) later that same year, at about the time he was beginning his translation of *Don Quixote* (published in 1755), here blends the Cervantine with the Spanish picaresque as being "the same method"; moreover, he holds *Gil Blas* up as a model, though no generic concept of the picaresque should fail to come to grips with the fact that Lesage in his work radically transforms the essential characteristics of the original Spanish genre. But then Smollett qualifies his model by emphasizing a major difference between his own work and that of Lesage. Instead of the lightness and frivolity of *Gil Blas*, his fiction offers a worldview in which "the sordid and vicious" is the norm and against which literature should stir readers to react with "generous indignation." Thus, ironically, his explicit rejection of some aspects of Lesage's fiction is also an implicit criticism of eighteenth-century alterations of the picaresque, while his overt assertion of a much darker worldview is also a covert reassertion of characteristics essential to the original Spanish works.

It is not clear how generically conscious Smollett actually was in making refinements in his perception of his narrative heritage. But he makes a similarly roundabout argument in both the dedication to and the first chapter of *The Adventures of Ferdinand Count Fathom* (1753), a work that is picaresque in content but not in technique or characterization. In the dedication (actually written to himself), he gives a definition of the novel that is very close to the *Raumroman* structure:

A Novel is a large diffused picture, comprehending the characters of life, disposed in different groups, and exhibited in various attitudes, for the purposes of an uniform plan, and general occurrence, to which every individual figure is subservient. But this plan cannot be executed with propriety, probability or success, without a principal personage to attract the attention, unite the incidents, unwind the clue of the labyrinth, and at last close the scene by virtue of his own importance. (2–3)

In the first chapter, the narrator rails against the readers who might raise objections to the depiction of low life in native fiction while tolerating—indeed, praising—it "when imported from another clime" (7), alluding specifically to such works as Petronius's *The Satyricon* (q.v.), Apuleius's *The Golden Ass* (q.v.), Aleman's *Guzmán de Alfarache* (q.v.), as well as *Gil Blas, Don Quixote,* and Scarron's *Roman comique* (1651, 1657). Without full generic realization, then, Smollett in both works is criticizing a kind of trivialization of the picaresque and arguing on behalf of the English novel the right to full portrayal of the sorts of social, economic, and moral conditions that were essential to the original Spanish picaresque genre but had been refined out of it by such writers as Lesage.

This unconscious generic confusion—whose most obvious symptom is an indiscriminate mixing of the Cervantine with the picaresque—on the part of writers themselves in the latter part of the seventeenth and the first half of the eighteenth centuries has left a troublesome critical legacy, making it necessary for any meaningful usage of the term *picaresque* to be accompanied by heavily qualifying adjectives. In fact, we may pay a heavy price in both the understanding of the picaresque narrative tradition and our readings of individual works themselves. Despite attempts, for example, to find picaresque elements in such works as Fielding's *Jonathan Wild* and *Tom Jones*, "we are, in *Tom Jones*, not only closer to *Don Quixote* than to the picaresque, but also closer to the world of the Greek romance. I suggest that if we wish to apply the term picaresque to eighteenth-century English fiction we must do so at the cost of such qualifications as to negate its usefulness" (Kearful, 389).

Nonetheless, the association of "picaresque" with eighteenth-century English fiction is so pervasive in both general treatments as well as studies of the picaresque that we have to confront the problem. It is hard to find a treatment of Smollett's *Roderick Random* that does not, however briefly or indirectly, place the book in the context of the picareque. "In all but his last fiction, *The Expedition of Humphrey Clinker,* Smollett added nothing to this primitive form of the novel [that is, the picaresque as practiced by Lesage]" (Allen, 64). "His general scheme invites comparison with Fielding and the picaresque tradition" (McKillop, 147). Among the more sustained considerations is the following, which begins with a survey of the picaresque in Spain and France and which also serves as a good summary of *Roderick Random*'s major lines of action:

If you are fashioning a novel upon the tradition of picaresque fiction and spicing it with a romantic turn of events, you can cause a surgeon's second mate to jump overboard and be rescued by a former schoolfellow who has become the master of a Rhode Island schooner. You can land your hero in France and have him at once come upon one of the two men there that it is important for him to encounter—in this case his uncle and former benefactor. When it is time for another change of scene, and you wish to return to England, you can rub the lamp and a genie will appear in the form of Strap, a stupid fellow but wonderfully supplied with money and devotion to bestow upon his underserving idol. You can see to it that the woman whom your hero had once befriended reappears as the maid of the woman he has since come to love. You can, if you wish, bring your novel to a happy conclusion by conjuring up from the fabulous land of South America a father rich enough to make all reasonable dreams come true and thus enable your hero, no longer a friendless orphan, to shine before his friends and to triumph over his enemies. (McCullough, 65–66)

Such an assessment could easily describe a romance or a satire, and thus it really does not illuminate either *Roderick Random* or our sense of the picaresque. As a final example of this kind of approach, there is the theory by Ronald Paulson that sees Smollett primarily as a formal satirist making use of his inherited narrative forms as they fit his purpose and discarding those conventions that do not: "Smollett unashamedly attempts to write satire in the most conventional form of his time. . . . He rationalizes certain picaresque conventions in terms of their satiric usefulness and abandons others because they detract from the satiric design" (166–67). Both the preface to *Roderick Random* and the dedication to (and first chapter of) *Ferdinand Count Fathom* present us with a writer who is aware of generic impulses shaping his fiction but is determined also to escape the tyranny of tradition by shaping it to his individual ends. In this view, Smollett ends up owing more to Lesage's *Diable boiteux* (1707) than to *Gil Blas:*

In the run-of-the-mill narrative satires of the seventeenth and eighteenth centuries, the Picaresque relationship between two people dwindled to the relationship between an eye and an object. A decided shift of emphasis took place from the master-servant relation to the master or (since the master as such tended to disappear) the character, object, scene, or place observed. As a relatively uninvolved observer, the picaro could assume any tone from urbane Horatian to savage, sarcastic Juvenalian, from ingénu to *vir bonus* and heroic defender of the faith. . . . The satirist's skill went undivided into the tableaux that were framed. Recognizing the convenience and flexibility of the picaresque form, satirists tended to overemphasize its satiric lines, turning it into a close approximation of formal verse satire. (Paulson, 175–76)

Picaresque is modally close to satire on the spectrum of fictional modes, and incidental satire is one of its essential characteristics as far back as the trickster myths (q.v.), but when the satiric impulse becomes the sustaining fictional vision, the balance is shifted in the direction of the satiric mode. It is the "large diffused picture" that matters much more than the picaro's act of seeing. "As a panoramic novelist, Smollett has never been surpassed" (Allen, 66).

G. S. Rousseau has examined the problems that result when Smollett's works are indiscriminately labeled picaresque. As can be seen in the preface to *Roderick Random*, "the term picaresque was in Smollett's era much more inclusive than it has been at almost any time since then: a catchall for literally any variety of literature depicting low-life characters and characters as they are rather than as they ought to be, and more often than not merely a muddled synonym for romance. . . . The label, not altogether unlike satire, was so overwhelmingly muddled and inclusive that upon occasion it accommodated most prose works, except Richardson's" (1900). Rousseau goes on to demonstrate that the term is still entirely muddled in its usage by contemporary critics, who will call all, some, or only one of Smollett's works picaresque, depending on their particular concepts. Thus, both our awareness of Smollett's specific fictional achievements and our knowledge of the development of narrative kinds suffer. (The resulting frustration is particularly evident in the book-length study by Giddings, in which the "tradition" is never satisfyingly defined: "The influence of the picaresque tradition which concerns us in this study, the branch of the tradition which provided Smollett with a tradition in which to write and which in turn produced its unmistakable effect on Dickens, came to England across the Channel, from France. The French writers of the seventeenth century were among the earliest to attempt to exploit the possibilities of the picaresque kind. . . . Smollett developed the picaresque novel to a level of perfection never equalled again in our language" [17–18].)

The problematics of linking Smollett, however qualifyingly, with the picaresrque from the larger perspective of the development of English fiction are not lessened in any way when the approach is from the perspective of the picaresque itself, by critics with a thorough knowledge of the Spanish picaresque genre. Parker gives *Roderick Random* only perfunctory treatment because it "is in no sense an exploration of human delinquency" (127), according to his major criterion (which *Ferdinand Count Fathom*, however, meets fully). Chandler had somewhat contradictorily concluded his treatment of Smollett by putting him among the few "who have contributed so much" (320) after having begun by pointing out that he "fell far short of his model": "Though [Smollett] relied on the picaresque formula, he used it but clumsily, and the worth of his novels consists less in their form and spirit than in their matter" (309). And Blackburn, like Parker, prefers *Ferdinand Count Fathom* over *Roderick Random* but for the major reason that in Fathom Smollett created a satanic figure on the order of Fielding's Jonathan Wild: "[*Ferdinand Count Fathom*] presents in its protagonist an interesting link between the picaro and the romantic Satan" (138).

The studies by Alter, Bjornson, and Miller are the most sustained, analytical, and thoroughly grounded in a knowledge of the Spanish genre. And, most significantly, they acknowledge, though in varying degrees and with differing judgments, the polygeneric makeup of *Roderick Random*. Alter sees the turn toward sentiment in the last third of the book as "strained and incongruous": "The decline from the picaresque of Roderick Random foreshadows what was soon to occur on a wide scale in European literature. Born in the flowering of the Renaissance, the picaresque novel is the characteristic expression of a vigorously active individualism in a rugged, competitive world. But as the age moved toward sentiment in the latter half of the eighteenth century, before long it would be only the dissident spirit who could feel at home in the picaresque tradition of hardship and adventure" (79). Miller, reconciling the romance ending of *Roderick Random* with what he sees as otherwise a thoroughly picaresque fiction, points out that "Smollett creates a picaresque world but puts a partially nonpicaresque character into it. . . . One genre exploits another. In *Roderick Random*, however, the relations between the generic elements are not always clear, and the result is a certain incoherence. The genres are not perfectly fused by any shaping spirit—the work lacks, too frequently, an overriding unity of tone" (93). And Bjornson concludes:

> For Smollett, the picaresque format offered an opportunity to place a noble hero in contact with a corrupt world. As that hero proved himself worthy, he also illustrated the aristocratic assumption that one's nature is determined at birth and ought to govern one's place in a static social hierarchy. Some Spanish writers had based picaresque fiction upon similar ideological assumptions, but in general they did not endow their protagonists with a concealed nobility like that of Roderick Random. . . . When Smollett modified literary conventions developed in Spain and adapted to French taste, he succeeded in transforming the characteristically picaresque sequence of events and giving it a meaning just the opposite of that which it had borne in the earliest Spanish novels. (244–45)

The major obstacle in generic studies of *Roderick Random* is the character of Roderick himself. He is high born and, unlike Simplicissimus (*Simplicius Simplicissimus*, q.v.), he always knows it; this knowledge governs both his behavior and his vision of the world. The restoration of his status, his fortune, and his happiness results in a romance ending that is difficult to reconcile with the picaresque unless we go to great lengths to qualify the work with statements about its transitional status or its multigeneric composition—even its portrayal of Smollett's fear that "England's cultural heritage and moral values were being undermined by the rise of the bourgeoisie" (Bjornson, 244). But every explicit picaresque contains within it an implicit romance, clearly demonstrable in the prototypal fictions (*Lazarillo de Tormes, Guzmán de Alfarache*, q.q.v.) and made explicit in subsequent variations like *Memoirs of a Good-for-Nothing* and *Knulp* (q.q.v.). Seen from a modal perspective, *Roderick Random* is essentially a picaresque within a romance, a modal mix that is signaled from the very beginning, in both the preface and the first chapter.

In the preface Smollett explains his strategy for the dual condition of his protagonist:

> I have attempted to represent modest merit struggling with every difficulty to which a friendless orphan is exposed, from his own want of experience, as well as from the

selfishness, envy, malice, and base indifference of mankind.—To secure a favourable prepossession, I have allowed him the advantages of birth and education, which in the series of his misfortunes, will, I hope, engage the ingenuous more warmly in his behalf. (xlv)

The first chapter, which relates his birth, the death of his mother, and the disappearance of his father as a direct result of his grandfather's disowning them, tells of a dream his mother had during her pregnancy:

She dreamed, she was delivered of a tennis-ball, which the devil (who to her great surprize, acted the part of a midwife) struck so forcibly with a racket, that it disappeared in an instant; and she was for some time inconsolable for the loss of her off-spring; when all of a sudden, she beheld it return with equal violence, and earth itself beneath her feet, whence immediately sprung up a goodly tree covered with blossons, the scent of which operated so strongly on her nerves that she awoke.—The attentive sage, after some deliberation, assured my parents, that their first-born would be a great traveller, that he would undergo many dangers and difficulties, and at last return to his native land, where he would flourish with great reputation and happiness. (1)

As presented directly through the preface and indirectly through this image, the pattern of Roderick's life is essentially a romance plot. The difficulties that the romance hero has to overcome are presented in purely picaresque tone and vision, however. Just the title alone of the second chapter illustrates this: "I grow up— am hated by my relations—sent to school—neglected by my grandfather—mal- treated by my master—seasoned to adversity—form cabals against the pedant— debarred access to my grandfather—hunted by his heir—demolish the teeth of his tutor" (4). Later, before he and Strap have even penetrated much into London, they have been rudely initiated into the chaos of life. As Strap sums it up: "God send us well out of this place, we have not been in London eight and forty hours, and I believe we have met with eight and forty thousand misfortunes.—We have been jeered, reproached, buffetted, pissed upon, and at last stript of our money; and I suppose by and by we shall be stript of our skins" (72). The world will get even uglier, as the battle scenes and the squalor on board ship later graphically depict. But despite the degradation, pain, humiliation, and alienation Roderick will suffer in a world that does indeed demonstrate—and cruelly—that "vicious indignation" Smollett speaks of, Roderick will never forget his birthright, which colors his attitude toward everything that happens to him, no matter how horrible. He is more like a Candide (Smollett edited and in part translated Voltaire) than he is a picaro; Smollett has constructed him in such a way that the reader is reassured of his indestructibility. Although we feel the pains of injustice no less for that, we nevertheless know that an ultimately restorative ending lies ahead. When Roderick has been reunited with Strap quite by chance, he tells his life story to him; Strap's reactions might well parallel those Smollett expects his readers to have:

During the recital, my friend was strongly affected, according to the various situations described: He started with surprize, glowed with indignation, gaped with curosity, smiled with pleasure, trembled with fear, and wept with sorrow, as the vicissitudes of my life inspired these different passions; and when my story was ended, signified his amazement on the whole, by lifting up his eyes and hands, and protesting, that tho' I was a young man, I had suffered more than all the blessed martyrs. (253)

Roderick had originally parted from Strap because he felt the latter was beneath him, and being supported by him hurt his well-born pride: "for it is impossible to express the pangs I felt, when I reflected on the miserable dependance in which I lived, at the expence of a poor barber's boy" (95). Strap perceives this and says so. At their miraculous reunion, when Roderick must again depend on Strap, who is now well off, Strap reminds him of this and how much it hurt him at the time: "And though I did not complain, I was not the less sensible of your unkindness, which was indeed the only thing that induced me to ramble abroad" (252). At being reminded of his pride, Roderick reacts with more of the same: "I was nettled at the charge, which, though just, I could not help thinking unseasonable, and told him with some tartness, that whether his suspicions were well or ill-grounded, he might have chosen a more convenient opportunity of introducing them: And that the question now was, whether or no he found himself disposed to lend me any assistance" (252). The more picaresque perspective here is Strap's, which resembles in attitude and situation that of Lazarillo toward the *hidalgo* in the third chapter of *Lazarillo de Tormes*. Given this somewhat insensitive aspect of Roderick's personality, the reader finds it difficulty to sustain Smollett's announced strategy of sympathy for the protagonist, at least for the twentieth-century reader who is indifferent to class differences. (Roderick makes up for it by rewarding Strap when he himself has discovered his father.) Pride in his birthright is the stabilizing force in Roderick's often impossibly random life. That his rightful place must be restored eventually, despite all obstacles, is a given from the start. The overall vision of *Roderick Random* is that of romance.

Yet even in this the work proves troublesome, for the happy ending is not brought about by any vision of cosmic order intelligible to human beings, in which cause-and-effect relationships operate according to some meaningful structure. Roderick is reunited with his now-wealthy father entirely by chance, an "amazing stroke of providence" (416) that takes place, significantly, in the New World. He has not done anything specific to earn it; it is his by right and has only been temporarily withheld by misfortune (from Roderick's perspective) and by the exigencies of satire (from Smollett's perspective). He is not the heroic hero, questing for something and reaping reward; he has been evicted from his Eden only to return to it, in a completion of the circle of existence. When he tells his story to his father, we have the reactions of yet another built-in reader:

I recounted the most material circumstances of my fortune, to which he listened with wonder and attention, manifesting from time to time those different emotions, which my different situations may be supposed to have raised in a parent's breast; and when my detail was ended, blessed God for the adversity I had undergone, which, he said, enlarged the understanding, improved the heart, steeled the constitution, and qualified a young man for all the duties and enjoyments of life, much better than any education which affluence could bestow. (415)

Such pat-on-the-head moralizing is ludicrously inadequate for the horrors Roderick has actually experienced, and since Roderick's father does not seem anywhere else in the book an object of satire, we find ourselves hard-pressed how to react to this outlandish incongruency. This stock response, this let's-get-on-with-it summary, reveals the satirist's machinery at work: the cruelties of a genuinely picaresque rendering of world-chaos are whisked off into the wings while the scenery of romance descends quickly from the flies. Like them, Roderick is a device, more puppet than picaro. The voice we hear in *Roderick Random* may often resemble the upstart "I" of the lowly, unstable, yet nevertheless resilient picaro; but enclosing it is the self-assured voice of an insider who has been temporarily kicked out of his rightful place in the scheme of things; and around them both is the peremptory eye of the omniscient satirist, with his ventriloquist's "I," manipulating the fortunes of romance and the misfortunes of picaresque.

EDITIONS

The Adventures of Roderick Random, ed. Paul-Gabriel Boucé (Oxford: Oxford University Press, 1979); *The Adventures of Ferdinand Count Fathom,* ed. Damiam Grant (London: Oxford University Press, 1971).

SELECT BIBLIOGRAPHY

Walter Allen, *The English Novel: A Short Critical History* (New York: Dutton, 1954); Robert Alter, *Rogue's Progress: Studies in the Picaresque Novel* (Cambridge: Harvard University Press, 1964); Jerry C. Beasley, *"Roderick Random*: The Picaresque Transformed,'' *College Literature* 6 (1979): 211–20; Richard Bjornson, *The Picaresque Hero in European Fiction* (Madison: University of Wisconsin Press, 1977); Alexander Blackburn, *The Myth of the Picaro: Continuity and Transformation of the Picaresque Novel, 1554–1954* (Chapel Hill: University of North Carolina Press, 1979); Paul-Gabriel Boucé, *The Novels of Tobias Smollett [Les Romans de Smollett,* 1971], trans. Antonia White (London: Longman, 1976), and "Smollett's Pseudo-Picaresque: A Response to Rousseau's 'Smollett and the Picaresque,' " *Studies in Burke and His Time* 14 (1972): 73–79; Frank Wadleigh Chandler, *The Literature of Roguery* [1907] (New York: Burt Franklin, 1958); Alice Green Freedman, "The Picaresque in Decline: Smollett's First Novel," in *English Writers of the Eighteenth Century,* ed. John H. Middendorf (New York and London: Columbia University Press, 1971): 189–207; Robert Giddings, *The Tradition of Smollett* (London: Methuen, 1967); Ursula Habel, *Die Nachwirkung des picaresken Romans in England (von Nash bis Fielding und Smollett)* (Breslau: Pribatsch, 1930); Hershel C. Johnson, "Tom Jones and the Picaresque Tradition," *Studies in English Language and Literature* 26 (1985): 9–17; Frank J. Kearful, "Spanish Rogues and English Foundlings: On the Disintegration of the Picaresque," *Genre* 4 (1971): 376–91; F. McCombie, "Count Fathom and *El Buscón,*" *Notes and Queries* 7 (1960): 197–99; Bruce McCullough, *Representative English Novelists: Defoe to Conrad* (New York: Harper & Row, 1946); Aland Dugald McKillop, *The Early Masters of English Fiction* (Lawrence: University Press of Kansas, 1956); Stuart Miller, *The Picaresque Novel* (Cleveland, Ohio:

Case Western Reserve University Press, 1967); Alexander A. Parker, *Literature and the Delinquent: The Picaresque Novel in Spain and Europe, 1599–1753* (Edinburgh: Edinburgh University Press, 1967); Ronald Paulson, *Satire and the Novel in Eighteenth-Century England* (New Haven, Conn.: Yale University Press, 1967); G. S. Rousseau, "Smollett and the Picaresque: Some Questions about a Label," *Studies in Burke and His Time* 12 (1971): 1886–1904; Philip Stevick, "Smollett's Picaresque Games," in *Tobias Smollett: Bicentennial Essays Presented to Lewis M. Knapp*, ed. George S. Rousseau and Paul-Gabriel Boucé (New York: Oxford University Press, 1971), 9–23.

ROXANA

(1724)

Daniel Defoe

Its full title is *Roxana, the Fortunate Mistress, or, a History of the Life and Vast Variety of Fortunes of Mademoiselle de Beleau, afterwards Called the Countess de Wintselsheim in Germany. Being the Person Known by the Name of the Lady Roxana in the Time of Charles II,* and its protagonist is one of the few full-fledged picaras in a line of female picaresques that begins with *La pícara Justina* (q.v.). Written two years after *Moll Flanders* (q.v.), it has been much neglected in favor of its predecessor, not only in the picaresque narrative tradition but in Defoe scholarship generally. Virginia Woolf wrote that on any monument to Defoe "worthy of the name of monument the names of *Moll Flanders* and *Roxana*, at least, should be carved as deeply as the name of Defoe. They stand among the few English novels which we can call indisputably great" (90). Since she wrote that in 1919, *Moll Flanders* has come at least to rival, if not replace, *Robinson Crusoe*'s position as Defoe's masterpiece, but *Roxana* is often treated as a minor variation on the picaresque condition rendered in *Moll Flanders*. But beneath the superficial similarities of character, situation, and narrative technique, there are some essential differences that reveal *Roxana* to be in some crucial ways a much deeper and ultimately darker foray into the picaresque condition than *Moll Flanders* offers.

A composite of several real-life confidence women, Roxana comes to England from France as a ten-year-old with her parents, who are Protestant refugees fleeing persecution. At age fifteen, she marries a brewer for his looks but soon realizes he is a fool; after eight years, he disappears, leaving her and their five children destitute. The rest of her narrative describes the succession of liaisons she makes, each of which leaves her economically better off, so that eventually she is quite rich. She becomes a scandalous figure in London society. Finally she marries the Dutch merchant whose arduous proposal she had previously rejected, but her outwardly quiet and contented married life is inwardly troubled by anxiety that her real reputation might be uncovered and by guilt over her maid Amy's having murdered one of Roxana's children, a daughter who could have revealed that past. To all this, Defoe prefaces a typical disclaimer that insists on negative examples in the story, which is designed to "discourage and expose" vice and should be read with "Profit and Delight": "If there are any Parts in her Story, which being oblig'd to relate a wicked Action, seem to describe it too plainly, *the Writer says,* all imaginable Care has been taken to keep clear of Indecencies, and immodest Expressions; and 'tis hop'd you will find nothing to prompt a vicious Mind" (2). Like Moll Flanders, whose essential condition in the world can be summed up in the prayer she herself inserts into her narrative, "give me not poverty lest I steal," Roxana's situation is one of absolute survival, summed up in the lesson Amy taught her: "*Comply and live; deny and starve*" (110). But while Moll's economic fortunes rise and fall precipitously, Roxana's wealth allows her moral transgressions of another kind; she enjoys being a mistress.

In stating her position, Roxana is more polemically articulate (though no more comfortable morally) than Moll. When the Dutch merchant entreats her to marry him, Roxana rejects him because her primary concern is preserving her own freedom: "I thought a Woman was a free Agent, as well as a Man, and was born free"; marriage reduces a woman to the status of servant or slave, forcing her to give "herself entirely away from herself" (147). Moreover,

I added, that whoever the Woman was, that had an Estate, and would give it up to be the Slave of *a Great Man,* that Woman was a Fool, and must be fit for nothing but a Beggar; that it was my Opinion, a Woman was as fit to govern and enjoy her own Estate, without a Man, as a Man was, without a Woman; and that, if she had a-mind to gratifie herself as to Sexes, she might entertain a Man, as a Man does a Mistress; that while she was thus single, she was her own, and if she gave away that Power, she merited to be as miserable as it was possible that any Creature cou'd be. (149)

The merchant replies that Roxana "had started a new thing in the World" (153), and she herself says, "but surely it was the most preposterous thing that ever Woman did" (157). In the narrative present, she interprets this action as a mistake in the light of what is still to happen to her before she finally does marry him. Ironically, she has rejected a man for his honesty of intention ("He would have taken me as a Wife, but would not entertain me as a Whore"); preserving her freedom from marital slavery only makes necessary her compromising other freedoms as she accommodates herself to a life of deceit in appearances.

Defoe's feminism in *Roxana* caught Virginia Woolf's attention, though she acknowledges that "the advocates of women's rights would hardly care, perhaps, to claim Moll Flanders and Roxana among their patron saints"; Roxana is a significant character

because she is blessedly unconscious that she is in any good sense an example to her sex and is thus at liberty to own that part of her argument is "of an elevated strain which was really not in my thoughts at first, at all." The knowledge of her own frailties and the honest questioning of her own motives, which that knowledge begets, have the happy result of keeping her fresh and human when the martyrs and pioneers of so many problem novels have shrunken and shrivelled to the pegs and props of their respective creeds. (95)

And Roxana's defense of her freedom against yet another suitor makes clear, in the force of her convictions, that she is acting out of some primeval need of her own that precedes any formulated ideology:

I told him, I knew no State of Matrimony, but what was, at best, a State of Inferiority, if not of Bondage; that I had no Notion of it; that I liv'd a Life of absolute Liberty now; was free as I was born, and having a plentiful Fortune, I did not understand what Coherence the Words *Honour* and *Obey* had with the Liberty of a *Free Woman;* that I knew no Reason the Men had to engross the whole Liberty of the Race, and make the Women, notwithstanding any desparity of Fortune, be subject to the Laws of Marriage, of their own making; that it was my Misfortune to be a Woman, but I was resolv'd it shou'd not be made worse by the Sex; and seeing Liberty seem'd to be the Men's Property, I wou'd be a *Man-Woman;* for as I was born free, I wou'd die so. (171)

While Virginia Woolf admires Moll and Roxana above all for their veracity—"For them there were no excuses; no kindly shelter obscured their motives. Poverty was their taskmaster" (96)—Chandler, writing specifically in the context of the picaresque narrative tradition, comes down hard on *Roxana* as a "sombre story" that "is not enlivened by a ray of humor. It is bloodless and unnatural. . . . Roxana is almost without emotion. She certainly wins no sympathy. Her passion is controlled by avarice" (296). Refuting Walter Scott's claim that it is one of the legitimate heirs of *Lazarillo de Tormes* and *Guzmán de Alfarache* (q.q.v.), Chandler concludes that *Roxana,* "in brief, lacks unity, plan, and interest" (299). Yet such an assessment takes little account of narrative distance as it functions in *Moll Flanders* and *Roxana.* While in the former we may have our problems with the sincerity of Moll's repentance, Roxana's passionate feelings about freedom charge her professed repentance with a credulity that is well beyond the merely tacked-on lip-service Chandler says it is. Chandler cites the momentary effect of fear of death during a storm on board ship that makes Roxana and Amy repent of their wicked ways, and then the following passage a few pages later:

and in this State, and on that Account, I look'd back upon my Wickedness with Abhorrence, as I have said above; but I had no Sence of Repentance, from the true Motive of Repentance; I saw nothing of the Corruption of Nature, the Sin of my Life, as an Offence against God; as a thing odious to the Holiness of his Being; as abusing his Mercy, and despising his Goodness; in short, I had no thorow effectual Repentance; no Sight of my Sins in their proper Shape; no view of a Redeemer, or Hope in him: I had only such a Repentance as a Criminal has at the Place of Execution, who is sorry, not that he has committed the Crime, as it is a Crime, but sorry *that he is to be Hang'd for it.* (129)

Chandler complains that "Roxana persists in her evil courses almost to the last" (298), but he neglects to take into account the fact that this passage comes after "the last," during the narrating act, and the insight Roxana has now into her own false repentance then emphasizes that moral growth has indeed taken place. Although she does not continue her story to show us any moral behavior, the fact that she can write such an analysis is itself evidence of considerable moral awareness from the narrating present. Moreover, through examination of narrative distance, we notice a tension between the implied author and his protagonist: "At times Defoe is in sympathy with his heroine, while at other times he is genuinely shocked by what she does" (Jack, x). This tension between sympathy and reprobation is evident throughout the book and is a major characteristic of the reader's relationship to all picaresque fictions. Unlike the conventionally moralistic ending of *Moll Flanders, Roxana* ends with a darker version of the tension that exists at the end of *Lazarillo* as well. Defoe likes her too much to end with her exposure and death (which is what he would have had to do had he followed his real-life sources), and yet she is too guilty to justify the relatively happy ending that a conversion implies. "And so he adopted the brilliant compromise of leaving her in physical safety and prosperity, yet in spiritual torment" (Jack, xi). With all her lust for freedom, Roxana is trapped in the end by total exclusion from innocence. She is a fallen woman in a much profounder sense than having been a mistress to many masters.

EDITION

London: Oxford University Press, 1964, ed. with an introduction by Jane Jack.

SELECT BIBLIOGRAPHY

F. W. Chandler, *The Literature of Roguery* [1907] (New York: Burt Franklin, 1958); Alan Dugald McKillop, *The Early Masters of English Fiction* (Lawrence: University of Kansas Press, 1956); Julio Rodríguez-Luis, "*Pícaras:* The Modal Approach to the Picaresque," *Comparative Literature* 31 (1979): 32–46; Virginia Woolf, *The Common Reader* [1925] (New York: Harcourt, Brace & World, 1953).

THE RUNAGATE COURAGE

(Die Landstörtzerin Courasche, 1670)

Hans Jacob Christoffel von Grimmelshausen

Her story begins in book V, chapter 6 of *Simplicius Simplicissimus* (q.v.), when Simplicius is keeping his dying friend Heartbrother company at a spa:

There was a beautiful woman at the mineral springs who said that she was a member of the nobility, but I thought that she was more *mobilis* than *nobilis*. I courted this mantrap intently, for she seemed to be rather attractive. It didn't take long before I not only got acquainted with her, but I also got all of the delights I could have ever wanted. But at the same time, I was disgusted by her wantoness, and so I looked for a chance to politely rid myself of her, for I suspected that she was more interested in fleecing me than she was in marrying me. Wherever we were, she went so overboard with her loving and fiery glances and other tokens of her burning affection, that I was ashamed of myself, and of her, too. (Tr. Adair, 389)

In chapter 9 of the same book, just when Simplicius's second wife and their maid are both giving birth to his children, this woman (whom he never names) deposits a baby on his doorstep, with a note stating that he is the father. "So I had three children all at once, and the fear that others would crawl out from every corner caused me some gray hairs! But that is the way it has to be if you lead the godless life I did by following my bestial desires" (400). This child, though named his heir in chapter 10, soon fades out of his story.

In her version of the encounter, Courage provides details that Simplicissimus could not have known and others that he has left out of his own rendition. She is at the spa recuperating from a bout with syphilis. Fitting herself out elegantly, she runs into Simplicius, and a mutual deception ensues:

I conducted myself very nobly, and because Simplicius made such a show and had many servants, I took him to be a proper nobleman and pondered whether I might throw my rope over his horns and make him my husband (as I had already done frequently with others). And he came sailing into the dangerous port of my insatiable lusts under full sail and before a strong wind, just as I had wished, and I treated him like Circe did the erring *Ulissem;* and soon I was confident for sure I had him safely in my net, but the tricky bird tore a hole in it with a pretty little trick, by which he showed his great ingratitude, ridiculing me and ultimately harming himself. By shooting blanks from a pistol and using a water-squirt full of blood in *secret,* he made me believe that I had been wounded, so that I was viewed, front and behind, not only by the leech who was supposed to bandage me, but also by almost all the people in Sauerbrunnen, who afterwards pointed their fingers at me, sang a song about it, and mocked me in such fashion that I was no longer able to bear the ridicule, but quit Sauerbrunnen and the spa before my cure was completed. (161–62)

This humiliation motivated her to play her own vengeful trick on Simplicissimus by leaving the child: the baby is not his, not even hers, but rather her maid's.

No one can believe how this deception delighted me, particularly when I heard that he was so well punished by his magistrate because of it and that his wife served him my pretty little trick every day with horseradish and mustard, *item* that I succeeded in making the simpleton really believe that I, a barren woman, had born a child, when if I had been of that kind I should surely not have waited for him, but should have accomplished in my youth what he thought I had done when I was approaching old age; for at that time I had seen at least forty years and was not worthy of such a rascal as Simplicius was. (162)

She is not done with revenge, however, and she compounds her trick in life by now playing another in art:

That booby Simplex calls me wanton in his biography, in Book V, Chapter vi, *item* when he says I was more *mobilis* than *nobilis*. I admit to both; but if he had himself been noble, or if there had been a decent bone in his body, then he would not have tangled with a baggage as wanton and as brazen as he took me to be, much less proclaimed and spread abroad to all the world, as he did, his dishonor and my shame. Dear Reader! What honor and fame is it for him now, that he (to use his own words) quickly gained entrance to her house and all favors which he might wish and desire from a woman whose wantonness he came to abhor? Indeed, from one who had but recently recuperated from the wood cure [for syphilis]? The poor devil certainly has won tremendous honors from bragging about what he might better and with greater honor have concealed. But that is the way it goes with these studs, who, like ignorant beasts, chase after anything in skirts, like a hunter does after any kind of game. (162)

She is thus writing her *vida* in refutation and revenge. In stripping off her masks, her goal is to undeceive the public about Simplicissimus's stupid gullibility, thus doubly punishing him. In fact, the original title of her account is *Trutz Simplex*— literally, "to spite Simplex"—and the rest of it runs: *Or, the Detailed and Wondrously Strange Life History of the Archfraud and Runagate Courage, How She First Was the Wife of a Captain of Horse, Afterwards the Wife of a Captain of Infantry, Further the Wife of a Lieutenant, Presently the Wife of a Musketeer, and Finally the Wife of a Gypsy. Expertly Carried Out and Excellently Described and Just as Entertaining, Agreeable, and Profitable to Contemplate as Simplicissimus Himself. All of It Dictated by the Person of Courage Herself for the Displeasure and Disgust of the Well-known Simplicissimus Directly to the Author.* However, it is usually referred to by the short title *Die Landstörtzerin Courasche* or, simply, *Courasche*.

In addition to providing her motivation for telling her story, Grimmelshausen also explains the means by which she did so. In a third work called *Der seltsame Springinsfeld* ("The Strange Hopalong," or "The Strange Skipinthefield"), which, together with still other works, is often grouped with *Simplicissimus* and *Courasche* into what are called the *Simplizianische Schriften,* or the Simplician Writings, Grimmelshausen has a young student tell the story of Springinsfeld, who first appeared as Simplicius's comrade-in-arms in book II, chapter 31 of *Simplicissimus* and who was one of Courage's husbands. The young student runs into Simplicius and Springinsfeld at an inn and tells them how Courage came to dictate her memoirs to him. Having read Simplicius's book, she takes the student (who encounters her by chance, on the road, where she is leading a band of gypsies) aside and asks him to write from her dictation, "for the sole purpose of spiting you, Simplicissimus, so that everyone should laugh at your folly" (192). As they listen, Simplicius and Springinsfeld react differently. The now one-legged Springinsfeld curses her, but Simplicius feels they should pray for her—"that the kindness of God may illuminate her heart and bring her to true repentance!" (200). But he is still vain enough to want to save face by claiming that he slept more often with Courage's maid than with Courage herself, and so he likes to believe that the child was his anyway. Thus the tricked trickster gets the last laugh, muffled in moral guise: "But here is an example of how those who think to deceive others often deceive themselves and of how God is wont to punish the great sins of those who will not reform with even greater sins, so that their final damnation is that much greater" (192)—which is also, chronologically, the last word on the whole incident.

This multiple view of the picara—which Cary tried for Sara Monday (*The Horse's Mouth, Herself Surprised,* q.q.v.) and which Defoe had promised for Moll by way of narratives by her governess and her last husband but never followed through (*Moll Flanders,* q.v.), and which is sometimes accomplished by shifting points of view within the work itself (for example, *The Tin Drum* and *The Family of Pascual Duarte,* q.q.v.)—creates an unusually vivid portrait. It is also a variation on Cervantes's metafictional sleight-of-hand in *Don Quixote,* when book characters discover the existence of a book about them and react as though they were not characters in a book. The result is aesthetic confusion about the differences between life and art, an effect inherent in the picaresque narrative stance of self recreation that complements the philosophical confusion resulting from the exploration of a major moral theme of most picaresques, and of *Simplicissimus* in particular: delusion deceives.

Grimmelshausen may have been influenced directly by *La pícara Justina* (q.v.), although a definite link has never been established. Nevertheless, much has been made of Grimmelshausen's choosing a female character, especially considering his incontrovertible misogyny. One traditional interpretation sees her as an archetypal temptress, an Eve, the *Urmutter* of sin. There is even speculation that Courage, because of her masculine characteristics, is really a homosexual self-projection. But a more objective approach has emerged, which pays more attention to the text itself and the actual portrait that emerges. Such an examination can reveal that "she is fundamentally what men have made of her," and her story becomes "a surprisingly modern study in the psychology of male-female relationships, not a conventional Baroque castigation of innate female immorality and *Unbeständigkeit*" (Jacobson, 43). Grimmelshausen "admired her. While condemning sex in all his writings, in this novel he succeeded in presenting at the same time the portrait of an irresistible woman, who reacts with lusty sexual abandon and revenge to terrible abuse by men and yet remains human and attractive to the reader" (Speier, 40). Her unity and strength of character emerge in spite of the allegorical framework within which she is serving as illustration for three typical baroque themes: "The first deals with the dangers of disturbing the harmony of nature; the second argues the proposition *mulier non homo* (women are not properly human beings); and the third demonstrates the vanity of the finite world" (Hiller and Osborne, 18). Offspring of an illicit union, raised by a lowborn woman of dubious morality, forced to wear male attire and act like a man in the war-ravaged world around her, Courage's whole being is a disruption of the normal rhythms of continuity and harmony. "From childhood on," she says, "it was my nature to like things best when they were all topsy-turvy" (36). The other two themes follow from this very condition she is born into: men are to blame for the world she must survive in, and her only means of survival is to appeal to the vanity of men by deceiving them. In her role as enchantress, she represents the world-as-sham, and as the action unfolds, "Courage is gradually unmasked, gradually stripped of her glamour, until we lose sight of her as an old gypsy queen who has blackened her face and no longer makes any pretense at allurement" (Hiller and Osborne, 20).

Parker says that Courage's story "is a typical picaresque novel not only in form but in the fact that the heroine has to fend for herself from an early age in a hostile world. It is particularly hostile in her case because she is a woman in a world of men at war'' (95); but by stressing impenitence and perverse wickedness, her story is "a departure from the Spanish tradition" (97). Rodríguez-Luis finds Courage—and indeed all other picaras before Moll Flanders—lacking in seriousness and depth compared to the picaros who emerged at the same time. He takes the socioeconomic ambition of the picaro and the verisimilitude of depiction as the two central traits of picaresque fiction. Measured in this way, such picaras as Justina, Teresa de Manzanares (*La niña de los Embustes*, q.v.), and Courage fall short as characters because the rules of contemporary society denied women the freedom to pursue ambition. "Consequently, we are left with empty characters, or at most with caricatures of the *pícaro*, until the time in history when it becomes possible for a woman of low birth to move up in society with a certain degree of freedom, thus allowing the *pícara* . . . to achieve real depth in her literary characterization" (43).

But just as she bursts forth from one book into two others, she breaks the confines of her merely mechanical function in an allegorical scheme, and she transcends even her relatively open-ended picaresque condition of being to attain the status of an archetype. Although from one point of view she quite literally descends in life—from being high born to being an old gypsy hag—from another she looms larger than life. There is something superhuman about her, which Grimmelshausen makes explicit in *Der seltzame Springinsfeld* when the student describes his encounter with the woman whose story he will be asked to write down. In her presence, he seems paralyzed and speechless as he takes in every minute detail of her appearance, seeing in her majesty a "spitting image of the Lady of Babylon" (189–90). She has been called a *virago* in the older meaning of the world, which is closer to *amazon:* "Whenever she fights men, whether with her fists as a young girl, with sword and pistol in battle later, with a cudgel after one of her many wedding nights, with a knife in the woods, or with wit, false tears, and pretty words—she almost always wins. Almost without exception men who oppose her are beaten up or humiliated, taken prisoner, killed, duped, or exploited by her" (Speier, 32). Her name itself (one of several she uses), as she explains its origin in chapter 3, refers to the male sex organ; when another soldier attacks her—she is dressed as a man—she beats him up "because he made a grab for my courage" (44), which of course she does not possess; but in giving herself that name, she in effect confers on herself masculine powers that make her, ironically, stronger than those who do possess it literally. This deflating of machismo is made even more explicit by the meaning and connotations—mostly lost in translation—of the German *Courasche*, which is "army slang, a rough equivalent of the English word *guts,* denoting the raw physical courage of the male animal. This soldier's term for a virtue particularly associated with men of action, but here applied to a woman, connotes an earthiness, even a vulgarity, in German which it is impossible to render into English without losing many word plays" (Hiller and Osborne, 20).

What creates this larger-than-life being is the remarkable narrative voice itself, which in sheer force exceeds that of Moll Flanders. Spite indeed fuels Courage's words, and from her first word to her last, she never takes her narrative eye from her goal of ridiculing him. Repeatedly throughout her narrative, she addresses him directly. But she also addresses the world of men in general, anticipating their every reaction and building a running argument into the narrative process. Her first words are, "Well (you will say, gentlemen) who would ever have thought that the old fool would ever presume to escape the impending wrath of God?" She admits that some will think "the old crowbait" is trying an eleventh-hour escape from the torments of hell. But then she concedes that others might think it preposterous that "this old slut" could seriously believe that she has any chance of mercy:

Yes, my good sirs! That is what you will say and that is what you will think, and therefore you will be astounded when the news of this, my great and general confession, reaches your ears; and I, when I hear your astonishment, I will forget my age and either laugh myself young again or laugh myself sick! Why that, Courage? Why will you laugh like that? For this reason: That you think an old woman who has enjoyed life so well for so long and who imagines that her soul has, so to speak, grown fast to her body should be thinking of death; that such a woman as you know me to be and to have been all my life should be thinking of saving her soul; and that she who, so the priests tell me, has trod a path bent straight for hell her whole life long should only now be thinking of heaven. I candidly confess that I cannot decide either to equip myself for the journey which the priests are trying to persuade me to take, or to give up that which, according to them, blocks my path; since for this journey I lack one thing and have too much of several, in particular two things. What I lack is repentance, and what I should lack but do not is avarice and envy. . . . You cannot teach an old dog new tricks. (31–33)

Why then is she doing it? To spite Simplicissimus because she cannot avenge herself on him in any other way. She will "tell him now what kind of honorable minx he was dealing with, so that he may know of what he bragged and may perhaps wish that he had kept silent about our *Historii;* by which, however, the whole reputable world may learn that just as horse and nag, just so whore and knave, are of the same breed" (34). She goes on unrelentingly until the end when she is satisfied that she has revealed enough to assure "the eternal shame of Simplicissimo" (182). By the time she is through, even the author himself is speechless, for the "Addendum of the Author" is an overtly preachy passage copied from another book.

As though the three books in which she appears were not room enough for her, the figure of Courage has been reincarnated in the twentieth century. Most people are probably much more familiar with Bertold Brecht's *Mother Courage* (*Mutter Courage und ihre Kinder: Eine Chronik aus dem Dreizigjährigen Krieg,* 1941) than they are with the original work. More recently still, Günter Grass in *The Meeting at Telgte (Das Treffen in Telgte,* 1979) describes an imaginary 1647 meeting of writers, among whom is Grimmelshausen, who lodge at an inn run by Libuschka, one of Courage's other names.

TRANSLATIONS

Quotations are from *The Runagate Courage*, trans. Robert L. Hiller and John C. Osborne (Lincoln: University of Nebraska Press, 1965). Hiller and Osborne provide an informative introduction and include from *Der seltzame Springinsfeld* those sections pertaining to Courage. Hans Speier's translation, *Courage, The Adventuress and The False Massiah* (Princeton, N.J.: Princeton University Press, 1964), contains an extensive introduction.

SELECT BIBLIOGRAPHY

John W. Jacobson, "A Defense of Grimmelshausen's Courasche," *German Quarterly* 41 (1968): 42–54; A. A. Parker, *Literature and the Delinquent: The Picaresque Novel in Spain and Europe, 1599–1753* (Edinburgh: University Press, 1967); J. M. Ritchie, "Grimmelshausen's *Simplicissimus* and *The Runagate Courage*," in *Knaves and Swindlers: Essays on the Picaresque Novel in Europe*, ed. Christine J. Whitbourn (London: Oxford University Press, 1974), 48–74; Julio Rodríguez-Luis, "*Pícaras:* The Modal Approach to the Picaresque," *Comparative Literature* 31 (1979): 32–46; Siegfried Steller, "Lebensbeschreibung der Ertzbetrügerin und Landstörtzerin Courasche" [1957] in *Der Simplicissimusdichter und sein Werk*, ed. Günther Weydt (Darmstadt: Wissenschaftliche Buchgesellschaft, 1969), 237–52.

THE SATYRICON

(first century A.D.)

Petronius [Arbiter]

Apuleius's *The Golden Ass* (q.v.) and *The Satyricon* are the only classical texts repeatedly cited as precursors of the Spanish picaresque tradition. Chandler quotes from an 1885 study by Dutch scholar Jan Ten Brink: "Encolpius in the *Satyricon* of Petronius Arbiter has been hailed as the forerunner of the Spanish rogues" (3–4). And Chandler also points out that Petronius was much in vogue during the sixteenth and seventeenth centuries, when picaresque fiction in Spain flourished. Nevertheless, he concludes, "the low-life adventures of the decadent voluptuary or the excesses of the feast of Trimalchio have little in common with the shifts of the unfortunate rascal in service" (4). Echoing Auerbach's criterion of dynamic interaction between individual and society in *Mimesis*, Blackburn claims that The *Satyricon* differs from fully picaresque fictions because "the fundamental situation of the literary picaro is the loneliness of an individual isolated *within* society," and Encolpius, though he comes into conflict with his environment, moves in a static, timeless continuum, not the active social reality of novelistic literature (19).

Yet the basic characteristics of the picaresque are here. It is an antiromance in its portrayal of Encolpius as a comic Odysseus suffering the anger, not of Poseidon, but of Priapus. Throughout there are jarring juxtapositions and incongruities that parody epic subject matter and style: frescoes combining scenes from the *Iliad* and the *Odyssey* with gladiator games, and a slave singing both

Virgil and obscene farce are part of the atmosphere at Trimalchio's dinner, itself a grotesque depiction of an epic feast. Later, a battle on board ship that is not at all heroic is described in a heroic style inappropriate to it; attempts at suicide or self-castration move uncomfortably from the serious to the comic, from the melodramatic to the farcical. In its savage portrayal of a world out of kilter, The *Satyricon* is more purely satire than it is picaresque; it is technically, an example of Menippean satire, which Frye says "resembles the confession in its ability to handle abstract ideas and theories" and "presents us with a vision of the world in terms of a single intellectual pattern" but differs from the picaresque form, "which has the novel's interest in the actual structure of society" (*Anatomy*, 309–10).

But it is also a good example of the mixture of narrative types, specifically the satiric, the comic, and the picaresque. Very early on, Encolpius, in pursuit of his rival Ascyltus, has forgotten where he lives and asks a woman selling vegetables beside the road: "Excuse me, ma'am, but would you happen to know where I live?" This preposterous question shifts the whole fictional world of The *Satyricon* into a disorientation from which it will never recover. Encolpius is the innocent, gullible, often victimized narrator of his own tale, which provides the confessional first-person narrative point of view with its built-in complexities of narrative distance. The naive Encolpius is constantly double-exposed through a more mature narrator who, like Lazarillo (*Lazarillo de Tormes*, q.v.) and other picaros, spouts proverbs and comments on the moral characteristics of fellow human beings. At the end of the surviving fragments of The *Satyricon*, when his impotence is cured, Encolpius experiences a conversion that is a parody of the more serious (though still problematic) conversions typical of the picaro prior to his narrative act of telling his life. Along the way, Encolpius discourses on fate in relation to his lot in life, a picaresque tendency of which chapter 25 is characteristicly representative:

And so we lived for some time at Croton. . . . Eumolpus, drunk with success, had so far forgotten the past that he began to boast to his intimates that no one in Croton dared to cross him and that, for any crimes we might commit, he could easily get us off through the influence of his new friends. For my part, thanks to the excellent food and the other gifts which Fortune showered on us in prodigious profusion, I had begun to put on weight again and had almost convinced myself that luck was no longer my enemy. Still, I couldn't help reflecting now and then on our present life and how it had come about. "What would happen," I used to wonder, "if one of these legacy-chasers had the wit to send off to Africa for information and then exposed us? Or suppose Eumolpus' hired servant got bored with his present luck and dropped a hint to his friends, or gave the whole show away out of spite? No mistake about it: we'd have to run for it, right back to our old life of poverty. Why, we'd have to start begging again. And, gods in heaven, an outlaw's life is a miserable business. Always waiting to be punished." (Tr. Arrowsmith)

This passage could easily have come from the pen of Lazarillo or Guzmán or Simplicius (*Guzmán de Alfarache, Simplicius Simplicissimus,* q.q.v.). The con-

tinuous dis-integration of the rendered world is fundamentally picaresque, as is
Encolpius's relationship to that world. (In his introduction, translator William
Arrowsmith uses the term *picaresque* half a dozen times.) And at least one
episode—the Widow of Ephesus, next to Trimalchio's Dinner the most famous
segment of *The Satyricon*—contains in essence the whole story of *Moll Flanders*
(q.v.).

Because only fragments of it are left, *The Satyricon* also raises the problem
of whether an incomplete narrative can be legitimately treated as a self-contained
artistic whole. As with Kafka's *Amerika* (q.v.), we can talk about only what
has survived and what is referred to secondhand by subsequent writers. *The
Satyricon* and *Amerika* are unintentional fragments, caused by the fortunes and
misfortunes of literary preservation and the author's death. Mann's *Felix Krull*
(q.v.) is yet another example. But even in its pure form, picaresque is inten-
tionally fragmentary. Continuations are not only hinted at but actually written,
in a narrative open-endedness that allows for infinite expansion, up to the point
when narrative distance is finally closed by the coinciding of the end of life with
the end of narrative. Ginés de Pasamonte, the self-conscious picaro in Cervantes's
Don Quixote, put this most succinctly when he says: "How can [my book] be
finished if my life isn't?" (pt. I, ch. 22). Moreover, the fragment as such is
entirely appropriate to the world rendered by the picaro (and to the picaro's
unique perspective itself). It is fitting that formal fragmentation (even if unintentional) be the container of the kinds of worlds and world visions and perspectives offered by picaresque narrative. Encolpius, subject as much to the
choppy reversals of his own personality as to the accidental and planned illusory
tricks the world sets up for him, can only tell a fragmented tale (though we
know him to be educated enough to write a polished, sophisticated account).
The narrative discontinuity or breaking of normative narrative rhythms is formally
suited to the mimesis of chaos, nightmare, and outsiderdom; it reflects the
continuous dis-integration and disorientation that are seminal to the picaresque
situation.

TRANSLATION

William Arrowsmith, *The Satyricon* (New York: Mentor, 1959).

SELECT BIBLIOGRAPHY

Erich Auerbach in *Mimesis: The Representation of Reality in Western Literature,* tr.
Willard Trask (Princeton, N.J.: Princeton University Press, 1953) is responsible for the
novel-focused view that has perpetuated the idea that picaresque fiction does not portray
the dynamic and problematic relationship of the individual to society. See also Angelo
Armendariz, "Petronius and Apuleius in the Spanish Picaresque Novel," *Fu Jen Studies*
(Republic of China) 3 (1970): 37–61; Alexander Blackburn, *The Myth of the Picaro:
Continuity and Transformation of the Picaresque Novel, 1554–1954* (Chapel Hill: Uni-
versity of North Carolina Press, 1979); Northrop Frye, *Anatomy of Criticism: Four Essays*
(Princeton, N.J.: Princeton University Press, 1957); Robert Scholes and Robert Kellogg

in *The Nature of Narrative* (London: Oxford University Press, 1966) belong to those who treat *The Satyricon* as "the first picaresque narrative" (73), and their analysis puts picaresque fiction in perspective with other narrative modes; A. Scobie, "Petronius, Apuleius, and the Spanish Picaresque Romance," in *Words: Wai-Te-Ata Studies in Literature*, ed. P. T. Hoffmann, D. F. McKenzie, and Peter Robb (Wellington, N. Z.: Wai-Te-Ata Press, 1966), 92–100; P. G. Walsh, " 'Nachleben': The Roman Novel and the Rebirth of the Picaresque," in his *The Roman Novel: The "Satyricon" of Petronius and the "Metamorphoses" of Apuleius* (Cambridge: University Press, 1970), 224–43.

SETTING FREE THE BEARS

(1968)

John Irving

This first novel is set in and around Vienna in 1967 and involves two failed students in their early twenties who take off on an aimless motorcycle trip across the Austrian countryside. The first and third parts are narrated by Hannes Graff, who has teamed up with Siggy, who makes meticulous plans to set free all the animals in the Hietzinger Zoo. Siggy narrates the middle section, a satirical "history" of his family before the Anschluss, during the war, and during the postwar Russian occupation, interspersed with excerpts from his notebooks detailing the twenty-two zoo watches he makes in preparation for his plan—a narrative intertwining made by Graff because "I felt, it was almost impossible to endure either the verbosity of Siggy's souped-up history or the fanaticism of his frotting zoo watches—if you were to read them whole" (259). After Siggy is killed in an accident, Graff completes his plan and lets the animals loose. On his way across the open countryside again, he encounters the bears; the last line of the book is, "For sure, I expect to hear great things of the Rare Spectacled Bears" (335).

The picaresque theme of freedom is explored ironically. These two picaros are hardly free, and the act of freeing the animals stands as vicarious atonement for the imprisonment of millions during the Nazi years (the night watchman at the zoo, O. Schrutt, appears to be a war criminal hiding his past). *Setting Free the Bears* also comments on the exhaustion of the Old World, a theme in picaresque fiction as far back as *El Buscón* (q.v.) and *Moll Flanders* (q.v.) and developed in *Amerika* (q.v.). In his notebook, Siggy writes:

I guess if you're twenty-one in 1967, in America, you needn't glut yourself with prehistory; in America I understand that there are crusades every day. But I'm not in America. I'm in the Old World, and what makes it old isn't that it's had a head start. Any place that's lagging, waiting again for The National Crisis—that's an Old World, and it's often a pity to be young in it. (107)

EDITION

New York: Random House, 1968.

SIMPLICIUS SIMPLICISSIMUS

(Der abentheuerliche Simplicissimus Teutsch . . . etc., 1668)

Hans Jakob Christoffel von Grimmelshausen

The first edition is actually dated 1669, and its title reads in full: *The Adventurous German Simplicissimus / Being the Account of the Life of a Singular Wanderer* [in the original, the genetive of *Vagant*] / *Named Melchior Sternfels von Fuchshaim / Where and How He Came into This World / What He Saw, Learned, Experienced, and Endured Therein / And Also Why He Willingly Quit It. Extremely Jolly / And Useful to Read for One and All,* followed by one of the anagrammatic pseudonyms with which Grimmelshausen fooled readers until 1838, when his authorship of the so-called Simplician writings was finally established. *Simplicissimus* was not a critical success, but it was very popular. By the end of the seventeenth century, not only had there been a number of reprintings and new editions (among them the inevitable piracy), but more than two dozen other works either imitating it or directly alluding to it had appeared. More than half of these incorporated, or were supposed to be written by, characters from the Simplician writings, including Simplicius himself. From the start, *Simplicissimus* has been a book-making book. Even Grimmelshausen himself continued to expand on his original material, at times using Cervantine shifts in narrative perspective, as in *The Runagate Courage* (q.v.) and *Der seltzame Springinsfeld,* in both of which Simplicissimus appears through the eyes of others.

Long ranked among the greatest of prose works in German literature, *Simplicissimus* and its major sequels continue to engender other books. Eichendorff's *Memoirs of a Good-for-Nothing* (q.v.) transfers Simplicius to a romantic landscape in which *Sein* and *Schein* confound in a manner not altogether different from the baroque exploration of the theme whose motto was inscribed into all the illustrations for early editions of *Simplicius Simplicissimus: Der Wahn betrügt* ("Delusion deceives"). The "wise fool" stage of Simplicius's early military career echoes in the outwardly naive, bumbling soldier type given exemplary shape in Jaroslav Hašek's *The Good Soldier Švejk and His Fortunes in the World War* (1920–1923). Brecht reworked Courage for *Mother Courage and Her Children* (1941). Hofmannsthal used the last chapter of book V (itself taken from Guevara) of *Simplicissimus* for what some consider to be his major tragedy, *The Tower* (1925, 1927), which is also heavily indebted to Calderón's *La vida es sueño.* Grass's *The Tin Drum* (q.v.) owes more than its structure and narrative technique to *Simplicius Simplicissimus,* and Grass has subsequently created a composite Grimmelshausen-Simplicius figure in the character of Christoffel Gelnhausen in *The Meeting at Telgte* (1979), an imagined gathering in 1647 of actual writers at an inn run by Courage; their concern with revitalizing language and literature after the destructive Thirty Years' War (1618–1648) parallels that of Grass's own Group 47 three hundred years later, after World War II. Grimmelshausen's portrayal of the devastation of war influenced Thomas Mann in *Doctor Faustus* (1947), which depicts the destruction of Germany in this century. He acknowledged *Simplicissimus* as a picaresque model when he was continuing *Felix Krull* (q.v.) And in his introduction to a 1944 Swedish translation of *Simplicissimus,* he described—on the eve of another annihilation of Germany— the enduring power of Grimmelshausen's work:

It is the rarest kind of monument to life and literature, for it has survived almost three centuries and will survive many more. It is a story of the most basic kind of grandeur— gaudy, wild, raw, amusing, rollicking and ragged, boiling with life, on intimate terms with death and devil—but in the end, contrite and fully tired of a world wasting itself in blood, pillage and lust, but immortal in the miserable splendor of its sins. (Quoted in Adair, xi)

From 1896 until its takeover by the National Socialists, one of Germany's leading satirical weeklies was called *Simplicissimus,* on the editorial staff of which Mann worked for a time and to which he was an occasional contributor. In its January 22, 1933, issue, as described by Ann Taylor Allen in her *Satire and Society in Wilhelmine Germany,* there appeared a cartoon in which Hitler as a shabby drummer entices innocent-looking customers into a disreputable circus: "Come in, come in, gentlemen—this time the Third Reich is really about to begin"; Goebels is standing behind a curtain, whispering, "But if we don't do anything, the whole audience will run away." (In book II, chapter 4, Simplicius is hastily dressed in borrowed clothes and given a borrowed drum for a military inspection by Swedish forces: "All I had to do was to beat on a drum because I was too small to be a musketeer" [104], an incident which in *The Tin Drum* expands to become Oskar's whole reason for being.) In postwar German literature, Grimmelshausen's unflinchingly graphic depiction of the random horrors war inflicts on the innocent and guilty alike in everyday life has served as a kind of literary rudder for interpreting the Nazi years, not only in *The Tin Drum* but in such directly allusive lesser-known works as Heinz Küpper's *Simplicius 45* (1963). The picaresque mode, with *Simplicissimus* as its model, has provided the major narrative means of expression for postwar German fiction, a phenomenon explored in such studies as Schumann's "Wiederkehr der Schelme" (Return of the picaros), Wilfried van der Will's *Pikaro heute* (Picaro today), and Günther's "Der ewige Simplizissimus" (The eternal Simplicissimus).

Books had gone into its making as well. While no direct link has been demonstrated between *Simplicissimus* and *Estebanillo González* (q.v.)—the only Spanish picaresque to have the Thirty Years' War as it setting (and in which the picaro also serves a stint as jester and eventually wanders to Russia, like Simplicissimus)—it is generally agreed that Grimmelshausen could not have failed to be influenced by Spanish picaresque fiction. "He had almost certainly read . . . the German *Lazarillo,* Albertinus' *Gusman* and Kuefuss' version of Luna's *Segunda parte*" (Bjornson, 166). The German rendering of *Guzmán de Alfarache* (q.v.) provides an interesting case study of translation as transition. As Parker summarizes the situation, when Albertinus published *Der Landstörtzer Gusman de Alfarche, oder Picaro genannt* in Munich in 1615, he did not know Alemán had already issued a second part in 1604, but he did know Martí's 1602 unauthorized continuation, which he incorporated into his translation of Aleman's first part. Albertinus wrote his own second part (published in the 1615 edition), in which Guzmán has a religious conversion and takes a hermit's advice to make a pilgrimage to the Holy Land in order to atone for all his sins. Although Albertinus never published his promised third part, someone under the pseudonym Martinus Freudenhold in 1626 issued a third part in which the picaro goes on his pilgrimage and then turns hermit. Alemán also never wrote his own promised third part, but around 1650 Machado de Silva, marquis of Montebelo, wrote a continuation (not published until 1927) in which Guzmán is released from the galleys, makes a pilgrimage to Santiago de Compostela, becomes a Franciscan monk, and retires to a hermitage near a hospital, where he takes care of the sick. While direct literary contact seems highly unlikely to have occurred, what unites these efforts is the strong established tradition of the medieval pilgrimage (Reynard makes one [*Reynard the Fox,* q.v.]). Thus the similarities between the German and the Spanish continuations—apparently independently arrived at but through a common cultural and literary heritage—suggest a natural final phase of existence for the picaro. As Parker concludes:

For all these continuators of Alemán there was the further point that a pilgrimage fitted into the peripatetic framework of the picaresque narrative. Alemán, if he had written his Third Part, would without any shadow of doubt have made Guzmán a pilgrim and, after that, a hermit. The line of succession from *Guzmán de Alfarache* to *Simplicissimus* is thus unbroken. (80)

Until relatively recently, *Simplicissimus* was much neglected in comparative studies of picaresque fiction. Chandler gave it barely a page: "This confused and formless fiction carries its naive anti-hero as fool, soldier, charlatan, and robber, up and down war-ridden Germany and to Paris. Magic and far journeys more and more invade the story, which concludes with an island shipwreck that foreshadows *Robinson Crusoe*" (29). With the exception of *The Runagate Courage* (q.v.), Chandler went on, all of the Simplician writings "are overweighted with moral reflections, yet in grossness they far outdo any novels of Spain. Their realism knows no subdual of detail, their range of observation is narrower than that of the Spaniards, and their satire is rude. The plots remain loose—travel, magic, and superstition confusing the true issues; and the characters are little removed from those of the jest-books" (30). Nevertheless, he conceded, Grimmelshausen's works were notable "for the freshness and epic quality of their portrayal of life." Not only do they throng with the stuff of popular native traditions, they "supplement the romance of chivalry, heroic romance, and the tale of adventure with a new genre, and if the form and inspiration for this be derived from Spain and France, its matter and manner are original." Their glory is "that they are thoroughly national." Their limitation is "that they lack the art which alone could have made them universal" (30). He saw Grimmelshausen's works as a natural consequence of the turmoil of the Thirty Years' War: "This period, with its intermingling of all classes in a struggle devoid of principle and its quick alternations of fortune, presented social conditions analogous to those that in Spain had given rise to the picaresque novel" (28).

Since the middle of this century, *Simplicissimus* has been somewhat more widely studied in comparative contexts. Bjornson's chapter title in *The Picaresque Hero in European Fiction*, for example, seems almost an explicit refutation of Chandler's judgment: "The Universality of the Picaresque: Visions of Truth in Grimmelshausen's *Simplicissimus*." Miller, in his formal analyses in *The Picaresque Novel*, considers it one of eight representative picaresque fictions. But Parker still observes (in the same year as Miller's book and ten years before Bjornson's), "Outside Germany *Simplicissimus* is unjustly neglected" (78), directly blaming this inattention for causing in turn a similar neglect by non-Hispanists of the importance of *Guzmán de Alfarache* to the picaresque tradition. And it is indeed a consequential distortion in the genealogy of picaresque narrative forms that *Simplicissimus* should share with *Guzmán de Alfarache* and *El Buscón* (q.v.) a generic prototypicality buried in relative obscurity outside the native literary tradition. Of the four exemplary picresques, only *Lazarillo de Tormes* (q.v.) seems to have achieved some kind of stature in world literature. Yet to construct a universal type of the picaresque without including *Guzmán, El Buscón*, and *Simplicissimus* is to omit significant dimensions of picaresque narrative.

Structurally, thematically, and narratively, *Simplicissimus* is a paradigmatic picaresque fiction. Its title contains the essence of the picaresque, condensing the life-into-art of the picaro into a sequence of six strong verbs: *came, saw, learned, experienced, endured,* and *quit.* In contrast to his direct descendant Oskar Matzerath in *The Tin Drum,* who is preternaturally conscious while still in the womb, Simplicius remains quite literally a tabula rasa until war separates him from his family and the hermit (who, unbeknown to him, is his real father) teaches him to read and write. "I knew neither God nor men, neither heaven nor hell, neither angel nor devil—and I didn't know how to tell right from wrong. So it is not hard to see that I lived according to the same theology as our first parents in Paradise. . . . Yes, I was so perfect and complete in my ignorance that it was not possible for me to know that I didn't know anything at all" (bk. I, ch. 1; 3). At the end (bk. VI, ch. 22), he and a carpenter, shipwrecked on a deserted island, "live like the first men in the Golden Age" (539); and when the carpenter dies and Simplicius is left the sole inhabitant, he "started to live like a hermit again" (540).

In between, he learns two crucial lessons in the chaos of existence as he alternates being victim and victimizer in a world that is never what it seems. He is exposed to these during his time with the hermit and then the pastor, but they are not absorbed until experience corroborates them and until self-perception allows their articulation. The first lesson, like Lazarillo's *solo soy,* is the essential coming to terms of the picaro with his landscape: fortune is fickle, or as he expresses it later, "nothing in the world is more constant than inconstancy" (bk. III, ch. 8; 226). When his pastoral existence is savagely interrupted by a troop of marauding cavalry, he at first takes rider and horse to be one creature, "just as the American Indians did the Spanish cavalry" (7). After the hermit dies and when he sees his new mentor, the pastor, led away by brigands after yet another pillage, he observes, "Oh, God! How full of pain and trouble is human life! One misfortune hardly ends before we are struck with another" (bk. I, ch. 13; 33). Yet on the same page, he describes letting himself be "overpowered by the desire to behold the world." Such perceptions will eventually grow into the self-knowledge that leads ultimately to repentance and renunciatiion. The Sisyphus rhythm (q.v.) of picaresque existence is the crude pattern that fortune imposes, as Simplicius comes to realize:

I also thought of how I'd changed from an officer to a peasant, from a rich peasant to a poor gentleman, from a Simplicius to a Melchior, from a widower to a married man, from a married man to a cuckold, and from a cuckold back to a widower again. Likewise, I'd gone from being a peasant's son to being the son of an honest soldier, and then back to the son of my knan again. I thought over how my fate had robbed me of Heartbrother and replaced him with two old married people. When I considered the blessed life and death of my father, the pitiful death of my mother, and the many different changes which I'd been subject to in my life, I could not stop myself from crying. (bk. V, ch. 11; 405)

The other crucial lession is Simplicius's learning to recognize the primal desire to be deceived, which half-sanctions the picaro's mode of operation by tolerating a mutually gratifying confidence game. After fooling those who intended to make a fool of him, he takes his troubled conscience to the pastor, who tells him, "The foolish world wants to be fooled" (bk. II, ch. 8; Schulz-Behrend, 80), an observed truth that is at the core of the picaresque vision and one that Simplicius's direct descendant Felix Krull incorporates into his very being. In one of his protean forms, Simplicius becomes quite literally an actor, in France, where he is known as "Beau Alman" (bk. IV, ch. 3). He gives it up after a stage fight turns real; "they battered me round more than you are supposed to do in a play" (299).

The first of these lessons helps the picaro to cope; it provides the equilibrium necessary to survive in a chaotic world that continually threatens the individual's right to be. The second lesson helps the picaro to manipulate; it provides the means by which he can alter his environment to his temporary advantage. Only by accepting the paradoxical constancy of inconstancy can the picaro befool, for the very nature of illusion is its transitoriness; yet, paradoxically also, the illusive provides a kind of stability for a world in which reality or truth is elusive. These two lessons are thus the two sides of the same coin, and they are emblematized in the figure of the satyr that appears in the frontispiece. A satyr, as Bjornson points out,

adopts many masks and believes in none of them. Like him, the narrating Simplicissimus has worn many disguises, and he is now describing them in an attempt to strip the facade of respectability from all the vices and follies of men. From his perspective, the entire world is a theater of masks: everyone wears them, and each person wears many different ones during a lifetime. Any individual's place in society is determined largely by historical accident, and as Simplicissimus' own experiences demonstrate, the same person can be master or servant, victimizer or victim. Capable of deceiving the mask-wearer as well as those whom he encounters, these masks are doubly harmful, and anyone who prides himself on his social role reveals a profound ignorance about himself. (172–73)

Parker has found in the macrostructure of *Simplicius Simplicissimus* the pattern for the "circle of existence," a concept from mystical writings, in which the individual leaves the hands of his Creator and is impelled through the world by successive loves (love of nature, love of men, love of ideas, love of the spirit, then love of God), eventually completing the circle of existence by a return to the Creator. "The affinity of Grimmelshausen with the Spanish religious writers is clear; the close connexion of the picaresque with the Counter-Reformation through *Guzmán de Alfarache* and *Simplicissimus* is indisputable" (83). In Parker's interpretation, war "replaces the Original Sin of *Guzmán de Alfarache* as the background for delinquent behavior" (86), showing all of humanity engaged in delinquency. For Parker, the religious quality of *Simplicissimus* "lies in the whole conception of the novel, in its circular structure a way from the home of a father, who is not known to be such, and back to it after experience of life teaches man from whence he has sprung. Above all it lies in the central symbolism, the contrast between the solitude of nature and the society of men, which is the brutality and the plundering of war" (91).

The closing of the circle of existence marks the beginning of the temporal point of narration, for it is here that Grimmelshausen depicts the actual narrating process. Alone on his island, Simplicissimus learns he can write by mixing certain juices together to make a kind of ink that shows up on large palm leaves. "I wrote down everything I could think of in this book which I have made from those palm leaves" (bk. VI, ch. 23; 543). In the twenty-fourth chapter of the *Continuatio,* or book VI, we get an external portrait of Simplicissimus by a Dutch sea captain named Cornelissen, whose ship is driven to the island in a storm. He and his crew find him hiding himself in the darkest recesses of a cave. He does not want to leave the island, but he gives them his manuscript of palm leaves, which the Dutch captain then turns over to his friend, "German Schleiffheim von Sulsfort," whose name appears on the title page as editor. The conventional device of the found manuscript serves to "authenticate" Simplicius's story, while Cornelissen's objective account of his piety and rejection of all worldly matters corroborates Simplicissimus's own self-portrait. The sixth book also foreshadows *Robinson Crusoe* and is the first of a whole series of so-called *Robinsonaden* in German literature. Grimmelshausen was inspired by Henry Neville's *Isle of Pines* (1668), based on a Dutch sailor's account of his experiences on the island of Mauritius in 1598, which was translated into German immediately after its publication in London.

Editorial framing of some kind is familiar in picaresque narrative, but there has been some controversy about the device in *Simplicissimus* because it is end-framed only, and the end was not originally published with the first five books. The *Continuatio* has come to be more and more accepted as an integral part of the work, however. Thematically and structurally, it provides the unity and coherence that the original ending—Guevara's "Farewell World!"—does not. Narratively, it is necessary too, for it creates authority, credence, and sincerity for a narrative voice that would otherwise remain anonymously uncharacterized, with little explicit detail about the motivation for narrating and none about the conditions of narration or the physical means of transmission of the narrative from writer to reader. The sixth book begins, in verse, with a recapitulation of that crucial first lesson about the constancy of inconstancy: "From this I pray you'll learn, that inconsistency / Alone consistent is" (452; Grimmelshausen's word in both cases is *Unbeständigkeit*). Here the frame of reference has shifted from the plane of experience to the plane of narration, from an observed truth about the nature of existence to a justification of writing and reading about that existence. Just as the paradisiacal island and the hermetic cave are necessary for structurally and thematically completing the circle of existence pattern, so the continuation is needed to fill out the full dimensions of narrative distance.

There has been much debate about whether *Simplicissimus* is a Bildungsroman, a question that relies heavily on the sincerity of the narrating attitude of Simplicius. If, however, the Bildungsroman is defined as depicting the complete inner and outer development of a character slowly achieving moral, spiritual, psychological, and social harmony with the surrounding world, then Simplicissimus in his total isolation at the end is not such a protagonist. While he may be at peace with himself, his life as a hermit is the antithesis of any kind of integrative existence. The Bildungsroman is dominated by the romance mode and by comedy, both of which posit attainable order, one cosmic, the other social. The picaro yearns for such orders but experiences them, when he does, only as fanatastic and unattainable improbabilities, as when Simplicissimus has his dream of the "people tree" (bk. I, ch. 15–16) or when he travels to the depths of the Mummelsee (bk. V, ch. 12–17).

Our last glimpse of Simplicissimus is the Dutch captain's:

As long as he had God for a friend, he wasn't worried in the least about being deprived of human consolation at the hour of his death. While he'd been among men in the world, he'd always received more trouble from his enemies than pleasure from his friends, who often caused more annoyance to him than anything he could hope for from his friendship with them. And even if he didn't have any friend here to love and aid him, he also didn't have any enemy to hate him. Both kinds of men could cause someone to sin; by being relieved of both, he could serve God more peacefully. (558)

The ambiguity of this problematic final image is disturbing, for it dramatizes once again the maddening paradox of picaresque freedom. Not only is the social and geographical mobility of picaresque existence an actual entrapment in a Sisyphean tug of war with life, the self-knowledge that that experience eventually brings leads only to total exclusion. To reject the follies and vices of the world is to have to reject the world. The vision is completely disintegrative—and typically picaresque. The narrative act Simplicius uses his island freedom for is as much bred of a desire to reconnect with life and the world as it is fed by moral and spiritual impulses. But the circle of narration, like the circle of existence, completes itself only in this troublesome final image. To free oneself from the "illusion that deceives"—to escape a world of mutually deceptive masks—is to negate oneself in the world. The only freedom Simplicissimus can achieve, short of death, is a form of self-imprisonment. The act of narration, despite some playful manipulation of narrative distance on occasion, does not integrate him in the end with any human order of being. Physically, psychologically, and narratively, Simplicissimus is almost solipsistically trapped, in his cave, in his thought, in his story. The contemporary reader who goes back more than three hundred years to *Simplicius Simplicissimus* will be startled to discover there the prototype for both *The Painted Bird* (q.v.) and *Invisible Man* (q.v.).

TRANSLATION

Quotations (unless otherwise indicated) are from *An Unabridged Translation of Simplicius Simplicissimus,* by Monte Adair (Lanham, New York, and London: University Press of America, 1986). Another complete translation is *Simplicius Simplicissimus* by Hellmuth Weissenborn and Lesley MacDonald (London, 1964), but it omits the *Continuatio* and reduces the many chapter divisions to twenty-seven. *The Adventures of Simplicissimus,* translated by John Spielman, with reproductions of wood engravings by Fritz Eichenberg, claims to be the first complete English text. Other versions (varyingly abridged and/or expurgated) are *Simplicius Simplicissimus* by George Schulz-Behrend (Indianapolis: Bobbs-Merrill, Library of Liberal Arts, 1965); *The Adventurous Simplicissimus* by A.T. S. Goodrick [1912] (Lincoln: University of Nebraska Press, 1962); and *The Adventures of a Simpleton* by Walter Wallich (New York: Frederick Ungar, 1963). Schulz-Behrend and Goodrick provide extensive and informative introductions.

SELECT BIBLIOGRAPHY

Werner Beck, *Die Anfänge des deutschen Schelmenromans. Studien zur frühbarocken Erzählung* (Zurich: Juris, 1957); Richard Bjornson, *The Picaresque Hero in European Fiction* (Madison: University of Wisconsin Press, 1977); Frank Wadleigh Chandler, *The Literature of Roguery* [1907] (New York: Burt Franklin, 1958); Maurice Gravier, "La 'Simplicité' de Simplicissimus," *Etudes germaniques* 6 (1951): 163–68 (in German as "Die Einfalt des Simplicissimus" in *Pikarische Welt: Schriften zum europäischen Schelmenroman,* ed. Helmut Heidenreich [Darmstadt: Wissenschaftliche Buchgesellschaft, 1969], 237–44); Helmut Günther, "Der ewige Simplizissimus. Gestalt und Wandlungen

des deutschen Schelmenromans," *Welt und Wort* 10 (1955): 1–5; Gerhart Hoffmeister,
"Grimmelshausens *Simplicissimus* und der spanisch-deutsche Schelmenroman: Beobach-
tungen zum Forschungsstand," *Daphnis* 5 (1976): 275–94; Jürgen Jacobs, *Der deutsche
Schelmenroman: Eine Einführung* (Munich: Artemis, 1983); Erich Jenisch, "Vom Aben-
teuer- zum Bildungsroman," *Germanisch-romanische Monatsschrift* 14 (1926): 339–51;
K. G. Knight, "The Novels of Johann Beer (1655–1700)," *Modern Language Review*
56 (1961): 194–211; Stuart Miller, *The Picaresque Novel* (Cleveland, Ohio: Case Western
Reserve University Press, 1967); María Navarrao de Adicenses, "La continuación del
Lazarillo de Luna y la aventura del Lego Mummel en el *Simplicissimus*," *Romanistisches
Jahrbuch* 12 (1961): 242–47; Alexander A. Parker, *Literature and the Delinquent: The
Picaresque Novel in Spain and Europe, 1599–1753* (Edinburgh: University Press, 1967);
Jürgen H. Petersen, "Formen der Ich-Erzählung in Grimmelshausens Simplicianische
Schriften," *Zeitschrift für deutsche Philologie* 93 (1974): 481–507; Franz Rauhut, "In-
fluencia de la literatura española en la literatura alemana," *Revista de Filología Hispánica*
1 (1939): 237–56; William Riggan, *Pícaros, Madmen, Naifs, and Clowns: The Unreliable
First-Person Narrator* (Norman: University of Oklahoma Press, 1981); J. M. Ritchie,
"Grimmelshausen's *Simplicissimus* and *The Runagate Courage*," in *Knaves and Swin-
dlers: Essays on the Picaresque Novel in Europe*, ed. Christine J. Whitbourn (London:
Oxford University Press, 1974), 48–74; Bertil Romberg, *Studies in the Narrative Technique of the First-Person Novel*, trans. Michael Taylor and Harold H. Borland (Stockholm:
Almqvist and Wiksell, 1962); Hans Gerd Rötzer, *Picaro—Landstörtzer—Simplicius: Studien zum niederen Roman in Spanien und Deutschland* (Darmstadt: Wissenschaftliche
Buchgesellschaft, 1972); Lothar Schmidt, "Das Ich im *Simplicissimus*," *Wirkendes Wort*
10 (1960): 215–20 (also in *Pikarische Welt;* see Gravier, above, 350–60); Rainer Schönhaar, "Pikaro und Eremit: Ursprung und Abwandlungen einer Grundfigur des europäischen Romans vom 17. ins 18. Jahrhundert," in *Dialog: Literatur und
Literaturwissenschaft im Zeichen deutsch-französischer Begegnung,* ed. Rainer Schönhaar
(Berlin: Erich Schmidt, 1973), 43–94; Edmund Schramm, "Die Einwirkung der spanischen Literatur auf die deutsche," in *Deutsche Philologie im Aufriss,* ed. Wolfgang
Stammler (Berlin: Erich Schmidt, 1962), 2: 147–99; Albert Schultheiss, *Der Schelmenroman der Spanier und seine Nachbildungen* (Hamburg: Sammlung gemeinverständlicher
wissenschaftlicher Vorträge, 1893); Willy Schumann, "Wiederkehr der Schelme," *PMLA*
81 (1966): 467–74; Harry Sieber, *The Picaresque* (London: Methuen, 1977); B. L. Spahr,
"Protean Stability in the Baroque Novel," *Germanic Review* 40 (1965): 253–60; H. H.
Weil, "The Conception of the Adventurer in German Baroque Literature," *German Life
and Letters* 6 (1953): 285–91; Arnold Weinstein, "The Unknown Soldier: *Simplicissimus,*" in his *Fictions of the Self: 1550–1800* (Princeton, N.J.: Princeton University Press,
1981): 50–65; Werner Welzig, "Der Wandel des Abenteuertums," in his *Beispielhafte
Figuren: Tor, Abenteurer und Einsiedler bei Grimmelshausen* (Graz and Cologne: Böh-
laus, 1963) (also in *Pikarische Welt;* see Gravier, above, 438–54); Gunther Weydt, ed.,
Der Simplicissimusdichter und sein Werk (Darmstadt: Wissenschaftliche Buchgesellschaft, 1969); Wilfried van der Will, *Pikaro heute: Metamorphosen des Schelms bei
Thomas Mann, Döblin, Brecht und Grass* (Stuttgart: Kohlhammer, 1967).

SISYPHUS MYTH

This son of Aeolus founded Ephyra, the ancient name for Corinth. He was called
"cunning" and "crafty" in the stories told about him and because of these
qualities was sometimes alleged to be the father of Odysseus. In *The Iliad,*

Sisyphus is described as "that sharpest of all men" (VI, 153; p. 157). Sisyphus drew down on himself the wrath of Zeus when he revealed to the river-god Asopus that it was Zeus who had carried off the latter's daughter, Aegina—an event Sisyphus happened to witness. In anger Zeus sent Thanatos for him, but Sisyphus trapped the god of death and bound him up, thus preventing anyone from dying. Ares, the god of war, had to set Thanatos free. Now Sisyphus had to submit to death, advising his wife not to pay him any final respects. In Hades he then complained about his wife's negligence and requested permission to return to earth in order to punish her. Sisyphus refused to return to the underworld, and Hermes (q.v.) had to intervene. For his deceitfulness, Sisyphus was punished by being eternally condemned to roll uphill an enormous boulder, which, every time it almost reached the top, would roll back down. His punishment is described by Homer in *The Odyssey* (XI, 593–600):

> "Also I saw Sisyphos. He was suffering strong pains,
> and with both arms embracing the monstrous stone, struggling
> with hands and feet alike, he would try to push the stone upward
> to the crest of the hill, but when it was on the point of going
> over the top, the force of gravity turned it backward,
> and the pitiless stone rolled back down to the level. He then
> tried once more to push it up, straining hard, and sweat ran
> all down his body, and over his head a cloud of dust rose." (183)

Sisyphus is linked in popular stories with another incarnation of the trickster archetype (q.v.), Autolycus, who was Odysseus's maternal grandfather and who "surpassed all men / in thievery and the art of the oath, and the god Hermes / himself had endowed him" (*Odyssey* XIX, 395–97; p. 292). Autolycus had stolen the helmet Odysseus wore for battle (*Iliad* X, 266–71; p. 225). Autolycus used to steal Sisyphus's cattle, but the latter turned the tables on him by attaching to his cattle's hooves lead tablets with the words "stolen by Autolycus," the imprint of which allowed Sisyphus to track them. The name of Sisyphus appears fairly often as a nickname for cunning persons.

But it is for his punishment, not for his trickery, that Sisyphus survives in the popular imagination. This image of futility was given wide contemporary significance by Albert Camus in his "The Myth of Sisyphus" (1942), a brief essay in which Camus emphasizes Sisyphus's scorn of the gods, his hatred of death, and his passion for life, which won him "that unspeakable penalty in which the whole being is exerted toward accomplishing nothing" (89). This "proletarian of the gods" is conscious of his condition when he descends the mountain to begin the task again. "The lucidity that was to constitute his torture at the same time crowns his victory. There is no fate that cannot be surmounted by scorn" (90).

Mateo Alemán had used the image hundreds of years earlier in *Guzmán de Alfarache* (q.v.) when Guzmán says, "volví de nuevo como Sísifo a subir la piedra," which Mabbe translated: "And being come now to the height of all my labors and paines-taking, and when I was to have received the reward of them, and to take mine ease after all this toyle, the stone rolled down, and I was forced like Sisyphus, to beginne the world anew, and to fall afresh to my work'' (pt. II, bk. III, ch. 4). This image reflects the picaresque condition, both experientially and narratively: *volver de neuvo,* ''to beginne the world anew,'' is the picaro's condition in life; *subir la piedra,* to climb again pushing the stone, is the rhythm of existence in the realm of the discontinuous, where the only continuity is the same thing over and over, paralleled narratively by a continuously dis-continuous (episodic) fictional form. ''Nothing in the world is more constant than inconstancy,'' says Simplicius (*Simplicius Simplicissimus,* q.v.). The primary structural characteristic of picaresque narrative is the Sisyphus rhythm, which renders the perpetual repetition of continuous dis-integration.

EDITIONS

Citations from Homer are from Richmond Lattimore's translations of *The Iliad* (Chicago: University of Chicago Press, 1951) and *The Odyssey* (New York: Harper Colophon, 1974). The whole story of Sisyphus is told by Félix Guirand, translated from *Mythologie Général Larousse* (1935) by Delano Ames in *Greek Mythology* (London: Paul Hamlyn Ltd., 1963), p. 140.

SELECT BIBLIOGRAPHY

Albert Camus, *The Myth of Sisyphus and Other Essays,* trans. Justin O'Brien (New York: Vintage Books, 1955); Ulrich Wicks, ''The Nature of Picaresque Narrative: A Modal Approach,'' *PMLA* 89 (1974): 240–49.

THE SONNE OF THE ROGUE

See LA DESORDENADA CODICIA DE LOS BIENES AJENOS

THE THIEF'S JOURNAL

(Journal du voleur, 1949)

Jean Genet

Like all other autobiographies that claim to be true to life, this book makes the already precarious distinction between fiction and nonfiction even more problematic, and ultimately futile. In the process of making a text out of the self, the historically existing ''I'' becomes a construct, a fictional character. As Eakin has written in *Fictions in Autobiography: Studies in the Art of Self-Invention,* ''The self that is the center of all autobiographical narrative is necessarily a fictive structure'' (3). Moreover, we realize that ''fictions and the fiction-making process are a central constituent of the truth of any life as it is lived and of any art devoted to the presentation of that life.'' We no longer believe ''that autobiography can offer a faithful and unmediated reconstruction of a historically verifiable past; instead it expresses the play of the autobiographical act itself, in which the materials of the past are shaped by memory and imagination to serve the needs of the present consciousness'' (5).

Picaresque narrative in its purest form must by its very nature be autobiographical-confessional, and from its beginnings (*The Satyricon, Lazarillo de Tormes, Guzmán de Alfarache, Simplicius Simplicissimus,* q.q.v.) it uses this form of presentation. Mainstream picaresque narrative has always played with our natural tendency to separate the invented fictional from the verifiable historical, and it has done this through the convention of the pretended or pseudo-autobiography—actually a redundant term. Just as reality is masked by a succession of appearances—a constant theme of picaresque fictions—so the narrative method of presentation masks the true self with a succession of self-constructs. Thus picaresque narrative teases us, much more than other kinds of fiction do, into pursuit of the question, How much of this really happened to the author? We can explore such matters with all the critical methodologies at hand, but as a critical path such investigations will lead us nowhere.

Genet constructs and explores himself in just this way, and on the broadest historical stage. His landscape includes Spain, which in 1932 ''was covered with vermin, its beggars. They went from village to village, to Andalusia because it is warm, to Catalonia because it is rich, but the whole country was favorable to us. I was thus a louse, and conscious of being one'' (18). And Nazi Germany

terrified all of Europe; it had become, particularly to me, the symbol of cruelty. It was already outside the law. Even on Unter den Linden I had the feeling that I was strolling about in a camp organized by bandits. . . . I was excited at being free amidst an entire people that had been placed on the index. Probably I stole there as elsewhere, but I felt a certain constraint, for what governed this activity and what resulted from it—this particular moral attitude set up as a civic virtue—was being experienced by a whole nation which directed it against others.

"It's a race of thieves," I thought to myself. "If I steal here, I perform no singular deed that might fulfill me. I obey the customary order; I do not destroy it. I am not committing evil. I am not upsetting anything. The outrageous is impossible. I'm stealing in the void." (123)

The disrupter of the social order is surprised to find himself in a realm that is disrupting the cosmic order. In this chaos, the picaro ought to feel at home, but Genet's thief realizes the limits of his own capacity for disorder. In this landscape he can no longer define himself according to the extremities of his own situation in the world. Born and brought up as a ward of the Assistance publique (his father unknown), he has always regarded himself in terms of his onlyness:

Whenever I come across *genêt* [broom] blossoms on the heaths . . . I feel a deep sense of kinship with them. I regard them solemnly, with tenderness. My emotion seems ordained by all nature. I am alone in the world, and I am not sure that I am not the king—perhaps the sprite—of these flowers. . . . I can regard all flowers without pity; they are members of my family. If, through them, I rejoin the nether realms—though it is to the bracken and their marshes, to the algae, that I should like to descend—I withdraw further from men. (44–45)

Without thinking myself magnificently born, the uncertainty of my origin allowed me to interpret it. I added to it the peculiarity of my misfortunes. Abandoned by my family, I already felt it was natural to aggravate this condition by a preference for boys, and this preference by theft, and theft by crime or a complacent attitude in regard to crime. I thus resolutely rejected a world which had rejected me. (86–87)

My being a foundling entailed a lonely youth and childhood. Being a thief led me to believe in the singularity of thievery. I told myself that I was a monstrous exception. In fact, my taste and my activity as a thief were related to my homosexuality, emerged from what had already set me apart in exceptional solitude. I was utterly astounded when I saw how prevalent theft was. . . .

  I wanted to oppose society, but it had already condemned me, punishing not so much the actual thief as the indomitable enemy whose lonely spirit it feared. (243–44)

His birth, his aloneness in the world, his withdrawal from men, his strange "family" of flowers (compare Pascual's family in *The Family of Pascual Duarte*, q.v.), his awareness of himself as a "monstrous exception," his "exceptional solitude," his initiation into the prevalence of theft (the world's corruption is a conventional surprise for the picaro in his second birth), society's fear of him (like that of the society that did not know what to do with Pascual Duarte), his rejection of the world, his ability through narrative to examine his onlyman condition, like Ellison's picaro (*Invisible Man,* q.v.)—in all these things, Genet's thief is one of those who take the extreme step from an already exceptional condition in a dunghill world and break reality's bounds by portraying themselves in a state of singularity and onlyness. He embodies Lazarillo's *solo soy* in contemporary terms. And in his extremity he rattles the social order. "Nothing jars the world's harmony more than men that break their ranks," says Meriton Latroon (*The English Rogue,* q.v.).

TRANSLATION

Bernard Frechtman (New York: Grove Press, 1964), with a short introduction by Jean-Paul Sartre.

SELECT BIBLIOGRAPHY

Paul John Eakin, *Fictions in Autobiography: Studies in the Art of Self-Invention* (Princeton, N.J.: Princeton University Press, 1985); Harry Sieber, *The Picaresque* (London: Methuen, 1977); Ulrich Wicks, "Onlyman," *Mosaic* 8 (1975): 21–47.

TILL EULENSPIEGEL

(fourteenth century; first printed 1515)

The variously titled collections of stories centering around Eulenspiegel (literally, "owl mirror") originate from the earliest surviving edition, published by Johannes Grieninger of Strassburg in 1515: *Ein kurzweilig lesen von Dyl/Ulenspiegel gebore uss dem land zu Brunsswick. Wie/er sein leben volbracht hatt. xcvi seiner geschichten* (An entertaining reading about Till Eulenspiegel, born in the country of Brunswick, how he spent his life, 96 of his tales—actually there are only ninety-five). The title character must have lived in the first part of the fourteenth century; the stories about him were first written in Low German and translated into Middle High German around 1500 by an anonymous author known as "N." (Some have ascribed authorship to Dr. Thomas Murner, who, among other known works, wrote *Die Schelmenzunft* [Fraternity of rogues] in 1516.) An English version appeared shortly after the Grieninger edition, probably in 1528 in London: *Till Eulenspiegel: A Merye Jest.*

By metaphorical extension (owl = wise, mirror = reflection), Eulenspiegel's name adds a satiric dimension to the otherwise crude pranks he plays on others. In chapter 40, for example, after working all day for a cruel smith who then shows him the outhouse and tells him to eat what is in there, Eulenspiegel spends the night forging the smith's tools and nails together:

> Now, Eulenspiegel had this custom whenever he did some mischief where he was not known: he took chalk or coal and drew an owl and a mirror over the door, and underneath wrote, in Latin, *Hic fuit* [He was here]. And this Eulenspiegel had drawn on the smith's door as well. (Oppenheimer, 103)

And yet the prank equals the injustice, as it does in many of the other tales as well, not much unlike Lazarillo's repaying the blind man at the end of chapter 1 by making him crash into a post *(Lazarillo de Tormes,* q.v.). Eulenspiegel—"jester, clown, rogue, sadist, skeptic, beggar, satirist, actor, thief, liar, savior, and even philosopher—was to become as perfect a mirror of a late medieval, and perhaps also very modern, German existentialist personality as of the everlasting foolishness of the lives of most men and women everywhere" (Oppenheimer, xvii). In his various adventures, he prefigures the picaro, as Chandler pointed out: "All in all, this little work may be regarded as the closest approach to the picaresque novel antedating the appearance of *Lazarillo de Tormes"* (10).

Till Eulenspiegel belongs properly to the type known in German as *Schwänke* or *Volksbücher,* jest books or folk tales, which Chandler calls "picaresque stories in embryo" *(Romances,* 8), various traditions of which he studies from a comparative perspective in his two-volume *The Literature of Roguery* (1907). Till Eulenspiegel is thus a close but human relative of the fox *(Reynard the Fox,* q.v.) and dozens of other such figures that have their origins in medieval folk literature. But he is also a direct descendant of Hermes (q.v.) and therefore a version of the trickster archetype (q.v.). A catalog of his escapades resembles that of any other trickster figure in any mythology, with the significant difference that Eulenspiegel lives in a time-bound world. His stories, though he does not tell them himself, are picaresque in tone and attitude and in their sharply satirical view of human foibles. The mirror of his name in fact reflects a concern for truth and the nature of reality that are major thematic preoccupations of mainstream picaresque narrative. In that same tale (ch. 40) in which Eulenspiegel leaves his "fool's coat of arms" over the smith's door, the revenge is prompted by the smith's original verbal deceit. Eulenspiegel had offered to work for food the smith would give him. When the smith then shows him the outhouse, he says, "Look, you say you're willing to eat whatever I wish, as long as I give you work. Now, nobody'd enjoy what's in here—so you eat it all" (Oppenheimer, 102). The truth of the promise (as perceived by Eulenspiegel) and the truth of actuality (as given by the smith) do not coincide, though each is real and not a lie. The nature of reality is muddled through language.

The extraordinary popularity of Eulenspiegel, according to Oppenheimer, resides in the "grand mockery of the human experience" that these tales depict: "It is man as a comical and foolish creature, rather than simply a corrupt society, that N. and Eulenspiegel want finally to reveal to us. For Eulenspiegel's is a book that belongs to what might be called the literature of middle-class escape, in which the hero, or anti-hero, succeeds in triumphing over the dull repetitiousness of much middle-class life, while implicitly acknowledging the futility of having been born a man in a universe that insists on cruelty, injustice, and death." Not only do these stories give us a picture of a world making the transition from an agricultural to an urban economy, they portray the transition "from medieval convictions that the universe must be harmonious to more modern suspicions that it might be ultimately chaotic" (xxiii, xxv).

Till Eulenspiegel has continued to inspire imitations and variations. Belgian novelist Charles de Coster wrote *Ulenspiegel* in 1869 (translated as *The Glorious Adventures of Tyl Ulenspiegel* by Allan Ross Macdougall [New York: Pantheon Books, 1943]), in which the popular figure is placed in the sixteenth-century revolution of the Low Countries against Spain. Richard Strauss composed a tone-poem, *Till Eulenspiegel's Merry Pranks,* in 1894. And Christa and Gerhard Wolf reworked the material in their *Till Eulenspiegel* (Berlin and Weimar: Aufbau-Verlag, 1972), a film scenario in which the character is "displaced" two hundred years, to the time of Luther, and in which class consciousness becomes particularly acute.

TRANSLATIONS

A facsimile of the 1528 (?) London translation was published in 1971 by Theatrum Orbis Terrarum in Amsterdam and Da Capo Press in New York. The Grieninger edition is translated by Paul Oppenheimer, *A Pleasant Vintage of Till Eulenspiegel* (Middletown, Conn.: Wesleyan University Press, 1972).

SELECT BIBLIOGRAPHY

Frank Wadleigh Chandler, *Romances of Roguery* [1899] (New York: Burt Franklin, 1961); Eugenio Suárez-Galban, "La caracterización en *Till Eulenspiegel* y en el *Lazarillo,*" *Cuadernos Hispanoamericanos: Revista Mensual de Cultura Hispánica* (Madrid) 319 (1977): 153–62.

THE TIN DRUM

(*Die Blechtrommel,* 1959)

Günter Grass

"I was too small to pass for a musketeer, so I took about an hour to become a drummer boy," writes Simplicius in *Simplicius Simplicissimus* (q.v.) in an episode in which he also receives his name. "They gave me a borrowed uniform . . . and a borrowed drum—probably because I was borrowed myself!—and that is how I passed the inspection" (bk. II, ch. 4). Hitler was known for some time before he came to power as *der Trommler* ("the drummer"). Dwarfs abound in German folklore, where they appear in various guises as mischievous pranksters, benevolent helpmeets, or malevolent manipulators. In the nursery-rhyme supplement to Arnim and Brentano's *Des Knaben Wunderhorn* (1806–1808) there is a verse called "Das buckliche Männlein" (The hump-backed little fellow) in which a hunchback dwarf plays irritating tricks throughout the household and at the end asks to be prayed for. Thomas Mann alludes to this rhyme in both *Buddenbrooks* and *The Magic Mountain*. In the former, little Hanno is upset by the song and tries to console himself by trying to believe that "he doesn't do that [disrupt the household] to be wicked, but only because he is unhappy, and it only makes him more unhappy still . . . But if one prays for him, then he does not need to do it any more!" (pt. VIII, ch. 3). In the latter, the antics of a fellow patient remind Hans Castorp of the dwarf in this nursery song, "with his pathetic wickedness and his craving for intercession" (ch. 7, "Highly Questionable"). (In this variation on the Bildungsroman, Hans is himself the quintessential German wanderer familiar from the nursery song "Hänschen klein," which Mann alludes to indirectly within the fairy-tale dimension of the story.) And the sinister figure of Pär Lagerkvist's *The Dwarf* (1944) explains his origins:

> We dwarfs have no homeland, no parents; we allow ourselves to be born of strangers, anywhere, in secret, among the poorest and most wretched, so that our race should not die out. . . . We have nothing to do with the perpetuation of life; we do not even desire it. We have no need to be fertile, for the human race itself produces its own dwarfs, of that one may be sure. We let ourselves be born of these haughty creatures, with the same pangs as they. Our race is perpetuated through them, and thus and thus only can we enter this world. That is the inner reason for our sterility. We belong to that race and at the same time we stand outside it. We are guests on a visit. Ancient wizened guests on a visit which has lasted for thousands of years. (15, 98)

Thus a partial portrait of the fragmentry and variegated ancestry of Oskar Matzerath, the hump-backed picaro-dwarf-artist of *The Tin Drum,* a work that blends the German narrative traditions of the Bildungsroman, the *Schelmenroman,* and the *Künstlerroman* into a grotesque vision fueled (in Grass's own words) by "linguistic showmanship, delight in changing forms, and the corresponding inclination of projecting counter-realities on to paper" (Grass, 84). Verbally, *The Tin Drum* shows considerable influence from James Joyce as well, and visually, it evokes the unsettling, often sadistic, almost diabolical behavior of children in such nineteenth-century German illustrated children's books as *Der Struwwelpeter* and Wilhelm Busch's *Max und Moritz,* familiarity with which is universal among German readers (their much tamer relatives on this side of the Atlantic were the Katzenjammer Kids). The fact that Oskar could spring directly from the pages of those disturbing books makes him an instantly accessible but simultaneously repellent figure. Oskar calls himself "the little demigod of thieves" (130) when he shatters jewelry store windows with his voice and lures passersby to steal, thus linking himself directly with Hermes (q.v.) and indirectly with Mann's Felix Krull (*Felix Krull,* q.v.), who shares with Oskar this direct Hermes identification as well as the phallic attributes associated with that god, which give Felix the sexual power he calls "The Great Joy" and which in Oskar grow, unlike the rest of him, "ultimately taking on Messianic proportions" (61). Oskar insists that his mother's cousin and lover, Jan Bronski, is his father, and not the German Alfred Matzerath; Felix, whose parents and sister behave with abandon, hints that his real father may well have been his godfather, the artist Schimmelpriester, who "was to intervene in my destiny decisively and providentially" (bk. I, ch. 4) later, but Mann never got that far. Having two fathers is a situation both share with Guzmán (*Guzmán de Alfarache,* q.v.), who never knows "which of these two did beget mee, or whether I were the sonne of a third" (pt. I, bk, I, ch. 2). Oskar is further influenced by other father figures, from the two formative reading experiences that constitute his education: Goethe's *The Elective Affinities* and an illustrated volume, *Rasputin and Women.* "The conflicting harmony between these two was to shape or influence my whole life" (90). Goethe and Rasputin are paralleled by Oskar's allegiance to two gods whom Hermes served and tricked and who form an important dichotomy in Nietzsche and Thomas Mann: Apollo and Dionysus. "If Apollo strove for harmony and Dionysus for drunkenness and chaos, Oskar was a little demigod whose business it was to harmonize chaos and intoxicate reason" (323).

With all this literary, mythic, and folkloric baggage, to which must be added the historical and political framework of the Third Reich, as well as the nostalgic evocation through folk legend of Poland's past and the irrecoverably lost edenic "home" of Danzig, *The Tin Drum* is probably the most allusive of modern picaresques. Thickened also by its problematic symbolism (the drum, Oskar's glass-shattering voice, Oskar's hump, the Onion Cellar, the Black Witch), *The Tin Drum* almost lumbers along, burdened, like some great Teutonic beast, by the sheer weight of its own intertextuality. (On the other hand, Thomas Mann, who has been criticized for the Germanically thorough bulk of some of his books, wrote a relatively unburdened work in his foray into picaresque, *Felix Krull*— though we do not know what he might have gone on to do with Professor Kuckuck.) Oskar's frequent bouts of logorrhea, like Céline's (*Journey to the End of the Night,* q.v.), result in a verbiage that is often far in excess of anything meaningful being said. But this, too, like the weightly intertextuality, is justified by Grass in both the deifying presumptuousness of the gnomic Oskar himself as character and in the narrative distance at work in the book. Self-reflexive disclaimers are built into the narrative situation itself. Oskar is first of all a mental patient in an asylum:

Granted, I am an inmate of a mental hospital; my keeper is watching me, he never lets me out of his sight. . . . So you see, my white-enameled, metal hospital bed has become a norm and standard. To me it is still more: my bed is a goal attained at last, it is my consolation. (15)

Like Ellison's picaro (*Invisible Man,* q.v.), like Simplicissimus in hermetic renunciation of the world on his deserted island, Oskar has withdrawn from life. He wants to complete the circle of existence by returning to the womb: "Oskar's aim is to get back to the umbilical cord; that is the sole purpose behind this whole vast verbal effort" (179). But the picaro's always implicit and often explicit romance impulse toward unbirth is transformed narratively into a rebirth of sorts, a metamorphosis of which Oskar is highly conscious and for which he will pull out all the stops:

You can begin a story in the middle and create confusion by striking out boldly, backward and forward. You can be modern, put aside all mention of time and distance and, when the whole thing is done, proclaim, or let someone else proclaim, that you have finally, at the last moment, solved the space-time problem. Or you can declare at the very start that it's impossible to write a novel nowadays, but then, behind your own back so to speak, give birth to a whopper, a novel to end all novels. (17)

His narrating technique resembles his childhood reading habits, when he tore out the pages of his Goethe and his Rasputin and "would shuffle the loose leaves of *Rasputin* and *The Elective Affinities* like playing cards, so creating a new book" (93), or the grotesque photomontages he likes to create with his friend Klepp out of passport pictures of themselves:

We bent and folded the pictures, and cut them up with the little scissors we carried about with us for this precise purpose. We juxtaposed old and new pictures, made ourselves one-eyed or three-eyed, put noses on our ears, made our exposed right ears into organs of speech or silence, combined chins and foreheads. And it was not only each with his own likeness that we made these montages; Klepp borrowed features from me and I from him: thus we succeeded in making new and, we hoped, happier creatures. Occasionally we gave a picture away. (52)

In his old family album, he uses ruler, triangle, and compass to plot the compositions "because I needed a point, a point of vantage, a point of departure, a point of contact, a point of view" (55). Later he will describe Mother Truczinski's cheeks as looking "as if they had been pasted on" (176) and Maria's beauty as seeming "to have been pieced together" (417). Omniscience as a narrative point of view, or as a worldview, is impossible for Oskar except ironically: "May our Father in Heaven, the untiring amateur who each Sunday snaps us from above, at an unfortunate angle that makes for hideous foreshortening, and pastes our pictures, properly exposed or not, in his album, guide me safely through this album of mine" (49–50); later he will refer to "our Sunday painter who art in heaven" (438). His problems as a combined fictor and histor in the narrative present are paralleled by others' portrayal of him in the past when he served as an artist's model in postwar Düsseldorf:

I, Oskar, [the professor] maintained, was the shattered image of man, an accusation, a challenge, timeless yet expressing the madness of our century. In conclusion he thundered over the easels: "I don't want you to sketch this cripple, this freak of nature, I want you to slaughter him, crucify him, to nail him to your paper with charcoal!" (463)

After he sees the results, Oskar finds that neither the sixteen students nor the professor turn out an acceptable portrait. "These sons and daughters of the Muses, I said to myself, have recognized the Rasputin in you; but will they ever discover the Goethe who lies dormant in your soul, will they ever call him to life and put him on paper, not with expressive charcoal but with a sensitive and restrained pencil point?" (463). With a tall female model named Ulla as Mary and Oskar as Jesus, an art student named Raskolnikov paints *Madonna 49,* which Oskar calls a masterpiece and which "was purchased for a considerable sum by a Rhenish industrialist and today it is hanging in the boardroom of a big business firm" (472). They pose for other surrealist paintings by Raskolnikov, in which "Oskar's face became a honey-yellow dial like that of our grandfather clock; in my hump bloomed mechanical roses which Ulla picked; Ulla, smiling on one end and long-legged on the other, was cut open in the middle and inside sat Oskar between her spleen and liver, turning over the pages of a picture book" (471–72). But when he poses alone, "they would always distort me horribly and paint me in the blackest colors" (511). These passages are all analogues to the narrative technique of *The Tin Drum,* in which distortion is the governing force. Oskar distorts in the telling, just as much as he feels others distort him in their perception and representation of him. In *The Tin Drum* distortion is the functional mode of behavior and perception for a world in which quotidian normalcy—conventional existence, inherited narrative forms—has lost any meaning it may have had. By willfully deforming himself, by stopping his growth at age three, Oskar rejects accommodation to a world he perceives as deformed. And from his hospital bed at age thirty, with the war now long "over," convicted of a murder he claims not to have committed, Oskar finds even less coherence to his world. Far from getting back to the umbilical cord, he finds himself in a condition that is "the exact opposite" (586) of his grandmother's skirts, under which his mother was conceived. The opposite to the womb is the feared "Black Witch" (*die schwarze Köchin*), and Oskar's narrative ends with an acknowledgment of a darkness that is the opposite of the darkness of the womb; it is an affirmation of negation: *Ist die schwarze Köchin da? / Ja! Ja! Ja!* misleadingly rendered by Manheim with strong overtones of defiance ("Here's the black, wicked Witch, / Ha! ha! ha!" [589], but literally, "Is the black cook there? Yes! Yes! Yes!"). As her disintegrative shadow begins to subsume him experientially, Oskar has nevertheless given narrative form to the deformed existence he has tried to chronicle, using both restrained pencil point and expressive charcoal.

The Tin Drum is a book of tensions. It is always wanting to explode and reassemble itself. Intertextually inflated, it seems to want to burst beyond all narrative forms, including the hybridization it is itself creating. Like Oskar's voice shattering the eyeglasses of Miss Spollenhauer, his first-grade teacher (83), *The Tin Drum* narrates to pieces our received literary conventions. Like Oskar's rhythm-making and rhythm-breaking drum at the Nazi rally (120–22), *The Tin Drum* mixes romance and picaresque modes in a dizzying simultaneity of order and chaos. The following key passage is a microcosm of these tensions:

I saw and heard all sorts of things in my fever; I was riding a merry-go-round, I wanted to get off but I couldn't. I was one of many little children sitting in fire engines and hollowed-out swans, on dogs, cats, pigs, and stags, riding round and round. I wanted to get off but I wasn't allowed to. All the little children were crying, like me they wanted to get out of the fire engines and hollowed-out swans, down from the backs of the cats, dogs, pigs, and stags, they didn't want to ride on the merry-go-round any more, but they weren't allowed to get off. The Heavenly Father was standing beside the merry-go-round and every time it stopped, he paid for another turn. And we prayed: "Oh, our Father who art in heaven, we know you have lots of loose change, we know you like to treat us to rides on the merry-go-round, we know you like to prove to us that this world is round. Please put your pocketbook away, say stop, finished, *fertig, basta, stoi,* closing time—we poor little children are dizzy. . . .

But God our Father, the merry-go-round owner, smiled in his most benevolent manner and another coin came sailing out of his purse to make the merry-go-round keep on turning . . . and every time my stag . . . carried us past our Father in heaven, the merry-go-round owner, he had a different face: he was Rasputin, laughing and biting the coin for the next ride with his faith healer's teeth; and then he was Goethe, the poet prince, holding a beautiful embroidered purse, and the coins he took out of it were all stamped with his father-in-heaven profile; and then again Rasputin, tipsy, and again Herr von Goethe, sober. A bit of madness with Rasputin and a bit of rationality with Goethe. (411–12)

The immediate situation is this: after having indirectly caused his father's death (as he had indirectly been responsible for the death of his other father, Bronski), Oskar has decided to grow a little, which puts him to bed with swelling, joint aches, and a fever. The attending doctor, who has dozed off while examining him, tells him she has been unable to sleep regularly since witnessing the death of four thousand refugee children trying to cross the river Vistula. What Oskar here describes is his feverish hallucination during the ensuing weeks. This image of the dizzying merry-go-round becomes a collective metaphor for the book's narrative technique, the landscape it renders, and the vision that emerges from the telling and the told. However they are dichotomized—chaos and order, night and day, dream and existence, Rasputin and Goethe, Dionysus and Apollo— opposing energies run the merry-go-round and pay for its rotation. Ruled by a force that removes a Goethe mask to reveal a Rasputin mask behind which there is a Goethe mask ad infinitum, Grass's fictional world is a world rendered through deformation of forms. Just as the book's intertextuality simultaneously creates and destroys all of its narrative frames, so the rendered landscape, with its excess of human galleries, is always bursting the bounds of normalcy, like one of Brueghel's populated canvases. There is a crowd sense in Grass's fiction, which makes the social panorama seem peopled with normative beings busy at the tasks of keeping their society running smoothly. But from the picaro's point of view (which is traditionally from below and outside and which in Oskar's case is literally from underneath), these beings turn out to be inhabitants of a community of rogues, of norm breakers, of social rhythm breakers. Tenderly felt nostalgic reminiscence of a Sunday stroll convulses into an emetic description of biological

processes (the eels feeding on the horse's head, followed by the cataloging of
Oskar's mother's vomit); appearances are not to be trusted (storekeeper Greff,
scout leader, exemplar to youth, is a homosexual who commits suicide); middle-
class family life is a sham (Jan Bronski, proper postal employee, commits
adultery with Oskar's mother); the therapeutic power of legend and myth erupts
into derangement (Herbert Truczinski's mounting the Niobe statue with a double-
headed axe); and so on. This all takes place amid the real historical chaos that
was World War II, a landscape described by Genet's thief as "already outside
the law," in which "the outrageous is impossible" (*The Thief's Journal,* q.v.).
The specific action takes place in a borderline no-land, half-Polish, half-German,
where many of the inhabitants are Kaschubes, a rootless Slavic people living in
the northeastern part of Pomerania and speaking a language that is transitional
between Polish and the Pomeranian dialect. Oskar thus grows up with a fragmented cultural, historical, linguistic, even genealogical identity, among a whole
group of people suffering from a similar loss. The legendary heritage of the past
wants to assert itself to give form to this shapelessness, but it fails in the onslaught
of the Nazis and the subsequent postwar redefining of borders. Even historically
and geographically, this landscape changes its frames. The resulting rendering,
like the distorted view from the revolving merry-go-round, is grotesque in all
the senses of that word. The grotesque "instills fear of life rather than fear of
death" by invoking the daemonic aspects of the world and thereby trying to
subdue them (Kayser, 188). In *The Tin Drum,* the whole landscape, not just the
picaro, is in extremis; abnormalcy is its norm and deformation its form.

"I show [my characters] in particular, grotesque or extreme situations," Grass
has said, "because such situations make people free from circumstance. As
themselves, as ordinary people, they are prisoners of the world; in their fantastic
incarnations, they are free to see everything" (Botsford, 68). But as Oskar's
whirl on the merry-go-round shows, this release into a demonically reassembled
reality becomes in itself an imprisonment in the very grotesque and extreme
forces that unleash the characters from order and circumstance to begin with.
The tryptical three-book structure of *The Tin Drum* resembles three distorting
mirrors facing one another like the sides of an equilateral triangle, in which the
prewar, wartime, and postwar portraits both project and reflect each other's
grotesque images and inside of which Oskar is trapped. Ultimately Oskar would
like to burst forth from history itself.

The merry-go-round is also emblematic of a distinctive aspect of Grass's
narrative technique: the combination of first- with third-person points of view.
In narrating his tale, Oskar gives us not only the autobiographical "I" and the
visionary "eye" fundamental to picaresque narration; he also speaks of himself
as "he." Grass thus compounds the problematical reliability of the recollecting
self by appearing to add an omniscient voice, though the source of that voice is
Oskar himself. This I-He narration confuses the relationship between the telling
and the teller, between the landscape and its inhabitant. Which Oskar (the Rasputin or the Goethe, the Dionysus or the Apollo) at any one point is talking

about which Oskar at any one point in the past: the one who "lurks with Satan
in doorways" or the one who believes himself to be Jesus? Is the Goethe-Oskar
the one who says "he" and the Rasputin-Oskar the one who says "I"? At least
two Oskars are telling a tale about two Oskars. On occasion there seem to be
three Oskars: "Who was doing all this: Oskar, he, or I?" (280) Like his drum,
Oskar's narrative voice is rhythm making as well as rhythm breaking; and like
the merry-go-round, it combines Dionysian as well as Apollonian energies in
the narrative task that Oskar sets himself: "to harmonize chaos and intoxicate
reason." Driven by the centripetal forces of Goethe-Apollo and Rasputin-Dion-
ysus to keep it turning in its vicious circle, the merry-go-round symbolizes the
mad world Oskar lives in, but its centrifugal force impels the rider outward,
toward the fixed vantage point that will allow for contemplation and narration.
Oskar wants to be on the carousel wanting to get off while keeping it going with
his Goethe and Rasputin selves. The whirling mixture that results makes it
difficult to measure narrative distance in any meaningful way. Even the modal
tension between picaresque and romance intensifies into a frenzy, as it does in
the I-He narration of Donleavy's *The Ginger Man* (q.v.). Grass, like Donleavy,
focuses on the protean character of the picaro and on the confusion that results
when he is unable to choose a role. In this I-He-Oskar instability, in this Apol-
lonian-Dionysian blur, the picaro seems to have lost even the fragile stability of
his lonely "I."

Oskar's situation, both narratively and experientially, is fittingly described by
Robert Jay Lifton, who characterizes twentiety-century human beings in terms
of Proteus, who had no real existence of his own but became a succession of
beings. Lifton sees the protean style not as pathological but as the functional
pattern of our day. Two historical developments are especially important for
creating protean man: a worldwide sense of historical (or psychohistorical) dislocation, a break in the sense of connection that human beings have long felt
with the vital and nourishing symbols of their cultural tradition—symbols revolving around family, idea systems, religions, and the life cycle in general;
and second, the flooding of imagery provided by mass communication. Modern
man, Lifton says, is thus a being of "omniattention"—having the possibility of
"receiving" and "taking in" everything. He is thus vulnerable to a flux in
emotions, and, intimately bound up with this, he has a profound inner sense of
absurdity. (Lifton names Donleavy's *The Ginger Man* and Grass's *The Tin Drum*
as the two works of fiction that best express this situation of protean man.) *The
Tin Drum*, he points out, is a fiction "in which the protagonist combines protean
adaptability with a kind of perpetual physical-mental 'strike' against any change
at all." Also, protean man

is profoundly attracted to the idea of making all things, including himself, totally new—
to the "mode of transformation." But he is equally drawn to an image of a mythical
past of perfect harmony and prescientific wholeness, to the "mode of restoration."
Moreover, beneath his transformationism is nostalgia, and beneath his restorationism is
his fascinated attraction to contemporary forms and symbols. Constantly balancing these

elements amidst the extraordinarily rapid change surrounding his own life, the nostalgia is pervasive, and can be one of his most explosive and dangerous emotions. (25)

This situation has been, in milder form, inherent in the picaresque from the beginning. Guzmán de Alfarache was the protean man of his time as much as Oskar is of his. And as a fictional mode, the picaresque represented transformationism—we recall Simplicissimus's "constancy of inconstancy"—with its built-in romance yearnings for order. Simplicissimus can order his discontinuous life through narrating it, through the mode of restoration. But for Oskar, the mode of restoration, the act of narration, is as disturbing in its way as was experiencing the life he seeks to narrate, and the act of narration thus exhibits "explosive and dangerous emotions." Moreover, his drum is both restorer of the past and of childhood (he evokes the past with it, he makes people wet their pants with it) and transformer (he disrupts Nazi rallies with it). Transformationism and restorationism finally blend so thoroughly in this narrative merry-go-round that it is impossible to tell where one begins and the other leaves off. When does Goethe's coin stop and Rasputin's begin? We cannot tell one mask from another, one role from the next. It has been said that the grotesque "is primarily the expression of our failure to orient ourselves in the physical universe" (Kayser, 185). In *The Tin Drum*, the picaro's protean adaptability does not suffice experientially or narratively. "Words fail me," Oskar says on the final page (589). In the original German, this is said of himself in the third person (literally, "he's run out of words"). And so this Teutonic monster of a book, with all its drumbeat sound and fury, huffs and puffs under its intertextual weight and manages only the refrain of a simple nursery rhyme. By the time Oskar reappears, at age sixty, in Grass's *The Rat* (*Die Ratte,* 1985), he has become a silent filmmaker.

TRANSLATION

Ralph Manheim (New York: Vintage Books, 1961).

SELECT BIBLIOGRAPHY

Paul F. Botheroyd, *Ich und Er: First and Third Person Self-Reference and Problems of Identity in Three Contemporary German-Language Novels* (The Hague: Mouton, 1976); Keith Botsford, "Günter Grass Is a Different Drummer," *The New York Times Magazine,* May 8, 1966; Edward Diller, *A Mythic Journey: Günter Grass's "Tin Drum"* (Lexington: University of Kentucky Press, 1974); G. Richard Dimler, "Simplicius Simplicissimus and Oskar Matzerath as Alienated Heroes: Comparison and Contrast," *Amsterdamer Beiträge zur neueren Germanistik* 4 (1975): 113–34; Ralph Freedman, "The Poet's Dilemma: The Narrative Worlds of Günter Grass," in *A Günter Grass Symposium,* ed. A. Leslie Willson (Austin: University of Texas Press, 1971), 46–59; Günter Grass, "On the Lack of Self-Confidence of the Literary Court Jester without a Court," *American-German Reivew* (June–July 1966): 20–22, and "Looking Back at *The Tin Drum*," *Encounter* (July 1976): 84–89; Helmut Günther, "Der ewige Simplizissimus: Gestalt und Wandlungen des deutschen Schelmenromans," *Welt und Wort* 10 (1955): 1–5; Henry Hatfield, "The Artist as Satirist: Günter Grass," in his *Crisis and Continuity in Modern German Fiction: Ten Essays* (Ithaca: Cornell University Press, 1969), 128–49; Thomas

R. Hinton and Wilfried van der Will, *The German Novel and the Affluent Society* (Manchester: Manchester University Press, 1968); Jürgen Jacobs, *Der deutsche Schelmenroman: Eine Einführung* (Munich: Artemis, 1983); Wolfgang Kayser, *The Grotesque in Art and Literature* [1957], trans. Ulrich Weisstein (New York: McGraw-Hill, 1966); Manfred Kremer, "Günter Grass, *Die Blechtrommel* und die pikarische Tradition," *German Quarterly* 46 (1973): 381–92; Pär Lagerkvist, *The Dwarf*, trans. Alexandra Dick (New York: Hill and Wang, 1945); Robert Jay Lifton, "Protean Man," *Partisan Review* 35 (Winter 1968): 13–27; David H. Miles, "Kafka's Hapless Pilgrims and Grass's Scurrilous Dwarf: Notes on Representative Figures in the Anti-Bildungsroman," *Monatshefte* 65 (1973): 341–50, and "The Picaro's Journey to the Confessional: The Changing Image of the Hero in the German Bildungsroman," *PMLA* 89 (1974): 980–92; Brigitte Neubert, *Der Aussenseiter im deutschen Roman nach 1945* (Bonn: Bouvier Verlag Herbert Grundmann, 1977); William Riggan, *Pícaros, Madmen, Naïfs, and Clowns: The Unreliable First-Person Narrator* (Norman: University of Oklahoma Press, 1981); N. L. Thomas, "Oskar, The Unreliable Narrator in Günter Grass's *Die Blechtrommel*," *New German Studies* 3 (1975): 31–47; Wilfried van der Will, *Pikaro heute: Metamorphosen des Schelms bei Thomas Mann, Döblin, Brecht, Grass* (Stuttgart: W. Kohlhammer, 1967); Hans Dieter Zimmerman, "Günter Grass: *Die Blechtrommel* (1959)," in *Deutsche Romane des 20. Jahrhunderts: Neue Interpretationen*, ed. Paul Michael Lützeler (Königstein/Ts: Athenäum, 1983), 324–39; Theodor Ziolkowski, "Der Blick von der Irrenanstalt: Verrückung der Perspektive in der modernen deutschen Prosa," *Neophilologus* 51 (1967): 42–54; Norris W. Yates, *Günter Grass: A Critical Essay* (Grand Rapids, Mich.: William B. Eerdmans, 1967).

TRICKSTER ARCHETYPE

An archetype is the original model, form, or pattern from which something is made or from which something develops (from a Greek word meaning "molded first as a model; exemplary"); in this sense, it is nearly synonymous with *prototype*. Since Jung, however, and in the subsequent literary theory and criticism based on his ideas, the word has come to refer to primordial images that recur in dreams, myths, and other constructs. In diverging from Freud, Jung posited the existence of a collective unconscious in addition to Freud's theory of the personal unconscious composed of individual and personal contents, derived from repression. The collective unconscious is not a personal acquisition; it consists of the blocked-off memories of our racial past, including our prehuman experiences. The personal unconscious comes from individual experience and consists for the most part of complexes; the collective unconscious has its origin in heredity and is made up of archetypes. Jung said that the collective unconscious "has contents that are more or less the same everywhere and in all individuals. It is, in other words, identical in all men and thus constitutes a common psychic substrate of a suprapersonal nature which is present in every one of us" (in Bennet, 66). To describe the content of this collective unconscious, Jung wrote: "*Archetype* is apposite and helpful, because it tells us that so far as the collective unconscious contents are concerned we are dealing with archaic or—I would say—primordial types, that is with universal images that have existed since the remotest times'' (in Bennet, 69). These archetypes ''represent all the general human situations; any universally human mode of behavior is an archetype. Inevitably these have taken innumerable forms, and they become perceptible as images in the mind'' (Bennet, 154). A pure archetype has no form as such; it is the possibility of form. Jung said that ''an archetype in its quiescent, unprojected state has no exactly determinable form but is in itself an indefinite structure which can assume definite forms only in projection'' (*Psychological Reflections*, 70).

In a 1934 essay, ''Archetypes of the Collective Unconscious'' (subsequently modified and expanded to become *The Archetypes and the Collective Unconscious*, volume 9 of *The Collected Works of C. G. Jung*), Jung tried to classify the archetypes he encountered most often in his patients. In addition to the Anima, the Animus, and the Shadow, Jung's system of archetypes included the Mother, the Wise Old Man, the Child, the Hero, and the Trickster Figure.

In his essay ''On the Psychology of the Trickster Figure'' (originally written for Paul Radin's *Der göttliche Schelm* [literally, ''The Divine Rogue'' but translated as *The Trickster*] in 1954), Jung expands on the nature of the trickster archetype beyond his immediate context of the Winnebago trickster cycle of North American Indian mythology. After describing the various medieval manifestations of the trickster, including the alchemical figure of Mercurius (and related fairy tale and folklore characters such as Tom Thumb, Stupid Hans, and Hanswurst), and such remnants of the ancient saturnalia as the *festum stultorum* (fools' feast) and the *festum asinarium* (the ass's feast, in memory of Mary's flight into Egypt) during which the whole congregation brayed like a donkey, Jung writes:

In picaresque tales, in carnivals and revels, in sacred and magical rites, in man's religious fears and exaltations, this phantom of the trickster haunts the mythology of all ages, sometimes in quite unmistakable form, sometimes in strangely modulated guise. He is obviously a ''psychologem,'' an archetypal psychic structure of extreme antiquity. In his clearest manifestations he is a faithful copy of an absolutely undifferentiated human consciousness, corresponding to a psyche that has hardly left the animal level. (200)

In its origins, the trickster myth was supposed to have a therapeutic effect by holding ''the earlier low intellectual and moral level before the eyes of the more highly developed individual, so that he shall not forget how things looked yesterday'' (207). The trickster intrudes still today:

Now if the myth were nothing but an historical remnant one would have to ask why it has not long since vanished into the great rubbish heap of the past, and why it continues to make its influence felt on the highest level of civilization, even where, on account of his stupidity and grotesque scurrility, the trickster no longer plays the role of a ''delight-maker.'' In many cultures his figure seems like an old river-bed in which the water still flows. One can see this best of all from the fact that the trickster motif does not crop up only in its original form but appears just as naively and authentically in the unsuspecting modern man—whenever, in fact, he feels himself at the mercy of annoying ''accidents'' which thwart his will and his actions with apparently malicious intent. He then speaks of "hoodoos" and "ginxes" or of the "mischievousness of the object." Here the trickster is represented by countertendencies in the unconscious, and in certain cases by a sort of second personality, of a puerile and inferior character, not unlike the personalities who announce themselves at spiritualistic séances and cause all those ineffably childish phenomena so typical of poltergeists. I have, I think, found a suitable designation for this character component when I called it the *shadow*. On the civilized level it is treated as a personal "gaffe," "slip," "faux pas," etc., which are then chalked up as defects of the conscious personality. We are no longer aware that in carnival customs and the like there are remnants of a collective shadow figure which prove that the personal shadow is in part descended from a numinous collective figure. This collective figure gradually breaks up under the impact of civilization, leaving traces in folklore which are difficult to recognize. But the main part of him gets personalized and is made an object of personal responsibility. (201–2)

The trickster is a forerunner of the savior, and, "like him, God, man, and animal at once," both subhuman and superhuman, "a bestial and divine being, whose chief and most alarming characteristic is his unconsciousness" (203). According to Jung, outwardly people are more or less civilized, but inwardly they are still primitives: "Something in man is profoundly disinclined to give up his beginnings, and something else believes it has long since got beyond all that" (208). We experience the living effect of the trickster "when a higher consciousness, rejoicing in its freedom and independence, is confronted by the autonomy of a mythological figure and yet cannot flee from its fascination, but must pay tribute to the overwhelming impression."

The trickster is a collective shadow figure, an epitome of all the inferior traits of character in individuals. And since the individual shadow is never absent as a component of personality, the collective figure can construct itself out of it continually. Not always, of course, as a mythological figure, but, in consequence of the increasing repression and neglect of the original mythologems, as a corresponding projection on other social groups and nations. (209)

The so-called civilized man has forgotten the trickster. He remembers him only figuratively and metaphorically, when, irritated by his own ineptitude, he speaks of fate playing tricks on him or of things being bewitched. He never suspects that his own hidden and apparently harmless shadow has qualities whose dangerousness exceeds his wildest dreams. As soon as people get together in masses and submerge the individual, the shadow is mobilized, and, as history shows, may even be personified and incarnated. (206)

Among the great trickster figures in mythology is Hermes (q.v.), who belongs wholly to the divine realm of the Olympian gods but who is also active in the realm of mortals. Hermes was born in a cave that "was a place of primeval chaos" and from which "the father of all cunning" commits his first trick, stealing Apollo's cattle; but, as Kerényi goes on to point out in "The Primordial Child in Primordial Times" (1940–1941), "His first encounter in the Homeric world brings something very primitive, mythologically speaking, to light. The fortuitous nature of this encounter is typical of Hermes, and it is primitive only insofar as chance and accident are an intrinsic part of primeval chaos. In fact, Hermes carries over this peculiarity of primeval chaos—accident—into the Olympian order. Hermes meets a tortoise, a primeval-looking creature,'' which he then makes into the lyre that he gives Apollo (57). This dual function of being both disrupter and orderer seems to be at the heart of the trickster archetype. ''The fundamental goal of initiation lies in taming the original Trickster-like wildness of the juvenile nature. It therefore has a civilizing or spiritualizing purpose, in spite of the violence of the rites that are required to set this process in motion,'' writes Henderson in ''Ancient Myths and Modern Man'' (146). And Joseph Campbell, surveying the many trickster figures in world mythologies, writes:

This ambiguous, curiously fascinating figure of the trickster appears to have been the chief mythological character of the paleolithic world of story. A fool, and a cruel, lecherous cheat, an epitome of the principle of disorder, he is nevertheless the culture-bringer also. And he appeared under many guises, both animal and human. Among the North American Plains Indians his usual form was Coyote. Among the woodland tribes of the north and east, he was the Great Hare, the Master Rabbit, some of whose deeds were assimilated by the Negroes of America to an African rabbit-trickster whom we know in the folktales of Br'er Rabbit. The tribes of the Northwest Coast knew him as Raven. Blue Jay is another of his forms. In Europe he is known as Reynard the Fox [*Reynard the Fox*, q.v.]; but also, on a more serious plane, he appears as the devil. (273)

Paul Radin, whose study of the Winnebago trickster cycle occasioned Jung's and Kerényi's writings on this archetype, says that trickster is the symbol for ''vague memories of an archaic and primordial past, where there as yet existed no clear-cut differentiation between the divine and the non-divine.'' Moreover,

The symbol which Trickster embodies is not a static one. It contains within itself the promise of differentiation, the promise of god and man. For this reason every generation occupies itself with interpreting Trickster anew. No generation understands him fully but no generation can do without him. Each had to include him in all its theologies, in all its cosmologies, despite the fact that it realized that he did not fit properly into any of them, for he represents not only the undifferentiated and distant past, but likewise the undifferentiated present within every individual. This constitutes his universal and persistent attraction. And so he became and remained everything to every man—god, animal, human being, hero, buffoon, he who was before good and evil, denier, affirmer, destroyer and creator. If we laugh at him, he grins at us. What happens to him happens to us. (168–69)

In the widest, most universl sense, then, the trickster archetype is present whenever the spirit of disorder erupts our consciously shaped daily regimen, from the most minor ''freak'' accident to a major catastrophe we may be part of or witness to. Trickster is there in Mardi Gras and all the other sanctioned disorders in which we reenact primordial chaos. And trickster is recapiutulated in Reynard the Fox and Till Eulenspiegel (*Till Eulenspiegel,* q.v.) and every other rogue, clown, fool, and buffoon of folklore and popular entertainment. Even the practical joke is a manifestation of trickster. ''Disorder belongs to the totality of life, and the spirit of this disorder is the trickster,'' writes Kerényi in ''The Trickster in Relation to Greek Mythology'':

His function in an archaic society, or rather the function of his mythology, of the tales told about him, is to add disorder to order and so make a whole, to render possible, within the fixed bounds of what is permitted, an experience of what is not permitted.

Picaresque literature has consciously taken over this function. . . . In Spain the picaresque novel constituted itself as a literary genus and remained the sole means of revolt against the rigidity of tradition. (185)

According to Kerényi, the Winnebago trickster cycle belongs to "a species of the genus mythology, just as the picaresque novel without national or temporal limitations, . . . dating from Petronius, is a species of the genus novel" (175). Behind the picaro is the trickster archetype, whose origins can only be speculated about:

How are we to conceive that unrecorded, original situation in which a story was told about him for the first time? There is much trickery at large in the world, all sorts of sly and cunning tricks among human beings, animals and even plants, which could no more remain hidden from a story-teller whose inner life was as much bound up with the world as his outer one, than they could from an observer at a distance. Did he ask himself the specific question: "Who played these tricks first, who introduced them into the scheme of things?" Was his story, like so many other mythologems, the answer to this question of origins? At any rate his story dealt neither with particular observations nor with slyness and cunning in general, but with a figure clearly envisaged by the eye of the myth-maker, pre-existent to any definite question: the arch-trickster himself, no matter whether he appeared in human form, or as a cunning animal, the prototype of Reynard the Fox, whose equivalent for some tribes was the coyote, for others the raven, but who in all his manifestations was a primordial being of the same order as the gods and heroes of mythology. Suddenly he must have sprung forth, the trickster behind all tricksters, and have been there so compellingly that all who heard tell of him recognized him at once as the figure whom the story-teller had in mind. (174–75)

Following Kerényi's train of thought, then, we might say that every picaro and picara, themselves role players and shape shifters in their specific fictions, is a metamorphosis of the trickster archetype, which, in turn, has many metamorphoses in many mythologies. In approaching picaresque fiction through the trickster archetype, we not only illuminate its narrative nature both diachronically and synchronically, we also begin to explain the stubborn persistence of *picaresque* in critical and even popular usage well beyond and outside of the historically identifiable and self-conscious tradition of the Spanish *novela picaresca*. It seems that Spain gave us the name we needed for the literary form in which the primordial image of the trickster is reenacted and reperceived from age to age. From this perspective, we might well speak, as Kerényi does, of a "picaresque mythology." Claudio Guillén has used the term "picaresque myth" as part of his definition of the picaresque, by which he means "an essential situation or structure of meaning which has been derived from the [picaresque] novels themselves" (253). And Alexander Blackburn makes a distinction between genre and myth by adopting Guillén's definition for the latter and defining the former as "a traditional model or conventional pattern" (7); a generic focus is more concerned with technical characteristics, while a focus on myth is more concerned with cultural characteristics.

SELECT BIBLIOGRAPHY

E. A. Bennet, *What Jung Really Said* (New York: Schocken Books, 1967); Alexander Blackburn, *The Myth of the Picaro: Continuity and Transformation of the Picaresque Novel, 1554–1954* (Chapel Hill: University of North Carolina Press, 1979); Joseph Campbell, *The Masks of God: Primitive Mythology* [1959] (New York: Penguin Books, 1976); Claudio Guillén, "Toward a Definition of the Picaresque," *Proceedings of the IIIrd Congress of the International Comparative Literature Association* (The Hague: Mouton, 1962), 252–66 (revised in his *Literature as System: Essays toward the Theory of Literary History* [Princeton, N.J.: Princeton University Press, 1971], 71–106); Joseph L. Henderson, "Ancient Myths and Modern Man," in *Man and His Symbols,* ed. Carl G. Jung, with M.-L. von Franz and John Freeman [1964] (New York: Dell, 1968); Carl G. Jung, "On the Psychology of the Trickster Figure," in *The Archetypes and the Collective Unconscious,* vol. 9 of *The Collected Works of C. G. Jung,* ed. Sir Herbert Read, Michael Fordham, and Gerhard Adler (London: Routledge and Kegan Paul, 1959), pp. 255–72 (also in Radin, below); Karl Kerényi, "The Trickster in Relation to Greek Mythology" (in Radin, below) and "The Primordial Child in Primordial Times," in C. G. Jung and C. Kerényi, *Essays on a Science of Mythology: The Myth of the Divine Child and the Mysteries of Eleusis* [1940–1941], tr. R. F. C. Hull (Princeton, N.J.: Princeton University Press, 1969); Paul Radin, *The Trickster: A Study in American Indian Mythology* [orig. *Der göttliche Schelm,* 1954] (New York: Schocken Books, 1972); see also Oliver Evans and Harry Finestone, eds., *The World of the Short Story: Archetypes in Action* (New York: Knopf, 1971).

THE UNFORTUNATE TRAVELLER, OR, THE LIFE OF JACK WILTON

(1954)

Thomas Nashe

There is considerable controversy about this book's place in the picaresque narrative tradition, and about its being a picaresque at all, which in turn reveals much about the failure of theory to come to terms with a universally acceptable concept of the picaresque. As a result, the shortcomings of critical terminology turn into value judgments of both picaresque fiction in general and of the particular work at hand; thus, a critic can praise a book for belonging to the picaresque, while another is relieved to find that same book lacking in the characteristics of his concept of the picaresque.

Among the first to suggest that *The Unfortunate Traveller* belongs to the picaresque was J. J. Jusserand who in his *The English Novel in the Time of Shakespeare* (1890) argued that Nashe was consciously imitating *Lazarillo de Tormes* (q.v.), which had been translated by David Rowland in 1576. (A similar, though less speculative, line of influence exists between the first English translation of *Guzmán de Alfarache* [q.v.] and Head's *The English Rogue* [q.v.].)

Bjornson says, "It is probable that the cosmopolitan Nashe knew *Lazarillo* in either the original text or in one of the extant translations; in fact, there must have been a general familiarity with the blind-beggar episode, for Shakespeare alluded to it . . . in *Much Ado About Nothing*." Despite differences between Jack Wilton and Lazarillo, "late sixtenth-century English readers undoubtedly placed their fictional autobiographies in the same categories of humorous literature; they wanted witty, entertaining stories, and that is what they apparently found in *Lazarillo* and *The Unfortunate Traveller*" (143).

Blackburn, on the other hand, states that Nashe has no place in the picaresque, deferring, first, to McKerrow, editor of Nashe's *Works,* and, second, to Hibbard in his study of Nashe. McKerrow finds no evidence for Nashe's having followed any model at all, much less *Lazarillo*: "Jack Wilton . . . was not intended to be a rogue at all. His behavior is indeed far from being in accord with present-day standards of propriety, but he is rather wantonly mischievous than depraved. Had Nashe meant to depict a vulgar rogue and trickster, he would hardly have shown him to us treated on such confidential terms by a nobleman of the rank and attainments of the Earl of Surrey" (23). Hibbard finds that the two were written "in entirely different spirits," with *Lazarillo* being essentially realistic in its portrayal of a boy who becomes a rogue because he has to. "The story is factual, unemphatic, makes no attempt to be sensational and does not moralize. Rowland gave to his translation of it the sub-title of *The Spaniard's Life,* and that sub-title is fully justified; *Lazarillo* has a representative quality, it depicts a general state of affairs. But it would be ridiculous to call *The Unfortunate Traveller* by any such title as *The Englishman's Life*. It has no representative quality at all, and, although the word 'realism' has often been used about it, no pretensions to any such thing" (146).

Neither McKerrow nor Hibbard has a clear conception of the picaresque, which makes Blackburn's automatic acceptance of their dismissal surprising. Equally problematic in his concept of the picaresque is Arnold Kettle, yet he finds the picaresque central to the rise of the novel in England and Nashe its most important practitioner before Defoe: "It was natural that Nashe, a writer responding fully in his sensibility to the new world, but not yet fully conscious of what it meant to be a bourgeois, should write a book like *The Unfortunate Traveller,* perhaps the most remarkable picaresque story in our language" (22–23). The contribution of the picaresque tradition to the development of the English novel, Kettle says, should not be underestimated: "Even though it made for a neglect of pattern it did demonstrate that the novel must draw its vitality from a concern with the actual life of the people. It made impossible any serious attempt to move back to the pastoral and courtly traditions of the early romances" (58). He then goes on to list a sequence of English fictions—*The Unfortunate Traveller, Moll Flanders* (q.v.), *Roderick Random* (q.v.), *Kim,* Joyce Cary's *The Horse's Mouth* (q.v.)—of which he says, "It is not a line that anyone who delights in the novel will despise." But his inclusion of Kipling's work and his readiness to accept prevailing critical commonplaces about the picaresque lacking "a controlling intelligence, a total significance" (58) make his concept of the picaresque a relatively unexamined embellishment on received critical opinion.

Even Chandler, with his obvious enthusiasm for Nashe, treats *The Unfortunate Traveller* with one eye focused on its importance as a precursor of the English novel proper. But he does respect the book for its narrative power, its realism, its vivid character sketching, its humor, and its style, and he plays down the question of direct influence: "There is little or nothing in Nashe's novel that may not be indigenous. Those who have remarked the analogy between it and the Spanish tales have usually exaggerated the analogy, and have interpreted it as necessarily the result of causal connection" (198). But the argument nevertheless continues, complicating the problem of conceptual inadequacies with the historical reality of the apparent misreadings of the Spanish picaresque works at the time they were being translated: "English writers and the English public were amused by the Spanish picaresque novels without comprehending the fundamental criticism of life which lay at their core. Even at the close of the seventeenth century the picaresque novel was considered not much more than a glorified jest book or criminal biography given a more connected and literary form" (Bowers, 26). But this argument, though more sympathetic to the universality of the picaresque mode across national boundaries, nevertheless still relies heavily on differences in social conditions between Spain and England and on a dubious analogy that equates literary qualities with cultural tempers: "The Elizabethan temper was too sanguine to be affected completely by the Spanish picaresque novel; and Spanish cynicism, at the root of the humor and the survey of manners in the *Lazarillo,* could not be Anglicized" (Bowers, 20).

Perhaps the search for a specific literary ancestry for *The Unfortunate Traveller* has not gone back far enough. It may well be that Nashe's models are much earlier in the evolution of the picaresque mode, before the emergence of the historically identifiable genre in Spain. Walsh has suggested that Nashe's work is "in the manner of Petronius and Apuleius. . . . The structure of the story, in which Jack meets a succession of characters satirically depicted, is similar to that of the Roman novel, and some episodes are reminiscent of Petronian or Apuleian scenes" (241). In its witty nonchalance, Jack Wilton's narrative tone does have some resemblance to that of Encolpius in *The Satyricon* (q.v.).

It is not difficult to see how arguments both for and against Nashe's work as a picaresque can be easily marshaled, even without the question of direct influence. On the one hand, *The Unfortunate Traveller* depicts trickery that is far more gratuitious than it is essential to survival; it portrays only one master-servant relationship, emphasizes exotic locales and adventures rather than the fringes of society, and only pays lip-service to the picaro's conversion at the end. Moreover, Jack Wilton is not really a social outsider, being relatively well taken care of in the upper levels of the social hierarchy. On the other hand, the book's structure and vision reveal essential picaresque characteristics such as role playing (Jack cross-dresses and changes places with his master), the vivid social panorama that includes historical figures such as Luther, the dance pattern that reveals coincidence and recurrence, and the narrative technique itself. Moreover, as Stuart Miller points out, its jagged narrative rhythm imitates "the hopeless whirl of Fortune" (29) that produces the vision of disorder that underlies all picaresques: "For the tale is as drunk as the teller—digressive, self-commenting, reader-addressing. It is a tale that refuses to get on with the business of narration. . . . Because the narrator quite gratuitously refuses to tell his story straight, his tale is chaotic not only in structure (plot and character) but also in texture" (104). This in turn demonstrates the attitude of the narrator toward reality: "he cannot try to describe it in a serious and continuous way. It is as though life were so ugly and horrible in its chaos that the only thing to do is avoid looking at it" (104).

This vision of disorder is most effectively rendered in *The Unfortunate Traveller* by the plague in Rome:

Within three quarters of a yeere in that one citie there died of it a hundred thousand looke in *Lanquets* chronicle and you shall finde it. . . . The clouds like a number of cormorants that keepe their corne til it stinke and is mustie, kept in their stinking exhalations till they had almost stifeled all *Romes* inhabitants. Phisitions greedines of golde made them greedie of their destinie. They would come to visit those with whose infirmitie their art had no affinitie, and even as a man with a fee should be hired to hang himselfe, so would they quietly go home and die presently after they had bin with their patients. All daye and all night long carre-men did nothing but go up and downe the streets with their carts and cry, Have you anie dead bodies to bury and had many times out of one house their whole loding: one grave was the spulchre of seven score, one bed was the alter whereon whole families were offered. The wals were hoard and furd with the moist scorching steame of their desolation. Even as before a gun is shot off, a stinking smoake funnels out, and prepares the way for him, so before any gave up the ghost, death araid in a stinking smoak stopt his nostrels, and cramd it selfe ful into his mouth that closed up his fellows eyes, to give him warning to prepare for his funeral. Some dide sitting at their meat, others as they were asking counsell of the phisition for theyr friends. I saw at the house where I was hosted a maide bring her master warme broth for to comfort him, and shee sinke downe dead her selfe ere he had halfe eate it up. (324–25)

This eyewitness experience, composed from the vantage point that narrative distance provides, is emblematic of the merciless unpredictability of human existence and experience in the world. Despite his moving in aristocratic circles, Jack finds the world as full of violence and horror as does any low-born picaro trapped in the unprotected outer fringes of structured existence.

The problem in interpreting Jack's conversion at the end may well be the result of its relative meaninglessness in a world such as the one he renders. Having witnessed a torture-murder, Jack says:

Unsearchable is the booke of our destinies, one murder begetteth another: was never yet bloud-shed barren from the beginning of the world to this daie. Mortifiedly abjected and danted was I with this truculent tragedie. . . . To such straight life did it thence forward incite me, that ere I went out of Bolognia I married my curtizan, performed many almes deedes, and hasted so fast out of the *Sodom* of *Italy,* that within fortie daies I arrived at the king of *Englands* campe. (356)

As in the ending of *El Buscón* (q.v.), the narrative haste of the presentation is incongruous with the claimed extensiveness of the actual experience. With a still unreformed part of himself casting a glance at the reader's taste for the unreformed, Jack leaves his options open:

All the conclusive epilogue I wil make is this, that if herein I have pleased anie, it shall animat mee to more paines in this kind.

Otherwise I will swere upon an English Chronicle never to bee out-landish Chronicler more while I live. Farewell as many as wish me well. (356)

This not only casts doubt on the reality of the rendered lived experience; it calls into question the sincerity of the narrative recollection of that experience. It winks at the readers and burdens them with collaborative responsibility: if you want it, Jack implies, this can go on and on, even if I am not the chronicler. As Miller puts it, "Jack has not . . . escaped the picaresque world, because such a world is clearly inescapable. All he has done in concluding the tale is to stop at a convenient place" (105).

EDITION

Everyman's Library edition of *Shorter Novels: Elizabethan* (New York: Dutton; London: Dent, 1929), with an introduction by George Saintsbury and notes by Philip Henderson.

SELECT BIBLIOGRAPHY

Richard Bjornson, *The Picaresque Hero in European Fiction* (Madison: University of Wisconsin Press, 1977); Alexander Blackburn, *The Myth of the Picaro: Continuity and Transformation of the Picaresque Novel, 1554–1954* (Chapel Hill: University of North Carolina Press, 1979); Fredson T. Bowers, "Thomas Nashe and the Picaresque Novel," in *Humanistic Studies in Honor of John Calvin Metcalf* (Charlottesville: University of Virginia Press, 1941), 12–27; Frank Wadleigh Chandler, *The Literature of Roguery* [1907] (New York: Burt Franklin, 1958); Ursula Habel, *Die Nachwirkung des picaresken Romans in England (von Nash bis Fielding und Smollett)* (Breslau: Pribatsch, 1930); G. R. Hibbard, *Thomas Nashe: A Critical Introduction* (Cambridge: Harvard University Press, 1962); Arnold Kettle, *An Introduction to the English Novel* [1951] (London: Hutchinson & Co., 1969), vol. 1; W. Kollmann, "Nash's 'Unfortunate Traveller' und Head's 'English Rogue,' die beiden Hauptvertreter des englischen Schelmenromans," *Anglia* 22 (1899): 81–140; Ronald B. McKerrow, ed., *The Works of Thomas Nashe* (Oxford: Basil Blackwell, 1958), vol. 5; Stuart Miller, *The Picaresque Novel* (Cleveland: Case Western Reserve University Press, 1967); Marcelino C. Peñuelas, "Algo más sobre la picaresca: Lázaro y Jack Wilton, " *Hispania* 37 (1954): 443–45; P. G. Walsh, " 'Nachleben': The Roman Novel and the Rebirth of the Picaresque," in his *The Roman Novel: The "Satyricon" of Petronius and the "Metamorphoses" of Apuleius* (Cambridge: University Press, 1970), 224–43.

ZELIG

(1983)

Directed by Woody Allen

In her review of this film (which Allen also wrote), Pauline Kael said: "If it's a masterpiece, it's a masterpiece only of its own kind; it's like an example of a nonexistent genre, or a genre from another country" (84), though she does suggest Melville's Confidence Man as a literary precursor (*The Confidence-Man*, q.v.). *Zelig* is indeed so unlike any other film that we have trouble placing it into a generic context within our accumulated narrative experiences. To consider *Zelig* a picaresque may at first appear as disorientingly inappropriate, but the more we examine it in such a context, the more we see that what Allen explores here is the most significant characteristic of the picaro's makeup: his shape-shifting or metamorphosing skills, honed through practice into effective survival tactics in his repeated attempts to integrate himself into a hostile and resistant world. As the "human chameleon," Leonard Zelig embodies both the protean adaptability of the picaro and the picaro's apersonality. Being, in essence, no one, the picaro has the potential for becoming everyone. In his many metamorphoses, Leonard Zelig is a comic extension ad infinitum of Felix Krull's notion of interchangeability and his observation that "he who really loves the world shapes himself to please it" (*Felix Krull*, q.v.), which in turn echoes Simplicius's insight during his early role as a court jester: "The foolish world wants to be fooled" (*Simplicius Simplicissimus*, q.v.).

Before he more or less fades away, Leonard Zelig has "been," among other things, a boxer, pilot, rabbi, opera singer, SS officer, psychiatrist, clerk, trumpet player, and baseball player; he has metamorphosed ethnically and physically into an Oriental, a Greek, an American Indian, a Frenchman, a black man, a fat man. He has traveled from Long Island to Hollywood, from Chicago to Texas, from New York City to Florida, and through Mexico, Germany, France, Spain, and Italy. He becomes a celebrity and is seen in the company of the famous and prominent; the world mimics him with dances and other fads. F. Scott Fitzgerald remembers meeting the "curious little man" at a party. Then ex-wives materialize with children and tell of his having been a fur trapper, a painter, and an actor. Former patients claim he performed unnecessary dental extractions and delivered a baby with ice tongs. A fickle public drops him: "In keeping with a pure society, I say lynch the little Hebe." Only after his psychiatrist, Eudora Fletcher, who eventually "cures" and marries him, tracks him down at a Hitler rally and thus sets off a slapstick chase that embarrasses Hitler, does the American public take Zelig up again as a hero. Like Lindbergh, he is given a ticker-tape parade (his second) for breaking the transatlantic flying record—upside down. By the time he settles down and virtually disappears again, his horizontal and vertical travels have taken him through a wide geographical and social panorama.

Zelig comes from a broken home and grows up with a mean stepmother and a father whose only deathbed advice is to tell him that life is meaningless and "to save string." When anti-Semites beat him up, his parents would side with them. For punishment, Leonard's parents put him in a dark closet; when they were really angry, they would get in with him. The family lived above a bowling alley, and it was the bowling alley that complained about the noise. Zelig grows up with a strong sense of displacement: "I want to be liked," he says, "to be like the others." It is out of this radical instability, this need to belong, that Zelig develops the ability to change his selves in order to blend in—quite literally—with those around him. That he controls his metamorphoses is made clear in a tricky role-playing standoff between himself and Eudora Fletcher when the latter faces the problem of having her patient mime her role as the psychiatrist. By pretending to be a patient pretending to be a psychiatrist, Fletcher apparently gets Zelig to see through such a reflection his own role playing. As a result, he becomes receptive to her attempts to hypnotize him, but whether he is playing a role even in these sessions is left ambiguous.

Zelig's name echoes the German *selig* (at one point Zelig calls himself "Dr. Selig"), which means "blessed," "happy," "blissful," and which in turn is etymologically related to the English *silly,* which originally carried the German word's meaning. Leonard's half-sister Ruth takes up with a man named Martin Geist, who engineers the media hype that forces the world to watch when he and Ruth show Zelig off profitably around the world as a freak. *Geist* is German for "spirit" and "wit," as well as "ghost," and Martin may well represent the spirit of a gawking and fickle media-manipulated age. In Spain, Ruth falls in love with a cowardly bullfighter, whereupon Martin in jealousy kills Ruth, the bullfighter, and himself. As a result, Leonard Zelig's life is "turned upside down." *Eudora* means "good gift" (from the Greek *eu* and *doron*), and she becomes his surrogate mother, sister, and wife. All this deliberate playing with names suggests that Woody Allen is after big symbolic game with the figure of Zelig as an ironic portrait of the twentieth-century personality as all-being in nonbeing, an entity so unstable that its identity shifts with every external circumstance, all reflected in an inconstant public that is as chameleon-like in its taste for fads as Zelig is for identities. Eudora Fletcher's "cure" is thus a gift of dubious goodness, since it turns Zelig into a nobody, a cipher. Allen undercuts symbol seeking while simultaneously inviting it. When Zelig visits Paris, French intellectuals pronounce him "a symbol for everything." As the son of a Yiddish actor who played Puck in an "Orthodox version of *A Midsummer Night's Dream,*" Leonard Zelig needs his roles; they represent the "constancy of inconstancy" that Simplicissimus discovers early on. Not to play roles is not to be. The horrible anxiety at the core of *Zelig* is that when we take our masks off, nothing will be there. Symbols are everything, and yet they are not anything. Such a use of the *desengaño* theme is purely picaresque.

Zelig's narrative technique is itself as uncentered, unstable, and fragmentary as its ephemeral subject matter. Presented in the form of a documentary, *Zelig* is put together out of bits and pieces of old newsreels, snapshots, home movies, newspaper articles—all intercut with present-day interviews with Susan Sontag, Saul Bellow, Irving Howe, Bruno Bettelheim, and John Morton Blum, as well as a much older Eudora Fletcher. These Zelig "experts" are presented in their real names, though they are playing roles as themselves (Blum is credited with being the author of *Interpreting Zelig*). On the one hand, Allen mines the documentary technique for all its conventions that give the status of reality to whatever is depicted; and on the other, he undermines that credence, which the audience has come to expect from the genre, by calling attention to the process of filmmaking itself by forcing us to become aware of the painstaking piecing together of fragments that is necessary to create illusion. *Zelig* establishes reality when it shows us the real Calvin Coolidge and the real Herbert Hoover; it undermines that same reality when it manipulates Zelig into the same picture.

In the end, the film *Zelig* is as ephemeral as an old newsreel. The experience of watching it is the eighty-four-minute equivalent of one of Zelig's many roles. (Inside *Zelig* the film we see clips from the 1935 Warner Brothers dramatization of Zelig's life, called *The Changing Man;* and even Zelig's first sessions with Dr. Fletcher are filmed.) As Zelig disappers, he is reborn through the cinematic narrative retrospection of *Zelig*. When Zelig's masks are gone, he fades away, just as the film leaves only a blank white screen behind: there is, after all, nothing there.

SCREENPLAY

The script of *Zelig* is available in *Three Films of Woody Allen* (New York: Vintage, 1987), pp. 1–141.

SELECT BIBLIOGRAPHY

Vincent Canby, review in *The New York Times,* July 15, 1983, and "Woody Allen Continues to Refine His Cinematic Art," *The New York Times,* July 17, 1983; Richard Feldstein, "The Dissolution of the Self in *Zelig*," *Literature/Film Quarterly* 13 (1985): 155–60; Pauline Kael, "Anybody Home?" *The New Yorker,* August 8, 1983, 84–87.

Chronology of Basic Picaresques

Prehistory	TRICKSTER ARCHETYPE
	Hermes
	Sisyphus
first century A.D.	Petronius, *The Satyricon*
second century A.D.	Apuleius, *The Golden Ass (Metamorphoses)*
twelfth century	*Reynard the Fox*
fourteenth century	*Till Eulenspiegel*
1509	*Liber Vagatorum*
1554	*Lazarillo de Tormes*
1594	Nashe, *The Unfortunate Traveller*
1599	Alemán, *Guzmán de Alfarache I*
1604	Alemán, *Guzmán de Alfarache II*
1605	Ubeda, *La pícara Justina*
1612	Salas Barbadillo, *La hija de Celestina*
1613	Cervantes, "El coloquio de los perros" ("The Dogs' Colloquy"), "La ilustre fregona" ("The Illustrious Kitchen-Maid"), "Rinconete y Cortadillo"
1618	Espinel, *Marcos de Obregón*
1619	Carlos García, *La desordenada codicia de los bienes ajenos*
1624	Jerónimo de Alcalá, *Alonso, mozo de muchos amos (El donado hablador)*
1626	Quevedo, *El Buscón*

1632	Castillo Solórzano, *La niña de los embustes, Teresa de Manzanares*
1637	Castillo Solórzano, *Aventuras del bachiller Trapaza*
1642	Castillo Solórzano, *La garduña de Sevilla*
1646	*Vida y hechos de Estebanillo González*
1665	Head and Kirkman, *The English Rogue*
1668	Grimmelshausen, *Simplicius Simplicissimus*; Francisco Santos, *Periquillo el de las gallineras*
1670	Grimmelshausen, *The Runagate Courage*
1680	Bunyan, *The Life and Death of Mr. Badman*
1715	Lesage, *The Adventures of Gil Blas of Santillane, Part I*
1722	Defoe, *The Fortunes and Misfortunes of the Famous Moll Flanders*
	Defoe, *Colonel Jack*
1724	Defoe, *Roxana*
	Lesage, *The Adventures of Gil Blas of Santillane, Part II*
1735	Lesage, *The Adventures of Gil Blas of Santillane, Part III*
1748	Smollett, *The Adventures of Roderick Random*
1816 (1830)	Lizardi, *The Itching Parrot (El Periquillo Sarniento)*
1826	Eichendorff, *Memoirs of a Good-for-Nothing*
1844 (1856)	Thackeray, *Barry Lyndon*
1857	Melville, *The Confidence-Man*
1885	Twain, *The Adventures of Huckleberry Finn*
1911	Mann, *Confessions of Felix Krull I*
1913 (1927)	Kafka, *Amerika*
1915	Hesse, *Knulp*
1932	Céline, *Journey to the End of the Night*
1933	Orwell, *Down and Out in Paris and London*
1934	Mann, *Confessions of Felix Krull II*
1938	Rubén Romero, *The Futile Life of Pito Pérez*
1941	Cary, *Herself Surprised*
1942	Cela, *The Family of Pascual Duarte*
1944	Cary, *The Horse's Mouth*
	Cela, *Nuevas andanzas y desventuras de Lazarillo de Tormes*

1949	Genet, *The Thief's Journal*
1952	Ellison, *Invisible Man*
1954	Mann, *Confessions of Felix Krull III*
1955 (1963)	Donleavy, *The Ginger Man*
1957	Kerouac, *On the Road*
1959	Grass, *The Tin Drum*
1962	Burgess, *A Clockwork Orange*
1964	Berger, *Little Big Man*
1965	Kosinski, *The Painted Bird*
1968	Irving, *Setting Free the Bears*
1969	Schlesinger, *Midnight Cowboy*
1973	Anderson, *O Lucky Man!*
1974	Blier, *Going Places*
1980	Jong, *Fanny*
1983	Allen, *Zelig*
1984	McInerney, *Bright Lights, Big City*

Index

Items from the bibliographies are indexed only where they are mentioned in the text.

About the Author

ULRICH WICKS is Associate Professor of English at the University of Maine, where he has also served as department chair and directed the Honors Program. His previous publications include articles on the picaresque in *PMLA, Genre, Mosaic,* and *College Literature*; on *Don Quixote* in *Approaches to Teaching Cervantes'* Don Quixote (Modern Language Association, 1984); and on film and fiction in *The Rhetoric Review, Literature/Film Quarterly,* and *Narrative Strategies: Original Essays in Film and Prose Fiction.* He has also contributed review essays to *Novel* and *Komparatistische Hefte,* and is the author of the entry on picaresque in *Dictionary of Literary Themes and Motifs* (Greenwood Press, 1988).